STRANGER MAGIC

STRANGER MAGIC

Charmed States and the Arabian Nights

Marina Warner

The Belknap Press of
Harvard University Press
Cambridge, Massachusetts

First published in Great Britain in 2011 by
Chatto & Windus

First Harvard University Press paperback edition, 2013

Printed in the United States of America

Library of Congress Cataloging-in-Publication Data
Warner, Marina, 1946–
Stranger magic : charmed states and The Arabian nights / Marina Warner
p.   cm.
Includes bibliographical references and index.
ISBN 978-0-674-05530-8 (cloth : alk. paper)
ISBN 978-0-674-72585-0 (pbk.)
1. Arabian nights—Influence.   2. Magic in literature.
3. Myth in literature.   4. Orientalism.   I. Title.
PJ7737.W37 2012
398.22—dc23   2011047124

For my sister Laura, and for Graeme's sisters,
Lynne and Barbara

A Note on the Text

The book is chiefly known in English as the *Arabian Nights* or, simply, the *Nights*, both contractions of the title of the first English translation, *Arabian Nights' Entertainments*. *Alf Layla wa-Layla* is the title in Arabic, more accurately caught by the popular alternative, found commonly in French and in other translations: *Tales of a Thousand and One Nights*. I have used these titles interchangeably. My readings and brief retellings of stories draw on many of the many editions and translations; the list can be found in the Bibliography, with a table of the variant titles of those tales (I hope useful to readers). Arabic has been transliterated as simply as possible, and again, a table at the end gives alternative spellings and names for some of the most familiar personae. I have chosen 'Shahrazad' and 'Dunyazad' for the heroine and her sister, and 'jinn' for the plural of jinni and jinniya. Orient has a capital letter when I am referring to an imaginary place, most often – but not always – in the interpretations of non-orientals; orientalist refers to a scholar of the orient, and with a capital O to ideologies and dreams inspired by that imaginary zone. Where not specified, the translations are my own. The notes are keyed to page numbers by brief phrases; some passages in their original languages can be looked up on my website *www.marinawarner.com* as well as fuller notes, bibliography, further material – and, no doubt, *errata*.

It is only by putting it into words that I make it whole; this wholeness means that it has lost the power to hurt me; it gives me, perhaps because by doing so I take away the pain, a great delight to put the severed parts together [. . .] From this I reach what I might call a philosophy; at any rate it is a constant idea of mine; that behind the cotton wool is hidden a pattern; that we – I mean all human beings – are connected with this; that the whole world is a work of art; that we are parts of the work of art [. . .] We are the words; we are the music; we are the thing itself. And I see this when I have a shock.

Virginia Woolf, A Sketch of the Past

Contents

List of Illustrations

Colour plates

Plate section I

Note: Some plates are reproduced in the following works: Plates 1 &
9 in J. M. Rogers, *The Arts of Islam: Treasures from the Nasser D. Khalili
Collection* (Sydney: Art Gallery of New South Wales, 2007), cat. nos.
251, 308; Plate 2, in *Dancing to the Flute: Music and Dance in Indian Art*,
ed. Pratapaditya Pal (Art Gallery of New South Wales, 1997), cat. no.
67; Plate 4 in *The Arabian Nights, The Book of The Thousand Nights
and One Night,* Vol. I, trans. Powys Mathers after J. C. Mardrus (London:
The Folio Society, 2003), f. p. 29; Plate 5 by Moleiro publishers:
http://www.moleiro.com/en/miscellanea/the-book-of-felicity/
miniatura/756.

Illustrations in the text

Ornaments in the text

Title page, Abbreviations: 'Antique Lamps', *The Gentleman's Magazine*
    (1751). My thanks to Karin Littau for this thoughtful present.
Contents, List of Illustrations, Introduction and Story headings: from
    Edward W. Lane, *The Arabian Nights* (1850).
Part-titles and chapter headings (specimens of panel work),
    Acknowledgements, Glossary, Notes, Index: from Edward W. Lane,
    The Manners & Customs of the Modern Egyptians (1836).
The Stories: Bird-woman by J. Carelman (1958).

Every effort has been made to trace and contact all holders of copyright
in illustrations. If there are any inadvertent omissions or errors, the
publishers will be pleased to correct these at the earliest opportunity.

Acknowledgements

Every book is made of the insights and learning of others, and many people have helped me write *Stranger Magic*. I am especially grateful to the University of Essex, where I teach, and to all my colleagues and students there who have collaborated on the development of the ideas in this book, most especially, Peter Hulme, for giving me periods of leave when I was able to concentrate on writing. I have also been fortunate to have peace and quiet in inspiring surroundings: at the Remarque Institute, New York University; in Paris, where my dear friend Irène Andreae lent me her apartment, and in Stony Brook, Long Island under the auspices of the Simons Institute for Geometry and Physics (where my partner was visiting).

My research was spurred by invitations to write reviews and essays and give seminars and lectures, and I am always glad of such incentives, and most grateful to the following: Mary-Kay Wilmers and Paul Myerscough at the *London Review of Books*; Sina Najafi and Graham D. Burnett at *Cabinet* magazine; Jackson Lears and Stephanie Volmer at *Raritan*; Terry Castle and John Bender, Stanford Institute of the Humanities, who asked me to give a Presidential Lecture; Mariam Said, Jacqueline Rose and the committee, Edward Said Memorial Trust; Jonathan Barker, Cathy Costain and all at the British Council, Cairo, and above all to Radwa Ashour, and the organisers of Cairo Book Fair, 2009; Lorraine Daston and the Siemens Foundation, Munich; Michael Holly at the Clark Art Institute, Williamstown; Dror Wahrman at the University of Indiana, Bloomington; Lieselotte E. Saurma and Anja Eisenberg, University of Heidelberg; Richard Kaye, CUNY Institute of the Humanities; Elizabeth Cullingford and the Harry Ransom Center at Austin, Texas; Alessandra Violi and Richard Davies, University of Bergamo; Florian Mussgnug and colleagues at the Synapsis conference on Shadows at Bertinoro; Prof. Daniela Corona and Valentina Castagna and the Universities of Palermo and Enna in Sicily; Alberto Manguel who included me in his series at the Centre Pompidou, Paris, and my co-panellist Abdelfattah Kilito; Hermione Lee, Wolfson College, Oxford; Caroline Van Eck for 'waking the Dead', Villa Médicis, Rome; Gervase Rosser for the invitation to give the Hussey Lecture at Oxford; and Mike O'Hanlon, the Pitt Rivers Museum, Oxford for the Beatrice Blackwood Lecture; Mary Beard for the Jane Harrison Memorial Lecture; Trevor Dadson and other colleagues at Queen Mary, University of London; Joan Ashworth, Professor of Animation at the Royal College of Art for the chance to take part in her courses, and to all conference and seminar convenors who have invited me over the last few years.

I have also been helped and inspired by the participants in three conferences which I was involved in organising: *Staging the East*, organised with Elizabeth Kuti at the Theatre Royal, Bury St Edmunds, 2010; *The Compass of Story* at the British Academy, London in 2008, and its expanded version the following year, *The Arabian Nights: Encounters and Translations*, created in collaboration with Philip Kennedy, the director of the Institute of the Humanities, New York University at Abu Dhabi. I learned a great deal from all, but am particularly indebted to Ros Ballaster, Aboubakr Chraibi, Elliott Colla, Anne Deneys, Angela Escott, Ferial Ghazoul, Rebecca Johnson, Donna Landry, Gerald Maclean, Ulrich Marzolph, Vaya Naidu, Tetsuo Nishio, Bridget Orr, Wen-chin Ouyang, Karl Sabbagh, Rosie Thomas, Yuriko Yamanata. My special thanks go to Mariët Westermann, Vice-Provost of NYUAD at the time, to Gila Waels, the co-ordinator there, and to Philip Kennedy, whose deep but lightly worn knowledge of the field of research has been invaluable, as well as a source of great delight.

I began reading the *Arabian Nights* again after I was asked to review Robert Irwin's classic study of the book, *The Arabian Nights: A Companion*, for the *TLS* in 1994. Everyone who now works on the *Nights* owes Robert's dervish wisdom a huge debt, and although he and I have our differences (chiefly over Edward Said), I could never have written this book without his work. Nor could I have done so without Edward Said's; and it is a matter of great regret that this generous man is no longer here to argue vehemently with us all about my interpretations here.

Libraries are under threat in the UK, while in other countries, the people are braving tanks and guns and prison in order to gain such access to knowledge. I have benefited from the incomparable resources of many magnificent institutions: above all the Warburg Institute, both in its Library and its Photographic Collections, where Elizabeth McGrath and Paul Taylor have been endlessly patient and inspiring in helping me find and identify images, and the British Library, with its inexhaustible riches and remarkable openness of access to rare materials. I am most grateful to Alastair Hamilton who introduced me to the exceptional Arcadian Library, London, and to Andrea Ludowisy-Meyer, and her successor Camilla Thomas, and also to Willem de Bruijn and Karem Ibrahim; and at the Bodleian Library, Oxford, to Julie-Anne Lambert in the John Johnson

Collection and Alasdair Watson, in Middle Eastern and Islamic Manuscripts. Michael Molnar guided me with his unsurpassed knowledge of the archives of the Freud Museum, London; Marcia Reed and David Brafman at the Getty Research Institute Library, showed me many rare alchemical manuscripts, and at the British Museum Venetia Porter revealed to me some of the treasures in the collection of amulets and talismans. I am always very grateful to the staff of the Albert Sloman Library, University of Essex; and of the London Library.

Drafts of parts of the book have been kindly commented on by Elizabeth McGrath, Peter Dronke, Roger Pearson, Laurent Châtel, T.J. (Jim) Reed; their critical attention has been stringent and invaluable. The whole final draft was read by some courageous spirits. It is difficult to express how much they helped me: I am grateful above all for the expert scrutiny of Jan Geert van Gelder, whose care in nuancing my perspective and saving me from various errors went far beyond anything I could have expected. It goes without saying that all the false notes and mistakes that remain are my fault.

Jenny Uglow, my editor at Chatto & Windus, has been firm, incisive and kind, an unusual combination; she has stimulated me with her ideas and knowledge as well as giving persevering support. I would never have brought the book to a conclusion without her. At Chatto I would also like to thank my copy-editor Beth Humphries; Parisa Ebrahimi; and Clara Farmer, the successor as publishing director to Alison Samuel, who commissioned this book in an earlier incarnation. John Kulka at Harvard University Press took it on early in a surprising act of faith; Gabrielle Townsend and Jasmine Richards helped me unflaggingly in the final stages; my agents Gill Coleridge and Cara Jones in London, and Amanda (Binky) Urban in New York have shown cheerful perseverance and understanding throughout.

Many friends, colleagues and chance encounters have contributed in numerous ways, provocative, illuminating, open-handed and eye-opening. I wish I could acknowledge each of them fully. But I would like at least to express my thanks to Isobel Armstrong, Lisa Appignanesi, Omeros and Betty Aridjis, Jeremy Barlow, Christiane and Tony Besse, Gillian Beer, Omar Berrada, Birgit Beumers, Duncan Bull, Terence Cave, Mary Carruthers, Lucia Boldrini, Peter Brooks, Penelope Brown, Wynd Bucknell, A.S. Byatt, Billy Chambers, William Christian, Jr., Ian Christie, Wendy Doniger, Evelyn Fishburn, John Forrester, David Freedberg, Jane Garnett, John Isaacs, Mary Jacobus, Joan Jonas, Berta Joncus, Jonathan Lamb, Christopher and Angela Legge, Pippa Lewis, Roger Luckhurst, Joanna MacGregor, Rogert Malberg, Philippe-Alain Michaud, Jane

Moody, Victoria Nelson, Jacqueline Rose, James Runcie, Malise Ruthven, Victor Sage, Aura Satz, Wolfgang Schivelbusch, David Scrase, Hanan al-Shaykh, Catherine Simmonds, Rebecca Solnit, Maggie Staats Simmons, Craig Stephenson, Tim Supple, Sadika Tancred, and Jack Zipes. Robert Chandler and Dubravka Ugresic generously advised on the Russian elements. Rita Apsan kindly provided photographs from the Freud Museum. I am especially grateful to Paula Rego for allowing 'Flying Children' to be included, and to Luca Buvoli for the image from his book, *Flying: Practical Training for Beginners*. I also wish to express my thanks to all the individuals, institutions and galleries who have given permission to reproduce illustrative material, as noted in the List of Illustrations.

At home, Beatrice Dillon has supported my work in a thousand thoughtful ways: I owe her immense gratitude. My son Conrad has left home but is always in my thoughts; Graeme Segal has been patiently full of loving kindness, while setting the highest standards; the pursuit of a vision of the best is worth the grief of falling short, inevitably.

Marina Warner
Kentish Town, 2011

Introduction

There is a kind of Writing, wherein the Poet quite loses Sight of Nature, and entertains his Reader's Imagination with the Characters and Actions of such Persons as have many of them no Existence, but what he bestows on them. Such are Fairies, Witches, Magicians, Demons, and departed Spirits. This Mr. *Dryden* calls *the Fairy Way of Writing*, which is, indeed, more difficult than any other that depends on the Poet's Fancy, because he has no Pattern to follow in it, and must work altogether out of his own Invention.

Joseph Addison, *The Spectator* 1 July 1712

That story of which I spoke – I, too, remember the beginning well, but I have forgotten all the rest. It must be a story of the *Arabian Nights*. I am collating the various editions, the translations in all languages. Similar stories are numerous and there are many variants, but none is that story. Can I have dreamed it? And yet I know I will have no peace until I have found it and find out how it ends.

Italo Calvino, *If on a Winter's Night a Traveller*, 1979

I Shahrazad's Way

THROUGH ALL THE TWISTS AND turns the *Arabian Nights* have undergone, the central theme remains, and remains known to every hearer and every reader: Shahrazad has been sentenced to die in the morning by the Sultan Shahriyar who, in revenge for the infidelity of his Sultana (he found her and all her handmaidens cavorting with slaves), has decided to marry a virgin every night and cut off her head in the morning. The vizier is ordered to find the bride and then, in the morning, to take her away to die; candidates are running out, but his eldest daughter, Shahrazad, volunteers. He tries to dissuade her by telling her two animal fables, one inside the other, amounting together to a nasty, threatening rigmarole about proper feminine obedience; a cock lords it over his hens, a merchant beats his wife till she faints. To this patriarchal show of authority backed by violence, Shahrazad is undaunted; she simply repeats that she will still do as she wishes, and her plan will go ahead. Her father the vizier gives in. But she still insists. She asks if she may bring her younger sister Dunyazade with her to the palace, for she has a plan: on the fated first night, after she and the Sultan have made love, Dunyazade is to ask her sister for a story – a bedtime story – and Shahrazad will begin to tell her one, and will continue until dawn breaks, when 'speaking was no longer permitted', as the enigmatic refrain puts it. The Sultan, who has been listening in, will want to know how that story ends, will want to hear more stories like it, and will give Shahrazad more time, sending away the vizier who arrives in the morning to take away the bride (his daughter) to the scaffold. In this way, she will be able to put off the day of her execution until the Sultan relents.

'The night is for ourselves, but the day is for God,' the writer and film-maker Nacer Khemir says, offering one way of explaining these mysterious arrangements. Profane stories can only continue in the privacy and darkness of night, the time and place of dreams. There, Shahrazad can wind the vengeful ruler into an exchange of confidences between one young woman and another: he is placed in the position of the male eavesdropper on their women's knowledge, tantalised into discovering more about the greater complexities and subtleties of human psychology – male as well as female – in response to the vicissitudes of fate.

Shahrazad plays the part of an Arabian Penelope, delaying her fate by weaving an endless tapestry of stories. She does not unpick her work, however, but lets it grow. From the vast store in her memory, she holds his curiosity, wins her reprieve and, through her heroic practice, vindicates her sex.

There is a paradox here, because so many of the stories told by Shahrazad in *Alf Layla wa Layla,* the *Tales of a Thousand and One Nights* reiterate the frame story's message that women are not to be trusted. Women's wiles (Arabic has words for this danger: *makr* and *kayd*) know no end – or do they?

For the Sultan is not alone in his plight: his brother Shahzenan, the Sultan of Great Tartary in other versions of Sanarkard, has also found his wife in flagrante with a black slave from the kitchens. The insult to his honour struck a deeper wound than the blow to his heart. Instantly, with one stroke of his scimitar, he cut off both the lovers' heads and threw their bodies out of the window. He then quit his country and his throne in his misery and set out on his travels. Visiting his brother, Shahriyar, the Sultan of the Indies, he comes across by chance even more riotous disorder in his harem; this accidental discovery has wonderfully rallied Shahzenan's spirits.

The beautiful (human) wife of a jinn takes advantage of his siesta to seduce the two royal brothers, and demands rings from each of them to add to her string of trophies Robert Smirke 1806).

The two brother-widowers commiserate and complain together and set out to roam the world, abandoning fame and fortune to live quiet lives of sorrow in obscurity. But settling down in a meadow by the shore, they see a huge jinn materialise out of the sea like a waterspout: on his head he is carrying a glass box, loaded with four padlocks, which when he puts it down and opens it reveals a beautiful young woman inside. The two kings hide in terror, climbing up a tree; they overhear him say how he stole her on her wedding day, and made her his wife. She settles his massive head in her lap, and as soon as he falls asleep, extricates herself and solicits the two kings, whom she has spied in their hiding place. She demands that they make love to her. Or she will wake her master. When they give in, she takes a ring from each of them in trophy and adds them to the string – she has already won ninety-eight in the translations, or 570 in the Arabic *Nights*. Her lust and treachery reinforce the brothers' opinion of the wicked *makr* of the female sex, and Shahriyar's vengeance – his serial marriages and murders – merely mirrors what women do if given a chance (*Così fan tutte*).

Although the narrator of this frame story allows no chink of doubt as to the truth of the brothers' experiences, it is possible that the Sultan and his brother have gone down into that dark rage that Shakespeare later dramatises in Othello's murderous jealousy and in Leontes's fury against his wife Hermione in *The Winter's Tale*. It is Shahrazad's role in the *Nights* to clear this anger and remove the rationale for the men's hatred. Her stories will gradually introduce maltreated wives, subjugated daughters, faithful female lovers, clever and courageous slave girls, courageous loving mothers, intelligent teachers, loyal sisters and devoted peris or fairies in an increasingly shining procession of women: refracting the virtues of the storyteller herself and her audience – but not so undilutedly or obviously that her purpose shows too much. By the end, the reader, like the Sultan, can agree that she deserves to live and that her stories should be inscribed in a book in letters of gold – the book we readers are holding in our hands, even if the letters are not always written in gold.

Within the stories-inside-stories, several tales dramatise other protagonists saved by storytelling. These 'ransom tales' include the tales told within the two opening cycles of 'The Merchant and the Genie' and 'The Fisherman and the Genie', and many others later in which the narrators subdue their enemies by fascination, like legendary snake charmers. Characters thrive on stories, and their accounts of their woes (for woes they most often are) nourish us, the listeners and readers who, like Shahriyar, will be lifted from our misogynist – and misanthropic – depression. Negativity will be overcome and unexpected possibilities will open before us. For in the event none of the woes matters – in the classic happy ending sometimes (but not always) provided, Shahrazad's sister Dunyazad marries Shahzenan, and Shahrazad herself presents Shahriyar with the three children to whom, unnoticed by her groom, she has given birth during her three or so years under sentence of death. This conclusion, in all its preposterous, cruel unlikelihood, accords of course with the fairytale conventions of the kind of stories Shahrazad herself knows and has been so busy spellbinding him with, and it still has the power to work its charm of release and contentment on the reader.

When I was young I found the scene in the cruel Sultan's bedroom a picture of the world, and the two sisters' conspiracy, with Dunyazad urging her elder sister Shahrazad to tell her a story, seemed to me the fullest metaphor for love against death, expressed through the alliance of girls against men in power over them, and ultimately for imagination over experience. That dot dot dot which intervenes between one break of day and the next night, that ellipsis which the French rightly call *points de suspension*, packs all the excitement of an unknowable future that is nevertheless thrillingly and inevitably round the corner.

The power of stories to forge destinies has never been so memorably and sharply put as it is in this cycle, in which the blade of the executioner's sword lies on the storyteller's neck: the *Arabian Nights* present the supreme case for storytelling because Shahrazad wins her life through her art. 'Her stories are white magic,' writes the novelist Naguib Mahfouz, speaking through the character of Shahriyar. 'They open up worlds that invite reflection.'

Shahrazad echoes the actions of Esther in the Bible, in her role as advocate for her fellows; Esther speaks to another tyrant, Ahasuerus, to save her people, while Shahrazad acts on behalf of women. But does a threat lurk inside the salvific purpose: is there an implication, when Shahrazad pleads with her father to let her marry the Sultan, that if she fails, she will avenge her predecessors? Is she a Judith, too, who seduced Holofernes in order to assassinate him, the enemy of her people, the Jews?

A related tale, found in some recensions of the *Nights*, dramatises a variant on the story: a king called Saba takes a virgin bride every week and kills her. No motive is given – he is a prototype serial killer, an ogre, a Bluebeard. He then marries Bilqis, daughter of his vizier and a genie, and does not realise that she, too, is a jinniya; she turns the table on the bloodthirsty king, and does away with him. Solomon's messenger bird, the hoopoe, brings back news of this exploit when he reports that a great queen rules in the south; Bilqis is her name, and in these Middle Eastern legends, Jewish as well as Arab and Persian, she is the Queen of Sheba, her kingdom is Saba, and she has the suspect nether parts (ass's hooves, shaggy legs?) of a non-human creature. Mahfouz picks up on the ambiguity of a wife's relation with such a husband in his stories, *Arabian Nights & Days*: his heroine, Shahrzad [*sic*], is unhappy. 'Whenever he [Shahriyar] approaches me,' she tells her father in despair, 'I breathe the smell of blood.'

In the literature of the Middle East, *'aja'ib* – meaning marvels, wonders, astonishing things – describes a genre that ranges from fantastic travel yarns to metaphysical myths. *Alf Layla wa-Layla* contains wonders of all kinds on this narrative spectrum, and aims to produce precisely that condition of '*ajab* – astonishment – in the reader and listener. Dinarzade gives us our cue when she exclaims each dawn at the splendour of her sister's tale, and Shahrazad then counters that she knows another, even more astonishing. These exchanges between them, with the Sultan concurring with Dunyazad's desire to hear more, provide a musical refrain that cadences the flow. (Some of the early European readers found it repetitious, and several translators dropped the interruption.) When someone in the *Nights* wants to convey how astonishing his – or her – story has been, they sometimes reach for an extreme image: 'If you inscribed [this tale] with a needle in the corner of the eye, it would give matter for reflection to those who can understand its lesson.' The extended metaphor raises shivers as it searches out an area of ultimate sensitivity, but it also works with the symbolism of the eye, as the organ of discernment and a vehicle of power. The story earns its place among sacred, apotropaic texts and the ranks of amulets and talismans: like an Egyptian *wadjet* eye or the eye of Fatima inscribed with sacred formulae, it can protect against the evil eye.

The experience of reading the stories and reflecting upon them is open-ended; surprise is an essential trait, but as we, the audience, quickly learn that surprises must be sprung, it becomes more difficult for the story to catch us off guard. The narrator is put on her mettle by the expectation: we find ourselves in the position of the Sultan with his jaded appetites. So when a story takes yet another imaginative leap and brings about the desired effect of *ajab*, the pleasure becomes more intense: this is a literature that intends to produce open mouths, shaken heads and inward chuckles. Hyperbole, wild coincidence, arbitrary patterning and illogical chains of cause and effect, all contribute.

As in a Borgesian library, the arabesque structures ramify in infinite recession, offering numerous repeats and recurrent motifs, but this repetition – the recurring formulae as well as the repeated plots and characters – opens the book up to the listener/reader's transference and hence identification. This 'openness as self-foundation', as the Japanese scholar Etsuko Aoyagi writes in *The Arabian Nights and Orientalism*, is a basic principle of fairytale, a genre which does not explore individual psychology or interiority. The word 'arabesque' was first applied to Moorish decoration in Spain in the seventeenth century and evokes an ornamental, branching line. Unlike Hogarth's 'line of beauty' and its sinuous symmetry, the arabesque intrinsically involves a pattern efflorescing on all sides, hence the term's meaning in ballet, when it invokes a pose with one leg and both arms fully outstretched. Though arabesque has not become an aesthetic term as widely understood as 'grotesque' or 'carnivalesque', a figural relationship does exist between it and the structure of the *Nights*. Endlessly generative and cyclical, arabesque embodies vitality, resourcefulness and the dream of plenitude (no surface left bare) towards which the frame story and the ransom tales themselves are moving.

The stories in the book are not confined by the texts they inhabit, or by the nights over which they are told. They form a book, but also a genre which is still changing, still growing. The tales spill out from the covers of the volumes in which they appear, in different versions and translations, and escape from the limits of time that the narrative struggles to impose. They keep generating more tales, in various media, themselves different but alike: the stories themselves are shape-shifters.

II

Like one of the genies who stream out of a jar in a pillar of smoke, *Alf Layla wa-Layla,* the *Arabian Nights,* or the *Tales of a Thousand and One Nights,* has taken many forms and has answered to many masters. Now in this version, now in that, it has no known author or named authors, no settled shape or length, no fixed table of contents, no definite birth-place or linguistic origin (India, Persia, Iraq, Syria and Egypt, have all contributed since the earliest vestiges of such tales were found in the ninth century). Late antique myth forms one deep layer of the palimpsest (the Greek *Romance of Alexander,* in the second or third century BC, features many motifs that will appear in the *Nights* – including one of the earliest examples of a flying vehicle, thought out in practical detail); the stories strike frequent echoes of the Bible and the Koran. The sacred folklore of the three world religions that flourished in the eastern Mediterranean creates another stratum: stories carried by pilgrims, traders and crusaders, criss-crossing by land and sea, and the bustling culture of political and economic centres constellate into the layers nearest the surface.

As different stones and fossils from aeons of geological strata are tumbled pell-mell on to a beach by a landslide, the stories contain traces of the Babylonian Epic of Gilgamesh, and of Indian, Egyptian, Greek,

Latin, Russian and Turkish myths floating in the ocean of the streams of story, all of which have contributed plots, motifs, tone and literary forms. Allusions to analogous story cycles as well as to individual tales are sprinkled here and there before the book takes shape. There are however three principal streams flowing into the cycle in Arabic: Persian sources have nourished it: for example, Shahrazad's name, and those of the Sultan and his brother – Shahriyar and Shahzenan – allude to the Sassanian dynasty and are congruent with Shah, as in 'Shah of Persia'; from Persia also come the beautiful and elaborate fairy romances and journeys to enchanted territories like 'The Tale of Camar al-Zaman and Princess Badoura'. Secondly, the culture of medieval Baghdad, when the city was at the height of its wealth and learning, provides another identifiable seam – Harun al-Rashid, the legendary ruler in that heyday, haunts some of these stories, with his restless curiosity and his hunger for more marvellous things to think about. And thirdly, Egypt, with its capital Cairo in the Mameluke period, provides the ambience of innumerable tales, characterised by powerful enchantments wrought by jinn and often lodged in goods, and by low-life 'rogue' and comic episodes.

Homo narrans observes no ethnic divisions, and has more than one god before him; like Grimms' folk tales, which have a specific history in German literature and yet derive from other cultures and have migrated far and wide, the *Arabian Nights* present a polyvocal anthology of world myths, fables and fairy tales. But the book is also a masterwork of Arabic literature, distinctively arranged and told, with a flavour that is unmistakably its own.

The stories form a shaped book with an overarching plot, created by the frame story of Shahrazad and by certain powerfully sustained themes: alongside the wiles of women there is the injustice of tyrants, as well as the caprices of destiny, the perplexity of desire and the power of love, luck in money, and its opposite, misfortune. The book has commanded audiences everywhere, but its status is dubious, especially in its cultures of origin, where, rather surprisingly, the tales were for most of their existence not as highly appreciated as in Europe. One of the first references to them, in the work of al-Masudi, a tenth-century scholar, uses the phrase *Alf khurafas*, meaning a thousand trifles, tall stories, enjoyable but not worth serious attention. The *Nights* continued to be considered popular trash, written in an impure Arabic beneath the attention of proper literati; and as pulp fiction, the cycles of stories were excluded from the classical Arabic canon. In spite of numerous allusions to the Prophet, quotations and echoes of the Koran, and exemplary characters such as the brilliant and pious slave girl Tawaddud, the stories represented too colourful a spectacle of magic and jinn, pleasure, transgression and amorality, to be found orthodox or respectable, and have never reached high status in their countries of origin. This attitude only began to change in the mid-nineteenth century, since when some of the most eminent writers in Arabic (Mahfouz, Tayeb Salih, Gamal el-Ghitan, Radwa Ashour, Elias Khoury, Hanan Al-Shaykh) have also taken up the style and structure of the *Nights*.

The stories exist in a tangle of styles and a polyphony of vocal registers: poetry and prose mingle; high-flown court lyrics from the Persian tradition will interrupt a comedy. These passages of poetry act as rhythmic markers to the unfolding story, slowing it down like an aria in opera, and adding emotional accents to the events described (cursing, blessing, praises of the beloved). They also recall the world outside the story, bringing in voices from the larger culture to which the audience belongs. Such mise-en-abyme effects, as one narrator within a story picks up from another, dizzyingly plunge the reader from one level to another, sometimes at three or four or more removes from the voice of Shahrazad herself. The extravagant acrobatics and vertiginous flights of language and metaphor, the ingenious plying of action and reversal, does not so much suspend disbelief as bring the impossible into embodied life, and – the tales persuade us – the fantastic appears before our mind's eye.

The huge narrative wheel of the *Arabian Nights* parades the variety and ingenuity of narrative forms: proverbial anecdotes, riddles, lyric songs, love poems, epigrams and jokes lift the simple unfolding of the fable or fairy tale; it spins out erotic incidents, bawdy scenes, cross-dressed encounters, and devices such as that perennial comic subterfuge, often adopted by Shakespeare, of the bed trick. Magic flights and spells and fumigations and potions bring dreams – and disasters – at the whim of capricious powers. Spells and enchantments, soul and body migration, possession and disorientation give the tales their fantastic character, but also represent a vision of psychology, human volition and interdependency. Young women are changed into dogs, young men are turned half to stone, princes into apes and parrots and ugly beasts: the human shape is not constant, and souls can be spirited away to inhabit other forms. Hosts of genies (jinn) and fairies (peri) and other magical creatures (marids, afrits) appear and determine the action; they can fly to the zenith and dive to the depths of the sea. If rewards fall at random, so do punishments. Curses work. Luck holds, sometimes. Lessons are hard to draw, and often dubious. Cruelty and violence erupt at every turn, heads are lopped off, the earth opens and reveals buried treasure or swallows the unwary; kings practise summary justice, viziers plot and deceive, sinister 'magians' – the alchemists and sorcerers of the *Nights* – have designs on innocent young heroes, beggars become kings and dewy young brides turn out to be deep-dyed in the dark arts of sorcery. There is really no rhyme or reason for the unfolding of the plots. When a motive drives the action, envy often rules. Besides envy, lust is the principal catalyst.

The stories do not obey internal rules about character, motive, verisimilitude or plot structure; they do not easily fit existing theories about fiction, history or psychology. Their excesses of emotion, desultory and extreme violence, twists of fate and improbable outcomes, seem to flout the generally accepted order of things. This makes them exciting, alarming and compelling: why is one young woman, with every sign of reluctance and remorse, beating two bitches every evening till the blood runs? Why have all three wandering holy men, the three dervishes or kalenders, lost an eye? The inventions in the tales remain utterly fantastic and have an eerie compulsion: the magnetic mountain draws every nail from a ship that falls by ill fate within its sphere of attraction, and reduces it to splinters; the giant bird, the Rukh (or Roc), breakfasts daily on two Bactrian camels; in the frozen cities of past glorious civilisations, everyone is turned to stone and heaped in riches; and the dead queen with wide open eyes of mercury lies on a bier guarded by automata which slice off the head of anyone daring to steal the jewels that cover her body.

Once you start reading, the telling itself, as Shahrazad sets one story inside another, acts like metre and rhyme in poetry: your mind rushes ahead before you can put up resistance (just like the Sultan). Given the intricacy of the tales, as you lose yourself in the labyrinth, the prosody resembles something fiendishly patterned, more *terza rima* than heroic couplets, so it is interesting that one of the most exacting forms of all, the Malaysian pantoum, is based on Arabic lyric patterning. Also, though the book collages so many different materials and forms of literature, it does in the end – like a very long and complicated puzzle – come out. Shahrazad's tales gradually move on from the virulent, complacent cynicism of the frame story, and of many earlier tales too, towards a politics of love and justice that opens the cruel Sultan's eyes to another vision of humanity and to his responsibilities as a ruler.

Causality in the *Nights* breaks laws of science and plausibility; fate rules according to its arbitrary logic, incarnate in its sinister or benevolent agents – jinn, sorcerers, peris. The hero will forget the prohibition, and his destiny, as ordained, will take its course (in 'The Tale of the Second Dervish', the prince will have his eye put out). The inevitable will happen, however long and forked the journey towards it, and its unfolding will heighten the otherworldly atmosphere that provokes astonishment. Oracles decree a future that cannot be thwarted: several tales turn on human attempts to prevent the fulfilment of such prophecies (three men are warned they will meet Death under a tree and indeed, when they dig up buried treasure there, they kill one another; Chaucer reimagines the story in the Pardoner's Tale, as does B. Traven's *Treasure of the Sierra Madre*, filmed by John Huston). However deep the beloved child is hidden from the death that has been foretold, however far the doomed victim runs, the appointment with fate will be kept. Kismet surpasses the Greek *moirai* in fatality, shows even less mercy, and never explains, unlike the Olympians who always argue their position. The tales also break with the narrative conventions of romance and fairytale, which one might expect them to obey. Even a blessed youngest son, for all his virtue and courage, will not be spared (as in the story of 'Judar and his Brothers').

Jorge Luis Borges took his cue from the nested boxes and self-mirroring regression of the *Nights*. The great reader and fabulist once commented that all great literature becomes children's literature; he was thinking of the *Odyssey, Don Quixote, Gulliver's Travels* and *Robinson Crusoe* as well as the *Tales of A Thousand and One Nights*, but his paradox depends on the deep universal pleasures of storytelling for young and old: stories like those in the *Arabian Nights* place the audience in the position of a child, at the mercy of the future, of life and its plots, just as the protagonists of the *Nights* are subject to unknown fates, both terrible and marvellous.

III

Only twenty-two manuscripts containing stories from the *Nights* have survived. One collection, now in the Arcadian Library, London, gives a powerful sense of the way the stories circulated: 30 octavo notebooks, written in a variety of hands, with a sprinkling of red-letter headings, the boards have been softened by handling, the pages tatterred and torn, in some places patched and edged – these copies have been read to bits. As with paper money after long use, a smell of human hands and breath rises from these working copies – they have every look of a professional storyteller's precious resources. On the inside cover at the back of several volumes, sums and a kind of tally appear to have been kept: the number of listeners? Receipts?

As Florence Dupont has shown so fascinatingly in *The Invention of Literature*, some of the greatest works of human imagination were created as texts to be performed and heard. They belong to written literature, but their making precedes print and multiple copies, and their form as well as their transmission took shape in relation to audiences, not silent readers. The passage from oral to written and back again is much more complex than a simple contrast between literature and orature. *The Arabian Nights*, before their publication, can be placed in this context. The stories did not need to be read from the page to become known.

A notebook from a bundle of manuscripts containing stories from *Alf Layla wa-Layla* (*One Thousand and One Nights*) shows signs of much loving handling – of reading and re-reading with the owners' annotations – possibly for storytelling to an audience? (part of 'The Story of Ghanim ibn Ayyub, the Slave of Love', Turkey, 17th c.)

The stories flowed with the traffic across the frontier of Islam and Christendom, a frontier that was more porous, commercially and culturally, than military and ideological history will admit. The first translation, by the French orientalist Antoine Galland, came out in 1704–12. He is the first named author of the *Nights* as we know them, and his publication is the first print edition of *Alf Layla wa-Layla* – surprising historical facts which give a glimpse into the crossed destinies of the book. His version, urbane, polished, witty, assured the triumph of the oriental tale in eighteenth-century Europe.

Galland began work on what would become the *Arabian Nights* with a manuscript of 'Sinbad', which he translated in 1701; fatefully but erroneously, he went on to include the merchant's adventures in the *Nights*. *Les mille et une nuit* [*sic*] appeared in four volumes in the course of 1704, with another two following the year after, and a seventh in 1706. As was customary in the salons of the *précieuses* and their successors, the scholar-author dedicated his opus to a great lady, the marquise d'O, who was in the train of the duchesse de Bourgogne. These were stories in which women mattered, and they consequently mattered – and appealed – to women, a quality which caused some trouble in their standing as literature.

This French version was swiftly followed by anonymous, chapbook or journal versions in English, the 'Grub Street' versions, called *Arabian Nights' Entertainments,* which take Galland for their text. The stories began appearing in 1705, and continued to flourish: 445 instalments, three times weekly, over three years, were published in the journal, the *London News,* from 1723 to 1726.

In both countries, oriental fever swept through the salons and coffee houses, the broadsheet publishers and the theatrical impresarios; the book fired a train of imitations, spoofs, *turqueries,* oriental tales, extravaganzas, pantomimes, and mauresque tastes in dress and furniture: the sofa, the brocade dressing gown, coffee itself. No hero could be called Damon: instead he must be Zemir; Phyllis and Corinna were now Zelima and Badoura. The pages of *Le Mercure galant* in Paris and *Parker's Penny Post* in London sparkled with the tales and the 'odd out-of-the-way Titles' of their adulatory imitators. The diaspora of the *Arabian Nights* does in fact resemble the triumphant progress of coffee, as it multiplies and metamorphoses from brass thimbles of thick dark syrup, in Damascus and Istanbul and Cairo, to today's US and UK hybrids (skinny latte, macchiato, et al.). So it is rather neat that Galland also published, in 1699, a treatise in praise of coffee, one of the first if not the first of its kind.

Antoine Galland (1646–1715) was a scholar, an antiquarian, numismatist and orientalist – he had a gift for languages and travelled for long periods in the Middle East, where he was collecting manuscripts, coins and other antiquities for his French employers. On his first journey, he was attached to the mission to the Sublime Porte of 1670–75, in the train of the marquis de Nointel, and was under specific instructions to look for early Greek documents that would throw light on theological issues, especially the doctrine of the Real Presence which was coming under attack from the Jansenists in France. It is an oddity that while no doubt Galland brought back much valuable Byzantine learning, his most significant acquisition by far was the three volumes of manuscripts comprising *Alf Layla wa-Layla* in Arabic, Syrian in origin and variously dated to the fourteenth or fifteenth century which contains the 'core' body of the *Arabian Nights*, thirty-four and a half stories (it breaks off halfway through Camar al-Zaman and Princess Badoura). This manuscript is the oldest yet discovered and is now in the Bibliothèque Nationale (there may have been a fourth volume, but it has gone missing). The tales it contains have done far more to shape the modern landscape of spirits, the workings of the supernatural and divine providence, than any writings of the Greek Church Fathers about Eucharistic matters.

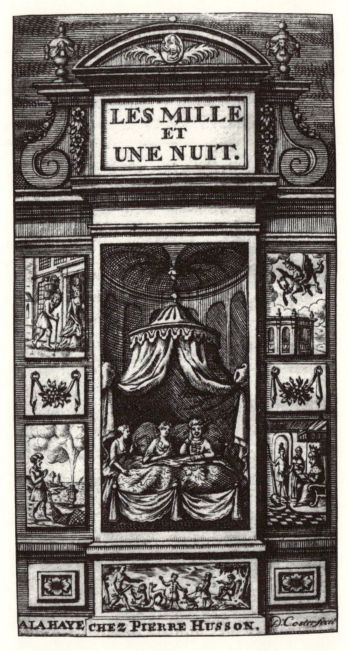

Shahrazad in bed with the vengeful Sultan keeps him enthralled, as night after night, at the prompting of her sister Dunyazad, she tells another story. Vignettes by D. Coster illustrate (clockwise, left to right) 'The Fisherman and the Genie', 'The Porter and the Three Ladies of Baghdad', 'The Ebony Horse', and 'The Greek King and Doctor Douban'. Antoine Galland, *Les Mille et une nuit* (The Hague, 1728–30).

Galland became an admirer and an advocate of Middle Eastern culture, returning to the region for two more long periods, the third lasting from 1679 to 1688, during which he continued to deepen his knowledge of Turkish, Arabic, Persian and Modern Greek, and gathered more antiques and manuscripts. When the great orientalist Barthélemy d'Herbelot died, Galland completed the vast encyclopaedia, the *Bibliothèque orientale*, for publication in 1697, and his preface to *Les mille et une nuit* shows that he saw the tales as continuing the work of illuminating oriental culture and thought to the West. He also started a course in Arabic at the Sorbonne (although nobody enrolled for his first classes). By contrast, from a literary point of view, he had chosen *le bon moment*, for the fashion for oriental romancing had a fair wind. The courtly embellished fairy tales by Jean de La Fontaine, Charles Perrault, Marie-Catherine d'Aulnoy, and others in the 1690s, reached for exotic settings – mauresque and arabesque – in the first decades of the eighteenth. Although Perrault does not say that Barbe-bleue is a Saracen in so many words, the earliest chapbook woodcuts pick up the echoes between the implacable and much-married Bluebeard and Sultan Shahriyar, and provide him with a turban and a scimitar, while the tradition was established, by the mid-eighteenth century, that his latest bride's name was Fatima. The abbé Bignon, a friend of Galland's, immediately gave his Beauty and the Beast names out of the *Mille et une nuit*.

Other orientalists and writers were soon busy creating their own 'translations' of oriental tales, and Galland took umbrage when his publisher combined two of these newfangled stories (by Pétis de la Croix) under Galland's name to make up an eighth volume of *Les mille et une nuit*. Then in 1709, a friend of his, another traveller in the Levant, Paul Lucas, introduced him to a cultivated Syrian living in Paris, a Christian – a Maronite – called Hanna Diab, who knew French, Arabic and Turkish and had a large repertoire of stories. Galland took notes of thirteen more from Hanna's oral recitations and gradually brought out another four volumes, the last two – Vols XI and XII – appearing in 1717 two years after his death.

This first European version of the *Arabian Nights* reads as a sophisticated, suavely romanced and ornamented fiction in line with fairy tales and romances by Galland's contemporaries, especially Marie-Catherine d'Aulnoy and Madame de Murat. The resemblances of style are marked: the frieze-like structural repetitiousness, exaggerated effects of splendour and luxury, heightened passions and other manners of the arabesque-baroque. D'Aulnoy declared in the preface to her collection *Histoires des fées* of 1712 that the stories came to her from 'une vieille esclave arabe' (an old Arab slave woman). Whether she was following Galland in identifying a real-life source, the equivalent of Hanna Diab, and had written up her stories, or offering a fashionable warranty for her own invented extravaganzas, in order to authenticate them as traditional, cannot be settled.

Galland transformed his sources, his fluent prose adding *politesse* and polish. He does not attempt the strongly flavoured shifts in tone and register of the original, which was not esteemed in its native places either. Bawdy and smut are left out altogether – none of the rude laughter here which later erupts at pantomime *Ali Baba*s or *Aladdin*s, nor the frank dealing with sexuality, as reflected, for example, in the mischievous 'naming of parts', in the bath scene in 'The Porter and the Three Ladies of Baghdad', or the designs the evil magician has on 'Aladdin of the Beautiful Moles' or those that Hasan of Basra's mother fears another Persian enchanter has on her son. Galland cleans up the bathing scene and includes neither of the last two stories in his translation and avoids explicit allusions to homosexuality. He expurgated the eroticism that heightens many passages in the original tales, and after readers had objected to the refrains that closed each session at dawn, he took out these crucial returns to the scene in the bedroom, where Shahrazad is telling the story to her sister and the Sultan. Galland also decided that the outbursts of poetry held up the narrative.

Galland's writerly interference does not stop there. The most popular tales of all, the ones which have since become synonymous with the *Nights*, excerpted again and again in children's books and retold on stage and screen the world over, such as 'Aladdin and the Wonderful Lamp' and 'Ali Baba and the Forty Thieves', might be his compositions, concocted of pomegranates and ebony, damask and jasmine, to pay a *précieux* tribute to the plots, motifs and style of Arabic storytelling. Scholars are now pretty much agreed that 'Aladdin' and these others are 'orphan tales', as Mia Gerhardt dubbed them in her fine study of the *Nights* of 1963; no decisive evidence, one way or another, has yet been found. Some of these orphans, like 'Aladdin', may have no Arabic literary parents: the earliest Arabic version of 'Aladdin' shows clear signs of being back-translated from Galland's French, so most of the leading scholars in the field are now fairly certain that he was their progenitor. The signs of bricolage are there: 'Aladdin' pieces and patches many elements from different tales in the book, especially from 'the true Aladdin' ('Aladdin of the Beautiful Moles') and 'Hasan of Basra'. Other scholars more bluntly call the poor orphans 'bastards', illegitimate cuckoos thrust into the nest of the *Nights* by Galland, who was taking to extremes the seventeenth-century practice of imitation or *belle infidèle* translation.

Yet the plot of 'Aladdin', which upholds the rise of a worthless orphan boy to princely fortune, fame and power, oddly replicates the fate of the book itself, as does the story of Morgiana the plucky slave girl in 'Ali Baba', for she too marries up; it is as if Galland were unconsciously confessing his own craft and luck.

Other much-loved stories, such as 'The Tale of Prince Ahmed and the Fairy Peri Banou', were composed from the live storytelling of Hanna Diab several years after Galland made his notes (he took time out to finish a translation of the Koran). A comparison shows how richly he embroiders them for the print versions. In this independent fashion, Galland set the trend which made the *Arabian Nights* into a kind of pattern book for later writers, artists, and film-makers. Borges defended this *belle infidèle* approach to translation in his magnificent essay, 'The Translators of the Thousand and One Nights': 'I think that the reader should enrich what he is reading. He should misunderstand the text; he should change it into something else.'

'Prince Ahmed and Fairy Peri Banou' has inspired marvellous interpretations since it first appeared in print in Galland's volumes, including the extraordinary 1926 silhouette film of Lotte Reiniger, but it is still considered inauthentic. (Neither the Miquel-Bencheikh edition of 2003–5, nor Malcolm Lyons's recent translation for Penguin, the first full English version from Arabic since John Payne's of 1882–84, include it. 'Aladdin' and 'Ali Baba' are often now relegated to an appendix. A similar cordon sanitaire keeps out other 'orphan tales', rather haphazardly.

Some scholars feel cheated by Galland's innovations – and apparent deception – but, on the whole, he is no longer condemned as an arch *traduttore-traditore*; instead he is emerging as a classic writer of independent significance to stand alongside his much more famous contemporaries. However much he interpolated and altered his sources, brought in his own values and his society's norms of decorum and, in the interest of armchair ethnography, underlined the local colour, customs and sights, Antoine Galland wrought a magnificent fiction for the West. He wrote with gaiety and grace, his enjoyment of his material glowing from the page. Many of the liberties he took offer us a model for the new global fiction of today, travelling texts made in the polyvocal echo chamber of literature beyond national boundaries, cultural taboos and different languages: the result of interactions and crossings between peoples, and their mutual curiosity. His stance inaugurates an ideal Enlightenment vision, extolling the virtues of openness, generosity and tolerance, and discovering them in an oriental guise. As one of his editors, Jean-Paul Sermain, writes, 'The invaluable contribution of Galland will have been that he not only emancipated himself from these conventions and managed to open up a double front, ethical and poetic, but also that he associated this change with Arab literature and the Orient.'

The subsequent story of the *Nights* is almost as tangled as the tales themselves. Later manuscripts were found and edited and have become the basis of new translations; these are fuller than Galland's but not as stuffed as some of the Victorian and *fin-de-siècle* editions, which excited heady orientalist fantasists to add their own material.

Two founding editions were created – in India – for the purposes of teaching Arabic: the so-called 'Calcutta I' in 1814–18, and 'Calcutta II' which appeared in 1839–42. The first derived from an Egyptian manuscript of the eighteenth century, and was packed with additional stories, in an attempt to eke out the required *1001 Nights*.

In the Victorian era, adventurer-explorers such as Edward W. Lane and Richard Burton, both ardent Arabophiles, produced translations that reflected their own attachments. Lane's, published in 1838–41, followed close on the heels of his ethnographical description of contemporary Cairo (*The Manners and Customs of the Modern Egyptians*, 1835); Lane added a huge apparatus of notes on Arab society (some of it densely researched and nostalgic, other parts rather fanciful). The three-volume set of 1850 includes 600 engravings based on Lane's experiences in Cairo; my copy, which came originally from my great-grandmother's library, is one of the few books that I've owned and read since I was a child, and though it is pretty fustian, with Lane tranquillising so much of the book's agitated emotions and adventures, it is readable to a degree that Richard Burton's lurid and archaising version, made fifty years later, never reaches.

Wilful translations have been an intrinsic, lumpy element in the *Nights'* history, a history that with its range, geographical, linguistic and picaresque, echoes some of the tales' own wandering vicissitudes. Translators like Lane expurgated, and Burton fantasticated, because the *Nights* have been treated throughout with an insouciant liberty. Burton's version is an almost Chattertonian exercise in auncient tongues, prolix and rococo, and is truffled with lore (much of it salacious, earning Burton his nickname, 'Dirty Dick'). Burton depended on John Payne's translation, which had come out in a tiny limited edition and was gleefully absorbed into Burton's rather unreliable and weird performance, without much credit being given to Payne, who was a friend.

Yet throughout the plethora of recensions and variations, Galland remained a blueprint. The poet Powys Mathers (1892–1939) produced his English version in 1923 from the lengthy and flamboyant French translation of J.C.V. Mardrus, which had appeared in 1899–1904. Mardrus (1868–1949), a *fin-de-siècle* aesthete and a friend of André Gide, had been born in Cairo in 1868 and spoken Arabic in his childhood. He claimed to be using Arabic sources, but the many traces of Galland throughout reveal how much he relied on his predecessor. Mardrus also followed Galland's example by introducing new stories, and some of his contributions have a decidedly decadent and Symbolist character, striking the French Orientalist note of Gustave Flaubert in *Salammbô,* and of Oscar Wilde in *Salome,* which relished Arabic images: a woman's breasts can be round like pomegranates, her sex like 'a husked sesame', her neck 'a cake for a king', her teeth 'a row of pearls set in coral'; lips are sugared and skin perfumed; fountains play and breezes lift the blossom in the inner courtyards of palaces; the local market overflows with scented oils and waters, ambergris, musk and rosemary. Young men's beauty can put the moon to shame, while the moon's beauty makes lovers ache. Mardrus gave rein to his fantasy, but he was not alone in enhancing the book's eroticism: in several languages, writers grasped the opportunity these images and scenes gave them – and often took liberties with the lush mode of the arabesque.

This languid, heady and sexy atmosphere, well captured by the *Yellow Book* prose of Mathers after Mardrus, epitomises the Western vision of a magical lost kingdom of pleasure, beyond classical and humanist rationality.

Writing this book, I have drawn on several different editions and translations, in the languages I can read (see Bibliography). I do not know Arabic (although I spoke it as a child, unfortunately nobody encouraged me to keep it up, and besides, I never could read it). However, the history of the *Nights'* reception makes its European fortunes very important, as I hope to show in the course of this book. The most recent *Arabian Nights* in English has been translated by the eminent Arabist Malcolm Lyons, and is invaluable in providing a lucid, full and scrupulous rendering of the vast array of the tales in the Calcutta II edition. It came out in 2009, when I was already deep in my research, and my favourite version of the *Nights* – the one I have used more than any others – is the French Pléiade edition of 2005–6 by Jamel Eddine Bencheikh and André Miquel. Their narrative style is ravishing, subtle and fluid, suave and carefree, light in touch or keyed up when desirable; their annotations marvellously learned and full of humanity, and they radiate unselfconscious delight in the stories. This is an incomparable account of the *1001 Nights*, and it would not be a mistake to translate it into English, notes and all, as Galland's version was three hundred years ago.

With this remarkable history of translation – of migration – between

East and West, the *Arabian Nights* or *Tales of a Thousand and One Nights* presents a unique key to the imaginary processes that govern the symbolism of magic, foreignness and mysterious power in modern culture. And the book's oriental origins, the arabesque interlace of the narrative, its voluptuous, ferocious, even sensational atmosphere, raise the live question of 'orientalism'. Is it possible to propose, as I am trying to do, that this book and the effect the stories had present a different perspective on the interaction of imagination and reason, on the history of intellectual inquiry and scientific invention in Europe, a move towards a reassessment of the exchanges that have taken place between Islamic and Christian, Eastern and Western culture?

IV

From its first appearance in print, between 1704 and 1721, in the French translation of Antoine Galland, the tales mirrored Arab civilisation and *mentalité* for the West, but at the same time communicated a fantastic European dream of Araby. As Robert Irwin vividly discusses in his foundational work, *A Companion to the Arabian Nights* (1994; rev. 2004), the stories convey the motley, mobile, tumultuous, polyglot and polymorphous urban culture of the Levant, which ravelled up different social and linguistic groups and religious allegiances, and conflicted value systems that jostled in a state of perpetual, energetic becoming. But the book's history has been a fabulous muddle, and it is fair to say, without colonialist aggression, that the work that appears in French as *Les mille et une nuit*, and in English, two years later, as *Arabian Nights' Entertainments*, is a hybrid, formed through cross-fertilisation over time between Europe, Asia and the Middle East. Some of the stories circulated before the book's print publication, and plot elements and motifs occur in Boccaccio, Chaucer, Camoëns, Basile, Ariosto and Shakespeare, amongst others. But it is in the eighteenth century that this medieval Arabic story collection became established in Europe as a masterpiece of imagination, inventiveness and wit, and took its place as a supreme fiction. A cycle of stories packed with ancient myths, fairytale romance, fantastic voyages, and comic folklore from all ages, gripped readers during the *siècle des Lumières,* the Enlightenment, when rationality was prized – the most contradictory possible time, one might think, for a book which is a monument to the torrential energies of the irrational.

From the start, in the midst of the enthusiasm, the *Nights* elicited complicated responses, in which horror, sympathy and passion were laced with laughter and irony. Some of its greatest emulators, like Voltaire, undercut their fascination with mockery. In Europe, the craze for the *Nights* met opposition: in Paris, Anthony Hamilton scoffed at their hyperbole and implausibility; in London the Earl of Shaftesbury, writing in 1711, found suspect romances' special popularity with women readers: 'the monstrous tales' excite them 'into a passion for a mysterious Race of black Enchanters: such as of old were said to *creep into Houses*, and *lead captive silly Women*'. His words unconsciously pick up on the Sultan's fears, and it will become more significant, in the history of East–West relations, that Shaftesbury could only understand the alien bogeys in terms of beliefs that enjoyed a long history at home (those black enchanters and Puck-like spirits of mischief).

Shaftesbury's response is typical, because the accepted opposition between rationality and irrationality has led to a customary disowning of magic and its influence and presence, while, partly as a symptom of this refusal to confront the question, popular beliefs in all kinds of magical traditions continue to proliferate. According to a prevalent view, magic processes either belong to a credulous, ignorant, pagan or medieval past, or such tendencies form part of cultures opposed to Western progress – primitive, retrograde cultures in Africa or Asia: voodoo, Islam. Both these assumptions relegate magic to a popular, uneducated cast of mind which will be transformed once the light of reason falls on it. This view underlies the disapproval the book excites in its own countries: in Cairo in 2010, the distinguished novelist and editor Gamal el-Ghitani was threatened by a sharia court for re-issuing a new edition of the Arabic version Bulaq II, first published in 1862.

Between the supernatural, which presumes belief in God and his providence, and the uncanny, which sees inexplicable, dreadful or wonderful things as dream products of the mind and, often, of personal disturbance, the *1001 Nights* opened up a vista of spirits that did not command the religious belief of the European reader. The Victorians dismissed fairies, elves, pixies et al. as belonging to the most primitive stratum of spiritual development, animism (or sent them upstairs to the nursery), but they provided no explanation for their stubborn appeal to some of the most highly philosophical intellects of the century. Coleridge's enraptured response to the capricious motions of fate in the tales, beyond logic, beyond ethics, can be felt in some of his most famous works. The 1817 version of the 'Rime of the Ancient Mariner', for example, strikes the same cold thrill as the *Nights* because it too conveys 'the inadequacy of human morality to comprehend the world in which we live'. Since then, the stories have gathered an ever more dazzling train of admirers

– and imitators: Marcel Proust, Gabriel García Márquez, A.S. Byatt, Salman Rushdie, as well as Borges and Calvino.

In *Stranger Magic*, I want to ask if it is possible to set the *Arabian Nights* in relation to the concerns of modern society and modern consciousness, as they were developing in the age of reason. How do such flights of fancy speak to reason? Shahrazad speaks truth to power, incarnate in the Sultan who wants to cut off her head – can it be said that the work of imagination in the *Nights* does something similar? I want to look without squeamishness at the contemporary uses of enchantment, at the continuing vitality of magic in literature as well as its structural presence in the everyday culture, and the reasons for its persistent survival – which is a source of perplexity, anxiety and even annoyance to some in a scientific, secular society. I also want to unpick a psychological stratagem that has made magic more comfortable for Western audiences: its progressive exoticisation since the eighteenth century through a continuing process of adopting and adapting oriental material. To do this, I explore the way contemporary culture has domesticated, commercialised, and given its consent to manifold expressions of magical thinking, but only designates it as such when it wears foreign dress.

Interest in magic is evidently growing and spreading in popular culture – look at the success of *Harry Potter* or Dan Brown, and at the spread of ideas about channelling, alien abduction, and false memory syndrome. This trend is alarming to most observers, who fear the tide of mumbo-jumbo swamping contemporary thought and dethroning reason and rationality in favour of superstition, barbarism and fanaticism. Can an intellectual position be developed that repositions the value of the magical tradition? For someone like myself, who is irresistibly attracted to myths in all their metamorphoses, from classical tragedy to the *Fortean Times*, from Ovidian scenes of enchanted shape-changing to the demons of Philip Pullman and the hybrid creatures of so many other inspired children's books in the past as well as today – the reason of myth beckons as one of the toughest questions to explore. 'The Reason of Myth' is the title of a key essay by the French classical scholar Jean-Pierre Vernant; before him, Jorge Luis Borges, the supreme performer of metafictional puzzles, who constantly troubles the boundaries between myth and history, truth and invention, declared that the greatest literature displays 'reasoned imagination'.

The oxymoron in Borges's phrase gave me the perspective from which to read the *Arabian Nights* and think about these questions. It did not seem enough to invoke escapism as the reason for the popularity of the *Arabian Nights* in the age of reason. Something more seemed to be at stake. Magic is not simply a matter of the occult or the esoteric, of astrology, wicca, and Satanism; it follows processes inherent to human consciousness and connected to constructive and imaginative thought. The faculties of imagination – dream, projection, fantasy – are bound up with the faculties of reasoning and essential to making the leap beyond the known into the unknown. At one pole (myth), magic is associated with poetic truth, at another (the history of science) with inquiry and speculation. It was bound up with understanding physical forces in nature and led to technical ingenuity and discoveries. Magical thinking structures the processes of imagination, and imagining something can and sometimes must precede the fact or the act; it has shaped many features of Western civilisation. But its influence has been constantly disavowed since the Enlightenment and its action and effects consequently misunderstood.

The issues remain, how do we live with the intrinsic, problematic irrationality of our consciousness? How do we make a helpful distinction between religious adherence and an acknowledgement that myth and magic have their own logic and potential, independent of belief in higher powers? Responding to these questions is the first step towards the ideal of 'reasoned imagination', towards the paradoxical vision granted by 'the necessary angel of earth,/Since in my sight you see the earth again . . .' (Wallace Stevens).

When Borges commented in an essay on the *Arabian Nights*: 'One of the chief events in the history of the West was the discovery of the East', his remark could seem just another reflex of Orientalism in its pejorative, complacent Western form. But could Borges have been making a comment based on historical fact, and one which offers – even demands – a movement towards mutual understanding? Is it possible that Borges's perception throws light on an alternative history to the *fable convenue*, the agreed fable (in Voltaire's phrase), about the conflicted relations between East and West?

'*Alf Layla wa-Layla* [*The Thousand and One Nights*] changed the world', write the editors of a recent book, 'on a scale unrivalled by any other literary text.' *Literary* text, note, rather than religious – the *Nights* would be outclassed by the Bible and the Koran. For while contemporary conflicts shadow the whole re-invigorated attempt to understand the *Arabian Nights*, the immediate and richest 'historical context' of the title remains Edward Said's *Orientalism* (1978), a cult bible of its own, as well as, in some quarters, a candidate for burning. Edward Said's ideas, as they themselves changed and developed since that polemical study, underlie the questions I put in this book, but I hope to give new bearings from the compass of story.

The advent of the *Arabian Nights* in Europe coincided with a period
of intense curiosity about Eastern culture, ranging from the Middle to
the Far East, as the French literary historian, Raymond Schwab, explores
in a monumental but sadly neglected study, *The Oriental Renaissance*
(1950). Schwab celebrates the orientalists who sought out and translated
manuscripts of the East – including Galland, whose biography he also
wrote. Schwab comments, in a wonderful phrase, that enthusiasm for the
East 'multiplied the world', and makes a powerful case for 'the Orient-
as-cause'. Among his cast of mediators, travellers, scholars and translators
are several of the same figures who appear in the history of the *Nights'*
dissemination. But Schwab's book chronicles the passage, in the Western
image of the Orient, from 'disruptive incredulous bedazzlement' to 'a con-
descending veneration'. There is a saddening impoverishment, obviously,
from one image to the other.

I am quoting Edward Said's essay on Schwab's work, where Said praises
both Schwab and Galland for bringing oriental literature to Western
readers. Said sums up the heart of the dilemma when he writes that
Schwab's book, *La Renaissance orientale*, 'is a virtual education in the
meaning of intellectual adventure . . . Schwab does not indict the desire
to know, but it goes wrong with the desire to control and to possess.'
(In general, Said's arguments about Western uses of Eastern literature do
not cohere nearly as ferociously as his detractors would have it.)

Said himself does not discuss the *Arabian Nights* as such in *Orientalism*,
but he does turn his scorn on several of the stories' scholars and translators, notably the English Arabist Edward W. Lane, and indicts them for
fostering prejudice; indeed, the story of the *Nights'* reception is inextri-
cably bound up with views of the Orient. Reading two opposed paths
of interpretation opens the stories: on the one hand, they reveal the
Orient, so called, and can be taken to represent the customs, beliefs and
passions actually held and experienced in the countries where the stories
are set: Iran, present-day Iraq, Egypt, Syria, etc. This approach – or rather
assumption – is the chief spur to Said's furious polemic against Orientalism,
and it has dominated perception of the *Nights* and related Orientalist
literature until now. The opposing way of approaching the tales, which
Hamilton and Voltaire exemplified early on and which was taken up by
many, including Jan Potocki, Calvino, Borges and Angela Carter, relates
to the *Nights* as a genre of dazzling fabulism, laying open infinite possibilities of fantastic invention and fabrication – the begetter of magical
realism. The two modes of reading have been confused at different times,
and dizzy flights of imagination taken for 'true reports', or documentary
evidence.

The *Nights* is a pre-eminent 'travelling' text, as evoked in Said's 1983 study, *The World, the Text and the Critic*. As a book of multiple transformations, putting on different guises and exciting different effects in various circumstances, it reveals how much translations between cultures can alter and even mitigate the costs of protracted and entrenched hostilities. Indeed, in literature, hostilities do not have purchase in a direct or simple way, and the *Nights'* multiple layerings show this. 'The Orient, in modernity,' Amit Chaudhuri comments, 'is not only a European invention but also an Oriental one.' The *Arabian Nights* holds out for scrutiny an extraordinarily productive case of cross-fertilisation, retellings, grafts and borrowings, overwriting, imitation, and dissemination back and forth between Persia, India, Iraq, Turkey, Egypt and Europe, and then back again into its homelands, over an extremely *longue durée*. The very concept of the sequence of narratives – the interlaced tales within the frame of a ransom tale – as well as individual story elements, became global nomads, travelled back and forth, camping and settling until they became indigenous throughout the world of literature.

The cross-fertilisation between our own culture and cultures which have been deemed irrational and unenlightened has been more pervasive and influential than has been acknowledged or understood. The dynamics of 'reverse colonisation', set in motion by the fascination of the Other, have been powerfully at work in many respects which the following chapters will explore. The reasons for this are not confined to exotic strangeness and seductively different mores and values; the attraction arises from encountering much that is revealing about ourselves and that then leads to 'something understood' at home. There is recognition of sameness at work, not only curiosity about difference.

I am not arguing a revisionist line on the political and economic and military relations between Europe and the Turks or the long history of enmity with points further south and east – Islam. But I am suggesting that the *cultural* picture has greater potential for enriching the historical view. Even when military and economic ambitions entrench protracted hostilities, different forms of arts – from literature to architecture – metamorphose in the fission and, as they do so, give a different angle on the enemy: as the Republic of Venice and the Ottomans were living in deep rivalry, erupting frequently into hostility, the most oriental city in Europe learned to make velvet damasks, blow gilded glass, and tell stories of astonishing wonders.

The story of the *Arabian Nights* and its impact is a story of complex attentions, themselves formed by complex historical and social interests, and that has intensified over the last thirty years. In the current state of conflict and flux, with domestic tensions, foreign wars, and also possibilities for change in the Arab world, pursuing the well-rehearsed racial and negative values of the past does not contribute to opening a dialogue; uncovering a neglected story of reciprocity and exchange can make for greater understanding. And one place where the conversation between East and West took a different shape was fiction, especially fabulist stories, packed with wonders, elastic in handling time and space, and plotted according to the different laws of fate and magic.

From its first success, the character of the *Arabian Nights* offered different ways of interpreting the European reader's own experience: on the one hand, it opened vistas of new freedoms – freedoms of form and of fantasy, with consequent effects on political and social imagination; on the other hand, as Shaftesbury's comment about its readers shows, it offered a stratagem of disavowal, by projecting magic, lust and cruelty as unknown, foreign and inimical.

This double dynamic unceasingly propels, sometimes in a single individual's response, both attraction to the stories and repulsion from them. In oriental costume, much could be enjoyed that was otherwise off limits, and the book became a playground for Enlightenment adventurers. An imaginary Orient, stimulated by the *Nights*, profoundly interacted with modernity's most characteristic expressions, cultural and social, even as it was being disparaged and repudiated, falsified and invented.

Reading the *Nights* as a case study in the contact zones of history offers a path towards changing preconceptions about Arabs, Islam, and the history and civilisation of the Middle and Near East. Contact or translation zones may be flashpoints for conflict and indeed fields of protracted oppression, but they are also areas of mingling and interfusion, of a process of Creolisation.

V The shape of this book

The title of this book, *Stranger Magic*, alludes to the *Nights'* emblematic character as a work of fantasy, packed with supernatural and unfamiliar wonders and founded in enchantments. But it also draws attention to the foreignness of many of the enchanters, who have since then shaped the exotic magicians in popular culture – conjurors, mediums, fairy godmothers and goblin kings are estranged in the wake of the *1001 Nights*, and acquire turbans and pointed hats and other Eastern features (is the magician's steeple hat inspired by the dress of dervishes, who play a lively part in the *Nights*?). The title also implies that there is a form of magical thinking, which is 'stranger' not because it is unfamiliar but because it is latent and denied. Confronting its workings in ordinary modern and contemporary processes will make us look stranger to ourselves. Imprinted but lying underneath the fantastic narrative intrigues of the *Nights*, a watermark can be made out which gives meaning to ways of irrational thinking in relation to contemporary experience; this is what is meant by 'representing before our eyes, in an intuitive way, the fact, the interior figure, of the exterior world'.

Overlooked and yet pervasive, magical thinking is structural to naming and language, ideas of self and property, and to visual representation, as the literature of the imagination has long grasped and conveyed. At the same time, the storytelling dynamics of *Alf Layla wa-Layla* are underpinned by a different form of magical thinking. This casts the writer/storyteller first as Shahrazad, whose art prevents harm falling on her own head and on all her sisters, under threat from the Sultan's decree and thus grants the story cycle itself charming powers. But secondly, the *Nights* inspires a way of thinking about writing and the making of literature as forms of exchange across time – dream journeys in which the maker fuses with what is being made, until the artefact exercises in return its own fashioning force. Both of these principles draw away from the prevalent idea of art as mimesis, representing the world in a persuasive, true-to-life way, and emphasise instead the agency of literature. Stories need not report on real life, but clear the way to changing the experience of living it.

Everyone thinks they know the stories (I did, before I began this book). But the tangled history of the *Nights* means that the stories are still not so easy to find in a readable (or portable) form. Some are known far better from stage and screen, pantomime and opera, hearsay, proverbial phrases, the design of boxes of Turkish Delight and hundreds of advertisements for holiday destinations. But many are not read well widely, or even very accessible, so rather than assume knowledge (which I did not have myself), I have written – in highly condensed form – fifteen of the stories for easy reference and interspersed them through the book.

Part I, 'Solomon the Wise King', focuses on enchantments in the stories, the jinn and the peris, their ways, habitat, powers and manifestations; Part II, 'Dark Arts; Strange Gods' explores magicians – particularly the magians, or sorcerers of the *Nights* – and their practices, including alchemy, astrology and dream divination. Attitudes have changed in response to religion and philosophy, and the *Nights* reveal how heterodox magic was exoticised, expelled beyond a boundary, and ascribed to strangers, according to a pattern that also took hold in post-eighteenth-century Europe (Faust is a German citizen, but Darth Vader or Sauron . . .). Recent developments, which include the rise in status of fairytale, as reflected in the success of the *Arabian Nights*, have however recast previous sorcery as shamanic and benevolent. Part III, 'Active Goods', turns to some distinctive loci of magical thinking, as expressed in the *1001 Nights*, and investigates the enchanted fixtures and fittings of a rich trading culture, and correspondences between charmed states and magical thinking in the tales and developments in modern experience. The *Nights* are fairy tales about property, in which things are literally alive and sentient and efficacious. Things talk, and the Ottoman empire became legible through its artefacts. I ask if our contemporary devices bear a relation to other classes of objects which have been ascribed power, such as relics, fetishes and talismans. Is the way things behave in the stories paradoxically illuminating for us, now?

Part IV, 'Oriental Masquerades', turns to the response of writers and other artists to the *Nights* soon after the book's appearance in print. This brings in my second principal argument: that the genre of far-fetched preposterous tale-spinning which the *Nights* represent created a perfect forum for another kind of liberty – of the imagination. The fantasy allowed them to conduct thought experiments – to take off on flights of reason.

Strictly speaking, such fantasy narratives of the eighteenth and early nineteenth centuries take the form of anti-fantasy, in the same way that the urbane fairy tales of the *salonnières* are so often mock fairy tales. This could be called a hairpin effect: the direction of mockery turns back on itself, and a frisson of wonder replaces the smile of raillery.

While many of the writers, like Voltaire, adopted the mode of the *Nights* and mocked and exaggerated it in an apparent spirit of levity, they also seized this chance for exuberant play to envision, as Shahrazad herself does in the stories, different régimes of authority, emancipated erotics, and prophetic technological innovations. In this respect they picked up on the deep dynamic of the book: that Shahrazad through her stories is persuading the tyrannical Sultan to think again.

For the generation after the *philosophes*, Eastern enchantments exercised a different, and darker attraction: where Voltaire sharpened the point of his satire on their absurdities, writers like William Beckford and Johann Wolfgang von Goethe found they laid out a stage for more personal, sexual and emotional freedoms. Projection on to a fantasy Orient also made deviancy a safer place. Beckford's supercharged imagination fills

Vathek and many other, lesser-known tales of his; he is usually spoken of as an eccentric, marginal figure, but his wild and violent fantasies reveal how the *Arabian Nights* now offered a space for psychological non-conformism – for the radical position of Romanticism and Gothic delinquency. The case of Goethe's late, intense cycle of love poems, the *West-Eastern Divan*, discussed in Chapter 15, brings Edward Said back into the argument, for he and Daniel Barenboim named the youth orchestra of Arab and Israeli musicians after Goethe's impassioned imper-sonation of a Persian poet and lover.

Almost eclipsing the literary descent, plays, operas and films have disseminated the genre of the *Arabian Nights*. In the final part of the book, 'Flights of Reason', I look at this history; or, rather, at a very small part of it. The freedom that the *Nights* gave to dream of possi-bilities included fantasies of human flight, and this feature especially inspired rich and entertaining speculation. Chapter 17, 'Why Aladdin?' inquires into the success of 'Aladdin' in particular, the rise of demo-cratic spectaculars in Victorian entertainment, and ingenious stagecraft. Early cinema learned all manner of tricks and illusions from the theatre, and turned eastwards, too. Chapter 18, 'Machine Dreams', focuses on Hollywood's most elaborate feature of that period, *The Thief of Bagdad* (1924), in many ways an uncomfortable film, which features an Aladdin-style hero and, while keeping to the jocular and romance traditions of panto, deploys many lavish special effects that would become synonymous with the cinema itself: vanishing and flying, for example. At the same time, in Berlin, a silhouette puppeteer of genius, Lotte Reiniger, was making one of the most memorable versions of the *Arabian Nights*, her beautiful 'shadow film', *The Adventures of Prince Achmed* (Chapter 19).

The coming of cinema and the invention of psychoanalysis form two of the most conspicuous identifying marks of modernity. It may be fanciful, but I hope it keeps to the spirit of *Alf Layla wa-Layla*, to wonder whether Freud, when he covered his couch with an oriental rug, was – consciously or unconsciously – creating an Oriental setting for the first psychoanalytical cures: talking as a form of storytelling, with the roles reversed (it is the narrator who needs to be healed, not the listener-Sultan). When I tested this hypothesis, the 'Smyrna rug' which Freud draped on his psychoanalytic couch turned out to be richer in symbolism than I had dreamed (Chapter 20).

I have taken the *Nights* as the starting point for capturing ideas of enchantments in the book's afterglow. *Stranger Magic* looks above all at the pleasure – the *'aja'ib,* the wonders and astonishments – which the

Arabian Nights give, and which the many variations inspired by the stories, in literature, and on stage and screen, continue to give, and asks to understand why.

Can stories be amuletic? Shahrazad acts to ward off danger, as an Egyptian Eye of Horus averts the harm of the evil eye.

Part I
Solomon the Wise King

Story 1

The Fisherman and the Genie

A
N OLD FISHERMAN LIVING IN great poverty with a wife, his
son and two daughters, throws his net into the sea one moonlit
night, and has no luck: his first haul is the carcass of a donkey,
his second an old jar full of sand and clay, his third a heap of bits of
glass and pottery, bones and débris. In between each throw of his net,
he rails against fortune and passionately laments his state:

'Here virtue cries for misery, and the good-for-nothing disguises
himself in his kingdom. The bird that soars high exhausts itself from west
to east, while the canary in its cage feasts on sweets.'

He then looks up at the sky, sees dawn is beginning to break and
prays that his fourth and last attempt will bring his family something to
eat from the sea, in the same way as God made it obey Moses.

This time, he fishes up a copper bottle, sealed with a lead stopper,
and is overjoyed because the copper will fetch at least six gold dinars
which he can use to buy wheat. Before setting out for the market, he
decides he must open it, and as he chisels away at the lead with his knife,
smoke starts rising up and up, and darkens the blue of the morning sky
before it rolls down to the ground again, gathers itself together to a great
rumble and takes the form of a huge afrit: 'his head, as high as a dome,
touched the clouds, while his feet rested on the ground. His hands
resembled gigantic pitchforks, his legs the mast of a ship, his ears shields,
his mouth a cavern, his teeth rocks, his nose a jar, his nostrils trumpets,
his eyes torches. He had a mane of hair, all tangled and dusty. A real
monster!'

The fisherman is seized by a terrible fear, as he hears the jinni – for
it is a jinni, of the fearsome species of the afrits – cry out a profession
of faith in the true God and in Solomon his prophet, and promise that
he will never disobey him again. The fisherman reproaches him, telling
him Solomon has been dead more than 1,800 years: 'We are living at
the end of time,' he says, and demands to know his story.

The jinni tells him to rejoice; but he is being cruelly ironic for
with his next breath he informs the fisherman that the hour of his
death is at hand, and he must choose the method and the tortures he
shall suffer.

The fisherman protests: he has delivered him from the bottle, and is to be rewarded by a terrible death?

'Listen to my story,' orders the afrit. He then tells the fisherman: 'Know that I am a heretical demon. I refused to obey Solomon, son of David. My name is Sakhr.' He relates how he was brought before Solomon by his vizier and ordered to embrace the true God, but persisted in his refusal, and so was captured and sealed up inside the flask with the lead stopper, inscribed with the name of the true God, and thrown by the faithful jinn to the bottom of the sea. There a hundred years passed, and the jinni promised to bring riches to his deliverer. No one saved him, and another hundred years passed, and he swore to make his rescuer even richer. Another four hundred years passed, and by this time the jinni inside the bottle had become so enraged, he swore that he would kill anyone who freed him now.

The fisherman begs for mercy, but his enemy remains obdurate.

'O master of demons,' cries out the fisherman. 'Is this how you return evil for good?' He recites a pious proverb which warns against such behaviour – and adds an allusion to the fate that overtakes the ungrateful hyena in a beast-fable.

'Stop dreaming,' says the implacable jinni. 'You have to die.'

The fisherman reminds himself that unlike this jinni, he is a human being, endowed with reasoning powers; he can work out a stratagem.

He invokes the name of God as engraved on the ring of Solomon and pledges the afrit to answer a question truthfully. His antagonist is agitated at the invocation of God and the ring, and agrees. The fisherman then asks him how he got into the bottle, since even one of his hands and feet would not fit.

'I'll only believe it when I see it with my own eyes,' says the fisherman.

(It is the end of the third night in the cycle, and Shahrazad breaks off: with the dawn she must stop. But the Sultan wants to hear what happens next and so she is reprieved for another day – and night.

On the fourth night, she resumes her tale.)

The fisherman watches the jinni shake himself all over and turn back into smoke which rises to heaven and then gathers together and enters the flask. From inside Sakhr calls out:

'You see, fisherman, I am inside the flask. Do you believe me now?'

The fisherman rushes to seize the flask and the stopper of lead imprinted with the seal of Solomon, and stuffs it back into the mouth of the bottle.

Now it is his turn to give the order that the jinni must die. He is going to throw him into the sea, he says, and build himself a house on the spot so that nobody else can fish there. The jinni struggles in vain to free himself, but he finds himself once more a prisoner of the seal of Solomon.

'No, no,' he cries out as his jailer walks towards the sea.

'Yes, yes,' replies the fisherman.

The rebel afrit tries to cajole him, sweetly and softly, and promises him wealth and blessings. But the fisherman does not believe his protestations. He knows another story about kindness rewarded with death, and it has made him wary.

And Shahrazad begins to tell the story of the fisherman telling that story . . .

CHAPTER ONE

Master of Jinn

I

THE FAMOUS TRICKSTER TALE OF 'The Fisherman and the Genie', at
once alarming and funny, so satisfying in its (first) neat resolution when
the pauper outwits the colossus, the enemy is hoist on his own petard,
and the jinni inveigled back into the bottle, has rightly enjoyed a long
and celebrated history (it was successfully restaged in the Disney *Aladdin*,
with Robin Williams voicing the genie). But when Sakhr remembers
the scene of his rebellion and punishment at the hands of Solomon, his
story provides the fundamental background plot for the cosmology of
the *Arabian Nights*, in which the wise king plays a pre-eminent role as
master of the book's magic, with the jinn at his command.

Unlike the biblical king, the Muslim Solomon understands the language
of beasts and birds and commands the winds and the elements; he rules
over the higher order of angels and, above all, is given mastery over the
innumerable spirits, the jinn, who exist invisibly alongside angels, humans
and animals and form a distinct order of beings, elemental and mortal,
metamorphic physically and morally, shifting between states of visibility
and invisibility, capable of redemption and goodness yet for the most
part, especially in the stories of the *Nights*, capricious, arbitrary and amoral.
The stories of the *Nights* take these aspects of Solomon for granted, and
treat them to no exclamations of wonder, giving the impression that
these qualities of his were generally known by the community of listeners
as well as by the makers of the literature. There is, however, so much
common ground between the Judaeo-Christian tradition about the wise
king and the Islamic and other Eastern material that it would be too
blunt to argue simply that something intrinsically Islamic fostered the
magus while Christendom preferred the wise judge.

Solomon belongs to the three monotheisms of the Middle East, appears
in the Bible and the Koran, and in Judaic folklore and Kabbalistic belief.
The wise king cuts a majestic yet enigmatic figure, and his deeds and
characteristics, as related in the scriptures of three faiths, provide the
seedstore from which the fantasies of the *Nights* have grown so richly.

The jinni Sakhr, shaggy and clawed, emerges from the bottle of the Fisherman, and
towers to the sky. H. J. Ford, for Andrew Lang's retelling, 1898.

The 'sagest of all sages, the mage of all mages', he combines kingship and prophecy with magic, and passes from mainstream religion into mysticism and hermetic lore, with numerous wisdom books from the Bible as well as medieval and later grimoires or magic handbooks claiming his authorship (such as the *Clavis Salomonis* – The Key of Solomon – and the *Ars notoria*); Solomonic wisdom, emerging from the Jewish-Hellenistic culture of the Middle East in antiquity, enjoyed remarkable longevity, and continued to be collected, copied and revised in manuscripts in various languages well into the eighteenth and nineteenth centuries. Solomon is credited with authorship of the Song of Songs, Ecclesiastes, the Book of Wisdom itself, and with the Book of Proverbs, books which include the most intense lyric passages of the Bible as well as the Wisdom tradition of the Middle East; both these strong strands weave through the *1001 Nights*, where the stories are cadenced by bursts of ecstatic poetry on the one hand and fabulist exempla on the other. His myth meets and combines with those of others – of the hero-kings and prophets, Alexander the Great, Merlin, Hermes Trismegistus and Virgil.

There are other figures of great wisdom in holy scripture – the three kings are called 'the wise men from the east' in the New Testament, and there are numerous prophets, of course, but Solomon surpasses them all because, when asked in a dream what he most desires, he does not ask for money and power or long life but responds by praying to God for 'an understanding heart to judge thy people and to know good and evil' (2 Chronicles 1: 7–12). As a result, God answers his prayer and 'Solomon's wisdom excelled the wisdom of all the children of the east country, and all the wisdom of Egypt' (1 Kings 4: 30). The reference to Egypt, the most fertile and ancient repository of magical wisdom, gives Solomon explicit superiority to that knowledge, as Moses (and Aaron) surpass Pharaoh's magicians in the Bible. The Middle Eastern scholar Chester Charlton McCown, commenting on Solomon's character as a magus, writes, 'Few [traditions] have a richer and more varied documentation than that which glorifies the wisdom of Solomon. It may well serve as an example of the manner in which the human mind works in certain fields.'

In the Bible, Solomon's wisdom translates into practical knowledge: he is no hermit or meditative philosopher, but pursues the *via activa* as an astronomer and natural scientist, as well as a judicious ruler handing out his celebrated and cunning decisions. God has given him knowledge of the stars and their relation to time, understanding of the properties of plants and roots; he can also read thoughts (Book of Wisdom 7: 17–22). The folklore that the king inspires in the Middle East, before Islam was founded, flows into the *Arabian Nights*. For example, *The Testament of Solomon*, a splendid phantasmagoria about Solomon drilling demons to build the Temple, is a Greek compendium composed in Jewish circles before AD 300, with some Christian additions and many affinities with later Koranic and Middle Eastern folklore. The New Testament scholar (and ghost story writer) M. R. James commented in 1899, 'No one has ever paid very much attention to this futile, but exceedingly curious, work . . . related to Greek magical papyri and . . . fairy and demon stories of East and West.'

Since then there has been more interest in this richly imaginative catalogue of demons, which is vividly cast in the first person of Solomon reviewing his life; it recounts a series of conversations between Solomon and the devils, whom he summons by power of his ring and the sign of the pentacle engraved on its gemstone, which has been given to him by the archangel Michael. The devils include some who have since achieved fame, like Beelzebub and Asmodeus, alongside scores of others who have not; they each have different very specific victims and ingenious – diabolical – ways of doing harm. One by one they are conscripted against their will and set to perform tasks that match their spheres of activity: the demoness Onoskelis, who strangles her victims in a noose, is ordered to spin the hemp to make ropes to haul materials. Later in the story, one of the demons whom Solomon tames links interestingly to the *Nights*: the king's help is requested in a pitiful letter by the ruler of Arabia, where the people are suffering from a demon wind ('its blast is harsh and terrible'). Solomon sets the request aside, as he is concentrating on raising the keystone of the Temple, but it is so huge and heavy that more help is needed besides Onoskelis's rope-making. But later, he dispatches a servant to Arabia with a leather flask and his seal, and tells him to hold it open facing the wind like a windsock and when it has filled out to close the neck with the seal; he is then to bring the devil wind back to Jerusalem.

He does so; and the wind duly dies down, to the relief and gratitude of the Arabs. Three days later, the servant returns to Jerusalem, and the story continues:

'And on the next day, I King Solomon, went into the Temple of God and sat in deep distress about the stone of the end of the corner. And when I entered the Temple, the flask stood up and walked around some seven steps and then fell on its mouth and did homage to me. And I marvelled that even along with the bottle the demon still had power and could walk about; and I commanded it to stand up.'

This demon tells him his name – Ephippass – and promises to do anything Solomon wishes. The king orders him to lift the keystone into place, which he does, later going on mysteriously to raise a huge column on a pillar of air.

With this miracle, the intermingling of air with spirits takes the form of physical currents – wind, even tornadoes – and the demon announces the feats of sprites like Ariel and the tempest he raises by enchantment. But the 'Testament' also provides some of the material that will be worked into the background of the *Nights*; its marked love of aerodynamic wonders – the flight of the jinn, of Aladdin's palace and other prodigious displacements and overnight sensations – can be seen taking shape in this storyteller's fantasy.

'The Testament of Solomon' takes the form its title suggests: at the end of his life the wise king is giving an account of himself, so, setting aside its anecdotal supernaturalism, the work makes a real attempt to make sense of Solomon's complex character as both a godly, wise man of sacred scriptures and an apostate who worships false gods. It does so by concluding with the story from the Bible that he fell in love with the

King Solomon in the Bible is led astray by women: the daughter of Pharaoh urges him to worship her gods (?Antwerp, sixteeenth century).

daughter of Pharaoh and 'many strange women' besides: 'And he had seven hundred wives, princesses, and three hundred concubines . . . For it came to pass, when Solomon was old, that his wives turned away his heart after other gods . . .' (I Kings 14). Among these gods, the Bible mentions Ashtoreth, and Milcom 'the abomination of the Ammonites', and how Solomon sacrificed to them. For this reason, the God of the Bible eventually prevents Solomon's son from inheriting his kingdom.

In relation to the *Arabian Nights*, this fall from grace gives Solomon an equivocal, even lesser status in the eyes of Western audiences. In the Muslim sacred book, by contrast, the wise ruler is tested by God and tempted in different, often highly ambiguous ways. But his character is steadier – there are no temptress women to lead him away from the true God. In one passage, his virtue falters:

> Remember when, on an evening, were displayed before him horses frisky and fleet.
> He said: 'I have a love of horses that makes me forget my Lord till the sun hides behind its veil. Bring them back to me.'
> And he proceeded to stroke their shanks and necks.(Qur'an 38: 31–3)

More crucially, he successfully withstands the lure of 'disbelieving devils . . . who taught mankind sorcery . . .'

> They know full well that he who deals in sorcery has no share in the afterlife.
> Wretched is the price they pay for their souls, if only they knew!
> (Qur'an 2: 101–2)

So his magical powers are clearly distinguished from the practice of sinners and apostates: theirs is goety, his theurgy.

Both holy books reflect legends and folklore circulating in the region before the stories about Solomon were written down, but with these careful discriminations the Koran establishes that some forms of magic can be divinely approved and benign. It presents Solomon as a man with a deep understanding of the heavens and the properties of things; it also describes the command God has given him over natural forces, embodied by jinn who inhabit distant kingdoms, worlds beyond this world often evoked as paradisal wildernesses filled with all kinds of rare and marvellous stones, animals and birds. These sides of Solomon's character subsequently give rise to yet more imaginative fantasies, ranging from the mystical to the scabrous.

Solomon's mythopoeic fertility has not come to an end. Hans Werner Henze recently composed an opera called *L'Upupa (The Hoopoe)* for which he wrote the libretto, where he improvises with evident delight on motifs from the *Nights* about Solomon and his messenger bird, while at the more popular end of culture, the World Wide Web today is packed, as one might expect, with Solomonic lore: the wise king is now identified as a shaman, and promises access to healing of mind and body.

II

The literature which gathers around his legend in Europe ranges through love magic, pharmacology, scatology, homespun lore, and rude common sense (when he finds himself in comic material, he plays the ultimate wise guy). But even in the most esoteric or coarsest passages, Solomon's supreme knowledge and insight remain his defining characteristics. Dante, who gives diviners and conjurors very short shrift in the *Inferno*, ignores any taint of necromancy, womanising, or other lapses in Solomon's legend, and places him unequivocally in Paradise in the sphere of the sun where he shines. Thomas Aquinas indicates his starry soul:

> La quinta luce, ch'è tra noi più bella,
>   spira di tale amor, che tutto 'l mondo
>   là giù ne gola di saper novella:
> entro v'è l'alata mente u' sì profondo
>   saver fu messo, che se 'l vero è vero
>   a veder tanto non surse il secondo. (*Par.* X, ll. 109–15)

(The fifth light, which is the most beautiful among us, breathes from such a love that all the world below hungers for news of it; within it is the lofty mind to which was given wisdom so deep that, if the truth be true, there never arose a second of such vision.)

Three cantos later, before another reverent evocation of King Solomon, Dante gives an elaborate account of the sphere of the sun, with the singing stars and their double dance (*Par.* XIII, ll. 1–27). The complex astronomical scheme which his dense verses evoke shows the poet's deep reading in hermetic and astrological texts, from Latin versions of Greek Neoplatonists which were transmitted – and preserved – through Arabic translations. But the harmony of the wheeling stars depends on Dante's identification of his own metaphysical strivings with the goals of geometry: in the closing lines of the *Divine Comedy*, he compares his awe at his vision of paradise to

Qual è 'l geomètra che tutto s'affige
  per misurar lo cherchio, e non ritrova,
  pensando, quel principio ond'elli indige,
tal era io a quella vista nova. (*Par.* XXXIII, 133–6)

(Like the geometer who sets all his mind to the squaring of the circle
and for all his thinking does not discover the principle he needs, such
was I at that strange sight.)

The biblical Solomon, who combines kingship with unsurpassed
wisdom, synthesises for Dante the ideal fusion of worldly justice, science
and metaphysics. But the topological structure of the universe in *Paradiso*
XIII, in which the shining soul of Solomon lives for ever, displays the
working of a particular practical mnemonic system credited to Solomon
the magus and to sages after him. Dante invites his readers directly to
picture in their mind's eye two turning gyres involving twenty-four stars;
in this way, he invites us to use fantasia to understand the heavens. Such
a practice of active imagination is central to magical thinking, invoked,
for example, in the life of the magus Apollonius of Tyana by Apollodorus
in the late second century AD, and adopted by such practitioners of
natural magic as Pietro Pomponazzi and Giordano Bruno, for whom
visualisation was an active force which can tune in to the forces of the
cosmos and penetrate the secrets of phenomena.

Dante always shows great sensitivity to the dangers of magic, and is
consistent in his repudiation: Virgil may be his guide to the underworld
because his epic proves his special access to such secrets, but the Roman
poet in Dante's poem bears no other trace of the many marvellous feats
of magic attributed to him by medieval tradition. In the same way, Dante
allows the associations of Solomon's occult wisdom to infuse the scenes
in which he appears in *Paradiso*, while he himself enacts mentalist methods
for committing knowledge to memory using geometrical forms, as
advocated in the tradition of natural magic, and then enjoins his readers
to follow the same process.

The glorious and blameless figure of Solomon in Dante's Paradise may
seem remote from the colourful folklore that fills the *Arabian Nights*, but
his Dantean character epitomises how acutely the poet needed to distance
his work. The strong contrast between this Solomon and the Solomon
who commands the jinn is crucial, I believe, to the eventual huge success
of the Eastern stories in Europe. While Christian orthodoxy, as defined
by Thomas Aquinas's thought, must reject magic, the cosmology of the
Nights gives magic space; it becomes a vision of natural order, and
the magus, symbolised pre-eminently by Solomon, takes up a role within

this territory of enchantment, which can be either beneficent or malignant depending on which story is being told. To contemporary readers, however, and to Jews and Christians whose angelology is more uncompromisingly dualist, Solomon's magical powers cast him in a very ambiguous light – in the realm of fantasy fit for (children's) literature rather than metaphysics. This alternative theology, however, does allow the concept of the good demon to flourish – and a demon who can be either good or bad, quite apart from the profound effects this possibility has on an ethics of redemption, is a catalyst of narrative surprise.

Even when absent in person from the tales (he often is) Solomon provides the basic structural plot on which Shahrazad's stories depend, and his powers underlie the whole narrative foundation of the magic in the *1001 Nights*. While the dominant frame of the *Nights* concerns Shahrazad's mission to save herself and all other women from the rage of the Sultan, that salvation story is itself contained within another larger myth about origins, analogous, but not identical, to the Judaeo-Christian account of the rebel angels. This relates that some of the jinn revolted against the true God and proclaimed allegiance to Eblis, the Satan of Islamic cosmology, were consequently punished by Solomon, and became the capricious and powerful agents of caprice and wickedness who work the wonders that transfuse the world of the stories. But unlike the biblical story, the Koran – and the *Nights* – include jinn who remained true to Solomon and Allah, as well as others who repent.

The jinns' double character in the stories opens a crucial space of possibility for them in the narrative: as the agents of fortune. As Pier Paolo Pasolini commented, 'every tale in the Thousand and One Nights begins with an "appearance of destiny" which manifests itself through an anomaly, and one anomaly always generates another. So a chain of anomalies is set up . . . The protagonist of the stories is in fact destiny itself.' Destiny is the chief character of the *Nights*. But destiny in the stories is multivalent and sets off the chain of anomalies which Pasolini describes: the jinn introduce a dynamic of pure chance which runs alongside the larger designs of fate, now meeting them, now parting from them, rather as the breeze on the sea will form cross-currents in the wave pattern on the surface, which sailors watch carefully to determine the direction of the wind they can catch rather than the current or the tide in the water.

III 'Beings of Shimmering Flame'

The jinn, good, bad and in-between, who flock in the *1001 Nights*, add the energy of unpredictability to the plots in which they appear. (Pl. 12)

They literally embody a tremendous narrative principle which gives the stories in the *Nights* their distinctive, enjoyable flavour. The jinn's role reflects how the collective poetic imagination that created the stories felt a need to identify intermediate agents, capable of both good and evil at whim; the invention constitutes an answer to the problem of evil existing in the monotheistic landscape, when a good, all-powerful deity allows terrible things to happen, including injustice.

Jinni is Arabic for genie or demon. Jinn resemble the daimones of Greek cosmology, neither angels nor devils but intermediate spirits. A human hero can fall in love with a jinniya and marry her – in some cases, happily. The Second Old Man, for example, in the cycle of 'The Merchant and the Genie' towards the beginning of the *Nights*, relates how he met a slave in rags on a quayside who asked him to marry her, which he did, and how, later, his brothers plotted against him, robbed him, and threw him and his young bride into the sea. Whereupon, revealing herself to be a fairy, she plucked him out to safety: 'She took me upon her shoulders and, carrying me to an island, left me and disappeared for the whole night. In the morning she returned and said: "Do you not know me? I am your wife. Know now that I am a jinniyah and that when I first saw you, my heart loved you, for Allah willed it so . . ."' She is in a rage against his brothers, she continues, and is flying off that very night to sink their boat and kill them. The old man pleads she show mercy towards them, and she agrees; she carries him up into the air and deposits him back on the roof of his home. There he finds his brothers leashed and weeping. They have been changed into bitches by his wife's fairy sister when she heard of their wickedness; the spell cannot be lifted before ten years are up. The old man is now wandering with his transformed brothers in search of his lost fairy wife.

Women – human women – can also become the spouses, reluctant or otherwise, of demon lovers. When Shahriyar and his brother Shahzenan come across the jinni's beautiful prisoner, they are astonished not by the relationship between him and a human woman but by her ferocious desire to avenge herself through sex. It seems that mortal men can marry jinn or peris, but the stories give warnings about the complexity of these unions, as in the tales of 'Hasan of Basra' and of 'Jullanar of the Sea'; as in the legends about selkies in Scotland, or the fairy tale of Undine or Rusalka in Europe, marriages to a fairy wife are fraught with danger and heartbreak. In the *Nights*, mortal women are less than happy with their demon husbands. (The 'woman wailing for her demon lover' might not be longing for him, as Coleridge's line seems to convey on the face of it, but railing against her fate as his prisoner.) Such unions rarely – if ever – lead to weddings, happy or other.

Several magical unions do, however, take place between human grooms and fairy brides, and these marriages can prosper and do not need to end with the separation of worlds again. Janshah, Hasan of Basra and Prince Ahmed are some of the heroes who, spellbound by the beauty of a fairy they have once glimpsed, pursue her through thick and thin, and eventually succeed in winning her and returning home to the world with her as their wife. Similarly, the otherworldly romance of 'Sayf al-Muluk and Badiat al-Jamal' dramatises Sayf's undying passion for the jinniya Badiat, daughter of the king of the true-believing jinn. Her portrait has been magically woven in gold into a jewel-studded robe, and given by Solomon himself to Sayf's father, the King of Egypt, as a reward for his conversion to Islam. Sayf unfolds the robe and sees Badiat's beauty and is lost – his life becomes an epic quest to find her. Through a tangle of bizarre and wonderful adventures (monstrous races, fabulous islands, many near-death experiences) he does so. En route he rescues a maiden – Dawlat Khatun; she is captive to a rebel jinni, son of the Blue King of the jinn, who has stolen her away to his castle, 120 years' journey from her home in Serendip. This demon prince has been warned at birth by his horoscope that he will meet his death at the hand of a son of a human king, so he has hidden his soul in the stomach of a sparrow, which he has shut up in a box, then put the box in a chest, inside another chest, repeating the manoeuvre seven times seven, until the last coffer, which is made of marble; this he has sunk by the shore of the ocean stream that encircles the world.

But Dawlat Khatun has learned the secret of her captor's vulnerability, and she confides it to Sayf, who, when he hears it, cries out,

"'I am that son of a king! And here on my finger is the ring of Solomon, son of David – blessed be their names! Come now with me down to the shore and we shall see if what is said is true!'"

With the magic of the ring he raises the marble chest from the ocean depths, breaks through all the boxes within boxes and extracts the sparrow. The demon jinni in the form of a huge cloud of dust pursues them, wheedling piteously for his life. But Sayf strangles the sparrow, and the jinni collapses in a heap of black ashes.

Dawlat Khatun is free: she turns out to be his beloved Badiat's milk-sister and she helps Sayf al-Muluk to find her. The romance ends in a double wedding which braids and knots together most satisfyingly the long tangle of the plotlines (I have hardly begun to comb them out here).

Solomon plays a distant role but his magic suffuses this epic romance, which stages a teeming population of jinn, both good and evil, inhabiting regions all around the world and far beyond its known borders. Dramatically capable of changing size, jinn have the edgeless forms of their elements, air and fire; whether rebels or not, they are intrinsically metamorphic beings and can take an infinite number of human, animal and monstrous shapes. Multiple, versatile, fluid and elusive, they incarnate energy in the stories. But they also feel things keenly, and they die: these mortal sympathies add depths and even pathos to their role (Pl. 7).

The poet and scholar Amira El-Zein has commented in a recent book, *Islam, Arabs, and the Intelligent World of the Jinn*:

> it is captivating that beings from the two realms of the visible and invisible worlds travel freely from one realm to the other . . . The movement from one dimension to another is constantly open both ways. From the perspective of these folktales, it is quite natural for humans and jinn to constantly circulate between the two realms as the scriptures and the tradition certify, while many folktales and fairytales in the West display rather preserved domains for each species.'

She goes on to compare this Eastern folk theme with the Mélusine legend, a tale which belongs in the family that inspired 'The Little Mermaid' by Hans Christian Andersen and the opera *Rusalka*, where the prohibition on mingling between the sea creature and a human prince demands that the heroine denature her fairy form: in Andersen's cruel imagination her tail is split to make legs. From Scotland to southern Europe, it is fatal to fall in love with a being of another world: the forlorn Merman in Arnold's poem pines for ever for his lost bride; the fisherman yearns for the selkie who vanished when he broke the prohibition and either looked at her on a forbidden day, or found her sealskin and tried to keep her from putting it on again.

Similarly, when the female jinn take the form of aerial beings and can also live in the depths of the sea, they resemble the swan maidens and sirens of European lore. But, again, they are not necessarily doomed to separation or death.

The daimonic, spiritual and enchanted interpenetrate the earthly like the twisting threads of a tapestry.

A remarkable legal treatise was drawn up in Syria in the fourteenth century to determine the status of such unions in accordance with the faith, with the Koran and the Hadith as well as the biographies of the Prophet. Though the theological evidence comes down on the side of disapproval of such marriages, they are not deemed inconceivable:

indeed the very disapproval expressed by these highest authorities admits their possibility.

Children can be born of these matches and the tales sometimes give warnings about their future; but the offspring of humans and jinn do not only occur in the fantasies of romances or the *Nights*: in Luxor in the 1970s, the Arabist Fred Leemhuis was told about a local man who had two wives, one a jinniya whom he saw every Thursday in the upstairs room of his house. They had five invisible children, while with his human wife, who lived on the ground floor, he had nine visible offspring. His transport business flourished as his jinn children lent a helping hand.

Some of the learned opinion oppose such beliefs arguing that, quite apart from the unlawfulness of such procreation, jinn cannot take the fully human form necessary to conceive a human baby – the existence of the jinn is not in doubt, but the suitability of their form.

Neither angels nor devils, jinn can move in both directions, as is clear from the romance of Sayf al-Kulut and Badiat: they can surpass the devil's works in wickedness and also act vigorously on behalf of the supreme God and goodness. In the sura called 'The Jinn' in the Koran, the jinn tell us,

'That among us there are the righteous, and there are the less so – of diverse persuasions are we'(72: 11).

In a plot, the supreme being can act as a narrative force embodied in providence, but there are limits to the spectrum of his behaviour. Even the furious God of the Old Testament does not possess the degree of idiosyncrasy and vitality that less strictly perfect beings, intrinsically various and unruly, can add to a story. It is not simply a question of the devil having the best tunes, but a reflection of the inherent demand that this kind of fairytale storytelling makes: for surprise, for wonder, for astonishment. The Greek myths could imagine gods and goddesses behaving badly and the stories correspondingly fizz with inventive plots: with the fairytale and the tales from the *Nights* this variety and spice, so necessary to a good story, moves out of the ranks of the divine into the intermediate world of spirits.

The myth of Solomon's relation with this distinctive order of being forms the deep and familiar backdrop of the *Nights*. It did not need to be spelt out by the storyteller but could be dropped into a plot where the focus lies elsewhere (on the fisherman's cunning and his ultimate salvation, for example). Shahrazad, and the real-life narrators who followed her, could assume the audience knew the backstory, just as Homer does not begin at the beginning with the story of the Trojan War, but plunges in, taking it for granted that his audience is fully aware of what took place at the Judgement of Paris.

Unexpectedly, the part of Solomon's story that concerns jinn in their bottles was known in the Middle Ages in Europe: a Middle English poem about St Margaret of Antioch includes her victory over the dragon sent by Beelzebub to destroy her. Beelzebub then appears; she binds him too. He plaintively reveals that the dragon was his brother and tells a variant of the story of their imprisonment by Solomon:

> 'Salamon the wyse kynge, whyle he was on lyve,
> He closed us in a bras fat and dalfe us in a clyve.
> The men of Babylon that bras fat gunne ryve;
> And whanne that broken was, oute we gan dryve . . .
> Some swyfter then the wynde and some as swyfte as roo,
> And alle that byleve on Jhesu Cryste we werke hem mychel woo.'

> ('Solomon the wise king, while he was still alive,
> Shut us up in a brass vat and buried us in the ground.
> The men of Babylon broke open that brass vat
> And when it was broken, we began to stream out.
> Some swifter than the wind and some as swift as deer,
> on all who believe in Jesus Christ, we work dreadful woe.')

The medieval poet may have heard the story as a pilgrim or a crusader, and it is after all from the same part of the world as Margaret of Antioch herself.

Just as it is no longer true that audiences know the Greek myths, so it is with the traditions of Solomon in the *Arabian Nights*, for his Koranic persona is unfamiliar beyond the world of Islam.

The translation 'demon' carries too strong an inference of evil in English; the alternative spellings 'daimon' or 'daemon', which derive from Greek, capture better the character of Solomon's followers, especially since Philip Pullman in *His Dark Materials* (1995, 1997, 2000) used 'daemon' for the metamorphic animal souls of his characters.

Solomon has been given control of these daemons or jinn, as is mentioned several times in the Koran: 'We created man from dried clay, from fetid mud. The *Jinn* We created beforehand, from the fiery wind' (Koran 15: 26–7). This fiery wind, close to the luminiferous ether of seventeenth-century New Science, becomes 'shimmering flame' elsewhere (Koran 55: 14–15), and the jinn make their appearance before human beings, who are made of clay. They are consequently close to the element of air, over which Solomon is also given mastery: it is the jinn who carry his flying throne, on which he can travel to the edge of the universe and encounter the angel who makes rain and the dragon who circles the world. (Pl. 2)

Jinn are also at home in the element of water and Solomon can command them there as well: 'And demons there were who dived deep at his command, and performed other, lesser tasks. Of them we took good care' (21: 82). In a more extended passage, from Sura 27, 'The Ants', the Koran gives more detail about Solomon's God-given gifts. It opens with apocalyptic passages about the plagues of Egypt obtained by Moses from God to punish Pharaoh and his people. The book then passes rapidly on to Moses's notable successors, and Solomon makes an enigmatic appearance in a sequence of compressed yet vividly coloured scenes which draw on popular legends about the wisest of wise men. The sura tells us that Solomon said:

> 'O people, we have been taught the language of Birds, and granted of all gifts. This is truly a favour most conspicuous.'
> To Solomon were mustered his troops of Jinn, and birds all held in strict order until, when they arrived at the Valley of the Ants, one ant said,
> 'O ants, enter your dwellings lest Solomon and his troops should crush you unawares.' (Qur'an 27: 15–18)

Solomon, understanding the warning, 'smiled in amusement at its words', and gives thanks for the gift, asking God to admit him to the company of his servants.

In a highly elliptical manner, the Koran does not expand on the episode, but implies that Solomon, as he has been given power to understand the speech of all creatures, was able to take care not to harm the ants who, as puny, anonymous and labouring creatures, serve to remind us of the importance of humility.

Another insect, sometimes a woodworm, sometimes a termite, makes a further, highly symbolic appearance in Solomon's legend: after the king has captured the most powerful of the jinn, including Beelzebub, and ordered them to build the Temple, but he realises that he will be dead before the work is finished, and that the jinn will down tools as soon as they see that he is near his end. So he sets himself up to lean on his staff and remain there, standing, until an insect gnaws through the stick and Solomon's corpse falls to the ground. The Koran refers simply to 'a crawling creature of earth' (Qur'an 34:14) and this is variously translated as 'worm' or 'beast', but in all cases the point is the paltriness of the agent in this episode when the great wise king's mortality is revealed. But Solomon's wisdom consists, however, in his appreciation of all human contingency, and his acknowledgement of his own littleness.

Sura 27 then passes swiftly on to the scene in which Solomon calls for

his messenger, the hoopoe, and when he does not come to his call,
threatens to kill him for this lapse. But the bird soon returns and brings
news of a queen living in the south — this is the Koran's account of the
Queen of Sheba's encounter with Solomon, given rather differently in
the Bible (1 Kings 10: 1–13). Solomon forgets about punishing the bird and
becomes curious; through a series of magical prestiges, he summons the
queen to come and meet him. The Koran then moves into phase briefly
with the Bible; but the two accounts of the meeting soon part again as the
Koran includes cryptic moments of mysterious magic, as when Solomon
conjures a floor of glass which the queen mistakes for a deep pool of water
. . . 'and exposed her legs'. Solomon then reveals to her that 'This is a terrace
burnished with glass.' (Qur'an 27:44) She instantly converts to his God.

The chapter then closes with stirring accounts detailing the doom
that will fall upon unbelievers at the Day of Judgment — in terms recognisably echoing both the Old Testament and the Book of Revelation.

As in the encounter with the ants, Solomon's reactions to the Queen
of Sheba reveal above all his defining persona as magus, a man endowed
with preternatural powers over living things and the elements, who can
interrupt time and vault through space at will. Yet he is also mortal, fallible
and flawed, while the Queen of Sheba's mysterious nether limbs identify
her as a jinniya in some versions of her encounter with Solomon. An
unusual moral twist on a ransom tale, told by the Persian romancer Nizami
in *The Mirror of the Invisible World*, has a compelling emotive charge:
Nizami relates how the child they have together is born deformed, but they
learn that they can heal him if they confess to each other the truth about
themselves. The queen admits she lusts after young men, while Solomon,
in this story, does not suffer from similar libidinousness but confesses he
covets lavish gifts in return for dispensing his famous wisdom. As the two
bare their weaknesses to each other, their child grows whole again.

This child, known by several different names, will himself enjoy a
great destiny, as the founder of the Ethiopian royal house, rulers of a
most ancient Christian nation, and the spiritual ancestor of Rastafarianism,
which traces itself in this way directly back to Solomon: Haile Selassie,
the last emperor, being the last earthly representative of the wise king.

In the visual tradition of Persia and India, where the ban on graven
images was less strictly observed than elsewhere in the Islamic world,
the Solomon of the Koran presides over a scene of paradisical enchantment, characterised by talking beasts and birds like the ants and the
hoopoe. For example, in a wonderfully opulent and richly detailed miniature from the Deccan in Mughal India, painted c. AD 1610–30 (Pl. 1),
the hoopoe is perched on Solomon's shoulder; Solomon is seated on his

throne with its seven steps and lions couchant; his deputy – the general in charge of the troops of the jinn, al-Dimiryat – stands on his right, next to his vizier. These are two of Solomon's four princes, with the lion as the prince of beasts and the eagle the prince of birds.

This Solomon of Islamic culture rules over animated phenomena, all obedient to his command, like the water that flows in front of the Queen of Sheba and takes on the appearance of a mirror. Some of the jinn's activities on Solomon's behalf – their diving into the sea and raising a wind – associate them with the elements, and in many ways they are closer to nature spirits, to the elves and fairies and sprites of English and Celtic folklore, than to the demons of the religious tradition. Many rich manuscript illuminations, painted in Persia or, again, in Moghul India, illustrate these passages of the Koran, and show Solomon presiding in his court, usually in a garden paradise, surrounded by angels and jinn, birds and animals – the harmonious and varied Edenic world at his disposal. Yet the jinn in attendance are monstrous, with hooves and tusks and tails and hairy bodies, often luridly coloured, spotted and ill-assorted with exaggerated, often comical faces, rolling eyes, drooling mouths. Visually, they are very close to the grotesque figures of devils in medieval Christianity, and to the fantasies of the witch-hunters in early modern Europe, and there may indeed be some cross-fertilisation from India and China, whose gods and demons influenced Christian artists' ways of depicting devils.

The Islamic vision of the jinn differs fundamentally, since the obedient jinn who have accepted the true faith are Solomon's servants and are absolutely not evil. They have their disobedient counterparts – the renegade jinn, who in the *Nights* appear in the form of ghouls, marids and afrits – the chief agents of the supernatural in the *1001 Nights*. They can cause sickness, epilepsy and madness. A particular foul species (*shayatin*) haunts refuse tips, lavatories, and other spots of defilement. These apostates adhere to the old religions and their gods; Zoroastrianism from Persia comes in for especially fierce condemnation in the *Arabian Nights*, far greater than Christianity and Judaism, as it constitutes a rejection of Islam by close neighbours and cultural affiliates. It is interesting that it does so, because Zoroastrian cosmology is dualist, with a powerful dark force contending perpetually with the force of good, Ahriman. The Muslim vision rejects any such arrangements, and this is important to the stories, which consequently do not condemn all jinn as diabolical; they are ambivalent, contrary, often intent on doing harm but easily fooled, cravenly servile to their master or mistress as well as entirely subject to whomsoever chance places in that role: to hear is to obey is the jinn's watchword. The Koran warns against praying to them for protection (72: 22) but custom over the centuries and into the present resembles rather the Catholic cult of the Virgin Mary, who must not be worshipped as such, while in practice . . .

Solomon may be the divinely appointed master of the jinn, but his very mastery often places his famed justice and wisdom in doubt. Besides, he is not in control of all of them all of the time: he has to go to war on an epic scale to maintain his authority, and many of the jinn with whom heroes fall in love exist in zones of enchantment, sometimes under the sway of fantastic demon kings who thrive beyond Solomon's reach.

The legends of Solomon form the warp on which the *Nights* are woven. His being helps define magic itself: it consists of occult knowledge. More particularly with regard to storytelling fabulism, Solomon becomes the chief model in fantasy for the white wizard, the beneficent natural philosopher inquiring into the nature of the universe, a theurgist as opposed to a sorcerer or goetist, the man of wisdom who sees into the secrets of life.

Such wisdom as Solomon possesses leads to power, magical power, and his mythic figure becomes intertwined with the figures of Merlin and Virgil in the Middle Ages, who usurp the credit for some of his feats and are given some of his best exploits, just as he himself took over some of his precursors – from Pharaoh's magicians in the Bible, and even from Gilgamesh. Prospero in *The Tempest* can be placed in the lineage, with Ariel, his airy spirit, very jinn-like; and much later, in current successes, the white magicians Gandalf from Tolkien's *Lord of the Rings*, and – to some extent – Dumbledore from the Harry Potter series (J. K. Rowling even mixes in some Solomonic ambiguities in the later part of the story).

The activity of jinn and their masters in myths and stories has explanatory force for the marvels that occur in them, but it also sets up troubling moral dilemmas for audiences in a monotheistic culture. Muslim theologians tackled the question of magic, jinn and Solomon's connection with them, and, in general, orthodox thinking remained uneasy and cautious, while popular belief and custom, as reflected in the *Arabian Nights* and other stories, as well as in hundreds of amulets and charms of other kinds, stood firmly with the jinn and their powers.

An equivocal consequence follows from this divergence between learned and popular approaches: the one whom the jinn obey seems not so different from the enchanters or sorcerers who can summon them at will through their dark arts. The world of the *Arabian Nights* may be enchanted, but the stories discriminate between forms of magic and their dramatic interest arises from the sharp and often cruel clashes of opposing powers.

Story 2

The City of Brass

IN DAMASCUS, THE CALIPH ABD EL-MALIK wants to know more about the great king Solomon; in response one of his court begins to tell him about the existence of old copper bottles which release, as soon as they are opened, strange forms of smoke. A traveller and treasure-hunter present, called Talib ibn Sahl, picks up the story, describing to the Caliph how his grandfather was once sailing to Sicily but was blown off course and fetched up in a land inhabited by a black people who went about naked, had not yet heard of the true faith, and spoke an incomprehensible language – with the exception of their king, who could speak Arabic. There Talib's forebear met a fisherman who in turn told him how he and his fellow fishermen often found in their nets copper flasks sealed with lead stoppers, which, when opened, released jinn in the shape of columns of smoke who cried to Solomon in repentance.

Others present in the assembly corroborate Talib's account, until the ruler is fired with unappeasable curiosity to see one of these vessels for himself, and wants to set out immediately on a journey to find them. But Talib tells him there's no need to stir, as his emir in the Maghreb, Musa, will be able to track one down for him with much less trouble. The emir's territory lies at the foot of a mountain deep in that part of north Africa which borders the sea which holds the jars. The Caliph duly sends Talib to give Musa his orders to procure him a jinni in a bottle; the Emir in turn summons another veteran traveller and wise man, the sheikh Abd el-Samad, but this ancient sage warns the company that it will take years to go and longer to return. Ominously, he adds a note of caution about the truth of these reports, and about the people who are said to exist in the famous, infinitely remote City of Brass. Only Solomon and Alexander, he goes on, have ever passed though these far distant wildernesses, and survived. But the emir Musa does not quail – and so the party sets out with one thousand camels carrying water and another thousand carrying supplies.

As they trek across the desert, they reach the first of the ruined cities and lost civilisations they will encounter, where only the inscriptions on the empty palaces proclaim 'the once living glory of Kush ibn Shaddad ibn Ad, surnamed the great'. This lost city is the first of a long, melancholy sequence of vanished kingdoms which the travellers will come across. The ruins provoke the emir Musa to a storm of weeping, and this city's fate foreshadows that of the even more magnificent and eerie City of Brass.

Soon after, the party encounters an automaton, a horseman of brass who swivels as soon as they rub his hand holding the spear, and points the way they should take to reach the City of Brass; they change direction accordingly, and come across a huge column of black stone standing in the desert on its own. Approaching it, they find it is the living tomb of an afrit who persisted in his rejection of the true God and Solomon. He is a dreadful sight: a monstrous being with a third eye blazing in the centre of his forehead, wings, and four arms, two of which are human but the other two bestial and tipped by metal talons, and they hear his terrible cries as he rages against his sentence of eternal petrification.

The afrit Dahesh is a half-living half-dead thing, and as he begins to tell his story on the 570th night, Shahrazad opens another narrative chamber, down another level, in the spiralling labyrinth of the book's structure. From his stone prison inside the column, he relates how he fought Solomon and lost, for the king mustered all his forces and flew them into battle on the magic carpet.

Dahesh was the guardian of an idol, he tells the travellers, an idol carved of red carnelian, which he looked after on behalf of a pagan king of the sea, a worshipper of Eblis with a multitude of rebel jinn at his command. It was Dahesh's task to slip inside the idol and give out the oracles from within the statue. One day, from his vantage point inside the statue, he saw the king's daughter come to the shrine to pray. He fell in love with her. But Solomon had heard of her beauty and charms, and he wanted to add her to his harem and so sent a message to the king her father to that effect. And in the same letter, Solomon ordered the king to convert and smash the idol carved in red carnelian that he and his daughter adored.

The sea-king was enraged at this presumption; his viziers and councillors likewise. With a great clamour, they argued that Solomon's orders should be defied. After all, the pagan king, Dahesh and their allies possessed a powerful idol to support them, they held a stronghold in the distant ocean, and they could marshal many thousands of jinn to fight on their side; with all this, the infidel king would be bound to defeat Solomon.

But, first, he needed to consult the idol.

When the king arrived at the shrine, Dahesh slipped into the statue of red carnelian once more, and urged the king to oppose Solomon without a qualm.

As Dahesh remembers the colossal and terrible cataclysm that ensued, he lashes himself for his folly and rashness. He tells the travellers how Solomon's army rode out against the King of the Sea with a vast host of jinn, wild beasts, reptiles and birds, whom Solomon's vizier al-Dimriyat had mustered from all over the world. They were 600 million strong, and this entire multitude mounted the flying carpet, on either side of Solomon, seated in the centre of it on his throne.

The flying carpet, woven of green silk and richly embroidered, 60 miles long on each side – 360 square miles – had enough room for all the campaign provisions, the whole host of cooks and batmen, an entire *batterie de cuisine*, as well as stables and cavalry. Every species of animal and bird also flocked to join Solomon – the beasts marching on the land beneath, while the birds formed a phalanx overhead to shade the host as they went. In this astonishing cosmic battle array Solomon set out. As they flew on this astonishing expanse towards the battle, they crossed the Valley of the Ants, where the Queen of the Ants expressed fear that if the carpet settled on them it would crush them all, and so advised her subjects to run deep into their ant hills.

Solomon heard what she was saying and understood; as a result, he ordered his army to make a very soft landing, and took the queen on the palm of his hand, and explained to her that he would never crush even an ant under his foot. The ants then swarmed out of their burrows, and he presented the Queen of the Ants with half of the leg of a locust, a gift which matched his resources, he said. In this way, he acknowledged the scarcity of his realm and the scanty numbers of his subjects, compared to her multitudinous ant subjects in their kingdom.

It will take Shahrazad two more nights to complete the recounting of Dahesh's fate. Solomon ordered his troops to do their worst; the beasts on his side were to lacerate their enemies with their beaks and claws. Finally, after prolonged, ferocious violence, Dahesh met the vizier al-Dimriyat in hand-to-hand combat, and for months they grappled, so that long after the King of the Sea and his forces had been horribly massacred, Dahesh was still being pursued by the vizier. After three months, he was at last captured and changed into a pillar of rock.

The rebel jinni finishes his story, and gives the travellers directions to the City of Brass, and so they continue on their way.

When they reach the city, it is buried in sand and they can't find any doors or windows in its walls of brass. One by one they attempt to scale them; the first of the travellers who are sent to climb in jump to their deaths from the top of the fortifications. Eventually Abd el-Samad the wise man decides to make the attempt and, protecting himself with pious invocations, he finds that his predecessors were lured to hurl themselves down by beautiful women beckoning to them – sirens conjured by the jinn who protect the place from intruders. Eventually, the party meet a living being who is not a jinni: an eagle, seven hundred years old, who remembers that his brother, also an eagle, and two hundred years older than him, once said something about a certain people who lived in the City of Brass. But when this ancient bird appears, he does not remember anything. Together the two birds then fetch their elder brother to talk to the visitors. They carry him, for he can no longer fly, as he is 1,300 years old; he remembers that his father told him there was once a door in a wall on the west side, now covered in the desert sands.

Again the emir Musa weeps bitterly and freely at the vanity of vanities that is the world.

The sage el-Samad finds the keys on the body of one of the many dead guards and opens the city gates, which give a huge groan after the long years when they have remained closed. Inside, all is utterly desolate and suspended in time – an eternal nightmarish present tense, in which everyone they encounter is imprisoned behind gates of iron, frozen in death, preserved for eternity looking as if they are alive but eerily stilled – in the markets, in the banqueting halls, and at their tasks. As the party penetrate deeper into the many-chambered city, they come across over-flowing evidence of its past opulence: heaps of jewels and precious metals, artefacts and trinkets and inventions and luxuries, all extravagantly and lavishly described. The party moves on through the markets and halls, palaces and streets, and find one gate after another, each of them iron-barred, stamped with warning signs like Hell's Gate in the *Inferno*, and guarded by talismans, automata and speaking images, which breathe fire and which summon, if touched or tampered with, hosts of devils to repel the intruders. Nothing moves, for everything has been captured at the moment of its ceasing.

The City of Brass represents the acme of magical art: it even includes a sea of mirror like the one which Solomon conjures in the Koran during the visit of the Queen of Sheba.

Finally Musa and his party reach the centre of the city and the most resplendently decorated pavilion of all. Lying in state there, the young queen is arrayed on her bier in pearls and red gold; she is a mummy, and her eyes have been replaced by quicksilver. A breeze plays on her face so that she seems to be alert, looking and moving. She is the ulti-mate illusory artefact, the enchanted effigy of Tadmurah, Princess of the Amalekites. A plaque at the foot of her bed urges wayfarers who have reached her to take the city's wealth, but not to touch her body.

But Talib the treasure-hunter is greedy, and loots the corpse. And the automata who stand guard over her – one white slave, one black, one armed with a club and one with a sabre – strike him to the ground and cut off his head.

Around the bed, inscriptions tell her story in her own words: after seven years of drought and famine, the inhabitants of the City of Brass, who had been struggling by every means to find sustenance and survive, gave up the ghost.

After the party has left with their camel train laden with all the plunder they have found (treasure they were allowed to take), and sealed the gates to the city as they had found them, the emir Musa and the wise man Abd el-Samad eventually find the people who had been described by the blasphemous Talib at the very beginning of the story, the black fishermen who often found copper bottles in their nets. Their king, speaking in Arabic, explains that they are not heathen at all, contrary to their reputation, but have the rudiments of the true faith, taught by a luminous being who once appeared to them. At the travellers' request, they fish up twelve flasks sealed with Solomon's seal to give the Caliph, and they warn that, before unsealing them, it is crucial to bang the vessels on the outside and call to the spirit inside to testify to his true repentance for his rebellion against Solomon. Their hosts also lay out a feast of their fresh catch, present them with some mermaids, and send them on their way back to Damascus.

The expedition makes a safe journey back across the deserts to Damascus, and are greeted by the Caliph with astonishment and delight at their success. He opens the twelve bottles one by one, and a plume of smoke streams out of each, taking shape as a colossal afrit, howling. The imprisoned jinn do not understand how much time has gone by, and they take the Caliph for Solomon himself and beg his forgiveness.

The mermaids suffer a grimmer and more practical fate, for although Abd el-Malik provides them with their own pool to live in, they catch tuberculosis and soon die of heat stroke.

CHAPTER TWO

Riding the Wind:
The Flying Carpet I

Therefore they shall be as the morning cloud, and as the early dew that passeth away, as the chaff that is driven with the whirlwind out of the floor, and as the smoke out of the chimney.

Hosea 13:3

I

SHAHRAZAD BEGINS TO RELATE 'THE Tale of the City of Brass' on the 567th night, past the centre of the vortex of her stories; it is a slow, magnificent, melancholy tale of a quest within a quest, a sober elegy to human littleness and mortality, condensing major themes of the *Nights*. The critic Andras Hamori has called it, a little unkindly, 'the gloomiest of travelogues', but its protracted, incantatory melancholy creates a lull – a *berceuse* motif in the midst of a vast symphony.

The Caliph Abd el-Malik ruled the immense Umayyad empire from its capital in Damascus from 685 to 705 at a time at the beginning of Islam when someone of his eminence could plausibly have been in ignorance about the fate of the rebellious jinn; Talib ibn Sahl is also an historical figure, a traveller who was famed for divining the whereabouts of buried treasure. The story covers a vivid expanse of territory, while the ruins encountered in the course of the travellers' quest invoke the past glories of civilisations both historical and legendary, including the vanished civilisation of ancient Egypt (Shelley caught this note in his famous sonnet 'Ozymandias'). Like the story of the Fisherman and the Genie, 'The City of Brass' embroiders a myth of origin for the magic powers in the *1001 Nights*.

The afrit Dahesh, imprisoned in his pillar of basalt, corresponds to other disturbing figures in the *Nights*, a book which continually tests the limits of animate life. Like one of the sinners whom Dante meets in the underworld, Dahesh is mocked by his punishment: just as he once impersonated a statue, he is now forced to live for ever as a block of stone. As he thinks

back on the circumstances that brought him to his pilloried state, his story
has a tragic dignity that inspires sympathy in the reader, in spite of the
caricatured grotesqueness with which his outer features are described.

The engraver William Harvey, illustrating Lane's 1850 translation of 'The City of
Brass', renders in detail the description of the monstrous rebel jinni, Dahesh,
condemned to live immured for ever in a pillar of black stone in the desert.

In contrast to his immobility, the story Dahesh tells is filled with
movement – with sound and fury. It also considerably complicates the
character of Solomon himself. The refined details which evoke the flying
carpet clash perversely with the bloodthirsty matter in hand, and throw
into stark relief the sophisticated, smooth and luxurious authority of the
magus against the heterogeneous hideousness of the demon army. But
Solomon travels by this prodigious means because, as the Koran says, he
can command the elements, especially the winds, as he can the water
he changes to glass when the Queen of Sheba comes.

The intuition is interesting: Solomon does not invent a zoomorphic flying machine after the model of birds or insects, as so many of his predecessors in myth and fantasy do: he is no Daedalus, no Alexander. By contrast Solomon's magic controls a natural source of energy, the winds. Aerodynamics need both to streamline the vehicle and to harness the power, but still the principle behind the flying carpet is not as absurd as it seems at first glance: a people of skilled navigators and sailors, the Arabs and other Middle Easterners envisaged a form of sailing through the air on a sheet like a kind of spinnaker. His carpet is a universe of itself; an airborne, mobile world.

Solomon is sometimes cast as the protagonist of the journey to find the abandoned city; in these variations on 'The City of Brass,' the tale is less a quest for the copper flasks than a warning to Solomon that responds to the ambiguities of his character. The apocalyptic battle over the idolatrous king's daughter reflects the legends about his womanising, explicitly condemned in the Bible, while the violence of the struggle against the sea-king amplifies, in popular apocalyptic mode, the brief, elliptical ambiguous hints in the Koran about the way Solomon was tested.

The encounter with the doomed afrit darkens the already sombre and God-fearing mood of the tale; as it moves deeper into the desert, the party is travelling back in time, finding the way strewn with exemplary acts of God in punishing his enemies and unbelievers. The quest for the City of Brass is also a journey towards understanding the implacable divine justice – anger – throughout history.

In both cases, when the travellers arrive at the City, its desolation achieves the same majestic notes of pity, lament and awe; it is a ruin like Thebes or Abu Simbel or ancient Babylon, a witness to past grandeur and an eerie site of phantoms and loss. The story swirls the reader deeper and deeper into lost ages when the people and the civilisation of the City of Brass flourished and produced their magnificent buildings and inventions. The descriptions of the city's multifarious wonders proceed through lists and numbers, accumulations and litanies, repetition and rhythmic incantation, in ways that echo the passages that evoke the splendour of Solomon and in particular of the Temple that Solomon builds in the Book of Kings in the Bible and in the Koran.

When Dahesh's account includes the mysterious offering of a locust leg to the Queen of the Ants, that sign of Solomon's wisdom offers another lesson in humility inside the larger picture given by the City of Brass, which stresses at every turn the fall of the most ambitious and grandest of civilisations, and the insignificance of even the greatest princes and sages.

In the versions which feature Solomon as the leader of the expedition, he clears the sands concealing the gates in the city walls by commanding the jinn to blow them away; when he enters the city, the magic image which has been guarding it for all these centuries raises the alarm: '"Come hither, ye children of Iblis, for King Solomon has come to destroy you!" And fire and smoke came out of its nostrils. Immediately there arose a loud and bitter cry among the demons and there was earthquake and thunder.' They take flight, rushing to drown themselves in the sea rather than capitulate to Solomon; he then leaves on his carpet 'away from the place of a vanished people'.

This cycle of Solomon's legends ends with prophecies of the coming of the Prophet Muhammad and the pilgrimage to Mecca. 'So great was the number of pilgrims that Solomon had a new and much larger carpet woven for him by the Jinns.'

In the story as told in the *Nights*, the entry into the city follows a different pattern, with the party of travellers depending on an alternative figure of wisdom, the old sage, Abd el-Samad.

The city itself is a work of craftsmanship and technology, raised and adorned by human skills and trades, overflowing with luxury and plenty – once upon a time; a specifically brazen city perhaps because brass, unlike gold or silver, is a metal alloy made by human craft. It brings before the mind's eye a bewitched castle that is also a Platonist nightmare – a civilisation entirely made up of illusions and artifice, where everything is dead though it looks as if it were alive. The city offers a mirror image of culture's ambitions, and a catastrophic warning to the story's characters and readers.

The method of the storyteller drops the imagination into a dizzying descent through what Shakespeare in *The Tempest* calls 'the dark backward and abysm of time' (1: ii.50); we fall through aeons, and yet, at the same time, the city's characteristic motifs – the details of sparkling gold and crystal and jewels, the infinite variety of objects that are somehow animate and kinetic, the invisible demon-infested atmosphere, the feeling of wonder and dread – spring vividly to life in the mind's eye, a presage of the Gothic imagination in its most contemporary forms in the cinema.

Intricately imbricated, the stories in 'The City of Brass' still involve fewer strands than most of the narrative skeins in the *Nights*. The tale has a marked unity of purpose: a grand, extended meditation on vanity, in the tradition of medieval 'ubi sunt?' writings and it echoes the Koran's harsh reminders of impious peoples and cities (Iram-of-the-High Columns, for example), which have also vanished. It is also a variation on the *vanitas* meditations in the Bible; as in the Book of Ecclesiastes, this Arabian night is cadenced throughout by outbursts of extravagant lamenting.

In the *Nights*, the story asserts the true faith of Islam, and urges conversion. A close, succinct counterpart, 'The Tale of the City of Labtayt', gives an eerie, laconic variation on the theme more tightly connected to history: every time Christendom sees a new king come to the throne, another lock is added to the gates of a castle to which nobody has gained entrance. A new king succeeds to the throne who wants to smash the locks of his predecessors and see what lies inside the secret castle. Against all the warnings and pleas of his subjects, he breaks down the gates and enters. Inside he finds statues of Arabs, armed and mounted; further on, a tablet warns that anyone who profanes the enclave will see his realm pass into the power of the people – the Arabs – he sees here.

That same year, says the story, when the king flouted the prohibition, Andalusia was conquered, he was put to death most horribly, and the treasures of Labtayt, including all those manuscripts containing Solomon's wisdom and knowledge of the sciences, were carried off.

In this way, the story recalls that, when they invaded Spain, the Arabs discovered the 'learning of Greek origin which Islam would then develop'.

In keeping with the spirit of the Koran – and the Old Testament prophets – the stories of the lost cities of civilisation, of Ad and Iram-of-the-High Columns, mentioned in the Koran (89: 5/6–7/80), lament the futility and transitory nature of human achievement, and insist on the fate of the profaners, the disobedient, the apostates and the unbelievers. The fate of great, vanished empires gives a vision of the past as inevitable failure: 'The City of Brass' and other tales emphasise not the empty desert of Shelley's 'Ozymandias', where once-mighty works stood, but the wreckage of those works when even supreme wisdom is tempted by complacency and excess of power.

II

The flying carpet of Solomon belongs to the mythology of the whole Middle East, originating at a time before the *Arabian Nights* was compiled. It has been eclipsed by much more popular later manifestations, in illustrated books and, above all, the cinema, but the qualities that made it a fitting vehicle for the great prophet and king persist in the much more familiar folklore that developed, in stories such as 'The Tale of Prince Ahmed and the Fairy Peri Banou' and 'The Tale of Aladdin of the Beautiful Moles.'

Certain traditional patterns signal a carpet's uses: a prayer rug often includes a schematic *mihrab* or niche for the owner to unroll and lay in the direction of the *qibla*, the Kaaba and Mecca. (Pl. 9) Sometimes the four rivers of Paradise are shown flowing from this *mihrab*. A beautiful pattern, under the generic title of the Tree of Life, unfolds paradisical scenes of flowers and fruit, with animals in harmony. Other designs from Persia in particular map the garden of Paradise, or offer schematic but rich of conceptions of the world. The carpets of China, India and Persia sometimes include scenes, occasionally even people, and decipherable stories. The Persian Emperor Chosroes, fabled for his opulence, commissioned a carpet in AD 562 to celebrate his conquest of the Yemen and the treaty he had concluded with the Emperor in the West, Justinian. The carpet became known as 'The Spring of Chosroes', and during the winter months when he could not wander in his own palace gardens it provided him with a flowering pleasance no less airy and spacious, no less sumptuous and efflorescent: it had *allées* where he could walk and flower beds filled with gems; the earth was of gold, the water features of crystal.

Compare this lost marvel with an Indo-Ispahan Carpet with mirroring zigzag meanders in the central panel, a border of interlaced floral garlands, and birds, each one different, perched on the innermost border against the rich red ground of the rug. In one highly unusual pictorial example in the collection of the Gulbenkian Museum, Lisbon, several Portuguese merchants in hats, smoking pipes and perched on the prow of caravels, appear in a magnificent piece thought to be of seventeenth-century Persian manufacture.

Such worldly and luxurious artefacts are each of them one of a kind, non-pareil; but ordinary carpets are also found everywhere in use in the *Nights*, and in the cultures where they originate they are more than floor coverings (although they do serve this purpose). Spread on the ground, they define a space – a zone for prayer, a ceremonial enclave, an official precinct. Their display is festive: it celebrates a presence, a special visitor, a holiday (Pl. 11). In Italian Renaissance paintings by Carlo Crivelli, Andrea Mantegna, and many others, rich oriental carpets are not only spread beneath the throne of the Madonna and Child, but also appear hung from the balconies of surrounding palaces to celebrate a holiday. The practice of displaying fine carpets and fabrics migrated to Venice (it can be seen in Carpaccio's cycle of Santa Ursula, for example) and to England, where Charles II's entry was greeted by such display. In Andalusia today, when the statue of the Madonna passes down the street on one of her feast days, the inhabitants still bring out their most precious textiles – shawls and tapestries and rugs – to honour her as she goes by.

Solomon enjoys command over the jinn, who carry him through the air on his luxurious, carpeted throne, while birds provide shade overhead. (Persian, sixteenth century)

So the carpet that transports Solomon on the back of the wind unfurls to include manifold meanings. 'Tapis' in the French translation hints at the broader sense – closer to tapestry. The flying carpet is above all a luxury, a ruler's unique and beautiful treasure, a hanging, a coverlet, an 'arras', and a screen. It belongs at the centre of the panoply that shows forth Solomon's status as prophet and king; it forms an intrinsic part of his enthroned glory, there to manifest his sacred dignity. (Vestiges of such ceremonial and symbolic associations of carpets have not disappeared: the customary red carpet was rolled out the length of the nave of Westminster Abbey and on to the pavement outside for the wedding of Prince William and Catherine Middleton, to awed commentaries from the press. Being 'carpeted', i.e. reprimanded, also conveys the power of authority. At airports, thin red mats mark the queue for first or business class, and at the Musée du Quai Branly in Paris in 2009 I noticed that the priority queue for ticket-holders is marked on the tarmac outside by a carpet – in red paint.)

In the Middle East, carpets have generally been too highly prized to be routinely trodden underfoot; unrolling one's prayer mat is central to daily worship, while taking off one's shoes is a sign of respect and correspondingly, as we have seen on the news, flinging one's shoes at someone is a powerful insult in the Middle East. Rugs cordon off a place of higher value to protect it from pollution, and their various uses carry memory traces of the nomadic makers. Carried into the countryside for picnics, and spread out beneath trees or beside springs and pools, oriental carpets become mobile pictures and ornaments as well as furnishings. They also transform somewhere that is outside into something domestic, as it were inside. When laid on rooftops on summer nights, for example, they move the salon or coffee room upstairs in order for the household members to enjoy the cooler temperatures: as recalled by Naguib Mahfouz in *The Cairo Trilogy*, for example, and Hanan al-Shaykh in her short story, 'The Persian Carpet'.

There are humbler carpets; but the humbler variety also does duty as a prayer mat, a portable precinct where someone can be contained, separated from whatever is happening around. In an essay on the poetics of the carpet, the Italian art historian Sergio Bettini rejects any thought of decoration and insists instead on the architectural function of rugs laid out on the ground: for the nomadic societies who make them, carpets demarcate their home. Not in the manner of a fence or a wall, but to build the dwelling itself. 'The true carpet,' he writes, '. . . isn't a garment that covers the body or a drape that adorns a house; for the simple reason that it is itself the house.'

A carpet can be hung as well; in function it can be used like an arras, a curtain, and a coverlet. Bettini censures those who blur these categories, but he is too severe: if the carpet rolls out the space of home on a plane, the nomadic tent institutes it in three dimensions by means of hangings, awnings, covers, canopies, which are also worked with intricate patterns. The fabrics create distinctive spaces, sometimes public, sometimes private. The Kaaba itself is screened by richly patterned curtains. But fabrics are suspended to screen private places of intimacy too – nooks, pavilions, alcoves. Shahrazad is depicted with the Sultan on the frontispiece of the Galland edition illustrated in Amsterdam in 1728–30 in such a bed-tent, and her sister Dunyazad, when her presence is invoked, is present but screened behind a curtain. Cleopatra – so famously delivered to Caesar rolled up in a rug, according to Plutarch's entertaining account – was not improvising on the uses of carpets, unusual as her mode of delivery has generally seemed to modern readers. The carpet carves a private world for its user; it is a kind of portable sanctum, a more than usually splendid mobile home.

III

When a carpet takes off, as Solomon's does when he carries his armies into battle with the King of the Jinn, the bird's-eye view gives him a vantage point of great power; from this height and synoptic angle, hitherto unknown experiences and information can be unified and displayed. The flying vehicle grants the flyer superior powers – to see farther, to know and control more. More precisely, a carpet or rug miniaturises the view, unfolding a full planar perspective: plan with elevation included. The aerial view defies the laws of time and space, and for the narrator in the story (and beyond him or her, Shahrazad who is telling all), flying gives a chance to lose those constraints and bodies forth a literal, dream pun on flight of fancy on the one hand, and the rush of enhanced knowledge – enlightenment – on the other. The analogies with storytelling are plain, especially with regard to fairy tales, where the narrator's knowledge of what is to come is assumed, and the witnesses to their own histories – such as both Sinbads, the three dervishes in the cycle of the Porter, the Eldest Lady and numerous other embedded story tellers in the book – are also in full possession of the facts of their narratives as they revisit their experiences retrospectively. Shahrazad does not provide the overarching viewpoint, however, because there is the unnamed narrator who begins the book and continues to appear, returning us to the scene in the Sultan's bedroom and finally resolving the story (technically the extradiegetic voice). This is the omniscient view, surveying all, and it correlates with supreme wisdom, as possessed by Solomon, embarked on his flying vehicle which gives him an overview. The unfurled carpet that rises above the action, spreads out level and moves over it, embodies features that distinguish epic, often unauthored narratives, originating in oral culture (Homer's bird's-eye view of the siege of Troy, for example); the repetition of motifs and their imbrication in bands and borders also reproduce graphically the layering of the narrative method and the repetitions and condensation of motifs in an anthology like the *Nights*.

Paradoxically, this heroic and often vast vision can allow small, personal glimpses of private scenes, and so become a vehicle for gaining entry to secrets – and for transmitting intimate communiqués to the viewer. Furthermore, an aerial viewpoint defies the laws of time and space, and gives the narrator a chance to fly free of these constraints. The vantage point magic makes possible grants the flyer superior powers – to see farther, to know and control more.

In traditional literature this view often contains a warning. Alexander the Great, whose legend intertwines with Solomon's, learns a bitter lesson in his *Romance* when he surveys the world beneath him from the flying machine he has rigged up with griffons. He realises that his vast empire is tiny by comparison with the expanses that unfold beneath him. A winged man appears and warns him of the folly of his ambitions. '"Look down on the earth, Alexander!"' he orders him.

'"I looked down, somewhat afraid, and behold I saw a great snake curled up, and in the middle of the snake a tiny circle like a threshing floor."' The angel then tells him, '"Point your spear at the threshing floor, for that is the world. The snake is the sea that surrounds the world."' The emperor understands his vanity, and when he lands, frozen and exhausted, from his aerial adventure, he finds himself seven days' march from his army.

The view from above miniaturises and flattens, compressing the cosmos on to a surface in order to inculcate a sense of human insignificance. But there is also, packed inside this lesson, the myth of Faustian hubris. When the devil takes Jesus up to the topmost peak to look over Jerusalem and offers him the world laid out below him, he is taking the opposing line to Alexander's angel, and tempting him to greater ambition. When Simon Magus the sorcerer boasts to Peter that he can fly, he summons a devil to help him as he begins his demonstration, but still he tumbles to his death. The *Arabian Nights* tells the story of the Queen of the Serpents, who carries Hasib to the summit of the legendary Mount Qaf to show him the wonders of the world. She is initiating him into magic and esoteric wisdom permitted only to the privileged wise man, prophet and hero.

In the *Inferno*, Dante reflects the tense, moral ambiguity with which visions of flight were associated, and interestingly his imagination turns eastwards, specifically to carpets and carpet-makers, when he describes the fabulous flying monster Gerione who appears to carry Virgil and Dante into the pit of hell.

Dante's Geryon bears the name of the Greek mythical creature, but he is an altogether richer and more alluring beast, a jinn-like being, aerial, vast and terrifying, a master of deception with a beautiful face, a terrible stench, and a scorpion's tail. His oriental, figured gorgeousness heightens his treacherous allure:

> La faccia sua era d'uom giusto . . .
> e d'un serpente tutto l'altro fusto;
> due branche avea pilose infin l'ascelle;
> lo dosso e 'l petto e ambedue le coste
> dipinti avea di nodi et di rotelle:
> con più color, sommesse e sopraposte
> non fer mai drappi Tartari nè Turchi,
> nè fuor tai tele per Aragne imposte.'
> (Dante, *Inferno* XVII: 10–18)

'His face was the face of a just man . . . and all the rest was a serpent's down his trunk; he had two paws, hairy to the armpit, and the back and breast and both flanks were painted with knots and circlets – Tartars or Turks never made such stuffs with such colours in ground and embroidery, nor were such webs laid by Arachne on the loom.'

It is one of Dante's characteristic comparisons: in order to bring out the particular grandeur of a phenomenon he is experiencing, he sets it beside the greatest instance he knows, and then exclaims that it far exceeds that limit. When he adds that Gerione's richly patterned body surpasses the brilliancy of colour and design created by carpet-weavers from Tartary and Turkey (the Ovidian figure of Arachne is a young woman of Lydia, hence also made 'Turkish' tapestries), he seems to be warning himself not to be seduced by the excitement of the flight. His fear of falling off clashes with the excitement conveyed by the adventure, the wheeling journey down into the abyss, and he leans on the imagery to give it moral ballast: he compares himself to Phaeton and to Icarus, both of them warnings against hubris; he builds up the physical sensations of flight into order to stress how terrified he was.

As the beast goes circling slowly on down, Dante turns to natural observation to evoke him, likening him to a falcon in a widening gyre who lands, exhausted. Then Gerione deposits his human cargo at the bottom of the pit and vanishes, bringing Canto 17 to a mysterious, open-ended close. The remarkable scene is a microcosm of the conflict, central to flight itself, between ascent and descent − and the allegorical meanings they bear.

Story 3
Prince Ahmed and the Fairy Peri Banou

THREE BROTHERS, SONS OF THE Sultan of the Indies, are rivals for the hand of the exquisitely beautiful Princess Nouronnihar, their first cousin and an orphan, who lives in the palace with them. The three princes are dispatched by their father at the beginning of the story: the one who brings back the greatest wonder shall marry her.

Prince Houssain, the eldest, travels eastwards in several caravans to a city of fabulous wealth, where a fabulous trade in carpets and jewels is being conducted, rose-sellers throng the streets, and its black inhabitants gleam from the gold, pearls and gems with which they are covered. He hears a tapestry cried for an inflated sum – it's a nondescript piece, on the small side, and besides, the fabric is poor. But the vendor reveals to him that if you sit on it, you can be carried in an instant anywhere in the world you want to be.

Prince Ali, the second brother, travels to Shiraz and there buys a telescope carved from ivory, through which you can see anything and everything, wherever it is happening in the world at the time.

Meanwhile Ahmed, the youngest, has taken the road to Samarkand; there he acquires for a very high price an artificial apple which exudes a perfume that can heal any disease.

Once the brothers meet again at an inn on the road as arranged, they see through Ali's telescope that the beautiful Princess Nouronnihar has been taken terribly ill and is on the point of death. The three brothers immediately mount the flying carpet and ride to her rescue – and then use the magic apple to cure her.

Revived, Nouronnihar still has no say in her choice of suitor, and the father of the three princes continues to declare himself undecided. So he sets a further test for his sons: the one who shoots an arrow the farthest will win her for his bride.

Ahmed's arrow flies out of sight and he's disqualified; Nouronnihar marries the winner, Prince Ali, while Houssain, in his fury at losing her, renounces the crown and becomes a dervish. Ahmed meanwhile sets out to find his arrow and finds himself straying far from any territory known to him, until he discovers it pointing the way through rocks to an iron door; through this he descends and enters . . . fairyland. Peri Banou comes to greet him, leads him into her palace where she sits him down and tells him that she has contrived to bring him to her by her magic arts, for the carpet, the glass and the apple were her handiwork, and she then carried off his arrow. If he seizes his chance with her now, she promises to make him happy. According to fairy law, she explains, women can be forward and choose their love; she has chosen him, if he'll agree. Prince Ahmed needs no persuading, and the ceremony takes place then and there between the two of them, contracted and sealed with a thousand kisses.

At court, the Sultan is pining for his lost children – Houssain has become a dervish, he knows, but Ahmed has vanished. He summons a sorceress to help him trace them, and she assures him Ahmed is alive. When Ahmed reappears, given permission by Peri Banou to visit his father, this wicked female magician conspires with jealous courtiers to excite the Sultan's suspicions. She then follows Ahmed on his return journey to Peri Banou, and feigning illness by the side of the road, tricks him into taking her with him into the kingdom of faery, where she is nursed by Peri Banou's kindly jinn helpers, and spies out the land. Once back in his court, this old and wicked maga is able to report to the Sultan on the magnificence and power of the fairy queen with whom his youngest son is living. Malignantly, she stirs up his envy and works on his insecurity, until he agrees to everything she proposes.

Through her magic arts, Peri Banou is to grant the Sultan one fabulous magic boon after another; just as she had provided the glass, the carpet and the apple, she now conjures an enchanted tent, light as a feather yet large enough to shelter his entire army; this does not satisfy him. Spurred on by the sorceress, he asks for the magic water from the fountain of lions, which she had been given when she was pretending to be ill. Ahmed sets out on the dangerous quest for this precious element, and with the help of Peri Banou's charms, manages to bring back a flask of it. Again, the Sultan is not satisfied. This time he asks his son to bring him a tiny man with the strength of giants, with a beard thirty feet long, carrying a huge heavy bar of iron.

Peri Banou reveals that this creature is none other than her unpredictable and violent brother, Schaibar, and with fumigations, she conjures him to appear.

When Ahmed takes Schaibar to meet his father, everybody flees from the terrifying sight of the dwarf; he marches up to the Sultan and demands to know why he has been summoned to his presence. But the Sultan covers his eyes in horror, insulting Schaibar, who lifts his iron bar and strikes him dead. He then lays about him right and left to the same end, killing the wicked sorceress as well. Prince Ali and Nouronnihar would have suffered the same fate, had Ahmed not intervened. Instead, they're given a good portion but dethroned; Prince Ahmed takes over as Sultan and the fairy Peri Banou is established Sultana of the Indies.

CHAPTER THREE

A Tapestry of Great Price: The Flying Carpet II

> . . . the upheaval will be complete as worlds are flung out of orbit, the
> magic chair will carry him [the sleeper] off at full speed through time
> and space, and when he opens his eyes again he will imagine that he went
> to sleep months earlier in another place.
>
> Marcel Proust, *À la Recherche du temps perdu*

I

THE STORIES OF THE *Nights* invite the Sultan to deepen his understanding – of wonders, secrets, human behaviour and the unexpected
twists of destiny – and we the readers find ourselves listening in and
learning alongside him. When human characters, as opposed to Solomon,
are given the chance to set off on a flying carpet, the double effects of
excitement and disorientation resonate very powerfully indeed.

The magic carpet does not attract special attention from the storyteller; it simply features as one of three magical gifts obtained by the
brothers. Yet, just as the glass extends the faculty of sight, the carpet
also undoes limits on human capacity – all three magic objects in the
story overcome human limits and the bonds of ordinary space and
time. The enchantments of a powerful fairy, numerous ordeals, extensive
globetrotting – including excursions to fairy realms – and a happy
ending for all, follow romance convention. But in spite of Peri Banou's
otherworldly nature, the atmosphere of this fairy tale does not evoke
a fairyland of fantasy, the far-distant islands of Waq-Waq or a kingdom
under the sea, as in the tale of Jullanar the Sea-Born and her brothers.
By contrast, the three princes' wanderings eastwards, through present
day Syria, Iraq, Iran and India, reveal a degree of first-hand knowledge
of the countries' cultures in a recognisable time period, often doubling
the tracks of Galland himself in his explorations of the Middle East
and farther afield. The story echoes several other romances from the
core corpus of the *Nights*, such as 'The Tale of the Vizier Nur Ad-din

and his Brother Shams al-Din', in which improbable coincidences follow one upon the other in rich circumstantial detail. 'Prince Ahmed' unfolds with similar enthusiasm a profusely detailed, admiring panorama of the traffic and bustle on their city streets, and inventories the abundant, ingenious, precious goods and services on offer in the markets and the buildings. This genre of literary survey – a cross between an auctioneer's catalogue and an explorer-scholar's true report – presents a realistic, synoptic view from above that will provide European scientific inquiry with a mode of writing. A twist on the imaginary voyage as a genre, the oriental adventure will open horizons in narrative methods themselves, to direct stories towards creative, scientific speculation.

It is not insignificant that Prince Houssain buys the flying carpet in one of these wonder-laden emporia: no jinn conjures it or sorcerer produces it (Pl. 19). A merchant offers it for sale for a high price: the story presents this marvellous thing as something that has been made, whose value is known and can be, in the way of modern markets, acquired by purchase. The humour of understatement suffuses the exchange, but does not erode the wonder, and this empirical curiosity about other peoples, their ways and their worlds, when combined with fairy tale invention, spurs the reasoning imagination.

Through another magical realist slippage between figurative and literal, the glass and the carpet in particular reproduce the effects of the imagination as it is stimulated by stories – by listening to them or by reading them. The princes can see the princess on her sickbed and they can displace themselves at whim. Perhaps the scented apple too communicates the restorative energy of literature and storytelling?

The magic gifts in 'Prince Ahmed' are toys: toys in the sense that automata are also toys – mechanical birds in cages, clepsydrae, and dolls or puppets that sing, dance and write. While they reflect princely passions for such ingenious devices in the seventeenth and eighteenth centuries, they also resemble the character of enchanted things in myth and romance: the magic mirror and the flying brass horse that appear in Chaucer's 'Squire's Tale', for example. Magic flying furniture is commonplace in the *Nights*: in the tale of 'Aladdin of the Beautiful Moles', the lovers embark on a flying sofa; in the tale of 'Hasan of Basra', the enchantress Shawahi sails through the air in a Greek amphora which she adapts with a harness of palm leaves for the purpose. The opening story of Jonathan Scott's collection of translations features a flying chair, which does duty for the charming rascal hero along the lines of Aladdin's lamp, until it is mistakenly chopped up and burnt as firewood by a diligent maid who thinks it is nothing but an old and broken bit of furniture. The mechanical flying horses are not entirely of the same order, but, being non-sentient, they are also distinct from Pegasus.

Aerial transport is otherwise provided in the *Nights* by animate means: by the giant Rukh bird, the arms and shoulders and backs of jinn, magic cloaks of feathers that change their wearers into birds. Flying is always charged with highly ambiguous magic power, and on some occasions jinn tremble at picking up a human being since they are only allowed to carry those who know the secret name of God.

The carpet has however eclipsed these other vehicles, and become synonymous with the *Arabian Nights*. Yet, if you search for its appearances in the book, it can prove elusive, for 'Prince Ahmed and the Fairy Peri Banou', the story in which it makes its clearest appearance, belongs to the cluster of tales which were first written down by Antoine Galland in Paris, as heard from Hanna Diab, his Syrian Christian informant. So it is one of the 'orphan tales', like 'Aladdin' and 'Ali Baba'. It was published in 1717, in the last, posthumous volume of Galland's *Mille et une nuit*. The first English Grub Street *Arabian Nights' Entertainments* includes it, and it later enters the anthologies by Lane and Burton and others keen to swell the number of tales to fill the three years and more that elapse in the course of Shahrazad's feat. But as it is not included in the Arabic editions (Calcutta I or Calcutta II), on which the most reputable recent editors draw, the story has been left out of many of the recent most scholarly translations.

The internal evidence of 'Prince Ahmed' strongly supports an attribution to Galland or another French author of the time: in structure and motifs, the tale matches closely fairy tales by Galland's contemporaries, especially Marie-Catherine d'Aulnoy; the stories she published a little earlier stage similarly protracted and outlandish romantic tests for lovers, as well as ingenious magical devices and aerial transport, in, for example, 'La Chatte blanche', 'Serpentin vert', and 'L'Oranger et l'abeille'. 'Prince Ahmed' is also shaggy and inconsistent, but whereas D'Aulnoy and her associates often bring off such weakness with a bravura flourish, the appearance of the herculean and capricious dwarf in the concluding episode of 'Prince Ahmed' has no satisfying emotional logic. There are other possible influences: a flying carpet, called a *samolyet* ('self-flyer'), also appears in Russia, casually invoked alongside magic cudgels, shirts and tablecloths; in the story of 'The Frog Princess', it belongs to an old woman, and Ivan and his beloved escape from her clutches by stealing it and flying away.

Nevertheless, in spite of its inauthenticity, 'Prince Ahmed' has rightly been a favourite with readers and imitators, and its opening plot has shaped numerous later interpretations of the *Nights*, including *The Thief of Bagdad* (1924; 1940) and Lotte Reiniger's *Adventures of Prince Achmed* (1926), three of the most significant films made of the *Nights* (see Chapters 18 and 19). If Galland pieced and patched together from other stories, he was only doing what storytellers have always done, before and since. The magic device of the carpet can take its place beside other emblems of fairytale fashioned by an author under a sudden inspiration, such as Cinderella's glass slipper or the wicked queen's speaking mirror. The symbol distils essence of Orient (*eau d'Orient*, as it were); it did so for the eighteenth-century audience, and it was to enjoy a stellar future as a symbol in the Western imagination of narrative dream-voyaging itself.

Besides its solemn role as Solomon's vehicle, the flying carpet is associated with lighter matters: it makes a brief appearance in a story from the *Nights* about a fairy bride, a mythic predecessor of Peri Banou, and this is a likely internal source for Galland. In the long, imbricated sequence told by the Queen of the Serpents, one of the oldest cycles in the book, the hero Janshah wins the love of Shamshah, and they return to his earthly home again on 'a throne so vast that two hundred male Jinn and two hundred females might stand upon the steps of it'; it is then picked up by a host of other jinn and wafted to Janshah's father's palace in Kabul.

The translator Mardrus, who took a leaf from Galland in his approach to the task, introduced his own variation, a story known only from his collection: a spirited princess who, like so many in the *Nights*, has sworn never to marry, happens also to be a prize wrestler, and manages to floor every one of her suitors in turn (and have their heads chopped off afterwards). She is ultimately vanquished, however, by the son of a poor flute player who has come by a flying carpet. He uses it to abduct her, but in midair she heartlessly tosses him overboard. It takes a few more bouts before they reach the happy ending – and bliss together.

It is nevertheless a surprise when editions of the *Nights* no longer include a fully functioning flying carpet, and, in spite of these examples, the fact remains that the magic carpet which can transport its owner through the air at his – or her – command does not dominate the Arabic collection of stories or its literary imitations and homages nearly as strongly as expected. Yet it has clearly emerged as the universally understood, contemporary symbol of the *Arabian Nights*, the enchantments in the stories, the pleasures and possibilities they offer. It acts as shorthand for dream, ecstasy and fulfilled desire, and for creating thrills with erotic and transfiguring resonance. More broadly, too, flying figures of different varieties, magical machines and automata, and fantastically imagined displacements in the stories perform a series of delighting puns on the very idea of transport – as both travel and rapture. (See Chapter 13.) Flying in most ingenious ways becomes central to the range of metamorphic experiences.

The Tales of a Thousand and One Nights were published in Europe during a century of experiments with flying vehicles, which would culminate in the first balloon ascents in the 1780s. The stories associate such views from above with the power and knowledge of flight brought about on behalf of humans by magic, either by jinn or by enchanters' devices. But they no longer condemn it, as in the tradition of Faust; in the later interpretations of the stories, both on the page and on stage and screen, flying has been disinfected of sorcery. It has come instead to stand for the action of the story, in whatever medium, in the minds of its readers or audience, for they themselves become transported on a fantastic journey alongside the heroes of the adventures, often airborne.

In the course of the nineteenth and twentieth centuries, the flying carpet gradually took over from Aladdin's lamp, which had dominated the theatrical spectaculars of the eighteenth, and from the figure of Shahrazad herself. The cinema took to the motif with gusto, and the kinship was recognised from its early years: a worthy Manchester doctor, writing in the *Guardian* in 1913, deplored the way the populace was idling at 'the pictures' when they should be turning an honest penny, yet even he allowed himself to see the promise of pleasure they brought, and he reached for the image of the flying carpet of the *Nights*: 'Every evening a magic carpet transports half of us, men, women, and children, to a region which we can explore with something of the joy of a traveller from chill northern lands in an unvisited country of tropical refulgence where it is always afternoon.'

The Disney cartoon *Aladdin* (1992) gives the carpet a role as Aladdin's best mate, and animates it/him with ingenious gestures of his tassel hands and feet. In the closing sequence, Aladdin and Princess Jasmine are embarked together on the flying carpet, rapturously soaring and swooping above the landscape as the song 'A Whole New World' plays in the background. The scene speaks of the lovers' rapture, but also of a glorious future ahead in other terms (the film is, absolutely, an 'American dream').

Legends have grown up around the carpet: a favourite internet urban myth spins a tall tale from elements of the *Arabian Nights* to tell of the secret sect who wove the magic rugs in eleventh-century Baghdad, where they were used in aerial warfare (as in Dahesh's story from the 'City of Brass'), commercial transport systems, and in the Library in Alexandria to reach the books on the top shelves. This is a spoof by an Australian-Iranian writer, Azhar Abidi, but it has been taken as a true report, in keeping with the tradition exemplified by Borges's *ficcion,* 'Tlön, Uqbar, Orbis Tertius', in which the real world is gradually absorbed into the fictive one. By contrast, in 2000, the artists Jem Finer and Ansuman Biswas, experimenting in a genuine spirit of inquiry, tried to ride small prayer mats in the gravity-free environment of a Russian astronaut training centre. The resulting film, *Zero Genie*, shows each artist, dressed in turban and caftan, cross-legged on a levitating rug, and hanging on for dear life while burly Russian astronauts now and then teasingly give them a prod to send them soaring. The footage has an absurd hilarity and pathos, recalling the harshly comic scene in William Beckford's novel *Vathek*, when Nouronihar and her companions in the harem push the Chief Eunuch Bababalouk higher and higher on their indoor swing until he begs for mercy and is unceremoniously dumped in the women's pool.

II

To understand the thinking that turned the folk motif of a flying carpet into such a prime symbol of fantasy today it is necessary to press a little further into the analogies between carpets, desire and narrative, specifically the narrative of dream-thoughts and fantastic, oriental plots. The history of the relations between text and textile, fantasy and flight provides remarkable instances of the logic of the imagination at work at a profound, unconscious poetic level, and the carpet of the *Arabian Nights* metonymically enacts the work of imagination in making up a story and perusing it; knotting a plot or following it, drawing on a repertory of elements in different, recurring combinations, adds to the satisfaction of the audience. The perceived 'figure' brings the pleasure of recognition, while the metonymies of rug, carpet and fabric condense many desired properties of fantasy narrative: a satisfying pattern, a defining frame, harmonic relations of detail and whole, significant ornament, pleasurable texture, atmospheric colour. The practical functions flower into figurative meanings, which have themselves changed in relation to material conditions.

Persian or other oriental carpets rarely tell stories or contain human figures. The whole surface is webbed and interlaced with abstract, geometric, ornamental elements and designs. The symbols used are ancient, familiar and conventional: the arabesques, circles and stars, palmettes and rosettes, the medallions and the paisley commas, the key and other border motifs, the creatures – angels, dragons, grotesques, birds and other animals – sprinkled here and there, are for the most part recognisable, (Pl. 10).

But the key to their relations is not given. The greatest connoisseurs and traders who have studied the patterns give descriptions both broad and vague: one kind of design symbolises Paradise, another the cosmos; flower vases appear in some designs, combats of beasts in another. Their symmetries and repetitions convey experiences, which have been condensed into symbols to present a harmonious vision in colour and form; but those paisley comma's, Greek key patterns and occult geometries – they are figures whose semantics elude pinning down. The hieroglyphs are stubborn, perhaps ultimately without significance, without ulterior referent.

The intricacy and system of a woven carpet imply a strong degree of predictability; the symmetry and recursive repetitions work like oracles: the patterns must come out in a certain sequence, so discerning them becomes paramount but not quite patent. It needs finesse to read a carpet's complexities. Many of the stories in the *Nights* establish such a pattern and follow it to its outcome; often the outcome is predicted, by a prophecy or a spell, or it can be anticipated by the reader from the character of the genre. Much pleasure for the reader arises when, like the protagonist or other characters, the story takes an unexpected turn and springs a different dénouement. Or when, as in some cases, the reader succeeds in foreseeing the end result of the characters' action when they fail to do so. In these ways, the story ties up its subjects and its audience in crafty knots and self-mirroring devices: the man who recognises his own house in another man's dream about a fortune hidden in a courtyard under the floor; the dervish who opens the forbidden door and meets the fate he was trying to escape. These come out according to preordained structural rules. Vladimir Nabokov catches this recursive character of time in the *Arabian Nights* when he brings in the image in his memoir *Speak, Memory*: 'I like to fold my magic carpet, after use, in such a way as to superimpose one part of the pattern upon another.'

Even when the pattern of a rug contains no representations of animals or people or things, 'A carpet tells a story,' writes the Moroccan poet Abdelkebir Khatibi, 'a secret, and is arranged according to one's wishes, for some erotic encounter, for some prayer, for some entreaty.' Aside from the cultural coincidence of carpet-making and storytelling among nomadic peoples, the flying carpet of the *Arabian Nights* embodies the fairy way of writing and the fairy way of telling. Scenes of pleasures taken in reverie and reading share features with storytelling as Shahrazad practises it. A Turkish rug or oriental carpet from Egypt, Iraq or the eastern Mediterranean, the heartlands of the *Arabian Nights*, above all consists of a formal abstract pattern into which a repertory of certain figurative elements has been woven. This abstract order accords with an analysis of narrative structure proposed by the Russian Formalists, like Vladimir Propp. Functions and characters recur in different permutations to produce strikingly different effects: every oriental carpet is like every other, yet no two oriental carpets are identical.

Italo Calvino, who undertook in his anthology *Italian Folktales* to create a corpus comparable to the Grimm Brothers' German collection, emphasised the correspondences with the weaving process in which patterns keep shifting and creating new patterns, each time producing a new story. Writing about Giambattista Basile, the seventeenth-century Neapolitan author of the *Pentamerone*, Calvino underlines the way ornament belongs in the essential structure of the narrative, and proposes: 'A reading in which metaphors, rather than being considered an ornament that adorns the fundamental interweaving of plot, subplots and narrative functions, move them forward into the foreground, as the true substance of the text, bordered by the decorative arabesque threadwork of fabulous vicissitudes.' (As Freud said of his own dream-analysis – as discussed in more detail in Chapter 20 – the weaver conjugates structural motifs 'in infinite combinations' within a basic structure of frame, ground and figure, and then inflects each one differently through variations of colour, dimensions, quality of materials.)

The sequence of imagery reveals correspondences: the work of building the story corresponds to the weaving and knotting from a repertory of elements whose recurrence in different combinations adds to the satisfaction of the audience, bringing with it the pleasure of recognition. Khatibi comments on the interplay in Arabic culture between writing and carpet-making; and alluding to the interconnectedness of text and textile in Latin languages, he notes that the word *bissat*, a term for rug in Arabic, also describes a poetic metre. He emphasises the role geometry plays in a range of media, especially the geometry of curved forms and loops – of stitches and knots – involved in 'the arabesque'.

The flatness of a carpet contains and orders all constituent elements at an indeterminate scale – large or small – in the same way as a story compresses and organises swathes of raw material. The Italian writer Cristina Campo evokes how an oriental rug unfolds a surface on which ornaments play in infinite recession, or mise-en-abyme. 'The borders themselves are eloquent,' she writes. 'Above all, the number of the borders speaks, for it can reach twelve or thirteen, enclave within enclave, discourse into discourse. A hierarchy of allusions is assigned to the succession of borders, from the inside towards the outside.' This structure rhymes with the storytellers' methods in *Nights*: stories within stories that give the

Nights its involuted structure, just as oriental carpets are often banded one frame set inside another. The sprawling vagaries of the tales are contained – sometimes barely so – by the storyteller who imposes limits; these take the form of internal structural devices, but are also affected by the fundamental outside frame, the space of a single night which begins with Dinarzade on cue prompting her sister to speak, but which ends when dawn interrupts the episode. Then the voice that remains above or outside the scene, in the position of the Solomonic narrator above, repeats the refrain, 'and speaking was no longer permitted and Shahrazad was silent'.

Cristina Campo was a religious thinker, and she concludes her meditation on the flying carpet of the *Nights* by linking the dream of Paradise with the activity of prayer performed upon prayer rugs in Islamic ritual – as Khatibi also does. The *Arabian Nights* however is a profane work; the transports and uplift it offers are of a different order from mystical ecstasy. But the stories are populated by dervishes, sometimes called calenders, mendicant holy men who were celebrated for their whirling – which is a form of levitation, and certainly designed to take the dancer out of his body into another world until he swirls in the ether. With a magical realist move between figurative and literal, saints and heroes can, as Simon Magus and Faustus wished they could, take flight. They rise in ecstasy.

The dancer Rudolf Nureyev (d. 1993),who could jump so high and for so long that you might say he flew, stipulated that after his death he was to be buried under a rug woven by his people, Tatars of the Steppes, Muslim nomads and carpet-makers, to whom he felt he belonged by birth and upbringing. He had always been a wanderer, he said, ever since he was born, unexpectedly, on the Trans-Siberian railway when his mother was on her way to visit his father in Vladivostok; the family, though they originated from further east, were settled in Ufa, the capital of Bashkiria, one of the Muslim Khanates absorbed into the Russian empire in the time of Ivan the Terrible.

Nureyev began dancing in performances of folklore in the early 1950s during the zenith of Soviet socialist pan-Russian celebrations: some of the stories he interpreted as a boy relate to local tribal storytelling, and many elements of these folk tales have migrated in and out of the *Arabian Nights*, as Diaghilev recognised with the richly orientalising scenarios of the Ballets Russes. Later, after Nureyev had made his historic 'leap to freedom' in 1961, he danced – and choreographed – several roles that showed him leaping through the veil of the visible world into that other zone, enchanted, ethereal and dream-like, which romantic ballets like *The*

Sleeping Beauty, *Swan Lake* and *Giselle* can conjure especially well (Odile/ Odette resembles one of the peris of the *Nights*, refracted through a Christian dualist lens so that union with her can only be fatal). The dancer's tomb in the Russian cemetery at Ste-Geneviève-des-Bois outside Paris is indeed draped, as he wanted, in a gold and scarlet and richly patterned carpet, made of mosaic but looking very real (Pl. 24). Among the silver birches and the Russian Orthodox tombstones, it blazes with defiant glamour – an oriental symbol of its occupant's many flights.

Part II

Dark Arts; Strange Gods

Story 4

The Prince of the Black Islands

T HE FISHERMAN RELUCTANTLY AGREES TO trust the jinni, Sakhr,
releases him from the copper flask for a second time, and lets
himself be led toward the promised fortune. After long days' and
nights' walking beyond all known territory, they reach a lake; the jinni
has explained nothing, but at his orders the fisherman casts his net and
draws up a haul of fishes, marvellously coloured white, red, blue and yellow;
he is to take them, the jinni goes on, to the nearby palace and offer
them to the vizier for the king of that country, who will find them
delicious and give the fisherman rich payment.

It turns out as promised; but then the king wants to eat more of the
same. This time, when the vizier gives the fish to the kitchen maid to
prepare – she is new, just arrived from Byzantium, we are told – something very strange happens. As soon as the girl starts frying the fish, the
wall behind her opens and a beautiful woman appears who strikes the
fish with her wand and imperiously commands them; they lift up their
heads from the pan, and cry out:

> If you come back, we shall come back,
> If you are faithful, we shall be too.
> If you abandon us, we shall do likewise.

This is a very ambiguous profession of allegiance; she acknowledges
it, but gives no mercy and vanishes. The cook finds the dish utterly
spoiled: the fish blackened to cinders.

The king will not be deterred; he demands more fish from the fisherman and gives him even more money for them – he showers him with
gold. The same mysterious scene takes place; and then again, for a third
time. On this occasion, however, no beautiful witch appears from the
wall. Instead, a giant who resembles one of the black men of Ad, one
of the pre-Islamic Southern peoples whose cities stand abandoned in the
desert, bursts furiously from the wall and commands the fish in the pan
to renew their promises. Piteously they do so, but again to no avail – he
upsets the pan with the green staff he carries and disappears. Again, the
servant faints, and the king finds the fish charred to ash.

The king decides to investigate the prodigy, and together with the fisherman returns to the lake, which neither the king nor his vizier nor anyone in his entourage has ever seen or heard of before. But the silent lake cannot on its own solve the mystery of the fishes that swim in it. The king decides to press on further, and signalling his desire to be alone, sets off in disguise across the desert and walks for three nights and days (when the heat allows) until he comes upon a citadel of great might and splendour. It is eerily, utterly empty. He passes through the gates, the courtyards, the interior halls, all of them gorgeously decorated, with fountains playing, silk curtains gleaming and billowing, inlaid marble ringing. Not a soul. Eventually he hears a thin sad sound: crying from the innermost chamber. There he finds a young man in his prime, the beautiful young prince of the country, who cannot move from the spot or rise to greet his surprise visitor.

He has been enchanted, he tells his royal visitor, turned to stone from the navel down, by his wife whom he had loved with blissful love.

One afternoon, he relates, when he was having a siesta but missed his wife so keenly that he couldn't rest, he overheard the chatter of their servants who were fanning him, and discovered that every night the young wife who loved him, or so he thought, and whom he loved so much, laced his drink and then cursed him, telling his senseless form: 'Sleep on! And may you never wake up again. How I loathe you and your whole body. When you touch me, I feel nothing but disgust. How I long for the day you'll die.'

The maids thought it was a crying shame, he heard them say, that their mistress would then set out to meet the man she loved and spend time with him; later, on her return, she'd rouse her husband with a different drug, so that he never knew what had taken place.

The next night, the Prince of the Black Islands spills the drugged wine so that he can follow his young and beloved wife, and taking his sword he reaches the place of her tryst. There he finds that her lover is a filthy black slave, diseased and foul-mouthed, lying in rags on a dirty bed of straw in a disgusting hovel; from the roof he watches her prostrate herself and promise him everything he wants, slavishly, until he relents and makes love to her and they fall into a lovers' deep sleep. Her young husband goes mad with rage and attacks the slave, making to cut off his head. But he doesn't succeed. He leaves his rival fatally wounded, speechless and immobile.

When his wife wakes, and finds her lover half dead, she doesn't realise at this stage that her husband is to blame for his wound; instead, she announces she has suddenly lost several family members and needs to mourn. For three years she mourns, dramatically, furiously, cutting her hair and wearing sackcloth; she builds her half-dead lover a tomb as if for a saint and visits him every day, weeping and praying for his resuscitation.

After three years of this, and no sign of her laments ceasing or even lessening, her husband breaks in on her devotions; he has had enough. He confronts her with his knowledge, reveals his part in her sufferings, and advances on her to kill her.

This was the moment when she blasted him with her evil spell, the frozen and immured young man in the abandoned city tells the king and the fisherman. Muttering nonsense words over him, she paralysed him from the waist down. She also took revenge on his whole kingdom, the young prince continues, and turned the city and its four islands into a lake and every one of its inhabitants into coloured fishes, the Muslims into green/blue fish, the Christians into white, the Jews into yellow and the Zoroastrians into red.

Laying waste to his country, turning its citizens into animals, and imprisoning him in an inert body have not been enough to slake her rage for vengeance. She still comes every day to beat him with whips made of ox pizzles till the blood runs down his back, and then throws a hair shirt over him to exacerbate the agony, all the while howling over her loss.

The visiting king decides to help: he locates the tomb where the moribund slave is lying, enters it and finishes the deed the wronged husband had begun. He then dumps the corpse in a well, and going back to the tomb, he takes the slave's place on the slab, covers himself in the slave's bedclothes and waits for the weeping wife to appear. When she comes as usual with food and drink for her wounded lover, he speaks to her, imitating the accents of a man of Ad, and she can't believe the miracle: in answer to all her prayers, her beloved has revived. Still in an assumed voice, the false double reproaches her. He would have been cured long ago, he tells her, if only she would stop tormenting her husband. In wild joy she rushes back to the palace, mixes a spell in a magic bowl and sprinkles the contents over her victim. The prince's stone limbs loosen and bend and he finds himself able to move again – and all the while she still keeps railing that the sight of him disgusts her.

When she returns once more to the mausoleum, hoping to find the miracle complete, the king there, still in his convincing assumed persona, heaps her with more reproaches, telling her now that his full recovery can never happen while the city is a lake and its people fishes. Immediately, she conjures the antidote. The fishes put their heads out of the water and turn back into human beings; the lake drains away and the bustling brilliant city with its streets and houses and markets reappears with no memory of the terrible time it has endured.

The beautiful wife turns to her lover hoping for his full resurrection, but finds the king instead, who throws off his disguise, runs her through with his sword and then chops her in two.

After this, the king and the young prince who was bewitched swear eternal loyalty to each other. The latter sets off on the Hajj for Mecca, but not before marrying one of the fisherman's daughters. The visiting king, who restored the city and killed the witch and her lover, makes the fisherman's son the royal treasurer, and marries his older daughter. The fisherman becomes the richest man of his time.

No more is heard of the jinn Sakhr: he has returned to his airy element.

CHAPTER FOUR

The Worst Witch

THE TALE OF 'THE PRINCE of the Black Islands', which is also known
in Burton's translation as 'The Tale of the Ensorcelled Prince', and in
the most recent French version, simply as 'The Tale of the Young Man',
closes the first cycle of stories in the *Nights*. With its happy ending (for
some), it ties and knots several threads, and proves the power of the
ransom tale. The next cycle, 'The Porter and the Three Ladies of Baghdad',
will drive home harder the salvific function of the storyteller's art. Every
story in both these groups plunges into depths of inexplicable, forbidden
desires, and features characters whose passions cause them to perpetrate
extreme savagery.

The unnamed sorceress is the worst witch in the book; she has no
motive for her protracted cruelty towards her young husband – except
her passion for the filthy and abject slave. She figures undiluted malice
and violence, the state of a person inflamed by a pure brand of negative
passion exceptional in the book (even the Sultan does not show such
sustained raging grief at the Sultana's betrayal), and the tortures she inflicts
cold-bloodedly at the same hour every day on her immured and helpless
spouse are unparalleled in their implacable repetition.

With this story, Shahrazad is continuing to unfold to the Sultan the
full range of behaviour and passions, and 'The Prince of the Black
Islands' is only one of several stories in which she tackles love *in
extremis*. By insisting on the brutishness of the slave, the story does
reveal at least two aspects of a passion that takes possession of someone
without rhyme or reason. The witch is the victim of her love; it drives
her to excesses of abjection, lust, grief and revenge. According to a
fairytale principle, mystery rules human drives. But to focus on this
aspect misses the deeper stratum: the story is also being told by a man
wronged by his wife's adultery, and the lurid features of her lover echo
closely the evocation of the slave(s) with whom the Sultan Shahriyar
and his brother Shahzenan find their wives cavorting in the opening
frame story. An adulterous object of desire will always be dyed deep
in dark deeds, lowest of the low and loathliest of the loathly: this is
the point of view of a wronged husband/wife and in many ways the

convention is psychologically acute. But in the *Nights*, this foul rival repeatedly takes on a black face and black skin in a chain of associations that ask for more reflection. Deep in this story of the Prince of the Black Isles, a mirror image is forming of the Sultan's causes for grief, and his revenge.

Coloured fishes from the fisherman's surprising catch lift up their heads and cry fealty to the enchantress. (Charles-Émile Wattier, 1864)

André Miquel has commented that the sorceress's unfailing devotion to her lover makes her one of the most constant hearts in the book, and that in itself is a kind of virtue. Miquel's is a merciful view, and it goes some way to softening the patent misogyny – and racism – of the story; but the plot's furious energy charges the enchantress's mysterious and terrifying behaviour, its effects carrying the reader over numerous non-sequiturs and gaps in the narrative on the momentum of her virulence.

The wicked enchantress turns her husband to stone from the waist down, and entombs him in a chamber deep in his palace; this punishment replicates, in the familiar interlaced structure of the *Nights*, the other tomb in the story, the one in which she has laid her wounded lover, where she visits him every day. Many sites of enchantment in the stories are underground or secret cells and labyrinths: the stories often mimic in their topography the characters' psychological descent into the abysses of passion. The prince's petrified state mirrors, with ghastly mimicry, the state of the half-dead slave over whom she weeps, and it inverts, in a grim, half-conscious pun, the potency she used to enjoy with her lover (some of the versions are strongly racist in their insinuations about the black slave's prowess). As in a Dantesque torment by talion, she is reducing her husband to the state to which he has brought her lover.

Like much of the fantastical tale-spinning of the book, this scene eludes rational analysis or construal; but as a cluster of images, it reprises the crucial metaphors through which the mixed culture of the Mediterranean in antiquity struggled to understand relations between humans, sexuality and love, liberty and licence, theurgy and goety; mortality and immortal beings. When the sorceress takes up obscene and bestial instruments to belabour and degrade her husband, her acts recall scenes of bitter carnival.

Lurid and violent scenes of an equally ritualistic kind take place in the embedded story cycle which follows. 'The Porter and the Three Ladies of Baghdad' and its intersheaved tales also move towards purification and restoration, the true faith regained and an end to magic. In these stories the enchantress is destroyed, the two bitches are metamorphosed back into women and married off by Harun al-Rashid to two of the three one-eyed dervishes, while all the other characters in the cycle, including Harun al-Rashid himself, are united in other marriages; the far horizons where they met with bizarre enchantments contract and they settle down to live a human existence. Only the Porter is excepted. Still, the closing ring of their relationships gives us, the audience, a sense that with the end of their travails all has been healed.

By contrast the enchantress in 'The Prince of the Black Islands' offers a picture of unregenerate sorcery rooted in a pre-Islamic, pagan faith. There is no saving this sinner, no ransom, no restoration: she is an adulteress and a dominatrix, and her act of turning all the citizens of her husband's kingdom into fish epitomises the evil uses to which she puts her knowledge.

At this early stage in the scheme of the whole book of the *Nights*, Shahrazad's tales feature many women who corroborate the Sultan's dim view of her sex, their lust and treachery. Is she cunningly displaying her sympathy with a husband who is a victim of his wife's adultery? Is she showing him a reflection of his own story, and inveigling him into trusting her by demonstrating, at this point in the task she has set herself, that she understands and approves his anger?

Is she winning his trust by seeming to agree with him? Do the stories reel him in slowly by beginning uncontentiously and then gradually introducing true and loving and resourceful wives, Badoura, Zumurrud, the girdle-makers Mariam and Tawaddud and many others of the later stories?

The picture of the kingdom, with the different faiths coexisting in such a climate of tolerance, is highly unusual in the *Nights*. Jews do not figure prominently in the stories, but Christians appear frequently, usually behaving unscrupulously. In 'The Tale of Ali Shar and Zumurrud', the clever heroine warns her beloved Ali Shar not to sell the embroidered cloth she has made to a man with blue eyes, but he fails to follow her instructions, and Barsum, who has blue eyes and is a Christian, then drugs Ali Shar and abducts Zumurrud to sell her to a villainous slaver. In this case Barsum is a generic figure of low greed, but in an epic like 'Aladdin of the Beautiful Moles' the Mediterranean setting gives vivid sight of the historical realities: the hero is captured by a pirate who carries him off to sell him in the market in Genoa, while this Mariam is a Christian princess who has converted secretly to Islam; she murders her father in cold blood on account of her new allegiance. On the whole, the *Nights* is dedicated to upholding the faith of the Prophet against all others, without quarter.

Black magic is as strongly disapproved of in the commentaries on the Koran as it is in Christian doctrine, and though the *1001 Nights* is steeped through and through in magic, some of it is licit and some of it is illicit. But the borders are tricky, and the *Nights* negotiates them ingeniously. Its generally low reputation in its own homelands nevertheless probably arises from the pervasiveness of this magic. In terms of storytelling not theology, it remains the case that these fluctuating limits on permitted magic in orthodox Muslim belief create the most wonderfully fertile ground for narrative, for conflicts, drama and plots.

Likeness in religion does not breed sympathy. Often, the creeds that provoke the greatest abhorrence belong to neighbouring cultures that follow very similar practices. In the *Nights*, these are often peoples who have historically been superseded or at least subordinated and weakened: ancient Egyptian pagans, medieval Zoroastrians. (The pattern of antagonism reflects similar struggles in the Bible: the enemies of the Israelites are the bordering nations: for example, the Canaanites who worship Baal.) Who controls magical forces matters desperately in these struggles: magic itself is ambivalent, dependent for its virtue – but not its power – on the faith of the person controlling it. Wrongdoing by the renegade jinn is easily condemned, but in the stories even the rebels can do good when ordered by their master. The effects do not reveal the authorship: blessings are brought by evil jinn on their masters quite indiscrimately; as the many ne'er-do-well heroes reveal, great destinies are brought about by magical means, regardless of deserts. But everyone in the stories and their readers need barbarians at the gates to know who they are.

Without the barbarians, without those Others, how can home ground be safely identified? The stories need to look at the enemy threats closely in order to discover how they differ, because frequently the similarities are striking and, without careful attention, confusing.

Several stories illuminate the differences; very few of them, like 'The Prince of the Black Islands', conjure a dream of the Mediterranean and Middle East as the pattern for multicultural, multi-faith societies. Does the name, the Black Islands, catch the volcanic islands off the coast of Sicily and their lava beaches and black crags? Is there a memory, here, of the period when the Arabs ruled and soon after them the Normans, who adopted their predecessors' tolerance and scholarship, uniting Jews and Greeks and Muslims?

The tolerance the Black Islands show towards Zoroastrianism, the religion whose followers are turned into the red fish on account of their worship of fire, is highly unusual in the *Nights*. The sorceress herself, acting independently against all the faiths in the kingdom, including the Zoroastrians, is also unusual: she does not command troops of (rebel) jinn nor is she herself a jinniya. She is rather a throwback, a descendant of the witches of antiquity, a dark enchanter whose ancestors are Circe and Medea or the wild priestess who performs fumigations and incantations around Dido's pyre in the *Aeneid* (as discussed in the next chapter). The repeated appearances of blackness in the story play insistently and rather obviously on the blackness of her arts, but they also point south.

With the allusions to the unconverted tribe of Ad, located historically in the Horn of Africa, the villains seem survivors from the pagan prehistory of Islam, who are perceived, in this book of stories, as stubborn apostates.

The apparitions in the kitchen when the maidservant is trying to cook the coloured fish remain unexplained and all the more powerful for their weirdness. But they sketch scenes of forced conversion: the enchantress and her lover are torturing the metamorphosed believers until they renounce their faith and come over to join them in their profanity. Many of the disturbing later scenes burlesque scenes of worship, in their ritual repetition, in the use of a tomb for profane purposes, and the woman's unreasonable, unwavering faith in her lover. When he lies half dead in the monument, an atmosphere of ancient Egypt hangs in the air.

This witch is one of the great monstrous witches of storytelling, and her lineage reveals that she represents the enemy, the pre-Islamic culture of antiquity with its magical knowledge and practices. With the furious passions of the possessed enchantress and her filthy lover, 'The Prince of the Black Islands' defines pagan magic as alien and abominable. However, because the magic bears a troubling resemblance to traditions which continue in the regions of the true believers, they must absolutely be expelled and rejected – even if it means allowing some space for other faiths. On the whole, the *Arabian Nights* are not a safe place for racial differences, but tends to show vehement suspicion of peoples from further east and further south. Frequently, the most potent magical knowledge originates in Egypt, while evil magicians are Zoroastrians from Persia, as in the story of Hasan of Basra, and practise alchemy or other magical arts. So the relegation of magic to 'Others' takes place in the *Nights* and related legends, doubling and reflecting the persistent later tactic of disavowal in the West, where magic presences at home are distanced from native rationality, and most vociferously denounced when they bear a resemblance to it.

CHAPTER FIVE

Egyptian Attitudes

O this false soul of Egypt! This grave charm,
[. . .]
Like a right gypsy hath at fast and loose
Beguiled me to the very heart of loss.

Shakespeare, *Antony and Cleopatra*

I

IN A PACKED ACCOUNT OF Egypt, a country which he admired and where he had travelled extensively, the Greek historian Herodotus declares: 'the names of all the gods have been known in Egypt from the beginning of time . . .' In a genial, idiosyncratic gossipy style, he inventories a *Wunderkammer* of knowledge, reviewing the origin and habits of the phoenix, the edibility of crocodiles and the processes used in mummification. Through all the fabulous lore, Herodotus stresses the primacy and the originality of the country: 'It was the Egyptians too,' he writes,

who originated, and taught the Greeks to use ceremonial meetings, processions, and liturgies . . . by their practice of keeping records of the past, [they] have made themselves the most learned of any nation of which I have had experience . . . The Egyptians were also the first . . . to foretell by the date of a man's birth his character, his fortunes, and the day of his death – a discovery which the Greeks have turned to account. The Egyptians, too, have made more use of omens and prognostics than any other nation; they keep written records of the observed results of any unusual phenomenon, so that they come to expect a smiliar consequence to follow a similar occurrence in the future.'

The Greek chronicler set the key for what followed – the undiminished fascination of ancient Egypt and its wisdom. Combining orderly and rational methods of book-keeping and archiving with curious customs and magic, Egyptian civilisation has been and remains identified with wonderful science: pharmacology, gemmology, sacred geometry, spells and incantations, and almost every divination ever invented (by dreams, by figures in the sand, by moles). These associations with the civilisation of the Pyramids and Pharaohs still dominate the culture of enchantment, including the *Arabian Nights*, for historical reasons – in part.

The country was the *fons et origo* of hermetic wisdom in antiquity and it remained so for Renaissance Europe: Marsilio Ficino revered the Egyptian Hermes (Hermes Trismegistus, Thrice-Greatest Hermes), as the messenger of divine knowledge; Athanasius Kircher found out the meaning of the hieroglyphs (or so he thought) and imagined they expressed a prophetic knowledge of Christian wisdom and ethics; Mozart and his librettist Emanuel Schikaneder modified Masonic Egyptian symbolism in *The Magic Flute* (1791), while nineteenth- and twentieth-century occultists ranged from the deadly serious (Madame Blavatsky) to popular showmen with their tales of curses and secrets of the pyramids. It is not happenstance that Giovanni Battista Belzoni, one of the prime movers of Egyptomania, began his career in the circus as a strongman. In 1821, in the Egyptian Hall, Piccadilly, his atmospheric installation, evoking the astonishing finds he had made at Luxor and elsewhere, drew appreciative crowds till the following year. The 'Egyptian Hall' was launched as the leading London venue for a new kind of entertainment: science mixed with mysticism, fakery and showmanship. Conjurors' magazines were called *The Sphinx* and *Genii*, and an Englishman born plain David Charles Lemmy took the stage name Ali Bey and wore costumes to match. In 1903, the writer E. Nesbit returned to the mummies at the British Museum to rekindle her inspiration, and went to see E. Wallis Budge, the Keeper of Egyptian and Assyrian Antiquities and a keen, prolific translator of magical papyri and ancient legends. He described to her the principles of Egyptian spells and the uses of the papyri and objects in the collections; his stories enthralled her (she also enjoyed a brief love affair with him). The result was *The Story of the Amulet* (1905), Nesbit's much-loved time-travelling adventure about children who summon a Psammead, or sand fairy.

Interest in the magic of Egypt never altogether ebbs: an exhibition of *The Book of the Dead* at the British Museum in 2010–11 was a popular success; it revealed the foresight with which the culture helped the dead to make the passage into the afterlife, how every eventuality was forestalled by a specific formula ('Spell for not doing work in the realm of the dead', 'Spell for assembling a bier', 'Spell for being transformed into a phoenix', 'Spell for preventing a man from going upside down and from eating faeces'). The show of these magical scrolls, some of them unrolled to their entire length for the first time, radiated a reverence for death that contrasts with today's violent and often heedless treatment of the dead in representations and, more seriously, reality.

Of all the countries that were to embrace Islam, it is Egypt that has dominated the fabulous geography of magic. It would be impossible to pick out all the threads that weave the narrative backcloth to the *Nights'* dramas of licit and illicit magic, but the sources are rooted in ancient myth and even scriptural history. The city of Cairo is a dominant, vital setting of the stories and the origin of the two most compendious and significant manuscripts after Galland's Syrian collection. The tales that eventually coalesced into the book are suffused with the strong flavour of Egyptian magic in the history of imagination.

II

When Moses and Aaron are summoned by Pharaoh to a contest with his magicians, Aaron the high priest of the Jews throws down his rod and it turns into a serpent. Then 'the magicians of Egypt, they also did in like manner with their enchantments' (Exodus 7: 11). But Aaron's rod immediately swallows up all the serpents the Egyptians make. Later, Moses and Aaron summon the plagues – frogs and lice – and their infidel rivals attempt to turn the magic back on them, but without success.

Among the models for the dark enchanters in the *Nights* are these Pharaonic 'wise men and sorcerers' from the Bible. With regard to the uneasy question of the heterodox and orthodox uses of enchantment, the biblical episode which recounts their defeat by Moses and Aaron is highly illuminating. The conjuring feats of the four contenders are identical; the difference lies only in the god(s) whom they worship; their feats are in effect trials of these gods' relative powers.

In the Middle Ages, the episode was retold as a cautionary tale against paganism, in a tenth-century example of oriental storytelling, *The Marvels of the East*, in which the two Egyptian magicians meet again: 'After the death of the wizard Jannes [*sic*],' writes the author, 'his brother Mambres opened his magical books and called up his ghost from Hell. Jannes said that he was justly judged for his resistance to Moses and Aaron, and warned his brother to do good in his life . . .'

Hellenistic fiction is also characterised by enchantments of a kind which reverberate in later secular literature of the region. For example, the last pharaoh, Nectanebo, is portrayed as a powerful, shape-shifting magician, and plays a crucial role in the *Romance of Alexander,* a book that puts a strong stamp on *Alf Layla wa-Layla.* Its historical hero, Alexander the Great, migrates into Arabic myth and literature; the stories attached

TAB. CXXII.

EXODI Cap. VII. v. 9-12.
Baculi Serpentes.

II. Buch Mosis Cap. VII. v. 9-12.
Stäbe in Schlangen verwandelt.

Pharaoh's magicians are defeated when their snakes prove no match for those conjured by Moses and Aaron (an Enlightenment illustrator, demonstrating the wisdom of the Bible, frames the scene with anatomical details of a snake's life cycle). (J. J. Scheuchzer, *Physica Sacra*, 1731–5) to this figure threading marvellous bright colours through the whole tapestry of folklore, including some of the tales Shahrazad tells.

The Greek romance was already forming in the third century BC, not long after its hero Alexander died, and continued to evolve until it was written down in the third century AD. It is packed with rich fantasies about Alexander, including an elaborate bedtrick that takes place at his very origins: Nectanebo has fled to Macedon after his reign in Egypt has been overthrown by the Persians, and established himself as 'an Egyptian prophet' and local astrologer. Olympias, wife of Philip of Macedon, has not produced an heir; fearing that Philip is going to take another wife on his return from campaigning, she consults Nectanebo, who casts her horoscope and advises her that her destiny requires her to avenge herself on Philip and sleep with 'an incarnate god', Ammon of Libya, who will give her a child. He describes him: 'hair and beard of gold' and gold horns growing from his forehead. Olympias listens carefully, and when she has gone, Nectanebo makes a waxen image, sprinkles herbal mixtures on it, and inscribes it with the queen's name; by this magic, he can enter and take control of her mind. He then appears to her in a dream in disguise as the god and she finds herself being made love to. The charm works, so that when Nectanebo himself, no dream visitor but the man himself, dressed up with the expected gold hair and beard and horns, visits the queen clandestinely in her bedroom, she yields serenely. 'It was very sweet with him,' she says, and allows it to happen again and again until from these acts of enchantment and impersonation, Alexander is conceived.

Later, in order to forestall Philip's anger about the son and heir surprisingly produced in his absence, Nectanebo stages further remarkable feats of oneiromancy and metamorphosis, until Philip of Macedon has to accept that his son's father is truly Jupiter Ammon.

This fanciful (and scandalous) story obeys the mythic principle that a divine hero like Alexander must be born in some miraculous way, but it also exposes it through the machinations of a magician. It also introduces, in an early work of romancing, a narrative device that becomes routine: to enhance magical mystery and potency, a storyteller invokes exotic, foreign enchanters, and an Egyptian origin is a hallmark of authentic magic power.

Nectanebo figures in the story as a powerful magus in other ways:

> This Nectanebo was skilled in the art of magic, and by his use overcame all peoples and thus lived in peace. If ever a hostile power came aganst him, he did not prepare armies [. . .] but took a bowl and carried out a divination by water. He filled the bowl with spring water and with his hands moulded

ships and men of wax, and placed them in the bowl. Then he robed himself
in the priestly robes of a prophet and took an ebony staff in his hand.
Standing erect, he called on the so-called gods of spells and the airy spirits
and the demons below the earth, and by the spells the wax figures came to
life. Then he sank the ships in the bowl, and straightaway, as they sank, so
the ships of the enemy which were coming against him perished. All this
came about because of the great man's experience in the magic art.

Nectanebo, the last of the Pharaohs and the secret father of Alexander the Great,
uses sympathetic magic to sink the fleet of his enemy. (*The Wars of Alexander,*
fifteenth century)

An illuminated manuscript of the *Romance* in the National Library of Wales
includes a vivid picture of the last Pharaoh's model navy. His spells are an
early and very successful instance of the practice of sympathetic magic,
manipulating large effects according to principles of microcosmic mimicry;
these often govern magical acts in the *Arabian Nights* and are central to
the humanists' scientific theories in Renaissance Europe. The magic of
strangers persists as a motif in the history of esoteric wisdom, and suffuses
the literature of *ajib*, astonishment. When Ficino, John Dee, Paracelsus,
Francis Bacon and Kircher invoked as their precursors magi, alchemists,
philosophers and wizards – mostly imaginary, but some historical – they

often saw them as oriental or African: Moses, King Solomon, and the Sibyls associated with the outer limits of the known world – the Persian, Hellespontine, Erythraean, Phrygian, Libyan sibyls and, sometimes, the Queen of Sheba as well. The prophet-god Hermes Trismegistus, who presided over the pursuit of divine wisdom, combined the powers of Thoth, the Egyptian god and inventor of letters, and Hermes, the Olympian whose sphere of influence embraces secrets, messages, and cross-roads, as well as the mysteries of writing. Hermes Trismegistus gives his name to hermetic studies, and he dominated Italian humanist studies in classical magic and science (he makes a famous, magus-like appearance in the beautiful graffito pavement of the Duomo of Siena, where the Sibyls are also depicted, including a young, graceful black Sibilla Libyca).

The pursuit of such knowledge bears on the *Nights* not only because the stories give the fullest dramatic expression to this kind of magic, but also because, while building fantastic systems, evoking visions and developing analyses of phenomena, European writers and thinkers were turning their heads away from their own culture and its magical tradition and looking outwards; it is as if they needed to think they were interpreting – even channelling – the ancient wisdom of dark and distant strangers.

In one of the fullest scenes of magical conjuring from classical literature, the death of Dido in the *Aeneid*, Virgil resorts to the same distancing manoeuvre of the imagination, to stage a scene of attempted sympathetic magic. After Aeneas has left her, Dido, Queen of Carthage, calls her sister Anna to help her build her funeral pyre and load it with mementoes of Aeneas, including the bed in which they have made love:

> Sister, Anna, congratulate me! For I have found the way which will either give him back to me or release me from loving him. Close to Ocean's margin and the setting of the sun lies the land of Aethiopia on the edge of the world, where giant Atlas holds, turning . . . the pole of the heavens. I have been told of another Massylian priestess living in that land. She guards the Temple of the Hesperides; it was she who fed the dragon . . . she can stay the current of a river, and reverse the movement of the stars. She can evoke the spirits in the night-time . . .

Dido is lying to Anna when she swears that the powerful priestess has given her a spell to recapture Aeneas by these magical means or exorcise him from her heart. For Dido has no love charm; instead she is preparing an elaborate death ritual, the ceremony of her suicide.

In the geography of the ancient world, the Garden of the Hesperides stood beyond the Pillars of Hercules, near the setting sun as its name suggests, somewhere near the Atlas mountains of present-day Morocco; Virgil is following Homer when he calls this region 'Aethiopia': it lies beyond the Ocean stream in the first book of the *Iliad*. 'Massylian', which Virgil uses to place the priestess, is another way of generically referring to Africa. (It is striking that the dark enchanters of the *Nights* predominantly come from these places, from Egypt, North Africa, 'Aethiopia', Egypt, Persia and India.)

Later, Virgil describes this African priestess circling the pyre with her hair unbound, calling in a voice of thunder, sprinkling with 'purported' water from the underworld; the magic of this mysterious figure includes connections to the powers of darkness. The poet is enjoying his dramatic scene-painting here: wild, dishevelled and raving, the maga calls on the gods of the underworld and its goddess, the Triple Hecate, as she performs her queasy spells around Dido's pyre.

Virgil's national epic, while it has entrenched a vision of female magic, both in the scene at Dido's pyre and in Aeneas's later encounter with the Cumaean sibyl, does not belong to the folk- or fairy-tale corpus. By contrast, Hellenistic romances in Greek and Latin, recognisably revel in marvels and wonders in a way that the *Nights* later make their own. The *Aethiopica* of Heliodorus, for example, ramifies and fantasticates, with many tales-within-tales of prodigies, coincidences, foundlings, and lovers' partings, misadventures and reunions; the plot is set in motion when the Ethiopian queen exposes her baby daughter Charicleia because she is white. In many ways, this romance in ten books, as it works its exuberant, many-sided way toward recognition and reconciliation, turns on the folly of reacting to appearances only.

Many critics now see the Greek romances as the precursors of the novel, but the *Aethiopica* is above all a forerunner of the meta-fictional and allegorical fairy-tale form, crystallised by the *Arabian Nights*.

The best-known wonder fiction of late antiquity, the *Metamorphoses* of Lucius, or *The Golden Ass*, a Hellenistic romance written in Latin in the second century AD, includes the tale of 'Cupid and Psyche', a template for the love stories of fairytale, East and West; its author, Apuleius, was born in Madaura, in present-day Libya, and was put on trial in AD 158–9 in Sabratha, also on the North African coast. He had married a rich widow who was older than he was; her family suspected his motives and brought charges that he had used magic to win her. Apuleius vindicated himself, composing a long and passionate plea, a kind of Verrine oration in its scornful ironies against his accusers and the imputation of goety. 'On Magic' presents itself as his defence from the dock; it is also one of the most pugnacious defences of magic as a form of epistemology, not the worship of false gods. He admits to a belief in intermediate spirit beings between gods and humans and calls on Plato for support; he also alludes to trance experiences that can carry the dreamer's soul back to its heavenly origins. He agrees that he practises healing and boasts of his successes. But they are rooted in pharmacology and psychology, he asserts, and he denies all sorcery. Accused of making statues of ghosts and skeletons to work deadly harm by sympathetic means, Apuleius produces an example of his art, and blasts his enemies: 'Is this what you call a devil? Is this a magic likeness, and not one of the holy images of the community?' He evokes the beauty and realism of the image, and continues, 'He who dares call this a skeleton certainly hasn't seen any divine images or holds them all in contempt. He who believes this to be a phantom, it is he who conjures phantoms.'

Apuleius's treatise is an unstable document – it is not certain that this was what he said at his trial (for a speech it seems rather long), or even that the trial took place. However, if it did, he must have been vindicated, as he seems to have continued to live happily with the wife whom he had protested he truly loved. His attitude to magic is much more familiar from the fantastic fiction of *The Golden Ass*, which twists and turns from wonder tale to farce to initiatory romance and metaphysical wisdom. The story stages a prodigious feat of witchcraft – the hero applies what he believes to be flying ointment and finds himself changed into a donkey. Although Apuleius's witch lives in Thessaly, a hotbed of magic in antiquity, and the story ends in Rome, the hero's fate has powerful Egyptian associations: it culminates in an intense vision of the Goddess Isis and the ass's restoration to human form at her mysteries, after which he is initiated into her priesthood. On the way, this irrepressible book unfolds a picaresque story packed with enchantments, mystery, erotic lyricism and spiritual dreaming; it also makes effective use of imbricated tales and switches of register from idealism to explicit bawdy; it is one of the most recognisable forerunners of the fabulist genre to which the *Arabian Nights* belongs.

III

Looking through the lens of the *Arabian Nights* at the emergence and character of dark magicians, we see a pattern emerge. Exoticism and magic knowledge are often fused, especially in the symbols of Egyptian hermetic knowledge. However, the historical picture is complicated: Dante inflicted torments on Muhammad in his poem, but he drew on Muslim scholarship and on scholars who themselves depended on the transmission of Greek philosophy through Arabic manuscript copies (the words algebra, alembic and alchemy carry the traces of this Arabic scholarship). Hostilities in religion and politics were ferocious throughout the rise of the Islamic empire and the Crusades, but during this long period the quest for knowledge in Europe did not despise and exclude oriental philosophy or science as infidel or heterodox. Genealogies of knowledge were drawn up regardless of their faith, to include all questors into mysteries, all seekers and lovers of truth. Later, however, exchanges of knowledge between East and West, and the impetus given by translations across borders in the medieval era and the Renaissance, weakened, and as Ottoman power grew and then declined, the cultural conversation was twisted into different shapes.

During the Renaissance, magic arts were pursued by Europeans – some of them the greatest scholars of their age (Marsilio Ficino was the first translator of Plato, rendering the Greek into Latin). Such a pursuit of knowledge through alchemy, numerology, astrology and other methods of magical tradition was nevertheless suspect. Ficino was investigated by the Inquisition (1489) and lucky to escape. Others were not so lucky: priests and scholars, most famously Giordano Bruno, who died at the stake in Rome in 1600, were burned or otherwise silenced for their attempted knowledge. The borders between faith or religion, magic and science were constantly in complex moves in relation to one another, like participants in a restless dance. What was sorcery or goety, theurgy or white magic, profane necromancy or sacred ritual? What were the proper methods and pursuits of science? These were questions fought over fiercely by theologians and lawyers, resulting in many victims. Yet it is the general case that up to and including the seventeenth century adepts of the esoteric arts including hermetic occultism were included in the intellectual classical tradition: Newton, as is now admitted, explored intensively, even obsessively, the possibilities of the alchemical corpus. But it is less commonly mentioned, let alone accepted, that an empirical scientist as important as the chemist Robert Boyle and the doctor, antiquarian and essayist Sir Thomas Browne staunchly withstood the new modern philosophers with their tendencies to agnosticism if not atheism: they refuted Hobbes's physiological explanations of visions, arguing that the Bible was full of spirits, signs and wonders, which Christians had to accept on scriptural authority. They attempted to prove the existence of spirit worlds on empirical grounds: 'It is a riddle to me,' writes Sir Thomas Browne, '. . . how so many learned heads should so farre forget their Metaphysicks, and destroy the Ladder and scale of creatures, as to question the existence of Spirits: for my part, I have ever beleeved, and doe now know, that there are Witches; they that doubt of these, doe not onely deny them, but Spirits; and are obliquely and upon consequence a sort, not of Infidels, but Atheists.'

Hermes Aegyptus (top, second left) presides over an ecumenical intellectual pantheon: Avicenna Arabus, Albertus Magnus, Raymond Lull, Francis Bacon and one woman ('Maria Hebraea', the inventor of the *bain-Marie*). (From an alchemical work by Michael Maier, 1617)

Unexpectedly, the emphasis on the sinister qualities of magical wisdom became more pronounced in Enlightenment and modern times than they were in medieval or Renaissance thought, when good wise men still came from the East. The splitting of magic and science that took place in the quest for rationality during the eighteenth century led to a new intensity in rejecting esoteric learning; whereas a pantheon of scientists drawn up in 1617 aligns Hermes Trismegistus, Avicenna, Maria Hebraea and Thomas Aquinas without regard for borders or faith, let alone complexions. By 1800 the Greek and Jewish scholars might be clinging on in the lists, but the Muslims and the alchemists have been banished to the margins – only weird occultists would continue to explore these branches of knowledge. Newton's inquiries into sacred geometry (with regard to Solomon's temple, for example), and his practice of casting horoscopes, were to become inadmissible and literally unspeakable – his voluminous notes in these matters are only being examined and edited now.

A famous watercolour by John White can provide a clear case history in attitudes to the magic. It is the first portrait of an Indian made by an English artist in the Americas, and shows a young man, *The Flyer*, dressed in bird's feathers and animal skins, and gracefully leaping on the page. Its many reproductions reveal a history of changing ideology in attitudes to magic. White was in Virginia in 1580–85 with the first, abortive colony of the Virginia Company, and his image belongs in a series of studies of local Indian rituals. The label, which he wrote on the painting, draws attention not only to the figure's leap but also to the bird fastened to the side of the flyer's head; he is imitating flight, his limbs spread, fingers fluttering like the wing tips of the bird he wears – even his big toe lifts, while the fringes on the pouch fan open, echoing the tail of the bird and adding to the sense of upward movement. The marked length of the eyelashes gives a hint of extended extremities, while the different animal skins he wears, carefully rendered by White to show their nap and furry contours, and his roached hair, rising in tiny tufts on his scalp behind the bird's wings, accentuate the liveliness of his animal impersonation.

In 2007, the image was catalogued as 'Watercolour of Algonquian Shaman in stylized pose.' But interpretations of the character were not always so accepting. When the printer-publisher Theodor de Bry, in 1590, commissioned prints for Thomas Harriott's account of the Virginia enterprise, *The Flyer* was renamed *The Conjurer*, the rhyme between the angle of the bird's wings and the man's *élan vital* was lost, and a caption explained:

'The Flyer', now identified as an 'Algonquian shaman', imitates the flight of a bird in a ritual dance (John White, 1580–85).

They [Virginians] have commonly conjurers or jugglers which use strange gestures, and often contrary to nature in their enchantments: For they be very familiar with devils, of whom they enquire what their enemies do, or other such things. They shave all their heads saving their crest which they wear as others do, and fasten a small black bird above one of their ears as a badge of their office . . . The Inhabitants give great credit unto their speech, which oftentimes they find to be true.

'Conjuror' was an Elizabethan term for one who practised magic arts for malign purposes; it carried overtones of diabolism as well as charlatanry, while 'juggler' increased the atmosphere of danger, being strongly associated with the devil's deceptions (near his death Macbeth exclaims, 'And be these juggling fiends no more believed,/That palter with us in a double sense' – *Macbeth*, V. viii). Later in De Bry's handsome publication, the flyer makes another appearance: his leap mutates into religious prostration, as he genuflects, hand on heart, to a monstrous god enthroned above an animal skull on the broken architrave of the monumental title page. This 'idol', which does not figure in John White's eyewitness images, shifted the Flyer's dancing motion on to the much more familiar home territory of devil worship, strongly credited in British Protestant circles. King James's believing and fearful study of witchcraft, *Demonologie,* was published six years after the engraved volume of Harriott's *True and Brief Report*.

Post-Reformation anxieties about Catholic practices run through the complex play of attraction and repudiation in the struggle over magic in the century preceding the European appearance of the *1001 Nights*. The fortunes of the Flyer illuminate how beliefs in conjurors and their powers – Marlowe's Doctor Faustus, Shakespeare's Prospero in *The Tempest* and Cerimon in *Pericles*; even Paulina in *The Winter's Tale* – were inflected during a period fraught by religious tension between different forms of Christian beliefs and cults, when encounters with the magical practices of other cultures, both in North America and in the Mediterranean, were increasingly fashioning a new awareness that other ways existed of thinking about and relating to the invisible and the spiritual. Dr John Dee, the great scholar and mathematician, was one of the instigators and investors in the Virginia enterprise. Dee was also widely reputed to be a powerful conjuror: the British Museum displays the polished basalt disc brought to him by angels, in which he and his acolyte Edward Kelley scried for revelations. The mirror is Aztec, and like many early objects in museums – before cataloguing – its passage to England remains unknown. It passed from Dee's hands into the antiquarian collection of Horace Walpole, the catalyst of English Gothic, and thence into the British Museum, where it now appears in the display of the Enlightenment. Interestingly, a magic table also used by John Dee can be seen in Oxford, in the Museum of the History of Science, in a replica that belonged to the astronomer William Lilly. Both institutions in this way recognise the hooks and crotchets which attach magic, cosmology, empire, science and enlightenment.

Supposed magicians like John Dee were not exotic themselves, but they took their place in a genealogy in which wisdom was identified with distant times and distant places. The imaginings of literature about a mysterious, learned East were reproduced in different media that circulated beyond scholarly milieux: an artefact such as the 'Ripley Scroll', named after the fifteenth-century English alchemist George Ripley, exists in various seventeenth-century copies. In richly coloured vignettes, the scrolls depict the alchemical process, with a fountain of rejuvenation and ovens for calcination and other stages of the process, a garden for simples and other necessary pursuits. Above all, they include lively individualised portraits of celebrated experimenters – philosophers, alchemists and magicians – from all over the globe, regardless of race or creed (Pl. 3). Although these images were made during an era of serious hostilities with the Ottomans, this angle of view on the history of knowledge does not exclude Islamic science: several of the sages are turbaned and bearded in the style of Muslim scholars.

The scrolls' uses are not known for certain, but the number of copies suggests that they might have been hung outside apothecary shops – a form of very beautiful advertising billboard. A copy in the Getty Research Institute, a splendid specimen, includes an ecumenical picture of alchemists at their labours – philosophical, scholarly types, Renaissance men and, usually, one woman: all, from East and West, are united over their alembics and retorts, their salamanders and their athanors in joint pursuit of the philosophical egg: Aristotle, Hermes Trismegistus, Abu Mazar, Solomon, Moses, Thomas Aquinas and Roger Bacon are represented as equal in the search.

But this ecumenical picture of a commonwealth of learning fades. A clear shift takes place when magic and science, imagination and reason, come to be seen as irreconcilable processes. Many of the sources (Neoplatonist, Arabic, Persian, etc.) from which medieval and humanist learning sprang were banished from approved research: astrology, numerology, sacred geometry, systems of correspondences, medical models of microcosm–macrocosm correlations ('mic-mac', as Wallace Stevens called it), all were swept out of view.

IV

In the course of the seventeenth century, the intellectual élite began expelling magic beyond the borders of the homelands of Europe, and disowned it within Christianity; the adepts of esoteric knowledge

became less ecumenically united, and Plato, Moses, Solomon and Virgil
were no longer classified with magi. Exotic foreigners, non-Europeans
– from Egypt, North Africa, the eastern Mediterranean, and farther
east into Persia, Iraq, India and China – commanded the territories
of the occult and the heterodox. The process was accompanied by a
figurative darkening of the arts in question: blackness slipped from
metaphor of diabolical agency to include physical attributes, and
'necromancy', with its root in the word for death (as in 'necro-polis'),
was confused with 'nigromancy', with its root in the word for the
colour black, *niger*.

In early uses, from the late fourteenth century onwards, the ambivalent
word evokes chiefly the symbolic darkness of apostasy, sin and death.
'Machometus, a fals prophete and nigromancier' is mentioned in the
fifteenth century. In the Bible and long afterwards, witchcraft is a danger
at home and although Medea is a notorious foreign sorceress, who
'murdered many a one/Through Nigromancie', in Richard Robinson's
*The Reward of Wickednesse: Discoursing the . . . abuses of wicked and ungodlye
worldelinges, etc.* of 1574, there are few directly ethnic ascriptions made by
the term. By 1600 English 'nigromancer' seems to be formed from late
Latin *necromantia*, though later the words become interchangeable. The
OED treats necromancer and negro- or nigromancer under the same
entry, a decision which reveals how the metaphors have invisibly collapsed
into each other; in this way symbolism institutes history, language becomes
act and reality (magical manoeuvres in themselves).

Writings on witchcraft and sorcery perpetuate the literal application
of this symbolism, through thriving figures of fantasy. Poets and dramatists
infuse the language with the dark arts to colour the complexion of their
agents, as rhetorical uses of darkness and light reveal. The term Moor
from Latin, *morus*, dark, is notoriously difficult, but as an imagined ethnic
description it overlaps with darkness figured as the ignorance of benighted
heathen. In his early play, *Titus Andronicus*, Shakespeare slips from identifying evil with Moors to associating their villainy with the dark arts.
Aaron the Moor, the complex antagonist and source of much mischief
in this most macabre and gory play, addresses himself in an aside after
some of his foulest deeds:

> O! how this villainy
> Doth fat me with the very thoughts of it.
> Let fools do good, and fair men call for grace,
> Aaron will have his soul black like his face. (III.i.202–5)

In *Othello*, Brabantio, the father of Desdemona, suspects that Othello has cast a spell on her with 'arts inhibited and out of warrant'. When Othello later demands that Desdemona produce the fatal handkerchief, he describes its provenance in elaborate detail, like a valuer enhancing the authenticity of his item. An Egyptian gave it to his mother, Othello tells her:

> . . . there's magic in the web of it:
> A sibyl, that had numb'red in the world
> The sun to course two hundred compasses,
> In her prophetic fury sew'd the work;
> The worms were hallow'd that did breed the silk
> And it was dy'd in mummy which the skilful
> Conserv'd of maidens' hearts. (III. iv. 68–74)

Shakespeare winds into the web of his magic language different means of strengthening the spell, and they pick up on Brabantio's suspicions about Othello as enchanter, and involve throwing the mind into far distant exotic places: the handkerchief was stitched by a two-hundred-year-old Sibyl; silk worms, presumably from the East, made the fabric, and it was soaked in embalmed, virgins' organs from ancient Egypt – a love charm of uncommon grisliness, and it is no wonder Desdemona exclaims at her husband's speech. Above all, however, Othello's evocation lays stress on the handkerchief's provenance in Egypt, a word which in the ear of Shakespeare and his contemporaries, resonates with 'gypsy', as Antony conveys when he speaks of the thrall in which Cleopatra holds him. The chain of associations creates an imaginary geography and genealogy for magical lore, the wisdom of Ancient Egypt transmitted to gypsies, 'internal Others', foreign exotics in Europe who were notorious for their fortune-telling, love spells and siren enchantments (the afterglow of this Renaissance mythology spreads to *Carmen*, in Prosper Mérimée and Bizet's vision of Spain).

In Webster's *The White Devil* (1612) the title itself draws attention to its more common shadow double, and the toxic cast includes the maidservant Zanche, the 'precious gipsy' and 'black fury' whose evil deceptions are constantly intertwined with the imagery of her origins and colour, not least by herself. When *Titus* and *Othello* and *The White Devil* first played before their audiences, the victims of the witch hunts, present and future, were still native Christians all, and in all innocence would remain so.

It is possible to see resonances in history of the metaphors' hostility in action: Elizabeth 1 had issued an edict in 1596 to repatriate Africans.

Solomon's fall in the Bible, when he consorts with strange women and allows them to persuade him to worship false gods, does not receive much attention until the Reformation, when his idolatry and marriage to the daughter of Pharaoh excited moral condemnation. Engravings which target the Catholic worship of icons, by Northern artists like Lucas van Leyden and Albrecht Altdorfer, press home lessons about the consequences of dallying with foreign women and their objects of devotion.

So the dark enchanters of *Alf Layla wa-Layla* had a history for eighteenth-century English readers when they appeared in the stories as the Persian enchanter Bahram, or the 'African magician' from 'Aladdin and the Wonderful Lamp'. In 'Judar and his Brothers', a Moorish magician controls a fantastical sequence of magic things: an all-conquering sabre, a clairvoyant sphere, a magic ring which summons a jinni, a saddlebag which never empties. He gives the hero, Judar, complicated instructions to reach a wonderful treasure-finding book. These include, impressively, the order that when his mother appears to him on the way, he must order her to undress, whatever she says or does. Only then will this apparition vanish — it is a counterfeit and he must ignore it. Only then will he be able to enter the treasure chamber. But Judar fails the first time: he cannot make himself dishonour his mother's image in this way.

Such exotic figures have their popular successors in figures like Svengali and Dr Caligari. The abhorrence in which they are held in the stories matched their estimate in the home tradition, and home-grown racism recognised a reflection of its own in the horror of the stranger magician in *Alf Layla wa-Layla*.

However different the Pharaohs were from the Mamelukes who ruled the country in the nineteenth century, however long ago the ancient Egyptians had created hieroglyphs, mummified remains and built the Pyramids, a dream of an unaltered and persistent tradition of magic dominated the perspective brought to reading the stories in the *Arabian Nights*. Edward Lane, in his hugely successful study, *The Manners and Customs of the Modern Egyptians* (1836), published just before he embarked on his version of the *Nights*, opens a chapter on 'Magic, Astrology, and Alchymy' by declaring: 'If we might believe some stories which are commonly related in Egypt, it would appear that, in modern days, there have been, in this country, magicians not less skilful than Pharaoh's "wise men and sorcerers" of whom we read in the Bible.'

Edward Said rightly points out that such an ahistorical perspective casts the East as perennial, static and primitive. However, Said does not tackle directly the question of enchantment, which is central to the view that the Orient is generally backward and effeminate.

There are aspects to Eastern magic which can go some way to changing understanding of this issue. The reception of the *Nights* has generally coarsened the portrayal of enchantments in the stories and leached them of complexity, definition and depths. The richness of several of the stories arises from the many varied enchantments they explore and the fine discriminations between their pleasures and their dangers. Arabic has several different terms for what we call more bluntly black and white magic, branching from the fundamental categories of *sihr* (magic) and *kihana* (divination).' Licit – pious – magical practices associated with *sihr* include the use of protective amulets and talismans, and of invocations and inscriptions as blessings, to ward off the evil eye, for example. But as the stories in the *Nights* dramatise so vividly, magic was also recognised as trickery, designed to deceive, and for this aspect, *nirandj*, a word of Persian origin was used; it means the making of illusions. Some forms of divination by chance were proscribed, others enthusiastically pursued with official approval. Astrology and numerology, geomancy and *firasa* (scrutiny of faces) were widely practised but under continuous review.

The whole territory was highly ambiguous, giving much work to philosophers. Significantly, *aja'ib*, the term so deeply connected with Shahrazad's tales, designates marvels of a magical order – natural wonders, artefacts of human contrivance, fabulous spells bringing about metamorphoses. The imaginative abundance of popular literature, like the *Nights*, enriches the picture as well as continuing the ethical inquiry, though that may sound a bit high-flown for such enchanting concoctions. Yet the tales continually discriminate between different forms of magic – between spells for finding treasure and alchemy, for example – and some of this subtlety has been damaged in transition from their homelands. The Islamic revulsion against sorcerers, embodied by so many sinister foreign enchanters in the *Tales*, does not read in the same way to readers in Europe or America, for whom all the magic in the *Nights* is exotic, and all the more alluring for it, imbued in general with the glamour of the heterodox. In the encounter with this stranger magic, writers and readers can revel there – to 'play in the dark' in Toni Morrison's fine phrase – and give themselves permission to savour the forbidden fruit of the Tree of Knowledge. For a sceptic, black magicians present a mooring to beliefs that do not have to be shared: through identifying with the fantasy magus, marvels can still be credited, at a safe distance.

'The Stranger was a sorcerer…': a classic illustration for 'Aladdin' by René Bull (1916) of a dark enchanter and his mysterious doings.

Story 5
Hasan of Basra

A SUCCESSFUL MERCHANT OF BASRA dies before his time, leaving his widow with two sons; one of them is calm and prudent and takes his half of the inheritance to follow in his father's footsteps and open a shop in the market. But the other, called Hasan, a boy of radiant beauty and charm, is a lazy good-for-nothing. His mother is determined, however, and she's made sure he knows the Koran and can write an elegant hand and express himself gracefully. Even with these gifts, he won't apply himself to anything serious but runs around in a gang of feckless youths. Soon he's gone through all the money his father left him, and, in his distress, turns for help to a friend, who's a goldsmith with a stall in the souk; Hasan becomes his apprentice, and soon shows such aptitude that his reputation spreads from Basra as far as Baghdad.

Three years pass, and one day a stranger, a visitor from Persia, comes passing through the souk; he's powerfully drawn to the beauty of the young man, and to the excellence of his work, and he stops to watch him, marvelling aloud, while other bystanders also have eyes for nothing else but the skill and the grace of Hasan. All the while, as the Persian lavishes compliments on Hasan, he's holding an old book in his hand, which he glances at now and then.

Then the call for prayer is sounded and the shop empties, leaving Hasan and the Persian together. The stranger offers himself to Hasan, promising to be a father to him, to replace the one whom he has lost. He tells him that he knows an ancient art whose secrets have been forgotten by the rest of the world.

'Many have begged me to tell them,' he says, 'but I did not want to pass them on to just anybody. I have come to you because I want to reveal them to you.'

The Persian swears to protect Hasan for ever from poverty and toil, and says that when he returns the next day he will change copper into gold under Hasan's very eyes.

In high spirits, Hasan goes home to his mother, who isn't used to seeing him so light-hearted after a long day's work. But when he tells her about his new benefactor, she begins to cry, for she knows his kind: 'They harbour secret designs on young people, whom they kidnap and kill and make disappear. Don't trust anything they say, especially if they are Persians. They are impostors who claim they understand alchemy. But they are liars and robbers and will strip you of everything.'

But Hasan is stubborn, and protests that this old man means to do them all manner of good.

The next day, the Persian performs his magic and orders Hasan to chop up a copper tray and feed it into the fire; he sprinkles some powder into it, and the mixture turns into a bar of gold. Pure gold, which the stunned Hasan takes to the gold market where it's sold for fifteen thousand times more than the value of the copper tray he's broken up. Hasan wants the Persian to repeat the trick, but he scolds him for his greed: the boy will have to show patience. He's to accompany his new-found father back to his country, and there he'll study to acquire the alchemical art.

Hasan agrees, and, before setting out, he takes the Persian home and they eat together and pledge their new relationship by the solemn bonds of hospitality, breaking bread and salt; then the stranger produces some more of the magic powder and gives it to Hasan, who finds an old copper cup and practises. To his utter joy, he finds that he too can change the base metal into another ingot of pure gold. While Hasan exults, quite beside himself with excitement, the Persian takes henbane from a packet secreted in his turban: there's enough of it that a mere whiff could have put an elephant to sleep for twenty-four hours. He slides a leaf of it into the pastry on Hasan's plate.

'You are truly my son now,' he says, 'dearer to me than my own soul.' Hasan puts the pastry to his lips, and instantly he tastes it, crashes to the floor.

The Persian exults, 'Now you are captured in my toils, you child of the devil, you Arab dog. For years I've been looking for you and now I have you.'

Bahram is a sorcerer – a magian – he is now named, and Shahrazade reveals the depths of his depravity: like so many of his kind in the *Arabian Nights*, this Persian scholar is an infidel, a fire-worshipper who is filled with hatred of Muslims, who blasphemes against the true God and schemes to destroy the faithful. Every year, when he runs out of the special herb he needs for his potions, he kidnaps a boy and sends him to gather it, then abandons him in that dangerous place to die.

Hasan is his latest victim: the alchemist ties him up, wrists bound to his ankles, stuffs him into a trunk, and sets sail for another country far away. There, the boy is roused at last from his drugged stupor when his abductor passes vinegar under his nose and gives him hellebore to drink to vomit up the poison.

The boy is frightened and hurt, but in his innocence he still tries to cajole the Persian. Bahram responds with furious invective, cursing Hasan and announcing he will kill him as he has killed ninety-nine youths before him. Fire has helped him in his wicked devices, and as fire is god, Hasan should bow down before him.

Hasan refuses; the magian hits him cruelly.

Matters continue in this way, as they keep sailing on; but one day, when a dreadful storm begins to batter the ship, the crew rebel and insist that the Persian stop maltreating Hasan or they will throw him overboard.

Bahram changes tack and sweet-talks Hasan, saying that all these torments were only tests of the boy's virtue, and that he has proved himself wonderfully. They are making their way, he reveals, to the Mountain of Clouds where the elixir necessary to alchemy can be found.

After three months, they disembark on a strange beach strewn with differently coloured pebbles; there the magian takes from inside his clothes a small copper drum and a drumstick, covered in silk and embroidered in golden talismanic characters. He beats it, and as he does so three black thoroughbreds materialise in front of them in a cloud of dust. They are jinn horses, and Bahram and Hasan of Basra mount them. There is one for each of them to ride and another to carry their baggage. They travel on, passing a castle where Bahram tells Hasan his enemies, demons and demonesses, live. When they reach the foot of the Mountain of Clouds, its summit is wrapped in mist. Bahram kills one of their horses, guts it and flays it, and forces Hasan into the hide; he gives him a knife and some food, then stitches up the carcass and exposes the boy on the ground like carrion. Enormous Rukh birds appear and seize him as planned, and carry him up to the summit of the Mountain of Clouds, where the herb grows. But when Hasan looks around him there, he sees the bones of his predecessors strewn all around the place where Bahram has left them to die.

The magian promises to bring him back safe and sound if he throws him down bundles of the precious ingredient. Hasan gathers six sheaves of it, and throws them down, but the Persian taunts him and roars with diabolical laughter at the boy's stupid trust.

In despair at all he has suffered, at the broken promises of the man who said he would be a father to him, and the dangers he has been subjected to, Hasan throws himself off the edge of the cliff.

But he does not come to grief. The ocean into which Hasan plunges carries him to the enchanted castle he had passed on his way to the Mountain of Clouds. He wanders in and finds two young girls playing chess; these are two of seven sisters, and all of them female jinn, daughters of the Blue King of the Jinn, himself the mere viceroy of the Jinn emperor, who also has seven daughters.

The seven jinn princesses loathe Bahram because they have witnessed the cruel stratagems he uses for gathering the herbs for his potions. Besides, they are among the faithful jinn, true to Islam, and they know that he blasphemes against Islam and denounces them as demonesses. So they take Hasan in their arms and kiss him between his eyes, and one of them − the youngest − swears she will be a sister to him. In this case she is telling the truth, and throughout the subsequent twists of the story she protects and helps Hasan, like an angel or a fairy godmother.

So when Hasan decides on revenge and returns to the fiery mountain to track down Bahram again, she and her sisters help him. He manages to confront his treacherous protector and though the magian wheedles and lies, Hasan holds firm this time, and cuts off his head with one stroke of his sword.

The jinn princesses take him home to their remote castle, where their father has shut them up to protect them; he knows how squalid and dishonest humans are and they are not to marry out of the world of the jinn. There, sequestered in the Valley of Birds, Gazelles and Wild Beasts, they enjoy a natural Eden far from human society and cities in the most beautiful gardens, watered by streams that cure leprosy, elephantiasis and other diseases. Inside the castle, crystal, jewels, spiral staircases carved from Yemeni onyx − every kind of splendid thing surrounds them. They can read and write; the story is studded with the letters and poems they compose. Some creature comforts which enliven the human world are missing − they have never eaten candied or dried fruits, for example. Later Hasan will fetch some back for them. For the time being, they are pleased to see him because he can strangle the game they have caught on their hunting expeditions and dress the animals for their table.

The jinn princesses are magical beings of great sweetness of character, and even after Hasan has opened a forbidden door with a key his new sister has given him and expressly warned him not to use, she does not punish or abandon him. Behind it he has a glimpse of a gorgeous, marble and bejewelled pavilion housing a pool; he hides and watches, and sees birds fly down to bathe in it. He realises, when they take off their feathers to swim, that they aren't birds but girls, and he goes on watching them as they wash and frolic in the water. He falls madly in love with one of them, the youngest, and when he sees her mount of Venus between her legs, he remembers a poem which invokes the desire that overcomes him.

And the storyteller continues to evoke her irresistibility: image upon image in verse and in prose distilled from the long tradition of Arabic love poetry over several pages as Hasan keeps peeping at the scene.

The girls put on their feather cloaks again and fly away, leaving Hasan mad for love.

He pines, he cries, he can't eat or sleep; eventually he confesses and his adoptive sister doesn't reproach him for disobeying, but helps him.

His love is another jinn princess whose father is of the highest rank of jinn, higher than their own, who is merely his viceroy. She lives with her six sisters on an even more distant and far vaster estate; they are Amazons, and her eldest sister is a powerful and dangerous witch. Hasan's sister has a plan, however, for Hasan to capture his love: she comes to bathe every new moon and next time, if he steals her magic cloak of feathers, she won't be able to fly away.

She warns him that he must not give in to her and let her have her feathers back, however much she promises she won't leave him; and that he must hide the cloak and never let her know where.

The next new moon, he lies in wait and captures her as planned. He does not give in to her cries of shame at her nakedness, but carries her off to his apartments, where his sister visits her and assures her that Hasan is a good man with no (further) evil intentions. After many more scenes of distress at her abduction, persuasion by the other jinn maidens in the castle, and a long period in which the ardent Hasan manages to show gentlemanly restraint until they are married, Hasan's mother appears to him in a dream. He realises what grief his disappearance with the magian all that time ago is causing her, so he decides to return to his home in Basra. He calls up the jinn horses again, and after describing his adventures to his mother, settles his family in Baghdad, because in his home town of Basra his sudden fortune would have to be explained.

Two sons are born, but now Hasan misses his fairy sister in the enchanted castle and he wants to show his gratitude to her by taking all kinds of human luxuries she and her sisters don't have: dried fruits, savoury and sweet, sophisticated fabrics and fabulous settings for jewels. Before he sets out on the long journey again, he tells his mother about his wife's nature and the suit of feathers hidden in a trunk which she must not let her find. Or she will fly away with the children, says Hasan, and break his heart.

One day in the capital, the Sultana Zubayda, the favourite of Harun al-Rashid, summons Hasan's wife to court because she has heard reports of her incomparable beauty from a slave girl who saw her at the baths. But Hasan's wife has overheard his last instructions to his mother, and she offers to show the Sultana something that surpasses her physical charms, if only she can put on her magic feathers.

When she demonstrates how she can fly, to the marvelling of the court, Hasan's fears are fulfilled: she ascends into the dome but does not stop there. With cries of distress at leaving Hasan's mother, she gathers her two children up with her and, taking wing, calls for Hasan to follow her if he loves her, to the islands of Waq-Waq.

Hasan's quest to regain his fairy wife will take him on many, many more journeys and adventures, involve him in complicated tussles with the laws that govern fairylands, and above all with the enchanters who make them. One is Abd al-Quddus, a learned sheikh, the kind and wise uncle of Hasan's little sister, and when she summons him to help Hasan, he arrives riding on an enormous elephant. His magic contrasts with the perverted knowledge of Bahram, and he insists on the terrible dangers and insuperable difficulties that reaching her will involve. He can't help directly, but he gives Hasan a letter for his master, Abu el-Ruwaysh, an even more learned magus than himself, who is the son of Bilqis, the Queen of Sheba. This supreme master of magic is black and robed in black, and he takes Hasan to meet a group of scholars in a library, each of them reading and surrounded by disciples: a vision of a fairy university. Abu el-Ruwaysh listens to Hasan's story and takes pity on him. Burning some incense, he conjures the jinn Dahnash, and orders him to put Hasan on his shoulders and carry him to the Land of Camphor where the king will be able to help him reach Waq-Waq.

The narrative keeps heaping up the horrors and pitfalls and the vastness of the task ahead. The numbers the King of Camphor invokes are delirious, excessive. Hasan will find his wife on the seventh island and there is a flotilla leaving for Waq-Waq the next night. At the harbour, Hasan watches from his hiding place as the ships are loaded with goods by the merchants who are as numerous as a host of grasshoppers and covered with layers of mail. Each of them is armed, and they give instructions to the market vendors and the dockers, selecting the goods, bargaining and ordering them on board. They are all women: the Amazons of Waq-Waq.

Hasan stows away; on landing in Waq-Waq, he puts on women's clothes so that he can pass among the Amazons, and hides in one of the tents erected near the port. He is discovered. The tent belongs to an old woman, a loathly lady, an Amazonian warrior and a blue-eyed hag, with a big, dripping nose, evoked by Shahrazad as a horrendous grotesque, her 'smooth and hairless skin like a brindled viper's'. But Shawahi Umm al-Dawahi is a skilled enchantress, a nurse who loves her charges, and a maga with a heart of gold. She takes a shine to the young man she finds has stolen into her tent wearing women's clothes. She likes him too much, perhaps (she later asks him to kiss her, not on her cheek, but on the lips). But she is the commander-in-chief of the Amazon army and is aware of the proper uses of her knowledge.

Shawahi paints the horrors that lie ahead of Hasan before he can reach the seventh island, where his wife is; there is the small problem of the Amazon queen, Nur al-Huda, who will be hostile.

But Hasan won't be deterred. On they go, through islands and islands where the trees bear leaves with human faces that cry 'waq waq,' amid praises to God. The woods are thronged with birds and wild animals, and the cities with beautiful young girls whom Shawahi orders to bathe in front of her tent so that Hasan can look for his lost wife among them. No sign of her. They continue their search until they come before the formidable queen, Nur al-Huda, who falls into a rage with Shawahi that she has allowed a man into their territory.

At this late point in the story, Hasan reveals that he does not know his wife's name.

She is the unnameable, a prohibited presence, a fairy over whom he does not have power. But his children, he tells the queen, are called Nasir and Mansur.

It dawns on the angry queen that the trespasser has married her own sister, Manar an-Nisa. She orders Shawahi to fetch her, with her two children, and bring her to court as she wants to meet her little nephews, whose existence had not been revealed to her before.

Manar trembles at these orders: nobody has ever seen her children. She cries, 'I am jealous of the breeze if it blows on them in the evening!' She does not say they are half-fairy, half-human, and that she has broken fairy law, but that is the reason for her fears and her caution.

And she has reason to hide them away, for her sister the queen's rage at her marriage to a man – a human man, at that – grows more ferocious the more she knows. When Manar arrives, she hurls abuse at her: 'Whore, strumpet, traitor, wantoning with a man who isn't even a vizier or the son of a vizier or a great merchant!' She will strangle her and her bastards. If she isn't married, she'll be severely punished. And if she is married, why did she leave her husband and take her children away?

The queen heaps curses on her sister, and then, in a long letter to their father, sets out all her crimes. She begins: 'A human being has penetrated our country. My sister has fallen in love with a huckster from Iraq . . .'

The demon king responds: Manar must be executed, along with her brats.

Her sister loses no time in obeying his order: first she beats Manar till she faints; then, not content with that, she rolls up her sleeves and lays about Manar with whips made for driving elephants in battle charges. When the distraught Shawahi tries to run away, the queen orders her slaves to seize her.

But this is still a romance, and Hasan is the hero, so fate intervenes. Hasan is wandering in despair at his situation when he comes across two jinn children – boys – fighting over two instruments their magician father worked on for thirty-five years before his death: a copper rod with power over seven tribes of jinn, and a cap of invisibility, both covered all over with talismanic inscriptions and seals.

Hasan thinks for a while, then suggests to the quarrelling boys a way of allotting the instruments fairly: he will throw a ball, and the one who catches it will have the rod, the other who comes after, the cap.

When the boys run off after the ball, Hasan puts the cap on his head, grasps the copper rod, and orders it to transport him back to the palace and, still invisible, to the quarters of his champion, the old woman Shawahi. When he reveals himself and tells her all, she recognises the magic objects he now has in his possession as the work of her own master in magic, and remembers that he had warned his sons that they would not inherit them, but that a stranger would come . . .

Shawahi and Hasan now know that they have the means of rescuing Manar.

They discover her, half dead, strung up as if crucified on a scaffold, bound by her hair to the top strut. Unable to brush away the flies settling on her open wounds she is crying out in agony for her loss of Hasan, and of her children – who are at her feet – and blaming herself for leaving him in the first place.

'A woman only knows the value of a man,' she says, 'when she has lost him.'

'I was at fault,' says Hasan, 'because I left you to go on a long journey.'

With the power of the rod and the cap, they plan their escape; Hasan takes the eldest child in his arms, and Manar the youngest. Shawahi appears and begs them to take her with them: she is riding a big Byzantine jar with reins made of palm leaves, which can go faster than a colt from Najd. She promises them that she knows many even more powerful spells, and that she has only checked herself till then out of fear of their father, the demon king, and of Manar's sisters, especially the queen Nur al-Huda.

Hasan strikes the rod on the ground and ten colossal jinn appear, their heads reaching to the skies, their feet in the depths; each of them has multitudes more jinn and spirits under his control. Hasan tells them he and Manar and their children and Shawahi want to go home, and to take them up and fly them to Baghdad. But the jinn quake: they are forbidden to carry humans. Trembling and shaking, they tell Hasan how amazing his adventures have been, and that he could only be carried by Dahnash because the sheikh Abu el-Ruwaysh is one of the few wise men who knows the secret name of God.

So Hasan beats his drum again and conjures up some jinn horses instead.

Shawahi abandons her Byzantine jar and they all fly away together. Leaving Waq Waq they come upon a horrifying colossus, who tells them he's the chieftain of the jinn of Waq-Waq, but he is one of the faithful to Muhammad, and he promises to help them escape.

They see a cloud of dust on the horizon behind them: the army of Waq-Waq is in hot pursuit. They're overtaken, and a dreadful battle follows. But the seven tribes of jinn ruled by the copper rod and the chieftain of the jinn who is on their side make it impossible for the queen to win; she's taken prisoner and brought before Hasan, Manar and Shawahi, whom she has made suffer so much.

Shawahi hurls abuse at her and threatens to have her dragged by horses and devoured by ravening dogs because she countermanded the law of God and of nature: that a woman should marry and live with a man.

But Manar takes pity on her sister, and even after all the tortures she's inflicted on her, she forgives her. She manages to reconcile her with the old woman Shawahi, who goes back with her to Waq-Waq.

Still on their way back to Baghdad, the party meet the two sheikhs, the two powerful, good magicians Abd al-Quddus and Abu el-Ruwaysh, who originally helped Hasan when he was looking for Manar. They ask Hasan to give them the cap and the rod so they can keep them safe from evildoers – while promising to look after Hasan from a distance. Hasan willingly gives up possession of these supreme weapons.

Back in Baghdad, Hasan's mother has not been able to sleep or eat or drink during his long absence; the worry has made her ill. When he and Manar and the children arrive home at last, he hears her grieving words behind the door. As she recites some of the poetry she knows by heart, he calls out to her,

'O my mother, the day has come at last when we can all be together again!'

And he went into the house and embraced her, and she greeted Manar with love and asked her forgiveness if she had done her wrong. Then Hasan began to tell his mother the entire story of their adventures.

CHAPTER SIX

Magians and Dervishes

To fall in love with what she feared to look on?
. . . I therefore vouch again
That with some mixtures powerful o'er the blood,
Or with some dram conjur'd to this effect,
He wrought upon her.

Shakespeare, Othello

I

THE *ARABIAN NIGHTS* CONJURED AN enchanted virtual world that could be safely entered and explored, accepted and naturalised by the Enlightenment and modern reader and writer precisely because they often unfold in an elsewhere that is different from the native habitat of Judaeo-Christian demons and eschatological visions. A home-grown practice of, and belief in, magic was set aside to be replaced by foreign magic – stranger magic, much easier to disown, or otherwise hold in intellectual and political quarantine.

The stories provide a stimulus to this legitimate – and hypocritical – pleasure. Powerful, fiendish enchanters appear in several of the tales to work their terrible will on their victims; in the book these characters are almost invariably magians, obdurate in their rejection of Islam. Their allegiance is to earlier gods, such as the Egyptian pantheon in half-animal form, or Fire, as worshipped by the Zoroastrians from Persia. If ancient pagan Egypt with its Pharaonic mysteries and science throws a long shadow across the enchantments of the *Nights*, it is the magians of Persia who wield the most sinister and potent magic, as the romance of Hasan of Basra shows through the hero's relations with the implacable Bahram.

'The Tale of Hasan of Basra' is a ravelled tapestry of a story, frame within frame, border within border, with knots and clusters and repeats of motifs; a performance of ebullient story-spinning fancy, an endlessly mobile picaresque romance, which increasingly breaks out into outbursts of verse and song that echo the erotic lyricism of the Song of Songs from the Bible. The tale is technically shorter than a *sira*, or romance of chivalry, and longer than a *khabar*, the equivalent of a fairy or folk tale. It combines many other literary modes: the travel yarn, a moral lesson in the conduct of wives, a recognition tale about parents separated from beloved children, and a romance of initiation.

The story also presents strands which the more famous 'Aladdin and the Wonderful Lamp' picks up and winds into a different overall pattern: the lazy, disobedient boy who brings nothing but grief to his widowed mother, and the stranger magician who uses the boy for his own purposes and abandons him to die when he does not comply. Interestingly, Borges, in one of his passionate essays about the *Arabian Nights*, recounts De Quincey writing that his favourite moment in the book took place in 'Aladdin', when the evil magician, looking for the boy who will help him obtain the lamp, puts his ear to the ground and hears, from the other side of the world in China, the footfalls of Aladdin and recognises that he must be the one.

Borges, having looked in vain for this scene in 'Aladdin', takes it for a marvellous example of an ideal response to the *Nights*, in which the reader or listener's fancy plays freely with the material. It is indeed an illustration of creative reading as advocated by Borges, but it does also suggest that De Quincey had read another story of fated pursuit from the *Nights*, for his memory echoes the scene when Bahram cries out to Hasan, 'It's been years that I've been looking for you and now I have you.'

But 'Hasan of Basra' is more than a complicated fairy tale: its picture of so many different orders of jinn, so many degrees of apostasy, fidelity, orthodoxy and heresy, and the teeming numbers of different magic adepts, wise men and women, Amazons, sorcerers and magas, bring into view a whirling and perplexing drama about how supernatural powers contend in the human world. The continual expansion of the enchanted horizons, as more and more mysterious jinn principalities and kingdoms are evoked, unfolds a natural world – of clouds and camphor, wild beasts and birds – in contrast to the home territory of Baghdad and Basra. But because it was not one of the *Arabian Nights* tales in the core corpus, and was not translated by Galland in the first volumes, this tale and others closely connected to it, 'Janshah and Shamshah' and 'Sayf al-Muluk and Princess Badiat al-Jamal', have not been told and retold, dramatised or adapted with the frequency and assiduity that greeted material from Galland's founding edition, though the many resemblances to 'Prince Ahmed and the Fairy Peri Banou', as well as to 'Aladdin', suggest he might have known these fairy romances. The pervasive enchantments in these stories convey the flavour of the narrative tradition differently from the raunchy and comic cunning of 'Ali Baba' or the 'Hunchback' cycle, but they are more wonderful, richer in invention, and packed with '*aja'ib*' (wonders) to inspire amazement.

Hasan's story is also thronged with powerful women of steadfastness, independence and selfless passion, from his mother to Hasan's adoptive jinn sister who loves him from the first. The Amazons are vividly if luridly depicted and the moral of the tale comes down emphatically against their choice of lifestyle – but individually they are fascinating, and in Shawahi, the ugly old nurse-cum-sorceress, the *Nights* have created a towering character. When she mounts her jar like a spirited steed, she suggests the later connections between the *Arabian Nights* and Russian fairy tales, in which the tremendous ogress, Baba Yaga, rides through the air in a mortar.

Although the Amazon queen, Nur al-Huda, rivals in cruelty the sorceress in the story of 'The Prince of the Black Islands' (she will be reprised by William Beckford for the portrait of Carathis, the mother of Vathek), the presence of the heroines provides a counterweight to the tales of female deceit, lust and cruelty in the opening frame story that incite the Sultan Shahriyar to revenge on womankind. It is one of the tales, suffused with struggle, hope and love, that strengthens Shahrazad's attempt to persuade the Sultan to think more carefully about human complexity and the range of women's characters. When Manar forgives her sister Nur, she offers a startling lesson in magnanimity.

So it is not surprising that the name Hasan of Basra comes from an historical figure in Sufi mysticism. Its appearance here directs the reader towards the metaphysical depths at which the hero's fantastic adventures are moving. Constant reference to books, and to book learning, occur: from the deviant knowledge of the alchemist to the accomplished calligraphy of Hasan himself, the tale assumes the powerful effects of scripture and scripts. The jinn princesses write letters and love poetry, while Hasan's mother, who has made sure her son is literate, has memorised a store of poetry which she recites to turn away further dangers, give herself courage and affirm her faith in providence however unpropitious matters are looking. This intensely literary quality of the story adds a layer of fable to the far-fetched vicissitudes of the adventures. The story's fantastic geography relates it to the travel literature of wonderlands, where fabulous beasts and monstrous races appear on medieval and early modern maps, but it also captures a shamanistic yearning for a dream world of knowledge and harmony beyond this one.

The story indicts alchemy used for material gain not only as wicked but also, interestingly, as patently fraudulent. The Persian alchemist is intent on deceiving Hasan; he is a child abductor, a paedophile, and the precursor of nursery bogeymen, like the child-catcher in *Chitty Chitty Bang Bang*. The strangeness of these enchanters lends weight to a structural impulse in fairytale to imagine dangerous magic as coming from far away. The Orient in the *Arabian Nights* has its own Orient.

The story of Hasan of Basra shows the Persian magician condemned as someone unable to grasp the principle, laid down by monotheism, that jinn are not only demons in the predominant Judaeo-Christian sense, but an order of spirit beings ranging in character, appearance and behaviour, sentient and individual. They can be good or otherwise, depending on their allegiance. Some jinn have remained fire-worshippers, hence infidels from the point of view of Islam, and those stubborn renegades follow their lord, Iblis, or Satan. But even they need not all be considered unregenerate devils and monsters; some of them have been perverted from their true destiny by various failings – rebelliousness rooted in pride above all and punished by incarceration in copper flasks. Surprisingly, many are spirits of virtue – and there are thousands upon thousands of them invisibly crowding this world and others beyond it.

II

Zoroastrianism predates Islam by a millennium at least, and survived the success of the new faith in Iran and, later, in India. It sets up two opposing divinities, Ahura Mazda, the source of light and good, who contends with Ahriman, the principle of darkness and evil. Although ultimately Ahura Mazda will prevail, the Zoroastrian cosmology imagines the two deities struggling in a state of continual battle. For this seemingly dualist dogma, the believers came in for sporadic persecution.

Counterparts of Bahram in 'Hasan of Basra' make their appearance in some of the oldest stories in the *Nights*: in the long chivalric romance 'The History of Gharib and his Brother Ajib', in some episodes of 'Sinbad', and in the tale of 'Jullanar of the Sea'. As in the case of Hasan's kidnapper, the Persian magians' expertise is vast; but through their associations with fire, which they are represented as worshipping at blazing shrines in their temples, they are chiefly associated with alchemy, blacksmithery, and other kinds of forging and metallurgy. These stories are wildly plotted, and bear all the marks of oral storytelling: multiple reprises and repetitions, doublings of characters, generations and incidents.

Like so many other evil sorcerers in the *Nights*, the magician is a passing stranger; before Hasan's eyes, he changes dross into gold. William Harvey, 'Hassan and the Persian' (1850).

Memories of the earliest years when Islam was conquering countries that professed other gods are embedded in the stories of renegade cities, wicked pagan queens, stubborn superstitious tyrants. 'Jullanar the Sea-Born', which is one of the earliest tales in the *Nights* and another loose skein of Persian origin, tells a story which in certain features – the underwater kingdom of the heroine, her mysterious silence, her marriage to a mortal human – resembles the fairytale group of Mélusine, the Little Mermaid, and Rusalka. But in one of the many offshoots in 'Jullanar', her child Badr Basim becomes the captive and lover of another Zoroastrian apostate and sorceress, Queen Lab. Circe-like, Lab lives in her fiery palace surrounded by animals and birds who are her former lovers: an inverted picture of Solomon with his court of intelligible creatures. Badr Basim tries – and fails – to resist Queen Lab's designs on him and is turned into a bird, until his mermaid mother rides into battle against her son's captor and defeats her.

Everywhere in the *Nights*, the magicians are linked to savagery and perversion – the stories are quite unrepentantly hostile. When the heroine,

Zobeide, the mistress of the house in the cycle of 'The Porter', is summoned to explain to the Caliph why she cruelly whips two black dogs every day while weeping as she does so, she describes arriving at a mysterious and deserted city – another of the stories' uncanny ruins – in which all the inhabitants are suspended at their business and turned to black stone. Finally, deep inside a splendid palace in an exquisite oratory, she finds a single, surviving inhabitant, a young man, who is reading from the Koran. He is so beautiful and smells so delicious that she is instantly smitten. He tells her she has reached a city of magians who refused to convert after numerous attempts to save them and turn them to the right path. They were stubborn and so have been punished; he alone has escaped because his old nurse taught him the true faith. For many years he has lived in complete seclusion in the ghost town.

Zobeide is an enterprising trader and she has a ship in the harbour taking on merchandise for Baghdad; she invites him to leave with her and marry her. They embark, in blissful happiness. She gives her sisters all her money, as long as she can have him. But her two sisters are envious – of their love, their happiness – and they throw them both overboard. Zobeide survives by clinging to a floating spar, but the young man has never had the chance to learn to swim, she tells her audience, and he drowns.

She finds herself on a strange shore, and sees a lizard, out of breath as a ferocious snake chases it; she kills the attacker by throwing a stone at its head, whereupon the lizard she has saved suddenly sprouts wings and turns into a beautiful jinniya who, when she hears her rescuer's story, immediately punishes the treacherous sisters by changing them into black bitches.

'By the truth of the words engraved on Solomon's seal,' she then cries out, 'if you do not give each of these two three hundred lashes every day you shall see me appear to render you just like them.' This is the explanation for the sadomasochistic tableau which the porter and the others have witnessed that afternoon in the lady's house.

Harun al-Rashid asks the story's heroine if she knows how to summon the fairy responsible. She replies that she can burn a lock of the fairy's hair – a reference to supposed Zoroastrian sacrifices. When the fairy reappears, she instantly professes her true faith as a Muslim, and promises to obey Harun al-Rashid. He wants the bitches back in human shape, and so she takes a magic bowl and sprinkles its water over them.

In the tidy outcome, the Sultan then marries off the sisters to the three one-eyed dervishes whose stories had also astonished him, and whom he installs in his palace as his chamberlains.

The anonymous fairy in this story emanates from the magians' profane society, but has seen the light and is able to end the degrading metamorphoses she inflicted on the two wicked sisters.

Zoroastrians survived – and still survive – in a small population in India, where they took refuge in the ninth and tenth centuries, fleeing Muslim persecution, and where they are better known as Parsis. André Miquel dates the epic tale of Gharib and Ajib to the ninth or tenth century; an earlier scholar dates it to before the establishment of Islam. 'In this respect, the romance's campaigns of conversion foreshadow Muhammad's revelations.'

It is astonishing how deeply these memories of remote and otherwise forgotten conflicts have bitten into the collective imagination. Here are stories which were first being told in the ninth century, and still there is Bahram flourishing as the archetypal figure of the dark enchanter, a naturalised species in modern and contemporary culture, dating from a time when his Anglo-Saxon or Celtic equivalent was admired for his cunning with runes. An enemy of the Muslim faithful before the first millennium has become the template for 'He who cannot be named' (Voldemort), Sauron the Dark Lord of Mordor, known in *The Hobbit* as 'the Necromancer', and for Darth Vader and, before them all, for 'the African Magician', as Galland calls the corresponding villain in 'The Tale of Aladdin and the Wonderful Lamp', and who is now known as Abu Mazar – the distinguished medieval astronomer Albumazar (d. 886), turned into a pantomime villain.

In popular culture, exotic strangers endowed with deadly powers catalyse many successful plots, as in the combat myths of antiquity; in James Bond thrillers, *Star Wars* films and the Harry Potter series they pit the forces of humanity against diabolical evil in an apocalyptic drama with roots in ancient biblical visions such as Daniel's of the Ancient of Days sitting in judgement (Daniel 7: 3–11) or Jesus's prophecy of the second coming (Matt. 24: 29–51). This Judaeo-Christian tendency continues, to a varying pulse, to inject paranoid passions into contemporary attitudes to foreign policy, for example, as well as into attitudes to the migrations of people in today's mobile, war-torn, economically critical world. Yet good magical beings – the faithful jinn – and the cosmos they inhabit have survived less well. This other order of spirits, whose counterparts might be the elves and fairies, often occupy a harmonious and benevolent region; but this realm gradually shrinks and fades from view in the course of the *Nights'* reception. If it does survive, in the fairylands of children's literature and films, it is belittled, infantilised and commercialised. Consequently, in appearance, enchantments keep their oriental character for sinister purposes, but become prettified when they divest themselves of it, while the full ambiguities of magic in the *Nights* lose their original definition, as the jinn and their masters are conflated with devils and simplistically opposed to one another – sometimes humorously, sometimes scarily, sometimes directly threatening. This gradual orientalisation of magicians amounts to a form of aesthetic rendition, by which the dirty work is done by strangers so that the home team keeps its hands clean and its smile all innocence.

III

Bahram, the Persian magician of the *Nights*, makes an appearance under a different guise in another corner of popular culture even earlier than these early elements in the book: the three wise men of the New Testament, the three magi, are his forebears. Their canny sky-gazing has discovered the new star and brought them to Herod, and they offer the newborn baby gold, frankincense and myrrh, precious Eastern gifts redolent of Arabian or Persian luxury, by contrast to the stable's ideal Christian poverty. By these offerings, they recognise the baby's divinity and sovereignty, and implicitly abandon their old gods.

The magi's coming fulfilled a prophecy that 'the kings of Tarshish and of the isles shall bring presents: the kings of Sheba and Seba shall offer gifts (Ps. 72:10) and so although the Bible only calls them 'wise men from the east' and never names them as rulers or says there were three of them (Matt. 2: 1–12) the Old Testament verse inspired the idea that at least one of them was an African – a Moor. The visit is also foreshadowed, in biblical typology, by the Queen of Sheba's visit to Solomon, and her conversion to his god is recapitulated in the scene when the gorgeous wise men from the east with their fabulous caravan of camels and mules, treasures and delicacies, prostrate themselves before the newborn Saviour. (Bosch includes Solomon and Sheba in the rich, encrusted embroidery on the robes of one of the magi in his painting of *The Adoration of the Magi*, in the Prado.) The magi's story expressed a fulfilled longing for religious triumph along identical lines to the romances of the *Nights*, though these tend to be rather more highly coloured as well as less laconic.

The nearer the painter of an Adoration of the Magi is working to the frontiers of Islam, the more profoundly the three wise men reflect the luxurious clothing and display of the way of life under the Ottomans in former Byzantium or the Mamelukes in Egypt. The scenes are a hubbub of activity, ceremony and celebrity display; huge turbans, billowing brocades and samite, numerous attendants and inordinate amounts of baggage point out the unmistakable worldly stature of the visitors, and justify their status as kings.

From as early as the second century, Christian theologians debated carefully where in the East the three wise men might have started their journey. St Augustine pointed out that dromedaries can travel forty leagues a day, but even so, with all the luxuries and train of attendants, Persia seemed too far away for them to have covered the ground in the interval between spotting the star and reaching the stable, as described in the Gospel of St Matthew. St Jerome and others proposed Chaldea, where astronomy was enthusiastically followed. India was also suggested, and Mesopotamia; but the most favoured point of origin was neighbouring Arabia Felix, where they were presumed to be local kings called Gaspar, Melchior and Balthasar.

One of them – it is not settled which one – is represented as a Moor according to a tradition first alluded to by the Venerable Bede, who described Balthasar as 'dark-skinned (*fuscus*), with a full beard . . .' The presence of a black wise man at the scene of Christ's nativity shifts this magus's identity across from Zoroastrianism (the religion to which Persians belonged at the time of Jesus's birth) to the territories taken over by Islam, including African countries more southerly and easterly that Persia. But neither his previous allegiance nor his geographical origin has ever been decisively settled.

Reports from merchants, soldiers and travellers provided rich circumstantial context for the map of their journey. An artist such as the remarkable Danish engraver and draughtsman Melchior Lorck – aptly named after one of the three wise men – published observations made during his travels in the Ottoman Empire and gives early glimpses of the culture's sumptuary dress codes. In the case of a Spanish artist, like Juan Bautista Maíno (1569–1649), his portrait of the black magus draws on the inhabitants of neighbouring territories in North Africa and Egypt (Pl. 8).

Individual 'Moors' inspired artists' images of the black magus: the imposing and startled figure painted by Rubens in the great altarpiece of the *Adoration of the Magi* in Antwerp was based on a Tunisian ally of the Holy Roman Emperor, Charles V: Mulay Ahmad, a Berber prince whom Rubens knew from a portrait; this 'African prince' in the painting wears Turkish clothes, a complete outfit brought back to Antwerp by a local merchant.

MVLEI AHMET PRINCEPS AFRICANVS FILIVS REGIS TVNSI

The Berber leader Mulay Ahmad was known as 'the King of Tunis', and partly inspired figures of the black king in Nativity scenes (Jan Cornelisz. Vermeyen, c. 1613–15).

Even as it is being noted by travellers and eyewitnesses, this Orient of the mind was stimulated by legends and the Bible; historically, it marches with the political dominions of Muslim influence, and so the many paintings of the Adoration of the Magi, offering tribute to the newborn Saviour, also implicitly communicate their capitulation to the incarnate God of Christianity and the long-desired conversion of Islam.

But can the black magus of medieval and Renaissance art relate in any other way to the *Arabian Nights*, which appeared in print so much later? Elizabeth McGrath writes, 'The Magi collectively epitomize pagan wisdom, combined with elevated status: they are rich and mighty kings come from afar to humble themselves before the true king . . .' She then goes on, making a different point: 'the feast of the Epiphany is above all the celebration of Christ's manifestation to and recognition *by the Gentiles*' (my emphasis). Such pictures offered a model for depictions of Solomon as well as for the three kings, and offered another lens, rosier than the legacy of nigromancy, through which the magical literature from the Middle East was read when the *Nights* first reached Western readers in translation.

Because magical thinking was gradually becoming interdicted, so 'modern' enchantment resorted to costume and dressed up *à l'Orientale, à la turque*, in silk pyjamas, which provided an excuse as well as a rationale and a site of pleasure. A small but precise example of the step change in attitude towards the mystical and magical aspects of Islam takes place in a traveller's report on the ceremonies of the dervishes in Istanbul published in Paris in 1717, and therefore coinciding with the first print versions of the *Nights*.

The ritual of the whirling dervishes in their temple in Istanbul was open to visitors, who marvelled at this mystical practice and its effects (J.B. Scotin le jeune, after J.-B. Vanmour, *c.* 1707–8).

Dervishes make their appearance in several marvellous stories besides the cycle of 'The Porter and the Three Ladies of Baghdad'. The caliph, Harun al-Rashid, who is also present at the scenes in the house that night, has adopted the disguise of a dervish in order to wander about his city with maximum impunity and listen in anonymously on his people's talk and doings.

Dervishes are Sufi mystics, vowed to poverty (their name means 'poor'): a dervish is an ascetic, dedicated to the higher life of the spirit. Like Christian monks, they can belong to many different orders. As holy men, they were held in high esteem in the seventeenth century, not suspicion. Pétis de la Croix, whose rival collection, *Les mille et un Jours*, 1710–12, piqued Galland to continue with his volumes of the *Nights*, attributed the stories in his five volumes to 'the celebrated Dervish Moclès, whom Persia counts among its greatest personages. He was head of the Sufis of Isfahan.' Pétis finds nothing to reject in this source, which is rather presented as impeccable; he adds that he was given the manuscript in 1675. His editors now believe that the stories are in fact Turkish in origin, and retold and embellished by Pétis himself with other intervening hands. The dervish Moclès was introduced to authenticate the work according to a pattern of impersonation and disguise that runs through the history of the *Nights*.

One celebrated order gained – or gains – an alternative state where the divine takes possession of the self through the ritual practice of whirling for hours in trance; they used to perform the rite in their own cult site in Pera, Istanbul, attracting audiences both local and foreign, many travellers reporting their astonishment. (Whirling dervishes still perform at festivals worldwide – I saw them in the 1970s when they visited the Round House, in north London, a temple perfectly made for their wheeling movement and the unfurling of their long circular skirts that seem to be lifting them literally off the floor.)

When the artist Jean-Baptiste Vanmour accompanied the French ambassador the marquis de Ferriol to Istanbul in 1707–8, he created an album of portraits, court ceremonies and customs, including the ritual of the whirling dervishes. His paintings were then engraved and published in the *Recueil de cent estampes*, or 'Album Ferriol', as the visual chronicle is now known. A sheet of music giving the 'Tune used by the Dervishes of Pera for their whirling' is tipped into the copy in the British Library which belonged to one of its founders, Sir Hans Sloane. The caption to one engraving is 'Dervish, or Turkish monk, who whirls out of piety', and the whole album closes with a magnificent, detailed, double-page spread, 'Dervishes in their temple at Pera, ending their whirling'. In this

engraving the focus has moved more intimately than Vanmour painting
into the throng of dancers. All the dervishes are wearing the tall cylinder
hats that, according to in the Ottoman empire's strict dress code, with
its especially significant millinery, denotes their profession. Their gracefully outstretched arms and tilted heads, set off by the chimney headgear,
give an impressive feeling of ecstatic transport – beyond pleasure or pain,
an intense state of convincingly altered consciousness. Some of the eight
dervishes in the ring are manifestly of a certain age, with long grey or
even white beards; one of the whirlers is beardless: 'the young ones turn
at an unbelievable speed,' says the French publisher and commentator,
Jacques Le Hay. This is an important detail, because the Parisian bookman
later directs the reader or viewer to appraise the images in a way that
captures the prevailing opinion in France. According to the caption, they
are coming to the end of their rite, and two have indeed fallen to their
knees – crouched on the floor, exhausted or overcome by dizziness when
they finally ceased to move.

In the first edition of the *Recueil*, given royal approval in July 1714,
the commentary describes very simply how everybody flocks to see the
astonishing show; how a reading from the Koran precedes the dance, and
how the inscriptions on the columns and around the dome come from
the Koran and utter God's praises, while the hoop above the dancers'
heads serves to hang lamps during Ramadan. However, the following
year, when high demand led to a second edition, the Parisian publisher-
editor added a preface, and an 'Explanation of the hundred engravings'.
In a fuller commentary on each of the prints he clearly warmed to a
new theme, and the factual tenor of the laconic first text has been
superseded. Although he adds that M. de Ferriol delighted in the dervishes'
musicianship and often asked them to play while he accompanied them
on the bass viol, he also gossips about them: 'There are other Dervishes
who move from country to country and often lead a libertine life. Many
come to Constantinople from Persia and the Indies. The dervish's bonnet
is a good passport for going wherever they wish; even for insinuating
themselves to the table of grandees, who would not dare chase them
away, for fear of seeming proud . . . although their presence is often
irksome to them.' The writer then moves into the realms of heterodox
fascination exercised by the *Nights*: 'Most Indian and Persian dervishes
adore Fire, and consequently the Sun which is its principle . . .' When
he returns to the subject of the image he is discussing, he amplifies his
earlier description with his own insinuation: 'It is the music that animates
them; they claim it has something of the divine.'

With the flagrant statement that dervishes adore fire, the writer cancels the distinction so fiercely set up between magians and the Islamic faithful in the *Arabian Nights*, and turns them into Bahrams one and all; while with the innocuous little phrase, 'they claim that it [the music] has something of the divine', the Parisian cordons himself off from the scene and the people in it in a way that had not been felt necessary by the ambassador, comfortable playing on his cello while the dervishes turned. The manoeuvre copies exactly those acts of rejection and repression of false magic – of pagans and Zoroastrians – in the *Nights*.

It would be a bit blunt to say French commentators learned tactics from the stories; but it seems to me that the *Nights'* great success does arise in part from its harsh treatment of some faiths and some practices and that this was an area where the oriental mode again provided effective camouflage.

When the radical philosopher William Godwin was compiling *The Lives of the Necromancers* (1834), an entertaining and sceptical potboiler about wizards throughout history, he expected to discover many oriental magicians, and revealingly confessed himself disappointed that they eluded him. His book is subtitled *An Account of the Most Eminent Persons in Successive Ages, who have claimed for themselves, or to whom has been imputed by others, The Exercise of Magical Power*. In a subsection called 'General Silence of the East respecting Individual Necromancers', he writes:

'Asia has been more notorious than perhaps any other division of the globe for the vast multiplicity and variety of its narratives of sorcery and magic. I have however been much disappointed in the thing I looked for in the first place, and that is, in the individual adventures of such persons as might be supposed to have gained a high degree of credit and reputation for their skill in exploits of magic.' Unlike the many cases in European history (and Godwin throws his net wide, taking in Circe and Medea, Daedalus and Pythagoras, Socrates and Apuleius, Merlin, Joan of Arc, Faust and Roger Bacon), 'the magicians of the East,' he writes, '. . . are mere abstractions . . .'.

He turns thankfully to the *Arabian Nights* and notices the importance of the Zoroastrians and the Persian presence; he then gives a brief but engaging account of some stories from the cycle of 'The Porter and the Three Ladies of Baghdad' (including 'The Tale of the Third Dervish') and the grisly story of Amina and her husband, who discovers she is a ghoul when he follows her to a cemetery and sees her gorging on human remains.

Godwin takes several steps which are highly revealing in respect of 'stranger magic'. He recognises without evasion that an irrational belief in instrumental magic fills the European classical tradition; he calmly proclaims that Christianity produced 'a revolution in the history of necromancy and witchcraft' by condemning magic and superstition, not noticing that deep belief in devils and magic was necessary to fuel witch-hunting in the first place. Above all, he expects to find in the record numerous Muslim enchanters, and failing that, turns to the *Nights* to identify them, using the stories as evidence. 'It is true,' he writes, 'that these are delivered to us in the garb of fiction; but they are known to present so exact a picture of Eastern manners and customs, and so just a delineation of the follies, the weaknesses and credulity of the races of men that figure in them, that, in the absence of materials of a strictly historical sort . . . they . . . may furnish us with a pretty full representation of the ideas of sorcery and magic which for centuries were entertained in this part of the world.'

Godwin's anthology is key to the late Enlightenment perspective on magic: he was writing in the wake of the Egyptomania unleashed by Napoleon's expedition and Belzoni's archaeological discoveries, and during the second high tide of enthusiasm for the *Arabian Nights* when Edward Lane was working on his translation. As the husband of Mary Wollstonecraft, father of Mary Shelley, father-in-law of Percy Bysshe Shelley, and author and publisher of children's fairy tales, Godwin was in the closest possible contact with the Romantics' involvement with fantasy, myth and enchantment, but he remained a staunch man of the earlier generation, committed to radical rationalism. Yet, even in a gallimaufry about magicians (written no doubt to pay the bills), his approach conveys the younger thinkers' new hope for the emancipatory imagination and its products.

Story 6

A Fortune Regained

THERE'S A LOVELY OLD HOUSE in Baghdad, built around a shaded and tiled courtyard with a square pool in the centre where a small jet of water pulses. It resembles many others in that old city. Doves fly down from their dovecote in the heat of the day to rinse their dusty wings in the little pool, and the small lemon trees breathe honey; beaded wooden interlacings on the windows of the house, both those overlooking the street and those facing the courtyard, mottle the cool inner rooms. It is not unlike many other houses in that city.

But to the owner it was not like any of them; it was his mother's family house, and the pleasure he felt living there was exceptional. Besides, his mother had lived there till her death two years before and over decades she had added distinctive touches – a carving on the lintel of the kitchen quarters with a special blessing for the bowls and dishes, pots and pans inside. His wife and daughters watered the potted flowers every morning in the courtyard and put out food for the birds at a table in the corner of the courtyard.

In the days when this story unfolds, the house is falling to rack and ruin, the wooden shutters are missing beads and leaning on their hinges, the pump no longer purls in the little pool, and nobody in the household thinks of feeding the birds since they themselves have to scavenge to survive.

After several difficult years, the owner's business has failed completely; he can't pay his servants, satisfy his creditors, or revive his trade and help his family.

One night in the depths of his despair, he dreamed. A form appeared in his bedroom and a voice announced to him, as clearly as if the speaker were standing in the room at his very ear, 'If you want to know how to live, go to Cairo.'

So the ruined man set out from Baghdad for the Egyptian capital, and reaching it at nightfall, with no money to pay for a bed, turned into a mosque and laid himself down to sleep.

As he lay there, it so happened that a band of robbers entered the mosque in order to break into the adjoining house. But they were rough and wild and made such a clatter and commotion as they were trying to break in that they woke the inhabitants in the house, who called the guards. They rushed to the scene. The robbers skedaddled on the instant, so the guards found only the Baghdadi, whom they hauled before their chief. He had him beaten. The beating was so severe the man's despair deepened, if that were possible, and he thought he would die of the blows.

Then they threw him into the cells.

For three days he languished there before he was summoned to appear before the chief of police.

The police chief demanded of the traveller, 'What brought you to Cairo?'

The man told him of his dream, adding ruefully that he'd now found a new way of life, which was to be beaten like an old donkey.

At this, the chief of police roared with laughter so widely that the man could see down his gullet to the wisdom teeth at the back.

When, in due course, the chief of police recovered his composure, he said to the ruined man from Baghdad:

'I have dreams, too. On several occasions I've heard a voice telling me to go to Baghdad. "There's an old house there," the voice says, "built around an inner courtyard and a little pool with a fountain – it must have been lovely, but now the whole place is dilapidated and abandoned." In my dream someone shows me the house, the lemon trees in pots, the shadows cast by the shutters and a funny prayer inscribed over the door to the kitchen asking for protection for the pots and pans.' He began laughing heartily again. 'The voice tells me, "Under the threshold of the doorway there, a fortune is waiting for you! Go to Baghdad and know how to live!"

'But I am not a fool like you! I am not going to bestir myself for a dream!'

Still merry, the policeman dribbled some small change into the ruined man's hands, and told him to go home.

The man from Baghdad took the money and travelled back as fast as he could, and when he reached his house, he called his family and household and they dug under the threshold of the kitchen quarters, and there was indeed a great fortune buried there. So he was able to pay his creditors and re-engage his household servants and start his business again and thrive till the end of his days, when the master of graveyards and the destroyer of all joys came to fetch him.

How weird and wonderful are the ways of destiny!

CHAPTER SEVEN

Dream Knowledge

Romeo: I dreamed a dream to-night.
Mercutio: And so did I.
Romeo: Well, what was yours?
Mercutio: That dreamers often lie.
Romeo: In bed asleep, while they do dream things true.

Shakespeare, *Romeo and Juliet*

Reality gave in on more than one point. The truth is, it longed
to give in.

Jorge Luis Borges, 'Tlön, Uqbar, Orbis Tertius'

I

THE *ARABIAN NIGHTS* STORIES ARE told in the night by a woman in
bed with her husband; her inspiration must not stop flowing or she will
die. She must continue summoning up stories, or she – and others – will
wake up to the reality of her danger. It is as if the dreamer must continue
to dream – on our behalf. Our survival depends on the continued processes of her mind.

Interestingly, Shahrazad does not make up the stories, as we are told
clearly from the start that she is clever and learned and has 'never forgotten
anything she had ever read. She had applied herself happily to philosophy,
medicine, history and the fine arts, and she wrote better poetry than the
most famous poets of her time.' She has a library of a thousand books,
and knows all the stories she tells from having read them.

At the end of the book of the *Arabian Nights*, according to some versions,
her library is brought from the vizier's house to the palace. So the stories
have already been collected – the *Arabian Nights* we have been hearing are
already in existence. Indeed now and then in the course of the book we
are shown the circumstances in which they are recorded, when for example,
Harun el-Rashid, after hearing the tales in the house of Zobeide, orders
them to be written in the official records and placed in the state archives.
Harun's orders are echoed by Sultan Shahriyar, when he joyfully reprieves

Shahrazad and tells the scribes to write down all her stories. However, as Abdelfattah Kilito points out, this command adds to the dizzy circularity of the *Nights*: this copy will be a copy of something which already exists in the library that Shahrazad collected as a young, unmarried woman. Except for the story of Shahriyar himself: that is the only one she has not told.

The prior existence of this vast body of stories adds to the oneiric quality of the whole: not exactly a collective unconscious, her library seems to stretch in infinite recession, an archive of all the stories. The '1001' in the book's title hints at infinity, and indeed the stories keep multiplying, podding off into different new stories, as well as into multiple versions and translations. The utopian fantasy of the book includes the possibility that someone could act as the keeper of memories on this vast and labyrinthine scale, that someone like Shahrazad, could fulfil the role described by the poet Derek Walcott: 'Every collection of human beings gathered for a long time in one place codifies itself, arranges rules of conduct, and makes a calendar for its celebrations of harvest, of the shapes of the moon, with tribal melodies, and preserves its fables and its history in the archives of the shaman and the griot and the bard's memory.'

This is a hope of survival, too. A wager against history, a stand against entropy and a sighting of a small light in the general darkness. Ferial Ghazoul has remarked how the darkness of the *Nights'* original setting extends narrative circumstances into metaphor, from the time of their telling to the dark skin of the slave with whom his wife betrays him to the black rage that overcomes the Sultan – ground keeps flipping into figure and back again. In Italo Calvino's *Invisible Cities*, in which he revisions many themes of the *Nights*, Marco Polo says to the Great Khan, 'This is also the aim of my explorations: examining the traces of happiness still to be glimpsed, I gauge its short supply. If you want to know how much darkness there is around you, you must sharpen your eyes, peering at the faint lights in the distance.' His Marco Polo is an alter ego, a male writer and teller of tales standing in for Shahrazad, who also tells her stories to the Sultan to pick out faint lights and dispel the thickest part of the darkness around him.

The immediate locale seems, however, to have proved a little too nocturnal for the first translators. Antoine Galland demonstrates seventeenth-century decorum when he clarifies the arrangements: 'The sultan went to bed with Shahrazad upon an alcove raised very high, according to the custom of the monarchs of the east; and Dunyazad lay in a bed that was prepared for her near the foot of the alcove.' It is fanciful to imagine such high beds in the Middle East in any period, and the illustrations to the *Nights* reveal the reasoning: embarrassment at the presence of the younger sister in the marriage chamber. In many of the illustrations, Dunyazad is concealed behind the bed-curtains, and all three are fully dressed besides. Indeed Galland introduces a small change, which has not been remarked on to my knowledge, but which reveals how disturbing the setting was to European readers. Galland specifies that Dunyazad, as requested by her sister, wakes up Shahrazad before dawn so that she can continue her story and then stop when dawn breaks, not because they needed to get some sleep, like partygoers, but because the Sultan has to go to work. Again, Kilito has noticed a puzzling crux here: clearly Shahriyar never sleeps.

H. J. Ford's story-telling scene casts the Sultan as eavesdropper on the two sisters' intimacy (from Andrew Lang, 1898).

The *Nights* are not much concerned with likelihood, it is true, but the scene of Shahrazad's storytelling could not possibly involve an early morning call, such as might take place in a boarding school or a monastery. The Arabic editions describe the three of them together all night long talking and listening till dawn – a much more recognisable situation (the two sisters are young women, after all) and a far more psychologically convincing way for the pair of them to beguile the Sultan than a wake-up call an hour or so before dawn which would most assuredly strengthen his resolve to have this wife beheaded. The night-time scene, as originally set, fulfils a crucial atmospheric purpose: it blurs the boundary between waking and dreaming, and plunges the frame story into that intense, in-between state which Caliban inhabits, yearningly, as he tells the shipwrecked crew in his famous lines about preternatural, poetic knowledge:

> Be not afeared. The isle is full of noises,
> Sounds and sweet airs that give delight and hurt not.
> Sometimes a thousand twangling instruments
> Will hum about mine ears, and sometime voices
> That, if I then had waked after long sleep,
> Will make me sleep again; and then in dreaming
> The clouds methought would open and show riches
> Ready to drop upon me, that when I waked
> I cried to dream again. (*The Tempest*, III. ii)

Readers of Galland's first two volumes objected to the interruptions between Shahrazad and her sister that ritually open and close each night's episode, so he decided to suppress them in the subsequent instalments and allow each story to run freely to its end. Again, this editorialising threw more daylight on to the book, and with this, faded the feeling of the dreamwork of the bedroom.

The first French illustrators at least show the couple in bed together, but wideawake, bolt upright and far apart, as well as fully dressed; scores of later illustrators indulge the lascivious possibilities, but very rarely, as far as I can see, show the trio in the post-coital intimacy as described in the book. In the nineteenth century, harem conventions prevail and a ripe artist like Adolphe Lalauze pictures Shahrazad as a siren, coiled around Shahriyar. But the mood is teasing (foreplay rather than the aftermath, 'the lover's ordinary swoon'). Dunyazad is often sidelined, sometimes absent altogether, and so the scene misses the feeling of conspiracy and initiation which the sisters' exchanges create. Later illustrators, often in de luxe editions aimed at children, lay the stress on threat and hierarchy, showing Shahrazad at the foot of the Sultan's throne, not in bed, but on a balcony or in the throne room. Kay Nielsen, for the Danish translation of 1917, created a striking image of Shahriyar's power when he imagined Shahrazad kneeling, a stark naked, diminutive and pearl-white suppliant nymph, at some distance on the floor below the dais on which the looming Sultan is enthroned. Such compositions draw attention to the male ruler and his disproportionate power, but lose the sense of the night voyage – the midsummer night's dream – that the two sisters embark on together with their adversary.

II

The dreams in the stories the Sultan hears see beyond appearances and into the future; through them characters in the stories can also understand something that has happened that until then was hidden from them. Oneiromancy, or divination through dreams, was a practice throughout the ancient world, and cultivated in Egypt: Joseph interprets dreams in both the Old Testament (Genesis 40–41) and the Koran (Sura 12). Many stories in the *Nights* enclose such prophetic dreams, and many more unfold in a dream-like way. But besides the high incidence of dreaming in the *Nights*, the book itself lights pictures in the mind's eye with the vividness of hypnagogic vision, while the storytelling scene itself in the Sultan's bedroom wraps the stories in the night. And more deeply than this intimate and darkened setting, the anti-realism of the stories matches dream experiences: suddenness and vividness, fragmentation, episodic and often entangling structures, displacements in time and space, the instability of bodies, and a recurrence of certain motifs, are all features of dreams.

The dream quality of the *Nights* depends on a feature of the storytelling mode itself, more fundamental than its optical magic. When the stories use language to institute impossible realities, images become reality and metaphors' status is dissolved so that any referent becomes fact. This mental slippage, turning the figurative into the literal, is typical of the dreaming mind, which happily – and often amusingly – makes puns, especially on homonyms and proper names. Such wordplay dominates the concept of causality in magical operations – verbal spells and charms as well as image magic using figurines. But the instability of metaphor, as it moves to denote a new, alternative magical reality, shows in the *Nights* when dream journeys involving out-of-body experiences take place in fact, as for instance in the story of Camar and Badoura, when the hero and heroine are carried off by jinn to meet each other in their sleep. They are literally transported through the air by the competing jinn, but they do not know it at the time, or afterwards. They wake up, smitten, the visions in their minds like experiences in a dream, except that they have a token left behind – a ring – to prove that something has taken place for real. The jinn can personify interior states, in this case sudden desperate passion, by analogy with the daimones of Greek myth.

Significantly, the twofold character of belief in dreams as they take form in the *Nights* – that on the one hand they reveal the truth of what is or of what is to come; and, on the other, that dream experiences actually take place, physically and for real – opens another angle of view on magic itself as conveyed by the enchanted character of the stories themselves, not by individual figures of good or bad enchanters. What the reality of mental experiences might be is a question the *Nights* continually raises, and the acceptance of the proposition became the defining premise of magical realism in its later literary manifestations.

Dreams in the *Nights* do not always appear at the bidding of supernatural powers, and it does not fall only to magians and dervishes to see through them to their meaning. They represent a magical power available to all, without special books or special knowledge of the properties of things. In the religious sphere, dreaming can reveal the divine plan to privileged individuals: for instance, in some versions of 'The City of Brass' Abraham appears in a dream to Solomon to prophesy the coming of the Prophet Muhammad. But in the generally more fairytale realm of the *Arabian Nights*, dreams occur in numerous stories, and have a dynamic role to play in the unfolding of the plots, leading towards the plenitude and comfort of recognition. Other stories contain dreams which work crookedly, like riddles, and mishaps can befall the dreamer who misunderstands the message. Yet others communicate straightforwardly and helpfully, and the outcome is happy: wrongs are righted, fortune restored and love regained. Hasan of Basra sees his mother in a dream and understands how much she has suffered since he vanished, so decides to return to her and introduce her to his fairy wife. As the stories are so often romances about love and money, moving towards reconciliation, our pleasure is sharpened as we know destiny must take its course and fulfil the dream.

Dreams can be exchanged between sleepers in the *Nights*, so that one dreamer can enter another's dream, as in the tale of the ruined man who gains a fortune. Sometimes, two dreamers experience parts of the same dream and discover what had been hidden from them till then, as in the love story of Prince Ardashir and Hayat al-Nufus, and another, inspired by an historical legend, 'The Tale of al-Mutawakkil and Mahbuba', in which the caliph and his favourite, who lived in the ninth century, become estranged, but during their separation both of them have the same dream, which restores their undying love. The inner life of characters in the *Nights* flows into their outer circumstances without resistance, and it is not always clear what is dream and what is not. What you dream looks ahead: perhaps the pattern of all things lying ahead has been set and can be descried in the right conditions, or perhaps dreaming itself makes things happen. Dreams can come true for anyone, for the knowledge they contain belongs in a supernatural realm, of prophecy and God-ordained destiny, and so they can reveal what is decreed (oracles fulfil a similar function in the dramatic ironies of classical literature: Sophocles's Oedipus; Euripides's Ion). The celebrated story of 'The Appointment in Samarra' has all the marks of a parable about ineluctable destiny from the *Arabian Nights*, but is not in fact found in the book. (The protagonist sees Death in the marketplace in the morning, and the encounter terrifies him so much that he flees immediately as far as he can to get away from him, and reaches Samarra, only to come across Death again, who says to him, 'I was startled to see you this morning as I knew I had an appointment with you tonight in Samarra.')

Such prophetic visions and dreams announce to us, the listeners and readers, where the story will be taking us, and often make us privy to more information than the characters in the story have about themselves; we as readers glimpse the resolution before it happens. However, by contrast, dreams are also shown to be active, capable of putting their stamp upon reality. If dream divination is the gift of prophets who have been admitted to share God's knowledge, then dream understanding is the wisdom of fairytale, a gift given to its heroes and heroines.

Confidence in the wisdom of dreams buoys up some of its most haunting and beautiful stories, emanating from the earliest strata of myth in the book, such as the initiatory romances of the heroes Buluqiya and Hasib. Their stories are enclosed in the long sequence narrated by Yamlika, Queen of the Serpents, and in their entirety form one of the most elaborate sets of Chinese boxes of stories in the book, revealing its eclectic composition over time. Mythological motifs from the Epic of Gilgamesh – of katabasis and the recognition of mortality – sound in these literally marvellous tales. The heroes voyage beyond the known world on their quests, and their experiences have the quality of dreams. The different realms they enter – natural, supernatural, human and social – retain metaphysical resonances of lost paradises, lost natural harmony, lost organic enchantments. In one of these imbricated tales, 'Janshah and Shamsah', also known as 'The Tale of the Fair Sad Youth', Janshah falls in love with a peri, who is also a bird, in a scene of powerful erotic lyricism:

'When I opened my eyes,' Janshah recalls,

'I saw three beautiful doves coming down to the basin to take their bath, ruffling their white plumes. They hopped gracefully upon the broad rim of the silver basin and then, before my marvelling eyes, when they had embraced and given each other a thousand charming caresses, each one threw from her her virgin mantle of feathers, and coming out of it, appeared in jasmine nakedness as a young girl fairer than the moon. They plunged into the water . . .

When the maidens saw me, each gave a cry of fright and, coming up quickly out of the water, ran and covered her nakedness with her robe of feathers. They all three flew up into the highest of those trees which fringed the basin and looked down upon me, laughing.

Later, when pursuing the youngest fairy, Janshah comes upon al-Nasr, who tells Janshah how to assuage his passion for the Princess Shamsah he has glimpsed: Janshah must steal her feathers while she is bathing and then abduct her passionately (not a proper hero's way to behave today, and certainly not in children's books). Al-Nasr is King of the Birds, understands their speech and rules harmoniously over them; he acts as a shamanic alter ego of Solomon, and his mastery over animals opens a conduit between Janshah's desire and its fulfilment, between the dream and reality. Eventually, when he wins her love, they return together to the ordinary world.

But as Janshah nears the end of his story he starts to cry, because one day, Shamsah went swimming and was bitten on her heel by a water snake, and died – the watery element with which she was associated in the enchanted world she came from has taken its revenge. This lyrical love story, echoing the myth of Eurydice, ends with the fair sad youth renouncing his life in order to mourn eternally.

The central drama of this story, one of the most ancient in the *Nights* (though it is not always included), of the love between a human hero and a divine, apsara-like bird-fairy, is reprised with variations in several other romances, especially 'Prince Ahmed and the Fairy Peri Banou' and 'Hasan of Basra'.

This conception of dream experiences can be placed on more familiar ground: what dreams are and what they do in the *Arabian Nights* corresponds to their role in Elizabethan and Jacobean drama, revealing the common foundations of stories and shared concepts of fate and consciousness in the larger Mediterranean world since the medieval period. From the bittersweet illusions of *A Midsummer Night's Dream* to the tormenting truth-telling of the weird sisters' pronouncements and Lady Macbeth's nightmares, Shakespeare's dream world reveals the shared belief of playwright and audience in clairvoyance, both individually and collectively. Calpurnia foresees in a dream the murder of her husband Caesar, but cannot dissuade him from going to the Senate on the Ides of March, and in *The Winter's Tale* Antigonus sees Hermione's ghost appear, also in a dream (or so he thinks), and command him to take her baby daughter Perdita into safety. Renaissance theories of dream possession, inspiration and imagination combine in Shakespeare (and in his contemporaries and successors) with other forms of belief emanating from sources closer to hand than classical myth. In Scotland in the 1690s, for example, the Reverend Robert Kirk compiled a handbook of his parishioners' theories of Second Sight, the 'gift' to see beyond the visible world and to travel to fairyland and back. The Highlanders' dream world reflects the redemptive, rather than nightmarish, dream voyaging of *The Tempest* and *Cymbeline*, for Kirk does not follow compatriots like James I in condemning the seers, but argues that their faculties are entirely compatible with the Bible's view of dream knowledge (numerous incidents of enlightenment through dreams take place in the Old and New Testaments; for example, besides Joseph in Egypt, Jesus's father, Joseph, receives a warning about Herod from an angel in a dream: Matthew 2:13). Kirk not only believes in second sight but approves it, on scriptural grounds, as a moral good in the community.

The dreams of the *Nights* tally with this view. However, there are exceptions, when dreams can mislead. One of the most famous of the stories, 'The Sleeper and the Dreamer', makes fun of the widespread belief in the reality of dreams: the protagonist, Abu 'l-Hasan expresses a wish to live like the caliph, Harun al-Rashid, which the caliph overhears. He has him drugged and brought to the palace, where the entire court is told to treat Abu 'l-Hasan like the caliph. After a day of this, he is drugged again and transported back home. When Abu 'l-Hasan wakes up, he thinks he is the caliph, and will not accept that what he experienced was merely a dream.

Although the tale is a joke it is also, in the way of jokes, rather deep, and it touches on disturbing areas of experience. Interestingly, Abu 'l-Hasan is of course correct: what he experienced was no dream. The ambiguity in the story points to the enigmatic truth status of dreams themselves, which take place vividly in the mind *just as if they were real*; dreaming can also have a proleptic effect and bring about what the dreamer desires or fears. But it also points to the reality of dreams in the *Nights*, as Abu 'l-Hasan knows. His story is light-hearted, but the same story attracted both Shakespeare in the frame story of *The Taming of the Shrew* (1595), and Calderón de la Barca in his play, *Life is a Dream* (1635), where the undercurrents are harsher. In Calderón's play, the deceived protagonist's confusion is cruel and terrifying: a dream can be very painful and literally maddening.

In his own nocturnal poetics, Marcel Proust aspired to the dream-like qualities of the *Nights*, both as a man who wrote to gain time, composing in bed his huge wheeling cycle of memories, and as a boy projecting images of legends with a magic lantern in his room: 'it substituted for the opaqueness of my walls an impalpable iridescence, supernatural phenomena of many colours, in which legends were depicted as on a shifting and transitory window.' After this scene, the passage segues into the narrator's longing for his mother's goodnight visit and her kiss; this intensity, pressing the boy Marcel's emotions to the edge of delirium, displays another feature that the *Nights* possesses – it is a continuum between reality and illusion, daily consciousness and night vision, which enfolds dream, trance, hallucination, ecstasy and anguish and renders distinctions between them blurred. A typical hero or heroine of the *Nights*, like the Proustian narrator, lives his or her destiny in a state of hyper-stimulated sensitivity which gives much of what happens the feeling of a waking dream.

With regard to dreams, the *Nights* stages ways of thinking which have increasing significance in the last century and this, when dreams entered scientific psychology through psychoanalysis to become a prime tool of personal understanding. Psychoanalytic theories do not claim dreams are clairvoyant, but that they are retrospectively revelatory for the individual dreamer. Freud placed dream analysis at the centre of his talking cure, and saw dreams as riddles of the individual's psyche, composed of past experiences and giving access to that person's unconscious, so that the process of interpreting dreams can help shape the dreamer's future conduct, can release him or her from damaging repression and repetition. Freud's one-time colleague and friend Carl Jung interpreted the matter differently (the disagreement was one of the causes of their split); Jungian psychoanalysis also recognises the interconnectedness of myth and fairy tale, but holds closer to the vision of dreaming in the *Nights* (and other fantastic literature) by positing a collective unconscious which dreamers tap, bringing them illumination not only of their individual psyche but of a larger wisdom; this exists beyond the individual as a form of universal lexicon or symbolic reservoir, and it colours and shapes the dreams and their messages. According to the Jungian view, shared dreaming is possible: your dream may tell me something I need to know.

In the 1920s and 1930s, the Surrealists responded to the new importance given to the idea of an unconscious mind, experimented with incubating dreams, and gave reverie, trance, suggestion, hypnosis and other states beyond consciousness a central role in creativity. They turned for their ideas to anthropology, and to alternative models of mind and the universe in cultures beyond Europe. In this way, neither the psychoanalytical theories nor the artistic movements altogether broke the connection to oneiromancy in the past, but refashioned it to develop a modern view of independent and particular subjectivity. Today, beyond the circles of psychoanalyis and anthropology, dreams at every stage of sleep, trance and intoxication are no longer swept aside as irrelevant ravings. Dreams and dreaming are the subject of intense inquiry and their activity remains a contentious question. Findings range widely, from the neuroscientific view dismissing their deeper meaning, as expressed for example in

J. Allan Hobson's useful study, *Dreaming: An Introduction to the Science of Sleep* (2002), to the deliberate dream practice of artists, like Jackson Pollock, Leonora Carrington and Paula Rego, to name just three who, in accord with the Jungian analysis they experienced, cultivated hypnagogic states and the vivid pictures they bring between sleeping and waking in order to work them directly into their art. It is startling how deeply these approaches were adopted in different milieux and disciplines from the 1950s onwards, and yet how overlooked the principles of magical thinking underlying these developments have been.

The changing understanding of dreams is bound up with a cultural phenomenon that has taken place over the same period as the literary success of the *Nights* and an accompanying rise in collecting and retelling myths and fairy tales: since the end of the eighteenth century, the idea of shamanism has spread from its origins in a different and farther east, namely the border of Siberia and Mongolia, and taken root. As writers began following the cue of the *Nights* (and of other traditional literature of enchantment) and exercising the power of words to institute dreams as realities, a new term for a magician – 'shaman' – was gradually naturalised throughout Western culture and applied far and wide.

The 'shaman' is the priest and doctor of the Tungus, a nomadic, reindeer-herding people on the Mongolian–Siberian border, and the term was first introduced into Europe through ethnographical literature by explorers, who were often travelling as part of the Russian empire's march eastwards. With evident fascination, they reported on the peoples who lived around the North Pole, from Lapland to Mongolia, and practised ritual disciplines in order to gain access to other worlds. Their priests – men and women – stimulated dreams with drugs, drumming and dancing, in order to summon an animal alter ego, who would allow the dreamer to walk between worlds and return with the power to heal bodily and mental ills. An early work, Johannes Scheffer's *History of Lappland* (1673), includes a dramatic woodcut showing a shaman lying face down under the drum after he had drummed himself unconscious. In this sense, the drum became his flying vehicle which carried him to another world (another instance of figure turning into statement). The animals whose spirit enters him – reindeer, bear, whale, elk, seal – are the tribe's staple, source of their food, fuel, clothing and shelter, and the magical exchange the shaman performs when he metamorphoses and becomes one with the animal not only commemorates the creature's gifts to the tribe and propitiates its ghost, but asserts the authority of the hunters to use it for their purposes. Dreams in this case are ritual acts to secure security: 'they become 'the "safety valve" of the clan'.

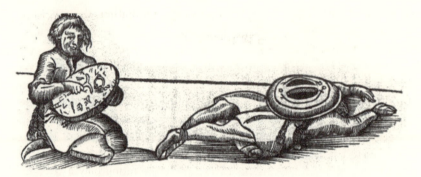

Travellers to the far north reported in fascination on shamanic practices. Here, a shaman drums himself into a dream state in order to walk in other worlds (Johannes Sheffer, *A History of Lapland*, 1673).

'Shaman' and 'shamanism' gradually established themselves as the preferred, alternative terms for sorcerers and sorcery, first through the appreciation of the German Romantics, Goethe and his friend Gottfried Herder, who in turn influenced Coleridge's concept of imagination and interest in native cultures and their beliefs. However, the word did not reach its current familiarity until the 1960s, and did so in the ambience of psychedelia (Mircea Éliade's influential study, *Shamanism: Archaic Techniques of Ecstasy*, was published in 1964), but it is now firmly associated with nature and beneficent ritual, healing and dream voyaging.

The psychology underlying shamanic dreaming is axiomatic to fairy tales: it fundamentally presumes a self that is fluid, shape-shifting, subject to transformation that might be disabling or degrading, as in the animal metamorphoses of the *Nights*. But aside from the animal metamorphoses, the shaman's soul-voyaging puns on the idea of levitation and flying. Overlapping geography must account in part for some of the convergence, for the circumpolar regions where shamanism was first practised border on and even coincide with the Muslim Khanates of Central Asia. But even more crucially in relation to the *Arabian Nights*, shamanism presupposes that dreams can be dreamed on behalf of someone else, that they can take place in common and communicate information of value to other people besides the dreamer for the larger good.

Some sense of the purchase of this interpretation of dreams can be felt in a significant passage from Barack Obama's 1994 autobiography, a remarkable and eloquent work of self-exploration. He gave it a title, *Dreams from My Father*, which plays on many layers of meaning in the word 'dreams' for a black politician in America. But the book also includes an arresting memory of a nightmare Obama had in Kenya on the way to the Luo township where his imposing grandfather, the patriarch of the family, came from:

> I finally fell asleep, and dreamed I was walking along a village road . . . I began to notice that people were looking behind me fearfully, rushing into their huts as I passed. I heard the growl of a leopard and started to run into the forest, tripping over roots and stumps and vines, until at last I couldn't run any longer and fell to my knees in the middle of a bright clearing. Panting for breath, I turned around to see the day turned night, and a giant figure looming as tall as the trees, wearing only a loincloth and a ghostly mask. The lifeless eyes bored into me, and I heard a thunderous voice saying only that it was time, and my entire body began to shake violently with the sound, as if I were breaking apart . . .

Writing in 1995, the future President of the United States has a dream. It calls him to act, on behalf of people endangered by a leopard, and its intensity affects him powerfully and induces in him the sense of a truth glimpsed in a state of heightened receptivity. Martin Luther King had expressed his vision in the cadences of biblical prophecy. Obama, four decades later, described a shamanic vision and communicated it as knowledge that came in a dream.

While it is unlikely that many people, if they stopped to consider the question, would assent intellectually to the concept of dreams as portents of the future (and Obama himself does not say as much), it has become deeply rooted in culture regardless, in every kind of film and in fiction even when the writers are not strictly speaking magical realists (a prophetic daydream is central to J. D. Salinger's *The Catcher in the Rye*, for example). This unremarked convention presents another vivid instance when the magical thinking which the *Nights* epitomises has radiated outward far beyond the book itself.

III

Shahrazad's ransom tale-telling could be described as a single, prolonged act of performative utterance, by which she demonstrates the power of words to affect reality – her own fate and by extension others'. As when dreams dematerialise in reality on waking, words are made flesh throughout the stories of the *Nights*. Such speech acts take place as part of the plots themselves, and they also constitute a strong claim for the effects of the storyteller or writer's methods. The enchantments of the *Arabian Nights* depend on this self-mirroring, magical technique, whereby the audience experience illusions summoned by the words on the page or in the ear, in the same way as the characters in the stories move in a landscape where magic keeps turning illusions into reality and inward apprehensions turn out to be truthful signs, propitious and cautionary.

'Open sesame!' the robber chief calls out, and is overheard by Ali Baba, who uses the magic formula to open the entrance to the treasure cave. The verbal form of this charm does not conform to other spells or charms in the *Nights*, which mostly depend on well-known sacred names, especially the 99 names of God, Solomonic allusions in words and ciphers, and other riddling and talismanic verbal combinations. Sometimes the words form mysterious images, as on the carnelian which Princess Maryam rubs to summon the flying bed in 'Aladdin of the Beautiful Moles'. By comparison, 'Open sesame!' is simple, and heightens the fun when the wicked brother cannot remember it to escape from the cave and keeps listing different cereals in vain. But the underlying principle, that words can operate effectively to do things in the world, remains. 'To hear is to obey, O Master,' says the genie of the lamp. Vows, blessings, curses, apotropaic and expiatory formulae, repeated and performed in the correct way, place language at the centre of ritual; these verbal rituals occupy the heart of fairytale. Just as the vow ('With this ring I thee wed') establishes the fact of the marriage, and the ritual phrase ('Hoc est corpus meum'), which a Roman Catholic priest pronounces over the bread to change it into the real presence of the body of Christ, effects the miracle, so spells and charms in the *Nights* bring about transformations. (The jibe, 'hocus pocus', was aimed at the 'trick of transubstantiation': 1694, *OED*).

Fabulist writers in the twentieth century have followed the cue of fairytale in their uses of performative speech. Metaphors are no longer comparative, but take up the foreground, as the fact of the matter. They shift from images into reality and institute another, impossible dimension of experience as if it were fact : Kafka's Gregor Samsa in *The Metamorphosis* wakes up to find he *is* a monstrous insect, an *Ungeziefer*, variously translated as 'beetle', 'bug', 'vermin'. Not a metaphorical bug, nor a bug in his own eyes only, for his bug-ness does not depend on likeness or analogy, or on observers' subjective impression. Kafka's style, its careful accountancy of detail and its measured verisimilitude, performs a sleight-of-hand to obscure the symbolic, allegorical and fairytale character of his tales. Gregor's metamorphosis is presented as an event that has taken place, and it involves a complete hypostatic change: species and substance into the real presence of a monstrous bug. No agents of the change are invoked, unlike the mythological tales by Ovid which Kafka echoes in his story's title, or the jinn who change men into beasts in the *Nights*, because this new, modernist supernatural does not presuppose a hierarchy of beings, higher or lower, divine or diabolical: the daimon occupies a here and now, curled up in the word that brings the thing – the bug – into being on the page for us, the readers.

Even more pertinently, the judicial machine in the story 'In the Penal Colony' moves likewise beyond the realm of the metaphorical into the literal, and in this case the harrow that carries out judgement on the condemned victim laid under its blades actually writes sentences on his body. Here the writer's process reflects in the tale in multiplying recession as Kafka places himself in the role of Shahrazad and tells a tale of a death sentence and its instrument. The harrow is a writing machine designed to kill, which starts operating on its own, malfunctioning in wild abandon as its staunchest officer, advocate and keeper attempts to demonstrate its perfection. The harrow, like the letter on the clay tablet which Zadig breaks in two in Voltaire's fable (more on this in Chapter 13), or the talismanic sabres at the start of *Vathek* (and more on this in Chapter 10), encloses significance and promises to deliver a message – the words are powerful but their meaning is not stable. Their efficacy can be abused. The word can be made flesh to perverted ends. So on the one hand the reader surrenders to the illusions that the writer creates and to the outlandish realities such storytelling persuasively conveys; and on the other hand, the world inside such literature casts material phenomena of all kinds as menacingly active. Like the word-magic of the *Nights*, 'In the Penal Colony' encloses a warning about the ways language binds and looses, speaks false and yet makes things happen.

One of the most celebrated fables of the Argentinian writer Jorge Luis Borges, 'The Circular Ruins,' was first published in 1946 in the collection *Ficciones* (*Fictions*) and it stages a dreamwork of great power when *el mago* (translations give 'wizard' or 'sorcerer') sets about his mission: 'He wanted to dream a man; he wanted to dream him in minute entirety and impose him on reality.' Limb by limb, organ by organ, over a cycle of several years, the dreamer fashions a boy, a child: 'Within a year he had come to the skeleton and the eyelids. The innumerable hair was probably the most difficult task. He dreamed an entire man – a young man, but who did not sit up or talk, who was unable to open his eyes. Night after night, the man dreamed him asleep.'

Borges's tale institutes an impossible reality and demonstrates how imagination at work in literature forges the impossible through language, and opens up meaning to depths beyond sense: the not-sense that magic unfolds. 'The Circular Ruins' is an allegory of writing, as are many of Borges's stories, for the magus's patient and methodical work is mirrored by the writer's activity as he painstakingly evokes it. The fable is also many other things, but in connection to dreams in the *Nights*, Borges is spinning his readers into a Shahrazadean vortex, for the man who dreams a boy into existence realises at the end that he is himself being dreamed: 'With relief, with humiliation, with terror, he understood that he also was an illusion, that someone else was dreaming him.' The magus belongs in a story inside someone else's story; as a dreamer generating realities through dreams, he is living inside the minds of other dreamers in infinite recession, who are themselves living inside the narratives the dreams relate. The writer, too, belongs in a line of writers, and Borges the reader makes it clear how much he owes to literature, and above all to Kafka, about whom he wrote an essay, precisely called 'Kafka and his Precursors', which looks at the lineage he established in metaphysical fabulism.

A possible source for Borges's story appeared in the wider circles of Surrealists in Paris, whose works he followed. Anatole Lewitsky, an ethnographer specialising in Russia, collected a myth about the first Buryat shaman – called Boholi-Hara. Like many of the *Nights*, it begins with a rich man lamenting that he has no son and heir, and a man claiming special powers appearing to grant his wish. Boholi-Hara

> went into the rich man's house and began to shamanize, but he did not address the gods or genies with the request that they grant this man with no descendants a son. He himself made a son for him, setting about it in the following manner: He made the bones of stone, the flesh of clay, the blood of river water. He still had to give him a soul, but Boholi-Hara was not at all at a loss: He gathered seventy different flowers and made the boy's soul out of them.'

The gods however became angry with the shaman for overstepping his authority and they 'sentenced [him] to sit astride a black stone until either the stone or he wore out. If Boholi-Hara wore out before the stone then he would no longer exist and shamans would be powerless. But Boholi-Hara put on iron boots that wouldn't wear out . . . and that is why, now, Boholi-Hara sits astride the stone and the stone is wearing away, is already halfway gone.'

The Buryat myth of male creation does not take Borges's hallucinatory, recursive twist and plunge the reader into a dizzy illusion, but it does also defer closure, gesturing instead (lightly, consolingly) towards an ever-receding vanishing point.

In the epigraph to his fable, Borges quotes a line from another of his favourite writers, Lewis Carroll, from the scene in which Alice comes upon the Red King snoring.

> 'He's dreaming now,' said Tweedledee: 'and what do you think he's dreaming about?'
>
> Alice said, 'Nobody can guess that.'
>
> 'Why, about *you*!' Tweedledee exclaimed, clapping his hands triumphantly. 'And if he left off dreaming about you, where do you suppose you'd be?'
>
> 'Where I am now, of course,' said Alice.
>
> 'Not you!' Tweedledee retorted contemptuously. 'You'd be nowhere. Why, you're only a kind of thing in his dream!'

Tweedledee is taking Bishop Berkeley's Idealist philosophy to a teasing conclusion, but Alice is perturbed by the thought that she might be 'only a kind of thing in his dream', and her trouble continues to reverberate in the contemporary context of mass media, technological reproduction, and other powerful forgers of illusion in modernity. The idea that you might be being dreamed, as Borges expresses it, continues to give a shiver of anagnorisis no matter how many times you have read his story, and its vibrations are still making themselves felt as they spread out in more circular rings. His story is the acknowledged progenitor, for example, of major commercial successes in the cinema, *The Matrix* (1999; written and directed by Larry and Andy Wachowski) and *Inception* (2010; begun by the writer-director Christopher Nolan in 2001), both of which posit one dream world inside another, until the notion of verifiable reality out there disappears into an abyss of multiple reflections. Such widespread intensity of recognition cannot be excited only by the consummate craft of Borges's original telling. The central proposition that reality is a phantasmagoria, that the individual mind creates its own reality, and that other consciousnesses are entering and controlling it, has become a central modern myth, paranoid, solipsistic, and deeply determinist. It has gained purchase because it matches the way many experience their lives.

Part III

Active Goods

Objects, particularly old ones, have witnessed all sorts of events and lives . . . First become a collector of old things. Listen to them. Never do violence to objects . . . tell *their* stories.

Jan Švankmajer, *Decalogue*, 1999

CHAPTER EIGHT

'Everything You Desire to Know about the East . . .'

These mute and sometimes inanimate beings rise up before me with such
a plenitude, such a presence of love that my joyful eye finds nothing dead
anywhere. . . . mute things speak to me.

Hugo von Hofmannsthal, 'Letter', 1902

I

INTERACTIONS BETWEEN THE SUBLIME PORTE and the capitals of
Western powers did not become very frequent – or indeed any friendlier
– but the degree of acquaintance grew. From assuming difference and
observing it with curiosity, travellers began to point to the differences
in order to keep a distance and exculpate themselves by association, as
we saw in relation to the whirling dervishes. When the *Arabian Nights*
appeared in French and English, the book was received as a Baedeker,
as it were, an encyclopaedia, a social handbook and a costume album. It
was seen as a far superior substitute to witnesses like Lorck and Van
Mour, since it originated in the countries in question.

In his Notice to the reader, the *Avertissement* at the beginning of his
translation of the *Arabian Nights* of 1704, Antoine Galland begins by
drawing attention to the marvellous inventiveness and wonders in the
tales, in which the Arabs surpass all other peoples, he says. But although
their composition of the stories took place several centuries before the
translations, he then passes on swiftly to propose another reason for
reading the stories:

> They should also give pleasure through the customs and the manners of
> the Orientals [they depict], the ceremonies of their religion, pagan as well
> as Muslim; and these things are better represented here than in those
> authors who have written of them and in the accounts of travellers. All
> the Orientals, Persians, Tartars and Indians, can be distinguished here, and
> appear just as they are, from the sovereigns to the people of the lowest

condition. And so, without having suffered the weariness of going to look
for these peoples in their country, the reader will have the pleasure here
of seeing them act and hearing them speak.

He closes with assurances that the moral consciousness of all readers will
only be improved by reading these tales (rather than works with similar
pretensions, he hints darkly, by certain contemporaries).

When the eminent man of letters and rationalist Fontenelle wrote to
commend the publication of Galland's translation, he did so warmly,
making the same point: 'These Arabian tales should also delight through
[their depiction of] the customs and manners of orientals.' For a caustic
opponent of irrationality and a lucid demolisher of myth, this practical
way of reading the *Nights* could be the only excuse for doing so.

These early promises of armchair travelling and its rewards appeared
after a small band of artists and explorers had visited the Levant, bringing
back stories of many difficulties arising from the explosive antagonisms
of different political powers in the region, as well as hardships on the
road. Galland was himself an experienced traveller in the territory, but
his framing of the stories is making a more significant claim: that the
Nights faithfully represents the countries where it is set.

Such emphasis on the stories' illuminating character strikes a reader
now as oddly blind to the fantastical contents, bizarre inventions and
general improbable tenor of the tales. But Galland set the rhetorical
ground for understanding the *Arabian Nights*, and his invitation to the
reader to read the tales as palimpsests of documentary information is
echoed by Mary Wortley Montagu's letters from Turkey of 1716–18,
almost coincidentally with the first appearance of the *Nights* in English.
(Indeed her husband brought back some manuscripts of the stories, now
in the Bodleian, which were to lead to the further translations and
re-tellings of Jonathan Scott and William Beckford.) Admitted to the
company of the great ladies of the Ottoman court, Montagu claims a
sisterhood of aristocracy, rhapsodises about the luxury of their apartments
and the splendour of their jewels, their dress fabrics, porcelain and glassware. She writes to her sister, Lady Mar: 'Now do I fancy that you
imagine I have entertained you all this while with a relation that has, at
least, received many embellishments from my hand. This is but too like,
says you, the Arabian tales; these embroidered napkins, and a jewel as
large as a turkey's egg! You forget, dear sister, those very tales were writ
by an author of this country and, excepting the enchantments, are a real
representation of the manners here.'

The comparison becomes a refrain: Edward Lane in the early

nineteenth century, the first translator to render the full cycle of the stories into English from the original Arabic, also presents the book as a faithful picture of life in the contemporary Levant; William Godwin repeats the claim in his *Lives of the Necromancers*.

The view is predominantly museological: the tales of the *Nights* become a catalogue of beautiful and picturesque elements, selected for their preciousness and splendour. It is a way of thinking familiar from the *Centro storico* conservation of the great Italian cities or heritage sites all over the world. It is brimming with aesthetic desire, antiquarian hopes, longing to step into the same river not merely twice but again and again. It flattens history to an unchanging and static horizon: historical meta-morphosis disappears along with differences and texture. Yet Galland was working from a fourteenth-century Syrian manuscript, and translating stories set in legendary days of yore in fairylands forgot, or during the fabled reign of Harun al-Rashid in the late eighth to early ninth century. So his idea of presenting the *Nights* as a kind of Baedeker to the Middle East of his time is like urging a contemporary setting out for Italy to read Dante, or pressing a copy of *Macbeth* on someone interested in the Highlands. Dante and Shakespeare would afford much pleasure and knowledge; there would be similarities of topography, culture, customs and language. But within limits.

This approach is also ideological, as critics have trenchantly observed: it presents the Levant as unchanging, a fossil rather than a living organism. Earlier reports had not adopted this angle of view. Even when orientalist antiquarians and collectors and travellers and artists were producing a vicarious experience of their exotic and unfamiliar subjects, and drawing attention to the luxury and gorgeousness of the East, they also reveal inquisitiveness about the exact means of wealth production and military effectiveness in the Ottoman empire. They are examining the success of a formidable rival. So, rather surprisingly, technology as well as tulips, engines as well as damasks, attract the attention of early witnesses. Utensils and contrivances, every kind of manufacture, from hydraulics to harnesses, tools to bibelots, were made visible and bore witness to the society in which they circulated, as useful or enjoyable. When the Arabic of the travellers concerned was non-existent, or so scholarly as to prevent easy communication with the local inhabitants, things were the chief media through which information and sympathy travelled between strangers who could hardly talk to one another.

The things the culture made not only kept captive the jinn of Islamic cosmology; figuratively, they came to embody the essence of the culture and its skills. The lamp, the flask, the casket, the box: if they could be opened they might yield something that would lead to greater understanding. Like the merchants cracking open the Rukh's egg in the story of Sinbad, visitors wanted to find the hatchling or jinn hidden inside. (Pl. 15) Edward Said's polemic saw this search for knowledge primarily as a quest for control and power. From the pages of the artist-explorers, from the cases of museums, things spoke to armchair travellers of their owners according to an impulse of acquisition that followed, imaginatively, the real acts of possession undertaken by the conquering colonial powers.

Another way of looking at this would suggest that the scholars and artists who observed and documented – and sectioned and measured – the things of the East encountered something which they recognised as a sign of their own changing relationship to things, and that what they learned can be instructive in our times as well. For, although these exchanges are taking place in modernity, the concepts describing the power of things were defined by concepts first shaped centuries before in Baghdad and Basra, Shiraz, Damascus and Cairo.

'The subject is born from the object,' the philosopher Michel Serres has pronounced, with gnomic gravity, and Bill Brown sets this maxim in pride of place as the epigraph to his essay, 'Thing Theory'. But Brown is not following Galland's example and treating things as mirrors, clues or evidence. He criticises this historical position: 'As they circulate through our lives, we look *through* objects (to see what they disclose about history, society, nature, or culture – above all, what they disclose about us)'. Instead, he asks for things' qualities to be attended to as active agents; he wants their interactivity with people explored, and the meanings that ensue from these relationships confronted, by paying attention to 'the story of objects asserting themselves as things . . . the story of a changed relation to the human subject and thus the story of how the thing really names less an object than a particular subject–object relation.'

Reading the *Arabian Nights* as an encyclopaedia of things reveals that imaginative writing has been observing the active life of things for a very long time.

Magic in the *Arabian Nights*, by casting common artefacts as agents of wonders and riches, captured ambiguities in relations with those things: mixed feelings, made of awe and admiration, on the one hand, scepticism and defensive emulation on the other. The artists and writers who documented the culture of Egypt and Turkey and other parts of the Ottoman empire in the Middle East attended to the things these cultures made, partly in a spirit of mercantile enterprise, but partly also from a new understanding of the marvellous in the banal. Attention which explorers and travellers had previously trained on flora and fauna, minerals and their properties, as well as other aspects of the natural cosmos, now extended to the built environment and the world of goods – to machines, lamps, carpets, flasks, caskets, and the various enchanted paraphernalia as found in the *Arabian Nights*.

In the centuries before the *Nights* were published, Ottoman splendour was exciting and terrifying: it was forbidden for outsiders to travel in the empire, and consequently dangerous; yet knowing the Other was a strategy as well as a compulsion. Curiosity was often a response to the military threat the empire presented to European powers: an historical map of the period shows that the empire's territories stretched from Algeria to the west, Mecca to the south, Baghdad to the east and the river Don to the north, all adjoining – and often aggressing – the Hapsburgs' own huge possessions. Suleiman the Magnificent besieged Vienna – twice – and though he had had to retreat, the threat persisted.

II

At the apogee of Ottoman power, a scant number of European artists made the journey, most famously Gentile Bellini, who visited the Sublime Porte in 1479–81; a Flemish artist, Pieter Coecke van Aelst, followed him in 1533–54 on a trading mission with tapestry weavers from Brussels (the connection to craft skills is important); but by far the most significant artist to travel in Turkey and perhaps farther – and stay for nearly four years from 1555 to 1559 – was the Danish-born Melchior Lorck (1526/7 – after 1588). Lorck was originally attached to the embassy of Archduke Ferdinand I, which was led by Ogier Ghiselin de Busbecq, who had been sent generally to help ease the tensions caused by Suleiman's ambitions and restlessness, and specifically to claim Hungary for his master and confirm him on that country's throne.

Essentially Lorck was working alongside the mission as a spy, and he was there to gather information about the Ottoman enemy, especially about their military organisation, armour and matériel. The resulting album of his observations is surprising for many reasons: first, because it is so little known, indeed almost unknown; secondly, because his Ottoman hosts gave him such freedom of access and movement in their military encampments, places of worship, and even, perhaps, their domestic quarters; and thirdly, because the spirit of his pictures of Turkish culture and Islam departs so categorically from the approach we now know as 'Orientalism'. For all his flamboyant fantasy, Lorck is not an Orientalist in that he disdains what he finds. He does not slaver nor does he despise. Rather the contrary. Page after page, he draws attention to the marvels of Turkish architecture, social arrangements, skills, technical processes and accoutrements. Significantly, the first publication of his Turkish work did not select one of his more arrestingly exotic figure studies for the title page, but a plain image of a water tower, a well and a trough – three different ways the Turks controlled water supplies. As a northern European with experience of the Netherlands as well as his native Denmark, Lorck knew the importance of hydraulic engineering. Many other prints show war tents large and small, military suppliers and transports – pack mules and dromedaries, one with a drummer boy gleefully banging away. In a series of astonishing figure studies, often placed with droll wit in juxtaposition with animals or monuments, Lorck inventories the range of rank and file and officers: janissaries, archers, cavalry, standard-bearers, blacksmiths, and a water carrier with a huge curved leather skin slung under his arm. The artist tracks obsessively the degrees and varations of insignia and armour – the wearers and bearers often completely concealed under huge curving bucklers embossed with monsters, their faces buried inside vast edifices crested with great bunches of ostrich feathers or trailing lyre birds' tails. The uniforms of the enormous and successful Turkish army had evolved according to intricate sumptuary laws, as the society was not stratified by blood ties (unlike Lorck's employers the Hapsburgs). Ottoman society arranged individuals in sectors and groups according to their rank and occupation, beliefs and ethnicity, with a fantastic dress code and a panoply of gear. For example, Lorck lingers, apparently mesmerised, by elaborate battle standards flowing with horsetails – trophies which were 'one of the most coveted booties from the combat'. This was a culture that valued artefacts as signs: communication took place by means of apparel and accessories, according to a dynamic of display and accumulation.

The corpus he compiled, of figures and scenes of life under Ottoman rule, remains a document of unparalleled witness. It belongs to that historical period defined by Raymond Schwab in *The Oriental Renaissance*, when Europeans were galvanised by what they found in the East. Can Lorck's images, for this reason, help rebalance the historical picture of relations between Europe, Turkey and Egypt, Christianity and Islam? Could his *oeuvre* and his activities, once restored to mind, even cast a different light on the past which stretches between his experience of the Ottoman empire and us today, during the rise of different Asian and Middle Eastern forms of power? In other words, can the artistic output of a neglected Danish artist provide, quite independently from his pay-masters' intentions at the time, intelligence of the past that might be valuable in the present?

Ottoman military might was highly codified, with every rank and order distinguished by elaborate uniforms (Lorck, 'Standing Soldier', 1626).

Lorck was a young artist, and he absorbed the aesthetics of his hosts as he created a new version of arabesque. He borrowed local visual material as models, from styles in portraiture to mapping and calligraphic ornament. 'Gothic', 'baroque', 'Kafkaesque', 'surrealist': such generic terms can apply to specific historical epochs and their styles; the characteristic works – whether a rose window or a razored eye – can be sourced and dated and placed within definite bounds. But these terms have also leapt clear of those bounds to designate something far less precise – a feeling and making which cannot be contained in a particular chronology; like other generic aesthetic categories – grotesque, macabre, carnivalesque, magical realist – they characterise a key and a mood, an approach to form and content. (Is that -esque suffix, foreign and spondaic, catching at the stylish vagueness in play?) Sometimes, the mode will define itself retrospectively, and an artist or a writer who has not been much visible before will materialise out of the forgettings of the past, and like a figure walking towards us in a haze, begin to gain definition and move into one of these areas of sensibility. Melchior Lorck is one of these oddities, with elective affinities to a Gothic sensibility like Henry Fuseli's and to the shadowed empty spaces of de Chirico, and even to the eerie objectivity of photographers like Eugène Atget and August Sander.

Lorck is one of the architects of arabesque as a European mode of expression. The art historian Peter Ward-Jackson noticed 'the strange atmosphere that pervades the whole scene', 'the hallucinatory quality' of his selection of topics and his rendering of figures and objects, 'the morbid trend of his imagination' and 'his predilection for the weird and the sinister'. The artist practised bizarre conjunctions: a tortoise in flight over the Venetian lagoon (Pl. 13); a Zoroastrian whose steeple hat rhymes with a smoking ziggurat in the background.

Lorck was briefly admitted to an audience with the Sultan, and no other artist captured the majesty of the Ottoman Sultan quite so awesomely as Lorck does in his portraits of Suleiman. In the full-length portrait, Suleiman is standing, effigy-like, and appears to be 12 feet high, erect and majestic, with a curved sword down to the floor, his whole frame flowing with gleaming silk, and dwarfing a caparisoned elephant which is entering the palace through the archway behind him. Beyond, the Suleimanye mosque, which was opened in 1557, can be seen – a monument of his reign. This image has a hieratic stiffness and almost eerie unearthly majesty that resembles the style of portraiture the Safavid Persian empire cultivated, and which would be perfected by the Mughals in India – Akbar came to the throne in 1556. These were Ottoman

Turkey's rivals to the east, and the cross-cultural conversations between the two great Muslim courts would prove very lively, and shape the human image in the East for centuries.

The Ottoman ruler, Suleiman the Magnificent, also known as the Law-Giver, built the Süleimanye mosque (behind him) to be his mausoleum. Melchior Lorck portrayed him in 1559, soon after it opened.

The artist boldly portrays the Sultan's face; by contrast, many of Lorck's subjects are turned away from the artist, or fully hidden under their headgear; other aspects of his work – the unpeopled urban spaces, the stylised patterning – are ultimately anti-realist and aniconic. Recording the customs and costumes of the society around him, he seems to be sensitive to the Islamic prohibition on lifelikeness in representation. Only God can make life, according to Muslim precept, so artists must refrain from making any image so lifelike that it looks real. It was during this period when Lorck was travelling that Reformation wrangling about the Second Commandment was still fierce; in Germany, Switzerland and England, iconoclastic passions rose and fell. The leaders – Luther, Calvin, Melanchthon, Zwingli – all argued about the permitted limits to artistic deception, for the devil is the ape of God and counterfeiting his strong suit. Luther recommended that artists condense images into signs and symbols to recall the Word of God; he abhorred the highly wrought illusionistic verismo which Spanish sculptors of the Counter-Reformation perfected.

By rendering human figures as unreal effigies, Lorck was likewise making signs by which to remember unfamiliar scenes. Lorck's impersonality, the equivalence between a pyramid and a person, to which he enjoys drawing the viewer's attention, his preference for depicting a plumed helmet rather than the face of the soldier wearing it, could also result from a constraint he felt – or had learned to observe – arising both from Reformed iconoclastic tendencies and from fundamental Muslim strictures against image-making.

In the greatest work Lorck produced, *The Prospect of Constantinople*, he made a panorama drawing over 11 metres long of the city of Constantinople and the Golden Horn. Signed and dated 1559, it is the first eyewitness view of the city organised from a unified viewpoint; it unfolds a vast, synoptic vista of Istanbul, magically and microscopically rendered from the heights of the fortifications in the Galata district on the European side of the Bosphorus, overlooking the Golden Horn. The channel is thronged with the graceful gaff-rigged dhows of the Turkish merchants, with fishing boats, naval vessels, ferries and skiffs plying the waters in a breeze that fills their sails. Lorck details the city's architecture with delicate graphic penmanship, and records the interlaced play of wind-filled sails in the Golden Horn. In his spiky handwriting, he identifies the palaces and mosques, classical antiquities, churches, aqueducts and schools.

In the foreground of the *Prospect*, the artist has included himself at work with a flourishing gesture of his quill; the scroll and a chalice for his ink and paint – there are washes of green and pink on the drawing

– are being held for him by a seated Ottoman grandee, who is wearing the huge rolled turban that marked out the status of a mufti or an emir, both pre-eminent definers and upholders of the law (Pl. 14).

The composition communicates to us that the sweeping view of the great Ottoman capital has been granted to a gifted humanist artist and gentleman traveller; his self-portrait shows Lorck, then in his early thirties, as a Renaissance courtier, a graceful youthful figure with elongated fingers, as in a painting by his contemporary Parmigianino, a suitable recipient of a king's bursary who has studied in Italy and garnered the benefits. He is executing his art with élan under the benevolent supervision of a high-placed protector. The Ottoman official is being helpful, even admiring, but he remains present and no doubt vigilant; the visiting artist from Europe is able to record the city, its layout, its dwellings, its fortifications, its trade and shipping, but by permission, and that permission is granted because the Turkish empire has nothing to fear from being revealed to foreigners, so confident are its citizens in what they have achieved and what they are. So the *Prospect* is triple-faced: an act of intelligence-gathering by a visitor from a hostile power, a reverent homage to a munificent and enthralling host country, and a message to the neighbouring European empire about what it has to reckon with.

However fanciful, or occasionally surrealist in character, Lorck's drawings extend an awed tribute to Ottoman wealth and efficiency: not a trace announces those notions of languor and effeminacy – that tendency comes a good two hundred years later.

When Lorck returned to his home territory, he did not find it easy to publish his work. The status of images was still one of the sorest issues; iconoclasm swept through the Netherlands in 1566. But at the same time, no Reformer in Europe could make common ground with Islam or invoke its principles, nor would want to, let alone recognise fellowship with its aesthetics, even though the churches of Germany and Holland hung blazons of scripture on their walls instead of saints, like the magnificent panels of the Names of God and of Koranic suras that decorate mosques.

In this climate, on his return, Lorck began editing his prints in significant ways. The first arrangement had opened with the page showing ways of managing water, as mentioned above. But later schemes give pride of place to a profile of Jesus Christ as Redeemer and to a mosque with storm clouds gathering above it, and the hand of God appearing in thunder and lightning. He composed a poem, ominously called *A*

Song of the Turk and the Antichrist, with a trumpeting angel of doom on
the cover. It laments the plight of Christian prisoners under the Ottomans.
He begins to complain vociferously of the hardships he endured in 'a
barbaric country' while away. To an image of the sanctuary of Mecca,
he adds a capriccio of buildings, including a Christian church. In a new
commentary on his portrait of Suleiman, he writes that the Sultan's
features are 'gruesome and evil'.

Two conclusions can be drawn from this: first, that religion was introduced as a structural motif of his narrative when it had been first and
foremost concerned with power and business – financial and military;
second, that the more an individual artist might owe to cross-cultural
inspiration, the less it could be acknowledged in a climate of fear and
antagonism. In respect of relations today between the West and the world
that was Ottoman, the Muslim religion was not seen as superstitious or
ignorant, and did not present the defining distinction – the artist is aware
of the antagonism, but faith was not of paramount importance to Lorck
in evoking the other culture. (After all, the Ottomans were well known
to employ Christians and to tolerate other religions as well.) The mosque
and the madrasa, as well as the church and the synagogue, come in later
to provide a cover story when the real dynamics of the plot are moving
at another level, to do with income, resources and status. The historical
recognition of points in common, even between such an unlikely pair
as Luther and Muhammad, is worth exploring more deeply in order to
grasp current twists in religious fundamentalism. The uses of images,
sacred and profane, still play an incendiary role in cultural confrontations,
for which Bruno Latour has coined the apt term 'iconoclash'.

Lorck made several attempts to persuade a patron to subsidise his
Turkish project. In a letter to the new Danish King Frederick II he wrote,
'I do not bring home gold, pearls, and treasures, for they were not the cause
of my travels . . . therefore I present what I have . . .' He then searched for
a metaphor for his motives, and hit upon an image: 'For (to speak what is
already on my tongue) if it were possible for me to move freely about in
the sea, then I would rather imitate the fish – especially the large ones –
than begin groping for pearls and precious stones . . .' After this expression
of idenfication with large marine creatures, he tries to persuade his prospec-
tive protector of his good faith, and switches to another metaphor: 'Indeed,'
he continues, 'could I bodily step in and out of heaven, neither effort nor
danger would restrain me . . .' Again he fumbles towards a vision of a zone
without borders, giving free passage – first the sea, then the air. In Lorck's
chain of images, the surprising sympathy he expresses for large fish swimming in the sea segues to another kind of freedom of movement, an angelic

mobility between earth and sky. These two points of identification are both embodied in the fantastic turtle he drew flying over the Venetian lagoon (Pl. 13). The airborne creature, so little a natural candidate for flight, conveys through the joking, punning conjugations of the unconscious, an ideal alter ego for a struggling artist-traveller, a lumbering grounded animal who wanted to find a different vantage point from the parti pris of his contemporaries.

III

With regard to the vitality of things, as depicted in the *Nights*, another stage of cross-fertilisation strongly shapes the reading and reception of oriental fiction, so that by the nineteenth century when the *Nights* come to be illustrated in ever more widely read editions, the documentary records of the scientific observers profoundly affect the way artists envision the stories.

A continuous colloquy takes place between orientalist painters, settled in Cairo or Istanbul in order to capture scenes of daily life around them, and the pictures that summon the stories of the *Nights* in print. The fantastic character of the tales are rendered by means of veracious scene-setting, with numerous objects introduced strategically to summon realistic tableaux. The effect is rationalising: the stories' wild implausibilities and dislocations of scale are tamed and ordered in well-furnished images in order to seem plausible and real. Two twists on reading the *Nights* then followed: first, the fantasy was pursued that objects held secrets which could be captured by intensive and scrupulous record-making; secondly, the fantastic tales were subsequently pictured in terms set by these documentary observations.

When Napoleon set out for Egypt he belonged to a generation that had grown up with orientalising fever in every field: readers had been devouring both the stories themselves and a spate of Oriental tales, rendered on page and stage. Imitations, *hommages*, satires, libretti and spoofs by Montesquieu, Swift, Voltaire, Dr Johnson, Frances Sheridan, Eliza Haywood, Carlo Gozzi and Lorenzo da Ponte (among others) combined with cultural tastes, fashions in smoking and coffee, dress and furnishings – and even garden swings. Napoleon's band of *savants*, accompanying his invasion of Egypt in 1798, were setting out to explore for themselves a world that had enthralled France – and England. Insistent themes in this craze for the *Nights* included unimaginable sumptuousness, ferocious tyranny, and meltingly amorous beauties: the Egyptian recorders of the French expedition noted with scorn the invaders' pursuit of these aspects. Works of imagination which mined these leitmotifs flourished as vigorously as the Enlightenment's pursuit of empirical, rational data.

Unexpectedly the cultural army mustered by Napoleon to work on the magnificent volumes of the *Description de l'Égypte* (1809–28), applied the same curiosity to the artefacts of 'L'État moderne', the Modern State of Egypt, as the archaeologists among them had brought to the monuments and temples or the zoologists to the dissection of living creatures: for example, a rice-whitening machine's innards are examined and exposed in an analogous way to the maw of the Nile fish, the Heterobranchus.

However, rather than looking at the analogy by stating that those living creatures were reified, it might be fruitful to think of the inert objects of their attention (irrigation gear, ironmongery, glassware, sugar mills) being ascribed animist powers. The *Description de l'Égypte* displays its findings by category of object, classified without regard for any single thing's particular origin or date, or even, most surprisingly, individual craftworker's hand or name. Although different skills and trades are eloquently captured in genre scenes, such as a group of young embroiderers at work on round frames, sitting on a balcony, or the knife-grinder using his feet as well as his hands to ply his whetstone (the French marvelled at the locals' dexterity in handling machinery), in general, the artefacts are tabulated separately from the workshops in which they were made, and are presented unattributed – as if they gave birth to themselves according to the mythic principles of autochthony.

The whole monumental sequence of the *Description de l'Égypte*, from the opening frontispiece of the pyramids, throws the emphasis on elegiac retrospection, and evokes the magnificence of ancient Egypt through its ruins. But the book does not collapse time as completely as Galland proposed. It tells a different story, and one that sprang numerous surprises on the makers of the vast encyclopaedia. Many critics have disparaged the *Description* for showing more interest in stones than in living people, but the aspersion, however justified, can be looked at differently. Mixed feelings, combining delight and dismay, arrogance and fear, form the psychogical and political ground from which rose the account of contemporary Egyptian customs, manners, social strata, etc. in these two concluding volumes of the *Description*. These set out to explain the contemporary society the French had invaded, and they assiduously compiled the precious evidence from the testimony of artefacts. The 'arabesque' can be made to talk.

These sober, technical plates possess an indwelling force of human curiosity and passionate attentiveness, which is sensory, even sensual.

Although the totalising, encyclopaedic ambitions that spurred on such projects as the *Description* have been convincingly ascribed to the colonialist ambitions of the European powers (and the condescension of the *savants* is at times audible in the text and accompanying letters), they also give an insight into the way such scholarly and objective visual records, following the scrutiny of an artist like Lorck, interact with the fictions of the *Arabian Nights*.

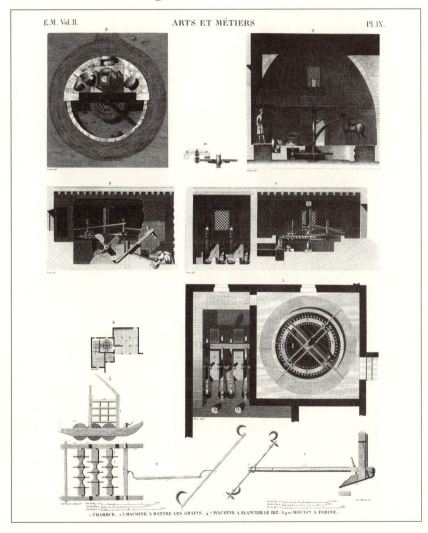

Napoleon's team of *savants* did not restrict their inquiries to Ancient Egypt, but catalogued technology in current use, such as this sugar mill, analysed in forensic detail by the engineer F-C. Cecile, and engraved by Mme de St. Morien (*Description de l'Égypte: L'état moderne*, 1809–29).

Goods became eloquent, and in this sense moved closer in character to the enchanted paraphernalia of the stories in the *Nights*. Merchandise and artefacts, both actual and fictive, became active and dynamic in the circulation of knowledge beyond the boundaries of entertainment. In a collection of essays, *Things That Talk*, Lorraine Daston comments, 'As seeds around which an elaborate crystal can suddenly congeal, things in a supersaturated cultural solution can crystallize ways of thinking, feeling, and acting. These thickenings of significance are one way that things can be made to talk.' But 'some things speak irresistibly', she writes. 'It is neither entirely arbitrary nor entirely entailed which objects will become eloquent when, and in what cause. The language of things derives from certain properties of the things themselves, which suit the cultural purposes for which they are enlisted.'

The formidable team of scholars, surveyors, architects and scientists, who were invited by Napoleon to join his conquering expedition in 1798, were nearly 200 strong. Many more hands, on their return, worked on completing the volumes. The *savants* included in their number the mathematician Gaspard Monge and the artist Nicolas-Jacques Conté, a keen pioneer balloonist, mechanical engineer, and the inventor of the pencil – and of the crayon named after him. They also took with them a printing press with fonts for different scripts, ancient and modern, as well as the latest, varied settings for different and extremely precise cross-hatching effects (the range, displayed in a series of rectangular abstracts, has the quiet intensity of a Sol LeWitt drawing). The *savants* compiled their findings over two decades; the prints circulated widely and found great success beyond scholarly circles, including among readers of the *Nights* and the many artists, designers, architects, impresarios and interpreters who were inspired by the tales and conveyed them in different forms to fresh audiences. They were intent on gathering evidence according to rational principles, but their work stimulated dreams.

This was a princely enterprise in more ways than one, a multi-volume publication with magnificent albums of plates which have become justifiably prized. The first 'Imperial' edition, with its plates illustrating the antiquities and monuments of Pharaonic Egypt, is familiar from numerous later editions and single framed prints (they can be seen on a splendid digitised and interactive website recently created by the Library of Alexandria). The closing volumes of *The Modern State* are not nearly as well known; they are 'elephant folios'. (Calling them up at the British Library caused quite a stir, requiring a special table and tremendously elaborate negotiations to have photographs taken.)

By the end of the Egyptian enterprise, over 80 artists and 400 engravers had been involved in working on the materials accumulated by the expedition and in supporting the research of the *savants*. The plates are organised in sections under headings such as 'Arts et Métiers' (Arts and Trades), including a harrow, a machine for blanching rice, and other devices. 'Arts and Trades' are followed by 'Costumes and Portraits', which unfold the culture of Mameluke Egypt in all its variety and industriousness, depicting the different tribes and peoples, their social ranks and offices as marked, as Lorck had earlier observed, by costumes and headgear. With assiduous and close attention, the images do more than pay lip service to the contemporary culture the French encountered, or put on a show of respect towards the people who now lived in the ruins of the civilisation they and other Europeans revered and coveted so lustfully. These are acts of epistemological penetration: cool, analytical, and wondering.

The clarity and intensity of the scrutiny that the plates convey does not lose force on the printed page, in spite of reaching the reader or viewer at several removes: the engravers were working from the drawings made *in situ* and from notes taken by engineers, architects, surveyors and painters who were deployed in the field by the emperor. For example, a dazzlingly scrupulous rendering of a sprinkling machine (*Roue à jantes creuses*, Wheel with hollow felloes), showing in section the gearing of its underground structure, was first drawn by F.-C. Cécile, one of the many engineers on the expedition, then painted in acqua fortis by a woman who worked on the project, Louise-Pierre Baltard, and later given to Mme de St Morien to engrave. Mme de St Morien shows exceptional abilities as a technical draughtsman: she also worked on a study of a blindfold ox turning a grindstone, and delineated the innards of a rice-whitening machine, a winnow, a flour mill, and a ploughshare – this last page includes a prancing Arabian horse, of a grace never seen on a farm in *la France profonde*.

This tremendous parade encompasses many of the precise professions of characters who figure in favourite stories in the *Arabian Nights*: barbers and tanners, belt-weavers and dervishes, attendants at the baths, porters and traders, singing and dancing girls, and wandering holy men or dervishes.

The sequence concludes with crowded pages of things . . . every kind of thing used by modern Egyptians: cradles and tents, turbans and lutes, locks and lathes and all manner of tools, pens, astrolabes, measuring devices, carpets, and bath towels, daggers and helmets, saddles, carpetbags and rugs, baskets and narghilehs or hookahs, and a whole enthralled page filled with scores of vessels – flasks and bottles, caskets and phials, basins and ewers, jars and pots. The shapes, the spouts, the ornaments, the delicacy, the variety of materials: the artist, working at the behest of the committee and the Institut d'Égypte, is clearly gripped.

The pages illustrate both specific examples of artefacts – board games and slippers – and the quest for universality: so many vessels testify to a longing to inventory everything, not to miss out on a single species. But the ambition to record objectively topples over under the excess of desire to have it all.

The *Description* sets an elegiac tone at the start of its survey: like 'The City of Brass', it too is the story of a princely expedition to a ruined civilisation. Is this book a memorial inventory, an evocation of an enchanted city of the past?

The vision in the *Arabian Nights* story warns against vanity and arrogance and hubris; but it also sings the splendour of that past and turns it into art, into effigy and monument, a hymn and an ode. 'The City of Brass' is a fiction about wealth and luxury and their penalties, but its glance is not turned only to the past. Like the *Description de l'Égypte*, the story's picture of the past transmits a picture of the present: the riches of Baghdad and Shiraz and Damascus and other great cities flourishing when the story was first told are captured in the performance of grief for the destroyed cultures of the predecessors; this reflects flatteringly on the present monumental lament for the vanished civilisations of the past. Nevertheless, the pictures in *l'État moderne* show few similarities to the Orientalist lusciousness that dominates the paintings of the Levant after 1850; the dynamics of their curiosity, in both the objects of their inquiry and in the mood they set, all predate the harem and snake-charming fantasies of Orientalism. However, subsequent to these encyclopaedic attempts at revelation, artists all over the world, from Norway to Japan, imagined Shahrazad and the host of dramatis personae in the stories in terms set by the circumstantial cornucopia on these plates.

IV Illustrators of the *Nights*

Edward W. Lane is one of the crucial hinges in this transmission. He comes in for a furious lashing from Edward Said, and Said is certainly right that such scholars fashioned the Orient in the imagination of Europeans. And yet, if the entanglement is unpicked with more sympathy, as Leila Ahmed does in her study of Lane, published the same year as Said's polemic, other qualities emerge.

Lane is one of the clearest examples of a charmed encounter with the Middle East, a forerunner of such romancers of Araby as Charles Doughty, Wilfrid Blunt, Robert Byron and T. E. Lawrence. A prompt reader of the *Description* and of Vivant Denon's *Travels in Upper and Lower Egypt*, fired up by the Egyptomania that followed the Napoleonic expedition and the exhibition, in London in 1821–2, of the fabulous discoveries in the excavations made by Belzoni, Lane set out almost immediately to discover Egypt for himself – and rectify the French view. His approach was empirical in the strongest English tradition: he would attain knowledge through immersion in the real thing – or rather things. He would be no armchair traveller, remote scholar or distant observer, but enthusiastically adopt the dress and use the instruments of the people he was studying.

In 1825, Lane landed in Egypt, acquired Arabic at great speed to a high level of fluency, found himself a house far from the 'Frankish' or European quarter of Cairo, arrayed himself in the robes of a Mameluke of the ruling class, and began working on a book. He called it, with an explicit gesture towards the French enterprise, *The Description of Egypt*; this ambitious work was illustrated entirely by Lane's drawings, executed with the help of a camera lucida which he expressly mastered in Egypt in order to be able to make accurate pictures.

The resulting magnum opus suffered many vicissitudes, and never appeared in his lifetime. But in 1836 he selected the part of it he had devoted to the contemporary society he had joined, and the richly detailed and admiring *Account of the Manners and Customs of the Modern Egyptians* was published by John Murray. It became a huge success, a classic work of Victorian anthropology, with all the defects as well as the assiduity of the genre. Again the title strikes a clear and defiant echo of the title of the French predecessor.

Lane was a great-nephew of the artist Thomas Gainsborough and had trained as an apprentice engraver, and his study is profusely illustrated, from his own sketchbooks, with help from his brother Richard J. Lane, a professional artist and printmaker. He sought out many of the scenes and subjects which the French *Description* had covered, but gave significantly less attention to technology, expertise, labour and trades; he shows greater curiosity about domestic arrangements, picturesque scenes, and a kind of oriental pastoral in the landscapes and cityscapes. He was especially fascinated by women's customs – and brought out to Egypt his sister Sophia Lane-Poole to investigate areas forbidden to men, which she wrote up in her book, *An Englishwoman in Egypt* (1844).

Through his command of the camera lucida, Lane excelled in rendering the intricate ornament of Cairene architecture, exterior and interior: his attention to the surface texture of the material world solicited it to speak, to communicate, in spite of the medium's silence, the ways of the culture he had adopted.

Lane followed *Manners and Customs* with a translation of selections from the Koran, and at the end of his life compiled a monumental Arabic–English Lexicon which he did not live to finish (it was published in parts from 1863 to 1893, the last three parts completed by his nephew Stanley Lane-Poole). In between these impressive undertakings, he produced a hugely influential, annotated translation of the *Nights* (1839–41) in three illustrated volumes.

In *Manners and Customs*, Lane describes how storytellers recited legends in the bazaar in Cairo, but reports that there were few survivors from the tradition – he mentions that they were reduced to six in number – and that their repertoire did not stretch to many stories from the *Nights*; he had heard one of them recounting the romance of Seyf Zu-l-Yezen, but he believes it to be an earlier work.

Manuscripts of the *Nights* and indeed of other texts were exceedingly rare and difficult for a foreigner to obtain, even one living in Arab style, he reports; and they were very expensive. Generally, Lane borrowed the materials he needed from mosques, applying through an intermediary of a sheikh whom he knew. For the translation of the *Nights*, he worked from a manuscript procured for him by his publisher, Charles Knight, but principally relied on the recently established Bulaq I edition (1835); he compared this with others, including Calcutta II, which appeared as he was working (1839–42) (see Introduction).

Purified of bawdy and salaciousness, violence and eroticism, Lane's version is the one I read, in the copy given to my great-grandmother by her father in 1850, and I still enjoy the stories in this version, because Lane is wonderfully capacious and includes scores of tales from the more expansive Egyptian tradition, many of which are still unfamiliar; he also restored the lyric poetry which Galland and his translators removed.

Lane the man has something of the omnivorous energy of the book itself, for he organised the astonishing portfolio of 600 illustrations which gives his translation its unforgettable character; they were made by the wood engraver William Harvey, who was one of the last and cherished students of Thomas Bewick. The list of illustrations in the book conscientiously names all the engravers who transferred Harvey's images to steel plates for the pages of the publication, but does not include Lane himself among the artists, or his brother Richard Lane, who provided Harvey with the necessary materials for imagining the scenes: Lane's own copious sketches and notes, the celebrated and popular album of Cairo by his friend and colleague Robert Hay, and many original views by other travelling artists of his acquaintance. Some of the vignettes and scenes are brought across from both Lane's planned *Description* and from *Manners and Customs*. In this way, Harvey was kept fully instructed in the furnishings, scenery, customs and dress of the times: very fine renderings of mosque lanterns, mule saddles, decorative wall interlace tiling and lattice screens (*moucharabieh*) punctuate the stories with a lively rhythm, giving an endless supply of triggers for the reader's mind-pictures.

Like Antoine Galland, Lane still advocates reading the tales as true reports of life in the Middle East in his time, praising 'the fullness and fidelity with which they describe the character, manners and customs of the Arabs'. But he took issue with Galland's perception, damning the great oriental scholar as ignorant and misleading:

> Deceived by the vague nature of Galland's version, travellers in Persia, Turkey, and India, have often fancied that the Arabian Tales describe the particular manners of the natives of these countries, but no one who had read them in the original language, having an intimate acquaintance with the Arabs, can be of this opinion: it is in Arabian countries, and especially in Egypt, that we see the people, the dresses, and the buildings, which it describes in almost every case, even when the scene is laid in Persia, in India, or in China.

By contrast, he, Lane, would give an accurate picture, and the far-flung geography of the *Nights* would be firmly mapped on the culture and country he knew best. No matter that the stories fly the reader to jinn's magical islands or to terrifying mountains – Lane 'had no trace of imagination', a surprising feature in a lover of the *Arabian Nights*.

The Victorian audience accepted this admiringly, one reviewer writing, 'It was not the lot of every man to see, as Mr Lane has done, with his own eyes, the streets of Cairo – to mingle in her feasts – to walk side by side with the sacred camel.' The effect, this critic continues, brings 'the reality bodily before us'.

Translators are not usually thought of as novelists in their own right, but as is clear by now, the history of the *Arabian Nights* in its European versions should warn against any such glib presumption. Like Galland, Lane is a fabricator, even as he compiles a valuable and monumental Arab–English dictionary and labours over footnotes. The heart of his fictive method involves lavish historicity, in keeping with Romantic uses of the past. Sir Walter Scott, in the prefatory letter to *Peveril of the Peak*

(1822), describes his method of intertwining real events with imaginary tales, and reaches for a metaphor from the scenery of an oriental garden: his work resembles, he writes, 'A Turkish kiosk rising on the ruins of an ancient temple. Not quite correct in architecture, strictly and classically criticised; but presenting something uncommon and fantastic to the imagination, on which the spectator gazes with pleasure of the same description which arises from the perusal of an Eastern tale.'

Illustrators of the *Nights* had no qualms about anachronism and liked adding fact to fiction: an accurate engraving of a mosque in Cairo serves to evoke the ruined and fallen City of Brass (William Harvey, 1850).

The drawbacks of Lane's Romantic bricolage and the consequent anachronisms can be felt in his placing of certain illustrations: a fine depiction of a mosque in Cairo accompanies the climax of 'The City of Brass', when the travellers finally enter the desolate place, which in the story is guarded by jinn and everyone is frozen in time. This is tantamount to modern-dress opera – setting *Götterdämmerung* in present-day Wall Street. Not altogether inappropriate, but tendentious. Evidence has a way of turning into eidola – and by not disclosing its fictive character it can bear false witness.

Orientalist fiction of the same period shares the hunger for the concrete: Théophile Gautier's fantasy fable, *La mille et deuxième nuit* (The 1002nd Night) written in 1842 (improbably published in the periodical *Le Musée des familles*) juxtaposes ancient and modern visions of the Orient in a mise-en-scène so detailed in description it could double as an interior decorator's sales catalogue. The first-person narrator, who presents himself as a *feuilletoniste* in the French capital, like Gautier himself, has cleared a whole day to give himself up to his favourite activity – daydreaming behind drawn curtains over his narghile (this is thirteen years before Baudelaire opens *Les Fleurs du mal* with a similar image of the man of letters dreaming of the scaffold as he too smokes his hookah). Just as he is settling himself down, someone calls at the door – it is Shéhérazade (as the French writers name her), blown in to ask for the favour of a story from the French *maître*; her sister Dinarzade has come with her, and they urgently need his help: Shéhérazade has run out of ideas and another tale must be found to save her from the block.

Our hero the Parisian journalist rises immediately to the occasion and makes her a gift of a pretty romance about a certain Mahmoud Ben Ahmed. Gautier's tone is arch, and he parodies the orientalist fad while playing it up for all it is worth. Shéhérazade appears:

> She was richly dressed in the Turkish fashion; a waistcoat of green velvet, overdecorated with ornaments, clasped her wasp waist; . . . a handkerchief of white satin, scattered with stars and spangled with sequins, served for a belt. Wide bouffant pantaloons came down to her knees; velvet greaves in the Albanian style adorned her slender and delicate legs with her pretty bare feet enclosed in little slippers of morocco, embossed, pricked, dyed and stitched with gold thread; an orange caftan, embroidered with silver flowers, a scarlet fez enlivened with a long silky tuft, completed the rather bizarre outfit for going out visiting friends in Paris in this sorry year of 1842.

The legendary storyteller is swallowed up in the gorgeous layers of her costume. But within its beautiful, buffed ironies, Gautier's fable interestingly fingers the unreliability of appearances: his hero is smitten by a glimpse of the Sultan's daughter Ayesha passing by in her palanquin; eventually, she gives him an assignation, and as he reads her his passionate love poetry, she metamorphoses: 'butterfly wings began sketchily to form on her trembling shoulders'. She is in truth no human being, but a peri. But Mahmoud Ben Ahmed does not notice, and Ayesha leaves the encounter displeased, realising he is more interested in his own raptures and their expression than in her, their subject.

Gautier introduces a third apparition of the beloved – in the form of a slave girl whom he rescues but ignores in his blind love of the princess. She too is the peri in disguise. In this hypersaturated ambience of visual opulence, the supernatural is what fails to be noticed: in many ways Gautier has noticed his own tendency to prefer furniture and fashions to interior landscape or dreaming; he expertly satirises this nineteenth-century attitude to the *Nights*, and its curious fundamental violation of the stories' magic nature.

Gautier's story ends with a haunting image: Dinarzade alone and bereft, crying into a handkerchief spotted with her sister's blood. The French journalist's story did not succeed in keeping the Sultan sweet.

For all its deflationary wit, the story conveys in this encounter a microcosm of nineteenth-century interest in the Orient, and the limits of scopophilia and of the hunger for evidence. That the evidence takes the form of artefacts presents a different way of delineating character, which has taken root in approaches to the Orient. Where a Renaissance humanist would anatomise an individual's personality by correlating each organ with the position of the stars at his or her nativity, the nineteenth-century realist assembled things around the subject of study, and charged them with conveying the qualities of that person and, by extension, their society.

This form of metonymy also governs Richard Burton's prodigal work on the *Arabian Nights*. He followed Edward Lane in translating the book largely because Lane's piety and politeness infuriated him; he also set out to outstrip him in antiquarian scholarship, adding detailed insider lore and expansive footnotes to his version in a spirit of full contradiction to the prevailing prudery of Victorian Britain; he expanded and embellished with attention to illuminating the customs of the Arabs, which he also documented with glee and a fair deal of invention, projection and transference. He is the Frank Harris of the desert and the bazaar. (A clever reviewer quipped: 'Galland is for the nursery, Lane for the library, Payne for the study, and Burton for the sewers.') It is still possible to meet people who, when I say I am working on the *Arabian Nights*, lean into my ear and impart some piece of extraordinary sexual information they have learned from Burton's specialist footnotes. To avoid legal action, Burton's magnum opus was privately printed and published under the alias of a learned society in India, the so-called 'Kama Shastra Society of Benares'. The first edition was illustrated by a friend of Burton's, the English artist Albert Letchford, who has vanished almost completely from view, partly because he died aged thirty-nine in 1905, before any of his work for Burton was published (with the exception of the frontispiece showing the two kings with the sleeping jinn and his fair captive).

Letchford's paintings were later printed for inclusion in the book; they take up the frank eroticism of the stories with a *fin-de-siècle* dreaminess – Letchford studied in Paris and was influenced by Odilon Redon and other Symbolists like Léon Bonnat, who taught him at the Beaux-Arts. Their influence shows in his smoky *sfumato* of a phalanx of dream children, for instance, in the opalescent flesh of his nudes, and the generally doe-eyed languor of his male characters as well. At times, Letchford's pictures are thrilling in their immense contrasts of scale between the jinn and humans: as in the scene from 'Gharib and Ajib' when the two human brothers are hauled off like dolls in the hands of their giant demonic captors. The chiaroscuro also gives them a sombreness unusual in illustrations of the *Nights*. But Letchford's images are interesting to look at and think about because they take their cue from Burton's historicising outlook and stage the *Nights* in realistic landscapes and cities; some of the scenery is not quite Levantine, as Letchford was living in Naples and used features of the Mediterranean coast as backdrops. But however supernatural and wondrous the tale, he pictures it as plausibly as he can manage, naturalising the jinn in vivid interiors with a pointed juxtaposition of objects in daily use in Cairo; these objects are treated with absorbed attention and glowingly lit to give them presence, such as the room of 'Dawlat Khatun', with a lute, an incense burner, a mirror, and books on the floor near her.

Significantly, the objects are frequently containers – vessels, bottles, boxes, placed prominently so that they hint to the viewer at their contents; their presence suggests latency, promises that more lies beneath the surface or that the surface is not all that it seems. (Hugo von Hofmannsthal once asked, 'Where is depth to be found?' And answered, 'On the surface.')

Once a week, her jinn abductor appears to the beautiful 'Damsel' whom he has sequestered in a remote castle, but she has a dulcimer and some other ways of whiling away the hours. (Albert Letchford for Burton, 1883)

1. Solomon listens to the hoopoe, his messenger, as he sits enthroned beside Bilqis, the queen of Sheba, in his garden paradise. His vizier is seated on his right, Simurghs and other birds, whose speech the wise king also understands, fly above, and a jinn commander stands guard over a flock of animals, real and imaginary. (*Falnamah*, or *Book of Omens*, Deccan, *c.* 1610–30)

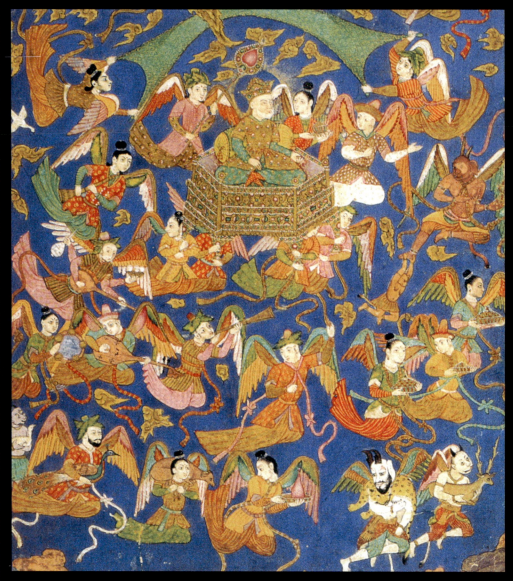

2. Through the heavens thronged with angels, apsaras and jinn, some carrying animals, some with hybrid human bodies, Solomon rides the wind on his luxurious divan. (Deccan manuscript, 1675–1700)

3. Magical knowledge was sometimes identified with Solomonic wisdom, not necromancy: a benign alchemist transforms a toad on a sixteenth-century 'Ripley scroll'.

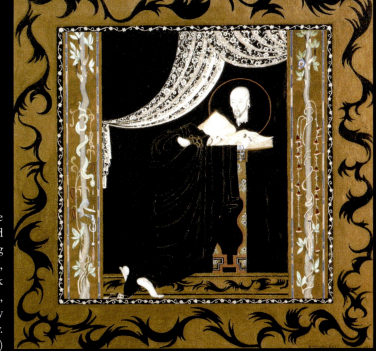

4. Magicians in the *Nights* can blight and bless: the Greek king falls to the ground, poisoned by the book of the doctor, Douban, whom he falsely suspected of treachery. (Kay Neilsen, 1917)

5. A sleeping child is assailed by the jinn of nightmares, but the image is a talisman and wards off the danger it represents. From *The Book of Felicity*, commissioned by Sultan Murad III in 1582 for his daughter Fatima and brought from Cairo to Paris by the mathematician Gaspard Monge, one of the savants on Napoleon's expedition.

6. The beautiful and faithful jinniya Miymuna contends with her rebellious rival, Dahnash, over the respective qualities of their protegés, Camar al-Zaman and Badoura (above).
7. In 'The Second Dervish's Tale' (left) the good fairy princess overcomes the enemy, but her flame-throwing scorches her and she too dies. (Edmund Dulac, *c.* 1910–1920)

8. The 'wise men from the east' of the New Testament were soon cast as three kings of fabulous wealth, with one imagined as a Moor. As the Muslim empire grew, the black king, resplendently arrayed here in multicoloured 'gipsy' silks, figured a contemporary hope of conversion. (Juan Bautista Maíno, *c.* 1613)

9. (Above left) Arabesques and inscriptions are interlaced on a carpet from Central Iran, woven *c.* 1570–80, figuring a prayer niche or mihrab. 10. (Above right) During centuries of conflict in the Mediterranean, cultural exchanges still took place and eastern luxuries were highly prized. One carpet pattern (known as 'Lotto' after the Venetian painter), distinguished by stars, meanders, and Kufic borders, was chiefly woven in Usak, western Turkey. This example is from the late fifteenth century.

11. The daughters of the Brescian house of Martinengo display with pride and pleasure the family's oriental carpets. (Moretto, *c.* 1543)

12. With the cry 'New lamps for old!' the wicked magician tricks the
Princess's maid, and commands the jinni of the lamp to carry off Aladdin's
enchanted palace, with the Princess inside. With this sumptuous image
of the colossal jinni, the British animator and artist Errol Le Cain
pays tribute to eastern manuscript illumination.

Letchford became close friends with Burton (some say, one of his only close friends) after meeting him in Trieste, where Burton was Consul and Letchford had been born. The illustrations were inspired by much intense discussion between them, with Burton monitoring Letchford closely with regard to the furnishings, dress, architecture and other material aspects; as in the notes Burton appended so copiously to his version of the stories, he wanted to parade the richness and ingenuity of the Arabs and their culture. So the promise of happy armchair travelling advocated by Galland and Lane remained unshaken, in spite of Burton's contempt for his predecessor: the *Arabian Nights* were documentary texts, historical, instructive and useful. Anachronism was not an issue; Arabic culture was essentially legible in the literature of the Middle Ages; it was eternal, enduring, and visible in present-day existence. There was no past, no change over time; there was to be no modernity.

Historical anachronism, as practised by Lane and Burton – as well as to some extent by their precursor, Galland – can be seen far more easily when the history is known, the culture familiar to the reader or spectator. Playing *Hamlet* in modern dress, with Claudius as a CEO and Gertrude as a brand-name shopaholic, can give new insights into the tragedy, but only because the stage company involved can count on the audience recognising that they are updating to a specific dramatic end. When Lane and Burton illustrate and footnote the *Nights* with the things of contemporary Egypt or Turkey they are effacing the place where they are themselves standing. This contributes to the picturesque effect but not to the historical veracity which the whole antiquarian apparatus claims to be intent on serving. Even the most static societies are not as static as that – it is an error born of wishful thinking and romantic nostalgia ('Orientalism') to cast the nineteenth-century Middle East as the perpetual 'golden prime/Of good Haroun Alraschid' (the accents of Tennyson's lilting refrain in his 1830 poem 'Recollections of the Arabian Nights' perfectly reverberate to his contemporaries' tune).

Many of the 'modern' aspects that Napoleon's team of engineers had investigated with curiosity and admiration are necessarily banished from the Lane edition's illustrations and from the vision of the Burton–Letchford version of the *Nights*. By eliminating all devices, machines and tackle, the pictures would then capture the surroundings of the protagonists in the period when the *Nights* was set. Although even this elision would be false, since many of the irrigation techniques and other devices which the *Description* reported are themselves ancient, as ancient as writing and astronomy. But such scientific processes would spoil the feeling of the image, the poetic atmosphere of mystery and time immemorial.

Even as they banish unpoetical machinery or other signs of modernity, the illustrations are nevertheless staging the stories in the contemporary Levant, in nineteenth-century Cairo. Both Lane and Letchford had collected items included in the images (on his return to England, Lane sold a few small objects to the British Museum – a figurine and a fragment of a lotus, among other things). Modern-day Egypt might exhibit a perennial picturesque, but it was not the selfsame place where the jinni touches down with Hasan of Basra.

The facts of history and the inventions of fiction fuse and react, both as a consequence of the *Arabian Nights'* wildfire success in the eighteenth century and as the supplement which rationalises and authenticates the supernatural fantasies in the stories. At the same time the *Nights'* charged landscape had naturalised a vision of an enchanted universe, in which artefacts were protagonists.

Story 7

The Greek King and Doctor Douban

THE FISHERMAN HAS MANAGED WITH his cunning ruse to trick the furious – and highly gullible – Sakhr back into the copper bottle and is walking back to the water's edge to throw him back into the sea when, from within, the jinni pleads for his life. The fisherman sternly refuses, while the jinni promises him every blessing. 'You are lying,' says the fisherman. 'Your promises are empty. You and I are like the vizier of King Yunan and Douban, the doctor. 'Tell me how we're like them,' says the jinni, and so sparks the next story within a story in the cycle.

In Byzantium, a king who has everything in the world – great riches, loyal followers, and vast armies at his command – falls ill with a disease, a kind of psoriasis, for which which none of his physicians or doctors can find a cure. A travelling sage called Douban happens to be passing through the king's territory; he's very old and very learned in Greek, Arabic, Persian and Syriac philosophy, medicine and astronomy, and knows the properties of herbs and other things: he is a natural philosopher, and his book, the Book of Nature. When he hears of the king's sickness, he arrays himself in his finest clothes and calls in all submissiveness on the court. When the king receives him, Douban offers to heal him, and in return Yunan, overjoyed, presents him with a ceremonial robe and promises to shower blessings on him and on all his descendants. The doctor begins his work, renting a house, studying his books; after consulting further, he prepares a mixture, fashions a ball and, into the shaft of a mallet which he has hollowed out, introduces the mixture; the next day he presents the ball and mallet to the king and tells him to go out to the polo field and ride as hard as he can, holding the mallet tight and swinging it vigorously until he's worked up a lather all over; the salve in the stick will transpire through his whole body. Then he's to return to the palace and, after bathing, he will be cured.

King Yunan does as the doctor tells him.

The following morning, when Douban presents himself at the palace, the king receives him royally because, as soon as he left the baths, he found all traces of his disease had vanished from his body. His skin has become as smooth as pure silver.

The passing old man is a foreigner, a stranger, and his magic is a form of practical intelligence, rooted in scientific learning.

In his joy and gratitude, King Yunan makes a fuss of Douban, sitting him by his side on his ceremonial divan, arraying him in splendid silks, feasting with him, showering him with money and other presents, and giving him his own thoroughbred to ride home.

The same happens the next day: more is lavished on the doctor who has cured the king.

One of the king's viziers looks darkly on these developments. He is particularly ugly, the fisherman says, with character to match, evil-tongued, jealous, and mendacious. He approaches the king and warns him that he is in danger from someone close to him.

'Speak,' says the king.

When the vizier names Douban, the king rejects the insinuation angrily, and reminds his advisor of the example of King Sindibad, who destroyed his favourite hawk when the bird kept overturning his cup, preventing him from drinking from a stream. But it turned out that a snake was in the tree above, pouring its venom into the water, and the bird had saved Sindibad's life.

'You are asking me to do the same,' says the king, 'and kill the man who has saved me.'

The envious vizier rejects the parable, and counters with another story of his own: a fairy tale about a prince who meets a young girl weeping in the forest. She says she's the daughter of an Indian king; the prince takes her up on his horse and prepares to rescue her. Seeing a ruined house, she asks to be let down, to meet a need of nature; he follows her, and finds she is in fact an ogress who has tricked him and is now rejoicing with her children that she's caught a nice fat young man for them to eat.

The doctor, Douban, says King Yunan's treacherous vizier, fits the part of the ogress in this story. 'If he cured you,' insinuates the vizier, 'he can kill you as easily.' The king is afraid, and the vizier advises him to execute Douban forthwith, before he can spring anything on him.

Summoned to the king's presence, in complete ignorance of the fate which lies in store, Douban salutes him with many fervent praise-poems about just providence, the wise ways of destiny, and the necessity of placing trust in learning and study.

The king tells him he is going to kill him – as abruptly as that. 'You are a spy, I've been advised, come to assassinate me.' And he orders the executioner to cut off the physician's head.

It is the doctor's turn to plead for his life, as the fisherman originally pleaded for his to the jinni whom he had delivered, as the jinni is now doing from inside the bottle, and as Shahrazad is doing throughout the 1001 nights to the Sultan who wants to execute her like all his other wives.

Douban pleads for justice; he compares himself to the crocodile in the fable – but he doesn't proceed to tell that story. There is perhaps not enough time left. The councillors and courtiers surrounding King Yunan uphold his innocence. The king is now blinded by suspicion and fear: 'You could kill me merely by giving me some perfume to smell,' he says. Douban protests that the charges are false and again begs for his life.

At this point, the fisherman interrupts the flow of the story and reminds Sakhr that these are the exact terms that he, the fisherman, had used to plead for his life, which the jinni had ignored.

'I shall only rest easy when you are dead,' continues King Yunan.

The doctor warns him, 'If you make me die, God will make you die.'

But the king remains implacable. The doctor weeps; the hangman binds his eyes and lays his head on the block. One of the courtiers rises and asks that he be spared. The doctor then asks for one last grace: to go back to his house, order his affairs, arrange his burial, and give away his books, especially his medical books. There is one book in his library, he adds, which he particularly wants to present to the king. It is full of a myriad secrets, only one of which is really singular and precious. He gives the king chapter and verse how to discover it, and tells him that after his head has been cut off, the king should place it in a basin, with a layer of kohl at the bottom to staunch the blood, and it will answer any question the king puts to it.

'Your severed head will speak to me?' the king marvels.

The following day, the court reassembles for the execution in their full splendour, so that, the fisherman says, 'The room seemed a bed of flowers.' The doctor Douban returns from his house with a book and a box of powder which he sprinkles on a dish, telling the king to place his head on the dish once it has been cut off, as the powder will staunch the flow of blood.

The doctor is executed. Yunan wants to open the book, but he finds that its pages are stuck together. He licks his finger and turns the first page, then a second, then a third. They can only be separated with great difficulty, and Yunan can see nothing written on them, so he keeps turning them, as the head on the dish urges him to keep doing, in order to find the place he wants.

The king continues, but at the end of a very short time, an evil has entered his entire body: the pages are poisoned. The king falls into convulsions and cries out, 'I am poisoned, I am poisoned.'

Then the head of the physician Douban recites another poem about the workings of destiny on the just and the unjust.

Hardly has he finished than the king falls down dead.

'You see,' says the fisherman to Sakhr the jinni, 'that if the king Yunan had allowed the doctor to live, God would have preserved him. But he refused, wanted to kill him, and God made him die. It is the same for you, jinni. If you had intended to keep me alive, God would have preserved your life.'

The jinni twists and turns, refusing this interpretation of his behaviour and promising, swearing to reform if only the fisherman will release him. After more toing and froing, the fisherman makes the jinni swear he will be good, true to his word and will do him no harm.

Sakhr swears, and the fisherman unstoppers the bottle; smoke pours out and the jinni materialises, horrible of aspect; he tramples the copper bottle in fury, and throws it into the sea.

The fisherman is terrified, and reminds the jinni of his promise, and of the lesson of the story of Yunan and Douban.

The jinni roars with laughter, and begins striding away, telling the fisherman to follow him – he is taking him into another country, another story and, eventually, fabulous fortune.

CHAPTER NINE

The Thing-World of the
Arabian Nights

When a person, an animal, or something inanimate returns our glance
with its own, we are drawn initially into the distance; its glance is dreaming,
draws *us* after its dream.

Walter Benjamin, 'Scrappy Paperwork', before 1940

I

IN THE BOX OF STORIES opened so far in the cycle of 'The Fisherman
and the Genie' the tales fit one inside the other with internal rhymes
and structural patterns, both matching and inverted. Remedies and poisons
alternate throughout the tales, instruments of healing with instruments
of harming; good deeds are rewarded by ill deeds and the ill deeds are
then punished according to the justice of providence (the king dies for
his treachery, but Douban also lies dead (Pl. 4), and we hear nothing of
the treacherous vizier). But as a ransom tale, told by the fisherman to the
jinni, the story has worked: he has won his own reprieve by means of
his parable and, furthermore, has himself taken in the lesson he was
teaching the jinni and has acted magnanimously, by trusting the demon
after all and setting him free.

'The Fisherman and the Genie' is one of the sets of stories-within-
stories which double in the mirror of Shahrazad's task: the sequence
consists of one ransom tale nested inside another which is its inverted
double, a lethal parable, whereas the true ransom tale is redemptive. Either
the story fails and an injustice is perpetrated, or the story succeeds, and
reprieve – justice – is achieved. The dizzy imbrication of the tales partly
conceals Shahrazad, yet, like her, the fisherman is simultaneously using
a story to put his case against violent reprisals, and threatening his inter-
locutor that a wronged victim can find a way to avenge himself – through
the pages of a book. With such narrative feints and passes, like a dancer
using fans and veils to make herself more vividly present through her

acts of disappearance, Shahrazad the maker of a book of tales is also expressing the possibility of her retaliation. Sultan Shahriyar stands well and truly warned by the tale of the Greek king and physician Douban.

The concatenation of stories so far – we have reached the sixth night when Shahrazad lets the fisherman set the jinni free and then segues straight into the story of the 'Prince of the Black Islands' – is masterly/ mistressly: succinct and tight. Shahrazad is telling stories to reinstate clarity in the enraged Sultan's mind, and bring back justice in his kingdom; the story of the physician Douban is one of a cluster of embedded tales within tales which reveal – among many other things – the terminal danger of mental blindness, arbitrary justice and ingratitude. Like the frame story in which Shahrazad pleads for her reprieve and for the salvation of all women, the story of the wronged doctor dramatises the active power of storytelling and animates a book as his avenger. The tale of Yunan and Douban is one of the greatest parables about the potency of literature, as Umberto Eco recognised when he borrowed it for the plot of *The Name of the Rose* (1981). It reveals how the character of a reader makes a difference, how the motives for wanting knowledge affect the act, and how book learning has power but no intrinsic moral value: a book (knowledge) can be used for evil purposes as well as good.

Understanding nature's properties forms the powerful knowledge in the stories: the hawk recognises the venom in the water just as Douban understands the combination of ingredients needed to purify the king's disease. Natural substances, however, do not play such an important part in the specialist magical knowledge displayed elsewhere in the stories. The fable about the hawk, the fairy tale about the ogress (and maybe the unheard story of the crocodile, too) ground their revelations in natural science. But Douban, while drawing on natural sciences, charges *objects* with power: the mallet, the powder, the book. His story is being told to a jinni inside a copper flask and though he does not use his scholarship to summon jinn or enchant objects, he takes his learning further when he makes the book the instrument of his revenge and his own severed head (that ghastly, uncanny thing) his active emanation after death.

The wicked vizier has not accused the doctor of occultism as such, but the cloud of suspicion that hangs around the wandering sage suggests as much, as does the astrology and the book learning the old man brings with him from his very first entrance into the tale.

His knowledge of the properties of things has given Douban esoteric powers over them: he can cause his own head to speak even after it has been cut off and his life has ended. In this way he refuses the thinghood imposed on him by the ungrateful king, who has used him as he would use his subjects, dealing with Douban as he would dispose of a slave. But although the doctor cannot overcome the sentence of death, he can prolong his subjectivity and his autonomy in this uncanny fashion. Like Orpheus, whose head keeps singing after his death, he speaks from the other side.

Homer suggests similar ghostly utterances in the *Iliad* (X. 457) and in the *Odyssey* (XXII. 329), and the image returns in numerous poems, consciously taking up Homer's image: Joseph of Exeter's retelling of the *Iliad* adds a passage when Hector, swinging the severed head of Patroclus, hears it (him?) eerily whisper, 'Where is Achilles, my avenger?' The speaking head in *Sir Gawain and the Green Knight* may owe something to classical antecedents and to many martyrs' legends, in which they provide proof of their sanctity by walking on after execution, holding their heads in their hands and continuing to speak.

The speaking head comes to symbolise on the one hand the irreducible freedom of the individual and, through that, supernatural powers, including occult prophecy. Legends attached to numerous reputed necromancers and magicians, including Virgil, Pope Sylvester II (Gerbert d'Aurillac), Roger Bacon and others describe their creation of a talking brass head which knows the future. Its powers gave it emblematic status, and such heads featured as the sign of a fortune-teller, as Daniel Defoe records in *Journal of a Plague Year*.

Douban's head is not made of brass; it is his real head on its way to becoming a skull, not yet fully changed to the condition of Yorick, though Yorick's is another head that is appealed to, and given eloquent presence when Hamlet talks to it so feverishly. Oscillating between a person and a thing, Douban's head can stand for the ambiguous condition of phenomena in the *Arabian Nights*: the stories continually test the border between persons and things. Slaves – persons reduced to things, to chattels – are omnipresent, their condition frequently evoked as loathsome, their presence threatening and polluting, as in the scene of lurid debauchery in the frame story (not an appealing aspect of the *Nights*).

A book and a severed head may not be the most obvious candidates in the *Nights* to exemplify the status of thingness in the stories. But for their very undecidability as objects, the head of the physician Douban and his murder weapon of choice illuminate the animist character of objects. Both of them belong in a debatable land: a person who is not a person, a thing that is not quite a thing. Or perhaps a very special kind of thing: a severed head that speaks, a book that kills. Sharing prescience and secret knowledge with the brazen head of medieval myth about magicians, and testifying to its owner's magical efficaciousness even after death, the severed head in the story epitomises how things stand in the thing-world of the

Nights. Its deathliness grows through its blankness: the king turns the pages because he finds nothing on them, and the more he turns, the deeper the poison from them sinks into him. So although the fable dramatises books-as-agents, it specifically empties its murder weapon of words and, in so doing, of live meaning. A blank book is a metonym for oblivion and passes sentence on the foolish and malignant king.

This type of live–dead thing infuses its baneful energy into many of the stories, as in the case of 'The Prince of the Black Islands', Dahesh the immured jinn, and the mummy of Princess Tadmoura of the Amalekites.

But books, whether grimoires filled with esoteric wisdom or blank and drenched in drugs, are analogues of mummies, and in their potency surpass most other things in the category. The *Arabian Nights* became infused with the glamour that such books radiate in the stories: for example the poet Coleridge, who read the *Arabian Nights* when he was a boy, was terrified by the sudden appearance of the enraged jinni in the story of 'The Merchant and the Genie' who rises up and demands vengeance when the merchant unwittingly kills his son by tossing a date pit on to the ground. Coleridge remembered afterwards:

> The book used to lie in a corner of the parlour window at my dear Father's Vicarage-house; and I can never forget with what a strange mixture of obscure dread and intense desire I used to look at the volume and watch it, till the morning sunshine had reached and nearly covered it, when, and not before, I felt the courage given me to seize the precious treasure and hurry off with it to some sunny corner of the playground.

His excitement grew so intense that he tells us his father burned his copy of the *Nights* for over-stimulating his young mind.

As Ros Ballaster has pointed out, in this memoir of the older poet the book itself takes on, for the child he then was, the character of a powerful living thing, exercising its thrall over him.

Besides books, automata and mechanical devices, eerily self-activating without benefit of jinn, move of their own accord, when sparked by a broken prohibition (as in 'The City of Brass') or at the command of their master or maker: 'The Tale of the Third Dervish', another oracular tale that announces a trap and springs it tight shut on the protagonist, and 'The Ebony Horse', to which it is connected (one of the most loved stories of pure fairytale enchantment in the book), both feature marvellous machines, flying automata in the exact likeness of a horse. But far less marvellous contrivances than these supply the vehicles of magic:

common furnishings and household goods are often the favourite lairs where jinn lurk. In 'Judar and his Brothers', the concatenation of magic comprises several instruments: an invincible sabre, a crystal ball that can set burning fires, a vase that can find treasure, a magic ring, a saddlebag that never empties, and so forth.

Things in the tales talk and move and appear to have consciousness and identity in ways which have played a part in the development of a new attitude to the world of goods in the contemporary Western imaginary. Anthropology on the one hand and psychology on the other can broaden understanding of a new relationship with the inanimate, and the literature on the topic is growing. As Bill Brown has written: 'Things quicken'. Enchanted things in the *Nights* ignite and speak, move and grow, pulse and radiate, displaying sentience and expressing feelings and developing attachments to their owners. All of these are signs of *qualia,* the particular properties of consciousness, even though to say that things have qualia is a contradiction in terms. European folklore and witch crazes may include fantasies about enchanted pots and pans and broomsticks, but the *Nights* does not single out instances as unusual. Its human world is quick with other lives. This vitality far exceeds the projective subjectivity of the things' users; things acquire a life of their own, a concealed but conscious, unfathomable existence spread through the surrounding air, invisible and independent of official divinities. Frequently, the more banal and quotidian the container, the more grimy and dilapidated it is and the closer it has moved to the condition of pure rubbish, worthy only of discarding, the more dramatic and exciting the sudden apparition of its indwelling, personal daimon, who spirals out of his prison with a great groan. Like the dull metal of magnets, objects pack inherent power.

A.S. Byatt's virtuoso fairy tale, 'The Djinn in the Nightingale's Eye', vividly captures the character of the magic containers of the *Nights*. The narratologist Gillian Perholt, attending a conference in Istanbul, buys a dusty bottle in the souk and brings it back to her luxury hotel, when

> suddenly it gave a kind of warm leap in her hand, like a frog, like a stillbeating heart in the hands of a surgeon . . . the stopper, with a faint glassy grinding, suddenly flew out of the neck of the flask . . . And out of the bottle in her hands came a swarming, an exhalation, a fast-moving dark stain which made a high-pitched buzzing sound and smelled of woodsmoke, of cinnamon, of sulphur, of something that might have been incense, of something that was not leather, but was? The dark cloud gathered and turned and flew in a great paisley or comma out of the bathroom.

The story rushes on, under the momentum of sheer storytelling energy, as the djinn of the story's title grants her three wishes, and becomes her lover and then her friend. As someone who is an expert in stories, Dr Perholt proceeds very cautiously and judiciously with her wishes: she knows from her reading how easily the chances are squandered.

Byatt's pastiche-cum-homage also reveals how the richest and most active relationships many of the characters in the stories experience arise from possession of an enchanted thing, for these possessions are themselves often possessed and exercise influence over their owners. Indeed, it is not always clear which way possession runs: even though jinn are commonly obedient to the thing that possesses them and its human master (they are slaves of the ring or the lamp), they are not invariably so, as in the tale of 'Judar and his Brothers', and, as we shall see in the next chapter, the story of 'Abu Mohammed the Lazy'. Gems and rings summon jinn but they can also act autonomously (as in 'Camar al-Zaman', 'Marouf the Cobbler', and numerous other examples); indeed, if the magic thing is stolen or lost – and many of the tales depend on these capricious twists of fate – the new owner can command the jinni inside it with as much authority as any predecessor, however more sympathetic and deserving: magic rings and lamps and gems, falling into the hands of scheming villains, keep the stories on the move.

The culture to whose belief system all these things belong, so suscep-tible to possession and enchantment, long turned on the making of things and the market in such things; Baghdad was the greatest city in the world when the stories were first being compiled, a city of manufactures and artefacts which it traded extensively by land and sea. Managing things – trading, acquiring, giving them away – occupies the lives of many protagonists whether they have come by their goods by luck or by diligence.

Like Zobeide and Sinbad and Marouf and so many other merchants and travelling traders, active and enchanted things also circulate in the bustling trade and traffic of the Mediterranean, the North African coast and the Middle East. This mercantile society, with its many tales of buried treasure and sudden windfalls, and its population of sailors, beggars, shopkeepers, craftsmen, tradesmen and every kind of shopper, endows goods with independent presence and vitality, while their enchanted state recognisably derives from a world of unique treasures on the one hand and a thriving market in series and copies on the other. An Egyptian legacy of magic activates the treasures which fill the pages: rings, jewels, stones, lamps, sofas and couches, statues, toys, weapons and other devices possess talismanic powers. These are distinguished less by differences in appearance or materials (so much silk, carnelian, fabulous fabrics) than by the magic power which emanates from *this* jewel, but not *that* jewel. The stories insist that these magic goods are individual examples of rare fabrication and value. But some other things issue in a plethora of like-nesses and do not have peculiar features: multiplicity rather than singularity defines them. And sometimes they have every appearance of being worth-less. In this fertile respect, the stories manifest their origins in cultures dedicated to artisanal repetition.

The stories Shahrazad and her embedded fellow narrators are telling resemble the goods that so often shadow the protagonists: they too are objects being traded and exchanged; she is bargaining for her survival, and her stories and others are both very like one another and yet have unique features. They are also artisanal in character, because she makes no claim to original invention but depends on her excellent memory, she says, where already existing examples are stored.

The serial nature of things in the stories developed, like them, in the great urban centres of Baghdad and Cairo and Damascus and Shiraz. They throw into relief the historic relationship of those communities to marketing and to objects – to things, to goods – circulating among them, and they make visible to us certain features that impinge on us now even more acutely.

Household goods and common furnishings are listed, numbered, and praised in a manner that parallels repetitive prayer and cumulative spells: lamps and carpets, weapons and wares, books and basins, luxurious and otherwise, supply the chief vehicles of magic and the jinn's favourite lairs. The stories present a cornucopia of objects, both manipulated by human agency and empowered with mastery over their owners. In this respect the enchanted things echo magic tales from the Hellenistic world: for example, a pestle plays tricks in the comic story by Lucian which Goethe revisioned in his celebrated poem 'The Sorcerer's Apprentice', changing the instrument to a broom, as Disney made famous with such sprightly brio in *Fantasia*. The live goods of the *Nights* belong in a tradi-tion of supernatural entertainments, and have their counterparts in the magic sticks and clubs and tablecloths and other domestic instruments of Western fairy tales, which act on their own accord at the command of their owner, as in several of the Grimm Brothers' stories. Cultural interminglings of Central Asian peoples in the Russian empire with their Middle Eastern neighbours can also be seen through such shared motifs. Aleksandr Nikolaevich Afanas'ev's anthology *Russian Fairy Tales* was published in 1855–64; there are numerous overlaps and resonances with the *Nights*, and enchanted, humdrum things feature strongly: not least the mortar which the ferocious witch Baba Yaga uses as a basket to ride across the sky, sweeping the way ahead with a besom as she goes. In other stories, a tablecloth which spreads a feast by itself is called a 'Self-Spreader', or 'Self-Victualler', which draws attention to the sense of the thing's self-activated inner life. But such objects are not imagined in quite the same way as they are in the *Nights*: individual jinn rarely dwell inside them.

The population of animate objects in fairytale and magic literature began to increase in the eighteenth century, under direct influence of the *Nights*, and has since exploded, to become indistinguishable from the genre: in cinema and new visual media, live things, alongside talking animals, have become the stock-in-trade of family entertainment.

II

Can any helpful distinctions be drawn between the classical myths, fairy tales and the *Arabian Nights*, with respect to magic things, their owners and manipulators? Although the generic rubrics of amulet, charm and talisman capture the function of enchanted artefacts in classical myth and romance, it seems to me they can be nuanced differently from their Arabic counterparts. The cap of darkness that Hades wears to render himself invisible, the winged sandals and helmet of Hermes, the mirror that Athena gives to Perseus to protect him from Medusa's petrifying stare, are made by the gods and goddesses, filled by them with power and passed on by them to chosen heroes; they are not intrinsically possessed of an animating spirit, a jinni. The symbolic language of magic in antique myths also draws more directly on natural forces for its imagery and its stories – on animals, birds, flowers, stones, as in Ovid's *Metamorphoses*. Magic still joins pastoral in *The Golden Ass*, Apuleius's great work of fantasy fiction, so however much its enchained narrative, its North African provenance, and its sophisticated urban scene herald the later concoctions of the medieval Egyptian and Arabic tradition which flows into the *Nights*, its author distinctively resorts to a vocabulary of organic substance, not inorganic manufacture, for the sources of supernatural power. (Lucius, the long-suffering hero, needs to eat roses in order to undo the charm laid upon him by the salve he took, which, when he rubbed it over his limbs, failed to turn him into a bird.)

In the Greek myths, the beneficiary of the enchantment – the wearer of the winged sandals or cap of invisibility – is usually an exceptional hero of inimitable prowess – a demigod, if not a god; but fairy tales, as we readers know (for we have been given heart by this tendency), whether

Eastern or Western, prefer to exalt insignificant figures – cowards and lazybones, female slaves and younger sons showing little promise – and give them the great good luck of a magic lamp or other wonder-working thing. The quickening of this pot or that rug in the *Nights* exists independently of its owner, as the objects in question are activated by jinni or other magical powers (the charm, the rite, the spell) and acquire a life of their own, a concealed but conscious, unfathomable vitality. The jinni in the old flask which the fisherman finds by chance in his net announces the indeterminacy of these magic things: the flask after all turns out to be a very live kind of flask. As we know, the famous lamp contains an all-powerful jinni who can transform Aladdin into a fabulously wealthy prince and win him marriage to the princess.

This magical underpinning of the narrative not only dramatises supernatural interventions; it also perceives the wayward power of goods in exchanges – 'the tournament of value', in the phrase of Arjun Appadurai – and it explores prophetically, through myriad tales, the spell they cast on us, on people in the era of branding and global markets.

Animism of this kind, according inert material things conscious vitality, has customarily been considered an aspect of past belief and primitive culture; contemporary civilisation has evolved beyond it, it is widely believed. However, there are many signs that this is not so, and that a new variety of animist thought has developed, principally under the influence of photography, film (especially animation), and communication technologies.

To look more deeply into this possibility, I need to explore the variety of ways things can be charged: relic, amulet, fetish, are some of the forms that charmed states take. (Among all the multifarious magic objects possessing power, talismans form a special class of active thing, specifically associated with the *Nights* and spreading into wider modern culture in their wake, and will be explored in the next chapter.) Susan Stewart's beautiful book *On Longing* (1993) meditates inspiringly on things transformed by attachment and memory, rather than by belief or superstition: souvenirs, toys, dolls, and mementoes such as lockets, photographs, casts. Many such things need play to become alive: and children's ways of playing provide a model for the animist character of things, for children infuse personality into lifeless and often lustreless things: a clothes peg acquires character and story, a stick becomes a forest, a piece of card a house, and so forth. The psychologists D. W. Winnicott and Melanie Klein underlined the importance of this work of imagination to the health of the individual child and future adult and to society as a whole. When Winnicott declares, 'Playing is reality', he is ranging himself with imagination as a good, and more particularly with the animating imagination which brings to life things that do not have it except through fantasy. Think how some children form attachments to a blanket or a rag, 'the transitional object'. Stewart proposes, 'The miniature relates to the personal, the gigantic to the collective.'

Can the multifarious uncanny phenomena in the *Nights* throw light on the changing status of objects in contemporary consciousness – in contemporary *cherishing* and personal value? Magic in the stories is by definition capable of imbuing lifeless things with vitality, which often endows single objects with power to affect the group and the whole society – the collective as well as the personal. But can these activated objects be more richly and deeply defined in relation to the secret life of things in present-day culture? Is it possible to sort out – in terms of today's meanings – relics from amulets, fetishes from talismans, and can an order of magic things be established? As Victoria Nelson has commented in *The Secret Life of Puppets,* 'the thingworld is rich in different kinds of animate things'.

Can the *Nights* tell us what these are?

III

Jan Švankmajer urges fellow film-makers, in the words quoted as the epigraph to this part of *Stranger Magic*, to '. . . become a collector of old things. Listen to them. Never do violence to objects . . . tell *their* stories'. His plea – his 'Commandment' – holds true beyond modern animation in the cinema. With regard to magic lamps, flying carpets and the function of imagination and its creative powers today, the questions have changed. They no longer take up the dreamwork of the couch ('What scenes does make-believe stage?' or, 'What stories does the unconscious relate?'). Instead, curiosity has changed direction and asks, 'What do these things or objects – these toys and talismans – tell us not about ourselves, but about themselves?' When we listen to the things that talk, to the voice of the toy, they become eloquent as vehicles of futurity – time machines of innovation, not retrospection or preservation but agents of prophetic science; as Walter Benjamin noted, a thing looks back at us, and draws *us* after its dream.

A number of thoughtful writers are exploring the secret life of things as their powers grow in the world of personal, electronic prostheses – mobile phones, iPods and laptops. Lorraine Daston, in *Things That Talk* (2004), and the psychologist Sherry Turkle, in both *The Second Self* (1984, rep. 2005) and *Evocative Objects* (2007), have probed the intense interdependency of people and their prosthetic devices. Oriental storytelling in the fashion of the *Nights* underlies this modern strain of animism, and its vision both foreshadows the eerie cybernetics of our hardware media and gives a way of understanding our relationship with them. The enchantments in the *Nights* dramatise – before the era of brand names and designer labels – the charmed states occupied, and transmitted, by certain things.

In any culture's taxonomy system, body parts such as the speaking head of Douban the physician, the relics of the saints and Egyptian mummies are things with a difference: their thingness was once ensouled and the disappeared person somehow hovers about them. The clash between their former state and their present inertness sharpens their unsettling and potent presence. Simone Weil, in her searing essay on the *Iliad*, keens over the violence that reduces and reifies bodies. 'Force is the true hero, the true subject, [and] the centre of the epic,' she writes. 'To define force, it is that x that turns anybody who is subjected to it into a *thing*. Exercised to the limit, it turns man into a thing in the most literal sense: it makes a corpse out of him.'

Stories in the *Nights* sing out against this ultimate reduction to thingness; it is the worst of fates to fall out of the vital zone altogether. Jinn trapped in copper bottles have been reduced to thingness which they rail against; they want their powers back, powers which challenge fundamentally the very existence of inanimateness as a state at all. The tales imbue many of the dead with a posthumous existence, metamorphosed into things that are more than things even though they are still less than life. Some of the most lethal sorcery in the *Nights* turns people to stone – just as the enchantress in 'The Prince of the Black Islands' petrifies her husband from the waist down, sentencing him to exist as an immobile, human–thing hybrid. At the same time, many machines and contrivances, moving statues and simulacra in the stories aspire to vitality: they simulate life-to-the-life.

Daston draws an illuminating distinction between 'idols' and 'evidence'. The word 'idol' comes from the Greek *eidolon*, and was applied to oracular statues, and to the magical doubles the gods and goddesses assume when they want to deceive humans. As phantoms, eidola are generally considered illusions – misleading, and fraudulent. Like puppets, which seem real even though the spectator knows they are not, these things that are not dead – neither dead wood nor dead meat – have inherent potency to fascinate, disturb, and quicken the pulse. The speaking head of Douban is an eidolon; so is the ebony horse which looks real but is a machine, and the stories of the *Arabian Nights* are packed with such ambiguous phenomena, from statues which speak to small humdrum objects which come alive. Eidola can include singing automata, like the doll of Thomas Edison that could recite 'Mary Had a Little Lamb', or, before Edison, Olympia in E.T.A. Hoffmann's short story 'The Sandman', which famously inspired Freud's meditations on things that are *unheimlich* (unhomely) – uncanny. Such things, he argues, are often familiar rather than exotic: they are *heimlich*, or homely, but have become estranged by repression.

By contrast with eidola/idols, another category of things that talk, according to Daston, acts as evidence; this category includes objects in geometry or forensic exhibits, such as photographs of the scene of the crime. However, Daston is of course quick to see that these two categories – eidola and evidence – are potentially interchangeable: imposture haunts everything and the forensic exhibit might be fabricated; it is also very susceptible to haunting, and can turn into a powerful eidolon. Observation, imaginative projection and interpretation transform objects of attention and can stimulate them to move and utter – subjectively. Remember how you kissed a photograph of a lover's face; or how Proust dramatised the scene in his novel in which Mlle Vinteuil desecrates her father's photograph?

The shifting opposition between idols and evidence can be translated into other pairings: for example, in Russian there is a word, *vesch*, which carries the implication that it is a *thing with a soul* in contrast to another word for a thing, *predmet*. This pairing reflects to some extent the implied difference between 'thing' and 'object' in English, where an object is more thing-like than a thing: you would never call a friend 'you dear old object'. Nor could you say anything other than 'I've a thing for Johnny Depp.' The word 'thing' comes from Old Norse and Icelandic where it means 'assembly', 'council', 'meeting'; it is still used in the Norwegian word for parliament – 'Storting', the Great Assembly. The derivation has led the psychologist Charles Fernyhough to gloss the word that a thing is 'where our minds go to make friends'. He offers this inspired definition in *The Baby in the Mirror*, a study of his daughter from birth to three, the period when a child begins to interact with the objects in her world – many of them toys. When children play Let's Pretend, they turn themselves into the things that surround them – Walter Benjamin remembered that he loved to imitate things: 'In me the compulsion acted through words. Not those that made me similar to models of good breeding, but those that made me similar to dwelling places, furniture, clothes.'

A comfort blanket, the familiar, smelly old cloth that becomes a toddler's necessary companion even as it grows ever grimier and more tattered, the one-eyed, limp-limbed and battered teddy bear – these adopted things and 'transitional objects', where the child's mind goes to make friends, have become for their child possessors far more than toys. The object exercises a shaping power over its subject; child and object grow together.

Relics and souvenirs, keepsakes, memorabilia, transitional objects and comfort rags belong in the order of things with souls, like *veschi*; they depend on the thought that 'A thing fallen out of signification creates a break in the network of connections with others and oneself.' The anthropologist William Christian, Jr. expresses the distinctions in terms of affect in an essay on the US custom of the 'yard sale': here former possessions are abandoned on the pavement; they have become 'trash' and 'junk' until they are bought and reinstalled in another household. (The equivalent in Britain is a 'jumble' or 'rummage' sale, often equal assemblies of melancholy, disaffected, once loved, now orphaned belongings.) Affective bonds change objects; they *charm* them.

In ways that throw light on the activity of jinn in the *Nights*, Christian identifies certain channels through which the affect moves: through a person, or other original source, and through associations with a time, a place, an episode. The state of enchantment, embodied in the jinn, offers both origin as a guarantee of the value of a thing, and associations which give it singular importance, distinguishing it from other like things (this lamp, not that one; this carnelian ring, not that one).

Many things are or can be *ensouled* by physical contact with an original body: the memento, the model, the mould, or cast. Relics also figure in this category, and they can be found in the secular zone as well, belonging to that category of strongly affected things that are enchanted independently of belief in a deity (I am not even pausing to consider things that have been hallowed or changed by a different process, consecrated through religious or sacred ritual). Such charmed things share affinities with children's miniaturised toys; they become microcosmic entities and personae imbued with special associations; these are established by personal connection through bodily contact, or by imaginative and emotional projection, leading to attachment, even dependency, in a virtual theatre of make-believe. The concept of the fetish also belongs here: an ordinary object such as a glove – the protagonist of Max Klinger's unsettling novella in pictures, *Ein Handschuh* (*A Glove*), (1881), or, similarly, Nadja's glove, photographed in André Breton's Surrealist classic of 1928. The essays by William Pietz on the fetish and, more recently by Caroline van Eck, provide a model to strive after in attempting this preliminary account of a related phenomenon, the talisman. Like the fetish, another import from the realm of the fascinating Other, the word's rich applications have valuable significance for illuminating modernity.

The power of the fetish: a mysterious woman drops a glove and a man, smitten by desire, picks it up. In Max Klinger's novella-in-pictures, strange creatures poke out their snouts in the glove's shrine (*A Glove*, 1881).

Photographs, above all, fill up with meaning in connection to their subjects. As things, they can be allocated to almost every category above: they are objects, they can be the dearest and most charged mementoes, they are often the object of idolatry, they are adduced as evidence, they are magically charged with something indefinable, arising from known connections or, in many cases, with the loss of connection. Photography and other modern tools of memory-work share the tie with the person who was there, in the flesh, at the time the image was made, and the medium has not only enhanced the potential for soulful things, but made their condition a crucial, familiar aspect of experience. As Christian has commented, a shoebox of old family photographs abandoned at the back of a charity shop by the house-clearance men, after the last person has died who could remember and identify the faces, is a box of orphaned things, now dis-affected, fallen out of the chain of signification.

This distinction between an ensouled or affected thing and its inert counterparts came home to me when I visited the house where the writer Mikhail Bulgakov lived in Kiev, in the Ukraine. The small museum, lovingly kept and animated by an enthusiastic curator, has gradually identified and retrieved a few things – a hat, a pen, some snapshots, a few manuscripts and notebooks – which Bulgakov himself or his family used; other miscellanea from the period and the milieu have been added to furnish the apartment in an atmospheric way. But anything which did not once belong to him, or has not been in contact with him or his family, has been painted white. These elements in the display stand blanched and leached of body and being, to show that they have not been imbued with soul by contact with the subject, with Bulgakov himself; in this sense they have remained mere *predmeti*.

In the house in Kiev of the writer Mikhail Bulgakov, objects that were his at the time have been left as they were and everything else has been painted white.

Story 8

Abu Mohammed the Lazy

ZUBAYDA, THE WIFE WHOM CALIPH Harun al-Rashid loves most of all, is making a head-dress of splendid jewels, but the central gem is missing and she wants a jewel bigger and brighter than any other. She sends a eunuch to the caliph and he immediately gives the order that the jewel she covets must be found; when he hears there are problems, he cries out in a rage, and is then told that the merchants have revealed that a certain merchant in Basra, nicknamed Abu Mohammed 'the Lazy', the son of a mere barber at the public baths, has a marvellous jewel of the size and purity required.

Harun instantly asks the executioner Mesrour to summon Abu Mohammed to the caliph's presence. While he waits in Basra, Mesrour tastes the unimaginable luxury and grace of Abu Mohammed's palace: his bathing pools of marble and gold filled with rosewater, his guest robes of brocade and precious stones, the feasts of delicacies he spreads at his table. The magnificence rivals the caliph's; Mesrour thinks darkly to himself that all this princeliness will have to be explained.

Saddling a mule with silver and jewels, Abu Mohammed sets out for Baghdad. In audience with Harun al-Rashid, Abu Mohammed lavishes gifts on the caliph: quantities of pearls and precious stones. Then, from another chest, he produces a brocade tent studded with jewels, its columns made of soft Indian aloe wood, the panels set off with green emeralds, with designs representing every kind of animal, bird, wild beast, all encrusted with yet more precious stones, 'jacinths, emeralds, topazes, rubies and others.' Abu Mohammed then offers to show some of the tricks he can perform: at a nod of his head, the crenellations of the palace bow to him; at a roll of his eyes, closed tents appear before the company; at a word, a concert of songbirds starts up.

Harun marvels that a son of a mere barber at the public baths can enjoy such powers and such fabulous wealth, and asks to know their source. Abu Mohammed shows no reluctance in telling him.

He was such a lazy boy, he says, that during the hot season if the sun reached him where he was dozing he was too indolent to move into the shade. His father died when he was fifteen, but his mother, who worked as a servant, provided him with what he needed, and he just idled and dozed, until one day she gave him a small sum and told him to give it to Abu al-Muzaffar, a travelling merchant and a man known for his generosity to the poor, who was leaving for China on a trading mission. Abu Mohammed was to ask him to buy something with it which Abu Mohammed might be able to use. In those days, he was so lazy that he needed his mother's help to set himself upright, dress himself, and then had to lean on her for support as he stumbled on the hem of his clothes on his way to the quayside.

Al-Muzaffar forgets all about the commission until the very last minute. But he's a man of his word and he orders the ship to turn back so he can use the small sum to buy something for Abu Mohammed, as he had promised. His fellow merchants refuse; he insists, but they still refuse, until he offers to reimburse them for the delay. This he does, handsomely. They set sail again and reach a populous island of pearl traders and jewel dealers, where al-Muzaffar finds a man sitting on the ground surrounded by monkeys; he keeps them chained and beats them as they fight among themselves. One monkey is mangy and miserable and the others turn on it with particular vengeance, which fills Abu al-Muzaffar with compassion. He buys the creature with the pittance Abu Mohammed's mother gave her son to help set him on his feet.

As they are leaving, pearl fishers approach the boat to sell more of their finds, and the monkey breaks free and dives with them, fetching up quantities of precious stones which it tosses into its benefactor's lap. At their next landfall they're unlucky and find themselves among cannibals. Some of the company are eaten; again the monkey demonstrates its prodigious nature and, when night falls, undoes the bonds on its new owner. Al-Muzaffar pays tribute to their saviour, endows the animal with a reward of a thousand dinars, and asks each of his fellow merchants to match his munificence. The monkey sets each one of them free, too, for an equal reward in every case.

Because he is an honest and generous man, Al-Muzaffar doesn't forget his original pledge to Abu Mohammed, and he doesn't plan to keep the marvellous animal. On his return to Basra from his voyages, now infinitely richer than he could ever have dreamed, al-Muzaffar seeks out Abu Mohammed, and finds him asleep. The young man bestirs himself reluctantly at his mother's pleas, and, still stumbling on the hem of his clothes, takes receipt of the monkey from al-Muzaffar's servants – cursing his mother for getting him out of bed just for this. But then al-Muzaffar arrives, and hands over the already vast treasure accumulated through the creature's cleverness.

And so begins the story of Abu Mohammed's powers and riches.

Abu Mohammed is revived by the money; he gives up his idle ways and sets up shop in the bazaar; helped by the monkey who brings him a thousand dinars every day at lunchtime, he begins to prosper. They become close, they live as one, eating and drinking together. Then one day the monkey opens its mouth and begins to speak, like a human being. He tells Abu Mohammed that he is 'a marid of the genii', and that his next boon will be to marry him to a beautiful girl, beautiful as the full moon, the daughter of a trader in provender. And so, clothed in gorgeous robes, riding on his mule with the silver jewel-studded saddle, and with ten slaves in attendance, Abu Mohammed sets out to ask for the hand of the merchant's beautiful daughter.

A poem interrupts the unfolding of the tale, a neat, icy piece of proverbial wisdom, commenting on the way riches give a different perspective to events:

> If a rich man talks all at sixes and sevens,
> people say, 'What a true opinion, quite beyond refutation!'
> But if a poor man speaks according to the truth,
> he's taken for a liar, his sayings are set at naught.

The merchant at first rejects Abu Mohammed, as he has no family and no social standing. But his money speaks, as the poem has noted.

The ape has given the bridegroom very exact instructions. When he collects his bride in ten days' time, he will find in her house a cupboard with a brass ring in the door. Under the ring he will find keys, which he must use to open the door; inside he will find 'a chest of iron, at the corners of which are four talismanic flags; in the midst is a basin filled with money . . . eleven serpents . . . a white cock with a lacy coxcomb tied up in string . . . and a knife . . .' He must take the knife and use it to sacrifice the cockerel; he must then tear up the flags, and kick over the iron chest. Then and only then will he be able to lay a finger on his virgin bride.

Abu Mohammed at first forgets the order of the monkey's commands, and only after the raptures of his wedding night, does he get up to fulfil them. As he comes to the end of his grisly business, his young bride leaps up and cries out,

'The jinn has taken possession of me!'

For Abu Mohammed the Lazy has undone the talismans her father has carefully contrived to protect her, and the ape appears and carries her off: he has been plotting for six years to abduct her 'to the City of Brass where the sun never rises'.

At first, Abu Mohammed abandons himself to despair, and wanders in the desert, bewailing his fate. There he comes across two snakes – one white, one black – attacking each other; he picks up a stone to break up the fight and kills the black one, and soon discovers that the survivor is a jinni as well, one of the good jinn who have repented. The good jinni's brother then appears, and in gratitude for the white snake's deliverance, offers to help Abu Mohammed in his quest for his lost love; he assures him they will overcome the evil ape in the end. More of his fellow jinn join forces, and they order one of their slaves to whisk Abu Mohammed into the air on his back – but he must remember not to call on the name of God while flying through the air.

Up they soar, 'so high that the world below disappeared to reveal to my eyes stars like mountains on their moorings, and in my ears angels singing the glory of God'. But he forgets the jinni's warning and when a divine apparition orders him to sing the praises of God, he does so; the jinni who is carrying him crumbles into ashes under his legs, and Abu Mohammed plunges headfirst into the sea.

More wanderings follow – through a country that's a dependency of China where the inhabitants speak Arabic, and farther, with Abu Mohammed still helped by the brother jinn of the snake he rescued. They show him the way at last to the City of Brass.

There, a jinni equips him with a magic sabre to keep him invisible among the huge crowds of monstrous inhabitants with their eyes placed in the middle of their chests. He reaches his bride, who tells him that the ape, in his mad passion for her, has revealed to her the secret talisman which gives power over all the jinn in the city. It takes the form of an eagle standing on a pillar with an inscription that she does not know. If Abu Mohammed fumigates it with musk, she tells him, the rebel jinn will muster and he will be able to command them to do whatever he wants. Abu Mohammed instantly orders them to seize and bind the ape, courteously asks his wife if she will consent to come back with him to Basra and, on her agreement, transfers his wife, himself and all the riches of the City of Brass to his house there. With the eagle talisman's power at his command, he then summons the monkey and shuts him up in a copper bottle sealed with a stopper of lead to keep him out of mischief for ever – or until another hero lets him out in the interests of another romance, another story.

The caliph is astonished by the adventures of Abu Mohammed, and makes him as many magnificent gifts in return as Abu Mohammed lavishes on him. The crown Zubayda was making is not mentioned again, and the story has been so stuffed with riches of every kind that the stone she coveted as the centrepiece has become a trifle.

CHAPTER TEN

The Word of the Talisman

'Tis true: there's magic in the web of it . . .

Shakespeare, *Othello*

.

I

THE TALE OF ABU MOHAMMED the Lazy combines two traditions: an Egyptian strand of eerie phenomena and powerful instrumental magic, and a story of trade and adventure in the East and the Far East which originates in Iraq. The monkey jinni begins as a poor maltreated creature, but changes into a malignant schemer; the effect is gripping, especially as his plans have been laid with such long-term foresight and have such a specific erotic purpose. By contrast with this wilfulness, our wastrel hero lacks all definition and volition; he is the plaything of chance, with no hint from the storyteller that he has been chosen for some reason of merit. Rather the opposite: there is comedy in the telling, with the scruffiness, the dopiness, the sheer hopelessness of the fifteen-year-old recognisable to most parents in any era. André Miquel points out that while Abu Mohammed's adventures coincide with Sinbad's in some respects, he is Sinbad's opposite in character: he drifts into things whereas Sinbad sets out with a goal. Abu Mohammed the lazy, the lackadaisical, the good-for-nothing who makes good, is one of the models that shapes Galland's Aladdin and all the comic disasters of pantomime Aladdins since. But he is also a living lesson in the ways of providence: what Allah gives, he gives according to his will, which is unfathomable. As Miquel wryly remarks, who is the caliph to deplore unmerited, unearned fortune beyond the wildest imagining?

The riches Abu Mohammed acquires are the true subject of the story, and al-Muzaffar is the ethical hero, the exemplary benefactor (a fairy godfather) who has no thought for his own gain. Throughout, the jinn occupy the ranks of the animals, in accordance with their heterogeneity in myth (monkey; cockerel; snakes; eagle). Through their agency, they bring the hero fabulous, manufactured treasures (money, jewelled mule saddles, brocade tents with jewel-encrusted skirts). Their connection to natural energies underlies the wealth they produce: the tale unfolds a story of international trade and literally animates the goods that form part of that trade. Jinn bring their owners measureless luxuries, as well as love and delight, a superfluity of pleasures and status made manifest in gold, jewels, fine cloths, perfumes and tableware. Yet the lists of riches punctuate the story so often that eyeskip sets in; listeners too would let their ears idle to the repetitions of jewels and the lovely words that name them. The flow is disrupted by the operation of talismans; these secure the natural forces which bring the riches, and they act as the instruments of reversal and counter-reversal in the narrative itself. The jinn and the talismans act in harness as the agents of the plot; they also embody happenstance itself, the workings of destiny.

By contrast with ensouled things like relics or fetishes, talismans form another class of charmed things, bringing luck or protection: things affected not by personal memories and feelings but by a kind of magnetic bond with an independent force – supernatural, divine or diabolical.

The word 'talisman' enters colloquial English principally by means of the translations of such stories of spell-binding, and their active, sometimes baneful, sometimes benevolent force irradiates the atmosphere of the most outlandish and impressive of the plots. In the same way as the fetish was imported from the imperial encounter in order to grasp attachments to inanimate things and shifting ideas of exchanges, financial and erotic, the term 'talisman', after it entered Western languages from the Middle East, also opens meanings accruing to things as they have circulated and exercised influence since the eighteenth century and into this new one.

The *OED* defines 'talisman' as 'an object imbued with magical power to offer protection or to inflict harm'. This limited definition could also apply to amulet, charm or periapt, but nuances in usage can be adduced to distinguish these magic objects and instruments. So how does a talisman differ, if at all? The derivation of the closely related term 'amulet' is not certain, but the a- here may be privative, from *a-moliri* meaning to avert or remove (soften?). Almost all dictionaries also characterise amulets as things worn on the person: the coral necklaces which baby Jesus wears in dozens of medieval and Renaissance paintings of the Madonna and Child, for example, linger from Egyptian and eastern Mediterranean magic practices. The rarer word 'periapt' also evokes something kept closely in contact with the body, from the Greek *peri-*, 'about' and possibly *haptein*, to touch. In both cases, the charms remain small and intimate and are not necessarily inscribed with verbal formulae. By contrast, talismans come in all shapes and sizes, and are imbued with their special properties and sphere of influence by the words written into them. Although they can be worn like lockets, they do not need to be kept about a person to work – indeed their efficacy even derives from their autonomy: their indwelling force can radiate regardless.

The use of protective and divinatory charms was widespread in antiquity before the establishment of Christianity and Islam, in the whole of the Hellenic and Judaic Middle East, though it is the Arabic word that has taken root since the Enlightenment. 'Talisman' was introduced into English in 1638 from French, where it was taken from Arabic *tilasm* (also *tilsim, tilism*, pl. *talasim*). These words were themselves adapted from Greek, *telesma. The Encyclopaedia of Islam* defines *tilsam* as 'an inscription with astrological and other magic signs or an object covered with such inscriptions, especially also with figures from the zodiacal circle . . .'

The word spread in English gradually in eighteenth-century Oriental tales, and became properly naturalised in the nineteenth century; a similar pattern occurred in French. It appears, for example, in the title of a lurid pamphlet of around 1770 about a magic gem belonging to Queen Catherine de' Médicis, who was widely suspected of necromancy. The term also took hold in other languages in the same period. The shadow of *telos*, Greek for goal, lingers in its meanings in these contexts: in ancient Greek, *telesma* surprisingly means simply 'money paid or to be paid'; other uses include 'tax', 'outlay', and, most significantly with regard to the development of 'talisman', 'a certified copy or certificate', often stamped with the symbolic power of a seal to give it specific value, significance and authority. A promissory note, an IOU, a wager, would fall under this first meaning. However, the stem *teles-* in Greek produced several related words applying in a religious context, as in *telesmos*, a consecration ceremony, for example, and *teles-ter,* a priest, or initiate, used by Plato in conjunction with *mantikos*, a seer. *Telesphorion*, still with the same root, describes a sorceress or ritual prostitute in the Greek translation of the Bible (Deut. 23:17/18). And that first attested use of 1638 simply adopts into English the word *telesmata,* used for consecrated statues set up in Egypt and Greece to protect city and community.

'Talisman' consequently entails something having been brought to fruition, completed, often a transaction or pact made for some sacred or religious purpose, with autonomous and often mysterious significance. Unlike the fetish it is not ascribed individual character or saturated with someone's presence. Instead it significantly settles into a European term for a charmed object in its own right, an amulet.

It is not difficult to see how the word eventually passed from practical acts of exchange towards a specified end, into the realm of the sacred where imagination is efficacious and changes reality. The connection remains especially strong in the case of seals: the power does not inhere in the object itself, but is released when it is used to stamp some other thing. This necessary act of transmission presupposes an inherent dynamic virtuality to the force inside the seal, easy to personify as a mobile energy force – a daimon, a jinni.

This origin of 'talisman' in forms of certification has rich implications. For looked at one way, money used to complete a payment possesses efficient power. The object's meaning radiates through the inscriptions it bears, often secret symbols authenticated by different, complex measures, like the emblems on banknotes and credit cards (I discuss this further in 'The Voice of the Toy', below). But its function shifts according to its referents. Consider the difference between a will and an indulgence – a will disposes of things in the world, while an indulgence guarantees the remission of punishment in the hereafter. Catholic indulgences, often profusely elaborated with many layers of official authentication and sanction, are indeed a form of talismanic certificate, and it is suggestive that the practice, enthusiastically promoted by cardinals and bishops in the fifteenth century, grew in the climate of crusading propaganda: is this an effect of contact? The new printing presses were not kept busy with learned works, but were pouring out hundreds of broadsides assuring the faithful that their sins could be ransomed by acquiring the document. The copy was as efficacious as the original: indeed the original did not matter.

Though the religious authorities of Islam did not use print to disseminate their reserves of grace, the talisman was essentially reproducible, and repetition did nothing to diminish its effects. Scribes made copies, and calligraphic expertise enhanced the value – and the power – of the document. In Mecca, certificates, some of them gorgeously illuminated, were sold to pilgrims to take home with an assurance of the grace they had received by doing the Hajj; some of them are substitutes for the pilgrimage itself. In cases when it could not be performed, their purchase could bring equal blessings.

The connection with writing as an act introducing meaning and value proves crucial to defining the talisman as distinct from the amulet; although talismans are seen as a subset of amulets by the leading scholars in the field, they are distinctively characterised by inscription. Sometimes enigmatic, sometimes expository, the texts written on them pack them with power; they also sometimes define their function, which varies in social contexts, as conveyed by so many stories in the *Nights*: protection against ill health, danger, poverty, nightmares (Pl. 5); success in childbearing, love, status; justice before the law and freedom from slander; luck in love, wealth and dreams. Remedies for specific purposes require specific formulae: to assure a flow of milk for a nursing mother, to withstand the onset of melancholy. Often the talismanic document is written out on paper, then rolled or folded into a wallet or a phylactery. (The exhibition of the Khalili collection at the Institut du monde arabe, Paris, in 2009 included a gilded talismanic wallet, signed by its maker and created specifically for a certain individual in 1712 to protect him against accidents and illness, and to liberate him should he be captured.)

The imagined outside forces, divine and usually benevolent, are activated chiefly by these words, and sometimes – but much less often – by depiction: word magic or image magic transforms raw matter into a symbolic object possessing power. These powers can be embodied in many different kinds of artefact, as long as the object is marked: words infuse the enchantment. And once done it can only be undone by applying immense knowledge of yet more powerful magic; the talismans' relationship to time appears to be central to their nature and they endure for aeons (Princess Tadmoura, and Solomon, have been lying there protected for hundreds of years). The jinn who animate things have transmuted into charmed things, activated by texts, which in turn become talismanic. In this way, the words of the story are translated into magic, into blessings.

II

The words on traditional talismans take many forms: the Ninety-Nine Names of God appear engraved on swords and scabbards; magic brass bowls are incised with prayers for the sick so that when filled with water, that water acquires healing powers by contact; sometimes such holy water was created by washing the hand-held blackboards on which children learned to read and write the Koran. Solomon is frequently invoked, his wisdom summoned by the pentacle or his seal or ring; sometimes all three combined. Storks and snakes and scorpions, powerful apotropaic symbols, are represented to secure the balance of the temperaments. The writings on the talismans need not be legible; indeed they gain in efficacy through their enigma and resistance to decipherment. The arabesque knots and imbrications are labyrinths to confuse the eye of enemies, as 'dazzle' camouflage bewilders aerial surveillance (non-sense is crucial to magic).

The British Museum general catalogue applies 'talisman' to a varied set of items ranging in time and in geography from North Africa to Asia: an astrological spell inscribed on a mid-tenth-century Daoist Chinese apron or girdle; a child's scarlet talismanic jacket from Ottoman Turkey embroidered all over with protective inscriptions; plaques from medieval Egypt with directions for finding treasure; and a painted flag by a contemporary Algerian-French artist, Rachid Koraïchi.

All these different kinds of thing – clothes, flags, school and household implements, medallions and stones – involve inscription; it is writing above all that defines the talisman and can consequently deepen our understanding of word magic in its currency today.

But it is not any text whatsoever that achieves the transformation of the thing in question from an ordinary object to a thing with talismanic power. The writings which charm it are magical, holy, and often hermetic and they frequently depend on underlying enigmatic systems, such as casting horoscopes and geomancy.

In Christian and Islamic cultures, the use of talismans was fraught, because magical devices were suspect, and black magic strongly disapproved of in the commentaries on the Koran as it was in Christian doctrine. With regard to Islamic amulets, Venetia Porter writes that

> Black magic as practised by 'illicit magicians' is condemned most strongly in the Hadith, while later Muslim lawyers attempted to clarify the separation between licit and illicit magic and what was tolerated. Although in general terms that which did no harm to others was accepted, the situation is highly complex, with Ibn Khaldun, for example, regarding all magic as illicit but distinguishing between charms and talismans in discussing magic, licit and illicit talismans.

The vast majority of Islamic examples in contemporary collections are pious and benign, but, as in so many apotropaic media, the danger that needs to be averted gives shape to the defence against it: the Gorgon head protects the wearer, the virgin martyr carries the weapons of her cruel death and protects against similar afflictions. St Apollonia carries the pincers which drew her teeth and is the patron saint of toothache and dentists. By analogy, a talismanic picture which protects children against nightmares reproduces a fearsome, blue, monstrous jinn flowing into the sleeping head of a child – the very scene which the image repels, or so it is hoped (Pl. 5). Talismans can turn hallowed or profane according to their maker or master, the powers invoked by them and the purposes for which they are made. They are ambiguous in the same way as the *pharmakon* – a remedy or a poison, depending on how they are applied.

The picture given in the *Nights* reveals a broader, less principled and far more capricious activity on the part of jinn, through the talismans where they sometimes dwell. But it is still writing that provides the particular and crucial characteristic, and writing figures in the *Arabian Nights* far more prominently than it does in the fairy tales of Perrault or the Grimm Brothers. The picaresque events in the life of a hero like Hasan of Basra move from document to document – this is an early epistolary romance, with the difference that fairies and sorcerers are letter-writers, too. The *Arabian Nights* often mentions without particular astonishment that a heroine can read and write – even when she is apparently a slave, like Zumurrud in the tale of her love of Ali Shar. In 'Hasan of Basra', we are told that Hasan is a good scholar, encouraged by his mother who cannot herself read and write, though she recites many poems by heart.

The Topkapi Museum in Istanbul holds the largest collection in the world of talismans in the form of clothes; nearly a hundred articles of dress, the earliest dating from the fifteenth century, such as the chemise made for Prince Djem (1425–95), and the most recent from the nineteenth century when the practice ended – officially – with the modernising of the Ottoman court. Shirts, skullcaps, tunics and other articles were worn for protection against every kind of harm – under armour in battle, for example – as well as for success in love and fertility. A child's talismanic shirt from Mogul India, fifteenth or sixteenth century, on exhibition in Paris, still shows dark stains of the child's sweat down the middle of the back, on the chest, and under the arms; stains also saturated with human hope, with parental wishing.

These talismanic clothes are astonishing artefacts: the robe of Sultan Murad IV (1623–40), for example, is richly gilded, patterned with circles and densely written all over in different coloured inks, with much gleaming decoration (Pl. 17a & b). Other Turkish noblemen's clothes from the same era have their entire surface damascened in exquisite geometric compositions, with diapers, medallions, and panels appliquéd on to the cloth, until the fabric becomes a different form of sacred illuminated manuscript or pilgrimage certificate.

The cotton from which the shirts are made has been treated with starch, so that they can be written on, indeed literally 'in-scribed', written *into,* and the serried, calligraphic ornament mingles different scripts – one so feathery it is called *ghubar i,* meaning 'like dust'. These inscriptions include the Beautiful Names of God, with certain ones emerging as the favourites; others reprise Sura 12, 'Joseph', from the Koran, which describes how Jacob, who had gone blind from crying over Joseph's disappearance, recovered his sight when he passed over his eyes a tunic which Joseph had sent from Egypt with his brothers. This passage gave clear approval to miracle-working garments, and was invoked especially for protection against such misfortunes as falling into wells and being held captive in dungeons.

These scriptural quotations and prayers are mixed with sacred emblems, such as Solomon's seal, and 'magic squares' in which numbers are substituted for letters to make arcane rebuses. The footprint of the Prophet, his sandals, his bow, arrows and sabre, the forked sword of Ali (for putting out both eyes of his enemy), and, sometimes, protector animals such as serpents and scorpions, are included to support the prophylactic value of wearing the chemise or other dress.

Talismanic garments form a group of magical instruments, but they are clearly each of them unique, carefully customised for their intended wearer. Court astrologers were instructed by the chief physician at the court when such a garment was needed in the palace, and they cast the wearer's horoscope in order to determine the exact hour propitious for the specialist scribes to begin the work of inscription; several years sometimes passed before it was completed, and again the time was carefully divined and met, the hour recorded on the fabric. The enchantment, like an individual jinn at their command, has been infused into them in every possible pertinent and particular detail.

The custom had travelled to Turkey from the East with astrology and, like the ornamentation of Ottoman damasks, bears the imprint of Chinese aesthetics and manufactures; the process of their making echoes the elaborate horoscopes and geomantic procedures of imperial Chinese traditions. The Turkish talismans, taking the form of articles of dress, are not trifles, but precious and sophisticated artefacts, élite articles produced by learning and skill, and credited with powers to hold sickness, death, disappointment and sterility at bay for the highest members of an intensely hierarchical society. They are above all produced as entirely characteristic artefacts by a literate culture which attaches very high value to the written word.

The counterparts of such talismanic clothes can be glimpsed in numerous tales of the *Nights* – from the many sumptuous magic garments bestowed by jinn on their favourites, to the flags which the father in 'Abu Mohammed the Lazy' posts at the corners of his spell. It is clear that talismans secure strong external guarantees for something that already has high value – the body of the Sultan or his child. But in the stories another valuable correlation often shows: the talisman serves to protect the virginity of a daughter (again, as in 'Abu Mohammed the Lazy') or the honour of a young woman, and it acts by synecdoche to figure her maidenhead.

As Wendy Doniger has discussed, an exchange of rings betokens the union of two lovers. In some of the stories of the *Nights*, a magic talisman takes the form of such a jewel. In the 'Tale of Camar al-Zaman and Princess Badoura', for example, Camar becomes curious and takes Badoura's gem from inside her clothes while she is sleeping; he discovers it is 'a carnelian engraven with unknown figures and characters'. The early English version of this much-loved story goes on:

> This carnelian, says the prince to himself, must have something extra-ordinary in it, or my princess would not be at the trouble to carry it with her. And indeed it was Badoura's talisman, or a scheme of her nativity, drawn from the constellations of heaven, which the queen of China had given her daughter, as a charm that would keep her from any harm as long as she had it about her.

So here the storyteller associates the Princess of China with astrological magic, inscribed on to her special protective charm.

Camar's act of curiosity is punished, an unusual occurrence with respect to a male protagonist, when a bird plucks the gem from his hands, and he finds himself wandering far from Badoura in pursuit of the bird. The talisman is evoked in other versions as 'blood-red jewels'; its privy place on Badoura's person, its hitherto unknown presence concealed in her clothes, ties it unmistakably to her most intimate and erotic persona, to her 'jewels' which have been stolen earlier in the story while she slept. (In European languages the stone's name actually points to its associations with flesh: it comes from Latin *caro, carnis*; however, the root of the Arabic word, *'aqiq*, comes from the verb to cut – perhaps on account of its aptness for carving?)

The stolen talisman keeps drawing a scarlet thread between Camar and Badoura, from one improbable episode to another, as it makes its way back to her and acts as the token which sparks the recognition when Badoura, in disguise as a male prince, rediscovers her jewel in the jars of olives in which Camar has shipped his treasure. She waits to produce it during the remarkable bed-trick seduction scene.

This was one of the most popular romances in the book, after Galland translated it for the first published volumes. (The story broke off before the darker second part, 'The Tale of Amgrad and Assad', in which each of Camar's two wives falls in love with the other woman's son, Phaedra-style.) The erotic reverberations of such gems are captured with wicked delight, for example, in Diderot's *Les Bijoux indiscrets* (1748), in which the jewels in question are the private parts of the Sultan's wives, and also, less salaciously, in *Le Saphir merveilleux, ou Le Talisman du bonheur* (The Marvellous Sapphire, or the Talisman of Happiness, 1803), a spirited parable by Mme de Genlis, in which the featured jewel changes colour if the woman who wears it is unfaithful (see more on both later).

Badoura's charm is made of carnelian, as are many other talismans in the *Nights*, for example Maryam's in 'Aladdin of the Beautiful Moles', which summons the magic flying bed for the newly wed lovers towards the end of the tale. Carnelian is the favourite material of such magic amulets, as can be seen from the collection in the British Museum, since the Prophet liked the stone best of all, it was said (though Muhammad himself recommended lack of ostentation) (Pls. 16a,d).

Venetia Porter's superb British Museum catalogue includes numerous talismans and amulets in carnelian in different strengths of glowing reds to browns, ranging from pine resin to cranberry relish to caramelised demerara sugar; such amulets can be very small, and exquisite in trans-lucency and workmanship – the engraving into the gemstone performed with fine pointed string-driven drills (Pls. 16a–f). The properties of stones were expounded in every aspect by the Arabic scholar al-Tifaschi in his book, *Best Thoughts on the Best of Stones*, written in the thirteenth century, but even without knowledge of this kind, the minerals in themselves offer richly satisfying surfaces and temperatures, for touching even more than contemplating: cool, dry, austere, almost lunar, pale or yellow-grey chalcedony, varied highly polished slippery streaked agates, sardonyx, jasper, obsidian, sard, jade. Rock crystal, perceived to be like frozen water, was especially suited to spells for finding wells and against dying of thirst or drowning. Amuletic stones, for putting in your pocket or wearing on your finger or dangling from your belt, could be made of all these varieties of rock, but also of silver, brass and gold. The list sounds the kind of litany that evokes earthly splendour in the *Nights*, and punctuates the wondrous fortunes that fall into the hands of lucky protagonists. In spite of the Prophet's warning against display, one group of amulets are medallions struck in gold, closely resembling Byzantine coins and pierced for wearing.

Like other imported terms – totem and taboo, fetish and shaman – the concept of the talisman, when it reaches Europe and takes root there, comes couched in a borrowed vocabulary in order to designate a form of other knowledge, developed in a non-Western culture.

III

In William Beckford's novel *Vathek*, written in 1782, the Giaour or heathen offers the Sultan mysterious talismanic sabres, which will lead him to the wisdom of Solomon and the pre-Adamite kings. The dramatic scene, turning on the magical inscriptions on the blades, assumes the reader understands the term. Genlis's enchanted stone, if acquired by anyone unworthy, will always be lost, or stolen; on the other hands it will assure 'a generous and just man . . . the fulfilment of his hopes and peace of mind'. Genlis uses the sapphire to set in motion a dramatic revenge plot with several recognition scenes: Zournea, the female protagonist, is a shameless hussy who throws over the love of the noble-hearted Aboukar for a rose pearl necklace an admirer offers her. But Aboukar unmasks her by means of the stone, marries instead the daughter of the Sultan, and becomes Grand Vizier. The tale ends by telling us that, since that time, the marvellous sapphire has passed through a thousand different hands, and been lost and stolen many times, but 'For a little while, it has been in France . . . for our happiness.'

The tale aims at our moral improvement as readers, as well as punishing Zournea and others who have done the hero wrong. But Genlis's more subtle targets include Diderot himself, for the action of the jewel, as it exposes one guilty woman after another, relates it to the device he had used in *Les Bijoux indiscrets* (*The Indiscreet Jewels*) in which the Sultan's ring makes the other jewels, his wives' vaginas, reveal their innermost thoughts. Both writers recognised the narrative efficiency of such a magic thing and revelled in it, but the stories they tell, while dressed in oriental costume, develop differently. Diderot's satire targets contemporary mores with outrageous boldness; Genlis slyly parodies the conventions of an *Arabian Nights* story, but chooses a traditional folk tale not found in the book about a magic truth-telling dress or some such object. In both their hands, the power of the talisman has a divinatory quality, which is applied to make psychological revelations.

Goethe, in the *West-Eastern Divan* (1819), his cycle of poems in the style of oriental lyric, invokes talismans at the start of the book; after the opening two poems in which he talks of himself and his 'hegira' – his flight to the east – he turns towards the world he is embracing and singles out 'Charms' as the first, defining element:

> *Talisman*, cornelian seal,
> Brings believers bliss and weal . . .
> It drives evil from the ground,
> Guards you and the earth around
> When the engraved words resound
> Purely Allah's name invoking . . .

He then compares engraved gems favourably with inscriptions on paper; a signet ring, he writes, fits the Most High into the smallest space.

In England, six years after Goethe's long orientalising poem appeared,

Walter Scott published *The Talisman* (1825), to much more acclaim and a far larger readership than either Genlis or Goethe had enjoyed. This novel presents a rich form of cross-cultural interaction, as Scott mingles beliefs from the Scottish Highlands with magical thinking of the Middle East. One of the most significant figures in the history of folklore and the re-evaluation of popular legends as literature, Scott chooses to set his story of high deeds of valour during a time of confrontation, the Crusades, and borrow from the imagery, vocabulary and beliefs of the historic enemy, the Saracens. He transmutes conflict into reciprocity, for he describes how, when Richard the Lionheart is lying sick in his tent, Saladin the arch-enemy of the Christians visits his enemy clandestinely and, with a powerful talisman, cures him, out of the magnanimity of his soul. In this way Scott rewrites history in order to stage a scene of exchange that projects into the past the eclectic way he, as a storyteller, keeps an open mind. Whether fairy lore from the glens or Islamic magic from the bazaar and the desert, Scott knew a good story when he came upon one and he recognised no barriers between cultures or faiths.

The story appeared as one of the Waverley novels, and was a huge popular success (there are dozens and dozens of editions, year on year, in the British Library). Scott explains in the preface, written in 1832, that 'A principal incident in the story, is that from which the title is derived. Of all people who ever lived, the Persians were perhaps most remarkable for their unshaken credulity in amulets, spells, periapts, and similar charms, framed, it was said, under the influence of particular planets, and bestowing high medical powers, as well as the means of advancing men's fortunes in various manners.' But Scott then leaves the Persians and their charms and turns to a local story of the heroic era of the Crusades, about the so-called Lee-penny, a healing charm belonging to the Lockhart family of Lee.

According to this legend, after Sir Simon Lockhart had captured an emir, the prisoner's mother came to the Crusaders' camp to ransom him, and spread out before Sir Simon a fortune of treasure. But as she was counting the gold, a dull stone set with a coin fell into the heap, and she instantly swooped to pick it out and take it back. The knight insisted that he wanted that stone and would accept no ransom without it. She agreed, and explained that 'The water in which it was dipt, operated as a styptic, as a febrifuge, and possessed several other properties as a medical talisman.' Sir Simon brought it back with him to Scotland, and its reputation grew. Scott professes himself surprised that the Church allowed it, 'when the Church of Scotland chose to impeach many other cures which savoured of the miraculous, as occasioned by sorcery', but added, without irony, 'there can be no reason for doubting that water which has been poured on the Lee-penny furnishes a congenial cure'. He does however add that 'Of late, [its powers] have been chiefly restricted to the cure of persons bitten by mad dogs . . .'

Scott's adoption of the word for his title holds even more interest in relation to the unacknowledged grafting of one concept onto another over time. For the legend of the Lee-penny touches the cult of the national hero, King Robert the Bruce, who on his deathbed asked Sir James Douglas to take his heart back to Jerusalem and bury it there. Sir Simon Lockhart was part of the embassy, and when Douglas died en route, Lockhart fulfilled the mission. The Lockhart family are also entangled in Scott's personal myth-making: in 1820, his daughter married Gibson Lockhart, who would become the author's monumental biographer.

The legendary Lee-penny, brought back from the Crusades, was evoked as a talisman by Sir Walter Scott, with protective powers, especially over mad dogs.

So the talisman of Scott's title travels back from a mythic pilgrimage to the Middle East; through a sequence of fictive substitutions, it leaves its place of origin and makes the transition to Scotland and into Scott's posterity. An emir's ransom against a penny set in a stone, a king's heart against a talisman, a story for a growing reputation. In this trail of different kinds of potent and charmed thing, the magic of Catholic relics joins the magic of the inscribed Islamic talisman, and gets thoroughly entangled.

In England in 1852, Henry Allen Wedgwood made up a long pica-resque fairy tale for his family, *The Bird Talisman: An Eastern Tale*, which was so much enjoyed by them that his wife Emma, who was Charles Darwin's sister, reprinted it for the next generation, as she reports in the preface to the 1887 edition. The book shows every sign of its origin in a household of wide reading and scientific inquisitiveness, as the author embroiders an effervescent adventure about a plucky and quick-witted young girl, the granddaughter of a King of Cashmere who has been usurped by his wicked son-in-law and the latter's even more wicked second wife, the heroine's evil stepmother. Murder plots, poisonous brews, narrow shaves, disguises, slave auctions, benevolent gypsies, talking parrots, and other high-spirited elements from the wonder tale and the travel literature of the time follow thick and fast, and the whole fantastic web spins out from a magic ring – the talisman of the title: 'it was with this ring that the famous enchanter, Moozuffer, ruled over the birds, and by their help worked so many wonders'. (His name has been borrowed from the benefactor who gives the monkey to Abu Mohammed the Lazy, while some of his other traits pick up on the powers of other theurgists – Solomon and al-Nasr, the King of the Birds from Sufi legend.) This Solomonic gem gives the wearer the power to understand the speech of animals, especially birds, and the wearer can then order them to do anything he or she wants. In this story, it has been given to the deposed king by a jackdaw he kindly saved from drowning, and when he realises his granddaughter is in danger, he sends it to her with a talking parrot to help her survive the machinations against her.

In spite of the supernatural presence of the ring, Wedgwood strongly shows the meliorist and pragmatic tendencies of Victorian children's writers, in stressing the good in everyone (except the stepmother and her sidekick the eunuch Baboof, a heedlessly racist caricature). He also chooses to avoid conjuring jinn or fairies and instead details the ingenious, natural devices the clever heroine and her staunch allies use to extricate themselves from a pickle. Their adventures are properly far-fetched, yet in keeping with the genre, they offer rationalising, quasi-possible moves by bringing in natural history (the family were not Darwins for nothing): for example, when the heroine is hidden in a tower without a staircase, she is too heavy for her friends the jackdaws to spring her by carrying her down, so they enlist larger and more powerful birds, first the parrot ('such a clumsy flier') and then an owl and his owl wife, who manage the airborne descent. Then, after several more excitements, the King of Cashmere rides to the rescue:

> High up in the air appeared a flock of mountain eagles, flying all close together, and in the midst of them was a large, dark object. They came rapidly over the plain; and, sweeping over the heads of the multitude, a man was seen, suspended in a sort of chair by means of long slender poles, and cords, which the eagles held in their claws, and [they] seemed to obey the voice of the old man – who wore a hermit's dress – and to follow his directions.

This vision from 1852 of a *deus ex machina* was inspired by the earlier fantasy flying vehicle Francis Godwin had illustrated in his book, *The Man in the Moone* (1638); the original woodcut was reworked for *The Bird Talisman*. It makes for a splendid rescue scene and represents vividly the way in which nineteenth-century uses of stranger magic, including the extravagant plotting and the magical devices of the *Nights*, attempted to domesticate and sweeten their strangeness into a normative, even feasible flying machine. (In Chapter 16, 'Thought Experiments: Flight before Flight', I explore in more depth the powerful desire of readers from the mid-eighteenth century onwards to match reality of some kind to the fantastic ideas of stories in the *Nights* and other like concoctions.)

How the imported word 'talisman' filled a semantic gap can be seen when reading Arrigo Boito's libretto for Verdi's *Otello*. The mischief-maker itself – the handkerchief Othello gives Desdemona – has become a talisman. In 1604, as we heard, Shakespeare's Othello had limned the love charm's potency, magnifying its dark provenance by stressing its origins in the far distant magic of sibyls, and the ancient Egyptian art of mummi-fication. But Shakespeare did not yet have to hand the word that came effortlessly to Boito in the late 1880s:

> Desdemona, woe if you lose it, woe!
> A powerful witch designed the secret thread
> In which is placed a talisman's deep bane.

By the end of the nineteenth century the word 'talismano' had arrived in Italian to give, as words do, a habitation and a name to something long intimated but not clearly designated.

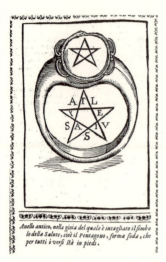

Anello antico, nella gioia del quale è intagliato il simbo lo della Salute, cioè il Pentagono, forma soda, che per tutti i versi stà in piedi.

Talismans carry magic inscriptions that release power: since antiquity Solomon's seal or pentacle has been a favourite cipher (Italian, seventeenth century).

Throughout the opera, the talismanic qualities of the handkerchief give it a quasi-autonomous power, greater than it possesses in the play. It becomes not only Iago's tool but in some way his emanation, his daimonic alter ego. Cassio and Iago sing a marvellous lilting duet to the transparent web, which takes on a spirit flimsiness:

> White and lighter than a snowflake,
> than a cloud woven from the air of heaven.

The thing itself dissolves: as with a talisman, the agent of its magical power lies beyond sensory perception, instilled into the material handkerchief by invisible arts that have transmuted its nature, just as a banknote or an IOU ceases to be a mere piece of paper.

The concept of the talisman may only shadow the character of modern money, but it emerges fully fleshed by contrast in other zones of experience, not least contemporary Catholic cult. The word offered oriental camouflage for concepts already in operation in modern Europe and the wider West. In the rue du Bac on the Left Bank in Paris, a street which follows an old crooked path to the river where a ferry (*bac*) used to ply the Seine, still stands the magnificent domed, glass and steel department store, Le Bon Marché. In 1838, when M. and Mme Boucicaut opened its doors, it inaugurated a new 'activité moderne', as Emile Zola called it: spectacular shopping – display, entertainment, combined with trade. The vast emporium heaped up its abundant goods all together; gone were the small specialist boutiques and individual market stalls: this was the beginning of modern consumerism – in a palace of superfluity and plenty. The pastimes of window-gazing, window-shopping and promiscuous serial acquisition began; they brought with them new forms of relationship between buyers and sellers, men and women, rich and less rich – a principal dynamic of urban life which defined the urban crowd, the aspirations and ease of the bourgeoisie and their glittering, phantasmagoric city. When other department stores followed, the names gestured eastwards: Le Bazar de l'Hôtel de Ville (known to Parisians as BHV) and La Samaritaine (named after a bas-relief of the Good Samaritan on the Pont Neuf). Modern mass consumption was cast in the language of the fabulous East.

Across the street from Le Bon Marché, a stone-built convent occupies a sizeable city plot, and a crowd also streams through its less fancy double doors into the paved *cour*, to enter the chapel on the side, where the supernatural events that took place in 1830 are pictured in pretty candy colours – frosted sugar silver, sky-blue, rose and gold mosaics and white marble statues. On an ordinary weekday in November 2009 the chapel was full for the afternoon mass, many people in the congregation with bandaged limbs, some using sticks or, several in wheelchairs.

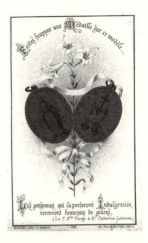

Catherine Labouré (1806–76), a young nun of little education and from a modest farm background, was in the first months of her noviciate in the order of the Sisters of Charity when she received her principal vision; it took place during the July Days of the 1830 uprising, and the fighting in the streets, close to the convent's site, terrified

'Have a medal struck according to this model . . .' said the Virgin Mary in a vision to a young nun, Catherine Labouré, in Paris in 1830. It was done, and the cult of the Miraculous Medal became an international, popular success.

the community. So in the same moment that Delacroix was inspired to paint *Liberty at the Barricades*, embodied by a passionate woman of the people, the Mother of God appeared in another street in Paris close by, in 'a rustle of white silk'. First she was holding a globe of the world but then she opened her hands and streams of light poured from the sparkling rings on her outspread fingers. She promised to protect Catherine and everyone in France and also in the rest of the world from all dangers; as an aureole appeared to outline the vision, she told Catherine to have a medal struck of her apparition: 'The graces will be abundant for those who wear it with confidence.'

Two years later, during a ferocious cholera outbreak in Paris, the medal was first struck, not through any action on Catherine's own part (she was then working in another convent, an old people's home, in a very menial capacity), but through the enthusiasm of a priest, Father J.-M. Aladel, a Lazarist (Vincentian) missionary who brought the medal to the attention of the Archbishop of Paris – who approved the practice.

The miraculous medal presents a cipher, made up of the initials of Mary and Jesus, stars and flames, two hearts, and the Virgin's promise. The resemblance to a seal or hermetic symbol is strong (it looks very like that infamous 'talisman magique et superstitieux' of the Queen Catherine de'

Médicis denounced by the abbé Fauvel in 1770), as the medal's efficacy derives from these intertwined and enigmatic inscriptions.

The cult caught on straight away: news of the medal spread through the networks of the missions, and the leaflets at the shrine in Paris today claim that ten million were adopted in the first ten years of the medal's approval – in the United States, China, Russia as well as throughout Europe. The practice was not confined to the unlettered or the poor: John Henry Newman had a special devotion to the Miraculous Medal. When he was preparing for the priesthood in Rome in 1846–47, he was lodged in the College of the Propaganda of the Faith, and could see from the window the church of S. Andrea delle Fratte, where Our Lady of the Miraculous Medal had appeared, four years earlier, to Alphonse Ratisbonne, a Jew from Strasbourg; Ratisbonne was fiercely loyal to his Jewish faith, but was instantly converted, subsequently becoming the founder of an active network of Catholic missions in the Holy Land.

Newman often expressed queasiness about Catholic superstition, yet this scholar and future cardinal, declared Blessed in 2010, was so impressed by the miracle of the medal that he included a statue of the Virgin's apparition in Paris in the portrait made of him in Rome in 1847. This was the year that Pope Pius IX officially recognised the association promoting the medal, the Sodality of the Children of Mary. The most industrious pontiff of the modern Church, he tirelessly consolidated church discipline around papal authority and reinvigorated symbols in the interests of worldwide Catholic unity; he followed up his endorsement of the Miraculous Medal with the related dogma of the Immaculate Conception seven years later, which declared the Virgin Mary free from original sin.

When I was about fourteen I became a Child of Our Lady after careful preparation with Mother Bridget, our headmistress, a woman of fierce, frustrated brilliance; my new inclusion in the Sodality was symbolised by the Miraculous Medal on a wide azure blue moiré ribbon over my uniform on feast days but under it, on a less splendid chain, in the ordinary course of the week.

On sale in the shop of the shrine on the rue du Bac, the Miraculous Medal is still rather tinny, and I remember how I found this disappointing when I was a child. However much the accompanying literature protests strongly that there is nothing powerful or divine in the medal itself but only in God to whom it connects, its affinity with talismans, in appearance as well as function, is patent.

The Church denies that it approves magic in any form: 'The medal, shown to Sister Catherine Labouré by the Blessed Virgin in this chapel, is only a piece of metal. We must not consider it to be a talisman or an amulet with magical powers, this would be futile gullibility . . .' But it then continues: 'The Blessed Virgin attached a particular efficacy to the medal. The Church has in fact always accepted that relics, statues, medals and scapulars produce miracles.'

The Miraculous Medal was not the only talisman I was given as a Catholic girl. We were also encouraged to wear a scapular, in this case an image of Jesus stamped and stitched on to two small squares of brown homespun attached by narrow blue ribbons, which I as a young girl wore round my neck and under my clothes to symbolise my devotion to Christ's sufferings. It was meant to copy in little the long contrasting overtunic worn by monks – white over black in the case of the Dominicans, lighter brown over darker brown in the Franciscan order, and so forth. Wearing it, we were imitating monks and nuns who were themselves imitating the poverty of Christ. The scapular came with all kinds of guarantees of protection: like the prayer book in the pocket of a soldier, which miraculously stands between him and the bullet which would have killed him, a scapular could ward off temptations and dangers, or so I believed when I was a young girl. I cherished the stringy brown thing – until I lost it, somehow. It was definitely amuletic, according to the dictionary definitions of amulets and periapts as worn around the neck, and it was not a relic. It was a charm – lucky, cheap, trivial – a fairing, but potent; more precisely, however, it was a talisman, in the sense in which I now understand the term, because it was charged with apotropaic power by the printed image and words inscribed on it and the elaborate chain of meaning stitched into it.

The Reformation extirpated the traditional talismans of Christian worship: relics, indulgences and charms. But such objects of Catholic cult, denounced as magic and heretical by Luther and Calvin, are treated far more mildly and inclusively today, in the new climate of ecumenical tolerance. Some Anglo-Catholic churches have restored the old ways: at Walsingham, the Catholic pilgrimage church is austere compared to its Protestant cousin in the same ancient cult site of 'Our Lady'. The relics of St Thérèse of Lisieux, who died in 1897 at the age of twenty-four, have been touring the world, and were welcomed into York Minster by the Dean. 'In my little way there are only ordinary things,' she said, and this assurance has more resonance than she may have intended. One of her relics was even taken into outer space by an astronaut. Pope Benedict XVI supports the revived practice of indulgences and has granted pilgrims to the relics a plenary indulgence, a complete relaxing of a sentence to hell for their sins to date.

Story 9
Marouf the Cobbler

MAROUF THE COBBLER'S LIFE IS made a misery by his wife, a harridan who subjects him to her whims and beats him when he fails to produce what she wants. He finds it hard to earn a living at his trade; nobody seems to have their shoes mended any more. One day, she demands that he bring her back a sweetmeat – shredded wheat drenched in wild honey. No work comes his way that day, but the baker takes pity on him and advances him the money he needs to buy the sweetmeat, nicely cooked in butter but steeped in cane sugar. 'It was worthy of a king's table,' says Shahrazad. But Fatima, Marouf's wife, flies into a rage at the sight of it and hits him so hard she knocks out a tooth. Seizing him by his beard, she drags him out and denounces him to the neighbours for his failures as a husband. They manage to calm her down. But once back home, she swears she will beat Marouf black and blue if he doesn't bring her back a honey-cake the following day.

He's barely set up shop again the next morning when he's summoned to court: his wife has issued a complaint against him. He finds himself brought before the magistrate, where his wife is weeping, claiming he beat her and nursing a supposedly broken arm; but the magistrate has compassion for Marouf after hearing his side of the story, gives him money to buy the cake and tells the couple to go home and stop quarrelling.

Matters do not improve: and eventually, unable to work after pawning his tools to pay his legal costs, and goaded beyond endurance, Marouf runs away.

There's a downpour and, soaked through, he reaches a ruined warehouse outside the walls of Cairo. He is about to settle for the night when the wall splits open and a huge jinni appears, crying out, 'Why have you disturbed me in this way tonight? I have lived here for two hundred years and nobody has entered and disturbed me as you are doing. Tell me what you are looking for and I'll help you – because my heart is seized with pity for you.'

Marouf tells the jinni his story, and the jinni asks him if he would like to travel so far away his wife would lose all trace of him.

'Oh yes,' says Marouf.

'Then climb on to my back,' says the jinni.

They fly all through the night until the following dawn when the jinni deposits Marouf on the summit of a mountain.

From this moment, his fortunes are altogether changed.

Marouf the cobbler discovers he has arrived at a splendid city that would normally take a year to reach from Cairo; its inhabitants are stunned by his account of his speedy travels. A merchant riding by scolds the crowd roundly for their discourtesy, gathers up Marouf and takes him home: he reveals himself to be Ali, son of Marouf's old friend from the Cairo souk, Ahmad the perfume vendor, who himself fled the city twenty years ago after his father beat him for stealing Christian books from their churches and selling them for pocket money. Ali begins to tell Marouf how he has prospered by borrowing money, buying goods on credit and cultivating his customers, and he advises Marouf not to tell the story of his real circumstances (as nobody will believe him) but to take a thousand dinars, which Ali offers him, and set up as a merchant waiting for his caravan to come in. Marouf is to come to the bazaar in the morning, where Ali will greet him like a long-lost colleague, and then they will banter together until it is clear that Marouf's awaited caravan is laden with fantastic fabrics in huge quantities 'And always give alms lavishly,' adds Ali. That way, people will be convinced of Marouf's great wealth.

Marouf follows his advice to the letter; he takes orders in advance for every kind of luxury cloth, and scatters the money here and there to the beggars in the streets and, later, to the petitioners who present themselves at his door. When at dinner with friends or in the market with colleagues, he boasts of the jewels and silks on their way; a debt of 60,000 dinars piles up, all distributed to the poor, and there is still no news of the caravan. Ali becomes furious: things have gone too far. But the ruler of the country believes that Marouf must be amazingly rich, or he would not throw away so much wealth, and decides, much to his vizier's disgust, to marry him to his daughter to secure Marouf's fortune for himself. The vizier observes, 'I believe him to be nothing but a crook, and crooks always bring ruin to covetous men.'

The ruler resolves to test Marouf by offering him a fabulous vast pearl. When Marouf appears before him, he continues to boast that he will give every one of his creditors double what they want in the form they want – gold, silver, jewels, goods. Marouf takes the pearl and it shatters; he expresses contempt for it – nothing but a piece of coral – and promises the king any number of pearls the same size.

The marriage to the king's daughter is planned: Marouf now asks the vizier to advance him, while he waits for the caravan to arrive, the dowry he needs – to lavish on the princess, her train of attendants, and on a thousand beggars. The king gives him the keys to his treasury, the sheikh is summoned to conduct the service and the wedding takes place.

Marouf and the princess make love in utter delight. But still no caravan, and the palace treasury is almost empty. The vizier eventually persuades the king that the princess must ask Marouf for the truth. As soon as she asks him straight, he admits everything – his termagant wife, his flight, his cobbling trade, his penury. But the princess does not want to be shamed, or married off to someone else, and besides, she loves her husband, so she orders him to escape, taking with him money from her private funds, and to set up in business in a town nearby and prosper. When her father dies, she will send him word to come home.

Marouf accepts, asking only to be allowed to make love to her one more time. He departs, and she presents her father with a letter which has been delivered to her, she says, by one of the guards of Marouf's caravan, reporting that it had been set upon by Bedouin bandits, hence the delay, and hence the sudden departure of Marouf, who has left to join them and bring back his cargo.

Riding out alone in the desert, Marouf weeps, sick with love and longing for Dunya – Shahrazad lets slip the princess's name for the first time in the story, a name very close to that of her sister Dunyazad, who has been her own accomplice night after night. After giving vent to his despair, Marouf meets a peasant ploughing a field with two oxen; the man offers to fetch food for him from the village and sets off. While he's waiting for him to return, Marouf decides to help him with the ploughing, to pay him back for his kindness; as he sets to work, the ploughshare strikes something, and the animals have to stop. Examining the ground, Marouf finds the blade caught in a gold ring attached to a marble slab the breadth of a millstone. When he lifts it, he sees that it leads to stairs; he goes down, and finds himself in a bathhouse giving on to four chambers, the first filled to the ceiling with gold, the second with emeralds, pearls and coral; the third with jacinths, rubies and turquoises; the fourth with diamonds, precious metals and other gems. In the middle of the chamber stands a casket of pure crystal filled with solitaire diamonds, each as large as a hazelnut. On this is placed a small golden box the size of a lemon. Inside it, Marouf finds a ring engraved with 'talismanic names and formulae interlaced like the tracks of ants on the ground'.

He rubs it, and the jinni of the ring replies, 'Here I am, your wishes

will be granted: do you want to make a country prosper, lay waste a
city, kill a king, dig a river, or other things of that kind? Whatever you
desire shall be yours by the grace of God, the almighty ruler, creator
of night and day. I am the servant of this ring, at the orders of whoever
possesses it.'

The jinni is one of a myriad of his kind: he informs Marouf of the
dizzy number of species of jinn under his command. His name is 'Father
of Prosperity' – Abu'l-Sa'adat – and the treasure Marouf has stumbled
on is the treasure of Shaddad, son of Ad, the legendary founder of Iram-
of-the-High Columns.

With the help of 800 of the jinni's beautiful young children, the treasure
is carried out of the subterranean chamber and loaded into coffers. The
children turn themselves into mules and Mamelukes to transport it in a
vast caravan escorted by a hundred outriders; other jinn are summoned
and metamorphose into splendidly caparisoned horses with saddles of gold.
Marouf asks if the jinni can obtain precious fabrics as well – from Egypt,
Syria, India, Persia, Byzantium? The jinni says that in a single night he can
load a hundred of his mule-children with all Marouf desires.

In the midst of all these dazzling wonders, the peasant returns with
a bowl of lentils and barley for Marouf, as he had promised. Marouf
welcomes him and tells him he will eat his lentils, and nothing else.
When the bowl stands empty, he fills it with gold and gives it to the
peasant, telling him to join him in the city later.

The following morning, after the mules laden with silks and fabrics
have duly arrived, Marouf writes to his father-in-law and sends the letter
with the jinni as messenger.

From this moment on, Marouf's glory grows: he's reunited wth the
princess and lavishes more and more fabulous riches on her and her
attendants, on the royal coffers, on the people. Eventually the vizier, always
suspicious, burning with envy and curiosity, persuades the king to take
Marouf out for a picnic and keep pouring the wine till he tells his story.

When Marouf reveals the power of the ring, the vizier seizes it, and
when Abu'l-Sa'adat appears orders him to throw Marouf into the most
desolate and distant wilderness where he will find nothing to eat or to
drink. 'May he die of hunger and grief without anybody knowing it.'

The vizier orders the jinni to dispose of the king in the same place
and manner as Marouf; he then summons the princess to marry him.
She asks that at least he wait for the legal period of widowhood to elapse
and for the marriage contract to be duly drawn up. He refuses, so she
decides to trick him and plays up sweetly to his every wish, her only
thought to regain the ring.

Which she does – and when the jinni appears, she orders him to bring back her father and her husband instantly. When they return, she takes charge, tells her father to make Marouf his Grand Vizier, and refuses to relinquish the ring. The former vizier is horribly tortured and executed.

For six years matters continue in this fashion until her father dies and Marouf becomes Sultan in his place. She now has a child, a boy. But when he is five years old, she falls mortally ill, and on her deathbed she hands over the ring to Marouf.

A few nights later he wakes, sensing someone in his bedroom, and sees a fright of a woman by his bed looking at him: 'Don't be scared,' she says, 'I am your wife, Fatima the termagant.'

She pours out her story: how after he vanished, she realised she had maltreated him, and had lived hand-to-mouth, reduced to the most bitter misery. But then, one day as she was crying and hungry, a being appeared and asked her the cause of her tears. When the being discovered she was married to Marouf, he offered to transport her to his side, where she now stands.

Marouf agrees to install her in her own palace, surrounded by her own slaves and courtiers, as long as she promises to give up her former ways, her malice and her complaints. He warns her that she won't be able to go to law against him, since he now is the law. In her palace, Marouf's little boy visits her, but he soon realises she hates him, and he begins to hate her in return. Shahrazad insists on the old woman's ugliness: 'her spotted skin is more repulsive than a spotted viper's.' Marouf would not have taken her back and treated her generously on account of any quality of her own, but only in the desire to please the Lord on high.

Dunyazad interrupts at this point – we are very near the story's end and the end of the book – to exclaim at the wonder of these strange tales, these rare and astonishing stories.

It is the 1001st night, and the vizier arrives as usual with a shroud ready and folded under his arm, for his daughter Shahrazad whom he expects to be beheaded.

Fatima, Marouf's former wife, filled with jealousy of the other women in his harem and of the son he has had with Dunya, is plotting to steal the ring which he always takes off when he makes love, to show respect for the names of God engraved on it, and does not put on again until he has purified himself at the baths. Fatima knows these habits of his, but as she sidles into his bedroom, his son is sitting on the lavatory and sees her enter, suspects her, and follows her with his short sabre, studded with jewels. As soon as she seizes hold of the ring, the boy strikes off her head; when Marouf comes back, he finds the bloodbath and the ring clasped in the hand of the corpse.

After this, Marouf sends for the peasant who helped him before he became Sultan and makes him his vizier; he marries again, and, eventually, sees his son married too. And they lived the most agreeable existence and their days passed happily, says Shahrazad, until the moment He carried them off, He who brings an end to all pleasures of this world, parts those whom life has joined together, ruins the richest houses and makes orphans of girls and boys.

After she finishes telling the story of Marouf the Cobbler, Shahrazad calls for the three children she has borne since she first became the Sultan's wife, of whose existence he knows nothing. The youngest is still nursing, the eldest already walking.

The Sultan bursts into tears, and tells her that he had already decided to repeal the death sentence because he realises how chaste, pure, pious and well-born she is. Joy spreads throughout the city.

CHAPTER ELEVEN

The Voice of the Toy

'But we are spirits of another sort.'
Shakespeare, *A Midsummer Night's Dream*

I

FORTUNE IS WEALTH IN THE story of 'Marouf the Cobbler,' and both arise without rhyme or reason and pour down blessings on him: no special qualities of personality single out the hero, except perhaps an unparalleled willingness to blag and go along with the scam once his friend the Egyptian merchant Ali has put it in his head. No unusual marks of favour from destiny, or exceptional piety or ability entitle him. The luck that comes his way when he disturbs the jinni in the ruined warehouse puts paid to any notions that virtues like hard work and diligence and cleverness earn their rewards in material goods. Rather, the point is that Marouf is not entitled, but the plaything of chance, which he understands very well: riches are phantasms, brought by a jinni who has no will of his own even though he commands legions of other jinn, some of them his children and all capable of prodigious feats of metamorphosis and of plucking fortunes out of thin air.

'Marouf' is above all a fable about the phantasmic character of wealth, brought about by a talismanic ring. It tells a story of a pre-modern pyramid scheme – a build-up of belief in a commodity (Marouf's phantom caravan) as in tulipmania or the South Sea Bubble – but one in which the perpetrator succeeds and everyone prospers; a gigantic Enron edifice of lies and dupes, feints and braggadocio – which does not collapse. It offers an early dream of capitalist triumph, set in a feudal scheme which incidentally discloses the feudal inequalities that have resulted from the triumph of markets since the nineteenth century. The story's only morality lies in its frankness: rewards do not accrue to the deserving, except to the peasant farmer who gives Marouf the lentils and barley.

This closing tale of the *Nights* shadows in many features the better-known story of Aladdin, and Antoine Galland, who does not include it in his edition, might have written up his famous tale of the wonderful lamp from a version of 'Marouf' told to him by Hanna Diab. But 'Marouf

The aerial imagination keeps the plot on the move: the jinni carries Marouf to
fame and fortune (William Harvey, 1850).

the Cobbler' is also strategically placed, as the closing tale of the whole
book: Fatima, the husband-bashing termagant who complains to the courts
about her husband, does have her head cut off. She is set up in conscious
counterpoint by Shahrazad and by the narrator who is telling Shahrazad's
story, since Fatima concedes to the bloodthirsty Sultan that shrews do exist,
and that a meek and willing husband, like Marouf at the start of the story,
can be unjustly treated. But at the same time, the story makes plain that
Fatima is an individual case; the misogyny of its appalling descriptions of
her behaviour and her ugliness does not extend to all women. Dunya, the
princess, belongs to the group of astute, enterprising and loving heroines
in the *Nights*, of whom Shahrazad is the *éminence grise*, dominating from
the wings. It is important that she takes control of the ring; with its

talismanic enigmas the ring is the source of fortune, and both she and her son after her understand the powers that it confers, as well as the limits of those powers; and they understand them better, it is implied, than the insouciant and feckless blaggers like Marouf, whom destiny in its capriciousness has favoured. If there is a moral to the story, it is that women like Dunya are to be trusted as they can interact more responsibly with the vagaries of destiny and the boons of jinn.

The operations of talismans in the *Nights* strengthened the freight of enchanted meanings carried by inert stones and other inanimate objects, and spread the exclusively instrumental, magical sense of the word through European languages. After the appearance of the *Arabian Nights* in French and English, the book excited a widespread craze for fabulism, as we have heard, for fantastic adventures, imaginary and preposterous stories, and while many of the writers who adopted its storytelling techniques parodied and exaggerated them in apparent frivolity, the freeing of imagination into exuberant play had extraordinary results, Not least, a shift began, which continues ever more decisively, towards attributing latent animate sentience to objects and matter.

One effect was to give voice to anything, especially to small moveable goods – tools, baubles, toys, love tokens and, most tellingly of all, to currency itself. Within the animation of inanimate objects in wonder tales lies a deep intuition about the functioning of financial – and erotic – transactions. In the early seventeenth century, the Neapolitan courtier Giambattista Basile enchanted the domestic interiors of his fairytale heroes and victims in a manner that follows the imagination of the *Nights*; directly inspired by him, the Venetian playwright and wit Carlo Gozzi, defender of the traditional stagecraft of the *commedia dell'arte*, added bizarre strokes of magic to the plots Basile had narrated, and animated wooden chests and fruits, trees and stones in his fairy plays, such as *The Love of Three Oranges,* later turned into an opera by Prokofiev (1919).

In many ways, the oriental imitations are born as anti-fairytales, for these early experimenters already wrote as parodists, aware of the inordinate demands of the genre on the audience's credulity. Yet they could not resist the opportunity the conventions gave them, and the possessed and talking things of the *Nights* were gifts to lively storytelling. At the same moment as Antoine Galland's versions of the *Nights* were appearing, the francophone Jacobite Anthony Hamilton, one of the first oriental fantasists in Paris, while proclaiming his horror of the new trend and piling on examples of their nonsense, clearly enjoyed himself by activating a whole cast of magic combs, cutlery, collars, harnesses, hats, mirrors, talking parrots and an enchanted mare (see Chapter 13).

The next generation of storytellers caught the animist tendency of the *Nights* and brought into play various bits of furniture, carpets, fob watches, and every kind of paraphernalia in order to voice their adventures from the most intimate recesses of a character's person. Claude Crébillon, *fils*, satirist, *conteur* and libertine, was one of the many authors to make fun of the *Nights*. In *Le Sopha, ou conte moral* (The Sofa, a moral tale, 1742), with his tongue making a fine bulge in his cheek, he tells the story in the first-person voice of the sofa; the angle of view is of course scandalous. *Le Canapé* (1714) and Crébillon's later diversions, *L'Écumoire* (or *Tanzaï et Néardarné; The Shaving Bowl*) continued to listen in on privy things. The salacious possibilities are clear from the titles.

The plot of *Le Sopha*, such as it is, is framed in jocular homage to the *Nights*, with the grandson of Schah-Riar (*sic*), Schah-Baham, demanding to be told stories to lift his terminal ennui; he longs to find someone with the skills of his grandmother Shahrazad, and his Sultana cannot satisfy him. He cries out, 'I want unusual happenings, fairies, talismans; for don't you make a mistake about this, it is the only truth there is.'

In the story that is then concocted to gratify his wishes, the eponymous sofa has begun life as a young rake – Amanzéï. But his escapades have brought vengeance on his head, and as a fitting punishment he has been turned into a piece of furniture – a sofa, and one that is moreover a rococo confection, 'rose-coloured, embroidered in silver'. Crébillon, here, is having fun with the eccentric metamorphoses in the *Nights*. Our hero will regain his human form only when two pure-hearted young lovers have made true love and given each other their '*prémices*' (their first fruits) – in all sincerity for the first time – while sitting on him.

Despite the flippant, licentious absurdism of Crébillon's *galanterie*, his sofa picks up on furniture's intimate – and animate – character in the stories of the *Nights*.

Crébillon's example was followed: in *Le Bidet* (1748), attributed to Antoine Bret, the hapless lover-protagonist, changed into a bidet by the angry fairy Grossopède, finds his penis transformed into a sponge, and alas, when he is changed back, it is still missing. The young Denis Diderot was also inspired by the trend. When he wrote *Les Bijoux indiscrets,* his first book, it appeared in 1748 and branded him as a libertine far longer than he cared for. The jewels at issue are twofold: an old hypochondriacal jinni, named with innuendo Cucufa, gives the young Sultan Mangogul the magic ring; when the stone is twisted on its bevel it can make women's 'jewels' speak. The Sultan is filled with glee at the thought of hearing his favourites' secret thoughts and opinions, and he begins to use the ring, awakening one after another the pudenda of thirty women whom he thought he knew well. They reveal themselves in tremendous variety and intensity, and they do not flatter or console the Sultan, nor indeed any other man.

This precursor of *The Vagina Monologues* is a pioneering work of philosophical comic fiction in the tradition that Voltaire would perfect. It is a long – perhaps over-long – prank; but it has remained scandalously funny, and a recent, spirited rereading by the French scholar Anne Deneys, for example, has argued for its loyalty to women's interests and its wit and frankness at the expense of men's pretensions and authority: 'It is in fact an investigation of sex that stages a radical critique of metaphysics, or more specifically, a radical critique of the dualism of soul and body'. Diderot nods with knowing mischief to many magic rings in the Eastern tradition and takes to the letter the synecdoche connecting talismans to eros. In particular his conceit is connected to the frame story in Galland's translation of the *Nights*, when the two stricken, royal cuckolds, Shahriyar and Shahzenan, fleeing from their wives' infidelities, fall into the hands of a jinni and when he falls asleep, find themselves peremptorily seduced by the jinni's captive wife, who demands a ring from each of them to add to her trophies.

The Orientalism provides a free forum for Diderot's frivolity and frankness and a pretext for indulging plenty of bad behaviour; it also lends glamour and fascination. But it is more than a patina and an excuse, because the conceit of the speaking jewels implicitly recognises that exchanges of goods, property and sex underpin social transactions, that some classes of persons are indeed treated as things ('reified'), and that, even more acutely, some parts of their bodies are bought and sold like things. In this attention to the falsehood inherent in systems of ascribed value in his day (and later), and in his indictment of commerce as it bears on the condition of women, denaturing and vitiating them for the most part, Diderot also picks up on the acceptance, in the *Nights*, of women's desire as fully incarnate, not ethereal. He conveys his analysis of society, as he observed it around him, by stretching a narrative device much used in the stories: that nothing can be depended upon to remain lifeless and that a stone or any other inanimate object might conceal a vital force.

When such writers related stories from the point of view of things, dramatising their cries and complaints and murmurs and gasps, they were also engaging in satirical exchanges with the fashionable 'true stories' and 'true reports' published by travellers, courtesans, libertines and servants which nurtured the fiction of the fake memoir, such as the titillating *Anecdotes sur Mme la Comtesse du Barry* and Mme d'Aulnoy's adventurous memoirs of court life. These were translated and very popular in England. Novels like Defoe's *Moll Flanders* and Fielding's *Tom Jones* in England, and Diderot's *La Religieuse* (The Nun) in France, are presented as the protagonist's true stories, fallen from their very lips. But with things that talk, instead of dramatising the eventual reprieve of human victim-heroes the writers are poking fun at the genre of misery memoir per se, and, at another level, revising the rules of fiction and displaying its artifice and range, exhibiting self-delighting pleasure in the play of realistic strategies against utter implausibility.

Writers took up the device of talking things to voice the plight of numerous ill-used and put-upon everyday objects: trinkets, toys, tools, a pincushion, a peg top, a corkscrew, a whipping top, sundry articles of dress (shoes, coats, waistcoats) and even a hackney coach. 'Perhaps you never thought,' writes Mary Jane [Ann] Kilner, who in 1780 published - anonymously - *The Adventures of a Pincushion*, 'that such things as are inanimate could be sensible of any thing which happens, as they can neither hear, see, or understand'. The protagonists begin, traditionally, with their 'birth and parentage', then fall victim to a catalogue of human folly and vice. The poor peg top falls from its proud place on a lady's table and ends up kicked under a water tub in a chicken yard. These parodies of *Moll Flanders* or *Tom Jones* set a pattern; unlike the gallant, directly orientalising French tales of furniture and objects, English variations are satirical, supposedly moralising, but their aims duplicitous: for example, is the writer for or against beating children in *The Adventures of a Whipping-Top. Illustrated with stories of many Bad Boys who themselves deserve whipping and of some Good Boys, who deserve Plum-Cakes*? In every case, secrets are the burden of the tale, the world is a spectacle of shame, and the outcome is disgrace: these are riches-to-rags stories at best, and mostly rags to trash.

Dickens's most popular story of all, *A Christmas Carol* (1843), also stages the awakening of Scrooge to his true nature by means of things which come to life and torment him. The apparitions are not Gothic, even though they strike chill and awe into Scrooge; the ghosts are entangled in quotidian objects – in door knockers and lanterns and padlocks and keys. The scene in which Scrooge struggles with the first spirit, and eventually forces him under a candle extinguisher, recalls jinn confined in their copper bottles; but the general mercantile setting imbues all these goods and ordinary objects with active memories, while the preoccupation with phantasmic money - with bills and letters of credit - illuminates, even under the folksy play of sentimental Victorian realism, the deep relation that such stories communicate between talismanic powers and presences and the illusions of commerce and economic value in the modern world:

'Spirit!' said Scrooge in a broken voice, 'remove me from this place.'

'I told you these were shadows of the things that have been,' said the Ghost. 'That they are what they are, do not blame me!'

'Remove me!' Scrooge exclaimed, 'I cannot bear it!'

He turned upon the Ghost, and seeing that it looked upon him with a face, in which in some strange way there were fragments of all the faces it had shown him, wrestled with it.

'Leave me! Take me back! Haunt me no longer!'

In the struggle, if that can be called a struggle in which the Ghost with no visible resistance on its own part was undisturbed by any effort of its adversary, Scrooge observed that its light was burning high and bright; and dimly connecting that with its influence over him, he seized the extinguisher-cap, and by a sudden action pressed it down upon its head.

The Spirit dropped beneath it, so that the extinguisher covered its whole form; but though Scrooge pressed it down with all his force, he could not hide the light, which streamed from under it, in an unbroken flood upon the ground.

He was conscious of being exhausted, and overcome by an irresistible drowsiness; and, further, of being in his own bedroom. He gave the cap a parting squeeze, in which his hand relaxed; and had barely time to reel to bed, before he sank into a heavy sleep.

With a keen sense of the cruel and banal grind of Victorian commerce, Dickens dramatised Scrooge's failure to subdue a jinni intent on doing good.

Scrooge encounters a troublesome Spirit and tries to snuff him out. (John Leech, from Charles Dickens, *A Christmas Carol*, 1843)

II

In a recent essay with the inspired punning title, 'The Crying of Lost Things', the literary scholar Jonathan Lamb discusses the eighteenth-century custom of advertising lost property in the broadsheets; the notorious fence, Jonathan Wild, set up a brisk business in the Old Bailey, restoring stolen goods to their owners – for a fee. In the advertisements he placed for his trade the goods identify themselves, speaking in their own voice in the same way as seekers after love and friendship or jobs or special services do in the 'personal ads' in the newspapers today. This stolen or lost property cries its own whereabouts, calling out in its orphaned state for its owners to come back and claim it: Lamb connects this to the growing literary fashion of the it-narratives, which give things a voice. In these 'it-narratives', things have their say, and their stories acknowledge the link between 'owning a thing in the sense of possessing it and owning a thing in the sense of confessing, relating or accounting for it'.

This popular device accords things what Lamb calls 'autonomous glamour': they are no longer meaningful by association alone but magic-ally empowered and efficacious, acting of their own volition. Entering Western literature as new characters, they embody an intuition about the industrial and post-industrial worlds, where the ways things acquire value will be irreversibly changed by machine replication and then digital reproduction: they glimpse a new 'régime of value' in the tournament of the empire's markets.

Lamb reads living toys, it-narratives and person-things in the light of Romantic ideas about sympathy. Sympathy has affinities with Aristotelian catharsis - but unlike the cathartic purging of pity and fear, sympathy demands continued connection with those feelings on behalf of other beings and other phenomena, not only on one's own account. It involves identification with suffering, to moral ends. Catharsis corresponds to a prophylactic use of magic – to ward off danger and undo evil; it glazes the objects of contemplation. Sympathy works another variety of magic, through identification. And it entails animating the objects of sympathy. Edmund Burke, in his *Enquiry into the Sublime and the Beautiful* (1757), defines sympathy as 'a sort of substitution by which we are put into the place of another man'. Coleridge took this further as he pondered art's effect on consciousness and its relationship to experience and developed his celebrated argument about 'that willing suspension of disbelief for the moment, which constitutes poetic faith'. The suspension of disbelief involves surrender to the words on the page; in Coleridge's view, a conscious act, though one might dispute this. His theory relates to ideas about the passions, and about sympathy in particular, which were developed in the ambience of *sentimentalité* on the one hand, and social reform movements on the other.

Jonathan Lamb, discussing *Gulliver's Travels*, sets out four stages of sympathy, which correspond to his contemporaries' psychology and apply illuminatingly to fairytale and to the *Arabian Nights'* cast of animated animals and things. The first stage is emotional – even sentimental - identifying with beasts, leading to anthropomorphism as in animal stories; this is a vast category of fantastic literature, and the *Nights*, besides including many fables, dramatises numerous animal metamorphoses of the protagonists. The second stage uses sympathy to unfold moral and ethical issues, to argue for animal rights and political justice (as in George Orwell's *Animal Farm*, or, more recently, Dick King-Smith's popular vegetarian manifesto, *The Sheep-Pig*, 1983). A third current of sympathy deploys figurative and imaginative expressions, playing on human–animal resemblances, as in 'Red Riding Hood' or 'Beauty and the Beast' or 'Jabberwocky'. Fourthly – and this is the form of sympathy most relevant to it-narratives and their successors – the writer immerses the reader in the object of sympathy to the point of complete identification. Lamb terms this 'realism', and he sums it up in this way: 'I know what it is like to be you, without reservation; not because I seem to be like you, or because I ought to feel as you do, or because it is as if I were you, but because to all intents and purposes I am you.'

One of the most influential storytellers to adopt techniques of sympathy from the *Nights* was Hans Christian Andersen, who was read the book by his father when he was a child. From this perspective, Andersen the fantasy storyteller is a realist writer. He works on our sympathies through many stratagems. Much has been written about his self-pity and his touchiness, his appeals for praise and reassurance and how these found expression in tales of vindication: the underdog's fate is turned into triumph in one story after another. He also solicits sympathy by pretend insouciance, by his breezy, vivacious storytelling manner, and his comic speed. These are only some of his techniques. Two further devices forge the bonds of sympathy with his protagonists: first, he has constant recourse to bodily states, but secondly - and this is where his realism is both highly wrought and paradoxical - Andersen animates inanimate things and turns them into active agents.

The magic mirror created by the troll demon in 'The Snow Queen' has 'the power to make everything good and beautiful that was reflected in it shrink to almost nothing, while whatever was worthless and loathsome would stand out clearly and look even worse'. After a shard from the shattered glass pierces Kai's eye, he sees the worm in the rose, and 'later, when [Gerda] brought out the picture book, he said that it was for babies, and if Grandmother told them stories, he would always come with some objection . . . it was the glass that had landed in his eye and the glass that sat in his heart; they were the reason he teased even little Gerda, who loved him with all her soul.'

When I was a child, Kai's frozen state captured my imagination as a terrible possibility in store for me; the Snow Queen enthralled me, as did the Robber Girl and Gerda, who were so adventurous and so spirited and fierce and loyal; they inspired me to dream of possible feats of generosity and daring. The mirror that deforms and perverts does not belong to the Queen herself, but it reflects inside the tale the malignant force that freezes love and numbs vitality. The mirror, followed by the kiss of the Snow Queen, numbs Kai, withers his joy and his human powers of connection to others. Like the shadow in Andersen's story of that name, Kai's very consciousness – composed of faculties like imagination and reflexivity – loses energy and substance. A.S. Byatt has commented, 'It took me a long time, as a puzzled child, to work out that Andersen meant, at some level, to frighten and even to hurt me, the reader . . . He crept into my heart like the splinter of broken mirror sliding into the heart of little Kai, making the child see the world as grim and terrifying.'

W.H. Auden, who was an admirer of Andersen's storytelling powers, pointed out that Andersen writes parables, not fairy tales, hence their frequent unhappy endings and absence of consolation. 'The Snow Queen' is an unforgettable parable about loss of self, through loss of lovingness; but like 'Snow White', which it resembles, it is also about representation and likenesses, about the mirror held up to nature, in Hamlet's phrase, of drama and art.

The magic mirror is a thing with real potency, like its enchanted counterparts in the *Nights* and other fairy tales. When Andersen animates other domestic items, and imagines a braggart of a shirt collar, who fancies himself loved by a garter and an iron, he is burlesquing the tradition. His objects do not necessarily produce magical transformations or marvels; the effects are humdrum, apart from their sentience and animation. He brings to life and gives voice to scissors and combs and lamps and brass knobs. He gives personality to a candlestick, and invents a conversation between a darning needle and a glass splinter in which his gift at catching social pretensions and self-deception is brilliantly displayed. The needle takes the glass for a diamond, and introduces herself as a brooch:

'I have lived in a box belonging to a young lady,' began the darning needle. 'She was a cook, and she had five fingers on each hand. There never existed creatures so conceited as those fingers; and yet they were only there to take me out of the box and put me back.'

'Did they shine?' asked the glass splinter.

'Shine!' sneered the needle. 'Oh, they were very haughty . . . They bragged and boasted day and night! That was all they could do well . . .'

'And here we sit and glitter,' said the glass splinter.

Auden compares these prosopopoeia with the devices used by Swift, who adopts a non-human angle of vision to bring about changes of scale and, by decentring the human observer, reorganises perceptions; as we have already seen, the supernatural world of the jinn also places human beings in perspective.

Many of Andersen's things bring down their ultimate fate upon themselves - in tune with the Netherlandish tradition satirising human folly. Like the traditional jester, he relishes the dreadful ends of his protagonists with the same deadpan heartlessness as writers of cautionary tales in a facetious, carnival mode. The foolish young fir tree opts to become a Christmas tree, and is tossed away on the fire; the proud candle burns down, still giving himself airs; the flying trunk is burned to ashes by the bundle of matches, and so on and so forth, terrible, brief jokes ringing out to the teller's glee: 'It was over, over, and that's what happens in every story!'

As with a fool's fooling, this kind of narrative technique requires an answer; it is brash clowning, that asks us to weep for its subject even while keeping up the pretence at light-heartedness. The critic Dinah Birch has commented that in 'Andersen's excruciatingly sentient world, nothing is excluded from the capacity to aspire, and to suffer'.

The intensity of Andersen's projection, through which the reader becomes sensitive to the vitality of all kinds of things, caused Auden to worry about the ethical consequences, especially in the case of violent fairy tales, which invite us to imagine the life of things, often to witness them smashed: 'Familiarity with the story by repetition,' he recognises, 'turns the pain of fear into the pleasure of a fear faced and mastered.' Words make the wicked witch leap up in the mind's eye in all her terrifying malignant vigour, but the deep pleasure of fairytale means that in the very midst of suspending disbelief, disbelief presents its reassurances. Auden wondered about the wicked stepmother in 'Snow White' dancing to death in her red-hot shoes or, he might have added, about Karen's feet cut off with an axe in 'The Red Shoes' to stop her dancing, or even about the forty thieves plunged into boiling oil by the clever Morgiana; or the many torments visited on the heroes and heroines of the *Nights* and not only on the villains. He concluded that the only real danger is that the reader will fail to grasp that the figure in the story is truly suffering and that he or she, unlike the reader, does not know the happy outcome ahead, and 'so [the reader] fails to feel the hero's trials as real'. Indeed, the perversity and cruelty of many *Arabian Nights* stories do not set out to stir empathy with the sufferings of their subjects, but pleasure in the strange scenes taking place. So Auden's note of warning is crucial: 'Imagination,' he went on, 'like reason, is a human faculty and therefore not foolproof.'

The act of animating the world through sympathetic projection may not be ethical or sentimental after all, but mimetic of its deeper structures. The child who makes believe her toy is talking to her may be moved by a need to cherish and value this specific peg top ('*My* doll Billie'), and that particular soft toy ('*My* teddy') and wrest them from the anonymous sameness of commodities by projecting stories on to them and building relationships with them. But she is also, as children do, mirroring the adult world's investment in the glamour of possessions. Significantly, thing-narratives often home in on the virtue of goods per se, and choose to dramatise the weird independent life of money which goods command.

CHAPTER TWELVE

Money Talks

Skilling: Here's the next big thing: trading bandwidth [. . .] If you're not using your bandwidth capacity, we could sell it on. It's tradeable. But people don't think in those terms because it's a virtual commodity. Well, Enron *gets* virtual.

Lucy Prebble, *Enron*, 2009

I

IN 1709, AN ANONYMOUS LAMPOONIST directly echoed the title of the first English translation, *Arabian Nights' Entertainments*, with the opening instalment of a satire called *The Golden Spy – The Introduction; or the First Nights* [sic] *Entertainment*. The author, Charles Gildon, dedicated his book to 'The author of *A Tale of a Tub*' and with scurrilous, Swiftian scorn, adopts the first person of a *louis d'or*, a gold coin from the luxurious spendthrifts across the Channel, to excoriate the abuses of contemporary society.

This penny morality about 'the power and progress of gold' starts in antiquity: the coin begins as no ordinary piece, but falls to earth in the golden shower which ravished Danae, an early instance of bribery and corruption perpetrated by the mighty. Gildon explains that he was wondering about the ideas which the Neoplatonist Tommaso Campanella expressed in *De Sensu rerum (On the Sense of Things)*, where he wrote that 'Chance . . . produced an Instance not only of the sensibility of things which we generally esteem mute but inanimate, but ev'en of their Rationality, and discursive Faculty, Observation, Memory, and Reflection.' Gildon relates this claim to the new science of 'animal, sensible, and perhaps rational Particles', and describes how he began to hear the coin whisper from under his pillow where he had secreted it. Like a contemporary magical realist – Gabriel García Márquez, Angela Carter or Salman Rushdie – this eighteenth-century satirist operates by returning a metaphor to its literal meaning, as the author comments that 'Gold would make the Silent speak, and the Loquacious dumb . . .'

Gildon's squib set a trend (and since then, a thousand, a million school essays on 'my life as a penny'). The popular narrative device grew out of new materialism, rooted in expanding world traffic and Enlightenment rationality. This appears to be a contradiction, but it remains consistent with the century's developments in public entertainment, such as Louther-bourg's Eidophusikon, dioramas, waxworks and, above all, the spectacular Phantasmagoria, which ratcheted up the spookiness while at the same time claiming to be showing it up for what it is – nothing but an illusion. But the dominant quality of this eerie materialism arises from its relationship to time, as conveyed by new media: it transforms the past into a perpetual present tense – be it Marilyn Monroe on the screen as she was in her salad days or the glister of gold – making this recollection into a prophecy.

In the *Tatler* in 1710, Joseph Addison published 'The Adventures of a Shilling', which begins:

> Methoughts the shilling that lay upon the table reared itself upon its edge, and turning the face towards me, opened its mouth, and in a soft silver sound, gave me the following account of his life and adventures: "I was born (says he) on the side of a mountain, near a little village of Peru, and made a voyage to England in an ingot, under the convoy of Sir Francis Drake. I was, soon after my arrival, taken out of my Indian habit, refined, naturalized, and put into the British mode, with the face of Queen Elizabeth on one side, and the arms of the country on the other. Being thus equipped, I found in me a wonderful inclination to ramble, and visit all parts of the new world into which I was brought.'

But the coin's happy wandering soon comes to an end; it falls prisoner to a miser, who shuts it up in an iron chest where it endures, jinni-like, a long period of captivity before thieves break open the chest and its adventures resume – with their need to launder it.

Other stories voicing coins and bills also pick up the dynamics of jinn-driven stories in the *Arabian Nights* in the way they foreground chance: stuff happens to Addison's shilling, over which it has no control. Sometimes a disaster turns out to be a blessing: the ways of chance are amoral and inscrutable. There is a kind of providence, but it operates remotely and impersonally. The critic Greg Afinogenov interestingly matches this view to political theories of commerce: 'the Whigs see trade as a life-giving recirculating stream interrupted at times by artificial blockages like miserliness and political upheaval. It is really only with [Adam] Smith and the political economists that commerce begins to be conceived in terms of rigidly defined categories of production, distribution, consumption, and their attendant fixing of subjectivity.'

A comparable economic fatalism runs through several more such stories in the course of the century: in 1760, a garrulous satire, a *roman-à-clef* in which historical characters are named and shamed, mobilised a coin as lead witness for the prosecution and explicitly borrowed a jinni to animate it: the protagonist, who inveighs against current despots, their folly and their evil deeds, is the spirit of gold imprisoned in a guinea. *Chrysal, or The Adventures of a Guinea* appeared first in two volumes, was into a third edition two years later, and was translated into French in 1768/9. The author was a Limerick-born lawyer, Charles Johnstone, who took himself off to India, continued to add volumes to his diatribe, wrote more ferocious satires, but died forgotten. Ever more garrulous money features in *The Adventures of a Bank-Note* by Thomas Bridges (4 volumes in 1770), and *The Adventures of a One Pound Note*, in 1819. The popular narrative device extends to the new virtual conditions of exchange, which are no longer effected by gold or silver or copper coin, but take place through paper money and other forms of inscribed documents. The development keeps march with imperial and colonial expansion and corresponding world traffic in goods; it also matches contemporary developments in banking, with the issue of bills and notes secured on government funds. In this way, money was dematerialised, and the writers who make it tell its story in fiction recognise the new conditions of its ghostliness.

Metals are matter, and their value derives from certain material qualities (the untarnished glister of gold!) and the symbolic dimensions attributed to those qualities. By contrast, paper money acquires value only through the authority backing the value it has been ascribed and the trust placed in that authority by the users, collectively. The first paper money, stamped 'Great Ming Circulating Treasure Certificate', was printed in China under the Ming dynasty in 1375. It carried a picture of heaps of coins to the amount it was worth and many inscriptions validating it from the emperor. The Chinese called it 'flying cash' and it proved to be so: in a process that has become familiar, more and more notes were issued to keep up with their spiralling loss of value until, in 1425, printing was suspended. As Neil MacGregor, the

Issuing '*assignats*', the revolutionary government in France inaugurated the modern printing of paper money; the earliest examples still bore the head of Louis XVI as a credible symbol of authority.

director of the British Museum, puts it, 'The fairies had fled – or, to put it in grander language, the faith structure needed for paper money to work had collapsed.' The first paper money in the West also depended on faith. The worth of certificates issued by John Law in his pioneering schemes to finance the Mississippi Company in 1716–20, of 'continental dollars' circulated by the United States during the War of Independence, and of *assignats* issued by the Revolutionary government in France to cover the debt, of share certificates, bills of exchange, cheques, IOUs, and all other forms of paper money, does not inhere in the materials in which they appear (even less so in the case of the phantasmic character of twenty-first-century finance). Value is inscribed into them, as it is with talismans: intricate graphic ornament, multiple lattices and complex sprinkling of letters, emblems, mottoes, names, symbols and distinctive numbers woven together, and embedded watermarks give the note such specificity that it cannot be forged. The symbols which still transform worthless paper into effective currency sometimes exactly repeat those on talismans, especially those associated with Solomon and the building of the Temple. The five-pointed star of the seal of Solomon is emblazoned on the US $50 banknote, for example, while the $1 note, itself a powerful symbol of the Union, carries the Great Seal of the United States, made up of hermetic emblems from the history of magic as well as scripture: the haloed eye of God at the summit of a pyramid with thirteen brick courses..The presence of such symbols reflects the success of Freemasonry since the seventeenth century, as a space where a secular form of ritual and esoteric wisdom could be pursued and a secular priesthood established within a rational state.

The processes involved in the object's certification resemble the repetitive inscription of talismans, while the transformation achieved likewise produces an enchanted and special object with active and powerful 'autonomous glamour', independent of who is handling it.

For financial dealings online today, encrypting the information is crucial: a plethora of codes – numbers, symbols, letters in jumbled series – is needed to protect the correct transfer of the monies. Nothing is ever quite enough to withstand the metamorphic antinomianism of lucre: 'Money is chameleon-like, ever-moving, ever-changing,

The one-dollar bill, a most potent symbol of the United States of America since Independence, presents a cluster of classical allusions and Egyptian, Solomonic, and Masonic emblems.

impervious to moral law'. Further invisible inscriptions, embedded in magnetic strips, also authenticate the card. In the United Arab Emirates, HSBC has issued a credit card inscribed with symbols to comply with the Koranic ban on usury. Is this a development of a talisman which protects against evil?

But the deepest, intrinsic quality of money and the new virtual uncanny arises from its mobility: money moves through space and time. Its liquidity takes it through the centuries as well as all over the globe. The Golden Spy in Charles Gildon's work declares at the end of his opening oration: 'But, to come to an end, Sir, I am the eldest Son of Time . . .' In this his protagonist, the *louis d'or*, resembles a jinni who emanates from a remote and ancient past and has not changed form or nature during the millennia he has spent incarcerated in a jar or a lamp or other thing: the talisman, into which meaning has been packed by a process of inscription, moves outside time and history. The power is captured and endures – by dint of the meaning and value written into it and attributed by common agreement of the users among whom it circulates.

Frozen Desire is the fine phrase chosen by the historian James Buchan for a compelling and original study of the meaning of money. 'Money is incarnate desire,' he writes:

> Money takes wishes, however vague or trivial or atrocious, and broadcasts them to the world, like the Mayday of a ship in difficulties. Unlike the Mayday, it appeals not to sensations of individual benevolence or common humanity . . . but offers a reward that is not in any sense fixed or finite – there is no objective or invariable value in money – but *that every person is free to imagine in the realm of his own desire* [emphasis added].
>
> That process of wish and imagination, launched or completed a million times every second, is the engine of our civilisation . . . In thus mobilising wishes, money sets people and matter in motion, has made great cities, railroads, satellites in the heavens, phantom warehouses of computing power, systems of law and equity, gardens, immense and long-winded corporations, sanguinary wars, monuments of architecture, teeming populations.

The movement of Buchan's own rhetoric, from imaginary wishing to lists of goods and products, even follows the pattern of fairytale plotting in many of the stories in the *Nights*. Even more pertinently, in relation to the prophetic character of the talisman in fairy tales, frozen desires can melt into thin air.

For while the magic inscriptions charm the thing on which they have been written, they refer to a power beyond the thing itself, a warranty of its trustworthiness: it is to be believed in, as the word 'credit' conveys. This ultimately depends on who or what is asking for belief. Islamic scholars, like the Doctors of the Church, distinguish good and bad magic not by its forms but by its sources and objects. The talismanic shirt of Sultan Murad IV invokes a range of godly, benign forces, and affirms its powers to protect its wearer through them (Pl. 17a & b). The illicit talismans of the *Nights* – the dark enchanters' instruments – draw their energy from Eblis and his servants, the unrepentant jinn.

So the power of the talisman is triangulated between, first, the external guarantor whose divine (or demonic) powers flow into it; secondly, the maker who inscribes it with invocations that draw down those powers into it; and, thirdly, the wearer or user who wishes by it. Unexpectedly, since virtual money is one of the most prominent signs of modernity, this fundamental magical structure underpins the workings of paper money and other forms of virtual value. Queens, presidents, famous men and women of the nation play the part taken by prophets and saints on talismans, as representatives of the principles and ideals underlying the body issuing the currency; when those are rejected, or the leaders fall, or the finance ministers and chancellors of the exchequer can no longer convince, the credit of that country can and will collapse. I have seen market vendors in the Far East use a former régime's banknotes to wrap goods; I have kept a bundle of joss sticks from Cambodia tightly wound with money that used to be worth a hundred times their cost. There is nothing more bleak than a bundle of currency which has become worthless. But they have a similar emptiness to lucky charms which have no purchase on our hopes.

II

The enchanted and phantasmic character of money in modernity inspired a scene of great inventive brio in the suffuse pageant of enchantments that is Johann Wolfgang von Goethe's *Faust: Part Two*, a drama that is part phantasmagoria, part exorcism, part tragicomedy of modern times. In the course of his struggle to unfold the meaning of his hero, Europe's most famous damned enchanter, Goethe stages the coming of paper money: it is a marvel, the salvation of the empire and social order, and the brainchild of Mephistopheles. This second part of his poem–play took Goethe decades to complete and did not appear in full in his lifetime. He was attempting a synthesis of science, culture and philosophy on a vast scale, and he poured into it his heterogeneous, often bizarre, fanciful and hallucinatory envisionings of every development he saw taking place around him in society and knowledge. The writing proceeded by fits and starts, but he returned to Act I after he had been sent, in 1825, the fifteen volumes of the German translation of *The Tales of 1001 Nights* by Maximilian Habicht (d. 1839). This very full selection and edition was based on Galland, but included stories from a Tunisian source of Habicht's own, and others brought in from Jonathan Scott's collection, amongst others. The scholar Katharina Mommsen has shown in her study, *Goethe und 1001 Nacht* (1960), and in subsequent articles and lectures, how this renewed encounter with the *Nights* re-ignited Goethe. He had known the stories from his youth, in Galland's translation. But re-reading them, in German, released his imagination; the *Nights'* structure and polyphony gave him a way of melding the disparate materials he wanted to bring into *Faust*, and a way of thinking about aspects of modernity. Between July 1827 and January 1828, and resuming again in late 1829, he kept bringing new fantasies into scenes set in the Emperor's Pleasure Garden.

The Emperor is being entertained with a mysterious, multifarious Carnival Masque, an alchemical dream and a fairy show, a Loutherbourgian spectacular, drawing on other stage techniques in vogue and involving many mythical characters as well as tableaux of the elements. David Lukes, translator and editor of *Faust,* comments that Goethe wishes to make a show of his own prodigious powers of poetic creation themselves; and it is during the course of this phantasmagoria that the Emperor, in the role of Great Pan, writes out the first paper bill.

After the Prospero–like visions of cloud–capp'd towers and domes of many–coloured glass have ended, Mephistopheles enters with Faust and makes an effusive speech about the Emperor's protean omnipotence. But the Emperor cuts him short:

> What lucky chance has brought you here, straight out
> Of the *Arabian Nights*? You need not doubt,
> If you can match Scheherazade's skill
> In story-telling, that I will
> Grant you high favour. Let me count on you
> When the day's doings bore me, as they often do.

In these few verses, Goethe invokes the original storyteller by name and parodies the proverbial ennui of the Sultan. But he also brushes in the analogy between storytelling (spinning yarns) and the miracle to come: actual payments secured by paper promises.

At that the Steward enters 'hurriedly', soon followed by high officials of the court, including the Treasurer and the Chancellor, and, marvelling, they announce that the army is being paid and the restive soldiers have calmed down, landlords have their rents again; the brothels are back in business. The Chancellor carefully describes the wonder:

> Hear then and see this fateful paper, which
> Has changed our poverty and made us rich.
> [*He reads.*]
> 'To whom it may concern: hereby be advised and told,
> The present note is worth a thousand crowns in gold . . .'

The Emperor has to be reminded of his actions in the night:

> *The Treasurer.* You wrote it, Sire, yourself, at Carnival time . . .
> You signed, and thanks to prestidigitation
> The night sufficed for ample duplication . . .
> We printed the whole series straightaway . . .

Between the Steward and the Treasurer, the picture builds: of a society restored, trade resumed, spending flowing again, shops and cafés, bars and pubs packed. As I read it in 2008–9 during the world financial crisis, with every Western nation's finance ministers and experts announcing larger and larger sums lost or borrowed, 'quantitative easing' declared a remedy, and vast private debts growing ever more vast, secured on credit-card plastic alone, Goethe's blackly humorous scene seemed truly a work of awful prophecy.

Mephistopheles exults:

> Such paper currency, replacing gold
> And pearls, is most convenient: you can hold
> A known amount, no sale or bartering
> Is needed to enjoy love, wine, or anything
> You please.

To which the Lord Treasurer gladly cries,

> Sire, there shall be no strife and no divisions;
> I like to have colleagues who are magicians.

Goethe was entranced by the form, structure and magical devices of the oriental narratives. The *Arabian Nights* struck him as the logical, appropriate setting for the Emperor's miraculous salvation through paper money, and his joy in the viewless horizons of credit which had magically opened before him at the stroke of a pen. So, with comic verve, Goethe succeeds in forging a dramatic (and amusing) connection between the talismans of the *Nights*, a wonderful stranger's oriental magic, and the demonic virtuality of modern money; the passage displays with powerful prescience the phantasmic character of modern financial arrangements. Goethe's mixed tone, lowering his metaphysical theme with broad satire, also imitates the mocking spirit of the *Nights*.

The journey from the talismans in the stories to the fabrication of money has carried this book from carnelians and cotton to paper and online banking, from physical quiddity to ephemeral virtuality, and has involved the argument so far in a contradiction. The gemstone or shirt, inscribed with spells or pious quotation in order to secure supernatural protection, materialises the wish in tangible form in a unique artefact – that is the whole point of its making. Paper money, credit cards and, even more acutely, online banking are intangible by comparison and exist in series. In the world of role-playing games, money circulates to obtain goods in the games' virtual economy, functioning in a mirror image of the actual world of financial transactions – and the GNP inside a game such as *Project Entropia* – now called *Entropia Universe* – is rumoured to exceed that of several nations. One form of such money, known as 'Open Metaverse Currency', or OMC, is accepted as legal tender across different virtual universes, a kind of hypergrid euro. Such economies are sufficiently 'real' to be used by criminals to launder money.

The analogy between these forms of frozen desire can only be taken so far. Yet Goethe was far-sighted when he did not congratulate modern financial arrangements on their ethics or their rationality but focused on their magical virtue – in the sense of their ascribed energy, their daimonic being.

III

Tales featuring objects with uncanny life which have been seized and not understood begin flourishing in the literature of imperial Gothic. Manufactured goods from distant trading partners, possessed by active and personal demons, emanate from the realm of the undead things: think of classic ghost stories about active, mobile, potent items such as 'The Monkey's Paw' by W.W. Jacobs (1902), and M. R James's unforgettable story, 'The Mezzotint', in which a work of art uncannily contains a living person, or the same writer's 'Oh, Whistle and I'll Come to You, My Lad' (both stories 1904) which features an enchanted whistle.

Such disturbing protagonists of the Gothic tale have sometimes travelled from far away in time and place, bringing ghosts with them and inspiring any number of museum horror vehicles in which talismans enthral and bind trespassers, and mummies walk. But the efficacity of charged or charmed things has familiarised another order of daily reality. Neither supernatural (underpinned by a god or gods), nor preternatural, since it is not an anomaly or an exception; neither surreal, nor unreal, it is firmly planted in science, of course. But not science that most users can understand. (This was not the case with crystal radio sets or the internal combustion engine.) We now exist in relation to any number of phenomena which work as if by magic. At least that is how it feels to use my BlackBerry, my laptop, my satnav, my blood monitor, my iPod, or to send you in Indonesia a photograph of Kentish Town from my mobile.

While we go about our ordinary lives in an ordinary way, film-makers, artists and writers pick up and broadcast back to us this state of weird connectedness. It is not surprising that the Harry Potter books and films, which take place in a parallel world and teem with inventive ideas about instrumental magic and fantastic gadgets – Quidditch sticks and Pensieves and portraits that wave at you – have crossed over to adult readers. In 2010, the Home Secretary of the UK was even considering punishing antisocial behaviour with confiscation – of mobile phones and iPods. Taking away gadgets might prove a greater incentive to better conduct, it is thought, than taking away other freedoms. The investment of the individual in these technological and immaterial extensions of our faculties now goes very deep.

This is where we can return to the idea that, unlike relics or mementoes, toys and talismans speak of the future not the past. The stories in the *Nights* captured the interest of eighteenth-century readers as soon as they appeared, because their motifs had – and still have – an uncanny applicability to modern experience as it was then forming. At a superficial level, the stories struck readers as wonderfully amusing through their bizarre, superstitious, 'backward' causality. But beneath that appeal, the animist imagination in the tales reproduced the brisk and eloquent traffic in goods across East-West boundaries, and the picture of despotism, sexual and religious conventions, and ideas of providence triggered brilliant parodic and satirical responses. The fabulous East became the rationalists' favourite arena, where their own reasoning imaginations could take wing.

Part IV
Oriental Masquerades

CHAPTER THIRTEEN

Magnificent Moustaches:
Hamilton's Fooling,
Voltaire's Impersonations

> Human beings are not born once and for all on the day their mother
> gives birth to them, but that life obliges them to give birth to
> themselves.
>
> Gabriel García Márquez, *Love in the Time of Cholera*, 1985

I

THE OPERA *COSÌ FAN TUTTE*, first performed in Vienna in January 1790, was Mozart's last collaboration with Lorenzo Da Ponte, most sparkling and inventive of librettists. Don Alfonso, the *éminence grise* of the drama, spurs on the two young male protagonists to test the constancy of their fiancées, Dorabella and Fiordiligi, and proposes they use the traditional romance device of a bed trick (as used in in several stories of the *Arabian Nights* and in *All's Well That Ends Well* and elsewhere). On this occasion it will take the form of an oriental farce, knowingly making fun of the craze for exotic settings which, by the last decade of the century, had taken hold of Europe for several decades.

When the two men reappear in their masquerade (the word is used often in the opera) the maid Despina, who is in on the plot, instantly draws attention to the new visitors' appearance, expressing horror at their outlandish moustaches (lots of opportunities for designers for pantomime stage business, with gigantic turbans, glittering damasks and swaggering seductiveness). But moustaches were also a mark of the stranger, Westerners then being clean-shaven (as Crusoe knows when on the island he finds he has grown 'a large pair of Mahometan whiskers'). Despina introduces the idea that they must be from the Ottoman empire – from the Balkans or from Turkey. Later, however, their identity settles down as Albanian, the closest part of the Muslim empire to Italy.

In a splendid comic aria, stuffed with amorous innuendo, Guglielmo asks the two women to admire him instead:

> Look at us,
> Touch us,
> Take stock of us:
> We're crazy but we're charming,
> We're strong and well made,
> And as anyone can see,
> Whether by merit or by chance,
> We've good feet,
> Good eyes, good noses.
> Look, good feet; note, good eyes;
> Touch, good noses; take stock of us;
> And these moustaches
> Could be called
> Manly triumphs,
> The plumage of love. (Act II: sc.11)

In the Italian original, these moustaches are '*pennachi d'amor*' – banners of love.

The mock-serenade reverses the usual direction of a singer's praise: the two male wooers vaunt their own charms, not the beauty of their love objects. Beneath the froth and mischief, the scene stages a double demand for recognition: the song asks Dorabella and Fiordiligi to look at the orientals without being prejudiced against their unfamiliar features (those moustaches), and to assess them for themselves, seeing through the men's disguises to their true lovers beneath. The women fail, but in doing so, come to realise their ignorance.

Such recognitions underlie the movement of fairy tales toward their happy endings: Cinderella is seen for who she is, not a slattern after all. In some ways, *Così fan tutte* also uses disguise, in this case oriental fancy dress, to warn that one should never trust appearances, not because they are deceptive but because they come burdened with prejudicial baggage. The Albanian disguises of their fiancés trigger out-of-character behaviour in the two young women: they fall for Oriental seductiveness, even when play-acted. Da Ponte and Mozart are exploring the self as changeable in relation to others, rather than atomised; identity does not possess fixed integrity, but alters as elective affinities work metamorphoses upon it. (In this respect, it is piquant to note that only a few decades later, every Victorian paterfamilias would be flourishing luxuriant whiskers.)

In his last essays, *On Late Style*, Edward Said explores his love of Mozart and especially *Così*, and he singles out this comic scene for praise.

One might have expected him to find it demeaning – Orientalist in the worst taste. Instead he points up the doubts the libretto casts on fixed identities. He chose to see past the light malice about the ways of all women and the farce about exotic strangers, and suggests instead that the scene offers a deeper insight into human character; for what then ensues in *Così* leads to a deeper state of understanding – of self and others. Said's concern with the fluidity of the self (and his own sense of himself as a man belonging nowhere and everywhere) returns again and again in his thoughts on late style, and often leads him to admire writers who explore shifting emotions and personal contradiction (Proust, Conrad). With respect to Mozart's *Così*, he perceives evidence of 'late style'. This productive stage in a creative life takes unexpected changes of direction, letting go of principles, experimenting with 'anachronism and anomaly'. 'Don Alfonso devises a game,' he writes, 'in which human identity is shown to be as protean, unstable, and undifferentiated as anything in the actual world.'

In the bed trick at the heart of Mozart and Da Ponte's *Così fan tutte*, does the irresistibility of the lovers' oriental disguise as 'Albanians' open their minds to a deeper understanding? (Hawaian Opera Theatre production, 2004)

The director Peter Sellars is notorious for his extreme updates, stretching favourite libretti to fit present circumstances: his Don Giovanni was a heroin addict, and he set *Zaide,* an early sketch towards Mozart's harem romance, *Die Entführung aus dem Serail* (The Abduction from the Seraglio), in an Asian sweatshop. Regarding Sellars's *Così,* Said found much to praise, emphasising the way the production illuminated this portrait of human personality as almost infinitely capable of mutations: 'What Sellars has picked up with great brilliance,' he wrote, 'is the void at the center . . . a void that allows an infinite series of substitutions, so long as each is internally consistent in its patterns and conceits.' *La donna è mobile,* as a later opera famously declares. But not only in the sense of fickle; thinking about the contrapuntal harmonies and forms of experimental liberty that belatedness makes possible, flightiness can be taken as flight in the strongest and best sense: flights of the mind.

Opera productions often now refuse a sense of completely serene closure at the end of *Così fan tutte.* The harmony of the final glorious sextet does not draw down the curtain on new vistas of happiness; what the lovers have discovered in themselves has unsettled their complacent sense of virtue. They have experienced contrapuntal consciousness and are changed.

Through such examples of mirroring, projection and exchanges of identity, the tangled and overworked concept of the Other can be unravelled and refreshed: the stand-off between Us and Them, built on the premise that 'You are Other', can be differently inflected by looking at this history. Said argued for such 'contrapuntal' readings. An exile's necessary mutations of persona could lead, Said argued, to opening up meanings: 'Most people are principally aware of one culture, one setting, one home,' he wrote. 'Exiles are aware of at least two, and this plurality of vision gives rise to an awareness of simultaneous dimensions, an awareness that, to borrow a phrase from music, is contrapuntal. For an exile, habits of life, expression, and activity in the new environment inevitably occur against the memory of these things in another environment.' The aftermath of the *Nights* saw a double-tongued mode of narration begin to flourish: ironical Orientalism, by which means writers – and artists in other mediums too, like opera – were able to have it both ways, to play-act seductive Albanians and yet remain masqueraders showing up the hollowness of the assumptions about them. Said's interest in fluid personality was bound up with his politics: dismantling the borders of the self could act to take down other borders.

II

Anthony Hamilton (1645–1720), an Anglo-Irish Jacobite soldier, minor aristocrat and courtier, is key to the afterlives of the *Arabian Nights* in their European border crossings, and to the later Oriental masquerades so brilliantly performed by Voltaire, Beckford and others. He was himself an exile, the condition Said sees as fundamental to contrapuntal consciousness, and a member of a family who served the Stuarts loyally after Charles I's execution. As a soldier, he fought in Ireland, leading the retreat of the Irish cavalry at the Battle of the Boyne, and then followed James II to France. And as a Catholic, he wrote in French chiefly to entertain the great ladies, the duchesse du Maine at the château de Sceaux, and the deposed royal family at Saint-Germain-en-Laye. His writing connects the *mondain* French entertainments of the late seventeenth century to the new wave of Enlightenment, rationalist satire, and, ultimately, to later English aristocratic Gothic: his literary lineage reveals cross-fertilisation between France and England and the *1001 Nights*, continues the fairytale tradition established by Charles Perrault, Madame d'Aulnoy, and Mlle de Lubert, and leads directly to Horace Walpole (who published him and also wrote spoofs of the *Nights*) and William Beckford, who was proud to be related to him by blood. Beckford was English-born and raised, but he, like Hamilton, chose to write in French; he had more reasons for this choice than his predecessor, as he had studied the French orientalists whose translations had established the language as the natural European host of arabesque.

Goethe, too, acknowledged Hamilton's inspiration: he was influenced by his *Faust*, left incomplete at the time of Hamilton's death. In England, Matthew ('Monk') Lewis (1775–1818) translated Hamilton's tales. Lewis also wrote sequels to several which Hamilton had left unfinished, rather missing the point, since Hamilton was a playful experimenter and deliberately resisted tidy conventions (one of his longer fictions, *Les quatre Facardins*, gives each of the four protagonists the same name in a kind of Oulipian *jeu d'esprit* ahead of its time). Lewis commented: 'It has been asserted that Hamilton's tales were written with the intention of turning the "Thousand and One Nights" into ridicule . . . but this I do not for one moment believe . . . Hamilton had too much good taste not to appreciate the merit of a work in which we find all the luxuriance of the Eastern imagination, so much more fervid than our own, with the striking simplicity of the early ages.'

Hamilton is best known today for the gossipy memoirs he wrote when he was staying with the duchesse du Maine at Sceaux. They mischievously impersonate his brother-in-law, the duc de Grammont, an unreformed *galant* of the *ancien régime*. Published in 1713, the book had a huge social and critical success, and was translated and first published in English by Horace Walpole in 1772, and again by Sir Walter Scott, who wrote of it:

> The *History of Grammont* may be considered as unique: there is nothing like it in any language. For drollery, knowledge of the world, various satire, general utility, united with great vivacity of composition, *Gil Blas* [by Alain–René Lesage] is unrivalled: but as a merely agreeable book, the *Memoirs of Grammont* perhaps deserve that character more than any which was ever written: it is a pleasantry throughout.

The same could be said of Hamilton's Oriental tales: they are pleasantries throughout, barbed entertainments composed with courtly nonchalance, written by a man who knows all about princes and powers, intrigue and scandal.

Even before Galland's translation was being composed, when the *Nights* were known by hearsay from the reports of orientalists, Hamilton was developing the parodic or 'mock' tradition; he treated the material of the *Arabian Nights* in the manner of the baroque comedians, Cervantes and Ariosto, but instead of mocking the gods of the Greeks and the heroes of the romances of chivalry, he made fun of the *Nights'* stock-in-trade, including the actual form of their storytelling. In spite of his declared impatience with fashionable ladies' addiction to the stories' improbable and tangled plots, the excesses of wonders and jewels, monsters and far distant lands of enchantment, Hamilton's stories succeed as sparkling confections, light soufflés baked for his friends. He helps himself liberally to motifs, bringing in beseeching animals who are enchanted humans that smile and gesture, unable to speak; arbitrary and sudden *coups de théâtre* which are accepted without demur by all concerned, and deadpan uses of summary justice. Of a supposed witch, he writes, 'It was first put out that the Mother of Sheaths needs must be burned alive, but the effort would have been in vain, witches in those days did not allow themselves to be burned as they do these days.'

In fairy tales such as *Fleur d'Épine* (*Princess Mayblossom: A Circassian Tale, c.* 1703), there is a luminous hat, a ringing mare and a prince in the shape of a parrot. The princess has eyes that kill any man who looks at her and turn any woman stone-blind. The hero battles against three hydras, ten rhinoceroses, fourteen elephants and twenty griffins, but scatters them with a blowtorch. There are also sunglasses, crimson unicorns, magpies who play cards, baby ogres, sudden deaths – and resuscitations, recognitions and transformations, of course. The whole thing is presented as the final story of the *1001 Nights:* not because Schéhérazade is reprieved but because Dinarzade has stepped in to stop her sister's endless storytelling, which has been driving her to despair. She tricks the Sultan into calling for a merciful release – without cutting off Schéhérazade's head.

For this reason, it is not impossible that the many unfinished stories intentionally refuse to tie together the efflorescing plots at the end and instead leave the reader tantalisingly in mid-air. Hamilton said he wrote his tales, 'to mark the absurdities of these badly made-up stories . . .'. Later, Voltaire, who admired Hamilton, also leaves stories dangling, squeezing a comic effect from letting them peter out.

Although Hamilton's fables are deliberately frivolous in tone and content and packed with adult innuendo, they are sustained by a genuine undertow of social and literary critique; and his approach was to prove an extraordinarily useful stratagem for writers with much clearer political aims. His appeal to reason against folly, his satire and levity, the suave confidence of his mocking tone, gave Voltaire the cue for his *contes philosophiques.* As the literary critic Ruth Clark observes, 'What Hamilton did bequeath to Voltaire was his manner of relating, his calm polite malice, his easy deprecating grace, the air of unconscious ridicule, that delightfully grave irony, so sure that it never exaggerates, so restrained it never gives way to laughter.'

Oriental disguises gave writers a cover for ironical philosophising and a satirical perspective on their own social mores and aberrant despots. The anonymous editor of one collection comments – and this author might well be Galland himself: 'The greater number of monarchies in the Orient were despotic, and the subjects in consequence did not see themselves as free; as those peoples are ingenious, they found this way of being able to give advice, without risking their lives, to their kings, who treat them as slaves and do not give them the liberty to say what they think.' The sentence significantly changes tense halfway through, to comment on the enduring motives of fabulists. Voltaire's acerbic Oriental *contes* provide an obvious instance of the West putting on Eastern dress in order to examine itself more clearly.

III

In the sly, naughty tale in verse, *What Pleases the Ladies* (1763–64) by Voltaire (1694–1778), the heroine, a loathly lady, will turn out to be 'wholly beautiful' ('toute belle') when given what she desires. She has Shahrazad's gift of 'verbal grace', ingenuity, pace and plotting, and is also a magical realist, a champion of antic fables and fairy toys. Voltaire, who mirrors himself in her prowess, concludes in mock solemnity with an insistence on the power of stories:

> And now they've banished spirits, fairies, too
> Reason rules, a story must be true.
> But the heart grows dull in a world of grey,
> Where sense and logic may not brook demur,
> And correctness is the order of the day.
> Believe me when I say: it can be right to err.

Voltaire learned the fantastic use of error from fantasy, fairy tale and the mode of the *Nights*: his development of the *conte philosophique* borrows its storytelling methods from this literary genre in general but from the *Mille et une nuits* in particular: incident-strewn plots, sudden and baffling reversals of boon and bane, absurd coincidences and flagrant improbabilities which provoke not a ruffle in their recipients; arbitrary switches of chance and mischance; prophetic dreams; scientific and metaphysical speculations; weird catastrophes and equally unexpected marvels. He adopted with glee the pulp fiction cast of characters, too: enchanters, genies, slaves, mutes, giants, dwarfs, often freakishly mutilated, as well as fairies, kings and princes galore, princesses of extraordinary beauty, fabulous caliphs and evil viziers. Voltaire drew on a large costume wardrobe and props cupboard through which he could rummage to furnish all his chief concerns and indict tyranny and arbitrary law, injustice, superstition, idolatry and unthinking conformity, curtailment of speech, and enslavement – mental as well as physical. And, not least, through the commitment of the stories to destiny, he could confront and grasp the dominant dilemma of his philosophy: the role of providence.

Of course he was twisting the material, ironically making fun of it even as he relished it. The bite of the satire depended on the low estimate his audience had of such preposterous literature (as Hamilton had shown), and also on the disdain with which arrangements in the Ottoman empire were generally viewed. 'Micromégas', a science-fiction-like tale written before *Zadig*, draws attention to cultural perspective and satirises those who, like earthlings, think their world is the only one and that their knowledge plumbs the limits of knowledge itself. Voltaire indicts this ignorance and complacency, attacking his own country by presenting it as Babylon or Mesopotamia or Turkey, whose inferiority was assumed by his contemporaries. He became the supreme exponent of Enlightenment parables, 'the authentic fables of reason', which communicate a powerful lesson concealed under sparkling wit; to do this he joined the fashion for Oriental fiction. He wrote, 'L'histoire nous apprend ce que sont les humains,/La fable ce qu'ils doivent être.' ('History teaches us what human beings are, Fable what human beings should be').

The fate that holds all in its invisible and unpredictable grasp – be it the Sultan who kills his wives in the frame story, or Solomon, who holds jinn prisoner in bottles – becomes Voltaire's obsessive subject; he perfected a caustic form of Oriental tale to create an arena where he could deal with the question of divine providence, as in the most famous of his *contes, Candide* (1759). Other tales are even more closely patterned on the sequenced adventures in the *Nights* and adopt the oriental stories' characteristic figures of speech, with intensive use of hyperbole, bathos, antithesis, zeugma to absurdist ends, and of narrative modes and motifs (strained coincidences, sudden reversals, burlesque, whimsy, fancifulness, flight).

Zadig, or Destiny is one of the earliest of the short fables which established Voltaire's huge readership in his own time and his lasting importance today. It was written in 1746–7 and published in 1748, over a decade before *Candide*; in many respects, it meditates on the themes that *Candide* targets with even more pointed wit: the workings of providence, predestination and free will, despotism and venality, corruption, public abuses and hypocrisies personal and other. Echoes of the *1001 Nights* sound at the very start: Zadig is subtitled *conte oriental*, and opens with a mock-solemn imprimatur from an oriental official, written with heavy tongue-in-cheek humour; this is followed by another prolegomenon, 'An Epistle Dedicatory' addressed by one 'Sadi' to the Sultana Sheraa and dated at length according to the Islamic calendar year of the Hegira. After this playful satire on pompous patrons and sycophants, Voltaire continues in his arabesque mode: 'It was originally written,' he tells the reader,

> in the Ancient Chaldee, which language neither thou nor I understand. It was translated into Arabic for the amusement of the celebrated Sultan Ouloug-Beg. This was about the time that the Arabs and the Persians were beginning to write the *Thousand and One Nights*, the *Thousand and One Days*, etc. Ouloug preferred *Zadig*; but the sultanas were fonder of the *Thousand and One Nights*. 'How can thee possibly,' wise Ouloug would say to them, 'prefer stories that make no sense and have no point?' – 'That is precisely why we do like them,' would come the sultanas' reply.

Sadi then goes on to assure his patroness that she is clearly different, and will follow Ouloug and prefer his story, 'Zadig', which by implication is full of sense and point.

This *conte* shows Voltaire still prepared to mull over the promises of Leibniz about a benevolent God and to entertain the notion that a higher power might be at work in mysterious ways. Towards the mid-point of his misadventures the innocent and virtuous hero meets an old Babylonian hermit who 'wore a white and venerable beard that came down to his waist. In his hand he held a book . . .' The old man offers it to Zadig for him to have a look. It is 'the Book of Destiny', he tells him, and it will guide Zadig out of his woes, as long as he submits to whatever the hermit asks him to do, unconditionally, for three days. Zadig agrees.

Incomprehensible and unspeakable things start happening: on the third night, for example, a philosopher treats them to wise conversation and houses them comfortably, but in the morning the hermit wakes Zadig early, tells him to start moving, and burns down their host's house. When the hermit's behaviour grows ever more erratic, Zadig cannot help himself and cries out against it.

'"You promised you'd be more patient," the hermit interjected.'

And he explains that everything he has done he has done for the best: for, after 'Providence' burned the good man's house to the ground, he found heaps of treasure there, and 'the young man, who's just had his neck wrung by Providence, would have murdered his aunt within a year, and you within two.' As the hermit is expounding his meaning, Zadig notices he begins to change: into an angel, with 'four beautiful wings and a majestic body that was radiant with light'. His companion is the angel Jesrad, and he closes his prophetic disclosure of the predestined future with the solemn axiom: 'There is no evil from which no good comes' – foreshadowing the Panglossian optimism of *Candide*. To this Zadig replies, 'Mais . . .' (But . . .) and then goes on, 'what if there were only good, and no evil at all?' Jesrad explains that there is an inscrutable order behind all things, and no such thing as chance. 'Feeble mortal,' he cries, 'cease to argue against that which rather you should worship and adore.'

Again Zadig cannot help himself, and blurts out, 'But . . .

'But', that nearly wordless objection to the exhibition of Western metaphysical rationality, is spoken by a stock ingénu from Oriental fabulism, the hapless put-upon hero. This type of Everyman from the *Nights* acts as Voltaire's alter ego and mouthpiece. Through fantastication taken to extremes of preposterous unlikelihood, Voltaire's *contes* set the reader on the ground of scepticism, dissent – and laughter.

This is considered a classical position of enlightened Western discern-ment, so it is worth underscoring that it was shaped by the encounter of the West with the East: straining credulity to the point when sheer entertainment ends and invigorating inquiry breaks out characterises Shahrazad's strategy as she continues, night after night spinning a yarn, to save her life and the life of all her possible fellow victims.

Voltaire in fact adapted the bizarre caprices of the hermit from a very similar series of baffling incidents in the Koran. But there the lessons in patience and submission are delivered by a mysterious 'Green man' who is never named, and the disciple who is tested is none other than Moses, standing in Zadig's place. Regarding the argument about magic arts and Enlightenment, it is significant that Voltaire lifts these 'koans', these meta-physical riddles, to convey his growing doubts about divine order: he is giving an arabesque character to his critique of faith, by making a démarche through Eastern wisdom literature. What he is doing is layered, as always, with irony, and his treatment of the sacred Muslim scripture shows his usual irreverence – an irreverence that Salman Rushdie, a fabulist of this stripe, learned directly from the eighteenth-century rationalists. But the man who was born François-Marie Arouet and had turned himself into Voltaire needed personae to crystallise his thought: through Zadig, Candide and other protagonists of the *contes*, strangers at odds with the world around them, the writer gives himself another pair of eyes.

At one point, Zadig is about to be executed because an enemy who is jealous of him – a Man of Envy, like many in the *Nights* – denounces him for a poem he has written in which he appears to insult the king terribly. However, with the help of a parrot and an astute, kind queen, all is revealed: the verses his accuser has produced are only half of the poem, written on a clay tablet which Zadig, thinking his lines no good, had broken in two, and then let fall in the garden. The two halves of the poem are reassembled, the blamelessness of its sentiments becomes clear, and Zadig is spared death. The poem is a kind of rebus or riddle, and it reads two ways; it is a Borgesian text, with a watermark, as it were, which alters its patent meaning when held up to another light. Voltaire is thereby presenting a succinct parable about the status of truth in any text, poem or legal deposition, historical record or fictional fantasy. The episode also directs us to look through Voltaire to the layers of meaning beneath his clever sallies.

The light, flagrant raillery and the blithely preposterous chain of events he concocts in *Zadig* and *Candide* conceal his earnest purpose; but they are also in some ways apparent insults which can be turned around by a different reading. The exotic places and fantastic oriental courts are all veils – and, not very thick veils at that – transparently draped over Western error, and, more specifically, French abuses of power. By setting his stories in a society that unthinkingly inspired horror, mirth or even contempt in his contemporaries, and showing they bear comparison with his (their/ our) own arrangements, he is relying on existing prejudice to back up his intended meaning. The costume and the geography heighten the comedy – and the critique.

But – to use Zadig's all-important word – in a European setting they also provide camouflage: although Voltaire did pay the price of his outspokenness several times, both in exile and in different prisons in France.

Roger Pearson, the Voltaire scholar and biographer, has vividly unfolded the background to Voltaire's adoption of the Oriental tale. When he was twenty, the duchesse du Maine took him under her wing at her château at Sceaux. Hamilton was one of the habitués, and indeed wrote his *Mémoires* there, where Voltaire may have met him and would certainly have read him. The duchesse was a sybarite of the old school, an aficionado and patron of the theatre, and deeply out of sorts with the puritan régime of Mme de Maintenon, who ruled over King Louis XIV's affections during his final years at Versailles. The pleasure-loving duchesse threw all-night parties with fabulous entertainments. One of these 'Grandes Nuits', held in 1714–15, may have been the setting for Voltaire's first excursions into the literary mode of the *Nights*, when he began making up stories for the company's amusement – and for his survival: the duchesse was his protectress.

An early tale, 'Le Crocheteur borgne' (The One-eyed Porter) picks up in ribald fashion the way one-eyed characters keep turning up in the stories; the hero, a porter, saves a great lady during an accident with her carriage, and instantly obtains satisfaction. This unsavoury hero turns out to possess Solomon's ring. (Given the libertine flavour, one-eyedness here catches the implicit erotic meaning hinted at in the *Nights*, where the stories of the one-eyed dervishes explore unusual sexual permutations, including incest.) Pearson thinks Voltaire was flirtatiously presenting himself as this low-born character, finding himself safe and admired in the duchesse's fabulous court.

Then, in 1747, Voltaire was once again in trouble with the authorities, and he rejoined the duchesse du Maine, this time at her château d'Anet. The writer was on the run because he had been overheard saying the queen had cheated at cards, and he seems to have recognised his own danger in the framing plot of the *Nights*. For a fortnight he remained in hiding, smuggled in under cover of night to sup with the duchesse in her bedroom, where he began to weave for her some of his most sparkling *contes*. 'Fearing royal anger, like Scheherazade,' writes Pearson, 'Voltaire was buying time by illuminating the dark winter evenings of his duchesse-sultana with the white magic of the oriental tale.'

With regard to the uses of the East in Voltaire's tales, clear procedures emerge: changing perspective can open the eyes of the audience, both inside and outside the text. An unfamiliar angle of view on familiar conditions will lift the pall of dull custom and conventional values: seeing the Inquisition through the eyes of a foreigner, for example, exposes its twisted reasoning and vicious procedures. Montesquieu, in *Lettres persanes* (1721), had used this device – the viewpoint of a foreign visitor – and Voltaire's defamiliarisation technique follows this model. By playing on his readers' assumptions about non-Western barbarity and inferiority and then presenting Western government, laws and society as superstitious, irrational and unjust, and their rulers, judges, priests as if they were just such barbarians, Voltaire is able to skewer iniquities at home that exceed iniquities commonly denounced abroad (are the pyres of autos-da-fé in Spain any better than the judicial beheadings of the Ottomans?) Of course, Voltaire's advocacy of tolerance did not include official churches, and all clergy, Eastern and Western, came under his lash: his tragedy *Le Fanatisme, ou Mahomet le Prophète* (first performed 1741) could not be produced today without provoking tumult.

Voltaire does, however, also introduce a positive angle to this ironical perspective: the Orient is important not only as a lens through which to observe his own society and its limits, its mores and prejudices, but because in itself it contains lessons to be learned. In *Zadig*, the hero comes upon a quarrel between believers from different faiths – each maintaining with threatening vehemence the superiority of the god or gods he worships. Zadig manages to calm them by demonstrating that they are all deists (after a fashion) and unanimous in their fundamental faith. Voltaire thus perceived common threads between diverse cultures, as well as distinctions that served his narrative ends of surprise and shock. In certain specific matters, the benevolent reformer in him also chose to dramatise other civilisations' laws, customs and discoveries, to, point the way to social and medical reforms. For instance, Voltaire followed his friend Mary Wortley Montagu in advocating the Turkish practice of inoculation against small-pox.

Of all the motifs of the *Nights* with which Voltaire plays, he warms most beguilingly to the wilful and plucky heroines who set out to rescue their beloved, come what may. When the ardent Formosanta, heroine of *La Princesse de Babylone* (1768), wishes to rejoin her lost beloved Amazon in his far distant realm, the Gangarides, she dons a beard and male garb to travel first to Arabia Felix, and there burn the ashes of her talking parrot. He rises from the flames in splendour, turning out to be none other than the Phoenix of myth, offers her help in her quest by summoning two griffins he knows, and makes up for her 'a comfy little sofa with drawers for your provisions. You will be very much at ease in this vehicle, with your lady-in-waiting. The two griffins are the most vigorous of their kind; each of them will grip one of the arms of the sofa in his talons . . .'

Voltaire is at his most mischievous here, with numerous targets in his sights. Slyly, he is parodying the supernaturalism of myth and romance by attaching giant mythical birds to a flying sofa and adding delicious incongruities: 'The drawers were filled with exquisitely delicate bread rolls, biscuits better than any found in Babylon, large lemons, pineapples, coconut, pistachio nuts, and wine from Eden, which surpasses Shiraz, as Shiraz surpasses the wine of Surinam.'

But, even as he makes fun of female passion, the philosopher shows his admiration for the determined heroines of the *Nights* like Zobeide, Mariam, Zumurrud, Dunya, Badoura – and indeed Shahrazad – who will not be stopped from acting in pursuit of their desires.

In one of the last tales Voltaire wrote, he uses magic against itself in a tour de force of brazen blasphemy. In 'Le Taureau blanc' (The White Bull), written in 1773–74 when he was in his eighties, he turned to biblical stories directly for the first time, rather than oriental or other foreign myths and legends, in order to mock Christianity out of its superior airs. In his old age, the stakes for him were no longer as high as they had been, and he could dare to attack his home targets without dressing them in Eastern costume.

'The White Bull' is the most hilarious of his *contes*; it makes merciless fun of the Bible, splicing together pagan, classical and infidel magic – talking beasts, visions, spells, bodily metamorphoses are blended to create a zany sheaf of wonders which would be deliciously silly if they were not so riskily outspoken.

In the story, the figure of the foreign enchanter returns, as the sympathetic *porte-parole* or alter ego for the author, 'wise Mambres, former sorcerer to the Pharaohs . . .' Why did Voltaire see himself in the guise of the obscure magician from ancient Egypt who had his snakes so ignominiously devoured by Moses and Aaron's? In some ways the reasons are obvious, but he has tremendous fun with the idea.

The joke takes off from the episode in the Bible when Nebuchadnezzar is punished for his idolatry, and becomes 'like a wild beast' with shaggy hair and long nails, condemned to eat 'grass like oxen' (Dan. 4:33). Princess Amasida is disconsolate because she is besotted with Nebuchadnezzar, but he has vanished she knows not where. Wandering in her grief on the banks of the Nile with her tutor ('Old Mambres . . . was at her side. Indeed he almost never left it . . . The Princess was 24 years old, while Mambres the magus was about thirteen hundred'), she comes across a crone surrounded by beasts and holding a fabulously beautiful white bull on a leash. This old woman is the Pythoness, the witch of Endor, who raised the ghost of Samuel in the Bible, and the animals surrounding her consist of all the wonderful creatures who star in the Old Testament: Jonah's whale, Balaam's ass, Tobias's dog, the serpent, and so forth. And the bull is Nebuchadnezzar himself, the princess's lost love – slyly given a touch more virility by association with Zeus in the shape of the beautiful amorous beast who abducts Europa.

The princess does not recognise him but feels inexplicably stirred:

'What an adorable animal,' she said. 'I would like to have him in my stable.'
　　At these words the bull went down on all four knees and kissed the ground.
　　'He understands what I say!' cried the Princess. 'He's showing me that he wants to be mine.'

Nebuchadnezzar has acquired the pretty ways of the metamorphosed victims of the *Arabian Nights*, who in their animal form understand language and give speaking looks to their masters, like the gazelle-wife of 'The First Old Man', and the clever ape from 'The Tale of the Second Dervish'.

The princess demands to be given the bull for a playfellow, but 'Miss Endor' refuses outright, and Mambres then confesses that with old age his powers are diminishing, so he recommends that the princess consult the serpent:

'He is clever, he knows how to put things, and he has long been accustomed to taking a hand in ladies' affairs.' When the princess obeys, she remarks that his reputation has gone before him:

'. . . you started with our common mother, whose name escapes me.'

The serpent answers:

'People malign me. I gave her the best advice in the world . . . Is it not necessary to know both good and evil that we may do one and avoid the other? There is no doubt about it, I should have been thanked.'

Voltaire's fable issues a manifesto for the uses of knowledge, spoken by a fallen angel in the form of a talking snake. He is imitating the irrational flights of traditional storytelling, as found in the *Arabian Nights*, to show that credulity and myth flourished just as well at home. When Zadig the ingénu observer and hapless protagonist is replaced, three decades later, by the older alter ego of Mambres, magus and eunuch, Voltaire is taking up a similar position on the periphery from which he can challenge lazy thinking and prejudice, awaken idle minds, and shake received ideas. But in another respect, the old sorcerer of the Pharaohs aligns the philosopher with prohibited speech, with heresy and outsider status from which he can voice his outrageous dissidence – with a little help from the serpent.

'The White Bull' decisively unmasks the oriental magician, for he has provided the most liberating point of identification for the philosopher, a role in which he can comment freely, beyond the constraints of orthodoxy; the ultimate escape route from every church and every club.

Hugh Haughton explores the dynamics of drollery in his introduction to *The Chatto Book of Nonsense Poetry*: he is talking about nineteenth-century English children's classics but what he writes throws light on Voltaire's methods too: 'This Victorian Nonsense Renaissance . . . forms part at any rate of the inspiring critique of seriousness generated by a culture with a huge investment in ideas of social and intellectual authority and a dedication to the ideal of moral earnestness – a critique played out in the children's books of Lear and Carroll . . . [and] the elegantly subversive dialogues and plays of Oscar Wilde.'

His comments apply equally to the earlier resistance of Enlightenment writers like Voltaire who adopted comic arabesque and silly nonsense to mount their deepest criticisms.

IV

Voltaire reached a huge audience in his day, and the fables affected – changed – more readers' minds than the rest of his *oeuvre*, and still do. The depth of his influence can be seen in the way so many different women writers wrote of emancipation in the Oriental mode. If the East was disparaged as effeminate, its subject condition could refract Western women's condition back to them; if by contrast the East (its male element) is castigated for tyranny and sexual abuses, Western women could again make merry use of this trope. As early as 1749, Mary Wortley Montagu took a cue from the growing vogue for the *Nights* and wrote 'The Sultan's Tale', a witty twist on a virginity test, which pokes fun at men who want to control women and at women who collaborate eagerly with them. As her editor Isobel Grundy comments, Montagu chose to speak through the Sultan, who was 'different in sex, race, creed, and country . . . showing how she felt out of tune with her own society's ways of writing and thinking.' The result is 'a surprisingly good-humoured, non-punitive story' from the pen of an author who was known for the sharpness of her wit.

During its first year, 1770, *The Lady's Magazine* ran dozens of poems, epistles, travel fictions and allegories in the Oriental style; the fashion colours its pages steadily thereafter. In this next generation, orientalising spreads beyond high society, and settles down as a recognised mask for satire and fun by jobbing playwrights working to please the public. Sometimes the form led to less light-footed didacticism: Frances Sheridan imagined the reform of a feckless and worldly young man in her tangled novella, *The History of Nourjahad: The Persian* (1767). The book was a hit in several countries, and reached the stage in 1813 as *Illusion or, The Trances of Nourjahad*; the plot, involving complex dreams, lent itself to stage machinery.

Voltaire's touch can be felt more surely in a different play, the effervescent 'afterpiece' called *The Mogul's Tale, or, The Descent of the Balloon* by the actress Elizabeth Inchbald. Inchbald was working up an earlier harem farce by Isaac Bickerstaffe; in a splendid stroke, she added a balloon voyage to her predecessor's version – the play was performed in 1784, the year of the first Channel crossing in a Montgolfier.

Three Londoners – a quack doctor, Johnny a cobbler, and his wife Fanny – have set off for Kent and landed by mistake in the Seraglio inside Topkapi after their vehicle of 'inflammible air' [*sic*] drifts off course. Inchbald then stages an adroit satire on the prejudices of her contemporaries, when the party from England imagine all kinds of torments and horrors they will suffer at the hands of the Mogul. But the Sultan knows that English folk will think him a despot, a barbarian, an abuser of women and a cannibal, and he enlists his chief eunuch to have a little fun with them: 'Aggravate their fears as much as possible; tell them I am the abstract of cruelty, the essence of tyranny; tell them the divan shall open with all its terrors. For though I mean to save their lives, I want to see the effect of their fears; for in the hour of reflection, I love to contemplate that greatest work of heaven, the mind of man.'

Inchbald's Mogul has been reading Voltaire.

So Fanny is seized for the harem; and the stake, boiling oil and other terrors are prepared for Johnny and the doctor. After much merriment – which shows up the depths of cowardice, faithlessness and generally low character of the English party – the Mogul reveals his magnanimous and enlightened nature and sends them on their way, with a safe conduct, in the repaired balloon.

Story 10

Rosebud and Uns al-Wujud
the Darling Boy

WHEN THE HERO (UNS AL-WUJUD the Darling Boy), at last arrives at the enchanted castle where his beloved, Rosebud (Felkanaman), has been imprisoned by her father, Ibrahim, vizier to the King of Hezan, he's been through thick and thin to reach her. The castle stands on the summit of the Mountain of the Grief-Stricken Mother, in the middle of the sea of Kenouz, one of the stormiest in the world, impassable. But Uns al-Wujud has been helped in his quest by many, for his sweetness and goodness and beauty inspire confidence in all who meet him, as well as a desire for love to succeed: a lion understands his speech and treats him gently, a hermit knows, from something that happened in his youth, just what it feels like to yearn for someone with one's whole heart and soul, and a fisherman shows Ansul how to make a coracle from a gourd tied together with reeds.

At his instructions, the Darling Boy has thrown himself on to the ocean wave when the tide was running towards the enchanted castle.

When the young man, who is as beautiful as the full moon in the black velvet sky of summer, and has the eyes of a gazelle and the waist of a pliant reed, reaches the prison where Rosebud is held, he comes across many caged birds of great beauty and varied species. To his astonishment they sing to him in his own language. Among the songs he hears a fierce dark bird of ill omen croak: 'She has given birth! For a vile maggot she has betrayed the lover whose beauty is beyond compare and whose love beyond measure! She has given birth! She has given birth!'

All around him, these terrible words are picked up by the other birds till the mountain rings to the echo. The words strike Uns to the heart; he falls face-down on the ground groaning and crying out. Wishing for nothing more than death, he tries to drown himself. But finding it difficult, he decides instead to search for his beloved Rosebud and at least reproach her with his death before attempting it again.

Rosebud fell in love with him when she first saw him from her window; he was playing polo with other young men in the grounds below her house, and she tossed an apple at him to capture his attention. He caught it, looked up, saw her, and lightning struck. With her nurse fondly conspiring with them, the two young people managed to write long mad letters of passionate lyric poetry to each other, pouring it out spontaneously then and there in response on the back of the same piece of paper, and sending it with the same messenger. Who was careless, and one of the letters fell into the hands of Rosebud's parents, the vizier Ibrahim and his wife.

Uns al-Wujud is the king's favourite, and so the vizier and his wife are scandalised. They are also scared: the king might not like it at all if Uns loves their daughter. They take extreme measures to prevent this danger, to protect her honour, to forbid her love; they order her to marry a savage oaf who is more convenient to their interests. When she rebels, they carry her off to the enchanted castle on the top of the Mountain of the Grief-Stricken Mother in the middle of the sea of Kenouz, and seal up the steel door with three seals on three great locks. Nobody will be able to find her there.

But Uns drifts across the roiling sea and reaches the castle where he hears the birds taunting him. He doesn't know that Rosebud has already torn her curtains of Damascus silk into shreds, knotted them together to make herself a rope, and let herself down from the turrets of her prison on to the shore below the castle. There, she met a fisherman, who took her at first for a jinniya; indeed, for the demoness well known to haunt the castle. But the young woman brushed aside his terror, forestalled his desire to tell her his life story, and commanded him to row as hard as he could and take her away from this terrible place so that she could be reunited with her beloved.

After missing each other so narrowly, the two lovers' quest now takes them far and wide, their stories becoming entangled in the lives of several other kings and viziers. Rosebud ends up in the country of the Sultan Dara, who recognises trueness of heart when he sees it. Her beauty and courage and the unswerving depths of her love for Uns inspire him, and he orders his vizier, Fakhrir, immediately to load twenty camels with musk and other spices, to pick fifty beautiful girls from his harem and fifty beautiful boys from his entourage, and offer all of this to the King of Hezan in return for his favourite, Uns the Darling Boy. If this prince's ransom does not persuade the King of Hezan to part with the young man, Fakhrir is to put on the table his own son and the sons of nine other viziers, if necessary.

The Sultan concludes his orders: 'If you come back without Uns the Darling Boy, I shall have your head cut off.'

When the vizier reaches the Hezan court, he finds that Uns has vanished around the same time as Rosebud was stolen away by her father. He does not dare return to tell Sultan Dara that he has failed in his mission. Instead he settles down to commiserate with his counterpart, the vizier Ibrahim, although he knows better than to let him into the secret that his daughter has escaped her island prison and arrived in Hezan and charmed the Sultan into helping her. So he agrees when Ibrahim suggests they set out for the enchanted castle, as they both expect that Uns might be looking for her there.

The two old men eventually arrive at the island in the roiling sea of Kenouz, and when they hear the caged birds crying out against the faithless lover who has borne another's child, Ibrahim recognises the story and begins to tell it to his travelling companion, the vizier Fakhrir, who is looking for Rosebud's missing lover, Uns the Darling Boy . . .

Story 11: The Jinniya and the Egyptian Prince

A king of Egypt had a son, Chemnis, for whom he wanted every advantage of upbringing and education, and to this end, he installed him in a quiet retreat on an island in the middle of a great lake. There the boy studied, and made great progress. On his eighteenth birthday, however, he told his father he wanted to taste the world; he had acquired deep learning, but no experience of life. The king offered him girls, but the young man asked instead to see the pyramid that his father was building for his tomb after his death. The father was flattered by this surprising filial devotion, and granted his wish.

On his finger, Chemnis had a magic ring of Solomon which protected him against maleficent jinn, but not, the father feared, against the wild animals – asps and crocodiles – which might have made a lair inside the pyramid. So he ordered a vast host of armed attendants to precede his son into the monument. But they could not pass: a wind arose at the entrance, felled them senseless to the ground, and drove their horses mad and ungovernable. Only the prince himself could enter, armed by the ring.

Inside, he found terrible darkness, mystery, and labyrinthine walls. In his confusion and terror, he lost consciousness and fell to the ground. There, a young jinniya discovered him – Fikelah, she was called, and her mother Roncai had given her the pyramid for her playground. She gathered the prince into her arms and flew up with him to her roost, which was lit by thousands of phosphorescent crystals and drenched in the most delicious and costly perfumes from the land of the jinn. She laid Chemnis in her lap and would him in her arms; her tears, spilling on to his face, woke him up.

For three hours they made love in total bliss. But the jinniya's mother Roncai burst in on them, and seeing them intertwined, exploded with rage. She railed and cursed the lovers, summoning snakes and reptiles and lizards and crocodiles, her faithful followers:

'Devour him, and don't leave a single crumb!' she screamed.

His crime? To make love to a young woman in the first place, but to make love – he, a human male – to a jinniya, daughter of Roncai the guardian of the pyramid!

Contrary to his father's understanding of the ring, it did have the power to repel the reptiles, and Roncai was stunned as she watched her army of monsters recoil from their victim, unable to fulfil her commands. She became determined to have the ring. Fikelah bargained with her mother: she could have the ring, but only if she allowed her to marry her sweet human lover.

Roncai's lust for the powers which the ring would give her surpassed her loyalty to the jinn species. She swore that she would allow the marriage and give the couple her protection; she swore it three times. But, as soon as Chemnis surrendered the ring and she was wearing it in triumph on her finger, she revealed that the resplendent multicoloured firebird, the Simurgh, loved Fikelah with a mad love. The Simurgh was so enraged at Fikelah's marrying at all, let alone marrying out of the world of jinn, that he was mustering every marvellous beast in the world to harass them in perpetuity. The only thing left for the lovers was to vanish: Roncai told them she would raise a magic castle on the summit of a mountain in the middle of the sea of Kenouz, where even the jinn would not be able to find them.

So, Ibrahim the vizier explains to his listener, the other old vizier, on their embassy to find Ansul the Darling Boy, 'We are now in that very castle, and the mountain is called after Fikelah because she was hidden there by her mother, as I later hid my daughter here − for similar reasons. Indeed, it is the old fairy story which gave me the idea.'

But the great bird-jinn Simurgh was not happy with Roncai's arrangements. He still wanted the young jinniya for his wife, and he now lusted after the magic ring as well. How was he to make the mother part with it? He commanded a monstrous afrit in his train to come up with a scheme. This demon, knowing how much Roncai liked to go fishing, patiently trained a very large and tempting fish by starving it and then giving it the finger of a human corpse to nibble. Every day he repeated this, and the fish learned to feed on the fingers, *faute de mieux*, until he had the trick pat. Then the horrid afrit slipped the fish into a pool outside the pyramid, and lured Roncai to put her hand out to catch it; she took the bait and the fish took her finger − with the ring.

Once he had possession of the ring, the afrit roared with laughter in the Simurgh's face: he wasn't going to let him have it, now that he was master of the ring. But the bird bent him to his will; they would combine forces.

In the meantime in the castle, the lovers were in seventh heaven, not knowing the doom that was about to fall on them. Fikelah conceived, and when she had the baby, jinn the world over broke out into a great lament, crying out,

'She's given birth! She's betrayed a lover whose beauty is beyond compare and his love beyond measure − for a vile maggot. She's given birth! She's given birth!'

At this ghastly din, the midwife receiving the baby took fright and dropped the newborn, and his tender skull broke into a thousand pieces.

This catastrophe left the lovers near to death. The prince, sensing how fast his end was approaching, begged his fairy wife to grant him one last wish, and carry him to see his father one more time, where he was still waiting, encamped outside the pyramid, wailing for his lost child. For the last time, Fikelah gathered up Chemnis in her arms, and flew with him back to Egypt; there, she laid him down beside his sorrowing father, who gave the lovers his blessing, just as Chemnis breathed his last.

The jinniya would never leave this place, she swore, but would haunt the tomb until ten thousand years had passed and Chemnis was resurrected from the dead. In the meantime the Simurg took his revenge on the jinn who had served the lovers during their brief time of happiness in the enchanted castle. He turned them all into birds and shut them in cages.

'That is what you see here,' says Ibrahim, the father of Rosebud, to Fakhrir his counterpart, who knows where his daughter is but is still not telling. 'The Simurgh,' he continues, 'not content with the destruction he has wrought, returns to the castle now and then in the shape of a dark bird of sinister omen, and here he cries his slanders to create more mischief in the world.'

After this romance, in which the wicked succeed and love is woe, the vizier and his companion set about searching the enchanted castle for the two young people. Ibrahim soon discovers, to his astonishment, that his daughter has managed to escape. Meanwhile, unknown to both viziers, Uns the Darling Boy is still there. He's weakened by sorrow and hardship, his beauty a little battered, but from his hiding place he has heard the whole story of the Mountain of the Grief-Stricken Mother, and he knows now what he always felt in his bones, that his beloved Rosebud is loyal, that she is not the young mother whose shame is being cried out by the uncanny speaking birds. He also knows that they are spreading shameful lies about a jinniya who loved her beloved faithfully, too.

So his hopes rally, and he stows away on the viziers' boat under a heap of tiger skins.

There he learns, from the anguished mutterings of the vizier Fakhrir, that the old man has been sent to find him by his master, Sultan Dara, on pain of death, and that Rosebud herself is in the court there, alive, and has told them the story of their love.

When the right moment comes to reveal himself, Uns al-Wujud does so. At first Fakhrir cannot believe that this skeletal stowaway, who hasn't seen the inside of a bathhouse for weeks, can be the same Darling Boy who was once as beautiful as the full moon. But Uns promises that if he's given enough to eat and provided with some soap, perfume and gorgeous clothes, he'll soon be himself again.

And so it turns out at last, once the party reach the court of Sultan Dara. The lovers are reunited, and Rosebud asks only for an hour or two to be alone with her love.

'As we have never spoken to each other,' she says, 'we have a great deal to talk about.'

The King of Hezan, whose favourite Uns was, now gives his permission with joy; Ibrahim, Rosebud's father, follows suit, but grudgingly.

The young marrieds make love madly for days, indeed for so long that the Sultan gets worried and calls on them. Uns eventually leaves their bed and brings Rosebud with him; when the Sultan congratulates them on their unsurpassed love story, Uns begins, 'But you don't know the story of Azora from Kashmir, whose happiness was almost equal to ours . . .'

CHAPTER FOURTEEN

'Symbols of Wonder': William Beckford's Arabesque

Stick to the East . . . The North, South, and West have all been exhausted
. . . the public are Orientalising.

Lord Byron to Tom Moore, 1813

I

THE STORY ABOUT ROSEBUD AND Uns al-Wujud the Darling Boy
appears in many different editions of the *Nights*, but none, as far as I
know, includes the story which the writer William Beckford (1760–1844)
interjects, 'The Jinniya and the Egyptian Prince'. The protagonists often
allude to a legend that gave the mountain its sad name, but their accounts
make little sense. (Lane has the jinn happily giving birth to 'hundreds of
children' – and it is their crying that passing sailors hear. But that would
hardly add 'Grief-Stricken Mother' to the mountain's name.) Beckford
paid attention to these inconsistencies and weaknesses in the fabric of
the narrative, possibly because he was working from an Arabic manuscript,
and the discipline of translation sharpens one's wits. But he supplied a
cogent story, one that provides a satisfying reverse image of the blissful
framing romance. It may contain autobiographical elements – Beckford's
wife, to whom he was very attached, died young in childbirth. It certainly
patches and pieces very adroitly figures and motifs and plots from the
Nights and the *Nights*' imitators – the human–jinn marriage, the talking
birds, the crossed lovers. In this approach, Beckford continues the work
of Shahrazad, and fits the profile of Borges's ideal reader of the stories,
as described in the essay on 'The Translators of the *Nights*', that every
reader can be, and should be, creative; that you can make up the stories
as you please. In the process, the translator is being translated.

Such translated writers are notable cases; they include Goethe and
Edward Fitzgerald, whose Omar Khayýam became a solid English classic.
Goethe took to wearing a caftan and turban, as many eighteenth-century
gentlemen, and women, had done before him; Fitzgerald did not 'turn

Turk' beyond the page. Although Beckford did not travel in the East and did not adopt oriental dress, his relationship with the culture and the languages was deep, especially in his youth when he was studying Arabic and Persian and reading the *Nights* in the Wortley-Montagu manuscripts. Laurent Châtel persuasively describes Beckford's approach to the *Nights* as a deep imaginative engagement beyond translation and imitation, dissolving critical distance in favour of 'fusion with the matter and structure' of the stories. The ventriloquy demanded by this relationship interestingly matches the multiple voices and shape-shifting forms of the stories' protagonists, both human and jinn; this conception of potential fluidity of identity presents one of the most influential psychological manifestations of magical thinking that took hold in modernity, offering a site of new meanings, alongside charmed things and phantasmic money. The Oriental masquerade meets the dream of labile performative personae, as represented by heroes like Marouf or Aladdin, and at the same time truly gave impersonators like Beckford the chance of metamorphosis.

For these reasons, Beckford emerges as a crucial figure in the history of the *Nights'* reception, aesthetically and politically. Yet this is unexpected, because, unlike Voltaire, Frances Sheridan, Mary Wortley Montagu or Goethe, nobody reads much of anything by Beckford the orientalist, except for his novel *Vathek* (1786). This work was published incomplete, and still appears without the several curious tales that he, like Shahrazad, wanted to nest one inside the other within the larger plot. He chose to write in French, adopting an exaggerated libertine and foreign persona the better to assault British class and sexual conventions, and out-*épater* the *épateurs*. His many weird and violent *Arabian Nights* stories are sublime and absurd, in earnest and in jest, Gothic in their exaggerations and black humour; they were not published in his lifetime and vanished after his death. They have only appeared haphazardly, from specialist publishing houses for the most part, and have still not been treated to scholarly editions. Beckford is one of a not inconsiderable number of great writers whom everyone knows, and whose fame rests on his extravagant and scandalous personality (a reputation only partly justified).

'Voici encore de l'arabesque . . .' (Here again is some arabesque . . .), he writes in the preface to oriental tales he wrote in the 1780s. The Beckfordian arabesque announces many shifts in the destiny of the *Nights*: his hyperbolic prose acts like the magician Bahram's burning glass, concentrating the heat and distorting what it claims to represent; at the same time, more reliably, the work looks into the distant future, and like Prince Ali's spyglass, reveals the theatrical destiny of the *Nights*, and the stories' closeness to games with fact and fiction and the arts of spectacle and illusion. He exaggerates, he lampoons, he derides, he postures, he romances; he breathes in everything he can discover and beams it outwards transmogrified. Imperial Gothic, grotesque fantasy, sublime pathos and flagrant profanities breach accepted decorum and native British manners; these excesses are combined with frivolous pastiche and burlesque exaggeration.

In 1776, on one of his European tours, the sixteen-year-old Beckford, accompanied by his tutor, visited Voltaire at Ferney, shortly before the philosopher's death; later, he remembered him as an 'old skeleton with eyes like carbuncles'. The younger man's dissenting imagination owes much to the rational ironies of both Voltaire and Hamilton. But, as a storyteller, he breathes a far more macabre and excitable atmosphere than either of them – the miasma of Romantic Gothic, of Horace Walpole and Mary Shelley, pervades Beckford's writings. However, he did learn from Hamilton and Voltaire a certain stylish lightness, and his rhetoric is packed with figures of speech deployed by his French predecessors to intensify absurdism and irony. He was keenly aware of their example: in a letter of 1782, he wrote, 'My Arabian tales go on prodigiously, and I think Count Hamilton will smile on me when we are introduced in Paradise.'

Even in his most smiling mood, however, the younger writer never attains Hamilton's nonchalance; his writing is strenuous, aiming at dazzling effect, and tinged with desperation. Yet the enchantments in the *Arabian Nights*, the stories' mix of excitement and languor, offered this edgy and complicated man a way of freeing his erotic fantasy, and in *Vathek* and other stories he singles out the sulphurous drama of fire worship to create his sorcerers and blasphemers and reprobates. Stéphane Mallarmé and Jorge Luis Borges prized *Vathek* very highly indeed, far more highly than Beckford's reputation in his own country yet stands. Mallarmé combed the reviews to see if anyone noticed the first edition of the novel in the original French; he is very funny about how he hunted high and low, but still found nothing. He raves against this neglect, heaps praises on the author and his style, compares Beckford with other Orientalising writers, to Flaubert and Gautier, and concludes that *Vathek* is 'one of the proudest gambles of the nascent modern imagination.'

Elinor Shaffer comments, 'It is not merely the exotic settings that bring Beckford and Flaubert together but the strange, charged, yet dreamlike atmosphere, fervid, sensual, with a streak of cruelty . . .' Beckford knows how to twist responses into lingering, horrible incongruities: a kind of experimental chef, an avatar of Heston Blumenthal in the realm of Enlightenment literature, he creates prose that reads like snail ice cream or seaweed custard.

Oriental Gothic, which Beckford practised to extremes, shares with
Imperial Gothic its response to the beliefs, demons and occult powers
of cultures beyond Europe; but the *Nights* originated in cultures that
were not directly subject to Europe or Britain, though they were in
tense and often ambiguous relations with Western powers. Egypt, the
Ottoman empire and Persia were established and independent states,
however ambitiously Britain and other nations fought over them, sought
to control them and offer 'protection'. They were also, strictly speaking,
on an enemy footing in a more formal way than the territories of the
New World in the first phase of colonialism. Beckford was the beneficiary
of a vast fortune rooted in slavery (he never visited his many sugar estates
in Jamaica), and when his father, a former Mayor of London, died, he
was left one of the richest young men in the country, if not the richest.
Like his younger contemporaries Southey and Coleridge, he gave expression to his personal complications in fantasies that mix Western fears
with animist and supernatural beliefs: possession, animal transformations,
demons and jinn.

The *Nights* opened a way of making literature, of being and living.
Beckford cultivated a plurality of selves, plunging himself into a delirium
of costumes, voices and metamorphoses. The resulting mix of flavours is
particularly strong in one of his tales: 'Messac la Négresse aux araignées'
(Messac, the Spider Negress), which is imbricated in the Oriental tale,
'Histoire de Darianoc, Jeune Homme du Pays de Gou-Gou' (The Story
of Darianoc, a Young Man from the Land of Gou-Gou). The hero travels
in a great caravan across wilderness and mountains to see the King of
the Snakes in his palace in the abyss; he has been allowed to join a vast
throng of magi and sorcerers, and like them is riding a gigantic ostrich;
alongside them, in baskets on other beasts of burden, they are convoying
hundreds of babies whom they have stolen and are fattening up for a
colossal sacrifice to the Snake King. The hero has won the grudging
tolerance of the profane company, in spite of his refusal to worship their
god, because he has confronted – and survived – a spell in the cave of
the sorceress of the story's title, a squalid and grotesque witch who feeds
her pet spiders till they reach a colossal size, and spins their silk and
bakes their webs into cakes she insists on feeding our hero. The words,
mossak, to hold, and *massakh*, to denature, sound in her name, Messac.

This is told by a typical Beckfordian first-person narrator, portrayed
as a committed unbeliever yet a true child of the Enlightenment, hungry
for knowledge, whatever horrors it holds, whatever terrors and ordeals
it inflicts. He quails before the ghastliness of what he finds, yet always
wants to know more and go further. If the story had not been discovered

among Beckford's *Nachlass*, it would be easy to think it was by Edgar Allan Poe or even H.P. Lovecraft.

The young Beckford 's enthusiasm for the exotic had been awakened by one of his many tutors, the artist Alexander Cozens, who had been appointed by his mother after his father's death. His mother, a devout Presbyterian, decided her brilliant son needed to be home-schooled, so he left Eton and was tutored by a combination of exceptional teachers, who accompanied him on several European tours. Another of them, the Reverend Samuel Henley, was an American who had taken the side of the British in the War of Independence and then left the new country for the former royal and colonial power.

Beckford started writing very young – an early piece, 'The Fountain of Merlin', finds him treating a faery legend with a Romantic touch; another work, produced at the age of twenty, is cast as a guide-book to Fonthill, his home (*Biographical Memoirs of Extraordinary Painters*, 1780), but the artists are all made up. He was already enjoying mocking genres and disturbing the boundaries between the elevated and the low, but the oriental tale dominated his imagination for a decade of productive, indeed frenzied writing.

His studies in Arabic and Persian began in his teens and were pursued in a circle around Lady Craven, later Margravine of Brandenburg-Anspach-Bayreuth (1750–1828), whom Beckford called his 'dear Arabian'. Elizabeth Craven was a spirited writer, theatre-lover, wit, traveller, society beauty and femme fatale; she knew several languages already and had been coached in Arabic by Dr Joseph White, the Laudian Professor at Oxford. During the 1780s, with the help of 'Zémir, the old Mohammedan', Beckford, Elizabeth Craven and others worked on reading the *Arabian Nights*, in the Wortley-Montagu manuscripts. Now partly deposited in the Bodleian Library, they include several bundles of tales, written in classical Arabic with some traces of Egyptian dialect. Some of these stories came to be known later from other manuscripts, but at the time, since many of them were not in Galland, they were entirely new to Europe. The bundles also contain numerous other tales which have not entered the familiar corpus, and one volume of the whole book is missing.

Because the manuscript transmission is so patchy, it is impossible to assess how much *Vathek* owes to this material. Beckford himself was very clear that he composed it as a fiction: 'I had begun to translate it literally. My Arabic teacher, an old Muslim born in Mecca, had recommended it as a language exercise . . . Zémir wanted to rein me in, quite rightly, but once I had the bit between my teeth, I hurled myself at a full gallop into the regions of my wandering imagination.'

This approach has absorbed Arabic ideas of authorship, which revere originality far less than an ideal originary voice, which, sounding in subsequent work by other hands, validates their efforts. *Imitatio*, parody, homages, ventriloquy and doublings characterise the classical Arabic literature Beckford was absorbing, while the popular stories are unauthored and multivocal, with porous borders and hospitable structures. He would draw from the materials he was studying – *il puisera'*, he wrote, using the word for drawing water from a well; he would not translate directly. So his oriental tales conduct a complicated, ultimately inscrutable dialogue with the originals: Beckford approaches the texts he was reading in multiple roles: as apprentice linguist, literary translator, cultural expositor, exhibitionist scholar, fantasist and forger – and impresario and party-giver.

Two legendary parties, for his twenty-first birthday in October 1781 and the Christmas that followed it, were thrown in spectacular style, with the Swiss-born artist and designer Philippe-Jacques de Loutherbourg, in charge of the production, instructed to make the party resemble something from the *Arabian Nights*.

That very year, Loutherbourg had been exhibiting his new invention in Lisle Street off Leicester Square, the Eidophusikon, a kind of son-et-lumière machine, which projected scenes of natural wonders. (Eidophusikon, meaning 'Form embodied', is an early instance of Greek terms for new science, as in 'panorama', 'kaleidoscope', 'phantascope'). Storms at sea, avalanches, conflagrations in battle, and the dark satanic mills of industrial England inspired Loutherbourg's works on canvas; for the miniature stage of his machine, he pioneered back lighting, made rollers on which back projections and floor pieces rose up and down, painted backdrops on veils and scrims, angled candlelight dramatically, and provided musical accompaniment. Between tasteful excursions into the picturesque, Loutherbourg staged what he called 'A Transparency'. These painted gauzes took a turn into terror and the supernatural, in particular with the grand finale, inspired by Milton: 'Satan arraying his Troops on the Banks of the Fiery Lake, with the Raising of Pandemonium'.

Loutherbourg had in effect taken the concept of the magic lantern and expanded it to fill a stage; so becoming one of the great proto-cinematic innovators, alongside Robertson and Philippsthal of the Phantasmagoria shows of the late eighteenth century.

Between the first run and second season of the Eidophusikon's performances, Loutherbourg was summoned to Fonthill to design the festivities. Later, Beckford looked back yearningly on his youthful friends' partying:

Even at this long, sad distance from these days and nights of exquisite refine-ments, chilled by age, still more by the coarse unpoetic tenor of the present disenchanting period – I still feel warmed and irradiated by the recollections of that strange, necromantic light which Loutherbourg had thrown over what absolutely appeared a realm of Fairy, or rather, perhaps, a Demon Temple deep beneath the earth set apart for tremendous mysteries – and yet how soft, how genial was this quiet light ... The glowing haze investing every object, the mystic look, the vastness, the intricacy of this vaulted labyrinth occasioned so bewildering an effect that it became impossible for any one to define – at the moment – where he stood, where he had been, or to whither he was wandering – such was the confusion – the perplexity so many illuminated storys of infinitely varied apartments gave rise to. It was, in short, the realization of romance in its most extravagant intensity. No wonder such scenery inspired the description of the Halls of Eblis.

Zémir was there ('A right old Mussulman . . . on hand to serve up tales hot & hot . . .'), and it was after the Christmas party, in the early part of 1782, that Beckford sat up for three days and two nights, and wrote *Vathek* in a delirious spate of fantasy: 'I was soaring on the Arabian bird roc, among genii and enchantments, not moving among men.' (Or so he claimed, later.)

Towards the beginning of *Vathek*, a stranger appears at the Caliph's court, 'a man so abominably hideous that the very guards, who arrested him, were forced to shut their eyes'. He bears with him some fabulous toys: slippers on springs, magic knives 'that cut without motion of the hand', and 'sabres, that dealt the blow at the person they were wished to strike ... the blades of which, emitted a dazzling radiance ... [with] uncouth characters engraven on their sides.' Beckford gives his name only as the Giaour (infidel in Turkish, derived from Persian), who identi-fies himself: '. . . know, that I am an Indian; but, from a region of India, which is wholly unknown'. He is variously referred to as 'the wonderful stranger', 'the frightful Indian', and other phrases in the same lurid vein. 'The man, or rather monster,' writes Beckford, '. . . opened wide his huge eyes which glowed like firebrands; began to laugh with a hideous noise, and discovered his long amber-coloured teeth, bestreaked with green.'

The Caliph throws him in irons, but by the next morning, the Giaour has flown and all the guards are dead. Vathek then proclaims his absolute need to learn the secrets encrypted in the talismanic sabres. A sage manages to decipher the mysterious inscription, and it promises that 'We, that is the swords, were made where every thing is well made: we are the least of the wonders of a place where all is wonderful.' Like the

Caliph in 'The City of Brass', Vathek becomes consumed with curiosity to travel to this wonderful place. The next day, the inscription on the sabres has changed; again, someone is found who can read it, and it now warns that a rash mortal should not seek to know 'that of which he should be ignorant'.

When the Giaour reappears, he commands Vathek to abjure Mahomet and worship his god, Fire, instead, and then promises him all the wisdom of Solomon, if he will only follow him to the infernal underworld of Eblis. 'It was from thence that I brought my sabres,' says this monstrous avatar of the jinn in the *Nights*, 'and it is there that Soliman Ben Daoud [Solomon Son of David] reposes, surrounded by the talismans that control the world.'

Indeterminacy and fluidity of reference and meaning characterise these charged opening scenes; as Rebecca Johnson has observed, the shifting messages on the magic swords embody the elusiveness of texts, and subliminally act as a warning to the reader not to trust too much in what is printed. 'The sabres dramatise indeterminacy,' writes Châtel, 'in a tale where perception is subjected to distortion and metamorphosis'. The material processes involved in making a text are necessary to magical formulae, whether incised into starched cotton on magic shirts or engraved on gems, or metal, as in curse tablets of lead or the scintillating sabres. Unknowability sets an unbearable limit on a man like Vathek, and the Giaour's mysterious promises lure him towards an impossible goal of stability and lucidity.

The Giaour is another dark magician, a descendant of the enemies of the *Nights*, and the various gewgaws which this strange magus presents to Vathek to tempt him are magic toys (the sabres with the labile inscriptions are specifically called talismans by Beckford, in an early use of the word). Vathek follows the sabres' call and sets out in a great caravan to the far-flung territories of the earth, with his beloved Nouronihar and her playmate Gulchenrouz, a girlish boy of great if sickening sweetness. Throughout the journey that takes him to Eblis and damnation, both the Caliph and his fantastic, Medea-like sorceress mother Carathis, perpetrate extremes of savagery on their slaves and on the populace. The novel heaps one horrendous incident upon another: the sacrifice of fifty little boys, enticed by the Caliph, the throng of 'deaf-mute negresses' around Carathis, even the mocking of the chief eunuch Bababalouk by the harem, keep twisting the responses of the reader from terrified recoil to hilarious, horrid laughter.

Eventually Vathek reaches the abyss of Eblis, the 'the first truly atrocious Hell in literature', Borges called it, where like Don Giovanni, Vathek and

Nouronihar will be consumed in fire for ever, their hearts kindled in excruciating pain. The good Gulchenrouz, by contrast, 'passed whole ages in undisturbed tranquillity, and in the pure happiness of childhood'.

Vathek summons a fantastic vision of orientalist tyranny and apostasy in a spirit of macabre humour which finally turns edifying and punishes the perpetrators of atrocity. Yet the book's targets remain out of focus: the author clearly sympathises – indeed identifies – with Vathek in his quest for knowledge, his lust to acquire curios, talismans, and manuscripts of magic power, his hunger for visionary knowledge, and his supreme contempt for ordinary belief and religious observance. But the self-portraiture goes deeper.

The book's conclusion joins this work to the Faustian corpus of myth: given its Orientalism, what Vathek discovers issues a warning, not so much against presuming against God, as in the Christian Faust story, but against imagining that there are no limits to knowledge of others. In other words, Beckford is reminding himself, as well as his readers, that the inscriptions on the sabres are hard to grasp – even after being read. Beckford's imagination is rooted in antiquarianism; and this warning against too much trust in bookishness itself connects him to the side of the Gothic that surfaces in Poe's tales of cryptography and occult texts, and, later, to M. R. James and the Victorian English ghost story. *Vathek* itself bears out this underlying mistrust, for its authorship is ambiguous, and the story's meanings and tone notoriously slippery.

Beckford held off publication because he wanted to include tales-within-tales in the Chinese box fashion of the *Nights*; these 'Episodes' were to be told towards the close of the book, when the Caliph and Nouronihar have reached Eblis. In a letter from Geneva in 1785, during his self-imposed flight from England, he wrote to his former tutor Henley: 'We have had a dismal winter, ground cracked, shrubs pinched, etc. the workmen numbed; but I have gone on sinking my princes to hell with active perseverance.'

As in Dante's poem, the sinners in this Muslim inferno speak of their folly and vice to the newcomers, but in this novel, there will be no return to the upper air for Vathek and his love. Three sufferers, whose hearts are burning visibly in their breasts, take it in turns to relate what they did on earth. Dante-like, Vathek listens to the stories of their sins and their punishment, before his own heart and Nouronihar's are kindled to the same torment.

II

After *Vathek* was rushed into print in 1786, without Beckford's permission, by his English translator and former tutor the Revd Samuel Henley, Beckford promised again and again to finish and include these extra stories, announcing their appearance in the second French edition of 1787 and in subsequent editions of the novel. However, these largely unread 'Episodes' are not the only oriental fictions he wrote. He produced a considerable number which have remained even more obscure, also written in French; these were collected in a volume in 1992, entitled *Suite de contes arabes.*

A tangled history of edition and publication has obscured Beckford's importance as a European writer with interests beyond European borders. Although the story has been told many times, some of the knots are worth unpicking here, as they bear on the psychological freedoms that oriental impersonation and masquerade made possible and the consequences for attitudes to the 'Orient'.

Henley's edition removed Beckford's name and presented the work under a multiple series of masks: first he added a subtitle on the title page – 'An Arabian Tale, from an Unpublished Manuscript: With Notes Critical and Explanatory' and then a Preface, in which he stated, 'The Original of the following Story, with some others of a similar kind, collected in the East by a Man of letters, was communicated to the Editor above three years ago. The pleasure he received from the perusal of it, induced him at that time to transcribe, and since to translate it. How far the copy may be a just representation, it becomes not him to determine.'

This is very sly: Henley rejects the use of the first person for himself, and then with sleight of hand fudges the manuscript's history – is the 'Editor' transcribing and editing 'the Original', or is he distinguishing it from 'the following story'?

Henley's act of annexation and his furtive editorialising collapse both Beckford's authorship and their joint industry of annotation into an act of faithful scholarly orientalism until both men disappear – an example of the Barthesian principle that myth presents itself as history. But Henley was not quite satisfied that this vanishing trick would work and a second title page precedes the text of *Vathek*, announcing 'The History of the Caliph Vathek, with Notes'. The repetition impresses the reader again with the authenticity of what is to follow: the book was a translation of an Arabic original, about the historical Abbasid ruler in the ninth century, al-Wathiq, grandson of Harun al-Rashid. The notes, all 122 pages of them, keep buttressing episodes, scenery, customs and costumes and other elements in the story with explanatory quotations and midrashic commentary. Henley insisted: 'to exhibit *Vathek* properly in English . . . to the story itself, should be subjoined notes to illustrate the costume: otherwise a very considerable part of its merit must be lost to 999 readers of a thousand'.

The supplementary material was the subject of intense correspondence between Henley and Beckford, with the latter audibly trying to restrain Henley's prolixity and at the same time passing on yet more wonderful and extraordinary details of oriental lore from his voracious reading; soon the pair of them were footnoting the footnotes. Henley wants to do justice to Beckford's erudition but he also wants to show off his own; and he is still playing the tutor, while his former pupil is struggling out of the role. At one point he adds a long digression on the history and use of fans – from Queen Elizabeth I's to their incidence in Milton, all accompanied by illustrations.

When Beckford produced his own edition, from his original French, the following year, he struck out all these digressions – contracting the first edition's Notes to 23 pages. In 1816, returning to the book again, he expanded them to 56 pages. He was also keen to elide history and fiction, fantasy and erudition; but while Henley was pushing *Vathek* to be read as a window on a real Middle East, Beckford was struggling to keep the reader's eyes on myths, wonders and sublime, imaginary horrors.

Henley's actions can be excused on the grounds that he was trying to represent Beckford's multiple roles accurately, and that he kept the work anonymous on account of Beckford's notoriety – Beckford had fled England after he was found in an apparent Sadeian tableau with William, known as 'Kitty', Courtenay, his sixteen-year-old cousin, and a boy of indeed kittenish prettiness, if his portrait is to be credited. But several other points can be made about Henley's framing of the book, as well as the mise-en-abyme of Beckford's work within them.

The protestations of *Vathek*'s authenticity, and the two men's protracted labours to ground the work in a rich humus of historical and ethnographic 'true reporting', places the whole construction on shifting sands. Yet the learning that presents itself so authoritatively does extend readers' knowledge against the grain. Both Henley and Beckford mined little-read materials about the East, and from the point of view of fiction, especially supernatural and magical fantastic fiction, many entries in the notes hold great interest: the entry on 'Genii', for example, quotes the Koran as the chief authority, and tells the story of how genies or jinn helped Solomon build the Temple, before helpfully likening genies to 'subtle' spirits in seventeenth-century philosophy. The entry for 'Gouls' expands with great enthusiasm: 'Gouls – Goul, or Ghul, in Arabick, figures any terrifying object, which deprives people of the use of their senses. Hence it became the appellation of that species of monster which was supposed to haunt forests, cemeteries, and other lonely places; & believed not only to tear in pieces the living, but to dig up and devour the dead.'

Comparing the two editions, Beckford shows he knows the *Nights*, and wants to cite the stories; Henley confesses that he read the book years ago and cannot remember it well enough. Beckford's notes on ghouls, for instance, bring in the story of Amina from the *Nights*, which Henley does not mention.

These annotations introduce key terms in magical thinking: 'ghoul', 'jinn' or 'genie', and 'talisman', as we have seen, provided an alternative lexicon for phenomena and practices which were already understood – there had been demons and charms and spells in England since the Romans at least – but they acquired nuance and modernity through exotic distancing and could re-enter the repertoire of the European imaginary in this guise.

The scholarship that frames *Vathek* has designs on the reader. Byron responded as desired when he praised Beckford for its accuracy as well as its fantasy: 'for correctness of costume, beauty of description, and power of imagination, *Vathek* far surpasses all European imitations,' he wrote in a footnote in his own oriental fantasy (partly inspired by Beckford), *The Giaour*, '. . . and bears such marks of originality, that those who have visited the East will find some difficulty in believing it to be more than a translation.' Byron's appreciation follows from the ways Galland and others had recommended reading oriental tales as documents of their societies. Their stance at least presupposed readers who dreamed of travelling somewhere they had never been. In contrast, while Byron rightly notices the ambiguity of *Vathek*'s generic status, it is surely alarming that he finds that this book, so extraordinary in its extremes, actually verifies experience of the East.

The fictive device of annotating a novel with a rich historical apparatus goes further than a self-delighting, pre-Borgesian playfulness with figments and reality. The Oriental character also gives readers a context which moves them out of their native habitat into an exotic realm where alternative ways become open to them. Presented as a real Arabic document, *Vathek*'s invitation to the voyage gains in persuasive permissiveness. Beckford's collaboration with Henley seduced readers into entering the Orient without an intermediary – the author or authors having been disappeared. That 'Other' place, with its different ways, also enjoyed a great advantage: unlike ourselves, it was *capable de tout*. The liberatory exuberance of Gothic, its pleasure in excess, its glorying in extreme passions, forbidden liaisons, in severe frissons and raised temperatures, found an Oriental landscape very hospitable.

But the ambiguous apparatus in which *Vathek* was embedded brought about a second effect, with more direct political consequences. By claiming the story to be a history from original sources, Beckford made his novel itself a source of information about the East and Islam, at a time when European relations with the Ottoman empire were strained.

Although Beckford was angered by Henley's actions, he continued to display great ambivalence on the question of *Vathek*'s status – mirror or illusion? The book is a forerunner of postmodern games, as played by Angela Carter in *Nights at the Circus* (1984), where Fevvers, the winged *aérialiste* heroine, keeps provoking the question, 'Is she fact or is she fiction?'

III

When Beckford hurriedly attempted to replace Henley's English version of *Vathek* with his original, written in French, he also kept it anonymous, so that the fiction appeared historical. If he had included 'The Episodes of *Vathek*', as he kept saying he wanted to, he would have upset the air of historicity that suffused the book, for these sinners' confessions are romances in close conversation with the *Nights*.

The first to speak to Vathek of his crimes is Prince Alassi, in 'Histoire des deux princes amis', where he recounts the hair-raising sequence of crimes he committed after falling under the spell of an enchanting child, Firouz, who has been given into his care after the death of his parents and who captures Prince Alassi's heart. Unlike Vathek, who does not repent until the very last moment, Alassi strikes the reader as sincerely contrite – and what seems his natural goodness of nature throws into more striking and virulent relief the unregenerate evil of his beloved catamite, Firouz, who, like a master in an S&M relationship, commands the abject older man to do whatever he asks of him, however evil. Deep into their spree of cruelty and vice, Firouz reveals to Alassi that he belongs to a master magus, a Zoroastrian called Zouloulou, who directs him to perpetrate all the dreadful things he does in order to garner tribute to his god, the God of Fire. This tribute takes the form of scalps – and beards. To shear believers desecrates them – one of the notes to *Vathek* draws attention to this. Firouz takes Alassi to visit the shrine of fire where his master presides, and in a scene of high drama, they throw the horrible holocaust of hair into the ever-hungry flames, while all around the blaze the walls are hung with more trophies from the cheeks and heads of the master's victims. In the same way as the Giaour offers Vathek knowledge of the secrets of the universe and the wisdom of the pre-Adamite kings, so Zouloulou promises Alassi boundless powers if he renounces his faith and solemnly binds himself to the God of Fire.

The protagonists' exploits resemble the possessed hero's in *The Private Memoirs and Confessions of a Justified Sinner*, by James Hogg, which was published in 1824, although Hogg does not manage, even in his antinomian, vice-addicted protagonist's experiences, to plunge him into a doomed passion for a creature of his own sex. Beckford's tale does not read like pornography of the time: the language used to describe the two friends' transports of bliss belongs to the realm of *sentimentalité*, not *galanterie*. Unlike a French eighteenth-century libertine novel, the narrative does not describe them having sex; only says that they cuddle and canoodle and delight in each other in every way, making vows of eternal fidelity. Firouz, Alassi keeps repeating, is a pretty, darling child whom he must protect. Perhaps Beckford even in the midst of staging this love does not altogether know what it is? And we should not be too quick to know either, since the interest of the story lies in this almost Jamesian ambiguity: what exactly are we being shown? Beckford describes Alassi as entirely enthralled, and implies here and there that he is not altogether powerless in Firouz's grip, but chooses to be so. So the story ranks as an exceptional, unblinking look at what an observer today would call paedophilia. It is not surprising that later, when Beckford wanted to publish the story in the 1837 edition, he reveals that Firouz is in disguise and is in fact a Princess Firouzhah, the guise in which Prince Alassi's young evil genius appears in the English version.

The story, the most heartfelt of Beckford's tales, pulls the reader into its coils. But one must move carefully with this writer and not forget the crucial part masquerade and irony – the rational glass – plays in his writing. Henley was a faithful amanuensis when he asked, 'How far the copy may be a just representation . . .?' Beckford's 'copy' of the two friends' passionate attachment and their consequent damnation was being begun, written, abandoned, picked up again and abandoned again during a period when he wrote – and published under female pseudonyms – two other, very different works: a novel called *Modern Novel Writing: A Rhapsodical Romance* (1796), and another, called *Azemia, a Novel . . . with Political Strictures* (1798). For the latter he called himself Jacquetta Agneta Mariana Jenks, and he interleaves a variation on 'Bluebeard'. Both fictions attack sidelong but with gusto the current fashion for sentiment by occupying the persona of just such an author — or, rather, authoress (Beckford's stepsister Mrs Elizabeth Hervey wrote romances). Impersonating a lady romance novelist, or a Zoroastrian necromancer, or a storyteller like Shahrazad, queered Beckford's vantage point on his material, and did not commit him, *in propria persona*, to whatever slant the reader could discern in the text. He was still concealed, still masked. But the mask frees his speech, giving him the chance to talk about infidelity to God, to virtue, to convention. He is above all committed to profanity: he found in Islam's blasphemers, its dark shadow, the threat of the fire-worshipping Zoroastrians, a way of reeling readers into a circuitry of outrage.

The story of the two friends, Alassi and Firouz, recapitulates the plot structure of *Vathek*, the framing novel, which in so many ways reflects the direct influence of the *Nights*: a panorama of human iniquity and passions where the potential for deep feeling and strong attachments needs to be understood and moderated. The second 'Episode', 'Histoire de la princess Zulkaïs et du prince Kalilah' (The Story of Princess Zulkaïs and Prince Kalilah), tells of another forbidden love, between a brother and sister; it is missing an ending. The third, 'Histoire du prince Barkiarokh', takes up the seamy side of Middle Eastern comic narrative. All three tales evoke in the first person the vile things for which the protagonists have been condemned for eternity. Their confessions add point to the authorial voice, at the very end of the book:

> Such was, and such should be, the punishment of unrestrained passions and atrocious deeds! Such shall be, the chastisement of that blind curiosity, which would transgress those bounds the wisdom of the Creator has prescribed to human knowledge; and such the dreadful disappointment of that restless ambition, which, aiming at discoveries reserved for beings of a supernatural order, perceives not, through its infatuated pride, that the condition of man upon earth is to be — humble and ignorant.

The geography of Beckford's magical universe places heterodoxy further to the east from where his characters stand, and in this he takes his cue from Muslim legends and lore, as well as from the *Nights*. Magic exists in counterpoint to faith, and faith, in *Vathek*, is Islam, the religion of the present, while magic emanates from the past, presided over by the pre-Adamic kings, no less, including Solomon, who are all condemned to eternal torment. The stories offloaded those troubling areas of magic, enchantment and the supernatural on to the foreigner, the stranger.

This counter-transference does not appear immediately to illuminate the question: How can it be that magical thinking continues to flourish when it is so fiercely expelled? But Beckford, while denouncing esoteric – infidel – wisdom, continues to root his imagery, motifs, plots and general storytelling power in the very texture of the *Nights* and related poetics of magical realism. In this, Beckford remains faithful and true to the *Arabian Nights* where the magicians, as we have seen, are followers of other religious systems and rituals.

So the effect of the *Nights* is that the old formulae that characterise the superannuated, now heretical religions – Persian Zoroastrianism – need to yield to a new terminology which will capture a modern vision of magical knowledge. Beckford is central to this process because he embodies the contradictory position of nineteenth-century attitudes to magic: on the one hand *Vathek*'s apocalyptic and tragic outcome disavows all seeking for something more than tradition and orthodoxy allow, but at the same time he retains fantasy as his principal means of expression. Some way has to be found to square this circle: some form of fantasy fashioned that will not fall under the stigma of the false gods of old. The discovery of alternative magical systems provided a way out of the impasse.

But Beckford's Islamophilia also plays into the hands of his natural adversaries, since *Vathek* laid out a spectacle of gross and grotesque acts which could not but flatter non-oriental ways of doing things by contrast, and to boost the opinion that the West was a calm, well-behaved and rational place in comparison. Luxurious, hedonistic, sexually polymorphous, as well as lubricious, cruel and heedless, the protagonists of *Vathek* and the 'Episodes' were avidly consumed as authentic depictions. Even when the Eastern origin was refuted by Beckford in his 1787 edition, and the fictions were presented as performances in the Oriental style, the stories could still be read, given the apparatus of notes, as representations of historical realities and so fall into the 'textual attitude' that Said deplores in the orientalists' self-validating and self-referential claims to truth.

In 1834, nearly half a century after *Vathek*'s first appearance, William Beckford was still negotiating for the first publication of the 'Episodes'. Bentley's Standard Novels had offered to publish the entire book bound together with Walpole's *The Castle of Otranto* (1764) and Matthew 'Monk' Lewis's, *The Bravo of Venice* (1804). To the editors at Bentley's the three works formed a perfect constellation, Gothic luminaries in dialogue with one another across the decades, with the expansion into territory east of Italy according happily with readers' appetite for colour and desperate passions in exotic settings.

Beckford haggled over the deal, because the 'Episodes' were not being re-printed, unlike *Otranto* and the *Bravo*. He held out for an author's first publication fees, and was rejected. So the 'Episodes' remained unpublished in Beckford's lifetime.

In a scene that stirs echoes of the Chatterton story, they were found, untouched, long after Beckford's death, by Lewis Melville, his first biographer, in two large chests in the Charter Room of Hamilton Palace, where Beckford's daughter had consigned them. An English edition of *Vathek*, uniting the novel with the 'Episodes', did not appear until 2001, bringing Beckford's work in line at last with its immediate inspiration, the *Arabian Nights*.

Beckford is oddly placed in relation to his reputation and the impact of *Vathek*. On the one hand, his Orientalising arose from a passionate fascination with the literature and culture of Islam; the involvement provided him with an alternative to English society and culture, and a refuge from the vested interests of his birth and the unusual circumstances of his upbringing. The reasons for this may be personal: he felt himself out of place, somebody who did not belong and could neither accept his fellow countrymen nor be accepted by them. As Donna Landry points out in a perceptive essay, *Vathek*'s blasphemies and salaciousness are directed, Voltaire-style, principally against his own country and its conventions. She recognises in the prodigious camel Alboufaki – the mount of Carathis, Vathek's malignant enchantress mother – the steed Beckford far prefers to the hunting horses of the rich landed gentry to whom he belonged by birth (he was fiercely opposed to blood sports, forbade hunting on his lands, and built a high wall around his country house to prevent the local hunt entering it). Landry even suggests that Alboufaki is a kind of self-portrait: with '[his] desire for solitude, and his nose for the pestilential and the ghastly . . . [Beckford] gives us a monstrous camel as also a type of the self . . . as a Romantic solitary'.

The multiple and shifting readings that Beckford's fictions demand do not end with a choice between realist representation and ludic parody; or between adopting a viewpoint in alignment with Islamic orthodoxy or the alternative, Western superiority and apartness. Beckford's deliberate impieties, even while cloaked in overt moralising rhetoric, offer emancipatory pathways – in a Voltairean style. Also, *Vathek* itself and the stories in the 'Episodes' develop plots that ultimately reveal how nothing is what it seems or claims, and that promises, vows, images, are not to be trusted, for they will turn out to be different from what was laid out, in every appearance plausibly, at the start.

This effect has many contradictory aspects: while the vision of excess chimes immediately with Said's critique of Western views of the Arab world, Beckford's own opinions and even political activity show little sympathy with imperialist views. He was nothing if not Islamophile, and he has many advocates in Middle Eastern studies, including the late Fatma Moussa Mahmoud, a feminist Egyptian scholar of English literature. Laurent Châtel similarly argues strongly for Beckford's political radicalism, and his understanding of, and antipathy to, colonialism. French readers, well used to raillery as rational analysis and freethinking from the writings of Diderot and Voltaire, recognise the antithetical mixture at work in Beckford: how seemingly ornamental trifling can wrap the knives of an irreverent and critical stance towards piety and received ideas of all kinds.

From 1790, architectural fantasies eclipsed literature in Beckford's activities and he specialised in collecting *objets de vertu* and rare bindings. It is interesting that he especially liked bindings – the revealing or misleading outer wrappings of a book. The themes of his Oriental fictions, themselves encased in many envelopes, trope towers and dungeons, crypts and cells and vaults, temples and inner sanctums, codes, documents and inscriptions in ways that announce the great towers and follies he built on his properties. He also remained an impresario – of houses and their décor – and in doing so spread his passionate orientalism deeper into English taste and culture. He razed the Palladian-style country seat, Fonthill Splendens, which he had inherited from his father, because he wanted something more fabulous, outstripping his father in magnificence. Horace Walpole's Strawberry Gothic at Strawberry Hill inspired him; he dreamed of a new, Gothic palace for himself: Fonthill Abbey. It was to be his mausoleum.

The new name alludes to the imaginative impulses at work; retroactive, performative, and distancing, the Abbey plundered another form of English apostasy – medieval Catholicism – and travestied its referents: a sybaritic palace for an unbeliever. James Wyatt was hired; the Norman Foster of his day, this most so sought-after of architects was involved in the new medievalism – the first phase of what would be called the Gothic Revival by the Victorians. The plans show an extended, cruciform building with very narrow aisles, an unusually extended transept, and the entrance in the west front, opening to a vista of the nave that stretched the whole length of the building. Beckford famously employed a young dwarf to open the massive front door. He had found him being maltreated in Spain, and brought him – or perhaps bought him – home. Stage effects still appealed strongly, and highly coloured incongruities of scale, taste and mood; a tendency to pastiche, a cult of transgression (guests were served by servants in monks' habits and hoods). The planned tower was to surpass St Peter's.

Fonthill was also created by a process of literary and antiquarian montage, Beckford devising every detail from his studies of buildings visited on his Grand Tour, with a greater inclination to the south, and its mingling of Gothic and baroque as in the Portuguese monastery of Batalha, which was a model for Fonthill. The high value he gave décor, theatricality, ornament, craft, costume, luxury and beauty stems from his early passion for the *Arabian Nights*. And all these aesthetic qualities and forms of expression are ranked with the applied arts, not the fine arts, with popular, even vulgar, pleasures, not refined high taste. In this respect, through his self-fashioning as an oriental, Beckford's inclinations are modern.

A certain mimetic narcissism can be felt in the interplay of the Caliph Vathek and his author. *Vathek* opens with the Caliph erecting himself a palace, laying out five pavilions, one for each of the senses, and then raising a tower 'in imitation of Nimrod' – a legendary builder of Babel. The jinn obey him, as they did Solomon during the building of the Temple. The tower gives him a vantage point higher than anyone has ever enjoyed before, and like Alexander the Great in his *Romance*, Vathek is overwhelmed by the vastness of the world and the paltriness of humans in comparison. The tower harbours the most fiendish enchantments of Carathis, Vathek's Medea-like mother, who brews her spells in a chamber at its summit. It acts as a dynamic in the plot as well as a symbol – a rather obvious symbol – of ambition and hubris. The story opens at its summit, and closes in the depths of the tunnels of Eblis.

Coda

The first tower at Fonthill was in fact a spire – a *flèche* of soaring slender flight, but it fell down in construction. Another, square, version was built to replace it. It crumbled as well, six years later. Yet Beckford persevered, and built a third tower of stone.

In 1822, having run through his fortune, he put Fonthill up for sale, and went to live in Bath where he designed yet another tower, the Lansdown Tower, which gives a view of five counties from the 'belvidere' (sic) at the top. Now that he had left Fonthill, it was intended to be his replacement mausoleum.

One day in 1825, when he was out riding round Bath, as was his custom, it is said that he noticed the third tower of Fonthill had disappeared from the horizon. It had stood for twenty-five years, but it too had now collapsed.

On a drizzly day in 2009, I went to visit William Beckford's sarcophagus, on its motte in the cemetery at the foot of the tower. A wet summer drowned the weeds and grass and dripped from the boughs of the yews. Suddenly between the tombs a doe appeared. She was a surprise, a lovely creature; she did not take fright but remained there, almost tame, it seemed.

The *Nights* are full of stories of gazelles; they are the pets of beloved and secluded princesses, or wives metamorphosed into animal shape for their sins. Beckford's revisionings of the *1001 Nights* insist on the ghoulish, voluptuary and perverse aspects of this fabulist tradition, but his passionate interest in the world that the stories summoned also offers glimpses of its different aesthetic and its marvellous enchantments.

CHAPTER FIFTEEN

Oriental Masquerade: Goethe's *West-Eastern Divan*

God has made the Orient!
God has made the Occident!
North and South his hands are holding,
All the lands in peace unfolding.

Goethe, *Talismane*, 1819

I

IN WEIMAR IN 1815, AROUND three decades after the first performance of *Così fan tutte*, Johann Wolfgang von Goethe came across translations of the medieval Persian poet Hafiz, by the orientalist Joseph von Hammer-Purgstall, some of the very first into a European language. They captivated him with an intensity that took him, in his mid-sixties, by surprise, and he wrote:

> And though the whole world sink to ruin, I will emulate you, Hafiz, you alone! Let us, who are twin spirits, share pleasure and sorrow! To love like you, and drink like you, shall be my pride and my life-long occupation.
>
> Now, oh my song, speak forth with fire of your own! For you are both older and younger than his.

The encounter inspired the *West-Östlicher Divan* (The West-Eastern Divan), a long, elaborate lyric cycle, in which Goethe rapturously turns his face towards the orient. Hafiz becomes his alter ego; through Hafiz, a poet who belonged to the historical world of the *Nights*, the German Romantic polymath could speak from behind a mask, and invite his readers to imagine an emancipatory change of identity – a psychological projection out of one old self into another, new being. As Goethe writes to Hafiz, the song he makes in response to his new 'twin spirit' takes on a life of its own, out of time, both older and younger.

Calligraphy and ornament: the title page and frontispiece of Goethe's lyric cycle continued his intense performance of oriental identity (*West-Östlicher Divan*, 1819).

The translator Hammer's biographical preface helped to spark Goethe's passionate identification, for Hafiz was religious, but also joyful and pleasure-loving, given to drinking and carousing and love-making – and wrote about these pleasures well into his seventies (he died in 1389). Hafiz lived in times of disaster and war, when Persia was invaded by the Mongol conqueror Timur (Tamburlaine), whom Hafiz met, and yet, like Goethe in Weimar during the triumphant campaigns of Napoleon, the poet stayed in his garden in Shiraz with his roses, able to keep his mind trained on beauty and writing. 'The Book of Hafiz,' wrote Goethe of his own poems, 'is dedicated to the description, evaluation and veneration of an extraordinary human being. It also expresses the German's relationship with the Persian to whom he declares he is passionately attracted and who cannot be equalled.' Although he recoiled from the puritanism of Islam (Goethe found in Hafiz a keen fellow tippler), he embraced it, writing of himself: 'The poet considers himself a traveller. He has already reached the Orient. He enjoys its ways, its customs, objects, religious beliefs and views.' And he continued with a flourish, 'he [the poet] does nothing which would rebut any suspicion that he himself could be a Moslem'.

The result of this enthusiasm is a dramatic spiritual – and carnal – odyssey told in exclamatory lyrics, by turns ecstatic and tender, comic and ferocious; the verse is highly wrought, lapidary, difficult to render into English without sounding like patter or nursery rhymes. Occasionally, the prosody steps to that rough music of the vernacular forms developed by Schiller and Heine as well as Goethe himself, inspired by popular European oral tradition: ballads, curses, spells, tales, dirges, lullabies, serenades and other kinds of love song. This quality of song inspired Goethe to compose some of his most effective, dazzling poems – such as *Erl-König*, set by Schubert. But Goethe chiefly adapts Persian and Arabic lyric forms, and through his enthusiastic *imitatio*, the Arabist Jaroslav Stetkevych comments, 'Arabic poetry was admitted in an unmitigated way into European literary sensibility, both practically-experientially and theoretically as a tributary to already existing or newly evolving poetics.' Stetkevych is careful here to distinguish this aesthetic and experimental movement from the study of the culture as a form of scientific ethnography designed to contain and control it, which came later and developed along a different path.

The Napoleonic Wars brought Goethe into further contact with Muslim culture, and in unexpected ways. The poet believed in omens, and took it for a sign when a soldier, just returned to Weimar from the Spanish campaign, handed him a manuscript page he had taken as booty, which contained the closing words of the Koran: 'Say, "I seek refuge with the Lord of people, the Controller of people, the God of people, against the harm of the slinking whisperer ..."' (Sura 114). This commandment spoke luminously to Goethe: he must take refuge from the gods and values of his own milieu. A little later, in January 1814, Bashkiri soldiers fighting on the Russian side reached Weimar and held services in the local high school; the following month, a valuable bundle of manuscripts was offered to the Ducal library, and Goethe became absorbed in them, filled with admiration for their Arabic calligraphy, remarking that no other language existed perhaps in which 'spirit, word and script were so primordially embodied together'.

Goethe was an omnivore and a polymath, and he threw himself into any number of subjects and sciences – botany, mineralogy and meteorology; he also became a dedicated and eccentric student of optics and colour theory. His enthusiasm for the literature of the Middle East inspired him to contact orientalists and to learn to read Persian; he even acquired enough Arabic script to pen two or three poems for his lyric collection.

His oriental studies were, he wrote, 'a kind of Hegira – one flees from the present into distant times and regions where one expects something of Paradisal quality'. He called an opening poem in the *West-Eastern Divan* 'Hegira'.

Goethe borrowed motifs and images from Firdusi and Rumi, and adapted their verse forms – paeans, epigrams, revenge-songs and, above all, the *ghazal*, the prime form of Persian lyric, a complex antiphonal song of around 7–15 lines, written in couplets with a refrain. Its closest counterpart in Western prosody would be a sonnet. But in a *ghazal*, each verse may start a new thought in a different direction, to jagged and colloquial effect, and the poet's name usually appears in the last line, as a signature. Other registers of the oriental voice attracted Goethe as well: he ventriloquises scathing Persian satire and epigrams and, while singing fervent praises to oriental attitudes to love, pleasure and ethics, he indicts his own era's state and church dogma and apparatus. As in Mozart and Da Ponte's opera, the act of writing the poems invites a reconfiguration of individuality as mobile, in a process of becoming and therefore able to change; and the whole cycle gives full expression to a concept of lyric hedonism in the style of the *1001 Nights*, with metaphorical power to create a visionary politics.

Hafiz, a near-contemporary of Chaucer, has been hailed as a Sufi mystic as well as a hedonist's patron saint, and holds his place in the canon as a virtuoso of rhyme and metre, a *poète maudit* and a great man, a figure in Eastern literature to stand beside Sappho, Horace, Petrarch or Keats. He is however a far more singular figure than this account conveys. He presented himself as an antinomian mystic, operating within profound contradictions: a Dionysiac drunkard extolling the wonders of wine, a blasphemer and a reprobate who raises delinquency and failure to saintliness, a dedicated lover – you could say, lecher – who proclaims he lives only for the moment. When illuminated in Persian manuscripts, Hafiz inspires images of ecstatic drunkenness, including at picnics in Paradise.

Hafiz is still a much loved and much quoted poet in Iran; his tomb in Shiraz is a shrine, and in the nearby souk there is said to be a fortune-teller with a pet pigeon that, in return for your rials, pecks out a screwed-up paper on which, as in a fortune cookie, a line or two of verse will guide you on your way. These are all lines from Hafiz:

> Like Hafiz, drink your wine to the sound of harp-strings:
> For the heart's joy is strung on a strand of silk.

The poet does not appear himself in the *Arabian Nights*, nor are his poems quoted – he was writing in Persian, not Arabic. But his predecessor and in many respects his precursor, the poet Abu Nuwas (d. 813/815), (who was raised among Bedouin) figures in a dozen or more stories, and his lyrics are sprinkled (though unattributed) throughout the book. He is presented as part of the entourage of the fabulously wealthy, munificent and doomed family of the Barmakids, who surrounded the Caliph Harun el-Rashid and feature in many of the *Nights*; this is the Golden Age in the Islamic imaginary, an apogee reflected and romanced in the *Nights*, as an era of civilised luxury and benevolent rule, when Baghdad was the richest and most populous city in the world.

The Abu Nuwas of the stories is a scapegrace, and a fool, in the Shakespearean sense, and gifted with eerie clairvoyance; his powers (not his poetry) spare him the Caliph's anger for his misdeeds and unruliness. In Pasolini's film *Il Fiore delle Mille e una Notte* (*The Arabian Nights*, 1978), Abu Nuwas plays a key role as the court poet, delightedly reciting scandalous poems at Harun al-Rashid's request; his words open new narrative chambers in the film, where insouciant scenes of erotic playfulness with girls and boys are taking place. Hafiz also appears to have set out to rival him in verbal music and the extravagance of his paeans to wine, roses and love of boys and girls).

Goethe's oriental masquerade projected him into an imaginary apartness from his home territory: the counterpoint position, as defined by Edward Said. No exile in fact, the poet chose to banish himself from his familiar compass points: he transmuted Weimar into medieval Shiraz out of a desire to be reborn. Impersonating an unfamiliar, exotic alter ego, accompanied by a form of throwing of the voice, was a creative necessity for Goethe. The Rimbaud axiom, '*Je est un Autre*' (I is an Other) crystallises a wider strategy, for to imagine oneself as Other lies at the foundation of the most fertile explorations of the Western self and selfhood; this changed angle of view, extending the range of person and personhood through a variety of different cultural modes, helped to put the questions about society and humanity that constitute the very ground of art and psychology in the West. As Goethe had given birth to a new self in Italy in 1786, he was now rebirthing himself again in oriental disguise.

The word 'divan', a novelty in German at that date, has many meanings in its origins: a Persian word adopted as 'diwan' in Arabic, it was first used for 'the process of recording, collecting and collating all kinds of information in writing'. It then was applied to other forms of assembly: the muster of soldiers in early Muslim armies, the departments of

government under the Caliph of Baghdad and the branches of admin-
istration under the Ottoman rulers (this meaning survives in related
words for customs house: French *douane*, Italian *dogana*). From this use,
it was transferred to the chamber where such offices were conducted by
the ruler, seated like Solomon on a carpet-strewn dais. Western witnesses
of Ottoman business may have been the first to apply the word to the
rooms' characteristic furnishings, cushions and couches, which come to
be called 'divans' in English in 1702.

The whole collection of the *Divan* has a grand, fugal shape, articulated
in thirteen 'Books'. The titles of each part – 'The Book of the Singer',
'The Book of Displeasure', and so on – are given in German and in
Farsi, and lend the sequence a scriptural feel, echoing both the Bible
and the Koran, even explicitly as with a 'Book of Proverbs' (prompted
mostly by oriental sayings, Goethe claimed). The book sequence begins
with a classic *ruba'i*, or quatrain, invoking the Barmakids, and the mood
is one of retrospective nostalgia:

> Twenty years I let time run
> And enjoyed the lot I drew;
> Unmarred lovely years, each one,
> Like the Barmecides once knew.

In this way, Goethe time-travels, sinking himself into his twin soul Hafiz,
and sounding as if he wants his readers to imagine that he is channelling
the poems rather than originating them.

Around fifty years later, the poet Edward FitzGerald experienced a
similar fusion with a twin soul in the past: in his case, with Omar
Khayyám, a predecessor of Hafiz, whom he absorbed and transmuted
into the famous *Rubáiyát*, an extended virtuoso performance of Persian
lyric which can also claim to be a Victorian monument. In his essays
Jorge Luis Borges returns frequently to the impact of the *Nights* and
oriental literature on Western culture, and he discusses what he calls
the 'miracle' of FitzGerald's *Rubáiyát*. He confesses himself stumped as
to how to interpret FitzGerald's achievement in communicating the
medieval poet to English readers eight hundred years after he was
writing. Borges hazards two explanations: that Edward FitzGerald was
the reincarnation of Omar Khayyám – and the proposal is only half
in jest: 'Isaac Luria the Lion taught that the soul of a dead man can
enter an unfortunate soul to nourish and instruct it; perhaps, around
1857, Omar's soul took up residence in FitzGerald's.' But Borges then

moves swiftly on to propose instead: 'a benevolent coincidence. Clouds sometimes form the shapes of mountains or lions; similarly, the unhappiness of Edward FitzGerald and a manuscript of yellow paper and purple letters, forgotten on a shelf of the Bodleian at Oxford, formed, for our benefit, the poem.' In a letter, FitzGerald offers a key thought on the process that he followed and that Goethe might have endorsed: 'a Thing must live: with a transfusion of one's own worse Life' . In his case, he transfused his own life into the persona of Omar Khayyám as Goethe transfused his own into Hafiz, and vice versa. They were able to formulate through their chosen Persian avatars an outlook, a world vision, a testament. When W. G. Sebald writes about FitzGerald, his work and his life in *The Rings of Saturn,* his perception could also be applied to Goethe's relation to Hafiz: 'FitzGerald described [. . .] translating this poem . . . as a colloquy with the dead man and an attempt to bring us tidings of him. The English verses he devised for the purpose . . . feign an anonymity that disdains even the least claim to authorship, and draw us, word by word, to an invisible point where the mediaeval orient and the fading occident can come together in a way never allowed them by the calamitous course of history.' Sebald is talking about the course of politics and military history, not the story of cultural crossings. Through the way Goethe and FitzGerald performed an eclipse of self to pay tribute to these poets in the past, they took Europe's voice into self-dissolving relation with the oriental tradition, in which lyric poetry – with or without music – dominates.

II

In *The Oriental Renaissance*, the literary historian Raymond Schwab declares that Oriental literature aims to transform everything, including words, into musicality. Stetkevych echoes this thought when he says that Goethe 'opts for the song, for the validity of the lyrical, for the expressive against the mimetic'. This dynamic affected the encounter immortalised in Goethe's poems, and helped form the Romantic impetus towards the fusion of music and words which culminates in the French Symbolists: Verlaine's 'de la musique avant toute chose' and Mallarméan ideals of nearly expelling sense from the harmonic sounds and shapes of the poem.

Comparing Goethe's emulation with the history of the *Arabian Nights* in translation before the *Divan* makes it possible to see how radical he was in his approach. A sample opening of any eighteenth-century edition of the stories conveys no sense of the verbal music that moves through the book, the sprinkling of poems and songs, verse squibs and proverbial wisdom throughout. Galland left these out and, until Lane, translators who worked from him followed suit.

The poetry breaks into the stories like the dawn itself, bringing respite but at the same time suspense and a desire for more: the digression into lyric or epigram, satire or drinking song can make a reader want to skip, but the delay sharpens the pleasure when the narrator resumes the thread. Sometimes fictive storytellers inside the stories recite or sing these works, as they give expression to their feelings, often at key moments of excitement and passion. Shahrazad is telling stories from memory, and within her stories, others tell theirs and as they do so reach into their store of memorised poetry, quoting to express more fully their passion, their grief, their anger: the stories picture a world where not only entertaining plots matter but also the music of lyric. Women have strong voices here, from the languishing of highly educated heroines to the sorrows of the illiterate.

Recent translators, such as André Miquel and Jamel Eddine Bencheikh, have restored this dialogue between prose and poetry, so that in a romance like 'Hasan of Basra', for example, the laments of the hero's mother when he leaves home take the form of classic elegies, and provide an intensely emotional continuo accompaniment to his adventures. When she gives voice in poetry, the storyteller implies that though the words are written by another, they communicate her anguish more deeply. In other stories, scenes of love-making metamorphose into rapturous language, given and taken on the page in the place of kisses and caresses. The lyrics here belong to the oral memory of the stories and sing out like music from the book.

Grief, desire, yearning and astonishment are the dominant notes. These lyric outbursts alter the texture of the experience of reading/hearing the stories; like the repetition of the refrains that open and close each night of storytelling, these poetic interludes sew together one tale to another through cross-echoes and reprises, composing a musical patterning that soothes and satisfies quite independently of the tumultuous twists and accidents of the narratives.

Lyric combines words and music to create a tempo that readers and listeners experience physically, as in dancing; poetry here struggles to free itself from constraints of reference and meaning, to reach a wordless state of transport (even of self-annihilation). In this way, lyric institutes an ordering of thought that might contribute to a realigning of values and a reshaping of alliances and allegiances, both personal and social.

The *Divan* is best known for the blazing sequence of love poems in 'The Book of Suleika'. 'Suleika' is another oriental mask for the young

13. 'If it were possible for me to move freely about in the sea, then I would rather imitate the fish – especially the large ones...', wrote the Danish artist Melchior Lorck, one of the first foreign artists to travel in the Ottoman empire. On his way to Turkey, the artist drew a turtle aloft over the Venetian lagoon.

14. Lorck included a portrait of himself embracing the whole sweep of the Golden Horn and the Ottoman capital. (Detail of 'Prospect of Constantinople', 1559)

15. On one of Sinbad's voyages, the travellers find an egg of the Rukh bird and break it open to see what is inside. Robert Swain Gifford's *The Roc's Egg* (1874), catches the nineteenth-century spirit of scientific inquiry into the mysteries of the East.

16. Amulets and talismans are incised with sacred words and symbols that charge them with power, and can be made of different gems; carnelian (a) was a favourite stone because the Prophet expressed his preference for it. Sir Hans Sloane, founder of the British Museum, owned (b), the heart-shaped chalcedony example; (c) is cut in garnet, (d) in lapis lazuli, (e) in carnelian and (f) in rock crystal.

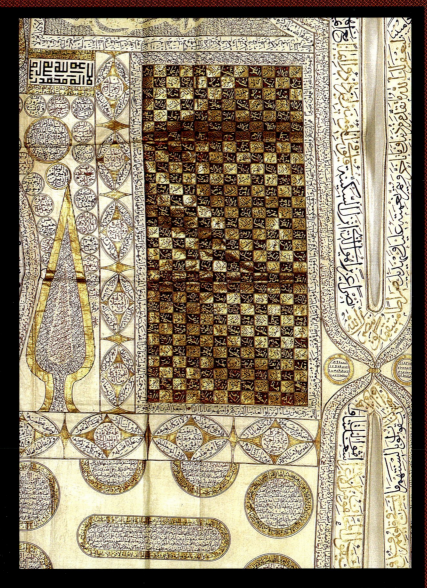

17a. (Detail above) and b. (left) Talismanic chemises and robes are turned into sacred manuscripts by dense inscriptions from the Koran, Solomonic signs, magic squares, invocations, saints' names, and other powerful symbols. The work began – and ended – on a propitious day to protect the wearer, in this case Sultan Murad IV (1612–1640).

18. Vehicles of wonder and pleasure: Jean–Etienne Liotard 'turned Turk'
during his years in Istanbul, and made many portraits of the city's residents,
including this *Woman Reading*, *c.* 1750, lying on an oriental sofa, lost in a book.

19. The three brother princes, armed with magic apple and spyglass, take off on the flying carpet
to save the ailing Princess. From a collector's card for a modern elixir, Liebig's Meat Extract.

20. Women's leisure and work both provide settings for exchanges of stories. John Frederick Lewis evokes the shuttered interior of a harem, with its pool, pet gazelle, sofas, carpets, cushions, and black servants in *A Lady Receiving Visitors* (*The Reception*), 1873.

21. By contrast, in the film *Gabbeh* (1996), women of the nomadic Ghashgha'i tribe are the spinners and dyers and makers of rugs.

22. The scene of the psychoanalytic 'talking cure'. Sigmund Freud's couch, brought to London from Vienna, is draped in a Ghashgha'i rug: was this to encourage the release of fantasy?

23a. and b. In 1929, Freud's niece, Tom Seidmann-Freud, made a children's book of magic transformations, *The Magic Boat*: with a square of red film, a child reading on a bed turns into a child flying through the air.

24. Rudolf Nureyev's tomb in the Russian Cemetery, Sainte-Geneviève-des-Bois, near Paris:
the dancer asked to be buried under a carpet woven by his people, the Tatars,
to symbolise his wanderings – and his ascensions.

25. 'You just think lovely wonderful thoughts,' Peter Pan explains.
'And they lift you up in the air.' Paula Rego's grandchildren inspired her
illustration (1993) of the Darling children carrying out Peter's instructions.

actress, musician and writer Marianne von Willemer (b. 1784), thirty-five years younger than Goethe, one of a long series of women with whom he fell rapturously in love. These erotic invitations encapsulate oriental lyricism in the Romantic era and have been much anthologised, giving a distorted sense of the whole cycle.

Marianne was the youngest performer in a troupe of travelling players when at the age of sixteen she was taken into the household of the Frankfurt banker Johann Jakob von Willemer to be educated with his daughters. She became his third wife in 1814 when she was twenty-nine, and he seems to have been the most complaisant of husbands, even offering Goethe a *ménage à trois* in his Frankfurt home (an arrangement to the poet's taste – this was not the first time).

The two began their love story in Eastern dress: the lovesick Goethe calls himself Hatem, after Hatem Thai, a poet to whom Hafiz perhaps refers, who was celebrated for his 'unsurpassed generosity'; Goethe also adapts the form of the 'Mohammedan rosary in which Allah's name is glorified through 99 attributes', in order to compose a litany of praise to the beloved. Marianne casts herself as Suleika, the Islamic name for the woman known in the Western tradition as 'Potiphar's wife'. In the Bible, she is smitten by the young Joseph and makes amorous advances to him; when he flees, leaving his torn coat behind in his eagerness to escape, she tells her husband he assaulted her (Gen. 39: 1–20). In the West, this story takes the form of a cautionary tale of entrapment and has a distinguished career in the annals of misogyny. In Christian moral exempla, in pictures and in stories, Potiphar's wife embodies women's lust and treachery; and remains nameless. By contrast, in Islamic legend she acquires her name Zulaykha, and in Sura 12 ('Joseph') of the Koran she calls her attendants together to witness the power of Joseph's beauty for themselves, and they too are so overcome that they cut themselves with fruit-knives – an odd but convincing insight into the perverse effects of desire and the springs of some self-harm. (This enigmatic episode has been beautifully depicted in some illuminated manuscripts). Her ardour captures a quality that burns in many a heroine of the *Nights*: they catch fire with love and desire as actively as any male protagonist in story after story, pursuing their beloved with resourcefulness and tenacity. They are not obliged to show the restraint or muteness of their maidenly counterparts in Western romance: patient Grisels are rare, perhaps non-existent, and so are the Snow Whites and Sleeping Beauties (I hesitate to say none can be found because the book is inexhaustible).

Later, Zulaykha agrees to put the love of God above her desire for

Joseph, and her self-restraint earns her a place in the highest rank of Muslim saints. But in the *Divan*, Goethe's beloved carries on like Princess Maryam or Badiat or Zumurrud in the *Nights*, and the poems are filled with caresses exchanged, with kisses given and taken on her face, her breasts; the lovers give rein together to ecstatic eroticism. The poems have become famous in Schubert's settings, in which the piano wafts and swells, and the voice, closely following the freight of metaphor in the verses, runs before the breeze and flows and ebbs, and transforms the lifting and freshening of the summer wind into kisses, fondling, and pent-up breath. She answers his delight, embodied in a wind blowing from the east; he in response sends her a message on the wings of the west wind:

> What means this stirring?
> Does the east wind bring me good news?
> The fresh moving of his wings
> cools my heart's deep wound.
>
> Caressingly it plays with the dust,
> chases it in light little clouds.
> Mildly it soothes the sun's heat,
> cools too my hot cheeks
> kisses as it goes the grapes
> that deck field and hill . . .
>
> Ah, the true heart's message,
> breath of love, life renewed,
> can be granted me only from his mouth,
> from his breath.

Brahms thought this was 'the most beautiful song . . . that has been written'.

This poem, along with several others, has since been attributed to Marianne von Willemer herself, and she has become a heroine of German Romantic women's poetry, although the authorship is still a matter of debate among Germanists. In either case, the lovers were caught up on the tide of projective sympathies flowing through their Oriental disguises: if Marianne wrote the lyrics and Goethe appropriated them, she seems to have taken this as part of the masquerade – at least at first (she claimed authorship in old age). If Goethe wrote them, Marianne was providing him with yet another Oriental mask, a female one.

Although the *West-Eastern Divan* is chiefly known for its erotic strain, to focus on this misses the truculent rebelliousness of Hafiz, which Goethe recognised and emulated in other parts of the work – 'The Book of Displeasure', above all, with its dyspeptic epigrams and savage cynicism, reminiscent of Ovid at his most worldly. Like Voltaire, Goethe bent his political views through the disguise of an Oriental, and besides the roses, moonlight and nightingales, he also makes rough music, both in the sound of some of his verse, and in its effects, shaking up received ideas, breaking through borders. Behind his identification with Hafiz lies a history of independent-mindedness and recusancy, for the Persian can write luminous erotica, but he also denounces adversaries in lyrics which rub against the grain, provoke and dissent. Hafiz flies from extremes of ecstatic pleasure to cantankerous fury and, in keeping with his spirit, Goethe's songs change their mood and bristle with furious anti-worldly scorn.

Goethe was writing during years of terrible bloodshed and conflict in Europe, and in the wake of Napoleon's defeat he found himself at odds with most of his contemporaries in his resistance to nationalism and sympathy for the French. Significantly, the *Divan* is a work born of international war and national struggles in divided peoples. In his oppos-itional sense of isolation, Goethe saw yet another bond between himself, who lived under Napoleon and had known him, and Hafiz, who had known Tamburlaine. Hafiz too had lambasted a local tyrant, Mubariz ud-Din Muhammad, a puritanical follower of extreme Islamic asceticism; he poured bitter witty scorn on his rule, on his lackeys and courtiers and sycophants and their hypocrisies.

It is not only the injustices of power, the corruption of rulers and officials that incur Hafiz's scathing wit, and inspire Goethe's imitation. Above all, Hafiz is a dissident Muslim. Although his name means 'Upholder of the faith', used to designate someone who knows the whole of the Koran by heart, Hafiz's lyrics seethe with loathing for devout ascetics, who forbid wine and frown on sex and pleasure. Preachers, cadis or judges, sheikhs or priests, he denounces them all (a bit like Jesus censuring the Pharisees):

> Don't kiss anything except the sweetheart's lip
> And the cup of wine, Hafez [*sic*], friends, it's a grave mistake
> To kiss the hand held out to you by a puritan.

Being divine, God does not desire such gestures of observance, or public protestations of rectitude.

Such an attitude to authority and to preachers of restraint appealed wonderfully to Goethe.

In the same *ghazal*, Hafiz describes God creating Adam out of clay as a potter throwing a wine cup:

> I said to the master of the tavern: 'Tell me, which is
> The road of salvation?' He lifted his wine and said,
> 'Not talking about the faults of other people.'

Alongside his caustic fury against religious oppressors and hypocrites, Hafiz inspired Goethe with a belief in the importance of contrition and mercy. Contentious as are some of his scathing pasquinades and accusations, his principal desire propels his readers away from blame and towards reconstruction. This politics of justice can be aligned with truth and reconciliation, acknowledgement of past wrongs and an agreement for a future made together.

It was ten years after writing the *Divan*, when Goethe was seventy-five, that the publishers of the first German translation of the *Nights*, knowing his orientalist interests, sent him all fifteen volumes of Habicht's great work of translation. Goethe had read the *Nights* long before, in Galland's French, but, as we heard in Chapter 12, the poet was newly enraptured. In numerous letters, Goethe praises the *Nights*, showing how the stories revealed to him how to give free play to his imagination, and to pass beyond reason's boundaries in order to express its ideals more fully.

Goethe's conception of Faust himself changes as a result. In *Part One* of Goethe's huge dramatic poem, the magician and his tempter Mephistopheles correspond broadly to the traditional medieval figures – the heretical enchanter led astray by the devil and the plot dramatises a Christian vision of salvation – and perdition. This part was begun in the 1770s. But in 1825, about six years after writing the *Divan*, Goethe's Faust is no longer a European necromancer, excited by forbidden knowledge and led by his appetites and desires; he is transformed into a seeker for oneness with all of nature, with the sylphs and gnomes and spirits that dwell in the airs and exist in all phenomena. This later Faust has abandoned dualism for a pantheistic mystical sense of the unity of all living things, a Wordsworthian 'sense sublime of something far more deeply interfused', and has become an opponent of modernity's own dark arts (industrialisation, mass production). The multitudes of spirit beings in *Faust: Part Two* are genies and sprites, and they animate everything – stones, trees, the elements – in tableau after tableau. Faust no longer embodies heterodox magic, but accedes to knowledge of the interconnectedness of phenomena, a Paracelsian and shamanic vision rather than a sorcerer's. The proleptic association with shamans reveals how developments in Romantic thinking about consciousness, imagination and ethics were triggered by the discoveries of other peoples and cultures that had begun the century before.

III

In 1999, the 250th anniversary of the birth of Goethe (1749–1832), Weimar was made cultural capital of Europe to honour the place where the national poet and polymath lived and worked and died. Weimar is a small city but huge in fame, for its connections to music – to Bach and Beethoven, as well as to Goethe and Schiller – and at a music school held there that summer, Daniel Barenboim and Edward Said founded their Arab–Israeli youth orchestra. It was 'a quite daring experiment,' Said wrote later. 'There was an assumption that this program might be an alternative way of making peace.' It was there, he remembered, that Goethe had composed 'a fantastic collection of poems based on his enthusiasm for Islam'. Said went on. 'He started to learn Arabic, although he didn't get very far. Then he discovered Persian poetry and produced this extraordinary set of poems about the "other" really, *West-Östlicher Divan*, which is, I think, unique in the history of European culture.' The West–Eastern Divan: the name of the orchestra was born; it was never discussed again.

It seems odd that Said, the fierce critic of European Orientalism, chose to use the title of a work that, on the face of it, belongs squarely in the Orientalist tradition. Goethe's poems are filled with roses and nightingales, beautiful boys, wine, women and song. Yet, as Said saw it, Goethe's lyric cycle is animated by a spirit of open inquiry towards the East, grounded in a sense of the past in art and culture, not in dogma or military or state apparatuses. Like Seamus Heaney, who famously put the question, Can poetry be strong enough to help? Said and Barenboim were asking, Can music be strong enough to help? In their case, the question applies more specifically to *music-making* and the live, embodied reality of the activity in real time. But it also involves a concept of the expressive, lyric voice and the deep associations of that voice with identity. In his later thought, Edward Said proposes that the arts of representation – the mimetic arts like fiction and history – yield pride of place to a lyric expressiveness and expansion; he also asks that historical perspective, while it must not be left out of the analysis, should not pin down the literary or cultural event to a defined moment in the past, but revisit it and reclaim it to fill a new present and shape a new future. Said's approach was always historical; his work as a critic and intellectual was rooted in an examination of context, both cultural and political, and the Orchestra embodies his commitment to the work of art as an actor in its time. In an essay of 1986, Said asks, 'how knowledge that is non-dominative and non-coercive can be produced in a setting that is deeply inscribed with the politics, the considerations, the positions, and the strategies of power.' His answer was to participate and engage. The word *theoria*, he liked to remind us, means 'the action of observing'; for him, theory was a dynamic activity, not a matter of passive reception. The theorist-critic affects the works he observes, and the works themselves are not self-created or autonomous but precipitated in the crucible of society and history. 'My position is that texts are worldly,' he writes; 'to some degree they are events, and, even when they appear to deny it, they are nevertheless a part of the social world, human life, and of course the historical moments in which they are located and interpreted.' The making of poetry and the making of music are events in this sense as well.

For Edward Said read the *West-Eastern Divan*'s calls for an understanding of individuality as a process of becoming and therefore fluid, the vision he also found in *Così*. Lightness, as in Mozart's music, does not have to be pliant or easy or smooth, as Calvino also discusses. (See the Conclusion.) It too can be an 'aesthetic of resistance'. So Goethe's impassioned lyric cycle represented for him – and represents for us – an alternative way of telling the story, presenting the history of cross-pollination that has occurred between East and West. The poems bear out the orchestra's principle that 'Ignorance of the other is not a strategy for survival.'

Part V

Flights of Reason

Omnes magiae prestant usum.
(All sciences allow the use of magic.)
Thomas Campanella

Story 12
Camar al-Zaman and Princess Badoura

C HILDLESSNESS IS A GREAT CURSE in the *Arabian Nights* and many kings and wealthy merchants suffer bitterly for it. But sharper still than lacking a child is the sorrow a child inflicts when he or she does not want to marry and bring grandchildren into the family.

Camar al-Zaman, the prince and heir to the Khalidan islands, is one of these young and angry voices raised up against marriage: he has heard the stories of women's *makr*, their wiles, lusts, perfidiousness and violence; and he refuses to marry, swearing he'd rather give himself up to die. As he is the only son of his father, King Shahriman is vexed to the depths of his being. Camar is beautiful, and any woman would be fortunate to have him; but he wants none of them. His mother begs him, but he tells her there is no woman like her in the world. More time passes. Camar grows more splendid, more graceful, and more troublingly desirable day by day, till the nightingale, maddened by his charms, sings only of his thighs – and his virtues, which out-dazzle all of humankind.

After three years of obduracy, even though his only son is the apple of his eye, the king has him held prisoner in a derelict tower to bring him to his senses. There, one night, a believing jinniya called Maimuna, daughter of Solomon's vizier al-Dimriyat, rises from the well where she has been lurking and, noticing the light in the ruined tower, slips in to find out what it is. She lifts her lamp, and comes upon the incomparable vision of Camar. Smitten, she blesses God for creating him.

She flies back to the heavens, where she meets Dahnash, one of the rebel jinn, and he issues a challenge. For he has just returned from China and there he found the Princess Badoura, daughter of the King Ghayur, and she has also vowed never to marry. She is more beautiful than any creature alive on earth, he swears. She surpasses Camar: her hair is dark like the moonless night when one sets out on a journey and parts from one's companions; her face as bright as the day one meets again. The rebel jinni limns every trait of her loveliness: from the nectar of her saliva to the littleness of her feet. Her father adores her with a passion, he goes on, but is grief-stricken that she is absolutely adamant that all other men are fools and villains.

'I am a woman of high rank,' she protests, 'and a reigning monarch. How could I tolerate a man ruling over me?' Her father has heaped her dowry with treasures, and built seven castles to house it. But she rejects every suitor.

Eventually, even though he dotes on her, the King of China also imprisons his daughter to bend her to his will.

The two jinn fall to quarrelling savagely about their different discoveries' superiority; to settle the matter, they decide to bring the young man Camar and Princess Badoura together so that they can be set side by side and compared (Pl. 6).

This is done – in a flash. Badoura is carried from China to the prince's ruined tower, dressed in her Venetian chemise trimmed in Egyptian brocade and North African gimp, and laid down next to him.

They look like twins, equal in beauty, so like to each other they could have had the same mother.

The two jinn start quarrelling again, but they finally decide to call in a monstrous old colleague to act as arbiter: the jinniya Qashqash, who has seven horns on her head, four locks of hair reaching the ground, lion's claws and elephant legs ending in ass's hooves. She decides that the only difference between them is their sex, and that they should wake them up, one by one, and whichever falls in love most desperately will have lost the contest. Dahnash turns himself into a flea and gives Camar a little nip. He wakes up and finds a young girl lying beside him in bed. Astonished, he looks at her – all over. The sight inflames him, he falls madly in love and covers her in kisses, but she does not stir. He decides that she must be the young woman his father wants him to marry and resolves to do so, the very next day. He's about to kiss her on the mouth, but stops himself, thinking he must not violate her. Instead he takes from her finger a ring she's wearing.

It is Maimuna's turn to change into a flea and bite Badoura, who wakes and finds Camar lying beside her. She too is seized by passion, crying out that if she had known that her father intended her to marry this young man, she would not have stood so firm. She tries to rouse him, shakes him, offers herself to him with passionate sighs and promises and caresses, but Maimuna with her dark wings keeps Camar snoring happily in his enchanted sleep. Then Badoura notices he is wearing her ring on his finger. She decides to leave it there and takes instead another, different ring from him and falls asleep again, their two bodies intertwined.

The jinn disentangle them, and, lifting the sleeping Badoura, Dàhnash carries her back to China.

When Camar wakes up, he rages to find her gone; his frustration drives him to such wild and intemperate behaviour that his father declares him insane and continues to keep him locked up. The same happens to Badoura, who behaves as if possessed, furiously assaulting her nurse and railing in rage against those who have hidden her beloved from her. She keeps telling her story, but nobody understands what she can be raving about, and she too is declared insane and put under restraint, an iron collar fixed around her neck and chains on her legs.

However, Badoura has a milk-brother, Marzawan, who recognises the symptoms of love and believes her story. He offers to track down her lost object of desire.

After a series of adventures – involving shipwreck, deceptions, and recognition by the rings they have each taken from the other – the lovers are eventually reunited at the Chinese court, and celebrate their marriage in jubilation. Soon afterwards Camar sees his father in a dream; he's missing his vanished son. So they ask permission from Badoura's father, the King of China, to visit Camar's father, Shahriman, the king of the Khalidan islands. After they've set out, their misfortunes begin again. They're resting en route in the heat of the day, and Badoura has fallen asleep in their tent; Camar, overcome by her beauty, begins to unfasten her clothes and finds a red gemstone knotted into her belt: it's her carnelian talisman, inscribed with letters he cannot decipher. He becomes curious: he carries it out of the tent to examine it in better light, and a bird swoops down on the gemstone, snatches it from his hand and flies away with it in its beak. Camar follows. But every time he is near enough to grasp the bird and retrieve the jewel, the creature eludes him and leads him on. In this way, he wanders from valley to valley till nightfall, and finds himself completely lost.

When dawn breaks, he thinks to himself, he will trap the bird.

But the morning comes, and still he pursues the coquettish bird, and so it continues for eleven days, until she – for the bird is a she – draws him to a strange city, and vanishes.

Camar finds himself in a desolate city, where the inhabitants are all magians, except for an old gardener who takes him on. A boat from the world calls only once a year. He sets to work helping the gardener by day; by night he cries for Badoura whom he has lost so stupidly.

When Badoura wakes up and finds Camar gone, she keeps her wits about her, realises she will forfeit all her liberty as a married woman who, for whatever reason, has lost her husband, and so changes roles with Camar, putting on his clothes, deepening her voice, and assuming his (male) authority. The two of them are like as like, as the jinn had declared, so her ruse works. She strikes camp and sets out again on her journey, reaching the Ebony Isles, where the ruler's daughter Hayat al-Nufus, is looking for a husband.

Badoura disguised as Camar finds to her embarrassment that she has every quality the princess and her father desire; he is old and failing and, seeing the handsome young stranger, gladly hands over his powers and his kingdom. Within a matter of days, Badoura finds herself officially united with Hayat and declared the ruler of the Ebony Isles.

After a few nights have passed since the wedding, Hayat is furious; her husband's indifference to her is an insult and unnatural and she explodes with reproaches so vehement and distressing that Badoura confesses: she speaks with her woman's voice, opens her robes and shows Hayat her breasts and her body.

Shahrazad breaks off at this point: the dawn is visible and speaking is no longer permitted.

Hayat does not take umbrage at Badoura's deception, but sympathises with her story and enters into the conspiracy with her: the next morning, she kills a chicken and shows her bloodied nightdress to her mother and her servants so that everyone can rejoice. Together they dispense justice in the Ebony Isles, while Badoura yearns to find Camar again.

Back in the city of the magians, the marooned Camar witnesses a strange fight between birds; one of them savagely beheads the other, but its fellows take vengeance on the attacker and murder the bird on the grave of the first victim. Camar notices something gleaming in the carnage: Badoura's magic gem. The portent is auspicious; he knows it means he will soon find her again. The next day, digging in the garden, he strikes iron, a sign of underground treasure. Under a copper trapdoor he finds stairs leading down to a chamber dating back to the era of Byzantium or even farther, to the reigns of Ad and Thamud. The hiding place is stacked with jars which, when he puts his hands in them, are filled with red gold of the highest purity.

He tells the old gardener what he has found, and wants to give him the gold, or at least half of it. But the old man tells him to keep it: 'I've lived in this garden for eighty years . . . and I never found anything. You arrived here less than a year ago and you've discovered this fortune. It's yours. It will help you struggle against adversity, to go back to your country and find your beloved again.'

But Camar insists on giving him half. Then he prepares to leave: he fills fifty jars full of gold with olives on top to conceal it, and in one of them he hides the talisman. The merchant ship is in harbour, loaded and ready to sail, but Camar can see that the gardener's health is failing; he must stay beside him in his last hours, and when death has come, give him a proper burial. This he does. But it means that the ship sails without him, and he will have to wait another year for it to return.

The jars are stowed, and the gold and olives arrive in the Ebony Isles, where Princess Badoura as ruler takes delivery of them, and finds her lost carnelian in one of them. Immediately, she orders a ship to collect the merchant who dispatched the jars from the city of the magians and bring him before her. When he arrives, she recognises that he is indeed her lost husband, Camar al-Zaman, whom she has longed for all this long gap of time they have been parted by destiny. But Camar does not recognise her – or rather, he does not see Badoura in the mirror-double of himself he encounters in the young King before him.

Badoura takes Hayat into her confidence, but she does not yet reveal herself to Camar. Instead she covers him with honours; she gives feasts for him, orders him splendid clothes, showers him with gifts and establishes him in offices of state. When he wonders at all this, the ruler of the Ebony Isles confesses that desire is the cause.

Camar blushes with shame: how could the king, who has all the loveliest women at his beck and call, feel such a shameful thing? He protests, he resists, but the king insists. 'Just this once,' says Camar. Weeping, he is led to the royal bedchamber, and there takes off his clothes.

'Pass your hand between my thighs as you must,' orders the false king.

'I don't know anything about these things,' sobs Camar.

But as his hand is guided to the place, Badoura bursts out laughing.

'My friend, how quickly you have forgotten the nights that we have spent together!'

In this way she reveals herself to her love, her husband Camar al-Zaman, who takes her in his arms.

All that night, they talk about what has happened to them since they lost each other.

The following day, Badoura discloses the true state of affairs to the king of the Ebony Isles, that his daughter Hayat is still a virgin. But all is sorted out: Camar al-Zaman marries Hayat as well, and takes his place as her consort to rule in Badoura's place; he throws open the jails, lifts the tariffs at the gates, abolishes all tolls and taxes and charges on moorings. As Hayat and Badoura remain the closest of allies, they do not mind when he spends alternate nights with them; everyone is happy.

A cloud falls on this happiness later in their lives, but that is a story for another time . . .

CHAPTER SIXTEEN

Thought Experiments: Flight before Flight

If you do not SEE, if you do not KNOW,
If you do not BELIEVE, then never fly –
And continue to walk, simpleton!
Félix Nadar, *Droit au vol*, 1866

I

THE STORY OF CAMAR AL-ZAMAN and Princess Badoura is one of the lovely long romances of the *Nights*, told by Shahrazad over many nights, from the 179th to the 217th night. Its heroine Badoura is strong-willed, ardent, capable and, above all, intensely loyal. She is a prime exhibit in Shahrazad's pageant of virtuous women: beginning as a stern, proud virgin, a fairytale princess who is wholly bound up with her royal father, she develops into a witty trickster who tests Camar in one of the frankest and most surprising bed tricks from a wide repertoire of variations on the motif: Shakespeare comes quite close to such a gay seduction in *Twelfth Night*, when Viola, cross-dressed as Cesario, passionately woos her beloved Orsino, but he does not go as far as the explicit sex of Badoura's deception. Camar belongs among the sweet and rather ineffectual heroes of the *Nights*, drifting along more passively than his wife, but he too shows strength of mind, true-heartedness, and generosity in his relation to the old gardener in the city of the magians. Enchantments and pragmatism mingle: travel by caravan, on foot, and by cargo ship, mapped on to a plausible geography, moves the story of the lovers' protracted double quest, but jinn in flight are the catalysts of the protagonists' passion. The twining of the stories resembles a dance: now meeting, now parting, the line of characters keeps turning and moving as the music of the scenes modulates the tune.

Flying happens in dreams, often for some, seldom for others; it can bring a sensation of ecstatic freedom, or dread and terror when you wake on the instant of crashing to earth. Long before flight became a reality and a commonplace way of travelling, it was part of the world of the mind and experienced, consciously and unconsciously, through phantasmata, pictures and stories. The idea of flying – like birds, like angels – opened a vista of metaphorical meanings for the human subject, associated with angelic bodilessness, sexual delight, fairy ethereality, untrammelled motion, uplift and intoxication – and also with vertigo, disorientation, the unbearable lightness of being. It was a property of spirits and animals but also of alarming things, of 'the invisible worm,/That flies in the night', insects, dragons, devils.

In the *Nights*, flying gives one of the most characteristic fantasy experiences of the stories. Through flying, the realm of the jinn touches and transforms the limits of the human body. Flight happens without any to-do; it is a dynamic of the plot, an element in the narrative material, a defining feature of its momentum (its time signature), and the key image in oneiric storytelling. In a self-reflexive narrative manner, flying mimics the motion of fantasy itself and of stories that seek to express it. Its agents are jinn and peris, machines and simulacra, and monstrous or wonderful creatures. Flying in the *Nights* acts as 'a fable of modernity', not of backwardness; its dreams of lightness have their eyes open to the future.

The jinn are the descendants of the daimones and the deities of antiquity, bodies that materialise in forms that defy materiality itself: in Apuleius's romance, Zephyr, the west wind, bears the sleeping Psyche to the castle that Cupid has prepared for her, just as the jinn bear up Solomon on his carpeted throne, or as Dahnash carries off the Princess Badoura in the *Nights*. Alongside the flying jinn, giant birds such as the Rukh, or different colossal raptors, even some with elephant's feet, also carry off heroes – Sinbad, Marouf, and many others. Hasan of Basra is also transported by sinister carrion Rukhs, but subsequently enjoys several other magical flights, on the backs of jinn and riding enchanted horses who come when he beats a magic drum. As in the enchanted meeting of Camar and Badoura in their sleep, such flights continue the series of high-spirited puns on transport in the *Nights* as travel and rapture.

Both meanings fill visions of flight: they are presented both as feasibility studies and dream states of ecstasy. The Renaissance scholar Brian Vickers has pointed out in an incisive essay about the character of magical thinking that 'in the scientific tradition . . . a clear distinction is made between words and things and between literal and metaphorical language. The occult tradition does not recognize this distinction: words are treated as if they are equivalent to things and can be substituted for them. Manipulate the one and you manipulate the other.' Vickers is exploring a specific historical period, but the axiom he defines continues to operate recognisably in contemporary understanding of the issue. However, the opposition gains nuance if we look at it through the lens of the monumental work of imagination that is the *Arabian Nights*, and its impact and continuing resonance. Flight offers a pre-eminent example of such slippage between literal and figural, and of the spectrum of metaphors that open from that indeterminacy; European fantastic fiction took up wonder as a dynamic of inquiry, enthusiastically recognising the potential of the device.

The meeting of lovers in a dream: while she sleeps, Badoura is carried to meet her future love, Camar al-Zaman, by the jinni Danhasch, who grips her fine Venetian drapery firmly between his teeth (J. D. Batten, 1893).

Whereas transformations above all mark the magic of European fairy tales before the *Arabian Nights*, flight distinguishes the fantasies of the latter, which present a more democratic view of flying: the jinn and peris are constantly aloft, and they frequently carry off the human protagonists too. Stories contrast this enchanted mobility with the practicalities of caravans, walking and shipping, which feature with historical vividness in the tales, alongside the wonders. The jinn, initiating the passionate love of the two young protagonists, Camar and Badoura, perform their volatile enchantments as metaphors for the mobility and surprise of the wonder tale itself.

In Christendom, condemnation hangs around the possibility of flight (think of the monstrous Geryon taking Dante and Virgil on his back down into the pit of Hell, in *Inferno* XVII: 10–18), and demons' powers are condemned in medieval and early modern literature: in the witch-hunters' fantasies, witches brew ointments to smear on their bodies in preparation for flying to the Sabbath, and take off on broomsticks or the backs of devils. On the whole, traditional fairy tales avoid scenes of flying, perhaps through anxiety of contamination by sorcery. Enchantments involve sudden and inexplicable changes of place, as when Beauty wishes herself back at her father's house and calls up the magic horse to carry her there in a trice; seven-league boots carry giants prodigiously far and fast until Puss or another clever young hero steals them; a bear will carry off a girl to a far country by impossible strides. Such wonders overturn the laws of physics and break all the boundaries on human possibility. But the protagonists of Perrault's fairy tales and the Grimms' *Children's and Household Tales* remain grounded. If one pauses to think about the nursery standards such as Perrault's 'Cinderella', 'The Sleeping Beauty in the Wood', 'Hop o'My Thumb', 'Puss in Boots', or the Grimm Brothers' 'Hansel and Gretel', 'Rapunzel', 'Snow White' and 'The Juniper Tree', one finds that flight does not feature significantly as part of the enchanted scene. The tales that take place in enchanted forests, like 'The Sleeping Beauty in the Wood' or 'Red Riding Hood', do not even feature daimonic sprites like Ariel from *The Tempest* or mischievous spirits of forest and lake like Puck, or Moth, Cobweb and Mustardseed from *A Midsummer Night's Dream*, let alone the Tinkerbell sort of fairy from *Peter Pan*.

It can be hard to see this difference in enchantment because the later tradition of fairytale has so gleefully taken off into the skies. Orientalising writers – Anthony Hamilton, Marie-Catherine d'Aulnoy – immediately begin to whisk their characters about in flying chariots, or on monstrous mounts; as Anne E. Duggan has pointed out, they were taking a cue from the stage machinery and effects used in court masques, operas and festivals in the fairy play or *féerie* tradition of France and Italy. But the aerial freedom emulates that of the *Nights*. The effect of Eastern levitation can also be seen in those European writers who, although contemporaries of the Grimms, prided themselves on original creativity rather than folkloristic fidelity: for example, Hans Christian Andersen and Wilhelm Hauff (1802–27). Hauff wrote *Der kleine Muck*, in the year after Habicht's translation of the *Arabian Nights* into German was published, and his fairy tales adopt the latest oriental trappings with enthusiasm: 'Little Mook' takes place in Nicaea, where the young hero becomes the servant of the predatory Madame Ahavzi, a sorceress. In a room which she always keeps locked, he finds 'only old clothes and vessels of strange and marvellous form', including some huge slippers.

Little Mook soon finds that the giant slippers behave like seven-league boots and whirl him wherever he wishes in no time at all, so that he can accomplish all kinds of impossible tasks and out-perform his larger, stronger, richer rivals and win the favour of the Sultan. In this ingenious way, Hauff spliced Western fairytale locomotion with Eastern soaring.

Another stratum of folklore, spreading from Russia and its Central Asian communities, intertwines with the *Arabian Nights* to deepen the bond between fairytale itself and the fantasy of flight. Interestingly, the magic carpet itself, which appears in 'The Frog Princess' and other tales, was called *samolyet* (self-flyer, by analogy with 'samovar', self-boiler); the word was also adopted to name the aeroplane when it was invented.

This is one of the few instances when a language does not create a new, learned word (aerostat, aeroplane), but borrows the term for a modern scientific innovation directly from folklore's prior fantasies.

The poet Velimir Khlebnikov cries out on behalf of fairy tales:

> Self-Flyer walks through the sky.
> But where is Tablecloth, Self-Victualler, wife of Self-Flyer?
> Is she by accident delayed, or thrown into prison?

And he continues,

> Now I always knew
> Fairy tales could come true:
> Today's hard fact was once a fairy tale.

Khlebnikov's wishful thinking, with its ironies about political promises of bread and plenty and its allusions to the repressions of the state, does however indicate a straightforward point of fact: that in the distant past fairy tales dreamed up possibilities that were to come about far ahead in the future.

II

Oriental fairytale becomes a preferred genre to communicate newfan-gledness; it often takes the place of the treatises and essays in which such speculation had more often been couched. Numerous *contes philos-ophiques*, imaginary voyages, utopian societies of fantasists and scientists display the rational author taking flight. When the spate of improvisa-tions on the *Nights* began to pour from the presses of eighteenth-century Europe, they gave impetus to the imagining of flight before flight. Parodies, satires, variations, admiring imitations, impressions in-the-style-of and mischievous forgeries seized the freedoms offered by the book's hyperbole and absurdities, its delight in extravagant plotting and fabulous enchantments and opened ways of storytelling with defined purposes. The 'new heuristic value of fiction' made it possible for thinkers to reject scientific orthodoxy and put forward their own ideas – in the guise of playful, comic romancing. The attraction of flight is allegorical, the freedoms of the body communicating an untrammelled spirit, too. For Anne E. Duggan, for example, the *élan* of Mme d'Aulnoy's fairy tales expresses a feminocentric riposte to male absolutism. Scenes of flight mark many of the most amusing, inventive and occasionally combative of these writings, which found that the dynamic of the metaphor moved thought towards new horizons – again both actually and allegorically. A strong intuition carries these wild imaginings: that these heroes may be overreaching the prescribed human lot, but they are moving towards something feasible; in this respect, the stories are distinguished from metaphysical speculations.

Lucian's *True History* tells of a journey to the moon, and in its absurdist hubris was a popular inspiration for the speculators about human flight. Another important source was the careful description in the *Alexander Romance* of the emperor's experiment; how he climbed into a basket, harnessed it to some griffins, hoisted red meat above their heads – some say it was ox liver (massive) – and fixed it out of their reach; in this way, as the dragon-birds soared upwards in pursuit of their quarry, the emperor succeeded in having himself lifted high above the earth. (The emperor's prototype Montgolfier balloon caught the imagination all over the world: he appears in it for example in the mosaic floor of the basilica of Otranto made by the monk Pantaleone in 1100BC; and there is a misericord carved with the scene in Gloucester cathedral.) Significantly, this flight is attached to the founding of Alexandria, and forms part of Alexander's heroic thirst for knowledge; it is just one experiment among many others through which he seeks to uncover for himself the wonders of the universe. In

Islamic sources, the same attempt becomes associated with another hero (Nimrod) and condemns him for folly and arrogance.

Scientific experiment features among Alexander the Great's many accomplishments: in his griffin-drawn flying machine he has a claim to being a pioneer of aviation.

Serious scientific speculation about the feasibility of human flight continued under the guise of tall-tale telling, partly to hide from the obloquy of religious authorities, partly to take refuge in trifling to protect one's own pride, and partly to divert and amuse. Francis Godwin (1562–1633), Bishop of Hereford, presented his radical ideas about the universe as the true-life memoir of a Spanish sailor: *The Man in the Moone, or A*

Discourse of a Voyage thither by Domingo Gonsales, the Little Spaniard . . .
In painstaking detail, Godwin describes how his hero, having fled various
misadventures in the second half of the previous century, reaches the
island of St Helena and there tames some colossal birds, ganzas (or gansas),
which have one eagle's claw and one webbed swan's foot. He trains them
to rise together at a signal, and then, in order to distribute the weight
between the birds, 'I fastened about each *Gansa* a little Pulley of *Cork*,
and putting a string of a just length through it, I fastened one end to a
block of almost eight pound weight, and tyed a two pound weight to
the other end of the string, and then causing the signal to be Erected,
they all Rose together, being four in number and carried away my block
to the place appointed.' He gradually increases the number of birds
harnessed and 'made Tryal of their carrying a Lamb, whose happiness I
much envied, that he should be the first living creature to partake of
such an excellent device'. In the edition I read, this tale was bound
together in a bundle with travel literature containing 'true' accounts of
monsters and wonders, and there are delightful illustrations by the anonymous engraver, showing a towering cascade of the birds, rather like a
stack of box kites, above the tiny figure of the seated Domingo.

More mishaps and shipwrecks follow, but in 1601 the birds take off.
It is time for their annual migration – to the moon.

Marco Polo's tales had brought news of the Rukh, while other stories
circulated motifs and plots from the Middle East before the *Nights*
appeared in print; Godwin's imagery bears marks of such tales. True to
the heuristic spirit of New Science in the seventeenth century, he blends
them with the empirical discipline of the traveller's log and works out
the detail, emphasising the size and might of the ganzas, and drawing
attention to the diminutive size – and weight – of his hero, Domingo
Gonsales, to make his method more plausible.

The writer is using the faux travel diary to communicate anti-Aristotelian,
controversial scientific theories: Godwin's moon stands for the New
World and his science fiction is a means of conveying new, dissident
knowledge: from his vantage point between the earth and the moon, the
hero observes the earth revolving on its orbit, and argues for Copernican
theory; once he reaches the moon, he rightly discovers that he is gravity-
free. Furthermore, he sees that the empyrean, the burning ethereal higher
heaven, does not exist. He also learns that the lunar people communicate
in musical tones, as in Chinese.

Throughout, he appeals to known authorities, to William Gilbert on
magnetism and Galileo on the heliocentric universe; for these reasons,
'fiction . . . is no longer synonymous with lying or pure fantasy. The

Bird-drawn vehicles dominated early speculation: Domingo Gonsales trained 'gansas' to fly him to the moon (Francis Godwin, *The Man in the Moone*, 1638).

playful narrative frame contains and integrates discursive elements which redefine the text as "serious fiction".' Godwin writes, 'So that what the ancient Poets were faine to put in a fable, our more happy age has found out in a truth, and we may discern as far with these eyes which Galileus has bestowed upon us, as Lynceus could with those which the Poets attributed to him.' The French critic Frédérique Aït-Touati neatly sums up: 'Fiction functions henceforth as a thought experiment, and takes the place of the impossible experimental proof [of the new philosophy].'

An early moon traveller ascends by the power of the dew evaporating in the sunlight from the vials around his waist (Cyrano de Bergerac, 1656).

Godwin was in other respects a dusty archivist, and compiled a useful catalogue of English bishops; but his startling flight of fancy was translated into French and read by Cyrano de Bergerac (d. 1655), who in turn couched a satire of contemporary thought in the form of a journey to the moon. In Cyrano's work, his pioneer aviator ascends aided by nothing more than phials filled with dew, which are slung about him from his belt; the dew evaporating in the heat of the sun causes him to rise bodily in the air. (In the illustration, the phials resemble the bottles from which issue forth the jinn of the *Nights*, with their spirituous bodies.)

The same year as Godwin's book, another English bishop, John Wilkins (1614–72), also took up the possibility of lunar travel. Wilkins was a genial mathematician and scientist, physicist and philosopher, one of the founders of the Royal Society, alongside Robert Boyle and John Hooke, and its first secretary (to start with, the group called themselves, rather suggestively, 'The Invisible College'). He believed in letting fantasy fly, gleefully, freely: 'Amongst the impediments of any strange invention or attempts,' he wrote, 'it is one of the meanest discouragements, that they are so generally derided by common opinion, being esteemed only as the dreams of a melancholy and distempered fancy.'

Wilkins investigated a fabulous range of questions with sober ratiocination: whether there is life on the moon; how the earth might be a planet; how to build a perpetual motion machine; the feasibility of a universal language; the transmission of thought and enciphered messages, and other issues packed with prophetic matters. His propositions foretell many wonderful things long before anything of the kind came about – the telephone and the wireless, the telegraph and the computer, Esperanto and even ringtones. Above all, he was concerned with flight. He pondered the difficulties that flying presented to humans, and offered detailed suggestions, advising that bats' wings be imitated: 'the continuate membrane rather than bird's feathers'. He grasped the principle – not apparent to many at that date – that things heavier than air can become airborne, from observing the flight of birds as large as eagles. He also invokes the case of the colossal Rukh, 'with wing feathers 12 paces or 3 score feet long . . . which can with as much ease scoop up an Elephant, as our Kites do a Mouse'. He deduces that a body does not need to be lighter than air to fly, but, just as a huge vessel floats as well as a piece of cork, and an eagle flies as well as the least insect, so it is simply a question of time before the obstacles that so far have prevented human beings from reaching the moon will be overcome. ''Tis possible,' he writes, 'for some of our posterity to finde out a conveyance to the other world, and if there be inhabitants there, to have commerce with them.'

He ends this book with a glad cry: 'Happy they who will be the first to succeed in this enterprise!'

In *Mathematical Magick; or, the Wonders that may be Performed by Natural Mechanicks* (1648) Wilkins significantly sets out his belief in the riches to be extracted from banal, everyday matters, by introducing an anecdote about Heraclitus frequenting tradesmen's shops which some of his fellow scholars were 'ashamed to enter . . . But Heraclitus told them that "the gods were well conversant in such places" . . . intimating that a divine power and wisdome might be discerned even in those common Arts, which are so much despised.'

Accordingly, from voracious reading, he reviews the history of toys and fancies, especially 'Automata, or Self-movers' – wind-guns, clocks, clockwork models, 'subterraneous lamps', and all the devices and gadgets made by 'artificers' (his term) which he has been able to excavate from chronicles, fairy tales, inventors and philosophers. He has heard of other ingenious contrivances: a head that speaks after it has been cut off, the Iron Fly that buzzes around and flies, a speaking statue. His fellow mathematician, Cardanus, has reported some fabulous stories of 'fighting images': one tempts you with the sight of a jewelled apple, but when you reach out to take it, a statue shoots arrows at you from several bows concealed in its body.

Among the Self-movers, objects that can fly detain him most, and he extrapolates from their existence to prophesy a flying future: 'on basis of such past inventions, imitating nature, it will clearly follow, that it is possible also for a man to fly himself: it being easie from the same grounds to frame an instrument, wherein any one may sit, and give such motion unto it as shall convey him aloft through the air. Than which there is not any imaginable invention that would prove of greater benefit to the world, or glory to the Author.'

Wilkins also continued to investigate, with calm deliberation, the possibility of human flight:

> These things that seem very difficult and fearfull at the first may grow very facil after frequent trial and exercise: And therefore he that would effect any thing in this kind must be brought up to the constant practice of it from his Youth; trying first only to use his wings in running on the ground, as an Estrich or tame geese will do . . . One of our nation hath proceeded so far in this experiment that he was able by the help of wings to skip constantly ten yards at a time.

He advised his readers to follow the example of acrobats and contortionists who can perform astonishing, unnatural feats, and start practising – from an early age. 'What strange agility and activeness,' he writes, 'do our common tumblers and dancers on the rope attain to by continual exercise?' He continues: 'circus riders, and swimmers – I mention these things to shew the great power of practice and custom, which might more probably succeed in this experiment in flying if it were but regularly attempted . . .'

Wilkins's book came out only five months after Godwin's, and it seems that he revised the first edition in the light of it, adding detail to the feasibility of lunar travel and lunar encounters: 'It is easily conceivable, how once a year a man might finish such a voyage; going along with these birds at the beginning of winter, and again returning with them in the spring.'

He brings in inimitable touches, too: moon travellers, like chameleons and birds of paradise, might nourish themselves only on the air, on aromas emanating from the ether. In his Preface, Wilkins declares, 'That the strangenesse of this opinion is no sufficient reason why it should be rejected, because other certaine truths have been formerly esteemed ridiculous, and great absurdities entertained by common consent.'

The worlds of science and fantasy do not invariably clash – one can nourish the other, and human minds are complicated jugglers and can believe many contradictory things before breakfast.

Wilkins is not presenting his work as fiction: his thoughts are set down in treatises, mathematical books and papers for discussion. Yet the fanciful-ness of his propositions makes his work read like fiction. After his death, Hooke wrote a tribute to him in his famous book *Micrographia* (1665): 'There is scarce one invention which this nation has produced in our age, but it has some way or other been set forward by his assistance . . . He is indeed a man born for the good of mankind.' Nearly three centuries later, Borges was so intrigued by Wilkins's experimental thinking that he wrote one of his most famous essays about him: 'He was full of happy curiosity: interested in theology, cryptography, music, the manufacture of transparent beehives, the course of an invisible planet, the possibility of a trip to the moon, the possibility and principles of a world language.' In his most deliberate, mock-pedantic way, Borges goes on to draw up the celebrated animal taxonomy of 'a certain Chinese encyclopaedia called the Heavenly Emporium of Benevolent Knowledge'. The list, made famous by Michel Foucault's totemic use of it in *L'Ordre des choses*, goes:

> . . . animals are divided into: (a) those that belong to the emperor; (b) embalmed ones; (c) those that are trained; (d) suckling pigs; (e) mermaids; (f) fabulous ones; (g) stray dogs; (h) those that are included in this classi-fication; (i) those that tremble as if they were mad; (j) innumerable ones; (k) those drawn with a very fine camel's-hair brush; (l) etcetera; (m) those that have just broken the flower vase; (n) those that at a distance resemble flies.'

Borges's mock learning was prompted by Wilkins's proposal for a universal language (it anticipates bar codes); it stirred Borges's thoughts about the arbitrariness of language and the mismatch between experience and words. When Swift satirises the philosophers in Laputa, whose language consists of the things themselves which they laboriously carry about and exchange rather than speaking in words, Swift is turning Wilkins's ideas topsy-turvy – he was one of the 'virtuosi' of the Royal Society whom Swift had in his sights.

Wilkins's scientific fantasies and his commitment to the wildest reaches of speculation make him, I think, a sympathetic predecessor of writers who in the next century began to imagine flying methods and flying in response to the jinn's aerodynamics in the *Nights*. The imagination of flight cannot be separated from the fabric of these fantasies. Yet, while Icarus and Daedalus figure in such histories, the various flying modes and vehicles of the *Nights* are left out as too far-fetched, preposterous, merely fanciful. (Wilkins would have relished the new machines, hang-gliders, windsurfers, and kite surfers, which unfurl sheets on the air not unlike the fancy of the flying carpet, a different concept of human flight than the ornithopters or bird-shaped vehicles of the Daedalus/Leonardo approach.)

Dr Johnson was an advocate of rational thought, and he opens his novella *Rasselas* (1759), a riposte to the oriental tale in biblical tones, with a glum warning against fantasy: 'Ye who listen with credulity to the whispers of fancy, and persue with eagerness the phantoms of hope [. . .] attend to the history of Rasselas prince of Abyssinia.' In a later chapter called 'A dissertation on the art of flying', the prince meets a Daedalus-like master craftsman who, in surroundings of unmistakable paradisical Orientalism, is building a 'sailing chariot'; as he informs Rasselas of its conditions and practicability, this 'mechanist' imports many suggestions about human flight from Wilkins's works. Rasselas longs to learn what is on the other side of the Happy Valley in which he is confined and so he encourages the man of science to try. He does so, and plunges into a lake from which Rasselas pulls him, 'half-dead'.

Rasselas, in the shadow of Voltaire's Oriental tales, borrows the fantastic clothing its author was resisting, and mounts a defence of reason in the motley of imaginary fooling. Its author's desire to dampen fancy in favour of moderation and proper scepticism had, however, little effect on fellow writers; crashes in fiction did not deter inventors any more than they did in the actual history of attempts to fly.

III

Human flight in fable and fairytale reaches a pinnacle of invention in *The Life and Adventures of Peter Wilkins, a Man of Cornwall*. Once a much-loved and widely known narrative, often interpreted for the stage and variety shows, the book has undeservedly faded in reputation.

Peter Wilkins first appeared in London in 1750 and the author carefully removed himself from view, in order to present his work as the true report of the narrator, a surviving seaman, as told to a faithful confidant, who took it down verbatim. Making claims to authenticity in the style of Godwin's *Domingo Gonsales*, or *Robinson Crusoe*, published thirty years before, it resembles Defoe's famous book in its freewheeling inventiveness; it rides on the kite-tail of *Crusoe*, one might say, to add plausibility to the far more fantastical claims it unfolds. *The Adventures of Peter Wilkins* combines travel yarn, exotic ethnography, science fiction speculation and romance. But it also overlaps with the *Nights* more directly than either Godwin, Defoe or Swift in their imaginary voyages, for the author creates a fairytale mood of sensitive and dream-like romance missing from these precursors.

The book sets out the story as told by Peter to one of the passengers on board the ship *Hector* which rescued him from a raft on the high seas off Cape Horn, and who, on hearing his extraordinary story, decides to act as his amanuensis; he not only writes it all down but also makes drawings from his detailed descriptions, which are engraved in the published book. In the preface, just to rub in the authenticity of what follows, 'R.S' adds that 'Upon a survey, he [Peter Wilkins] confessed that the very persons themselves could not have been more exact.'

The narrator gives chapter and verse of his origins and background: born on 21 December 1685, he lost his father when the latter supported the Duke of Monmouth's rebellion and was executed; Peter goes to sea, but is 'captured by a French privateer', the *Glorieux*, and sails down the west coast of Africa; terrible scenes follow when he and his fellow captives are put off by the French pirates and some of his companions resort to cannibalism; Peter himself wanders inland towards the Congo with a companion called Glaulipze, whose loyalty and bravery – he overcomes a crocodile by means of an ingenious trap – contrast starkly with the French slavers' savagery. The author's political allegiances appear in this portrait of the mutual respect between Peter and Glaulipze and segue smoothly into the eirenic utopianism of his later experiences of 'flying indians'.

The real-life author of this genial example of the imaginary voyage has been identified as one Robert Paltock (1697–1767), an otherwise unknown lawyer. The first edition of the book won little success but the French translator changed the book's fortunes when he gave it a new title, *Les Hommes volans* (1763), thus shifting the accent from travel yarn or political satire to fantastic fiction. When the book returned to print in England twenty years later, the publisher followed the French example; as *The Flying Indians*, the book struck a chord with the public, and joined the vigorous stream of orientalising fantasy combined with scientific magic already in vogue.

Peter Wilkins describes in circumstantial historical detail how, after he left Africa and joined another boat, the entire fleet was shipwrecked when, nearing the South Pole, they drifted into the force field of the Magnetic Mountain, which draws the nails from every timber of a boat in its vicinity. This reflects the century's curiosity about magnetic attraction, while the Mountain is a well-known hazard in the *Nights*: the Third Dervish describes how he too was overcome by disaster when his pilot told him the tempest had carried them

> so far out of our course, that to-morrow about noon we shall come near to that black place, which is nothing else but the black mountain, that is a mine of adamant, which at this minute draws all your ships; and when we come tomorrow at a certain distance, the strength of the adamant will have such a force, that all the nails will be drawn out of the sides and bottom of the ships, and fastened to the mountain, so that your vessel will fall to pieces and sink to the bottom. And as the adamant has a virtue to draw all iron to it, whereby its attraction becomes stronger, this mountain on the side of the sea is all covered over with nails, drawn out of an infinite number of vessels that have perished by it.

Compare this approach to the dramatic observations conducted by Peter Wilkins as he sits on deck musing on his life and finds that his shoes fly up into the air when he takes them off (in the early 1700s, he would be wearing shoes with metal buckles). He then experiments with other objects, with a pipe and a silver spoon and a bottle, and finds that some of these do not levitate. But when a key does, he surmises that the boat is approaching a lodestone. Throughout his manner is rational, calm and ingenious: he asserts that he knows the calamity to be no responsibility of spirits. In Paltock's scientific-fantastic imagination, causes are to be looked for in physical forces – natural, not supernatural magic.

Our hero enumerates the measures he takes to survive, first for three months on board the wreck, but then setting out alone in a rowing boat until he reaches, through dark passages under mountains, an inland lake, a paradise of 'the finest verdure I had ever seen . . .'

Robert Paltock then takes another cue from the *Nights*, one which made the fortunes of his book – though again it cannot be *asserted* that he had read the adventures of Sinbad or 'The Tale of the Third Dervish'). This last story, like that of Camar al-Zaman and Badoura, describes the hero's discovery of a region of fairy women.

He first sees them coming in from the sea in boats, and then taking off: '[they] flew . . . in a long train over the lake, quite out of my sight, laughing, hallooing, and sporting together'. Some time later, he hears a crash one evening outside his encampment. Taking his lamp, he finds someone has fallen and become tangled up in a tree; he lifts the lamp to discover 'the face of a beautiful woman'. Her hair was 'tucked up and twined' into 'a sort of brown chaplet . . . she seemed to be clothed in a thin hair-coloured silk garment.' He picks her up, and 'she felt to my touch in the oddest manner imaginable; for while in one respect, it was as though she had been cased up in whalebone, it was at the same time as soft and warm as if she had been naked.' This chapter closes with the annunciatory thrill: 'Little did I then think that she could fly.'

Peter Wilkins, a sailor shipwrecked at the South Pole, discovers a flying people and helps them overcome their enemies. (Robert Paltock, *Les Hommes Volands,* 1738)

After this mysterious and romantic start, Peter Wilkins comes to care for her and to learn her language (he appends a glossary). Once her injuries have healed, she takes to flying again. This comes in useful, and though he is worried she will not return, he dispatches her to the wreck to fetch back supplies. But she does come back with them, and shows off a few aerial turns and passes in the air. Ten minutes later, they marry and settle down in pastoral-colonial idyllic isolation and have children. Her name is Youwarkee, and she is a 'gauri', the name for a woman of her kind, not incidentally echoing the name of an Indian goddess, akin to the peris or fairies of the *Arabian Nights*.

The novel, for such it is, moves easily between lyricism and matter-of-fact travel writing; such flattening of the emotional register adds to the pragmatism of the prose and heightens the comic delight of the scene when Peter Wilkins investigates Youwarkee's body in the same scientific spirit as he used to test the lodestone, the subterranean passage to the lake and so on. Robert Paltock works out very deliberately how a flesh and blood woman would be able to fly; in a tender scene of love-making, Wilkins discovers that gauris like Youwarkee are tightly encased in a structure called a 'graundee', made of a silky elastic material which sheathes them like the wings of a moth, and equally can suddenly unfurl. The text is ambiguous about the organic character of this carapace, but it strikes the reader as a cross between a fan, a corset, a harness and a kite. Youwarkee is a hybrid creature, between woman and machine, a cyborg *avant la lettre* – not an automaton like a mechanical horse, but a natural woman capable of giving birth, yet still a kind of ingenious device, with a voice that is very sweet and musical, in spite of the Swiftian, cacophonous consonants in her language.

The males of the species are known as glumms (a direct echo of Gulliver's Brobdingnagian nurse Glumdalglitch); they are equipped to fly with a different carapace, possessing an extra fin between their legs. The couple's first child, Tommy, is born with a graundee and at first can fly too; but it fails to expand as he grows, and so he cannot take after his mother.

The idyll is interrupted when the plot veers into political allegory, and Youwarkee's people need to fight for their survival against an evil usurper from the unpronounceable state of Normnbdsgrasntt; Peter is cast as the saviour whose coming has been foretold. When he joins in the battle, he builds 'a machine', a raft which he then harnesses to several glumms; with this prototype bomber aircraft, a descendant of Godwin's gansa-drawn kite, they prevail.

During more than ten happy, productive and triumphant years in Brandleguarp, as his new country is called, Peter founds a new colony on enlightened lines and takes the opportunity to translate the Bible for Youwarkee and her people.

But Youwarkee is not a fairy and she dies; or rather, like a jinniya in the *Nights*, she is subject to physical laws. After her death, Peter decides to set out on his flying raft and return to his former life. The raft crashes into the sea, and off Cape Horn he is found and rescued by the passing ship *Hector*, which is where the story of his adventures began.

The Romantics especially responded to the story's charm: Robert Southey wrote that the winged characters Peter Wilkins encounters are 'the most beautiful creatures of the imagination that were ever devised';

Charles Lamb and Coleridge seconded him. Leigh Hunt agreed, but he could not help poking fun at Paltock's technology: 'We are to picture to ourselves a nymph in a vest of the finest texture and most delicate carnation. On a sudden this drapery parts in two and flies back, stretched from head to foot like an oval fan or an umbrella; and the lady is in front of it, preparing to sweep blushing away from us and "winnow the buxom air".'

Thirty years later he picked up his critique again: 'the wing, the graundee, or elastic drapery which opens and shuts at pleasure, however ingeniously and even beautifully contrived, would necessitate creatures whose modifications of humanity, bodily and mental . . . might have startled the inventor had he been more of a naturalist'.

Hunt has moved from his earlier understanding that the graundee is a manufactured artefact, like a whalebone petticoat, a sail, or a construction of wicker, a fan or an umbrella, and argued for more biological accuracy. By shifting the imagined model, he misses the interesting point of difference between fairytale fantasy and the progeny of the *Arabian Nights*. In the former, flying women are visualised on the whole by analogy with a bird or butterfly or dragonfly: many of Hunt's contemporaries enjoyed inventing fairy fantasias thronged with anthropomorphic insects – *The Butterfly's Ball and the Grasshopper's Feast* by William Roscoe (1807) or the artist Richard Dadd's later vision of a teeming undergrowth of elves and pixies in his hallucinatory painting *The Fairy Feller's Master-Stroke* (1855–64). Paltock, by contrast, is the inheritor of the age of wonder and New Science, and, as a writer, composes fantasies in the vein of early science fiction. He has become captivated by artificial contrivances rather than natural wonders. However, these artefacts are not all artifice; to fulfil the conditions of wonder, they must transform natural properties inherent in their component elements into another shape. While Youwarkee has a skin which is also a cocoon, it also possesses the qualities of a crafted and individual piece of workmanship, as caught by the illustrations, where the glumm's graundee resembles a square-rigged sail, and the gauri's a kite or flag.

The name Peter Wilkins is a likely tribute to the thought of John Wilkins, who represents reasoned imagination in the preceding century. Enough of the historical Wilkins's interests and suggestions have found dramatic expression in Robert Paltock's novel to support a conscious connection: magnets and magnetism lay at the heart of Wilkins's experiments with a perpetual motion machine, and his love of codes, ciphers and pre-Babelian speech informs the language that Peter Wilkins acquires with his new family.

But with the change of genre, from essay to fiction, Paltock's novel continues the decisive direction Francis Godwin also took. It signals the arrival of fabulism in literature as a paramount method of inquiry, critique and border-crossings. In order to open possibilities – or, as John Wilkins preferred to think – probabilities that there are other forms of life and ways of life equal to but different from our own, Paltock and many other writers in his time, now better known, chose to present fictions as facts. The airborne odysseys of the *Arabian Nights*, carrying protagonists to the ends of the earth where other worlds welcome them, are re-imagined to give ballast to an Enlightenment programme of passionate curiosity, leading to an embrace of the Other – a literal embrace since many of these stories involve erotic encounters and, as in the case of Peter Wilkins, marriage and children. In the *Nights*, mortal men fall desperately in love with jinniyas and sorceresses and suffer harsh treatment before their love is fulfilled; in eighteenth-century scenes of flight before flight to the new elsewheres, the demonic origins of the topos flower into erotic expression, as the authors seize freedom and, in some cases, licence to speak.

For example, in *The Voyages of Hildebrand Bowman*, published in London in 1778, the writer again assumes a mask and claims to tell a personal history of calamity and survival, in this case in immediate and highly newsworthy circumstances: he presents himself as a sailor who has survived the massacre of all his fellows on the *Adventure*, a ship of Captain Cook's fleet during the second voyage to Australia and New Zealand. One of the illustrations of his startling adventures shows a figure very like Captain Cook grappling with a monster, a half-man, half-beast with a pig's head. With an added metafictional flourish, the writer dedicates his work to the natural scientists Sir Joseph Banks and Daniel Solander who travelled with Cook and who were responsible for the wealth of hitherto undis-covered knowledge the expedition brought back, especially about undreamed-of peoples and their distinctive cultures and organisation.

Hildebrand Bowman comes across his tribe of flying women after many other strange encounters in the South Seas, which give him the opportunity to give rein to moral allegories about present-day society. Each world he discovers is dominated by a particular sense: Olfactaria and Audiante by smell and hearing, for example. In the kingdom of Luxo-Volupto, he finds himself surrounded by women who 'in general seemed handsome' but had odd bumps on their heads. Then, one evening as he is strolling through the town, one of these women – 'a tall, masculine figure – clasps me in her arms, mounts into the air, and flies with me about fifty paces; then set me down, and run away [*sic*] laughing like to kill herself; as did all that saw it'.

His companion explains that in Luxo-Volupto girls begin to grow wings when they commit 'a failure of chastity', and that the deeper they sink into a life of vice, the more their sexual appetite grows, the stronger and bigger their wings; conversely, as they reform their ways their wings shrink and can even eventually disappear (not a strong incentive, the reader feels). In the case of his ravisher, she is one of the Alae-putae – or, literally, winged whores.

This imaginary voyage belongs to the period's *littérature galante* in its scallywag pose, and happy trifling with conventional morality, but it also reveals how winged beings who are not conventional angels – or devils – began to take off in English fiction in order to stimulate certain pleasures in the reader and open new vistas.

The entertaining pseudo-memoirs of these imaginary voyagers, Peter Wilkins and Hildebrand Bowman, are followed, later in the century, by one of the most remarkable fantasies of flying to precede the first balloon ascents. Imitation did not arouse as much criticism in the eighteenth century as it does today, and Peter Wilkins's adventures directly shape the brilliant chronicles of more flying lovers by the libertine and pamphleteer Nicolas-Edmé Rétif de la Bretonne in a four-volume imaginary voyage, *La Découverte australe par un homme-voland, ou le Dédale français . . .* (The Discovery of the South Land by a Flying Man, or the French Daedalus, 1781). Even more acutely than Paltock and Bowman, Rétif epitomises the combination of parody and seriousness, mock-learning and genuine curiosity that forms the peculiar, mixed voice of this philosophical fictional genre, a voice which resonates so strongly with the mischievous narrative style of the *Nights*. *La Découverte australe* is a curio of Enlightenment thought, provocation and dissent: on the one hand a serious, didactic work sparked by the ethnographical and zoological findings of Cook and Bougainville on their journeys of discovery to the Pacific and Australasia in the preceding decades, and on the other an example of rationalist pornography, titillating and outrageous. It makes many bold, free-thinking assaults on the traditional hierarchy of living things, as our flying hero Victorin and his beloved Christine discover many different species of humanity on an imaginary scale of evolution, including hominid elephants.

The experiences inspire them to make protracted disquisitions on evolution, social reform of laws and liberty, as well as speculate about animal minds and the positive effects of miscegenation. All these questions are treated with scientific, omnivorous curiosity by the writer and would-be political reformer, in terms that live up to Rétif's scandalous reputation (he published the book anonymously, and it is still catalogued in the British Library with other forbidden books).

The new peoples range from the lower end of beastliness to utopian exemplars; from 'hommes-de-nuit' who stay awake by night and need to keep their eyes closed against the light by day, to rationalist paragons, the colossal Mega-Patagonians who live in tents suspended from trees, wear elaborate topsy-turvy dress (shoes on their heads and hats on their feet), and are attended by courtiers who have to climb on stilts to perform their duties; these Mega-Patagonians follow progressive social arrangements for which Rétif gives chapter and verse.

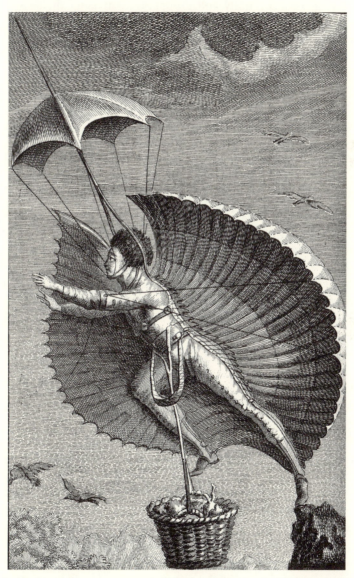

Victorin, the hero of a romance-cum-scientific disquisition by Rétif de la Bretonne, takes off with supplies for the flight to the unexplored south lands (*La Découverte australe*, 1782).

The couple also discover other forms of hybrids: monkey-men, bear-men, dog-men – on whom Victorin and his son Alexandre drop emergency supplies from the baskets they are carrying as they fly. Pigs, bulls, sheep, beavers, oxen, horses, frogs, snakes, lions have all evolved into hominids who use tools and even have guns. They have developed powerful loyalties to family and group, Rétif stressing their strength of feeling, their love, fierceness and sexual desires. There are traces of Ovidian imagination, but the overall effect belongs to a modern phase of natural history and biological theory, Lamarckian and pre-Darwinian. The elephants, for example, are granted anthropomorphic dignity according to the latest, advanced, materialist thinking about the relations of species to one another.

Eventually Victorin's eldest son, adopting a pair of stilts, marries the young Patagonian giantess Ishmichtriss. Miscegenation is upheld, and differences in scale, as in *Gulliver's Travels* and in Voltaire's 'Micromégas', teach readers to rethink the solipsistic view that takes themselves as the standard measure. The stilts point to Rétif's insistence on cultural forms of development rather than biologists' organic model: his heroes make the technology for flight (but not his heroines – Rétif's sexual libert-arianism did not extend to equal flying rights for women and Christine must be borne by her menfolk).

The *Découverte* is bound with a quirky, wittier work, *Lettre d'un singe* (Letter from a Monkey), a remarkable Darwinian vision *avant la lettre* of a 'monkey-baboon, of the main mixed-race species, having a jacket, no trousers, very little hair, white and fluffy'. He is pictured in the frontis-piece writing – with the pen held in his mouth. His metamorphosis from monkey to human, with its uncomfortable ironies and satirical anger against humankind, might echo the Second Dervish's tale from the *Nights*, in which a similar transformation takes place, but the tone eerily foreshadows Kafka's tales of Red Peter, 'A Report to an Academy' and the 'Two Fragments'.

In its four loquacious volumes of fantastic pseudo-science, *La Découverte* is also a preposterous, crazy and comic romance. As in Peter Wilkins's history, the sequence of over twenty engravings wonderfully enhances the supposed truth-telling of the writer since the peoples and episodes are carefully worked out in the style of a scientific illustration, with all details rendered and functioning. Rétif commissioned the images himself, and worked closely with the artist, who has been identified as his long-time collaborator, Louis Binet. Victorin's flying suit, as he swoops down like a profane St Michael to gather up the swooning form of his love in his arms, consists of full body armour, tight-laced the length of his elegant and slender limbs, with a harness under his chin that attaches to a small umbrella fixed rigidly to the top of his head; like the gauris with whom Peter Wilkins settled down, the suit unfurls into a vast ribbed canopy, like a crinoline petticoat.

It is striking that the novel was written in 1779 and published in January 1781, two years before the first manned Montgolfier ascents in 1783, and that these were made in balloons with a rigid, not collapsible, frame.

Parachutes followed, rather than preceded mechanical flight, and were invented in the twentieth century as an offshoot of aerial transport; the principle, easily understood from falling leaves, had however inspired many early experiments: some successful leaps from towers attached to awnings, kite-shaped structures, and inverted conical baskets as early as the fifteenth century; and some not so successful. But Binet's inspired rendering of Rétif's description reflects John Wilkins's recommendation that inventors should imitate the webbed wings of bats rather than birds' separate quills; there is indeed something prehensile and reptilian about the scalloped edges of his apparatus.

Rétif was rediscovered by the Surrealists, who appreciated his poly-morphous sexuality. He gave his name to the French word for shoe fetishism, *rétifisme*. His *Découverte australe* illuminates with lively originality the turn that fantasy took in the wake of the *Nights*; it transposes the *Nights'* motif of domestic trappings in flight, of enchanted kitchenware and soft furnishings, to the body of the flyers themselves, who become engines of alternative realities. Under the double influence of heroic Enlightenment individualism and mercantile exchanges of manufactured goods, Victorin and the male members of his family become artefacts, flying machines, 'artificial by nature', as Maurice Ravel acutely remarked about his own living toys. It is striking that these Western dreams of flight extend, in the imagination of both Robert Paltock and the shoe-fetishising Rétif, the techniques of corsetry and umbrella-making to solve the practical problems, while the oriental versions, dreamed up in cultures where men's and women's bodies were not constricted by close-fitting clothes, select instead the skills of carpet-weavers and upholsterers. The ecstatic – and erotic – imaginings of human soaring, before balloons and hang-gliders, draw on material culture and characteristic artefacts: sofas and carpets in the East, corsets and umbrellas and waterproofing in the West.

This form of make-believe was – and is – hugely enjoyable, and its claims led to even more sleight of hand to prove that its subjects were indeed not only possible but actual. The machinery of stage illusion began to fly backdrops, scenery, furniture, props – and actors, and as the possibilities grew for acrobatics with performers and dancers suspended on ropes and wires from the flies (the first use of the word with the specific theatrical meaning is dated to 1805 in the *OED*), so did literary inventions offer impresarios source material. Paltock's fantasy, *The Flying Indians*, was adapted as part of the divertimenti that punctuated the elaborate pantomimes of the Regency and Victorian periods. (A broadsheet from 1828 promises the sight of Flying Indians, alongside *Mother Shipton*, fairy tales, *Arabian Nights* and other fantasy vehicles). When it was adapted for the stage, the production promised machines to summon 'The Land of the Indies and its scenery with the descent of two gauris or flying women . . . romantic rocks, surrounded by cascades and waterfalls, in the midst of tremendous hurricanes and storms . . . the arrival of the island's flying inhabitants . . . and the extraordinary ascension of Peter Wilkins'.

Another, later broadsheet announcing the opening on 19 January 1861 of the Pantomime *Queen Topaze* at Her Majesty's Theatre, Haymarket, London, carried an advertisement on the reverse for the 'splendidly illustrated' 'Flying Women of the Loadstone Island . . . the Most Startling Romance of the Age', and 'Queen Topaze' ('a Gipsy'), a tongue-in-cheek, heterogeneous medley, full of high jinks, broad silliness and music-hall puns, which featured Grand Magic Metamorphoses and a Dénouement Extraordinary in which 'the Arabian Knights' (*sic*) were to be 'manfully active'. By this time, audiences were omnivorous, wanted to be entertained, and were comfortable to receive anything and everything in a spirit of light-hearted mockery. Impresarios and publishers targeted the same punters for pantomime, Oriental extravaganzas, imaginary voyages to far distant utopias – and dystopias. The theatre, the music hall and the circus became a playground for all, young and old, during the rise of public urban entertainments; Oriental extravanganzas provided a chance to perform magic illusions and feats of flying.

In some ways, Khlebnikov's proclamation has proved prophetic: the Self-Flyers of fairy tales have come true. But in another way, Dr Johnson has prevailed: the literature of fancy left the boudoir and the parlour for the nursery, and the scientific fancies of the seventeenth and eighteenth century became unsuitable for adult audiences. Children's authors then took off in the manner of the *Nights*: Peter Pan teaches the Darling children to fly out of the window of their bedroom, off to Neverland in the play and later in the book (Pl. 25). The motif of the flying carpet itself reappears in a wonderfully ordinary and contemporary London setting in E. Nesbit's story, *The Phoenix and the Carpet* (1904). (This magic carpet is bought for 22/9 in Kentish Town, a part of town where Iranian rug-dealers still heap their goods ceiling high in twilit emporia.) Nesbit followed this story two years later with *The Story of the Amulet*, where the magic is more obviously Egyptian and the child protagonists are teleported through time. By contrast, beloved Mary Poppins uses an umbrella. Her inventor (and alter ego), the author P. L. Travers, is another children's writer who, like Nesbit, read deeply in myth and magic (she was a regular contributor to *Parabola*, the Jungian journal). In the United States, Winsor McCay's *Little Nemo in Slumberland* (1910)

"'ARE YOU HURT?'
CRIED CYRIL."

Frontispiece

Bought in London for 22/9d, an oriental carpet changes Edwardian family life, in E. Nesbit's children's classic *The Phoenix and the Carpet* (H.R.Millar, 1904).

puts on his goggles and flying helmet and stretches out to fly off, still
in his bed, under no power except wishing and believing (as in *Peter
Pan*). His outfit acknowledges the first aviators, as his creator's imagination melded mythic fantasies with contemporary inventions. The
instances of flying in children's literature have proliferated furiously
since then: they would make a long list. Since Peter Pan taught the
Darling children how to fly, we all know how to, wings or no wings:
all we need are 'lovely wonderful thoughts' and a sprinkling of fairy
dust (Pl. 25).

   The era of machine dreams had begun, and it was in new spectacles
– in the theatre and the cinema – that the *Arabian Nights* found forms
that spread the genre so widely through the culture of pleasure and
entertainment.

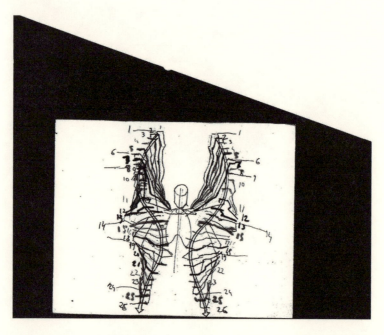

The contemporary artist Luca Buvoli continues to investigate the possibility that,
given exercises and perseverance, humans may be able to take off unaided. (From
Flying: Practical Training for Beginners, artist's book, 2000)

CHAPTER SEVENTEEN

Why Aladdin?

Take an Empire, an Alhambra, a Paris Opera House, take all the Lyric and
Terpsichorean Splendours of Venice and Constantinople; boil them down
and the Result is the Orient.

The Orient at Olympia, London, 1894

ON 26 OCTOBER 1831, IN the exquisite Regency Theatre at Bury St
Edmunds, Suffolk, England, 'under the patronage of Lieut.-Col. and Mrs
Rushbrooke', the *Grand Spectacular Tale of Enchantment, (interspersed with
Music) called Aladdin or, The Wonderful Lamp* was staged as the climax of a
varied bill of entertainments. The evening began with a comedy, called
Ups and Downs, or the Ladder of Life; this was followed by 'the popular
Farce of *My Wife! What Wife!*', and then 'A Comic Song, sung by Mr
Burton', as the curtain-raiser to the main attraction. This *Aladdin* was only
one in a spate of such Oriental entertainments up and down the country.
Harlequinades and pantomimes evolving from the *commedia dell'arte* of
Italian stagecraft, they offered laughter at the expense of perennial themes
(miserliness, foolish love, cuckolds), satire on contemporary, often local
issues, and 'New scenery, dresses, and decorations' – a vital part of any
theatrical success. The dramatis personae invoked the East in all its exotic
aura while simultaneously holding it up for ridicule: the Magician
Olmosnooko; the Princess Palmira, and Aladdin's Mother, Zulima.

For the Bury *Aladdin*, the playbill promised many fabulous changes
of décor: 'the Necromancer's Palace', 'the Cave of Albumanzor', 'where
'Mystic Rites and Incantations' would take place, a 'Magic Grotto, with
Gardens of Beauty and Golden Fruit', the Seraglio and Gates of the
Baths (*de rigueur* in an Oriental tale), and a 'Turkish Garden and Terrace',
where 'the Princess, disgusted at the coxcombry of Selim [the Vizier's
son], resolves never to be his'.

The whole thing culminated in the triumph of the lovers in 'The
Pavilion of the Fairies'.

The story of *Aladdin* on stage outstrips even its near rivals in popularity. *Ali Baba and the Forty Thieves* runs closest, with *Mother Goose* next;

but *Aladdin* and *Ali Baba* provided an opportunity for spectacle on a lavish scale – transformation scenes, trapdoor appearances and disappearances, flying, explosions, vanishings in puffs of smoke. Both stories also brought into play the themes of slavery and poverty, the feckless lad or clever servant who makes good, and the penalties of meanness, cruelty and tyranny. Even when ragamuffin Aladdin and wretched Ali Baba are not the ostensible protagonists of pantomime or farce, other plotlines borrow heavily from their exploits, while in the cinema, from its inception as a fantasy medium, Aladdin blended with Ali Baba emerged as its likeliest lad.

The play version of the story in the *1001 Nights* improvised on the original from the very beginning of its exuberant performance history: dramas and, after dramas, films, mixed and matched elements from several other stories until *Aladdin* became the handle to almost any amalgam of orientalising showmanship. Fundamental strands in the story – the lamp itself, the magician's antics, especially the powder he sprinkles on flames to produce fumigations and the flying palace in which he abducts the Princess – lent themselves perfectly to fulfilling the needs of audiences for fun and spectacle.

The *Aladdin* at Bury was playing to the gallery: part of a strong trend, solid and reliable for high ratings with young and old. Pioneering publishing ventures in children's literature, such as the New Juvenile Library, were producing Aladdin toy books by 1816. A tiny and seductive volume of that date, illustrated with copperplate engravings, it shortens the story considerably from the original, but the episodes it singles out for illustration echo the stage scenes: the 'famous African magician' seen from the back sprinkling something on the flames as he casts his spells. The mirrorings that take place between theatre and books, full-size stage productions to toy theatre cut-outs ('penny plain and tuppence coloured'), from élite architecture (Brighton Pavilion) and fashionable interior décors and clothes (the silk dressing gown, the turban and, later, the moustaches to go with them) to popular masquerades and vaudeville, children's chapbooks and colourful scraps for family albums: all these routes of transmission multiply from the late eighteenth century through the Victorian era. The Oriental mode did not observe boundaries of genre and style, and taste then as now moved with lightning speed from salon to street, and from private idiosyncrasy to public fad. The Orientalising genre was so popular that some stories became such English nursery standards – 'Aladdin', 'Sinbad', 'Ali Baba' – that they seem entirely to consist of hearty jollity and merriment in the John Bull swaggering style. Figures and backdrops and sets lay out an architect's pattern book of gazebos, pavilions, temples, palaces and pleasances, in some cases inter-changeable between the different plays. These playscripts interestingly give names to characters who remain nameless in the original: the 'African magician' who claims to be Aladdin's uncle is always called Abanazar, Albumanzor or variations thereof, and has a sidekick called Kasrac; such names can be found in a playbill of 30 May 1814 for Covent Garden, which announces that Mr Grimaldi will be playing 'Kazrac, his Chinese Slave'. The genies are sprites, and look like Tinker Bell, or, less surpris-ingly, like moustachioed paladins from a romance of chivalry. Some of the miniature theatre plays adapt lesser-known tales, but 'Aladdin' domi-nates the scene then as now.

Pollock's toy theatres ('Penny plain, tuppence coloured') evocatively distilled the characters and the plots of favourite stories; for many Victorian children they defined the landscape of enchantment. (*Aladdin*, 19th c.)

In the sequence of tableaux in the Bury play, armchair travelling mingles with fantasy: travellers' reports from the Ottoman empire intersect with dreams of distant places of a generic kind, and romancing submits to ironic teasing. Different visual techniques have produced a multiple

and shifting site of pleasure *à la turque*: made of gardens and baths, fountains, cascades, caves, the palace and the seraglio. The designs amount to
a kind of shopping catalogue of luxurious taste and amusing and preposterous exoticism; a fantasy zone which was home territory for the
Regency – with a very long life and an inestimable effect on the resonance of all allusions to 'the *Arabian Nights*'.

I

Besides 'Aladdin', other stories in the *1001 Nights*, also identified as 'orphan
tales', and possibly composed by Galland himself, have also won favour
with the public: 'Ali Baba', 'Prince Ahmed', 'The Enchanted Horse' and
the 'Two Envious Sisters'. Indeed, the Royal Shakespeare Company
dramatisation of the *Nights* (2009), although it was careful to avoid
'Aladdin' itself, selected stories from this later cluster in Galland's book.
And this is not adventitious: the stories are for several crucial reasons
historically closer to the Western fairytale than others in the *Nights*, as
Robert Irwin has suggested.

In his journal for 1709, Galland notes that among the thirteen stories
which Hanna Diab had told him were 'Les Finesses de Morgiane ou
les Quarante voleurs exterminés par l'adresse d'une esclave' (The
Stratagems of Morgiana or the Forty thieves exterminated by the skill
of a slave) and 'Aladdin', announced under the full title 'Histoire
d'Aladin, fils d'un tailleur, et de ce qui lui arriva avec un magicien
africain à l'occasion d'une lampe' (The Story of Aladdin, son of a
tailor, and what happened to him with an African magician because
of a lamp). Both these private advance notices draw attention to the
low birth and trade or menial status of the protagonists, bringing the
plots closer to fairy tales written in France by Galland's contemporaries.
Morgiane's 'adresse' echoes the cleverness of the youngest sister in Marie-
Jeanne L'Héritier's 'L'Adroite princesse' (The Skilful Princess), and her
'finesses' the ruses of the Cinderella figure Finette Cendron, by Marie
Catherine d'Aulnoy; both of these *contes de fées* in the French literary
tradition had appeared in 1697.

Two years passed before Galland wrote out 'Ali Baba' and 'Aladdin';
the interval would not have helped his memory of Hanna Diab's oral
performance. But when he did start working on them, he gave 'Aladdin'
his expansive attention – the story, in the Sermain paperback edition
(2004), is 118 pages long. It is one of the key works in the history of
exchange between literature of the East and West. Galland's act of *hommage*,
imitation and extrapolation drew from the genre of the *Nights* a structure

that emphasised growing Western European interests: talismanic things; binding verbal formulae; and infinite potential for inverting social status in a world of mobile capital and phantasmagoric wealth creation.

The story also refracts the psychological themes with which so many of the stories are concerned, but Galland intensifies the focus: on the hero's unlooked-for, undeserved high destiny, fulfilled love pursued freely across boundaries of status, and the caprices and faults of princes. These are highly familiar themes from 'Puss-in-Boots' and 'Hop o' My Thumb', two of Perrault's heroic fairy tales, which had been published with huge success in 1694, that is fifteen years before Galland began working on the tales Hanna Diab told him. Galland also adopts a tone combining warmth and flippancy, which tends to irony but never sarcasm or conde-scension towards his characters; the storytelling remains light, pleasant and insouciant.

Two terms are key to the story's popularity: multiplicity and mobility. Aladdin is a story of movement, of descents and dips, flights and ascents; and the material adventures and misadventures are mimicked in the volatile speed and cascade of the sentences and the images that appear in them. It is no accident that Italo Calvino, one of the great modern fabulists inspired by the *Nights*, singles out, alongside *Leggerezza* (Lightness), 'Quickness' and 'Multiplicity' as the qualities he most desired to find in literature.

Quickness is not perhaps the first characteristic that comes to mind when reading Galland's 'Aladdin', as the story is long and convoluted and ramifies wilfully and even tediously; the stage versions trim and truncate this garrulity. Robert Irwin also diagnoses, in the original, hypocritical French moral didacticism, as well as anti-Semitism; he is justifiably bored by the lists of jewels and treasures Aladdin covets (and gains) and alert to the Gallandian preoccupation with class and status: 'This is Galland using Scheherazade as a glove-puppet to address culti-vated French opinion.' Reviewing the Disney film, Irwin found that the film livened up the tale and stripped away some of its tedious obsession with money: 'The Disney version of the story,' he concluded, 'is actually less vulgar than Galland's, less obsessed with opulence, less sexist, and not at all anti-Semitic.'

But quickness and multiplicity are there in the dynamics of the written tale, in the unexplained and terrifying malevolence of 'the African magi-cian', in the apparitions of the slave of the ring and the slave of the lamp and the magic formulae associated with them, in the enchanted flights and metamorphoses, the doublings and redoublings of characters and plot.

II

In the story, the wicked uncle gives Aladdin a ring for protection, and when the hero finds himself abandoned in the jewel-strewn cave, he wrings his hands in despair and rubs it by chance, when 'a genie, of an enormous size and frightful look, rose out of the earth, and said to him, What wouldst thou have with me? I am ready to obey thee as thy slave, and the slave of all who possess the ring on thy finger; I and the other slaves of that ring.' This magic ring is then doubled by the wonderful lamp itself, and by its slave who declares the same thing. Towards the end of the story, the African magician's younger brother appears in a sinister episode that has not been rendered in any stage version that I have come across: the brother kills a holy woman, Fatima, assumes her body and then smuggles himself in this disguise into the palace. There he stirs up the princess Badroulbadour's dissatisfaction by telling her that one thing is missing from the totality of perfect luxury inside Aladdin's magic palace. This one thing is the egg of the Rukh bird. Clearly one of the wonders of the world, it must be hers, to be hung from the central dome of her palace. When Aladdin comes home she reproaches him bitterly for failing her in this respect.

He commands the slave of the lamp to produce the egg, but the jinni 'gave so terrible and loud a cry, that the hall shook so much, that Aladdin could scarce stand upright. 'What! Miserable wretch', said the genie, in a voice that would have made the most undaunted man tremble, 'is it not enough that I and my companions have done every thing for thee . . . ?' He reveals that the Rukh's egg is the dwelling place of his ultimate Master, against whom the two malevolent brother magicians are continually conspiring. He warns Aladdin about 'the counterfeit Fatima', but his request has exceeded their pact: 'His design is to kill thee; therefore take care of thyself. After these words, the genie disappeared.'

Galland's jinni, struggling against twinned enchanters, and enslaved to a mysterious and anonymous Master who lives inside the giant egg of a Rukh bird, distances the enchantments beyond the Levant itself into remote regions, geographically, mythologically. He foreshadows the way the British theatre exoticised magic – to make it more plausible and more fascinating, and to keep it at a safe distance as well – to estrange it. In the same way as the once-upon-a-time and the far distant country opened an arena for self-exploration in Enlightenment fictions, the theatre, even at its most apparently frivolous, also confronted darker issues by these exotic means. The obsessive themes of *Arabian Nights* spectacles reveal worries about freedom, both civic and personal, about power and responsibility, about the just grounds of authority and the nature of tyranny. The harem and the slave market pander to voyeurism, but they also, oddly enough, serve as arenas where we can think about sex and subjugation. Sentiment was then a prime conductor of ethics, and *Arabian Nights* stories turn up in the same playbill as *The Slave*, for example, and other titles, such as, in 1816, *Harlequin and the Sylph of the Oak, or The Blind Beggar of Bethnal Green*. The tradition has lasted: political raillery, sometimes quite daring, still livens up Christmas shows, also still accompanied by sentimental, soft romanticism.

Critics have discussed the harem as a paradise of erotic, often prurient fantasies projected on to the dreamed Orient, as in the bathhouse paintings by Ingres, but in some ways, focusing on this aspect of the freedom which Orientalising allows eclipses a general, larger liberty: to enjoy the irrational, the imaginary and the fraudulent.

One of the earliest staged retellings of *Aladdin* was put on at the Theatre Royal, Covent Garden in 1788, by the Irish actor turned playwright John O'Keeffe's who collaborated with the composer, William Shield, on 'the recitatives, airs, choruses' of what was a *féerie* in the courtly continental style, a Fairy Play.

The full script of O' Keeffes *Aladdin* was not included in the handsome four-volume subscription edition of his plays, published in 1798, but a handbook of the interspersed musical numbers has survived, and it shows that he melded 'Aladdin' into a wishful, comic morality fable, rather high flown in places, combining elements of Handel's *Alcina* with the legend of Faust, and introducing a female witch and an obedient sea monster in 'her subterraneous court'. The Aladdin of the book is unrecognisable: he has morphed into a pattern of virtue. The magus looking for the lamp is instructed:

> Seek a youth from av'rice free,
> Who can feel another's grief,
> Who is prompt to give relief,
> Bless'd with filial piety.
> If mortal win the Lamp, such must that mortal be.

Interestingly, the concern of the Galland story with crafts and trades continues here, with an English accent. A potter and a coachmaker are given jolly songs to sing, protesting then as now against imported goods over solid home manufactures:

And why abroad our money fling,
To please our fickle fair?
No more from China, China bring,
Here's English China-ware.

This period of ever-increasing commercial traffic over vast distances coincides with the growth of European colonial ambitions, too. The year this *Aladdin* was produced, 1788, was the year that the abolition of involvement in slavery was first moved in the British parliament, years before Abolition was passed there.

O'Keeffe kept far more faithfully to the *Arabian Nights* with a farce performed in 1789, called *The Little Hunchback, Or A Frolic in Bagdad*, in which he dramatises the knockabout story from the cycle of 'The Hunchback', about the tumbler who performs tricks at a dinner and chokes on a fish bone until he seems to be dead, and is then bundled from one party to another who each believe in turn that they have killed him. The story has a joyous outcome in the book: as one culprit or another is sentenced to death, another comes forward and confesses the crime – until the hunchback coughs and comes back to life again. O'Keeffe's version combines this with a romance about a Christian falling in love with a Muslim, and a tolerant Sultan who overcomes the wicked machinations of his vizier to prevent them marrying; as in so many of these harem comedies ultimately deriving from Marmontel, the Sultan is progressive, mild and clement. The playwright, in a by now familiar move, is making fun of the Orient in order to unsettle assumptions of superiority at home and attack religious bigotry: the theatre becomes a forum for pricking at prejudices, and the orientals are knowingly portrayed as far more complex and humane than their reputations allow.

The obsessive multiplication of slaves in the story of Aladdin, far more central to his wealth than in other tales of the *Nights*, forms part of the exotic fascination of the story, but also acts as a mask to express concerns of contemporaries. The Orient became a reflective surface in which to look at one's own face. The captive genie in the fairy tale or pantomime who announced himself as the slave of the ring or the slave of the lamp would have struck different resonances with the public then. The concept of an utterly subjugated, volitionless but powerful spirit communicates the soulless, dehumanised condition of enslavement decried by the abolitionists.

During the British struggles over the slave trade, the reversals that followed the initial French Revolutionary abolition, and the continuing practice in the United States, the theatre became a forum for exploring the trade's iniquities, and Romantic liberation melodramas in the Imperial Gothic mode evince deep embarrassment that 'we' are like 'them' in this business. Depicting the abuses of other societies – their treatment of women, their tormenting of slaves, their excesses of despotism – even a light-hearted impresario like John Rich was striking blows closer to home. One of the plays most in demand remained *Aladdin, or, The Wonderful Lamp*, which closes with the genies set at liberty, the spell of the wicked 'masters' broken, and Britain celebrated as the enlightened régime that has made this freedom possible.

The plays helped the English to feel aligned with the side of Enlightenment as people who would not use the lamp for evil ends by shutting up prisoners inside it and denying them humanity and liberty. The blame for this wicked perversion of the lamp's true purpose falls on the invisible Master, and his rival, the 'African Magician', both of them distanced, strange, ultimately alien figures who mask the slave traders in action (when children in the audience still boo them with great gusto they are keeping faith with this memory, but very faintly).

However, at the very same time, during the agitation for and against slavery, the pantomime participants might have unconsciously needed this kind of persuasion, since it might not be all that fanciful to think that the wonderful lamp itself bitterly summons up the ideals of civilisation, culture, enlightenment, with the slave trapped within.

The ethical issues raised by the powers of the lamp took a different direction in a little-known monument of Northern Romanticism, a poetic drama (*Aladdin, or the Wonderful Lamp*) by a young Danish playwright, Adam Oehlenschläger, in 1805. A Faustian dilemma about the limits of permitted knowledge dominates the conflict between the sorcerer Noureddin and the young lad, the play's hero. The sorcerer is unable to obtain full control of the wonderful lamp because his motives are base – ambition for self and greed. Aladdin on the other hand possesses the innocent natural wisdom of the Romantic child.

The curtain rises on the sorcerer, Noureddin, wearing a long black robe and a sash woven with magic symbols; he is helplessly scrying a tray of sand in which hieroglyphic marks appear for he cannot penetrate their meaning. They are acoustic 'Chladni' figures, or 'sounds made visible', so-called after the German savant who first reproduced them; using a violin bow to scrape a metal sheet spread with resin, Ernst Chladni made harmonious geometric patterns appear in response to the vibration of different notes. According to the scientist H. C. Orsted, friend and mentor to the young Oehlenschläger, these visual impressions made by sound revealed the invisible forces at work in the universe, including electricity.

His revelations inspired the dramatist to introduce Goethean twists to

Aladdin: the lamp becomes a symbol of untainted quest for knowledge and the magician a superannuated figure of false consciousness ('Science without consciousness is merely the ruin of the soul'). In an important move that combines empiricism with mysticism, rationalism with metaphysics, the Danish Aladdin transformed traditional hermetic ciphers into the organic language of matter itself, accessible to the initiates through study of the book of nature. This conjunction would heal the rift between god, nature, knowledge and human beings, bringing about 'an end of every dissonance'.

Such elevated concerns, epistemological and political, fade from view in the later rambunctious variations of *Aladdin* on stage; slaves continue to populate Oriental fantasies of all kinds, but the theme of their liberation vanishes altogether. Similarly, the lamp's power to illuminate natural mysteries is forgotten in favour of its money-making magic. Walter Crane, official artist to the Labour movement, portrays the 'wicked magician' crying his wares as a kind of pantomime dame crossed with a black minstrel, while Aladdin and his Princess trail entourages of dozens of slaves, black and white, in settings of spectacular luxury.

III

Since O' Keeffe's musical show, 'Aladdin' has inspired thousands of variations, including the Disney film and its many by-products, one of the production company's greatest successes since its founder's death. The tale's exotic locations created opportunities for fantastical stage effects: when the setting is a far distant place like Old Peking, or a vague and generalised Orient, anything goes. The explosion of the genies out of the lamp, the transformation of Aladdin and his mother and their hovel; the genies supporting the Flying Palace en route to Africa where the African Magician carries it after abducting the Princess: these key episodes sparked theatrical innovations. After Loutherbourg, the English theatre continued to produce novel special effects to match the fabulous fantasies of the stories. Flying on wires, explosions, vanishings, vast panoramas and 3-D illusions using scale models matched industrial ingenuity in the factories and mills; indeed they proceeded in symbiosis. New lighting made possible by Argand lamps allowed ever more vivid theatrical effects and, eventually, enabled designers to plunge the auditorium into darkness while the stage blazed with light.

Conjuring was incorporated into drama: 'Achilles changed into a sedan chair', promises one handbill. The fashion for Oriental spectaculars grew: the Great Exhibition in 1851 drew on theatrical scene-setting to create a fairytale atmosphere with exotic, oriental elements.

By the end of the century, spectacles had grown huge, designed to attract vast crowds with displays that involved showmanship of every kind. An impresario called Bolossy Kiralfy, for example, specialised in Oriental dreams and perfected a pioneering form of mass entertainment.

Bolossy Kiralfy was born in Pest in Hungary in 1847, the son of a haberdasher and a seamstress; he and his brother Imre began dancing as children, and were soon star performers: the story goes that when Bolossy was ten years old, they were smuggled into Belgrade, which was then still under Ottoman rule and forbidden to Austrians, to perform at court before the Pasha. The sight of Ottoman splendour on that secret visit inspired him, he wrote later, to stage the Orient for all to see.

The brothers brought in their other siblings – all nine of them – and the family became the Kiralfy troupe; they specialised in local folk dances – Hungarian, Russian – in popular plays. They featured for example in a Hungarian dance interlude during a harlequinade, *Humpty Dumpty* (1871–72), their first appearance in London (the cute child performers were brought in to revive the production's flagging fortunes). As travelling players, the Kiralfy troupe then began to tour entertainments inspired by the Bible, nursery rhymes, legends, Jules Verne's science fiction, fairy tales and the *Arabian Nights*, and they became famous and attracted large adoring audiences with their ingenious effects using limelight and muslin, tinsel and water, trapdoors, wires and revolves.

Enchantment, staged in New York in 1879, told the story of a poor fisherman who falls in love with a princess and is foiled by an evil magician; but with the help of a magic talisman he manages to win her in the end – a recognisable pattern, but not on this occasion called 'Aladdin', and not set in the East. 'So nonsensical was the plot,' according to one review, 'that it made little difference whether it was played backward or forward.'

Bolossy soon developed far larger ambitions; so large, he boasted, that generals praised him for his skills at marshalling thousands, literally thousands, of performers in enormous extravaganzas. In December 1893 he took over the vast space of Olympia to put on a show called *Constantinople, or The Revels of the East*, for which the orchestra was installed on an island in the middle of a lake in front of the stage. The spectacle was an opera, ballet, musical, world fair, theme park, waxworks and fairground ride, and climaxed with a grand aquatic pageant, including a boat trip for the audience around a miniaturised Golden Horn with a complete scale model of Topkapi and other sights of Istanbul. Among these featured 'An Arabian Nights Museum in the Hall of 1001 Columns', a mosque, and the Slave Market, where actresses were paraded on the quayside as 'the spoils of war'.

The harem was naturally a great attraction; rather startlingly, it was designed by a Mrs Murray Cookesley, by report an English society matron who had travelled in the East, and the performers were 'ladies of high birth, all the private friends of Mrs Cookesley'. (Disneyland's mixture of family fun and titillation was perhaps not as pioneering as usually thought, with classic early rides such as the famous Pirates of the Caribbean, showing the pirates auctioning their wives.)

'Mammoth Terpsichorean and Lyric Spectacle': an epic movie-before-the-movies with caravans and elephants, summoned a thrilling vision of Oriental splendour, wealth, and violence. (*The Orient at Olympia*, 1894).

What the programme for *Constantinople* at Olympia reveals is that the fantasies of 'illuminated perfumed fountains . . . dancing negresses . . . camels carrying loads of white and black moorish slaves' were meeting the appetite of the daytime strolling crowds in Kensington and were not confined to Wildean imitators, the decadent readers of the *Yellow Book* or the exclusive clientèle of M. Poiret's coutures or the Grosvenor Gallery.

In the midst of all this bedazzlement, Kiralfy also staged a series of *Arabian Nights* stories, and these show that his team knew the book and had explored farther than the usual repertoire. Aladdin features, and Morgiana pouring boiling oil on the thieves in their jars, but what he called his 'Plastic Groups and Decorations' placed many other far less well-known stories before the public in what must have been *tableaux vivants* ('Invented and Produced by Herman Hart') with sculptures, possibly waxworks. (Madame Tussauds also used to stage scenes from fairy tales and legends, as well as display celebrity effigies.) *Constantinople* at Olympia dramatised seventeen stories from the *Nights*: Shahrazad telling the tales; 'The Fisherman and the Genie'; the kitchen maid and the enchanted fish from 'The Prince of the Black Islands'; all three one-eyed dervishes and 'the prince, turned into an ape' was shown 'playing chess with the king' from 'The Second Tale of the Dervish'; 'The King Yooban and the Sage Dooban' was also staged. Unfortunately, no images of this spectacular survive. It would be very valuable to know how Herman Hart, Kiralfy's scriptwriter, interpreted these tales, and how the audience received them. Several of these imaginative plots and episodes in the *Nights* are rarely staged today and today's theatre producers could well rediscover them. Interestingly, some Victorian coloured scraps, those vignettes which were printed for children to collect and stick in albums, survive which also tell some of these lesser known stories.

Like dioramas and panoramas, the spectacle of the Orient at Olympia introduced movement in spectatorship: the public perambulated and boated past the tableaux, animating the waxworks or living statues through their own actions rather than the motion of the images. The effect was cinematic.

Kiralfy's work in the last decades of the century coincides with the coming of the movies and it presages the first cinematic blockbusters, directed by D. W. Griffith and Cecil B. DeMille, also in the style of 'military manoeuvres'. The scale of their vision was global – imagining deep vistas in time and geography, the more exotic the better. For the Christmas season in 1894–5 Kiralfy followed *Constantinople* at Olympia with *The Orient*, another vastly ambitious spectacle involving even more performers (2,500), including no fewer than 1,300 dancers, as well as 'a primitive tribe of snake worshippers, banditti, and a rogue elephant.' One critic commented, 'Mr Bolossy Kiralfy has let himself go with a prodigality almost reckless in the production of a stage pageant . . .' The final chorus sang the praises of 'Gold that rules the universe and makes the world go round.'

CHAPTER EIGHTEEN

Machine Dreams

Film is the folklore of the twentieth century.
Hein Heckroth, *c.* 1950

I

The film-maker William Kennedy Laurie Dickson was Thomas Edison's
assistant and collaborator in the early years of the Kinetograph. To make
the first experimental films, he built a set in their offices in Brooklyn.
Effectively a camera obscura, this pioneering film lot revolved so that
light penetration could be controlled; it was nicknamed 'the Black Maria',
and in a photograph that survives, it certainly has a grim look, as of a
detention centre. But for Dickson, the studio had different connotations:
it was itself mobile, tuned to the rhythms of cosmic revolutions as it
turned on its axle with the sun rather than bound to the earth. It was
a dream chamber, and uncanny: 'Its color is a grim and forbidding black,'
he wrote,

> enlivened by the dull luster of myriads of metallic points; its materials
> are paper, covered with pitch and profusely studded with tin nails. With
> its great sail-like roof and ebon complexion, it has a weird and semi-
> nautical appearance, like the unwieldy hulk of a medieval pirate-craft
> or *the air-ship of some swart Afrite,* and the uncanny effect is not lessened
> when, at an imperceptible signal, the great building swings slowly around
> upon a graphited center, presenting any given angle to the rays of the
> sun and rendering the apparatus independent of diurnal variations.
> (Emphasis added)

Dickson must have known the *Arabian Nights* through the translation
of Richard Burton: 'ebon complexion' and 'swart Afrite' have the unmistakable tune of his fancy, straining archaisms.

The allusions are not mere ornament. A pirate-craft is a mobile world
out of the pages of adventure and romance; 'the air-ship of some swart
Afrite' vividly over-determines the flights of jinn in the *Nights*: here

comes Solomon borne up by jinn, or some rebel jinni – Shakhr or Dahnash or Maimouna – sailing past in a Montgolfier. Dickson's construction is a vessel out of fantasies for the making of fantasies, where magic feats and vanishing acts will be performed for the camera, and preserved in all their fluttering evanescence. Yet Dickson senses, rightly, that the flying machines in the *Nights* eerily presage the character of cinema. All the various means of flying in the *Arabian Nights* – the giant Rukh, the magic horse automaton, bird metamorphoses, the carpet, and sometimes merely the arms or back or shoulders of a jinni – produce an effect of virtual lightness, the metaphor of pleasure, vitality, irresponsibility and beauty. The immateriality of the new medium itself, its *filminess*, met the conditions necessary to communicate this promise.

In 1894, cinema was still small scale, though its wonderful qualities were drawing crowds – often in halls tellingly called by Oriental names (the Alhambra, the Granada). The innovations of these Victorian spectaculars resonate further in the history of modern media; for several early experimenters with film began on the boards. As Ian Christie has discussed, the development of the cinema needs to be placed in this history of spectacle and drama, rather than seen as some sort of superior evolution of photography. The new moving camera was used to enter the same field of curiosity and performance as the old variety shows, fun fairs, world's fairs, halls of waxworks, and other miscellaneous entertainments of the showmen, and the interdependency has deepened in today's marriage between theme parks and films – the stars and the stories.

When moving pictures began, they did not break with the illusions and concerns of live entertainment at all; on the contrary, the unprecedented illusion of fluid movement achieved by the new medium made it a wonderfully versatile and apt dream machine. From the very first capture of people in moving images during the last decade of the nineteenth century, the movie camera was drawn to record exotic sights and fairy tales, frequently featuring strangers and their magic. The *Arabian Nights* continue to inspire rides and sideshows: flying carpet whirligigs, flights on the giant Rukh.

The cinema historian Philippe-Alain Michaud has proposed a deep affinity between the moving medium of film and the concept of the flying carpet: 'it can also be envisaged, contrary to the modernist credo, as a contrivance for setting surfaces in motion'. This animation of an unfurled, moving surface produces a particular relation to narrative: if you imagine yourself looking at the carpet, immersed in it rather than looking outwards from it, if you abandon the authority of aerial viewpoint

(Solomon's vantage; Shahrazad's omniscience) and place yourself upon it like a passenger or a reader or a spectator, then its planar quality unfolds the story in ways that the cinema has made familiar: 'the properties of expansion, rotation and succession produce effects of floating, disorientation or disequilibrium'. The movies, justly so-called, took to interpreting stories from the *Arabian Nights* with complete ease and sense of affinity; the carpet and other flying apparatus were models for many of the medium's own vehicles.

Dickson and Edison's new Kinetograph, by producing living, breathing bodies in the new light, transparent materials, no longer offered a tangible object that perdured in time like a daguerreotype or a print photograph; the first experimenters were consequently attracted by subjects that were in themselves evanescent. The medium could prise time out of time and create a sequence of vanished moments which would keep moving: this capacity granted it a deep affinity with the beliefs – about spectres, jinn and the spirit world – underpinning magic. In a variety of forms, early cinema gravitated to making its own astonishing new magic visible through different languages of enchantment.

The earliest film in existence was registered at the Library of Congress in 1894. Just over a second long, its forty-five frames capture a man in the act of sneezing. Michaud comments that

> through the expulsion of the breath, the *pneuma, Record of a Sneeze* exhibits, in the mythico-trivial register of the nascent cinema, the deployment of vital energy in an ecstatic convulsion . . . the point this time, was to demonstrate that life had been in fact captured in the images, that vital energy was being unleashed through the body and beyond it.

This historic sneeze was performed by an actor, Frederic P. Ott, liberally dosed with snuff and pepper.

After this achievement, Dickson continued to invite into the Black Maria circus artistes and variety acts, so that the camera could make visible movements that escape the ordinary limits of human vision and contravene everyday expectations of movement; feats and turns which can only be performed by a few who defy time and gravity. He filmed jugglers and contortionists, human dancers who appear to float, performing bears who stand up on their hind legs and dance. One of his subjects, the acrobat Sheik Hadj Tahar, turns a cartwheel and appears, in the surviving printed copy, to be hovering in mid-air.

Tellingly, among the performers who visited the Black Maria to be filmed were members of Buffalo Bill's travelling circus, playing in

Brooklyn in September 1894. The resulting films, one on the Indian
War Council (Buffalo Dance) and the other on the Sioux Ghost Dance,
have miraculously recorded the rituals of the tribes, only four years
after the Battle of Wounded Knee. These images are ineffably eerie,
giving a vision of ghosts. Ghosts three times over: the chieftain in his
eagle feather war bonnet in the foreground of the Sioux Ghost dance
has become a shadow of himself – through the historical disaster that
has destroyed his people and their way of life, through the re-enactment
he performs with his fellows, men and boys, of the ceremonies by
which they called on their gods for protection, and through the repetition of his image in motion then and in the century and more since
the film was made.

Film spectres: Sioux Indians re-enacted their Ghost Dance for the director W. K. L
Dickson on September 24, 1894, in Thomas Edison's mobile studio.

The very material qualities of the film intensify the transience of the
subject matter: literally ingrained with time, fugitive and vague, the
warriors stamp and turn in the confined cabin of the portable film studio.
It is no accident that Dickson's machine chose to fix for some kind of
eternity rituals whose purpose was the summoning of spirits.

And yet: the continued existence of the Indians in these films counters
the transitoriness they ostensibly announce. The medium has not
embodied them, even though they appear there still in their bodies; it
has rather ensouled them, seized their spirit beings. 'The *exoticon*, the
unfamiliar subject,' writes Michaud, 'places the cameraman . . . in a situation of discovery: an experience of remoteness was necessary to . . .
capture the visibility of a being in an image.' The Indians in the movie
are repeating, in a confined space, a dance that was intended to guarantee
their freedom; the sharp irony of their condition as subjects of Dickson's
camera echoes, replays and rejects their historical circumstances. This
interplay between images of freedom and constriction in the process of

the film's making will continually recur as the underlying motive in imagining flight. The cinema performs puns on movement, liberty, escape; it stages subjects trapped and restricted and dramatises their flying free. The Indians of the Plains roamed the great prairies, but when crushed, were penned in reservations. This model of tension between open spaces and constriction interestingly also structures the vision of the East in entertainment, from Mozart's *Die Entführung* (The Abduction) to Oriental movies, the 'Easterns': in films such as *The Sheik* (1921), *The Thief of Bagdad* (1924) and even later, *Lawrence of Arabia* (1962), the harem and the desert offer opposite poles for the development of plots about dreams of rescue and escape to freedom. Imagining flight takes the fantasy of galloping across trackless desert to new heights – literally and realistically with movie technology.

In the same decade as Edison and Dickson were making their films in Brooklyn, Georges Méliès and Alice Guy-Blaché in Paris and Robert Paul in Brighton were adapting legends and fairy tales, music-hall jokes and stunts, pantomime and variety shows, tumbling and juggling (the term 'trick films' retains the link to conjuring). Affinities also run deep between the smaller scale entertainments, puppetry, shadowplay, toy theatres, and the development of cinema.

Méliès had been a conjuror, and had taken over the celebrated magician Robert-Houdin's theatre in homage to the man and his art. The new medium allowed him to extend favourite gags and develop film illusions of vanishing, beheading, slicing in half, accompanied by lots of tumbling and juggling performed by himself and his wife Jeanne Diehl, also a variety artiste; he devised several ways of flying characters in and out of a scene, and together they made scores of ebullient fantasies, ranging from science fiction parodies to fairytale romances. Eclecticism was Méliès's method: in his approach to fairytale and literature he resembles his contemporary Jules Verne's exhilarating, limitless improvisation with materials old and new. He designed an aerobus to fly from Charenton to the North Pole, for which he grafted a griffin's head on to a wagon-lit rolling on little pram wheels. The poster advertising his workshop, 'The World within Reach' (*Le Monde à portée de la main*), visualised his own film-making as a way of flying round the world, which he pictured as the globe wafted by fin-de-siècle nymphs *en déshabillé* such as adorn many public buildings in France. Their job here resembles the work of the jinn as they bear Solomon or Hasan of Basra or another hero of the *Nights*. Several of his films made between 1896 and 1910 are set and costumed in a fabulous Orient: *Bluebeard*, *Alcofribas*, *The Master Magician*, *The Palace of*

a Thousand and One Nights, The Terrible Turkish Executioner (1905) and
If I Were King (Si j'étais le roi).

Méliès was not the only film-maker to feel the attraction of the book's
brand of fantasy. Because the medium enjoyed such an unprecedented
mobility and could conjure fictive spaces and happenings, it found a
natural home in the realms of enchantment, which from the eighteenth
century onwards, as we have seen, were clothed in Oriental dress. The
tendency towards embedding extravagant romances in assiduously created
historical verisimilitude continues, with early directors, like Fritz Lang
in Berlin, proudly announcing in the titles before his trilogy, *Der müde
Tod* (Weary Death, translated as *Destiny*, 1921), that 'authentic Oriental
artefacts and costumes were provided by the Heinrich Umlauf Museum,
Hamburg'. The mise-en-scène of 'The Persian episode' includes sumptuous curtains, carpets and sofas, and a voluptuous liquefaction of silks
and muslins, ribbons and gems sparkling and shimmering like the jinn
themselves in the superbly controlled chiaroscuro of Weimar cinema.

In England the enterprising Robert Paul (1869–1943) began screenings
in 1896 in the Alhambra, Leicester Square, operating new projectors he
had invented, the Theatrograph and the Animatograph. It was Robert
Paul who first staged a flight on a magic carpet on film, the medium in
which this device has enjoyed such a triumph. In 1901, in one of the
most ambitious 'trick films' to date, Paul joyously piles on incident after
incident to put on parade the medium's cleverness at conjuring illusions
– characters disappear in a puff of smoke, morph from one thing to
another, loom colossal and . . . levitate. In the catalogue which this genial
inventor, impresario and entrepreneur produced to advertise his line in
'trick and effect subjects' he gave *The Magic Sword* two pages, describing
it as 'a sumptuously produced extravaganza in three dissolving scenes,
with many novel and beautiful trick effects'. As in Méliès's films, enchantment meets absurdity, romance tangles with buffoonery, but the effect is

The first flying carpet of the movies: the good fairy changes the wicked witch into
a runner, on which the lovers make their escape in the grand finale of *The Magic
Sword* (1901), directed by Robert W. Paul.

whimsical, self-parodying, and wholly good-natured. The plot draws with promiscuous abandon on Gothic, pantomime, fairytale, circus and variety; it involves a pair of lovers and a jealous rival – a witch on a broomstick. Her tame hit man, a colossal ogre, snatches the bride and carries her off to the witch's cave, but as the bridegroom gives in to despair, a good fairy appears in tutu and tights and gives our hero a sword – a magic sword which does duty as a wand; he sets out to brave all dangers in his quest to regain his beloved. Eventually, after more magical appearances and disappearances, he tracks down the evil enchantress who is holding his love a prisoner; but she has turned herself into his beautiful beloved's double, so our hero does not know which is which; however, with a wave of his sword, he manages to turn his beloved back into herself. As he kisses her, he lets the instrument fall from his grasp; the witch seizes it but just in time the good fairy materialises again, and turns her into . . .. a carpet.

The even funnier aspect of this is that the mat in question is a runner, long and thin, which helps it to roll out with alacrity on screen; the lovers step on to it and it then 'floats upwards and out of sight'.

This gallimaufry of tricks and turns creates a cumulative comic effect, as in a nursery rhyme ('The House that Jack Built'; 'Green Grow the Rushes, O!'), but it interestingly draws on a repertory of stunts long performed in pantomime and vaudeville, which then come to a climax with a novelty that embodies the new medium's difference. The carpet is a *deus ex machina* which gives a new spin to predecessors (Alexander's griffin-drawn gondola, or the aerostat balloons on show at the end of the eighteenth century), because cinema does away with mass or weight altogether. In the final scene of *The Magic Sword*, the lovers 'drop down from the clouds' to join friends and fairies and celebrate their reunion.

Paul was more of a prophet of trends in magic than he could have imagined when he replaced a broomstick with a carpet. The light-hearted

ascension he stages at the end of *The Magic Sword* of 1901 brilliantly shows off the difference of film from its stage predecessors: it announces the future, in which the machine would vanish and, with the ultimate sleight of hand, film itself, in motion on the screen, becomes the magic vehicle.

From these experiments in the Victorian era, to the first major features, like *Destiny*, Vyacheslav [Viktor] Turzhansky's *Les Contes des mille et une nuits* (1921), Raoul Walsh's *The Thief of Bagdad*, and Lotte Reiniger's silhouette film *The Adventures of Prince Achmed* two years later, the fabulous East, and particularly the tales of the *1001 Nights*, beckoned film-makers.

In *Destiny* Lang dramatises three passionate romance quests in the style of the *Nights*, and sets them against Oriental dream backdrops – Persia, Venice and China; it looks as if he filmed some scenes in North Africa and/or Turkey, including documentary footage of whirling dervishes. In this respect, Lang precedes Pasolini in using the contemporary Middle East for stories in the tradition of the *Arabian Nights*.

The script, written by Lang with his wife Thea von Harbou, unfolds fables of young love cut short by Death (played with magnificent, sepulchral intensity by Bernhard Goetzke). Although the last, Chinese, story is comic, Lang's film conveys poetic depths of genuine passion on the part of the lovers, and in this respect keeps faith with the spirit of the *Nights*. He also introduces many clever effects – vanishings effected by dissolves, telekinetic scrolls, figures melting through solid walls, Lilliputian miniaturisation and consequent spectacular contrasts of scale and, not least, a scene where the magician and his two assistants lift off on an oriental rug he has conjured up with his 'best Sunday wand' and zoom across the Chinese landscape to the emperor's court.

Douglas Fairbanks was in Berlin in 1921 and saw both the Turzhansky and Lang *Arabian Nights*; he bought the rights to the Lang to study his

The magic carpet fuses with the moving camera: the magician and the lovers lift off to visit the Emperor of China in Fritz Lang's *Destiny* (1922).

techniques. Watching the flying carpet sequence now, it is difficult to appreciate how surprising – and exciting – such illusions would have been in 1921, and how much the producer and Hollywood star, like an envious vizier, would have wanted to have them for himself.

II *The Thief of Bagdad* (1924)

Douglas Fairbanks plays the hero, Ahmad the Thief, with expressionist swagger, balletic poses, and feats of conjuring. Still wrapped in the outlaw glamour of Zorro and of Robin Hood, two of his preceding roles, the hero combines Aladdin's poverty, and his instant passion for the Princess as soon as he glimpses her, with the Forty Thieves' treasure – and their jars – and the romance plot of 'Prince Ahmed and the Fairy Peri Banou'. Fairbanks visibly relishes playing the teeth-flashing, piratical hero, a quintessentially American dreamer, a poor boy who sees off great potentates. The film also takes up with zest the theatrical Aladdin tradition of special effects: the upward mobility of our hero inspires feats of ascension throughout. Soon after the film's opening sequence, the Thief is watching a street illusionist send his young assistant shinning up a rope to the sound of a flute and the swaying dance of a cobra; the magic rope has been 'woven from a witch's hair in the caverns of the djinn'; when the muezzin calls the hour of prayer, the Thief makes off with it while everyone is prostrating themselves. With the help of his stolen rope there is nowhere so high that he cannot reach it: a baker's balcony where some hot patties are steaming, the high and hyperbolically guarded palace walls (vast Nubians with vast scimitars, a gorilla on a leash), and, finally, the Princess's bedroom. In the last scene, when the wicked Mongol emperor seems to have succeeded in his machinations and has captured the Princess, the Thief appears in his magic cloak of invisibility, throws it over the Princess as well, and together they float, a light cone of spiralling light,

down the stairs and out of the palace and on to the magic carpet which is spread out waiting for them. Dropping the cloak, they are revealed rising higher and higher over Baghdad, hair, clothes, streaming in the wind, against a huge moon: an icon of ecstasy, escape, and romantic individualist bravura that keeps on recurring in cinema, making the magic carpet the famous emblem of the *Nights* it has become.

The Thief of Bagdad was directed by Raoul Walsh, but the film's particular flavour – a comic romance with circus acrobatics and music hall routines – was brewed by Fairbanks who, with his wife Mary Pickford, epitomised Hollywood in these early years. At 140 minutes long, *The Thief of Bagdad* was then the most ambitious and expensive feature film ever made; yet, although the critics appreciated its tonic energy, it did not succeed at the box office. Fairbanks also borrowed the stylised aesthetics of Lang's European Expressionism but gave them a Hollywood twirl of upbeat, crowd-pleasing self-parody very different from Lang's dominant mood of Gothic melancholy. *The Thief of Bagdad* takes place against painted sets, in dramatic lighting, with graphic décors, and anti-naturalistic, exaggerated scenery. The designs, by William Cameron Menzies and Mitchell Leisen (costume), were directly inspired by the Ballets Russes and Léon Bakst. They summon an imaginary Orient, an elsewhere of fantasy with no more historical depth in time than the pasteboard sets, which show such insouciance about their own reality and substance. One Ali Baba jar, in which the Thief's comic sidekick, his 'bird of evil', hides, is simply a flat, painted cut-out, which he moves in front of him like an adulterer escaping in a bedroom farce. The interior of the palace is a masterpiece of frivolous excess, and adopts the latest Hollywood art deco style, enhancing its tics and pretensions with touches of intended, ridiculous exaggeration; the costumes of the Princess, her attendants and her guards pay tribute to a whole cocktail of artists – to Edmund Dulac as well as Bakst, and to Paul Poiret's and Elsa Schiaparelli's fashions à *l'orientale* (at the 'Thousand and Second Night' party Poiret held for his collection of 1911, everyone wore the loose, layered, shimmering uncorseted look he championed, with harem trousers, turbans, aigrettes and long festoons of pearls).

Menzies and Leisen also modelled the designs on Aubrey Beardsley's profane and grotesque caricatures, with comic roly-poly eunuchs in top-heavy giant turbans. The scene in the Princess's bedroom outdoes the most languorous staging of *The Sleeping Beauty* in its seductive framing of the object of desire as she lies there, veiled in coruscating silks and gauzes and fanned by young women in diaphanous pyjamas. When she is startled awake by the sight of the Thief in her room, she sways on her feet, trailing her filmy draperies like a woman made of rainbows not of flesh and bone – Julanne Johnston, playing the Princess, appears uncommonly tall beside the compact, muscly Fairbanks and so intensifies the effect of preternatural willowiness.

Throughout, the makers' artifice draws attention to itself with self-pleasuring exhibitionism: there is in one sense no referent outside the set and the masquerade. The film presents itself as a simulacrum, a crafted thing of wit and beauty which does not want to make itself into a transparent window on to the world. It revels in its status as an automated vehicle, as it shows off its clever uses of pretence, deception, seduction, where illusion knows itself to be illusion and makes no apologies. Floors were painted black and polished to create depths of reflections, the cityscape of Baghdad was painted lighter at the bottom to make it appear to float, while the magic carpet, a huge sheet of steel, was swung from a crane high above. The production parades visual trickery (double exposure, glass shots, early versions of bluescreen), and pushes it to greater extremes across a far more ambitious canvas than Méliès or Paul ever attempted. As with earlier technologies of the spectacle, the machines were shaping the dreams.

Besides its aesthetic excess, the film is flagrantly Orientalist: it takes place in a named city, in a known geography and culture, not a fairyland, but it does not bother to discover anything about the history of the settings and stories which it has appropriated; it also feminises and eroticises the Middle East and then makes light of it. Even Fairbanks plays for maximum ironical impact; a parody of buccaneering virility, yet he does not seem altogether masculine: with his prancing and leaps, smooth, bare chest and curious tight harem pants, he conveys ambiguous sexuality. Above all, in its closing section, the movie portrays a dream of conquest: the Thief acclaimed by the adoring grateful multitude as he enters the city at the head of an army bent on rescuing Baghdad from the tyrant emperor.

Viewing the film during the war in Iraq in 2004 gave me very peculiar mixed feelings indeed. The grand entry of the Thief has something uncanny about it, a prophecy of a Western dream, while the whole film, viewed during the conflicts in the Middle East, becomes an unconscious parable of Western expansionism at the level of nations.

However, some of this unease can be dispelled, and the film can also be read differently – contrapuntally. While the plot stresses a rags-to-riches romance in the American mould, it exudes delight in the teeming Eastern culture it projects, and in this sense encapsulates a brief, early phase in the history of the Hollywood 'Eastern', when identification was strongly invited from the Western audience. The sympathetic East in question is Arab, Middle Eastern, and Muslim.

When love of the Princess has inspired the Thief to heroic idealism (smitten, he says, 'the evil in me died'), the mullah sets him the ordeals he must undertake to win her. Like Tamino in *The Magic Flute*, he undergoes trials by earth, air, fire and water, which are conjured in sequences of astounding novelty at the time; if lumbering and occasionally absurd now, they are still powerfully imagined: in the underwater encounter with the Old Man of the Midnight Sea, a colossal spider engulfs the screen in slow motion clouds of ink, and the race back to Baghdad on the winged white horse still realises a thrilling vision of riding on air. His quest has gained him the talismans he needs, which include a cloak of invisibility, the magic carpet, and a casket of magic powder which raises an army of spirit warriors.

The concept of the Arab world in the East emerges beside other Easts, personified in the film by the dastardly Mongol Prince, and his palace spy, played enticingly by Anna May Wong, who made her name with the part. They embody fascinating Oriental evil, and even practise a little necromancy with a crystal ball. The sinister Mongol Prince plots poison, abduction and death, and is played with zestful self-parody by the Japanese actor Sojin, a great Expressionist of the silent era, and another metamorphosis of the stock villain, the African Magician from *Aladdin*. He insinuates his designs on the Princess and her money with splendid silky gestures of his long hands, meaningful twitches of his eyebrows and nasty appetitious widening of his eyes.

In the 1920s, American audiences did not fear the Middle East but the Far East: the Chinese were stigmatised as backward, cruel and barbaric, the 'Yellow Peril', encapsulated in the popular pulp series. Then as now, these generalised prejudices fostered a politics of segregation and punishment, especially regarding coolie labour in California, as Maxine Hong Kingston has explored in her elegiac novel *China Men* (1980). So, among the various orients that the early Easterns explored, the Levant did not fare the worst. These early silent 'Easterns' can be distinguished clearly, the film historian John Eisele writes, from later movies that present Arab characters as exclusively villainous and marginal. He comments, 'The development has been away from identification with Arab characters as heroes, heroines, or love interests toward "disidentification" with them as antagonists, or "unseen" enemies.' By contrast, Indians, the enemy in the early Western, begin to be treated sympathetically. He cites many examples of the tendency to portray Middle Eastern villains, from John Ford's *The Lost Patrol* (1934) to

Raiders of the Lost Ark, Steven Spielberg's farrago of exotic magic of 1981. Eisele persuasively compares this repudiation of the Middle Eastern Other with the opposite, increasingly heroic appearance of Native Americans in Westerns.

Achmed Abdullah, the writer credited with the script alongside Fairbanks, has rarely been included in discussion of the film, although the life of Ahmad 'abd Allah, aka Achmed Abdullah (1881–1945) presents almost as extravagant a story as an *Arabian Night*. Even if only a little bit of what he tells us about himself is true, it still shakes preconceptions about *The Thief of Bagdad*. His entertaining memoirs, *The Cat Had Nine Lives* (1933), describe how he was born a Romanoff, a second cousin of Tsar Nicholas II, while his mother was the daughter of the Emir of Kabul. She tried to poison his father in revenge for his serial infidelities; after this, she returned to Kabul with Achmed, who was brought up by his grandparents or his uncle (sources differ) who changed his name to Nadir Khan al-Idrisi al-Durrani (his mother's family name), and converted him to Islam from his father's Russian Orthodoxy. After an education at Eton and Oxford, Abdullah became a soldier of fortune, then a spy, and subsequently joined various armies to fight throughout the Middle and Near East. These included the British army, which he left with the rank of captain in order to take up a prolific career in the US as a pulp fiction writer.

The territory where the *Arabian Nights* were made was not only well known to him, but a culture whose ways and riches he wanted to communicate and actively to promote: he followed the script for *The Thief of Bagdad* with a serious anthology of poetry from Central Asia, from cultures and peoples overlapping with the makers of the most famous carpets, too.

These works punctuate a career that saw dozens of titles promising much manly derring-do in exotic places, and includes an Oscar nomination for the script of *The Lives of a Bengal Lancer* (1935). Abdullah was after all a committed storyteller, in the imperial swashbuckling mode of G. A. Henty, Anthony Hope and John Buchan. In a period when Rider Haggard is receiving serious attention, Achmed Abdullah is worth critical notice: his 'novelisation' of *The Thief of Bagdad* outstrips even Richard Burton in purpling the Orient. If he had a hand in the shaping of *The Thief of Bagdad*'s storyline, the Orient imagined there owes something to his fantasy and his memories of his origins among a nomadic, carpet-making people. He lends evidence to Amit Chaudhuri's remark, 'The Orient, in modernity, is not, only a European invention but also an Oriental one'.

Douglas Fairbanks learned from Lang's virtuoso inventions, and created an iconic scene of the Hollywood dream in the closing sequence of *The Thief of Bagdad* (1924).

The Thief of Bagdad brought the flying carpet into being more than the stories in the *Nights* or the earlier, short films in which it featured. The final scene of the movie – the scene which has passed into cinematic vernacular – shows our hero renouncing power, majesty and celebrity. Instead, with his love the Princess, he sails up and away from Baghdad on the flying carpet to an unknown destination; he begins, standing arms outstretched to accept the future, while she is seated in front of him. They are no longer wound in each other's arms, but setting out together, and even as the flying carpet swells with erotic energy, it gives off vibrations about individual excitements in store; the image of the solitary daydreamer, the woman or man reading alone, vibrates through the intrepid questor aloft speeding towards terra incognita. This defining Hollywood film grants its Aladdin-style hero far greater nobility through his flight with the Princess away from worldly wealth. The carpet here asserts private life against public status; it enciphers the realisation of individual desires. It does so through the mobile world of a carpet that serves as shelter, habitation and bedroom for nomadic peoples, whose way of life was to acquire a different, crucial valency in the twentieth and twenty-first centuries when state persecution and civil conflicts, as well as natural disasters, would set more of the global population on the move than at any time in history.

This silent-era film also established certain tropes and even the panto-mimic, mocking style which would shape the continued fashion for gorgeous 'Easterns'– including a number of remakes of *The Thief of Bagdad,* like the lavish 1940 fantasy epic produced by Alexander Korda and directed by Korda with Cameron Menzies, Michael Powell and others; it is mindful of its predecessor, but determined to improve on it – in newfangledness of effects and in more complex plotting. It won Oscars for special effects, art design, and cinematography, and the whole joyful ride of the film has not palled. The mischievous and idolised Indian child actor Sabu stars as the hero, here called Abu; he rides on the carpet as if it were a surfboard, and is changed into a dog by the evil magician who has a version of the name of Harun al-Rashid's vizier, Jiafar, played mercilessly by Conrad Veidt. The jinni released from the bottle is a colossus, so huge that, in a memorable sequence, Sabu perches on the tip of his ear, small as a stud. The black actor, Rex Ingram, plays the part with unusual grandeur and solemnity.

In spite of disappointing responses when they first appeared, both the 1924 and the 1940 film have become standard models for a cinema of gorgeous Orientalism and pyrotechnics, projecting the idea of magic itself into a desired and dreaded East.

'Easterns' continued to be the medium of choice for the boldest inventions: Ray Harryhausen, legendary creator of the animatronic *King Kong*, returned again and again to the *Nights*, devising effects in *The 7th Voyage of Sinbad* (1958), *The Golden Voyage of Sinbad* (1974) and *Sinbad and the Eye of the Tiger* (1977). He planned to combine genres with a film of 'Sinbad Goes to Mars'.

When Achmed Abdullah describes the end of Douglas Fairbanks's trials by ordeal, he gives the magic horse a speech about enchantment, Eastern-style:

> 'When the impossible happens, it exists. A stone swims in the water, when eyes behold the fact of it. A monkey sings a Kashmiri love-song, when ears hear the fact of it. Only idiots, old spinsters, cats and learned profes-sors contradict the testimony of their own five senses . . .
>
> 'I am, as you know, the Horse of Winged Imagination.'

The stories in the *Nights* do not force the allegorical point in this way, when they feature horses that carry heroes and heroines to the stars. But film-makers like Lotte Reiniger recognised the magic automata as their alter egos; she opened her film, *The Adventures of Prince Achmed*, with the Ebony Horse, as conjured up by a sinister foreign enchanter.

Michael Powell (and others) powerfully re-imagined the story, casting the child star Sabu as the trickster hero and Rex Ingram as the magnificent genie (*The Thief of Bagdad*, 1940).

Story 13

The Ebony Horse

A KING HAS THREE DAUGHTERS who are as lovely as the moon at the full in the sky or as a spring garden in flower, and three learned men present themselves as suitors, bearing gifts: one has a brass trumpet which sounds whenever an enemy is approaching; the second offers a gold peacock which tells the time by beating its wings on the hour; the third presents a horse made of ivory and ebony which he promises will carry its rider wherever he wants.

The king tests the first two gifts. They work as promised, and the sages ask for the hand of his first two daughters; he grants their wishes, and nothing further is heard of them in this story. The third wise man asks to be treated as handsomely, but the horse has to be tried out first; so the king's son decides to mount it, and once in the saddle, spurs it on. It does not stir. This is not a living imaginary animal of myth like Pegasus: it is a machine, a wonderful contrivance. Its maker then shows the prince a key and tells him to rub it to make the ebony horse take off.

Straight away, the horse rears up and begins to carry its rider, not across the ground but mounting high, high into the sky, onwards and upwards until the prince fears that he's fallen into a plot to kill him. But then he finds another mechanism on the right shoulder of the horse, which looks like the head of a cock; when he rubs it, his magic steed continues to ascend. At last, he turns another knob on the left, and begins gently to descend to earth. In this way the prince learns to ride the ebony horse and decides to see the world . . .

Beneath him, a great city lies spread out and he decides to land there on the terrace of a splendid castle. He looks for something to eat, since he has grown hungry during his long flight. He's surprised not to find a single shadow of a human presence in the whole castle, until he sees a light and comes upon a princess and her attendants. She is visiting the castle – it is one of her retreats where she comes to spend a day or two when her heart is heavy. Peremptorily, he disarms the eunuch guard of his sabre and fells him to the floor; the princess has no other protection. Nor does she speak; at least, not yet. When the eunuch protests at the prince's rude entry, asking him if he is a jinni that he could penetrate this fortress, the prince demands to marry the princess, instantly.

The king her father comes hurriedly to the scene, and the princess speaks for the first time, to tell her suitor who her father is. The intruder is not daunted: boastful, impetuous, ardent, the prince declares his high birth and his descent from the fabled Persian Emperor Chosroes; he insists on a wedding; if not, he cries that he will fight the king in single combat or, failing that, his entire army, all forty thousand of his troops.

He sends for his magic horse to be brought from the battlements at the top of the castle where he left it, and a group of the king's servants, finding the astonishing contrivance of ivory and ebony, carry it down and stand it in front of the prince. He swears he will hurl himself at the king's troops, scatter them to the four quarters, and tear them to pieces. Settling himself in the saddle, he rubs the keys again until the animal begins to buck and rear and paw the ground. This time the storyteller gives more details about its working, for he describes how the magic horse fills with air and, as soon as it is fully inflated, takes off again into the skies.

The viziers and courtiers – and the soldiers – are glad to be rid of their challenger, whom they denounce as an exceptional, crooked magician. But the Princess of Sana'a – the prince has discovered the name of the city and the distant country – pines for him after he has gone and will not eat or drink or speak, whatever sweet words her father lavishes on her to comfort her.

When the prince returns home, to the joy and surprise and relief of his parents, he asks to see the learned man who brought the horse, and frees him from the prison where he's been held since the prince flew away; but the king does not give him his third daughter for a wife, and the sage's sense of grievance grows deeper.

The prince can't stop thinking of the princess, and he flies back to her on his horse: she tells him she would have died if he had delayed any longer. Then she agrees to follow him back to his country. So he places her on the horse, pressed tightly against him, and takes off into the air again while her mother and father below run to the terrace to watch in horror, making loud lamentation. En route, they stop over to picnic by a stream, but then complete the rest of the journey in a single flight. On landing, the prince wants to prepare the way for the princess, so he leaves her in a garden pavilion while he makes everything ready for her entrée and the festivities of their marriage.

There the magician – the sage, the learned man who bears a grudge – tracks her down and, pretending to be an emissary of the prince, cajoles the princess into setting out with him on the magic horse. Again it inflates; it rises, and her abductor reveals himself to her, tells her how passionately he regretted losing his wonderful artefact, and reneges on his promises. Soon they see the territory of Byzantium beneath them, where the king's men immediately seize him on landing and take the sage before their master.

Though he is beaten to within an inch of his life, he does not give up the secret of his magic horse and its wonderful workings.

Back home, the prince sets out to find his stolen beloved, and eventually he too reaches the land of the Christians, and he too is captured and thrown into prison, where the jailers, gossiping, soon reveal that the maker of the magic horse lies nearby, but that he cannot be nearly such a learned and brilliant man as he claims for he cannot cure the beautiful stranger with whom he was travelling, who has gone mad. The king has fallen in love with her, and is looking high and low for someone who can heal her.

The prince sees his chance; he recognises that his lost love is feigning folly (she has her wits very much about her in spite of her maidenliness). When he is summoned before the king, he claims he is a doctor specialising in madness: 'it is my trade,' he says. He's taken to see the princess, who is rolling on the ground thrashing her limbs and struggling against the bonds used to control her. When she sees the prince in his disguise she utters a terrible cry and faints, but the prince whispers his plans into her ear: he will say that she is possessed by a devil and that he can exorcise it if she's untied. He sets the king other conditions: they are all to gather in the field where she was first found with the ebony horse, and there he will perfom the necessary fumigations and incantations to reduce the demon to powerlessness and prevent him ever returning. The king agrees; the prince in disguise promises not only to heal the poor crazy girl but to deliver her to him when he has done so.

But the king is a king of dupes, and the lovers fly off once more on the ebony horse; after all the conventions for a legitimate, honourable and sacred union have been observed, and letters have travelled from Sana'a with formal permission, they give themselves to each other in bliss – until there came the One who brings an end to every joy, who parts those who have been reunited, lays castles in ruins and nourishes tombs.

CHAPTER NINETEEN

The Shadows of Lotte Reiniger

Even now I find the female puppets infinitely more real . . .
        Junichiro Tanizaki, *In Praise of Shadows*, 1933

I

The magic automaton from the romance of 'The Ebony Horse' gave
Lotte Reiniger her point of departure for *Die Abenteuer des Prinzen Achmed*
(The Adventures of Prince Achmed), which she made in Berlin in
1923–25; this 'shadow film', as she called it, is the first full-length animated
feature to survive. The story, an early peripatetic romance interrupted by
many unforeseen mishaps (reroutings, hijackings, kidnappings), is also
known as 'The Tale of the Magic Horse'. It is one of the most popular
in the *Arabian Nights*. It travelled on the sea of stories before the *1001
Nights* were printed: a mechanical horse – made of brass – appears in
Chaucer's 'Squire's Tale' among the marvels of newfangledness presented
to Cambuskan, the King of Tartary:

> Therwith so horsly, and so quyk of ye,
> As it a gentil Poilleys courser were.
> For certes, fro his tayl unto his ere,
> Nature ne art ne koude him nat amende
> In no degree, as al the people wende
>
> But everemoore hir mooste wonder was
> How that it koude gon, and was of bras.

The version in the *Arabian Nights* was told to Antoine Galland by Hanna
Diab, but unlike 'Aladdin', it also appears in one of the Arabic manuscripts,
and has therefore been retained in recent scholarly translations.

Lotte Reiniger was born in Berlin in 1899 and died in London in

1981. For a long time, she was forgotten and her films lost. But since a copy of *Prince Achmed* was rediscovered and restored by the British Film Institute in 1988–89 her masterpiece has become established as a classic of silent cinema. Though it has an epic feel, Reiniger worked almost single-handed, cutting out her shadow puppets with a tiny pair of straight nail scissors in her right hand, turning the paper in her left, moving with astonishing speed and accuracy and confidence (a 1970 documentary shows her at work in old age with undiminished dexterity). She was adapting a Victorian pastime, the toy theatre, with its long and deep connection to flights of the imagination. In 1894, Robert Louis Stevenson evoked, in an impassioned piece of nostalgia, the intoxicating other worlds that opened up through the miniature theatres of his childhood (published first by Skelt, then by Pollock): 'Every sheet we fingered was another lightning glance into obscure delicious story; it was like wallowing in the raw stuff of story-books. I know nothing to compare with it save now and then in dreams, when I am privileged to read in certain unwrit stories of adventure, from which I awake to find the world all vanity.'

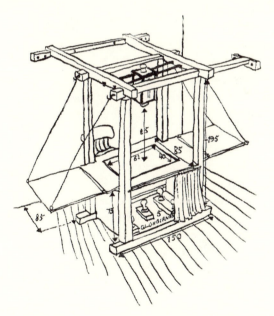

Lotte Reiniger invented her own dream machine: her 'Trick Table', equipped with rostrum camera, became an entire animation studio.

With her husband and producer Carl Koch, Reiniger devised a contraption, which she called her *Tricktisch* (trick table), a cross between a miniature proscenium, a sewing machine and an editing console, with a glass surface lit from below with two light bulbs; she covered this with layers of transparent tissue papers, sometimes coloured, to create the backgrounds to her shadow puppets. She then put the shadow puppets in place, articulating them 'with tiny wire hinges so that hands, feet, head and even each finger joint [were] capable of different motions'; she turned the score on rollers as she manipulated her puppets in order to synchronise the shots of their movements with the music.

Rather like H.G. Wells's visionary time machine, her trick table could transport her into another dimension of space and time; it was a device which made it possible for her to translate her imagination into another form of technology: film. As early as 1921, when Reiniger made a short (lost) cartoon, *Der fliegende Koffer* (The Flying Trunk), based on the Hans Christian Andersen tale, she intuited the way film could animate things, and specifically flying things – how it perfectly embodied and enacted flights of fancy. In this respect, the magic horse that carries off Prince Achmed to the stars presents the viewer with an objective correlative of the projector, from which the real film unspools, beaming visions on to the screen; the peg between the ears of the magic steed, and the brake on the tail that Achmed at last discovers, even echo the mechanism that controls the passage of the movie through the projector. The hero's delirious passage in the cosmos, against the translucent cobalt sky luminous with milky stars, also carries off the viewer on a dream journey.

The *Tricktisch* was Reiniger's own flying machine, studio, camera obscura and film set all in one. She was extending women's skills and children's games from the home. And her aesthetic was inspired by work (sewing, embroidery) and by play: finger shadow games, puppetry, doily-lace-making, Christmas frills and streamers. She was extending games of make-believe, when children dramatise their private interior world by activating lifeless and sometimes even invisible or nonexistent things, filling their immediate circumstances with a made-up story, play-acting the roles and turning the activity of 'let's pretend' into presence and action. 'The very young child,' wrote Jean-Paul Sartre, 'acts upon the world from his bed by orders and entreaties. The objects obey these orders of consciousness: they appear.' For a long time, Reiniger tried to buy the rights to Ravel's opera of enchanted childhood, *L'Enfant et les sortilèges* (The Child and the Spells), in which a naughty boy creates havoc in his nursery with his toys and finds that they all come to life and take revenge on him. She was drawn to the piece; she herself had 'an intensely felt connection to her puppets', the documentary film maker John Isaacs remembers: 'she always talked of them as though they were real people . . .'

Combining the imagination of make-believe with manual ingenuity, the director/animator was able to take flight on her own marvellous mechanical toy, which, like the magic horse of her hero Prince Achmed, transported her to fantastic regions. The animation process she developed illuminates the connections of that cinematic dreaming with the imagination of the *Arabian Nights*.

Her scissor-work initially attracted the attention of the impresario Max Reinhardt when she was a young, aspiring actress; she was making something to while away the wait on the set. It was perhaps through Reinhardt that she also met at this time the great actor and producer Paul Wegener, who then invited her to make silhouette sequences for the titles and subtitles of two early silent fairytale films, *Rübezahls Hochzeit* (The Wedding of Rubezahl, 1916) and *Der Rattenfänger von Hameln* (The Ratcatcher of Hamelin, 1918). With Wegener's help Reiniger became part of a group of experimental animation film makers in the new Berliner Institut für Kulturforschung. Other members included Barthold Bartosch and Walter Ruttmann, who helped with the hand-coloured abstract patterned effects in the background of *Prinzen Achmed,* in the sequence, for example, when luminous genies stream from the lamp to confront the demons of Waq-Waq. The flashing pulse of these forces of good radiate rapidly outwards to confound the forces of darkness, as if from a broadcasting tower or a lighthouse, and seem to beam out a message of hope, even of the potential of film to illuminate the darkness.

Prince Achmed was screened in Berlin in 1926. An *Arabian Nights* fantasia made entirely in cut-out silhouettes against illuminated backdrops, its overall mood is dreamy with touches of melancholy, and it includes some extended sinister passages, attuned to the dark, disturbing, phantasmagoric strain in shadow projection. Reiniger delights in the side of the *Nights* that summons monsters and devils and recounts devilish shenanigans; her film moves between lyric sweetness and fiendish caricatures of harsh ugliness. The symbolic rhyming and punning between underworlds and darkness, between evil and blackness, recur as leitmotifs. But on the whole the film is delightful in its inventiveness, exploiting the intrinsic kinetic liveliness of both shadow and film. With dazzling dexterity and a genuine sense of what charms, amuses and touches, without fuss or strain, Reiniger creates an enthralling adventure story in oriental dress, with Middle Eastern accents and a great deal of elaborately playful chinoiserie.

The famous frame story is set aside, and instead Reiniger places herself, invisibly, in Shahrazad's role: she is the mistress of the feast, and she snips and stitches her tales together, creating a lively cycle of romances from several other stories besides 'The Ebony Horse'. Abandoning the disconnected, episodic sequence of the original book, she trims and tidies the originals to bind elements from them into a series of adventures which close with happy endings.

The familiar villain of oriental fairytale, 'Der afrikanische Zauberer' (the African Magician) appears dramatically at the very beginning, conjuring the ebony horse during the credit sequence, shaping the automaton from a dark nothing, a sinister blob of antimatter swept and kneaded by his crooked fingers crowned with talons. A figure who combines the roles of Aladdin's uncle, Hasan of Basra's abductor and other wicked enchanters, he crystallises an image of pure cinematic evil that will last and last. Walt Disney learned from viewing the Berlin film-makers' work, and brought Walter Ruttman to Hollywood – very briefly – to help on *Fantasia*, for example, and he emulated the Magician's twitching expressiveness of eyes, eyebrows, nose and digits when he animated the wicked queen in *Snow White* (1937), which has often wrongly been praised as the first feature-length cartoon. More recently, in *Harry Potter and the Deathly Hallows* (2010), when Hermione tells the story of the Three Brothers, the animator Ben Hibon paid direct tribute to Reiniger's shadowplay.

The ebony horse is a magic artefact that looks natural. It is one of the many such charmed things in the *Nights*. The enchanter in the story promises that it exceeds its lookalike in nature: 'When it is mounted, it carries its rider through the air with the speed of light, taking him wheresoever he would go and covering in a day the year's journey of a horse of flesh and blood.' He demonstrates the marvel in action on its own, and then offers it to the caliph as a gift for his birthday. He desires it, but the magician asks in return for the Princess Dinarzade, his daughter. She objects from behind the lacy jalousies of her palanquin, in the submissive, melting manner of Reiniger's heroines. Her brother, Prince Achmed, is more forceful; but the African enchanter tempts him with the horse and Achmed mounts it and flies away, uncontrollably, until he finds himself beyond the stars and is whirled away in a thunderstorm. Reiniger uses different viewpoints: first we see the prince from the ground, where his father and the crowds of courtiers and spectators start up in alarm, and we then move in closer to the prince as he sails up against the darkening night sky, evocatively rendered by swirling clouds against transparent coloured papers. Eventually we, the audience, join the prince and see through his eyes again as he spots the islands of Waq-Waq and alights.

With this montage of images from different perspectives, moving freely both far from the scene and close to the action, as the prince climbs to the stars, Reiniger escapes the proscenium arch of the puppet show. The accompanying original soundtrack by Wolfgang Zeller swells and adds scale, changing from the tinkling carnival patter which had accompanied the caliph's festivities to more intense symphonic colour in the strings.

The film later intertwines strands from the adventures of Aladdin, but Reiniger did not confine herself to well-worn stories: she read deeply in the *Nights* to find adventures which would give her scissors gorgeous and intricate transformations, unfamiliar and ever more Eastern settings, flora and fauna. Following the various narrative threads as she picks them out gives a good sense of her storytelling predecessors, not only Antoine Galland but the original collectors and retellers, who picked out motifs and characters, reversals and exploits from the repertoire, and reworked them back into the fabric. Narrative as bricolage, as evident in the making of the *Nights*, also lends itself to film-montage techniques.

After many wanderings, including a lively episode in a harem with a Josephine-Baker-style dance from one of the houris, conveying much eagerness to retain him in their midst, Prince Achmed is united with his beloved, the fairy Peri Banou, and his sister Dinarzade marries Aladdin who has regained the lamp. In this way Reiniger's script brings both lines of her story to a traditional happy ending (a Shakespearean comedy's double wedding). By doubling the romance plot and casting her heroes and heroines as counterparts, Reiniger follows the mirror patternings of the *Nights*. But her storytelling also draws attention to the characters' uncanny presence as mere shadows. Although she staged them with astonishing precision and lifelikeness, their duplication recalls their status as pure illusion, the puppets of her fantasy.

Consistently, no doubt in the interests of entertainment, the film rejects the fatalistic turn many of the stories take in the original book. As early as the 1920s, an artist like Reiniger forestalled audience protests at down-beat endings. For example, an apocalyptic contest between a princess and a jinni, modelled on the epic struggle in 'The Tale of the Second Dervish', inspires a dazzling sequence of animal metamorphoses as Reiniger's witch (a benevolent power on the side of our hero) takes on the monstrous demons of Waq-Waq; during the course of this furious shapeshifters' battle, the adversaries morph from lion to scorpion to serpent, to eagle, to cat, worm, cockerel, and pounce on and ravage each other, flowing apparently seamlessly from one form to another. This sequence, the first of its kind on screen, exploits animation's potential for fluid metamorphosis in movement and has had a significant influence: for example, the witch's duel in Disney's *The Sword in the Stone,* of 1963.

The original story comes from the cycle of 'The Fisherman and the

Genie', where it provides the climax of 'The Second Dervish's Tale', as
he unfolds with hallucinatory intensity the deadly combat of the princess
with the jinni who has changed the hero into an ape, among other
mischiefs. In the book, the forces of good are embodied by a sorceress-
princess who is beautiful and young, not the grotesque old bat of
Reiniger's film, and she struggles against the evil jinni until 'all of a
sudden we heard terrible cries, which made us to quake, and a little
while after, we saw the princess and the jinni all in flames. They threw
flashes of fire out of their mouths at one another, until they came to it
hand in hand; then the fires increased . . .' A spark lands in the narrator's
eye and blinds him. But although the princess has devastated the evil
jinni, she herself has been touched too profoundly, and she dies, reduced
to a pile of ashes (Pl. 7).

Prince Achmed peeps at the fairy Peri Banou as she alights in her bird cloak to
bathe. (*The Adventures of Prince Achmed*, directed by Lotte Reiniger (1926).

    The fairytale romance from the *Nights*, 'Prince Ahmed and the Fairy
Peri Banou', gives Reiniger the name of her hero and the dream love
affair with a bird princess, the fairy Peri Banou, and her film touches
the mythical depths of the source stories, about Janshah and Hasan of
Basra, in the scene where her hero watches the fairies as they alight to
bathe in the pool. The dove-maidens, somewhere between a lyre bird, a

peacock and a bird of paradise, gave every chance to show off her scissor-work in the curling and fluttering detail of their feather cloaks.

The film communicates a heightened sense of magic as a separate sphere, distinct from human activities, one irradiated by natural plenty and beauty but fraught with danger: Prince Achmed sailing ecstatically up past the stars nearly meets his doom, and he definitely trespasses against the moral and natural order when he peeps at the fairies and steals their clothes. The flying beings in the film are supernatural: peris, demons, the monster guardians of the islands of Waq-Waq, and their enemy, the witch of the fire mountain; the enchanter who makes the magic horse practises dark arts. However, gaps open between the stories told in the book and the stories on celluloid. Unlike Janshah in the *Nights*, but like Hasan of Basra and Sayf al-Muluk, Achmed succeeds in prising Peri Banou out of the fairy world, and we are given to expect that they will survive happily ever after. So he is rewarded for his boldness in pursuit, and the human and fairy worlds meet and marry.

II

Cinema becomes a space where fantasies of fairyland are realised with ease and conviction. The enchanted horse in the story comes to life, and its image in film, a secondary artifice representing the first, makes it look real. The illusion depends on the interaction of the silhouettes with the audience's perception: we the viewers supply from our activated imaginations what is *non-finito* or missing, and fill in the illusion with what John Ruskin called 'second sight', projective imagination; we make appear without any effort of concentration or will the absent bodies which would have cast the shadows; we supply the missing dimensions and colour in order to realise – to animate – the dramatis personae and their settings. Shadows here represent a residue of something that never was, just as the animated film, which has no referents outside itself, manages to conjure persuasive realities. The shadows' volatility translates into the characters' anti-gravitational propensities; their own lightness of being as cinematic figments and cut-out silhouettes turns the medium's limits to advantage, mining the analogy of shadows with darkness.

The art of shadowplay, practised since medieval times by street entertainers from Japan to Baghdad, Djakarta to Cairo, entered Europe through the live arts of finger games, puppet theatres, magic lanterns, and related devices and diversions staged by travelling showmen; at the end of the eighteenth century, the newly invented Phantasmagoria also manipulated cast shadows to intensify spectral effects. In China and Japan and in parts of eastern Europe that belonged to the Ottoman empire at one time or bordered its territory, scissor-work on paper predominates, operating in tandem with origami to produce chains of paper dolls and intricate lacy silhouette designs. In Indonesia, shadow puppets are made of leather, painted and coloured and decorated in spite of being used only to project shadows; to this end, they are flat, with intricate perforations, and are animated with sticks moved by the puppeteer to give gesture and expression. Wayang Kulit puppet theatre is highly prized, and the dalang or puppeteers occupy high status in traditional society, acting as priest-like bards in recitations of the *Ramayana* and the *Mahabharata*.

Hans Christian Andersen recognised the origins of the craft in the Orientalising silhouettes and cut-outs he made for child friends and audiences. An adept at scissor-work, he created paper dolls and puppets as he performed his stories. Several of his surviving pieces feature Chinese elements. These paper figures extend the imaginative methods of a master storyteller: by his make-believe with flat outlines, he knowingly prompts his listeners' fantasies to work at supplying the missing elements. He was also adding to the delight because the illusion is patent: a shadow puppet or paper doll makes no pretence at being other than it is, and this intensifies the pleasure of belief, of surrendering to the movement of the story. This is not art that suspends disbelief, not exactly, but an art which tickles wonder at how much can be seen in so little. Andersen, who loved to give character to anything from animals to darning needles, dramatised his stories like a film animator before his time, and Disney also learned from him.

The uncanny vitality of shadows in their different forms – shadows as independent beings, silhouettes as active characters – pulses in a body of fiction emanating from Romantic circles in Germany and Austria, including E.T.A. Hoffmann's story 'A New Year's Eve Adventure' and Adalbert von Chamisso's novel, *Peter Schlemihls wundersame Geschichte*(The Wonderful History of Peter Schlemiel, 1814), which inspired several early films. The first cinematic version, *Der Student von Prag* (The Student of Prague), made in Berlin in 1913, involved original, memorable special effects: these featured Paul Wegener, who frequently appeared twice in the same frame. Seven years later, the Hoffmann tale on the same theme was revisited in *Der verlorene Schatten* (The Lost Shadow, directed by Rochus Gliese, 1920), another silent film that has become a classic; Lotte Reiniger created the eerie title sequence in which the violin casts a shadow on the wall and appears to move by itself, while the musician himself remains invisible.

Hans Christian Andersen made cut-out paper puppets, to accompany his story-telling. Here, a tumbler dances with swans and ballerinas – and his own double.

Shadows played a central role in these early cinematic experiments with optics, which were not only carried out in public: as the ideals of companionate marriage and domestic family life grew in the prosperous circles of the Victorian urban bourgeoisie, so parlour games began to take root, and fathers and uncles – and no doubt sometimes mothers and aunts – began to perform home entertainments: among them magic lanterns and shadowplay, sometimes known as *Ombres chinoises* (Chinese Shadows). Alongside parlour games, children's literature began to flourish, with a long-lasting effect on fairy tales and their reception.

In England, the foremost artist in silhouette and shadowplay was the illustrator Arthur Rackham (1867–1939), who produced a flow of fairy tales from different lands, including several volumes of *Arabian Nights*.

He decorated his pages with borders, vignettes and endpapers made of paper cut-outs, as supplements to the sumptuous full colour paintings of the main text, and created lasting silhouette images of grotesque and terrifying monsters, genies, elves, giants and witches. His illustrations have entered the collective memory of childhood through the sheer numbers of editions that appeared during his lifetime. Rackham's imagery suffuses the Gothic imagination of Tim Burton, for example, who is himself an artist in this vein. Lotte Reiniger quotes directly from Rackham's 'Fairy Books', especially in the short, lively films for children she made after she came to live in England in 1949, commissioned by British and American television.

Lotte Reiniger took pleasure in her chosen medium and the minimalism of its resources. In a short essay on *Shadow Theatres*, she begins by describing the parlour game of making portraits from profiles cast on a screen, and recalls the legend that they were named for the marquis de Silhouette. After he was appointed Comptroller-General under Louis XIV and had instituted an austerity regime, his cheese-paring ensured that his name passed to the cheapest – and least substantial – form of portraiture.

Silhouettes are characterised by details of their edges and their holes, and arabesque ornament lends itself richly to this intrinsic necessity. In *Prince Achmed*, the cities of Baghdad, Sana'a, and other more fanciful settings, proliferate in crescent pinnacles, ogive windows, lacy minarets, finialled domes, harem swings, palanquins and other exotic pointers: this superfluity of Oriental elements marks out a geography of enchantment, a strange and glamorous Other place. Similarly the cast of characters are intricately detailed as to their clothes from top to toe – bobbles, feathers, tassels, pommels, pennants and other elements dance on the edges of their forms. Reiniger observes carefully, borrowing from the collections in Berlin's museums. Just as the translator-editors of the *Arabian Nights*, like Habicht, Lane and Burton, supplemented translations with copious scholarly footnotes and additional volumes of commentary, so Reiniger particularises her fairy realms with Persian and Ottoman artefacts. But this saturated circumstantial and material detailing, engaging with the spectator's imagination to surpass the limits of the silhouette, interplays in the film with dizzy plunges into space and sweeping passages of time, dreamlike in their fluid disregard for realism.

Although the term 'Shadowfilm' is the one she used and it appears in the titles of her work, her films – and the medium itself – do not involve shadows, strictly speaking. A shade, a shadow, or a reflection is not the same as a silhouette. While the latter is made from drawing a cast shadow, it acquires an independent existence as an artefact, and is no longer attached to the person or object it represents. Reiniger's silhouettes are neither ghosts nor shades, but have material presence and a certain solidity, however two-dimensional. When Odysseus puts out his arms to embrace his mother Anticleia, when Orpheus reaches out to grasp the vanishing form of Eurydice, they find they are clutching empty air: no resistance. But this is not the case with shadow puppetry or Lotte Reiniger's shadow films; it would strike viewers as wholly incongruous and unconvincing if the Sultan could pass through Prince Achmed or the wicked magician seize Princess Dinarzade and find his hands empty.

Or would it? The images on a screen resemble light falling on a cathedral floor from a stained-glass window, or a rainbow, or looping light playing on the ceiling of a swimming pool: they are there but not there, like shadows. Yet they are not created by a solid object blocking the light source. At the time of the arrival of cinema, the philosopher G.E. Moore put the question, 'What is this thing thrown on the screen in the cinema?' He did not provide a reply – at least not fully. Picking up on Moore, the analytic philosopher Roy A. Sorensen recently proposed a new, useful coinage, 'filtow', by analogy with 'shadow', to describe a cast image through which light is filtered. A film is a filtow, made by 'a beam of light modulated by the film passing across it'. These qualities of the medium are intensified by Reiniger's techniques: we are caught up into a shadow of a shadow, or rather, a filtow of silhouettes made from people and things which were never there in the first place but only made up, like the ebony horse. For all these reasons, even when they remain unconscious to the audience, Reiniger's classic realised for the screen a foundational equivalent of fantasy storytelling as performed in the *1001 Nights*.

III

After the war, Reiniger's iconography, with its occasionally racialised, cartoonish aspects, betrayed the prejudices of her times: the caricatured Chinese, the African features of her witches and goblins, the apparently exaggerated Semitic profile of the enchanter himself became uncomfortable stereotypes in the post-war period. When Reiniger began reusing footage and figures from *Prince Achmed* for her fairytale shorts, she redrew her characters. The African Magician in *The Magic Horse* (1954), for example, lost his hooked nose and became a more cuddly, comic figure from Western nursery lore, a mad scientist with a bobble nose and big horn-rimmed specs, like the wizard from Disney's episode 'The Sorcerer's

Apprentice' in *Fantasia* (1940). Such revisions reveal how a problem arose from the qualities of *non-finito* in shadow, and from the operations of 'second sight' in the reading of silhouette theatre or film. The images fill with the imagined projections of the spectator, and this means that shadows draw on to themselves the values, opinions and attitudes of the individual and the community. Consequently, the appearance of 'the African Magician', as she had first drawn him, had changed meaning; the sinister spectres haunting earlier films, such as the Expressionist masterpiece *Nosferatu: A Symphony of Horror* (1922), were 'accidental stereotypes' latent in hidden networks but then emerged to define an enemy within and were used to entrench anti-Semitism.

There is no move in that film to identify the vampire as Jewish, but the figure bore enough resemblance, visually and psychologically, to Svengali, the mesmerising evil genius of George du Maurier's novel *Trilby* (1894), for the link to be made by Nazi propagandists. As Daniel Pick has explored in his powerful study *Svengali's Web*, illustrations of the novel, a bestseller since its appearance in 1894, and even more popular through subsequent films, draw attention to the menace of Trilby's mastermind by figuring him as 'Oriental'.

As a result, signs of retreat can be seen in Reiniger's post-war, fairytale shorts. Aladdin from the original *Prince Achmed* looks east African – an origin which would fit well with the map of maritime trade that the stories in the *Nights* cover. However, in the later *Aladdin* Reiniger made in 1954, the same slender elongated limbs, high-domed cranium and tight curly hair continue to appear but mixed in alongside a new puppet, who is younger, shorter, sturdier, with a snub nose, and more loosely wavy hair. Reiniger was stepping back from racial associations, it seems – the prejudice of the Nazis had altered, retrospectively, the terms in which she had expressed herself and circumscribed her range.

In *Prince Achmed*, the exoticism follows the stories' origins and travels, even if the geographies are eclectic and vague, and it is not only the evil characters who are drawn as non-white. But the language of shadows, combined with the oriental settings of the *Nights*, drew the artist filmmaker into a universe of different kinds of dark, not all of them touched with evil. By contrast, as the twentieth century wore on, the viewer began to read shadows according to the darkest developments of the times. The properties of mobility, impermanence and porousness soaked up perceptions as wet paper draws ink – and then another kind of darkness began to cast its shadow on what she had created.

Story 14
Aladdin of the Beautiful Moles

ONE OF THE RICHEST AND most powerful merchants in Baghdad grieves that he has no children, and a passing magician rallies him by giving him a wonderful mixture of stuff to thicken his sperm. The potion is a placebo – its power lies wholly in the believing, and the merchant does believe. A baby is born. He is the most beautiful boy ever seen, like the summer moon in its fullness on the horizon, with jet black hair and on his fair cheeks some beauty spots – *shamat* – which give him his name, Ala al-Din Abu 'l-Shamat, Aladdin of the Beautiful Moles. The overjoyed parents are terrified for him, and hide him away in fear of predators. But when he grows up, he chafes at his captivity and emerges – at a coffee morning of his mother's – and provokes the most excited admiration among her friends. The boy insists he wants to see the world, and his reluctant parents give in. But having set out as a merchant like his father, he's attacked by robbers and left for dead.

Adventures and misadventures pile up. He is married, blissfully and briefly, to the beautiful lute-player Zubayda, but she dies; he is subsequently framed for a serious crime by a professional thief, and hanged. Neither of them will prove to be altogether dead. Eventually, after several more reversals and surprises, Aladdin's destiny comes to a spectacular dénouement, engineered by a gigantic sparkling jewelled talisman. A 'red and shining' stone first appears mysteriously among the stock in Aladdin's shop in the bazaar in Alexandria: its six facets bear secret signs which look like insects. Aladdin of the Beautiful Moles agrees to sell it to a ship's captain for a vast sum, only to find that the purchaser is a dastardly Christian pirate who abducts him, transports him to Genoa, and puts him up for sale in a slave market. There he's bought by an old woman who sets him to work cleaning and guarding a Christian church. In due course of this demeaning – and, to him, defiling – labour, he meets a sorceress, Maryam, a princess and a Christian; but she is in fact a crypto-Christian, a Muslim in disguise. He also discovers that his long-dead beloved wife, the lute-player Zubayda, has survived by another quirk of fate (a jinniya was substituted for her corpse in the tomb), and she has become none other than Maryam's lady-in-waiting. They are joyfully reconciled, but their reunion does not prevent the accomplishment of the oracle which decreed that Maryam should marry Aladdin.

Indeed, it turns out that throughout the whole of his recent troubles – his capture and slavery – Maryam has been conspiring by her magic arts to become his wife, ever since a grimoire foretold that this was her destiny. When she finally manages to find him, she declares her love for him. She then reveals to Aladdin her role in his troubles, and having admitted everything, the oracle is accomplished and they are married.

When the ceremony is over, the princess asks Aladdin if he wants to return to Alexandria. 'As Allah lives, I do!' he answers, and so she takes the carnelian talisman and turns towards the sky one of its faces, where the image of a bed is engraved. She rubs this representation with her thumb, saying, 'In the name of Solomon, O carnelian, I order you to bring me a travelling bed!' As soon as she utters the words, a bed appears before them, made up with a quilt and cushions. All three of them – Aladdin, Maryam and Zubayda – settle themselves on it, and the princess continues her commands, rubbing another face of the gem, on which a bird is depicted: 'Carnelian, O carnelian, I conjure you,' she cries, 'in the name of Solomon, to carry us safely to Alexandria, by the direct way!'

At once the bed rises in the air, and with a smooth and steady motion, sails out of the great window in the dome. After a while, the party makes a stop for refreshments in the desert, which instantly bursts into blossom when the princess rubs another facet of the magic jewel. A river springs at their feet, a banquet is spread out before them, and a magic automaton knight appears to put to flight Maryam's villainous Christian brother. When they reach Alexandria, Aladdin returns to his shop in the bazaar and, like the good businessman he is, sells up for a good price. He also incidentally rediscovers his son, now twenty years old. In unsurpassed joyfulness, they all now re-embark on the flying bed to return to Cairo to find his mother and father. After a blissful reunion and a pause of three months to rest, the entire happy family settle themselves once more on the flying bed, and return in triumph to Baghdad. There the caliph brings out the master thief who framed Aladdin all those years ago, and presents him to Aladdin to do as he wishes. He lops off his head with his sabre.

On their wedding night, Maryam turns out to be a pure pearl of a virgin.

CHAPTER TWENTY

The Couch: A Case History

A symbol is something of a time machine.

Paul Valéry, *Mauvaises pensées*, 1899

I

THE LONG AND TANGLED ROMANCE, 'The Tale of Ala al-Din Abu 'l-Shamat' (Aladdin of the Beautiful Moles), is one of the most extravagant of all the *Nights* in its wayward plotting, far-fetched coincidence, and peculiar, unexplained emotional reversals. Told over nineteen nights, it proves a rigmarole which Shahrazad barely keeps under control; no summary can capture its corkscrew shape. It is, however, 'the true Aladdin', as Philip Kennedy has written, and it plies together multiple strands from different romances and different periods, so that 'a single tale has a complex stratigraphy of distinct kinds of stories that, in their tone, are not quite of a piece with each other'. Elements of the misadventures of Joseph and his Brothers, from the Old Testament and the Koran, several strands from other tales in the *Nights*, including one of the fables that aggrandise Harun al-Rashid, are all twined together, relating Aladdin's extreme ups and downs. Chivalric ideals jostle with low cunning; enchanted romance weaves in and out of comic and even occasionally lewd derring-do on the high seas; a pious and bloodthirsty moral exemplum about conversion pokes out of absurdist wool-gathering. The dénouement races to its end: just two pages cover a flurry of rewards, revenges and reconciliations in a bravura act of narrative *sprezzatura* which calls attention, hilariously, to the plot's contempt for plausibility.

The recognisable historical setting is unusually detailed: in a lawless Mediterranean rife with piracy, slavery and profiteering and convulsed by religious hostility, the tale features unmitigated violence against Christians. This religious intolerance is characteristic of a later layer of narratives in the *Nights*. In several tales, such as 'The Prince of the Black Islands', as we have seen, and in earlier romances, medieval in origin, for example 'The

Tale of Camar al-Zaman and Princess Badoura', the characters observe Islamic precepts of tolerance and hospitality, while interfaith marriage is not interdicted. But in later, urban and maritime adventure stories, like this 'Aladdin', antagonism has hardened under the influence of historical conflicts.

If the original romance was in earnest, translations have heightened its absurdities, and Voltaire borrowed some of its tropes (the resuscitation of Zubayda, for example, echoes in the many returns of Cunégonde from the dead). The whole of the final part of the romance, containing the marriage with Princess Maryam, feels grafted on to the earlier material, extending the earlier branches of the plot into improbable resolutions and trailing attendant inconsistencies – a feature of tales woven together and transmitted orally. As Kennedy comments,

> There is also much magic in this episode quite distinct in register . . . Aladdin and Maryam (and Zubayda too, now as a tag along third in effect) are transported home by sorcery and build palaces instantaneously with a dull stroke of magic. It all ends with a kind of absurd intensity of events. One wonders if the writer is not parodying his sources. Improbable recognition is often a parodic gesture in fiction.

He goes on to note that 'It is a matter of taste whether such effects are successful and enjoyable.' Such a double-tongued storytelling manner however became a signature of Oriental fabulism, as voiced by European writers almost immediately after the first translations. It allows the fabulist to have it both ways – at one level charming the reader with a romance ending that sends off the hero to happiness ever after, and at another claiming a conclusion so arbitrary and unlikely that the audience will laugh aloud. Like the magic potion at the very beginning, which is nothing but a placebo, this tale seems to wish to undermine its own claims to enchantment and set a mood closer to contemporary cartoon epic than traditional romance.

An oriental 'flying bed' makes a spectacular appearance, long before translations of the *Nights*, in the *Decameron*, in the ninth story of the last day. A high-spirited and happy tale, also partly set in Alexandria, it features Saladin as a magnanimous ruler and a loyal friend: Messer Torello has been taken prisoner on a crusade but is noticed by Saladin for his skill in training hawks; the Sultan has not forgotten that Torello once gave him shelter and so he treats him lavishly. When he learns how much Torello misses his wife, he summons a magician to help spirit the Italian knight back to Pavia.

The magician says it can be done, but Torello must be asleep. So Saladin orders for him a fabulous bed 'fashioned in the style of the east, with mattresses covered all over in velvet and cloth of gold, and Saladin had it bedecked with a quilt, embroidered with enormous pearls and the finest of precious stones geometrically arranged . . . and finally he had two pillows placed upon it . . .'

When Messer Torello wakes up the next day, he finds to his joy – and to the general astonishment of all – that he has landed in this sumptuous style in the nave of his parish church, just in time to forestall his wife's wedding to another man.

The hero, Princess Maryam and his first wife Zubayda (long lost but since recovered), fly back home on the magic bed summoned by the carnelian talisman. (William Harvey for Lane, 1850)

This is one of the many examples from the ocean of stories which show how 'the fairy way of writing' set up cross-currents against antagonisms in the political and religious realms. The translator Powys Mathers may have had Boccaccio in mind in 1923, when he translated the magic vehicle in 'The Tale of Ala al-Din Abu 'l-Shamat' as a 'flying bed'. When Mardrus describes the bed leaving Cairo, he writes, '[it] began to sail through the air more quickly than a bird, but with an easy and riding motion. In less time than it takes to piss, it came to earth in Alexandria.' Although his fanciful, *belle infidèle* rendering has been roundly criticised, it is polished and enjoyable and often astute in its choice of expression: 'flying bed' is no exception. However, in the hands of other translators the bed is not a bed as such, but a flying *sofa*, and in the Oriental tales which followed the *Nights*, a sofa becomes the coded site of passion – sometimes licit, sometimes illicit.

II

The *Arabian Nights* is a book of stories told in bed: the various beds in the stories are not only the site of storytelling but also embody the pleasures and freedoms of the stories themselves.

The word 'sofa' from *suffah* in Arabic, a bench, is recorded in English from 1717 onwards; in French, the orientalist Guillaume Postel in 1560 first mentions 'Un lieu fait de tables ou ais qu'ils nomment sopha' (a place made of tables or boards which they call sopha), while the Littré dictionary gives a letter from Voltaire as the first citation. Originally describing the raised section of the floor, round the edges of a room, designed for sitting on or lying on and covered in carpets and cushions, the concept of long and comfortable seating was adopted – with some differences. In Europe and America, the sofa presented a softer alternative to the carved settee or settle. Other words imported from the Near and Middle East were also borrowed to name novel seating arrangements: besides divan (1702 in English), there is the word 'ottoman' itself (introduced 1806 into English). Usage in English and French summons visions of luxuriating on a kind of daybed, and associations with other Eastern comforts, such as garden swings, sometimes draped and upholstered, colour the appearance of the sofa in both fact and fiction. Such places for lounging and loafing turn up with almost comical insistence in scenes of bliss in Orientalist picture-making, images produced by foreign and local artists alike; domestic interiors show rooms that are lined with sofas, covered in carpets and scattered with brocade throws, satin cushions and figured tapestries. Sofas became the epitome of oriental hedonism, of Mameluke and Ottoman culture, luxury and sophistication, the place where daydreaming readers lie, bringing up imaginary voyages in their mind's eye, stimulated by the words and images on the printed or illuminated page.

In a Turkish or Egyptian interior, as recorded by the Swiss-born artist Jean-Étienne Liotard (*A Woman Reading*, *c.*1750 Pl. 18), and, later, pictured by John Frederick Lewis (*A Lady Receiving Visitors*, 1873, Pl. 20), the oriental sofa becomes a nesting place for dreams and pleasure, a daybed, a low-lying couch for reclining and abandoning oneself, alone or with others – to love-making, autoeroticism, smoking, gossiping, daydreaming, to storytelling, reading and studying, and to quietness and reflection. Such sybaritic mores excited Western admiration and the furnishings were much copied, as were the fashions, the traveller Mary Wortley Montagu lavishing praise on the loose dresses of Turkish women – on the merciful absence of constricting foundation garments, stays and corsets.

The bliss figured by the image of a flying bed in 'Aladdin of the Beautiful Moles' suffuses some of the earliest licentious parodies of the *Nights*: sofas become a cipher for forbidden intimacies in works like Crébillon's *Le Sopha*. The seating became such a fashion in London society in the 1780s that when the poet William Cowper (1731–1800) was suffering one of his severe depressions, his friend, Lady Austen, thinking that writing something light would help him to rally, set him 'the sofa' for his theme. Cowper, who was devout as well as depressive (he wrote the famous hymn, 'God Moves in a Mysterious Way'), rose loquaciously to the occasion in a sequence of poems he called *The Task*:

> A Lady, fond of blank verse, demanded a poem of that kind from the author, and gave him the SOFA for a subject. He obeyed; and having much leisure, connected another subject with it; and pursuing the train of thought to which his situation and turn of mind led him, brought forth at length, instead of the trifle which he at first intended, a serious affair – a Volume.

He begins *The Task* as a mock-Virgilian epic, in the spirit of raillery and innuendo associated so strongly with the piece of furniture:

> I sing the Sofa . . .
> Thus first Necessity invented stools,
> Convenience next suggested elbow chairs,
> And Luxury th' accomplished Sofa last.

But the sympathies of the poet tend to the stool: the sofa soon turns out to be synonymous with metropolitan dissipation, dissolute living, idleness – and 'the toe of libertine excess' (i.e. gout) follows as a consequence of all this lolling about. Cowper sternly renounces it in favour of rural rambles in country lanes, and rounds off his poem with a fervent denunciation of London and the vices of the age (the famous line, 'God made the country and man made the town' appears here).

In her lively musings on literature, the critic Elif Batuman diagnoses in
Cowper an example of literary evasion or palinode which she has encountered elsewhere and much dislikes: writers taking flight on a subject and
then clipping their own wings out of a sense of guilt at making literature
enjoyable, or morbidly punishing their best characters in the interests of
improving the moral value of the work. She picks out another passage in
The Task, about the fantastic Palace of Ice built in St Petersburg by the
Empress Anna Ivanovna, which Cowper first invokes with gorgeous lyricism and then sternly denounces. 'Why does Cowper turn the poem
against itself,' she asks, 'cancelling out some of its loveliest lines?' (She finds
the same reflex in Tolstoy's *Anna Karenina* and in Thomas Mann's *The
Magic Mountain*.) It is interesting that Cowper targets a sofa, with its oriental
overtones, for a retraction of this kind, as wishing to have it both ways
generally characterises the eighteenth-century relationship to the figures
and features of arabesque. Quite often inside the Orientalist, the hymnodist
is waiting to make his appearance – and his excuses.

Despite the flippant licentiousmess of Crébillon's concoction, compared
to the mock-solemn loftiness of Cowper, the character of the sofa in both
authors' works picks up its link with sex and secrecy – with pleasure and
carnal knowledge, as in the romance of 'Aladdin of the Beautiful Moles'.

When lovers embark on a flying carpet or bed in the *Arabian Nights*,
a constellation of objects forms, communicating pleasure, luxury, intimacy,
magical powers and enchantments. Together, they assemble a space for
love, and in some ways they reflect the original setting of the storytelling:
the bed where Shahrazad, the Sultan and Dunyazad are secluded. Those
tales are unfolding in the night-time, whereas the flying sofas in a tale
like 'Aladdin of the Beautiful Moles' are strictly daybeds and as furnishings suggest a specific form of consciousness, the state of reverie that
arises when someone is still awake or rather semi-awake, a receptive state
of consciousness – reverie and daydream, rather than dream; subconscious-
ness rather than unconsciousness (even a hypnagogic condition when
mind-pictures are most vivid). These are indeed times open to 'l'invitation
au voyage', to travel towards 'luxe, calme et volupté'.

This relation between couch, confession, erotics, daydreaming and
storytelling reverberates wonderfully in the figure of the most famous
daybed in modern culture and a prime site of modern fantasy, the couch
which Sigmund Freud covered with oriental rugs and cushions. Were
there reasons for his choice? No other analyst imitated him, as far as
records show, then or since: clinical austerity is the note most of his
colleagues and followers prefer to strike. Are they deliberate, these confes-
sional and erotic associations of the oriental sofa? Perhaps something of

these remain, from a sense of mischief and provocation on Freud's part. As Lydia Marinelli wrote in her catalogue to the exhibition *The Couch: Thinking in Repose*, Freud's choice of 'examination bed' 'opens a wide spectrum of experience between dreaming and waking, dissoluteness and moral control'. It serves as a therapeutic instrument, as a site of free association and as a vehicle of poetic production. From a prone position, 'the clear certainties of thought can be diverted from their course into a twilight state of drowsiness and further into the anaesthetised state of sleep or into the depths of illegitimate sexuality'.

There is plenty to analyse in the stories of the *Nights*, but I am more interested in interpreting the symbols Freud chose to set the scene for his wisdom and hermeneutics (it is tempting to bring in his given name in Judaism, Schlomo, Solomon). Nothing was accidental for Freud in the psychopathology of everyday life, so his choice of furniture for the treatment of his patients was designed to help them tell him their stories and their dreams. He covered his couch with 'the Smyrna rug' that he had been given by a cousin, Moritz, for an engagement present, and added other oriental rugs and cushions. Does Freud's consulting room present a careful mise-en-scène for the modern variation on Shahrazad's talking cure, for continuing the 'nocturnal poetics' of the Arabic fantasy tradition? The multiple borders and interlace of an oriental carpet, as we saw earlier, mirror the narrative architecture of the *Nights*. Other aspects of this couch – of the sofa as symbol – deepen the connections between the character and function of the stories and the methods of psychoanalysis: encipherment and decipherment.

III

Sigmund Freud called the couch an ottoman or, at other times, his examination or consulting bed, but it is referred to now as 'the analytical couch' – in German (*Die Couch*) as well as in English. It is the prime symbol of psychoanalysis, and its presence in his final home, 20 Maresfield Gardens, Hampstead, London, currently the Freud Museum, is truly auratic. This sofa has taken on all the qualities of a relic; saturated with historic memories, it stands as a powerful witness, a thing changed and affected by its uses; charmed. The curtains are drawn to preserve Freud's *Wunderkammer*, his collections of books and works of art, prints, pots and statuettes, fabrics and carpets including rugs on the floor and on the furniture, and, most notably, 'the Smyrna rug' on the couch (Pl. 22).

Freud's library-study has become a modern shrine, where the presence of the great man can be felt, conducted through his possessions, his things;

the couch is its centrepiece, and now lies beyond a barrier. In a secular
spirit, the room offers a prophet for veneration, and assembles attendant
genii around his twin cenotaphs: his seat at the desk with a swivel chair
which was made for him by a friend to look like a Cycladic goddess,
with a violin-shaped body, and the armchair positioned behind the head
of the couch. He called his collections 'my old and dirty gods' in a letter
to his friend Fliess. They stand in cabinets and on bookshelves and tables
all around in both the library and the study, and include divinities from
Egypt, Greece and India, many of them oracular, scribal, channellers of
wisdom, solvers of riddles: Thoth, the counterpart of Hermes Trismegistus;
Oedipus and the Sphinx; Athena; several more sphinxes and griffins and
other monsters associated with riddles, their hybrid limbs embodying a
puzzle asking to be decoded. Among them, also tellingly, stand *shabti*
figures or Answerers – the surrogate figurines from ancient Egypt who
work in the afterlife on behalf of another.

The poet H.D. was analysed by Freud in 1933–34, and his collection
of antiquities plays an active and vivid part in her memoir (Freud
commented that she was the first visitor ever to look at his things before
looking at him). H.D. wrote twice about the experience, the first time
from memory in *Writing on the Wall*, the second time in *Advent*, which
was composed from her notes, notes which Freud did not want her to
make, fearing such conscious activities would interfere with the deeper,
spontaneous processes of her mind. H.D.'s own mystico-poetic interests
shape her accounts of the sessions, and she collided with Freud over her
interpretations, but her own hermeneutical processes accompany in fascinating ways his different enterprise of patterning and enciphering. She
sensed the living quality with which Freud had imbued the objects with
which he surrounded himself in his professional role: 'length, breadth,
thickness,' she writes, 'the shape, the scent, the feel of things'.

H.D. remembers the figurines forming a hemisphere facing Freud at
the desk, whereas today the protective phalanx watches over the ashtray
and cigar end, the pen and the pair of spectacles which stand in metonymically for the man himself. The shadowy interior, dimly wrapping so
many deities and seers, figures of curiosity and desire, the monochrome
prints on the walls, the twilit bookshelves, the terracotta and black figure
pots and bronzes in their wooden-framed vitrines, intensify the sense of
something holy about the room, and elicit exchanges in hushed voices
and reverent behaviour from the museum visitors, turning them into
pilgrims. The study was Freud's last consulting room; the accumulation of
his things a darkling mirror of the furnishings of his mind, and by instinct
H.D. reached eastwards to capture their mystery: 'today, lying on the famous

psychoanalytic couch, I have a feeling of evaporating cold menthol, some form of ether, laid on my morbid brow. Wherever my fantasies may take me now, I have a center, security, aim. I am centralized or reoriented here in this mysterious lion's den or Aladdin's cave of treasures.'

The allusion to the prophet Daniel, one of the most prominent interpreters of dreams in the Bible, precedes casually a clichéd allusion to the *Nights*. But H.D. is coasting here, not creating a poem, and responding to the combined divinatory and oriental atmosphere of Freud's inner sanctum.

With the help of Marie Bonaparte, Freud's collections were salvaged and brought to London from Vienna. The Hampstead address may not be the birthplace of psychoanalysis, but Freud's collections carry the aura of those origins. The couch is the selfsame piece of furniture from the beginning of Freud's talking cure, the same 'old-fashioned horsehair sofa that had heard more secrets than the confession box of any popular Roman Catholic father-confessor in his heyday, the homely historical instrument of the original scheme of psychotherapy, of psychoanalysis, the science of the unravelling of the tangled skeins of the unconscious mind and the healing implicit in the process.'

Hard and lumpy by all accounts (although the lumpiness may have developed over time), Freud's couch is a Victorian chaise longue, but with a difference. It does indeed have the classic raised end, ornamented with a sausage cushion which the carpet covering it conceals from view. H.D. was propped up somewhat like Mme Récamier, she recalled. Freud was certainly not aiming at associating his new treatment with the notorious rest cures of his contemporaries in the United States, as was prescribed for neurasthenics, notoriously in the case of Charlotte Perkins Gilman, whose ferocious parable, 'The Yellow Wallpaper' (1892), dramatises a woman going mad under the constraints of such treatment. His couch does not resemble the daybeds on which reclined young ladies of good family who might be given to the vapours, nor is it a lookalike of those divans which several contemporaries, creative and hypochondriacal female intelligences such as Florence Nightingale or Alice James, would take to for life. Were these current associations, well known in *fin-de-siècle* Vienna, repulsed by design by the doctor who pioneered his treatment by studying cases of hysteria?

With regard to a thinker celebrated for singling out the meaningfulness of the slip, the pun, the double entendre, it is funny and crucial that, far from sweeping things under the carpet, Freud lifted his carpet off the ground. The couch, in fact, does not have legs, but sits on an art deco box-like support flush with the floor, and from the start was covered with a carpet and several cushions, and, on top of the Persian rug, another plain blanket, embroidered with the interlaced initials of Freud's monogram. The effect creates a kind of nest and brings this stiff Western piece close in style to an Eastern furnishing – it becomes a divan. But the carpet on Freud's couch looks too much like the floor covering it was originally, too thick and bristly for the purpose he has given it. Victorian interiors, in Vienna and London and New York alike, were notoriously bedizened with bows and frills, and it was customary to drape everything from the parrot in his cage to the piano. It was only in certain aesthetic milieux in western Europe that oriental carpets were draped on sofas, namely, in the richly ornamented and luxurious interiors of Symbolist Paris and the *Yellow Book* circles of London. (The young Oscar Wilde, during the period he was Orientalising the necrophiliac perversities of *Salomé*, similarly cushioned and covered his sofa and salon with Persian carpets.) In *fin-de-siècle* Vienna, the inspired art historian and theorist Alois Riegl (1858–1905) became Curator of Textiles in the Austrian Museum of Art and Industry in 1887 (a position he held until 1898), leading the way in raising appreciation for the applied arts and particularly carpets; the first international exhibition of oriental rugs was held in Vienna in 1891.

Freud had already begun collecting rugs: in 1883, his cousin Moritz Freud gave him the carpet he used to drape over his couch. On the wall above it in Freud's study, beside the analytical couch, another small, browny-grey patterned rug hangs on the wall. Woven in two sections, the half towards the head of the couch is worn and faded compared to the other half: one patient after another must have stroked or rubbed or patted it with their left hand as they lay there and talked. Below it, the rug on the couch glows by contrast, the most opulently coloured and richly patterned object in the room.

Freud sat behind the head of the couch when listening to his patient talk. In London, in the last months before Freud's death, the patient would lie stretched out under the celebrated print of Charcot displaying a female hysteric to his class in the hospital of La Salpêtrière in Paris, during the lectures which made such a deep impression on the young Freud. This print replaced the engraving of the temple at Abu Simbel which hung above the couch in Vienna, offering – rather less provoca- tively – an image of colossal guardian deities. At the foot of the couch, and striding towards the analysand, hung the bas-relief of Gradiva, a key figure of inspiration for Freud. Visitors are not allowed to lie on the couch, but I was given permission to touch it, and the carpet turns out to be unexpectedly soft and silky, with the thick nap running down from the head to the feet of the person lying on it – H.D. found it slippery and slid down it from her propped position.

The rug was a modern piece when Moritz gave it to Freud; he was a trader in oriental antiquities, who travelled widely in the Middle East. A photograph of him in one of the Freud family albums shows him wrapped in a white djellaba, with his head covered; like many orientalist scholars, explorers and artists as well as traders, he took to native dress the better to pursue his profession as he travelled throughout the eastern Mediterranean and beyond. Experts have since identified the rug as a Ghashgha'i piece (not from Smyrna, as Freud thought), woven farther east by that great nomadic tribe who herd sheep and goats in the changing prairies and valleys of Fars province, on the borders of Iran and Turkey. Women and young girls do the weaving in this tribe, by contrast to most of their neighbours (Pl. 21). The Italian art historian Sergio Bettini quotes an Iranian informant who told him an old local proverb: "'Up to the age of eleven girls are good for carpets; after the age of eleven for love.'" He went on,

> There wasn't a young girl in the past who did not know how to make rugs: it was an essential precondition of marriage, more important than beauty. And girls made rugs everywhere, in the pastures, under the tents, in the harems. It was domestic work, not done with commercial intent or for gain. The rug served for weddings, for the birth of a son; there was a rug for funerals, and rugs for praying. Millions of Persians are born, have lived, and died on rugs.

The weaving was sometimes done in workshops, where the pattern of the rug was given out by a man, often an old man, chanting; each colour, each motif called out, strand by strand, knot by knot, to the girls and women at the looms.

In a film called *Gabbeh* (1996) after a traditional style of rug woven by this same people, the Iranian film-maker Mohsen Makhmalbaf opens with a scene of the final stages of the process, as a new piece is being rinsed over and over again by an old woman in the dancing waters of a mountain stream. Her husband is looking on, and as she works, he begins to sing, in a cracked rough voice; the old ballad invokes the spirit of the carpet, and she appears, stepping out of the stream, an ardent young woman with straight thick dark brows, a powerful gaze, a water pot on her shoulder, wrapped in brilliant ultramarine. She names herself 'Gabbeh', like the carpet. The singer also directs his song to his wife, the maker of the carpet, and it may be that the apparition is her younger self. Accompanied by his ballads and love songs, Gabbeh then tells a story from tiny images which appear in the weave – two blurry figures on a pony, for instance, or a line of dancing children.

Emblems and vignettes of this kind punctuate the rug on Freud's couch, too: zigzag white birds with long necks are knotted into the deep blue ground of the central panels, some of them facing the same way, some of them facing outwards, mirror-style, while at either end, in the deep brown-red of the outer field, are four winged creatures with majestically fanned tails, close cousins of the riddling griffins and sphinxes with which Freud surrounded himself.

Every carpet made by the Ghashgha'i tribe tells a story: in the film, the old man unfolds this *gabbeh*'s story of yearning passion, as a young man begins following the tribe as it pastures its sheep and goats. Howling with love from the mountain ridges under the moon, he calls to the young woman Gabbeh night after night, until she at last agrees to run away with him. But then her father, dishonoured according to tribal tradition by her disobedience and unchastity, pursues them both and shoots them. The tragic romance unfolds in the ballad sung by the old man to the beautiful young emanation of the carpet.

The film exemplifies the rich interplay of carpet-weaving and storytelling in the culture where Freud's rug was made. Given the history of the couch and its occupants, this is a highly suggestive convergence. *Gabbeh* was originally commissioned to promote tribal handicrafts, and the romance ballad is spliced with documentary footage recording the annual early summer transhumance of the flocks from the valleys to the pastures above. Against a huge, empty, volatile landscape, with long grasses as silky as hair, rushing streams, and fierce snows, the Ghashgha'i people's costumes, especially the children's and the young women's, blaze with colour: hot pink and acid lime, dazzling lemon and orange, with silken lights playing in the veils and drapery, and sparkling trimmings of silver and gold thread. In this vast scenery of clouds, mountain passes and vivid green river valleys, the close-ups of faces, the hypnotic tribal voices and accounts of their stories and dreams reach an almost hallucinatory intensity. The gorgeous display not only conveys the character and beauty of Ghashgha'i culture; it proclaims defiance against an Iranian oppressive regime, draws on the folk tradition of ballad, tale and fantasy against dogma and censorship, and it ignores pious bullying that all dress should be black or grey. The whole film vibrates with unspoken resistance to the bringers of death and despair, to the forces of intolerance and injustice, and the destroyers of fantasy.

The Smyrna rug on Freud's couch has a story to tell, like *Gabbeh*. Freud shows awareness of these relations between the structures of the unconscious and the patterning and weave of a rug. The Persian rug, the *Arabian Nights* and the psychoanalytic process are all forms of storytelling: examining their interactions can open up the function of narrative itself, oral and textual, as a prime activity of human consciousness.

IV

The magic carpet was already proverbial in Freud's lifetime, as can be seen in the letter he wrote to Martha in 1882:

> If only I knew what you are doing now. Standing in the garden and gazing out into the deserted street? Ah, I am no longer passing by to press your hand, the magic carpet that carried me to you is torn, the winged horses which gracious fairies used to send, even the fairies themselves, no longer arrive, magic hoods are no longer obtainable, the whole world is so prosaic, all it asks is: 'What is it you want, my child? You shall have it in time.' 'Patience' is its only magic word. And in saying so forgets how things get lost when we cannot have them then and there, when we have to pay for them with our own youth.

With this reference to the magic carpet in the English translation, it would seem we have 'struck oil', to use the ugly phrase that H.D. noticed, with something close to dismay, Freud liked. (She preferred older, mythic tropes, such as tapping a well of living water or salvage from the sea depths.) However, the original German of Freud's letter does not invoke a *Zauberteppich* but a *Zaubermantel*, one of those enchanted instruments from northern folklore, which Mephistopheles gives the hero at the beginning of Goethe's *Faust*.

The exclamation comes from one of the best known and most quoted speeches in the dramatic poem, when Faust cries out:

> In me there are two souls, alas, and their
> Division tears my life in two.
> One loves the world, it clutches her, it binds
> Itself to her, clinging with furious lust;
> The other longs to soar beyond the dust
> Into the realm of high ancestral minds.
> Are there no spirits moving in the air,
> Ruling the region between earth and sky?
> Come down then to me from your golden mists on high,
> Give me a magic cloak to carry me
> Away to some far place, some land untold,
> And I'd not part with it for silk or gold
> Or a king's crown, so precious it would be!

The imagery implies a form of transcendence, of otherworldly subli-mation, as well as unfulfilled dreams and desires. But at a deeper level,

this love promises a realm where fantasies can be plumbed and allowed
to flourish, where magic words give access to pleasures and knowledge,
to be possessed now, not deferred. Speaking in the persona of the most
mythopoeic of magi, the enchanter Faust, Freud lists the magic cloak
alongside other legendary paraphernalia, to express his ardour to Martha.
The English translator responded instinctively, when he changed Faust's
magic coat into the flying carpet of the *Nights* in order to bring out
Freud's intention – his desire – to fly to Martha's side. A young man
trying to express his passion to his fiancée, Freud does not want to be
invisible; he wants to be beside her.

The two magic instruments, the flying carpet and the magic cloak,
have become intertwined in storytelling (as shown by Douglas Fairbanks's
use of both in *The Thief of Bagdad*), through their common metaphorical
bond, fabric and fabrication. In *The Interpretation of Dreams* (1900) Freud
returns to Goethe's *Faust* and, quoting Mephistopheles, reflects on the
imagery:

> Numerous trains of thought converged upon it [a dream]. Here we find
> ourselves in a factory of thoughts where, as in the 'weaver's masterpiece'
> > . . . a thousand threads one treadle throws,
> > Where fly the shuttles hither and thither,
> > Unseen the threads are knit together,
> > And an infinite combination grows.

Freud describes how his method requires him to look intently at the
threads and, he continues, at 'the nodal points' where they meet.

The lines connect to H.D.'s 'tangled skeins', and to her own finely
spun metaphor about Freud's voice dipping the grey web of conven-
tionally woven thought 'into a vat of his own brewing' and drawing
out scraps of thoughts in new colours to become flags and pennants
and signs. The imagery is hardly original, but it gave Freud and H.D.
a way of speaking about a deeper layer beneath conscious and
deliberate utterance. In the same decade Freud pressed it further, to
provide a metaphor for the unconscious order of expression. He analyses
his own dream-thoughts, and invited his patients to express theirs
as they lay on the couch; in collaboration with them, he tried to
discern the patterns and connections in the weave, the figure in the
carpet.

In relation to the concept of the psychoanalytic method, it is worth
reconnecting the linguistic uses of this figure of speech to the material
properties of carpets. A carpet-maker conjugates structural motifs 'in

infinite combination', as Freud wrote about his dream analysis, within a basic structure of frame, ground and figure, and then inflects each one differently through variations of colour, dimensions and quality of materials. The presence of the borders within borders, to which Cristina Campo drew attention has been explored in relation to the *Nights'* structure by the literary scholar Ferial Ghazoul. She distinguished three orders of imbrication, which she calls subordination, coordination and superordination, a consciously Freudian arrangement, patterned on the relations of id, ego and superego. The orders contain the sprawling vagaries of the tales – sometimes barely so – as the storyteller tethers the expanding pattern. In some of the stories, this is a struggle. These restraints take the form of internal structural devices – repeats, recursive plotting, mirror pairs, interlace – but are also conveyed by the fundamental outside frame, the space of a single night.

The three central diamond medallions of the rug on Freud's couch are framed inside several borders of different width and elaboration, one set inside the other. I counted ten, but others may distinguish them differently. This structure echoes the unfolding of significance in psychoanalysis, as one circle of meaning encloses another, moving in towards the core. It is as if Freud chose to give his patients a place to lie and dream and speak, which itself reproduces the modes of patterning, knotting, repeating, interlacing and combining that he was there to decrypt as he listened in. He then imposed a time limit on the analysis in order to set a temporary border around the desired play of free-floating thought until the next session, when the narrative would be picked up again.

As H.D. recounts her memories of Freud, or Virginia Woolf captures the flashing epiphanies of consciousness, time is made to curl up end to end so that distance draws near and the past becomes present; depth disappears in a flattening effect that brings up to the surface what once lay buried. The seating arrangement Freud devised, still practised in analysis today, interestingly sets up a scene of eavesdropping, not conversation, which places the analyst in the position of the Sultan in the frame story of the *Nights*. The potential for truth-telling this possesses was already understood, as seen in George Crabbe's poem 'The Confidant' (1812). This takes up the form of an oriental morality tale to create a parable about a loving marriage: the heroine, Anna, has had a child before she married, but has never told her husband. Only one friend – Eliza – knows her dreadful secret, and while watching Anna rise in society, she has fallen on hard times. After Anna becomes Countess of Stafford, Eliza blackmails her mercilessly, tormenting her with the possible revelation of her past, until the poor woman begins to waste away.

The husband, the Earl of Stafford, enters the plot, and he begins to tell another tale, according to the manner of the *Nights*, about the legendary caliph Harun al-Rashid who threatens anyone poaching from his gardens with the most dire punishments. But one day, while walking in his garden, the caliph overhears someone blackmailing a young boy for stealing an apple and threatening to expose him.

The outcome springs a surprise, for the caliph punishes the blackmailer and forgives – and saves – the thief.

Anna's agitation in her supposed friend's company had not remained unnoticed by her husband and, concealing himself, he had overheard their conversation and discovered that Eliza the confidante was blackmailing Anna. Like Shahrazad warning the Sultan about the consequences of injustice and anger, the Earl of Stafford has decided to show his wife and her friend that he knows about her former life and does not hold it against her. In 1812, this rejection of the double standard was indeed extremely tolerant and magnanimous. Like Harun, he denounces her blackmailer and sends her packing.

The tale within a tale ransoms Anna from her fate. But in relation to sofas, secrecy and sexual experience, Crabbe's poem captures the structural importance of eavesdropping in the *Arabian Nights*: Dunyazad, present throughout the night in the bedroom, prompts the stories Shahrazad tells, and they are first told to her, and only to the Sultan when he asks. He overhears them being told by one sister to another, as the younger keeps vigil beside the bed, and his curiosity is all the more aroused.

Crabbe reached for a story form that is inherently suited to the telling of guilty secrets: the literature of the harem. Secondly, he moved a scandal of fallen female sexuality into the territory of the morality tale, and specifically the genre of morality literature called 'The Mirror of Princes', in which potentates, like Harun al-Rashid, receive instruction in how to rule justly. The princely behaviour in this story, in which the Earl of Stafford issues a Solomonic judgement on two women in conflict, involves eavesdropping. Spying, telling tales against others, gossip and whispering behind closed doors, and other forms of clandestine information-gathering were considered endemic in oriental society, and whatever the historical status of the stereotype, this association persisted.

It is piquant in this respect that Freud's prescribed arrangement for the consultation required the analyst to sit out of sight of the analysand on the couch, as if overhearing her private or his private utterances – addressed not to the analyst per se. Above all, the very idea of the ransom tale bears on the uses of storytelling in the talking cure; the patients' narratives were primarily aimed at releasing them from sexual repression, and at helping them psychically to survive through interpretation of elements, symbols, motifs in the stories.

The image of the carpet as a site of enigma returns in Henry James's famous parable of writing, the short story actually called 'The Figure in the Carpet' (1896), which can be placed in relation to the emerging science of psychoanalysis rather fruitfully, and read as a warning against Solomonic hubris. In the context of psychoanalytic history and late Victorian thinking about the unconscious – home territory for the James family – the figure in the carpet interplays teasingly with the premises of Freud's theories: that there is a key to the plot of an individual, that the meaning of the dream can be found encoded in its images, emerging from the nodal points that attach one to another. It also casts doubt on Freud's claims: in the novelist's landscape, James is hinting, the riddle may only uncover yet another riddle.

James's difficult allegory – his dark conceit – has inspired volumes of exegesis, but the story relates how a famous and successful writer claims to have concealed some device in the design of all his work. The narrator longs to discover it, yet it eludes him, a terrible teasing enigma, driving him mad with curiosity and frustration over a painful, protracted period of time. The Olympian view, James warns, does not allow for parallax which might obscure something (as in the French warning, 'Un train peut en cacher un autre'). James's own narrative manner, with its occlusions and obliquities, shows special sensitivity to restricted view, to exploring glimpses from the wings.

Alongside the structural analogies between the narrative of the *Nights* and the experience of psychoanalysis, corresponding metaphors of flying operate at an unconscious level around the function of the couch. Everything the stories in the *Arabian Nights* communicate when jinn magically whisk the heroes and heroines through the air – gravity-free mobility of mind and body, desire's dominion over time and space – are objective and literal happenings that are sought after, metaphorically, in the state of consciousness the couch is designed to produce. The flashing fugitive passage of thought matters: the psychoanalytic hour demanded that the recumbent subject move, and move through time without regard for the drag of the present, like Gradiva stepping forward with such élan. H.D. refers twice to a moment when Freud, sitting behind her head, suddenly thumped the high end of the couch, and the interruption is also shocking for the reader, who has been travelling swiftly and weightlessly with H.D. and her reverie; we too experience the unexpected hardness and material irreducibility of the couch as Freud strikes it, and its physical properties, solidly standing in the room on the floor, seem incongruous. The page, the woman's voice speaking from it, have paid out a surface that seems light and gravity-free, and Freud has broken into this with his enfleshed fist on the hard hair stuffing.

Levitation was above all associated for Freud with sexual delight, occasioned by the literal, physical rising of the penis – and of the clitoris. Dreams of flying, he considered, translate erotic impulses. Discussing such experiences, the psychoanalytic circle in Vienna in 1912 was aware of the comical but highly regarded amulets of the classical world which represent genitals as birds – winged phalluses and vulvae – and were worn as lucky charms. This widespread symbolism inspired the psychoanalyst Paul Federn to comment despondently, 'we encounter an ever more universal symbolism, in the analysis of which infantile material proves useless'. Erections can fail, the Vienna analysts glumly recognised. Fears of falling, as in vertigo, offered more fertile ground for psychoanalytical probing.

Vertigo is the penalty of rising; the sensation of plunging to one's death a consequence of dreaming too far. The connection of flying and fantasy has long excited opprobrium, for such dreams trail error and pride, lies and illusions in their wake; after all, Faust's desires will be granted by none other than Mephistopheles. These are the attitudes to fantasy that Freud wanted to explore, in order to liberate the psyche from repression, overcome vertigo, and alleviate dysfunction in sexual fulfilment. The process of psychoanalytical reverie did not lead to rapturous flight all the time: often it took a hard and bumpy road.

V

The case history of the couch has a tragic postscript. Moritz Freud, the original giver of the Smyrna rug, said of himself that his love of stories and 'hunger for knowledge' led him to 'swallow up ships' libraries,' and when he and Freud's sister Marie, known as Mitzi, got engaged in November 1883, Freud wrote to his wife Martha Bernays that Moritz was 'a fantasist, but . . . he will bring some lighter blood into our pessimistic self-tormenting family manner'. Moritz was away – in Egypt, St

Petersburg and Greece – when his children were born, but made it up later to his youngest daughter, born in 1892, by taking her on his travels. This child decided, rather in the manner of the loving heroines Zumurrud and Badoura, to take on a male identity in life. She called herself 'Tom', became a designer and writer for children, and married Jankew Seidmann, a scholar of Kabbalah, who ran Ophir, a small publishing house in Berlin which specialised in orientalist books and Judaica. The *Verwandlungsbücher* (Books of Transformations) which Tom Seidmann-Freud made include tabs to pull and discs to revolve and other imaginative, early interactive stimuli. In the first of these, *Das Wunderhaus* (The Magic House, 1927), the house in question shelters an extended family not unlike the Freuds; in the sequel, *Das Zauberboot* (The Magic Boat, 1929), a tab when pulled reveals her uncle at an upstairs window, smoking his signature cigar. Later, a picture of the interior comes with a piece of red film which changes what you see. In one room, a child is lying tummy down on a couch looking at a picture book; he is dressed like a boy, but the features are pretty, with long eyelashes, bright red cheeks, and a 1920s bob, so could be a girl (a 'tomboy'?). When you cover the image with the red film, the couch disappears: the child reading is no longer lying face down, but flying. In this children's picture book, Freud's niece gave graphic expression to the idea that reading – and reverie – can fly you away (Pls. 23a,b).

Tom Freud's husband committed suicide in late 1929; she followed him a few months later, in 1930. The Crash of 1929 and the looming political storm clouds had disastrously affected his business. *The Magic Boat* was published a few months before her death: the copy in the Freud Museum Library is inscribed to Anna Freud in September 1929. The picture book, resourceful and delightful, gives no sign of the impending double horror. Tom's history is sad enough, but because she died before the war she never knew the fate of her mother Mitzi who, like three of Freud's other sisters, was deported to the concentration camps, where they died in 1942–43.

The fate of Tom Freud adds to the knowledge conveyed by Freud's last consulting room, that all of this would have been destroyed – if he had not left with his collections (and the couch) when he did. The mise-en-scène speaks above all of Freud's method, of the uses of fantasy, the interactions of myth, imagination, narrative and consciousness. It speaks of a way of thinking and living that was denounced and (nearly) destroyed; it testifies to the ravages of intolerance and fanaticism and, more hopefully, to the richness of conversations between cultures across huge stretches of time and geography.

A couch is a couch is a couch. Or is it? As Gertrude Stein implies through the celebrated repetition, more lies under the rose than a rose.

Story 15
Prince Ardashir and
Hayat al-Nufus

ONE KING IN THIS STORY is childless; he rules in Shiraz, in Iran. At last in his old age, the doctors in his entourage mix him the right medicine, and a son is born, Ardashir, a boy as beautiful as the full moon and very good at his lessons, too. The other king in this story rules in Basra, in Iraq. He has a daughter, Hayat al-Nufus, who is equally accomplished and beautiful as Ardashir, if not more so. But she is set against marriage, and indeed declares that she will kill herself if her father tries to make a match for her. When Ardashir hears about this fierce princess and her resolve, he wants nothing more than to persuade her otherwise. His father sends an embassy, and when the proposal of marriage to his son is refused, he falls into such a rage he declares war on Iraq: he will lay the country to waste.

Ardashir is sensitive and civilised and also wise and he pleads with his bloodthirsty and vengeful father not to set out to win the love of the princess in this futile way; instead, he, Ardashir, will disguise himself as a merchant, he says, and try his luck with the haughty but adorable young woman.

Ardashir's parents agree, and load him with goods to trade in his new role, and he sets out for the White City of Basra with his father's vizier in attendance. When they reach their destination, they set up shop in fabulous style and very soon attract attention, for the splendour of their goods and the magnificence of Ardashir's outfits and his splendid good looks. Everyone is talking about the newcomer, and one day, at last, luck visits him: an old woman appears in the shop and wants to buy something very special − for her mistress.

On inquiring who that might be, Ardashir discovers that this old woman is none other than the nurse of his longed-for princess, Hayat al-Nufus.

Slowly but surely, he wins the loyal old servant woman to his side, and although she protests that the errand will come to nothing, that the merchant will have to aim lower, she does eventually agree to carry a billet-doux, inscribed with languishing love lyrics, from the young man

to her mistress; he also presents her with a robe of such glorious workmanship that when Hayat unfolds it, its luminousness irradiates every
nook of her apartments in the castle.

But she won't be swayed by a mere thing, and she is outraged that a
common tradesman would dare approach her: she will have his nose slit
for his contumely, she cries, and worse besides (she will have him crucified in the marketplace, right there, next to his shop).

Her old nurse urges her to write to him in this vein. Hayat worries,
'Won't it encourage him, if I reply?' 'Oh no,' says the go-between. 'We're
only writing to him to destroy his hopes and intensify his fear.'

And so a lively correspondence springs up between them, lasting for
days and weeks and months, with Hayat waxing ever more outraged at
the young man's uppitiness – after one intense declaration of undying
love from the unknown merchant, she tries to denounce him to her
father, but he is away hunting. Her old servant, hearing of this attempt
to tell all, advises her to be careful and not to speak of the matter, since
'honour is like milk, which the lightest dust dirties, or like glass, which
cannot be mended once it is broken'.

Hayat al-Nufus has reasons for her rage against all men and her adamant
refusal to marry anyone, let alone a common shopkeeper. The old
go-between on one of her visits to Prince Ardashir lets him into her
confidence.

The princess had a dream one night when she was growing up, which
she has never forgotten:

In her garden, the lovely garden of her family palace, a birdcatcher
comes in uninvited and unwanted, scatters seed on the ground and
then spreads his toils to catch the birds that begin flying down to eat;
among them a pair of doves, billing and cooing. As she dreams, Hayat
sees the male bird fall into the trap and begin struggling unavailingly
to free himself; seeing him captured, the other birds all take flight. Soon
after, however, the female dove, his partner, returns and, pecking with
her beak and unpicking with her claws, she tears the meshes of the
net and succeeds in freeing him. Meanwhile, the birdcatcher wakes up
from a nap he was having under a tree, mends the tear in the net,
spreads more seed and lies in wait a little farther off. Soon enough, the
birds are fluttering back and beginning to peck at the grain, the pair
of pigeons among them. This time, the female gets tangled up in the
net and begins to struggle – and all the birds, including her companion,
fly away . . .

A little while later, the birdcatcher rouses himself from his slumbers,
finds the female pigeon captive in his nets, and wrings her neck.

At that moment in the dream, Princess Hayat woke up in terror, her nurse tells Ardashir.

'Look!' cried Hayat al-Nufus, 'how men treat women! The female of the species came back to rescue her man, she had pity on him and she risked her life for him! But when she falls into the same snare, he leaves her, as if her good deed and their partnership counts for nothing! God abandons everyone who is stupid enough to put their trust in men! Men never recognise what they owe women! Curses on each and every one of them!'

At this, Ardashir's feverish love only grows hotter. And the nurse is complicit: she lets him know where Hayat walks in her garden in the cool of evening, and she plots with him how to smuggle him in. He swears to himself he will carry off the princess, throw her across his pommel, and gallop off into the desert and the unknown. But Hayat has had enough of the nurse's advice and she has her savagely beaten for her pandering efforts, and then sends her home, forbidding her to come near her again.

Meanwhile, the vizier of Ardashir's father has not lost the initiative.

By dint of much largesse – gold, food and drink – poured into the right hands, the vizier manages to suborn the keeper of the princess's garden and he musters his maintenance team. The vizier instructs them to restore a tumbledown pavilion that stands in one corner of the grounds; inside, they are to paint the walls with a sequence showing a dream:

A birdcatcher is spreading his nets and catches a pigeon who is extricated from the toils by his female companion; they both return and this time the female is captured in the mesh. Her mate is startled and flies up, and there he is caught by a waiting windhover, his neck broken, his flesh eaten and his blood drunk by the bird of prey.

Ardashir, waiting in the garden hoping to accost his love, Princess Hayat, sees the tableau painted on the walls of the pavilion and is amazed that it tells the story of her dream – but with a different ending.

'It is so extraordinary,' he says to the vizier, 'that if it were inscribed with a fine needle in ink on the corner of the eye, it would present a lesson worth pondering.'

'Yes, indeed,' says the vizier.

Ardashir continues, 'If only my love could have dreamed her dream until the end, she would then know that the male bird couldn't come back to save his companion, because a bird of prey had caught him, killed him, eaten his flesh and drunk his blood.'

'Why yes, indeed,' says the vizier.

It remains only for the picture to be seen by the princess, and for her to realise too that her dream might have led to a different conclusion about the nature of men, husbands, and the character of the male in general.

And so it turns out: when the summer brings ripe fruit on the trees in the garden, she goes out picnicking with her friends, who beg her to forgive their former companion, the old nurse, and bring her back to court. Eventually she agrees, and so the nurse can again help Ardashir, who has been waiting all this time, a secret tenant of the garden, for the princess to come and take the air there of a summer night. The vizier and he have kept their funds flowing into the right hands, and at last, one day, Ardashir realises he can at last meet Hayat in the flesh – after she has come across the painting, read the story of the dream it tells, and thought again about her prejudice against all men.

Their love grows from the moment they meet, and the romance explodes into passionate song and passionate love-making and passionate blazons of the two young people's beauty and charm.

Among many other things, Ardashir says to her:

> . . . your saliva is wine, the sweetest wine in the world,
> or the purest musk, water that's limpid and fresh.
> O gazelle of the fields, soothe my sorrow,
> be kind, come and see me in my dreams!

But they still have many dangers before them: angry parents, jealous courtiers. They too have to struggle in the tangled nets of envious conspiracies and moral obloquy. Ardashir manages to remain with Hayat in her palace for a while by disguising himself as a girl: the nurse plucks his hairs, paints his face, and provides him with pretty clothes so that he can be smuggled in. But the lovers are betrayed by a court eunuch, and Ardashir's neck is on the block when, just in time, his father arrives at the head of a vast army.

In the serene close, after forty nights of storytelling, the furious fathers have relented and let both of their children continue with their choice of a loving mate, have heaped rich gifts on them and announced weeks and weeks of holidays for everyone.

They all then lived in complete harmony until their love was ended by the One who destroys all pleasures, separates lovers who have been reunited, ruins palaces and fills the graveyards.

Conclusion:
'All the story of the night told over . . .'

I should need many nights, a hundred perhaps, or even a thousand. And I should live in the anxiety of not knowing whether the Master of my destiny might not prove less indulgent than the Sultan Shahriyar, whether in the morning, when I broke off my story, he would consent to lift my death sentence . . . Not that I had the slightest pretension to be writing a new version, in any way, of the *Arabian Nights* . . . or of any of those books which I had loved with a child's naivety and to which I had been as superstitiously attached as to my loves . . .

Marcel Proust, Time Regained (1927)

Now that the book is finished, I know that this was not a hallucination . . . but the confirmation of something I already suspected – folktales are real.

Italo Calvino, Italian Folktales (1956)

ANYONE WHO REACHES THE END of the tales of the 1001 Nights will die, the legend says; but the danger is not very serious, since it is not possible to say, as you might about another book, that you can put it down because you have finished it. The reason does not lie in its length, but in its myriad variations and the efflorescence of the structure. On the 602nd Night, Sultan Shahriyar finds himself listening to a story . . . about the son of a king, a young prince with no name, who climbs a tree and then sees a colossal and hideous afrit lie down to rest, laying his huge head in the lap of a beautiful young woman whom he has let out of a padlocked chest . . . When the prince returns to court, his father the Sultan is so furious that his son has lost the precious ring which he had given him that he sentences him to execution. But the young prince starts telling his father stories to defer the hour . . .

Shahriyar, listening to Shaharazad past the midpoint of the *Nights*, finds himself looking at gathering shadows in the mirror of his own story of almost two years before: will he fall for ever into the pool of Shahrazad's memory, and we the readers with him? 'By Allah, this story is my story and this case is my case,' he cries out in Burton's translation, where the story eerily matches his even more closely, as it runs on, pulling in Shahrazad and Dunyazad and their father the vizier. The possibility of recognition presses the fanciful tale towards ethics: we the listeners may realise, with a flash of illumination, that we are the subjects – the villains – of the drama.

In Habicht's version, the story returns on the last night of all, the 1001st night, thereby producing an endless loop. Borges, lover of labyrinths, paradox, and of the law of eternal return recognised, in this recapitulation, a defining and compelling instance of the fabulist imagination in action. A book of stories about liberation, flight, caprice and desire enmeshes us, imprisons us, its audience, in a *regressus ad infinitum*.

In another way as well the book cannot ever be read to its conclusion: it is still being written. Robert Irwin reviews the many writers all over the world who have responded – by echo, imitation, variation – to the stories of the *Nights*, from Robert Louis Stevenson to Salman Rushdie (Irwin calls this chapter 'Children of the *Nights*' in homage to Rushdie's *Midnight's Children*). Sequels have been woven into the fabric: in *When Dreams Travel* (1999), the Indian novelist Githa Hariharan imagines Dunyazad returning to Shahriyar's palace after her sister's mysterious, premature death; this is a fiction by a storyteller that will not accept the received story, but remains suspicious that the happy ending is peddling lies. Late twentieth-century reworkings of the *Nights* draw earlier political meanings into contemporary shapes: Rushdie effervescently parodies the talking beasts, magic rides and capricious genies in *Haroun and the Sea of Stories* (1990), a children's adventure story that is also his sharpest and most condensed political fable, about dictatorships and the freedom of art and the press. In the countries where the stories are set and where they were originally composed and told, previous disdain has lifted: the Lebanese writer Elias Khoury uses the structure of the *Nights* in *The Gate of the Sun* (1998), in which a chain of stories, interlinked and looped one inside the other, are being told to an old Palestinian freedom fighter as he lies dying. The Lebanese-American Alia Yunis, in *The Night Counter* (2010), relates the diasporic adventures of her grandmothers and aunts and mother and herself through another web of interlaced stories. In Egypt, Radwa Ashour, a scholar who, with Ferial Ghazoul, has compiled a survey anthology of women's writings in Arabic, also projects herself into the role of Shahrazad with a fierce novella, *Siraaj* (2007), in which she refracts present-day feudal arrangements and repression in the Gulf through a refashioning of Sinbad against a backdrop of slave trafficking in the fourteenth century. In the performing arts, the stories continue to show the expansive vitality of jinn: Hanan al-Shaykh has retold them for Tim Supple's pan-Arabic production, premiered at the Edinburgh Festival in the summer of 2011.

So the carpet continues to unfurl – like Solomon's, it will bear the population of a city of stories.

But if it is not feasible to finish reading the *1001 Nights*, it is possible to conclude this book, *Stranger Magic*, although the enjoyable nature of the work involved in making it invites the writer to put off the day. And coming to the end does not close the windows or draw the curtains against daybreak. As Paul Ricoeur writes, 'The first task is not to begin but, from the midst of speech, to remember; to remember with a view to beginning.'

My starting point was the perplexing passion of the Enlightenment for a collection of medieval fairy tales from another part of the world, and the continuing vitality and presence of the *Arabian Nights* in literature, entertainment and the arts. Why the attraction? And how did the book take such hold? The tales that I have chiefly explored consist of many elements of magic and enchantment common to belief systems in other cultures besides the ones invoked by the stories. Many are pure fairytale, and, as the great historian R.G. Collingwood remarked, in relation to a study of fairy tales he was planning to write, these are 'traditional stories about all sorts of magic'. But magic, he warned, 'is merely a convenient label by which we designate a variety of beliefs and customs found among savages'. There are many other strands of the *Nights* which are not dominated by enchantment – animal fables, comic genre tales of low life, historical anecdotes and legends, tales of pranks and jokes – but I have not dwelt on these. I am chiefly attracted by the implausible, impossible, and fantastic stories. This attraction puzzles me, for I was once a fervent Catholic and know what it is like to yield fully to verbal transformative magic, miracles, and other demands on faith beyond reason, and I struggled free (lost my faith) a long time ago. So why do I still like to think and read about jinn and animal metamorphoses, conjured palaces and vanishing treasures, deadly automata and flying sofas, ghastly torments and ineluctable destinies?

We cannot know if the Greeks believed in their gods, and it is no longer certain to what extent bishops – at least Anglican bishops – hold to the mysteries of the Christian credo, but on the whole we impute a different relationship of the original makers and receivers of the *Nights* to the *'aja'ib* – the astonishing things – which colour the stories. So how to characterise the pull of these stories which Proust loved with a child's naivety? (He does not write that he loved them only as a child.)

Pleasure is one quick answer – the tales gave and give pleasure. But what does this pleasure consist of, for adults? I hope the preceding chapters have exhibited some of their qualities. Various theories, however, have been proposed to explain the uses of enchantment in a sceptical age, and the continued interest of magic for the unbeliever. Simon During, in *Modern Enchantments*, rings a change on Coleridge's celebrated theory of 'the willing suspension of disbelief', and emphasises the know-ingness of contemporary audiences, who revel in illusions while in full possession of the knowledge that they are being taken in: according to this angle of view, the distance of disbelief adds a frisson, almost a perverse shiver, to the magical logic unfolding. With a deeper, more metaphysical sense of wonder, Wallace Stevens put forward a comparable paradox with his lines about the truth of metaphor, 'the nicer knowledge of belief, that what it believes in is not true'. This state of double-think, while recognisable intellectually, accounts for responses to the prodigious illusions of Computer Generated Imagery – the soaring dinosaur-like steeds, plugged in like appliances and then ridden through the sky like surfboards, for example, in the 2009 record-breaking cinema spectacular, *Avatar*. But the tinge of cynicism – and superiority – that such knowingness presup-poses fails to capture the intensity and raptness of experiencing enchant-ment, as produced by any number of tales in the *Nights*, or, for that matter, by Shakespeare's fairy plays. Hippolyta's reply to Theseus, towards the close of *A Midsummer Night's Dream*, evoking 'all the story of the night told over', rightly draws our attention to the characters' 'minds transfigur'd so together'. Their spellbound state, she declares, 'more witnesseth than fancy's images/ and grows to something of great constancy;/ but, howsoever, strange and admirable' (V.i).

The strange and admirable pleasures of magic are connected to the uses of enchantment and the transfiguring effects of imagining possibilities, but not in a directly functional way; rather the force of their explanatory potential sharpens the savour. 'All understanding, like all interpretation' continues Ricoeur, is 'continually oriented by the manner of posing the question and by what it aims at.' Regarding the *Nights*, the question that needs to be put is not an equivalent of J. M. Barrie's treacherous dialectical trick ('If you believe in fairies, clap your hands!'), but what do the stories show, what knowledge do they bring, especially at a time of such political turbulence?

That phrase of Borges's – 'reasoned imagination' – can help us live with these contradictions between dream/reality, belief/disbelief, ration-ality/irrationality: such stories display, with untrammelled exuberance, the oxymoronic activity of 'reasoned imagination' which communicates prophetically when it imagines things that have not yet come to be (paper money; lunar travel), as well as psychologically and emotionally (the significance of dreams, the terrors and joys that fate springs on us, the consequences of love, of breaking prohibitions, and travelling far away).

Taking up the question of a rationale for magic, Italo Calvino, in his classic essay on the quality of *leggerezza* (lightness), wrote, 'Whenever humanity seems condemned to heaviness, I think I should fly like Perseus into a different space. I don't mean escaping into dreams or into the irrational. I mean that I have to change my approach, look at the world from a different perspective, with a different logic and with fresh methods of cognition and verification.' Calvino's thoughts on lightness shift between magic and physics, fact and fiction, without clear demarcation, in the manner of such literature of enchantment: 'I am accustomed to consider literature a search for knowledge,' he continued. He then entered different, revealing territory:

> In order to move onto existential ground, I have to think of literature as extended to anthropology and ethnology and mythology. Faced with the precarious existence of tribal life – drought, sickness, evil influences – the shaman responded by ridding his body of weight and flying to another world, another level of perception, where he could find the strength to change the face of reality . . . These visions [of flight] were part of the folk imagination, or we might say of lived experience . . . it is this anthropological device that literature perpetuates.

This is a manifesto for literary imagination, and the passage enacts the way the imagery of flying in the *Nights* cannot remain grounded but keeps taking off into metaphor. How strongly Calvino wished to press the metaphor of flight to communicate the storyteller's ideal is moot – but the slippage between object and metaphor, as occurs in the case of talismans and other magical devices in the *Nights,* where the literal materiality of a thing dissolves into the virtual reality of its powers, is also happening here. More crucially, with regard to the reasoning imagination, Calvino relates literature to the quest for knowledge, and adduces the practical purpose – healing, security, survival – of the shaman's role, and then segues into the fantasy of the shamanic voyage to another world. He draws attention to the role anthropology has played, with its reports on peoples who operate according to different logic and apply different methods of cognition and verification. They will supply the means to rid ourselves of that weight of preconceptions and prejudices that we own, whether we like it or not. Through their eyes, the frame in which we are caught can be broken open. 'I think that the deepest rationality,' Calvino continues, 'behind every literary operation has to be sought out in the anthropological needs to which it corresponds.' The way Calvino uses mythic and magical imagery allows for its truth; not for its metaphorical value, but for something more, something deeper and more valuable: a symbol in action

Through the dream-like stories of the *Nights*, I too have been looking for a fable that would meet anthropological needs, 'a fable of modernity'. A reading of the *Nights* from this perspective opens up the stories' relations to these contemporary conditions. At a level beneath the surface of the narratives, a meaning gathers definition, the watermark in their fabric. Not as schematic or didactic as allegory or emblem, though related to encryption, these watermarked meanings do not have a specific design on the reader/receiver. They are not fixed, and indeed they change from one generation of readers to another, and from one individual to another, as the variety of media and interpretations of the *Nights* reveals. Symbols in the stories – the feather cloak of Peri Banou, the carnelian talisman of Princess Badoura, Aladdin's lamp – do not stand for something else, beyond the story, which can be pinpointed, but act in their own right within the story to provoke the imagination, and with imagination, thought.

Again, Paul Ricoeur is illuminating: 'If we can no longer live the great symbolisms of the sacred in accordance with the original belief in them, we can, we modern men [and women, and children], aim at a second naiveté in and through criticism. In short, it is by *interpreting* that we can *hear* again' (emphasis in the original). Naivety as openness, not simple-mindedness. The stress on the importance of interpretation takes us back to Edward Said, and to his view that the critic's vocation is to engage with a book or text as an agent of meaning in the world. Magic agency, as constantly dramatically in operation in the *Nights*, also offers a vision of what a literary or artistic artefact does as it moves in a society, a role that is crystallised by Shahrazad's mission and the ransom tales that she tells.

The acceptance of a potential meaning in magic won an unexpected supporter in the philosopher Ludwig Wittgenstein, when he wrote a response to *The Golden Bough*, J. G. Frazer's classic study of folk religion and worldwide animist beliefs. After Wittgenstein began reading Frazer, he made some notes towards his next book. This was in 1930, when he had published the *Tractatus*, a great work of logical positivism, and was now embarked on the research that would become *Philosophical Investigations*, which would appear in 1953 and give a very different approach to language and meaning.

In the notes inspired by his reading of Frazer's religious anthropology, Wittgenstein grappled with the question of what to do about illogical, irrational, mythic thinking. He jotted down three remarks:

> I think now that the right thing would be to begin my book with remarks about metaphysics as a kind of magic.
>
> But in doing this I must neither speak in defense of magic nor ridicule it.
>
> What it is that is deep about magic would be kept.

As these musings reveal, the comparatively new science of anthropology introduced ideas from other cultures about every aspect of human experience and knowledge, and produced a rich cross-fertilisation. Wittgenstein then began puzzling out how self and world are connected through language and, by extension, stories, and how the magical conception of the self, expressed in so-called primitive ritual, unites us with the world through a family of resemblances across history and geography. The philosopher was setting out to modify the general disparagement in Frazer's outlook, not only in the interests of tolerance and equality, but also through a more nuanced understanding of the human mind and the act of utterance, the agency of language. 'It is a wide variety of faces with common features,' Wittgenstein writes in the *Remarks on Frazer*, 'that keep showing in one place and in another. One would like to draw lines joining the parts that various faces have in common. But then a part of our contemplation would still be lacking, namely what connects this picture with our own feelings and thoughts. This part gives the contemplation its depth.'

Where shamanic lightness for Calvino leads to literature as a way of knowledge, for Wittgenstein the depths which such primitive belief systems allow us to glimpse reveal a way of ethics: 'Man has the urge to thrust against the limits of language. Think for instance of one's astonishment that anything exists. This astonishment cannot be expressed in the form of a question and there is no answer to it . . . This thrust against the limits of language is *ethics*' (emphasis in original).

So in the philosopher's view, the 'fairy way of writing' reaches out through its own linguistic inventiveness towards an ethical vision. This is what the emulators of the *Nights* recognised. Each story is an event, an event related to another story in a pattern at once mysterious and satisfying. It shows its links with a past of oral performance, with ritual associations, and it can revivify that effect, that function even, of the work of art.

The research for this book began during the first Gulf War, and

continued during the many, appalling and unresolved conflicts in the
regions where the *Nights* originated. I wanted to present another side of
the culture cast as the enemy and an alternative history to vengeance
and war. Since then, the Arab Spring, beginning in Tunisia and Egypt in
late 2010 and early 2011 and spreading with various degrees of success
throughout the region, has given hope of change. While the situation
remains unpredictable and fragile, the protestors are making heard their
call for a different politics and culture from the oppressive, sclerotic
governments of the past. The voices which are being raised include those
of many writers, storytellers, musicians, film-makers, artists and teachers
who have been struggling to continue to weave the marvellous fabric
of common civilisation, equal justice and daily freedoms in their countries.
In full hope against hope, the work of interconnectedness, of intercultural
and intergenerational exchanges is of paramount importance, in order to
give us knowledge and exchanges of one another ('to multiply the world',
in Schwab's phrase), to lift the shadows of rage and despair, bigotry and
prejudice, to invite reflection – to give the princes and sultans of this
world pause. This was – and is – Shahrazad's way.

Luxor, Egypt, 2010.

Glossary

afrit	a species of rebel jinni
'ajiba	(pl: 'ajā'ib) astonishment, wonder; marvellous or astonishing things
Abu-Maaschar (Albumanzar, Albumazar, Abu Mazar)	Astronomer, fl., in Baghad 9th century. Name of African magician in stage versions of *Aladdin*, including pantomime, since Victorian era
Alf Layla wa-Layla	Arabic for *The Thousand and One Nights*
apsara	a beautiful flying woman, often musical, with siren-like qualities, originally from Sanskrit mythology
Barmakids (Barmecides)	Clan in the entourage of Harun al-Rashid, celebrated for their wealth and largesse
calender	a dervish (q.v.), wandering, mendicant monk
Dahnash	a rebel jinni
dervish (darweesh)	a holy man, vowed to poverty, member of order of mendicant monks
al-Dimiryat	Solomon's vizier; his second-in-command over the jinn
Dunyazad, (Dinarzade)	Shahrazad's sister
Eblis, Iblis	Satan, by extension, his realm or hell
ghazal	a Persian lyric form
ghoul, ghul	haunts graveyards and eats flesh of the dead.
Giafar (Jafar)	Harun al-Rashid's vizier
Harun al-Rashid (Haroun)	Caliph who reigned in Baghdad 786–809
Hayat al-Nufus	Name made of words meaning 'life' and 'breath'; a character of this name appears in both 'The Tale of Zumurrud and Ali Shar' and in the tale of her love of 'Prince Ardashir and Hayat al-Nufus'
jinni (sing.), jinniya (female) and jinn (plural)	Named jinn include: Shakhr, Maimuna, Dahesh, Dahnash
magians, sometimes Magians	magicians or sorcerers of the *Arabian Nights*, often Zoroastrians. Word probably formed from magus, magi, or mage, as in the Three Kings of the Christian nativity story
marid	a species of jinni

peri	a fairy
rubai, rubaiyat (plural)	a lyric form in quatrains
Rukh, or Roc	colossal bird capable of carrying an elephant
sheikh (sheykh)	a religious scholar, often a leader, sometimes the ruler; sometimes used for an old man as a term of respect
Simurgh, the, or Simorg	fabulous birds, like the Phoenix
Solomon	Arabic: Suleiman, Sulayman; Hebrew: Schlomo; wise king, magus, in both Bible and Koran
Waq-Waq	islands to the east, sometimes identified with Japan
Zobeide (Zubayda)	Name of the 'Eldest Lady' in the cycle of 'The Porter and the Three Ladies of Baghdad'
Zulaykha (Suleika)	the name of Harun al-Rashid's favourite wife; also of 'Potiphar's wife' in the story of Joseph in the Koran

Abbreviations

ANE Anon, *Arabian Nights' Entertainments* [1706–21], Mack, Robert L. ed., (Oxford, Oxford University Press, 1998)

ANEnc *The Arabian Nights Encyclopaedia,* Van Leeuwen, Richard and Marzolph, Ulrich, 2 vols, (ABC Clio: Denver and Oxford, 2004)

BFI British Film Institute

Bencheikh/Miquel *Les mille et une Nuits*, trans. and ed. Bencheikh, Jamel Eddine and Miquel, André (3 vols, Paris: Gallimard, 2005)

Burton Burton, Richard, *The Arabian Nights*, (13 vols, manybooks.net, 2010)

Chraïbi *Les mille et une Nuits: Histoire du texte et classification des contes* (Paris: L'Harmattan, 2008)

Description de l'Egypte: *ou, Recueil des observations et des recherches qui ont été faites en Egypte pendant l'expédition de l'armée française. Publié par les ordres de Sa Majesté l'empereur Napoléon le Grand* (Paris: Impr. Imp., 1809–28), ed. E.F. Jomard. 20 vols.

EI *Encyclopaedia of Islam* (Leiden:Brill, vol. 1, 1913;Vol. 3, 1938; Supplement 1960, New Ed.,Vol. 1, 2007)

ELH *Journal of English Literary History*

Galland/Sermain Galland, Antoine, *Les mille et une Nuit: contes arabes*, ed. J.-P Sermain (3 vols, Paris, Flammarion, 2004)

Haddawy/Mahdi I Haddawy, Husain, trans., *The Arabian Nights* (New York, 1990)

Haddawy/Mahdi II Haddawy, Husain, trans., *The Arabian Nights II: Sindbad and Other Popular Stories* (New York, W. W. Norton, 1995)

Irwin Irwin, Robert, *The Arabian Nights: A Companion* (London: Allen Lane, 1994; London and New York, Tauris Parke, rev. ed., 2004)

JAL *Journal of Arabic Literature*

JJC John Johnson Collection, Bodleian Library, Oxford

JWCI *Journal of the Warburg and Courtauld Institutes*

Kennedy/Warner *The Arabian Nights: Encounters and Translations*, ed. Kennedy, Philip and Warner, Marina (New York: New York University Press, forthcoming, 2012)

Lane Lane, Edward William, trans., *The Arabian Nights' Entertainments* (3 vols, London, 1850)

LRB *London Review of Books*

Lyons Lyons, Malcolm C. with Lyons, Ursula, trans., *The Arabian Nights: Tales of 1001 Nights* (London: Penguin 2009)

Makdisi/Nussbaum *The Arabian Nights in Historical Context. Between East and West*, eds. Saree Makdisi and Felicity Nussbaum (Oxford: Oxford University Press, 2008)

Marzolph *The Arabian Nights Reader*, ed. Ulrich Marzolph (Detroit: Wayne University Press, 2006)

Mathers/Mardrus Mathers, Powys, from the French trans. by Dr J. C. Mardrus, *The Arabian Nights: The Book of the Thousand Nights and One Night* (6 vols, London: Folio Society, 2003)

MT *Marvels & Tales Journal of Fairy-Tale Studies*

NYRB *The New York Review of Books*

OED *Oxford English Dictionary*

RES *Journal of Anthropology and Aesthetics*

RSÉAA XVII-XVIII *Revue de la Societé d'etudes anglo-américaines des XVII et XVIII siècles*

SOAS The School of Oriental and African Studies

TLS *The Times Literary Supplement*

WED/Whaley Goethe, Johann Wolfgang von, and trans., Whaley, John *Poems of the West and East: West-Eastern Divan* (New York, 1998)

Yamanaka/Nishio *The Arabian Nights and Orientalism. Perspectives from East and West*. Yamanata, Yuriko and Nishio, Tetsuo, eds (London: I.B. Tauris, 2006)

The Stories

These are my sources and the alternative titles of the stories as they appear in the various editions consulted for this book (see Abbreviations and Bibliography).

1. The Fisherman and the Genie
The Fisherman and the 'Ifrit (Lyons) Vol. 1, 19–24.
Conte du Pêcheur et Démon (Bencheikh/Miquel, 2005) Vol. 1, 29–64.
The Story of the Fisherman and the Demon (Haddawy/Mahdi I) 30–35.
The Fisherman and the Jinni (Mathers/Mardrus) Vol. 1, 23–56.
The Fisherman and The Jinni (Burton) Vol. 1, 47–80.
Story of the Fisherman (Lane) Vol. 1, 32–71.
The Story of the Fisherman (ANE), 30–65.
Histoire du Pêcheur (Galland) Vol. 1, 65–112.

2. The City of Brass
The City of Brass (Lyons) Vol. 2, 566–78, 518–546.
La Ville de cuivre (Bencheikh/Miquel) Vol. 2, 553–581.
The Extraordinary Tale of the City of Brass (Mathers/Mardrus, Vol. 3, 339–346, 206–228.
The City of Brass (Burton) Vol. 6, 74–103.
The Story of the City of Brass (Lane) Vol. 3, 1–37.

3. Prince Ahmed and the Fairy Peri Banou
Prince Ahmad and the Fairy Perí-Bânû (Burton) Vol. 13, 208–254.
The Story of Prince Ahmed and the Fairy Pari Banou (ANE) 820–860.
Le prince Ahmed et la fée Pari Banou (Galland) Vol. 3, 267–325.

4. The Prince of the Black Islands
The Story of the Semi-Petrified Prince (Lyons) Vol. 1, 41–50.
Histoire du jeune homme (Bencheikh/Miquel) Vol. 1, 54–64.
The Tale of the Enchanted King (Haddawy/Mahdi I) 22–27, 56–66.
The Tale of the Young Man and the Fishes (Mathers/Mardrus) Vol. 1, 47–56.
The Tale of the Ensorcelled Prince (Burton) Vol. 1, 71–80.
The Story of the Young King of the Black Islands (Lane) Vol. 1, 61–71.

The History of the Young King of the Black-Isles (ANE) 54–66.
Histoire du jeune roi des îles noires (Galland) Vol. 1, 98–112.

5. Hasan of Basra

Hasan of Basra, the goldsmith (Lyons) Vol. 3, 145–261.
Conte de Hasan al-Basrî (Bencheikh/Miquel) Vol. 3, 149–301.
The Adventures of Hasan of Basrah (Mathers/Mardrus) Vol. 4, 271–346.
The Adventures of Hasan of Basra (Burton) Vol. 8, 20–123.
Story of Hassan of Balsora (Lane) Vol. 3, 213–356.

6. A Fortune Regained

The rich man who lost and then regained his money (Lyons) Vol. 2, 119–120.
Conte de la fortune enfouie (Bencheikh/Miquel) Vol. 2, 68–69.
The Ruined Man Who Became Rich Again Through a Dream (Burton) Vol. 4,
    218–219.
'*The Story of the Two Dreamers*' (1935), in Borges, *Collected Fictions* (1998), 56–57.

7. The Greek King and Doctor Douban

The Story of King Yunan and Duban the Sage (Lyons) Vol.1, 24–34.
Histoire du roi Yûnân, de son vizir et du médecin Dûbân (Bencheikh/Miquel,
    2005) Vol. 1, 34–46.
The Tale of King Yunan and the Sage Duban (Haddawy/Mahdi I) 36–41.
The Tale of the Wazīr of Yūnān and Rayyān the Doctor (Mathers/Mardrus) Vol. 1,
    28–40.
The Story of the King Yûnân and the Sage Dûbân (Burton) Vol. 1, 52–64.
The Story of the Grecian King and the Sage Douban (Lane) Vol. 1, 39–52.
The Story of the Grecian King and the Physician Douban (ANE) 36–46.
Histoire du Roi Grec et du médecin Douban (Galland) Vol. 1, 72–85.

8. Abu Mohammed the Lazy

Abu Muhammad the Sluggard (Lyons) Vol 2, 13–27.
Conte d'Abû Muhammad le Paresseux (Bencheikh/Miquel, 2005) Vol. 1,
    1099–1115.
Abu Muhammad Hight Lazybones (Burton) Vol. 4, 125–138.
Story of Abou Mahomed the Lazy (Lane) Vol. 2, 265–286.

9. Marouf the Cobbler

Ma'ruf the Cobbler (Lyons) Vol. 3, 690–731
Conte de Ma'rûf le savetier (Bencheikh/Miquel, 2005) Vol. 3, 761–1001.
The Tale of the Honey Cake and the Cobbler's Calamitous Wife (Mathers/Mardrus,
    1923) Vol. 6, 319–349.
Ma'ruf the Cobbler and His Wife Fâtima (Burton) Vol. 10, 12–52.
The Story of Marouf (Lane) Vol. 3, 488–549.

10. Rosebud and Uns al-Wujud the Darling Boy

Uns al-Wujud and al-Ward fi'l-Akmam (Lyons) Vol. 2, 3, 148–178.

Conte de 'Uns al-Wujûd et Ward fi' 'l-Akmâm (Bencheikh/Miquel) 2, 104–133.

The Tale of Rose-in-the-bud and World's-Delight (Mathers/Madrus) Vol. 3, 358–392.

Uns Al-Wujud and the Vizier's Daughter Al-Ward fi'l-Akmâm (Burton) Vol. 5, 37–59.

Story of Ansal-Wajoud and Rose-in-Bloom (Lane) Vol. 2, 378–406.

Histoire d'Edouard Felkanaman et d'Ansel Hougioud, in Beckford (1992) 97–144; 164–179.

11. The Jinniya and the Egyptian Prince

Histoire de la ginne Fikelah et du prince Chemnis, in Beckford (1992), 145–170.

12. Camar al-Zaman and Princess Badoura

The story of King Shahriman and his son, Qamar al-Zaman (Lyons) Vol. 1, 693–807.

Conte de Qamar az-Zamân, fils du roi Shâhramân, (Bencheikh/Miquel) Vol. 1, 745–962.

The Story of Qamar al-Zaman and His Two Sons, Amjad and As'ad (Haddawy/Mahdi II) 165–266.

The Tale of Kamar al-Zamān and the Princess Budūr, Moon of Moons (Mathers/Mardrus) Vol. 2, 324–397.

Tale of Qamar al-Zaman (Burton) Vols 3–4, 170–238, Vol. 3: 183–295, Vol. 4: 10–31.

Story of the Prince Camaralzaman and the Princess Badoura (Lane) Vol. 2, 1–77.

The Story of the Amours of Camaralzaman, Prince of the Isles of the Children of Khaledan, and of Badoura, Princess of China (ANE), 357–410.

Histoire des amours de Camaralzaman Prince de l'Isle des enfants de Khalendan, et de Badoure Princesse de la Chine (Galland) Vol. 2, 145–215.

13. The Ebony Horse

The ebony horse (Lyons) Vol. 2, 127–148.

Conte du cheval d'ébène (Bencheikh/Miquel) Vol. 2, 81–103.

The Magic Tale of the Ebony Horse (Mathers/Mardrus) Vol. 3, 392–424.

The Ebony Horse (Burton) Vol. 5, 69, 11–37.

Story of the Magic Horse (Lane) Vol. 2, 348–377.

The Story of the Enchanted Horse (ANE) 796–820.

Histoire du Cheval enchanté (Galland) Vol. 3, 231–266.

14. Aladdin of the Beautiful Moles

'Ala 'al-Din Abu 'l-Shamat (Lyons) Vol. 1, 832–884.

Conte de Alâ'ad-Dîn Abûsh-Shâmât (Bencheikh/Miquel) Vol. 3, 813–920.
The Tale of Alā al-Dīn Abū Shāmāt (Mathers/Mardrus) Vol. 3, 1–52.
'Ala 'l-Dîn Abû 'l-Shâmât (Burton) Vol. 4, 31–78.
Story of Aladdin Abushamat (Lane) Vol. 2, 150–220.

15. Prince Ardashir and Hayat al-Nufus

Ardashir and Hayat al-Nufus (Lyons) Vol. 3, 3–52.
Conte du Prince Ardashîr et Hayât an-Nufûs ((Bencheikh/Miquel) Vol. 3, 3–54.
Ardashîr and Hayât al-Nufûs (Burton) Vol. 7, 167–210.

BOOKS AND APPARATUS FOR WRITING.[2]

Notes

Epigraph

vii   Virginia Woolf, *Moments of Being: Autobiographical Writings*, ed. Jeanne Schulkind, pp. 78–160: 85.

Introduction

1   **'Fairy Way of Writing':** Joseph Addison, *The Spectator* 419 (1 July 1712), dedication to John Dryden, *King Arthur*, 1691, quoted in Châtel (2010). Many thanks to Laurent Châtel for giving me this article.

    ...how it ends: Calvino (1998), 257.

2   **...till she faints:** 'The Story of the Donkey, the Ox, and the Labourer', included in the tale of 'The Merchant and His Wife', Bencheikh/Miquel, Vol I: 12–13.

    ...the day is for God: Nacer Khemir, private communication, Dec. 2009, Abu Dhabi.

4   **Men's hatred:** Mistaken jealousy is the theme of the Tragic 'Story of the Lady that was murdered, and of the young Man her Husband', *ANE*, 182-186; of Amine, Zobeide's sister, and one of the three Ladies of Baghdad, *ANE*, 133-140.

    ...purpose shows too much: Ghazoul, 18.

5   **girls against men:** Ros Ballaster, *Fables,* 1–7; also 'Playing the second string: the role of Dinarzade in eighteenth-century English fiction', Makdisi/Nussbaum, 83–102.

    ...invite reflection: Mahfouz (1995), 2. Quoted by Roger Pearson in 'White Magic: Voltaire and Galland's Mille et Une Nuits', Kennedy/Warner, forthcoming.

    ANEnc I: 354 ff. 'The Story of King Saba'.

6   **non-human creature:** Warner, *Beast* (1994), pp. 110–128.

    the smell of blood: Mahfouz (1995), 4.

    'aja'ib Roy Mottahadeh, (1997), 29–39; 29; see also Kilito (1992), 105–7.

    '...understand its lesson.' From the preamble to 'The Tale of the Young Man' ('The Prince of the Black Islands'), Bencheikh/Miquel I: 54; also in preamble to 'The First Kalender's Tale', in 'The Porter and the Three Ladies of Baghdad', ibid. I: 82. Sometimes translated as 'fine pen' not 'needle'. André Miquel, 'Preface', in Kilito (1992), 7–8; Kilito, ibid., 104–111. Colla translates the sentence as 'Mine is a tale that, if it were written in lessons at the corner of the eye, would be a needle for those who would consider', or: 'for those who would be pricked'. See Chapter 10 on Talismans, pp.; Elliot Colla, 'The Ladies and the Eye . . .', Kennedy/Warner.

'openness as self-foundation': Yamanaka/Nishio, 68–92.

7   **arabesque structures**: Naddaff (1991) is a magnificent study of the Cycle of the Porter and the Three Ladies of Baghdad.

like one of the genies: The knotted history has been combed out by many inspired commentators on the Nights. See Gerhardt (1963); Robert Irwin (Irwin, 1994, 2004) gives a lucid, lively and unsurpassed account; Ros Ballaster (2005a, 2005b) fills in the history of the book's English and European context and influence superbly; Ulrich Marzolph and Richard Van Leeuwen and the contributors to the indispensable *Arabian Nights Encyclopaedia,* 2 vols, [ANEnc], and other Arabists and literary scholars, especially Aboubar Chraïbi, editor of *Les Mille et une nuits en partage* (Actes Sud, 2004) and author of *Les mille et une nuits: Histoire du texte et classification des contes* (Paris: L'Harmattan, 2008) [CHRAÏBI], and Abdelfatah Kilito (1992, 2001, 2010). See also the successive entries in *The Encyclopaedia of Islam*: J. Oestrup, 'Alf laila wa-laila', *EI,* Vol. 1 (Leiden, 1913), 252–256; Duncan Black MacDonald, 'Alf laila wa-laila (A.)' *EI* Supplement (Leiden, 1938), 17–21; E. Littman, 'Alf laila wa-laila (A.), *EI*, new edn, Vol. 1 (Leiden, 1960), 358–364; Ulrich Marzolph, 'Arabian Nights', *EI*, Vol. 3 (Leiden, 2007), Preview, *Brill's Encyclopaedia of Islam* (ibid)., 30–40. See also Robert Irwin's Introduction to Lyons, 1. iv–xvii; 2:1; 3: ix–xx.

Late antique myth: [Alexander] (1991), 35.

Epic of Gilgamesh: Stephanie Dalley, 'Gilgamesh in the *Arabian Nights*', *Journal of the Royal Asiatic Society*, 1991, 1–17.

three principal streams: Victor Chauvin, *Bibliographie des ouvrages arabes ou relatifs aux arabes*, Vols 4–7 (Liège 1900–03; repr. London, 2003) gives a magisterial comparative overview of Arabic sources.

8   **not as highly appreciated:** 'It is unfortunate that the Arabic world has never regarded [the *1001 Nights*] as belonging to polite literature': MacDonald (1950).

9   **eminent writers in Arabic:** Ahmad Faris al-Shidyak, *Leg upon Leg: Concerning that which is al-Faryak* (1855); see Rebecca C. Johnson, article in Kennedy/Warner; Mahfouz (1995); Tayeb Salih, *Season of Migration to the North* (New York: Random House, 2009); Radwa Ashour (2007).

variety... of narrative forms: Ulrich Marzolph, 'The *Arabian Nights* in Comparative Folk Narrative Research', in Yamanaka/Nishio, 3–24. See Warner, review of Yamanaka/Nishio, *TLS*, 2006; see Hasan El-Shamy, 'A Motif Index of *Alf laylah wa-laylah*', *JAL* 36 (2005),

3:235–68; also H. El-Shamy, 'Mythological Constituents of *Alf laylah wa-laylah*' in Yamanaka/Nishio, 25–46: 30–32.

10   **till the blood runs:** Proust (mis)remembers this story in his account of what he sees happening in the house of Jupien. Marcel Proust, *À la Recherche du temps perdu* (Paris: Gallimard, 1998), IV: 411.

causality in the *Nights*: Todorov, (1973) 107 ff.

Pasolini collaborated with another distinguished writer, Dacia Maraini, to create *Il fiore delle mille e una notte (The Arabian Nights)*, dir. Pier Paolo Pasolini (1978), a gorgeous and frankly erotic film which skilfully braids many tales together to a marvellously rich effect.

11   **children's literature:** Irwin, 290.

not silent readers: Dupont, 11, 248–9.

13   **Grub Street versions:** Ballaster Ros 'The Sea-Born Tale: Eighteenth Century Translations of *The Thousand and One Nights* and the Lure of Elemental Difference', in Kennedy/Warner; also Makdisi/Nussbaum, Introduction, 1–25; Robert L. Mack, intro, *ANE*, IX-XXIII; idem, 'Cultivating the Garden: Antoine Galland's *Arabian Nights* in the Traditions of English Literature', Makdisi/Nussbaum, 51–82.

adulatory imitators: *Le Cabinet des fées*, Vols 37–41 (Geneva: 1789–93) are dedicated to Oriental tales, many 'translated' by the Syrian monk Dom Denys Chavis and the fabulist Jacques Cazotte. See Irwin (2004), 262–263.

treatise on coffee: Antoine Galland, [De l'origine et du progrez du café. Sur un manuscrit arabe de la Bibliothèque du Roy], *Elogio del caffè*, ed. Ispano Roventi (Palermo: Sellerio, 1995).

French employers: Schwab (1964), 11 ff.

Jansenists: Alastair Hamilton, 'From East to West: Jansenists, Orientalists, and the Euchararistic Controversy', in Hent de Vries et al., *How the West Was Won: Essays on Literary Imagination, the Canon, and the Christian Middle Ages for Burcht Pranger* (Leiden: Brill, 2010), 83–100.

'core' body: Muhsin Madhi argued strongly that these stories form the genuine *Arabian Nights*, and all the rest, which Galland began adding, others later following suit, are cuckoos and should be tossed out of the nest. See intro., Haddawy/Mahdi; Irwin (2004); and idem, Introduction to Lyons I, ix-xx, ix-xxix.

15   **illuminating Oriental culture:** Irwin, Introduction to Lyons II: xii.

bride's name was Fatima: Elizabeth Kuti, 'Blue-beard and Theatrical Curiosity.' Paper given at 'Staging the East: Oriental Masking in the British Theatre, 1660–1830,' Theatre Royal, Bury St Edmunds, 11–12 June 2010, in Kennedy/Warner; Casie E. Hermansson, *Bluebeard: A Reader's Guide to the English Tradition* (Mississippi UP, 2009).

Bignon: Abbé Jean-Paul Bignon, 'Histoire de la Princesse Zeineb et du roi Léopard', in *Aventures d'Abdallah, fils d'Hanif etc.*, in Raymonde

Robert, *Il était une fois* (Paris: Presses Universitaires Nancy, 1984), 225.

to make up an eighth volume: Jean-Paul Sermain and Aboubakr Chraïbi, Présentation in Galland/Sermain I: xiv-xvi.

16   **old arab slave woman:** D'Aulnoy, *Contes des fées* (1710), quoted Warner (1994), 163.

orphan tales: Gerhardt (1963).

their composer: Galland/Sermain III: i-xiv 7–17

17   **change it into something else:** Borges, *Other Inquisitions*; quoted Irwin, 284; see also Madeleine Dobie, 'Translation in the Contact Zone: Antoine Galland's *Mille et une nuits: contes arabes*', in Makdisi/Nussbaum (2008), 25–50. Jorge Luis Borges, 'The Translators of *The Thousand and One Nights*', in Borges (1999), 92–109.

Since Payne's: See Irwin, Intro., Lyons II: xiv-xvi, for more detail.

18   **'Arab literature and the Orient':** Galland/Sermain 3: VIII.

on editing: See Irwin, 43; and idem, Intro. Lyons. II: xiii-xviii; see 'Editions', ANEnc. II, 545–6

additional stories: 'Thus authentic came to mean complete and, ironically, spurious,' Haddawy/Mahdi: xiv.

19   **On Miquel see:** André Miquel, with Gilles Plazy, *L'Orient d'une vie* (Paris: Payot, 1990); Miquel is the subject of a 2011 film by Nacer Khemir, *En Passant avec André Miquel.*

20   **elements circulated before:** Cf., for example, the apparition of the monstrous giant Adamastor from the sea, to the jinn in the frame story of the *Nights*. Camoëns, *The Lusiads*, Canto V, trans. William C. Atkinson (Harmondsworth: Penguin, 1952), 128–129. The poem, published in 1572, deals with conflicts with Islam.

21   **'silly Women':** quoted by Khalid Bekhaoui, 'White Wine and Moorish Fancy', in Makdisi/Nussbaum, 154.

Gamal el-Ghitani: *Economist*, May 13, 2010.

world in which we live: Tim Fulford, 'Coleridge and the Oriental Tale', Makdisi/Nussbaum, 213–234.

22   **'reasoned imagination':** Vernant, 'The Reason of Myth' in Vernant, *Myth and Society*, 186–242; Borges, intro. to Bioy Casares, *The Invention of Morel*, 5.

23   **'the necessary angel':** Wallace Stevens, 'Angel Surrounded by Paysans', in *The Collected Poems* (NY: Vintage, 1982), 496–7.

discovery of the East: Borges (1985) 42–57.

unrivalled by any other...text: Makdisi/Nussbaum, (2008), 1.

24   **one image to another:** E. Said, 'Raymond Schwab and the Romance of Ideas', in Said (1983, 1991), pp. 248–267: 252, 259. Schwab (1964), 252.

25   **preeminent travelling text**: Said, 'Travelling Theory' in Said (1983), 226–47.

The Orient in modernity: Amit Chaudhuri, 'The East as a Career' (first published *New Left Review*, 2006), in *Clearing a Space: Reflections on India, Literature and Culture* (London: Peter Lang, 2008), 91.

27 **'...the exterior world':** Franz Roh, 'Magical Realism: Post-Expressionism [1925], in Zamora and Faris, 15–32.

28 **often mock fairy tales:** Cf. 'literary Gothic is really anti-Gothic', as Chris Baldick points out with regard to the famous works of Horace Walpole and Mrs Radcliffe. Chris Baldick, Introduction to *The Oxford Book of Gothic Tales* (Oxford: Oxford University Press, 1992), xi–xxiii; xiii.

Chapter 1: Master of Jinn

36 **Robin Williams:** *Aladdin* [1992] DVD. (USA: Disney, 2008).

grown so richly: See McCown (1922), 1–24; Butler (1996), 104–113; Seymour (1924), 81–94; A. V. Rodriguez, ed., *Leyendas aljamiadas y moriscas sobre personajes biblicos* (Madrid: Editorial Gredos, 1983), 42–49; Torijano (2002); Shalev-Eyni (2006), 145–160; Morton Smith, *Jesus the Magician* (London: Gollancz, 1978), 79–80. The cult of Solomon has drifted ever southwards - he is now incarnated in the Emperor of Abyssinia, the direct descendant of Solomon's son with the Queen of Sheba, according to the beliefs of the Rastafarian Church, which from its beginnings in Jamaica in the 1930s has spread through the world with the Caribbean diaspora. Marcus Garvey prophesied 'Look to Africa when a black king shall be crowned for the day of deliverance is near.' Peter B. Clarke, *Black Paradise: The Rastafarian Movement* (Wellingborough: Aquarian Press, 1986), 34–44.

38 **'...mage of all mages':** Butler (1996), 104–113; Jan M. Ziolkowski, trans., *Solomon and Marcolf: Harvard Studies in Medieval Latin* (Cambridge, Mass and London: Harvard UP, 2008), 16–31.

human mind in certain fields: McCown (1922), 1–24.

39 **'demon stories of East and West':** See 'The Testament of Solomon', ed. and trans. M. R. James (accessed 25/11/10).

The devils include: For a learned (and entertaining) edition of the *Livre des esperitz*, the earliest demonology in French, see Jean-Patrice Boudet, 'Les *Who's who* démonologiques de la Renaissance et leurs ancêtres médiévaux', *Medievales*, 44 (2003), http://medievales.revues. org/document1019.html (accessed: 22/3/11).

harsh and terrible: 'Testament of Solomon', trans. Conybeare, 1898), 117.

to stand up: Ibid., 121.

on a pillar of air: Ibid., 122.

41 **'...his wives turned away his heart':** A nursery rhyme remembers the episode:

> King David and King Solomon
> Led merry, merry lives,
> With many, many lady friends
> And many, many wives

But even here, the verses prefer the picture of virtue:

> But when old age crept over them,
> With many, many qualms,
> King Solomon wrote the Proverbs
> And King David wrote the Psalms.
>
> (James Ball Naylor, attrib.)

41   **Sura 38:** [Koran] trans. Khalidi, 38:31–33: 291–292.

Sura 2: [Koran] trans. Khalidi, 2:101–2, 370.

to the scabrous: Torijano (2002), 192–224; see also Ziolkowski, *Solomon and Marcolf*, 1–50; Malcolm Jones, *The Secret Middle Ages* (Gloucestershire: Sutton, 2002), 122.

42   **Hans Werner Henze:** *L'Upupa und der Triumph der Sohnesliebe (The Hoopoe, or the Triumph of Filial Love)*, 'A German comedy after the Arabian,' commissioned by Salzburg Festival, with Deutsche Oper Berlin, Teatro Real Madrid, and Teatro Massimo Palermo. The work was reprised by Hans Werner Henze in an instrumental piece, *Five Passages for the Queen of Sheba.*

ultimate wise guy: Ziolkowski, *Solomon and Marcolf*, 1–50.

Dante: *The Divine Comedy*, trans. Sinclair, 3: 152–153.

43   **'...at that strange sight.':** Ibid., 3: 484–485; see Peter Dronke, 'The Conclusion of Dante's Commedia', in Dronke (1997), 131–155; 150–151.

the secrets of phenomena: Alison Cornish quotes the disagreement between Thomas Aquinas and Siger of Brabant (who are dancing together harmoniously in Dante's heaven): Siger rejects Aquinas's condemnation of all magical effects, and prefers the explanation from natural science offered by al-Kindi in *De radiis*, that the influence of the stars worked such effects. Quoted in Alison Cornish, 'I miti biblici. La sapienza di Salomone e le arti magiche', in *Mito e poesia*, ed. M. Picone and T. Crivelli (Florence: Cesati, 1999), 391–403: 398; she cites A. Maurer, 'Between Reason and Faith: Siger of Brabant and Pomponazzi on the Magic Arts', *Mediaeval Studies*, 18 (1956): 1–18.

feats of magic attributed: Warner (2008), 17–31.

44   **'destiny itself':** Willemen (1977), 74, quoted in Irwin, 200.

45   **story of the Second Old Man:** ANEnc, 26–29; Lane, 25–30; Bencheikh-Miquel, 'Histoire du deuxième vieillard', 1: 23–26. (I have followed this one in which the brothers are explicitly metamorphosed into female dogs.)

'**...Allah willed it so.**': Mathers/Mardrus, 'The Tale of the Second Sheikh', 1:18–21, 20.

46   '**...if what is said is true**': 'Sayf al-Muluk and Badiat al-Jamal', Bencheikh-Miquel, III: 94–148: 126.

47   **domains for each species:** Amira el-Zein (2009), 117.

a remarkable legal treatise: Badr al-Din al-Sibli, cadi of Tripoli, *Kitab akam al-margan fi ahkam al-gann* (The Book of the hills of coral on the juridical judgements concerning the jinn), in Fred Leemhuis, 'Épouser un jinn? Passé et présent' *Quaderni di Studi Arabi*, 11 (1993), 179–192. Leemhuis found a modern edition (1983) of the book in Cairo, and subsequently others, published in 1988, 1990–91 and more, which led him to conclude that the question of jinn-human relations was still live.

48   **lent a helping hand:** Ibid., 184–185.

of diverse persuasions: Qu'ran, trans. Khalidi, 72: 11, 482 'Some of us are righteous and others less so: we follow different paths.' Qu'ran, trans. Abdel Haleem, 72: 11, 393.

49   '**We work dreadful woe.**': 'Stanzaic Life of Margaret', from the Auchinleck Manuscript, in *Middle English Legends of Women Saints* ed. Sherry L. Reames (Kalamazoo: Medieval Institute 2003), http://www.lib.rochester.edu/camelot/teams/22sr.htm (accessed: 27/9/10). Cited in Weber (1812), 1: xxxi-ii.

'**...fiery wind**': Qur'an, trans. Khalidi, 206; 'The jinn, whose substance is not flesh, but made of "the fire of scorching wind"'. Qur'an, trans. Abdel Haleem, 15: 26–27, 163.

'**...shimmering flame**': Qur'an, trans. Khalidi, 441; 'smokeless fire'. Qur'an, trans. Abdel Haleem, trans. 353.

made of clay: El-Zein (2009), 32. She quotes Qur'an 15: 26–27.

'**circles the world**': 'Story of King Saba', ANEnc, 1:354 ff.

50   '**...took good care**': Qur'an, trans. Khalidi, 263.

'**...crush you unawares?**': Qur'an, trans. Khalidi, 305.

Solomon gives thanks: Qur'an, trans. Khalidi, 305.

'**creature of earth**': Qur'an, trans. Khalidi, 347; Abdel Haleem, 273. Al-Tabari (d. 923), in *Lives of the Prophets*, elaborates the story: Solomon studies the plants growing in the Temple as it is going up and realises that one of them will be the destruction of the building, so he cuts it down and makes the staff on which he leans after he has died. See Shalev-Eyni (2006), 146.

51   '**...burnished with glass**': Qur'an, trans. Khalidi, 307, 'and bared her legs. Solomon explained "It is just a hall paved with glass"', trans. Abdel Haleem, 307.

converts to his God: 'Bilqis visiting Solomon', c. 1530, Iran, from *Assembly of Lovers* (Bodleian Library, Oxford), MS Ouseley Add. 24, f. 1270. I have written before about this episode and the rich folklore about the queen's lower limbs, in Warner (1994); see Chs. 7 and 8, 97–128.

grows whole again: Chelkowski (1975), 82.

This child…: Hugues Le Roux, 'Introduction', in *Magda Queen of Sheba (Kěvbra Nagast),* trans. Le Roux (French) and Mrs John van Vorst (English) (London and New York: Funk & Wagnalls, 1907), 11 ff. The son here is called Bainelekhem, but he is also known more commonly, for instance among the Rastafarians, as Malek.

52   **Solomon's court:** Seymour (1924), 81–94: BL MS 4383, f. 143v, H. in St John Philby, *The Queen of Sheba* (London: Quartet, 1981), 67.

depicting devils: See Luther Link, *The Devil: A Mask without a Face* (London: Reaktion, 1995), 63–65; also Warner (1999), Ch. 11, 246–261.

agents of the supernatural: Some Muslim theologians found manifold classes of jinn and arranged them in hierarchies, Al-Masudi in the tenth century, for example, listed 31 different types. See El-Zein (2009), 139–145.

spots of defilement: Leemhuis, 'Épouser un jinn?', 185.

53   **charms of other kinds:** For example, in the Sackler Museum, Cambridge, Mass., a haematite cameo shows Solomon on horseback overcoming a female demon, with a Greek prayer on reverse. In a later version in bronze, the horseman becomes St Sisinnos. Probably from Syria/Palestine 6–7th c. Later images of emperors spearing their prone enemy were adopted as amulets because of the resemblance.

Chapter 2: Riding the Wind: The Flying Carpet I

59   **'gloomiest of travelogues':** Andras Hamori, 'An allegory from the *Arabian Nights*: The City of Brass', in Marzolph (2006), 283–297: 283.

vivid expanse of territory: see Gerhardt, pp. 195–235

myth of origin: Kilito (1992) 86–103. 'La ville de cuivre', Bencheikh/ Miquel II: 562–566; Lane III: 556–578, gives a more elaborated translation.

61   **no Alexander:** Kay Ka'us in the *Shahnama*, or Persian *Book of Kings*, by Firdausi, also contrives an early ascent by fixing raw meat above in his prototype vehicle and harnessing birds of prey so that they pursue the prey and lift him. See Kwiatkowski, *The Eckstein Shahnama:* no 12. f.129V: 61.

62   **'earthquake and thunder':** Seymour (1924), 85.

'…vanished people': Ibid., 86.

'…woven…by the Jinns': Ibid., 89.

human craft: 'Cité de cuivre' (copper) in Bencheikh/Miquel, not *airain* (brass). (In French 'cuivre' is also used for brass.)

Iram of the High Columns: 'The Dawn', in Qur'an, trans. Khalidi, 89: 6–14:509.

63   **City of Labtayt:** ANEnc I: 265–6 Bencheikh/Miquel I: 1029–32.
    'Islam would then develop': Miquel, notes, Bencheikh/Miquel, 1: 1203.

64   **'Spring of Chosroes':** Philippe-Alain Michaud, 'Mouvements de surfaces', in Michaud (2006), 178.
    rich red ground of the rug: Griffin Lewis (1920), between pp.318 and 319.
    merchants in hats: 'Portuguese' Carpet, Persia (?), 17th century, wool, (Gulbenkian Museum, Lisbon) inv. no. T.99. http://www.museu.gulbenkian.pt/obra.asp?num=t99&nuc=a4&lang=en (accessed 1/5/11)
    Charles II's entry: Jenny Uglow, *A Gambling Man: Charles II and the Restoration* (London: Faber & Faber, 2010), 49.

66   **'The Persian Carpet':** in Denys Johnson Davies, trans., *Arabic Short Stories* (California: University of California Press, 1994) 106–110; see also Hanan al-Shaykh, *The Locust and the Bird: My Mother's Story* (London: Bloomsbury, 2011).
    'itself the house': Sergio Bettini, "Poetica del tappeto orientale" [1962–63], from his *Tempo e Forma. Scritti 1935–1977*, ed. Cavalletti; in Riegl (1998), 224–242.

67   **mobile home:** Riegl (1998), 224–242. Quoted by Philippe-Alain Michaud, notes towards an exhibition about oriental carpets and cinema, kindly lent by the author.

68   **'The snake...surrounds the world':** [Alexander], 123.
    tumbles to his death: S. Francesca Romana, built in the Forum on the spot where this happened, displays a stone marked by Simon Magus's fall.

69   **Gerione:** [Dante], trans. Sinclair I: 214–5.

Chapter 3: A Tapestry of Great Price: The Flying Carpet II

74   **Epigraph:** Marcel Proust, *A la Recherche du temps perdu,* trans. Scott Moncrieff and Terence Kilmartin, 12 vols (Paris: Gallimard, 1954), I: 16; (London: Hogarth) I: 4. [Moncrieff has 'the world will go hurtling out of orbit'.]

75   **improbable coincidences:** 'Conte du Vizir Nur ad-Din et de son frère Shams Ad-Din', Bencheikh/Miquel 1: 158–208, 1174–1177.
    bit of furniture: ANE, 829. Jonathan Scott, 'Story of the Labourer and the Flying Chair', in Scott (1800), 7–37. See Ballaster (2005), 332–343.

76   **'La Chatte...l'abeille':** D'Aulnoy, Contes I: 525–60, 243–270; II: 163–214.
    'The Frog Princess': in Afanase'ev, (1973), 119–123.

77   **'The Story of Janshah':** ANEnc I: 238–41, 'The Tale of the Fair Sad Youth,' Mathers/Mardrus, 3 : 250–269: 283–4.

bliss together: 'Histoire de Baibars et les capitaines de police', Mathers/Mardrus, 8:1; Mardrus took the story from Guillaume Spitta Bey, *Contes arabes modernes* (Leiden E. J. Brill and Paris: Maisonneuve, 1884); see 'The Eighth Captain's Tale', ANEnc, I: 139.

78 **'...always afternoon':** Dr Edward Rees, 'Rosalie Street and "The Pictures"', *Manchester Guardian*, 26 Feb. 1913. I am most grateful to Karin Littau for this reference.

'Whole New World': The song was awarded a Grammy and an Oscar in 1992.

secret sect: Abidi, Azhar, 'The Secret History of the Flying Carpet,' first published in *Meanjin*, 63:2 (2004). http://secrethistoryflyingcarpet. blogspot.com (accessed 16/4/11). Abidi was interviewed and the story featured in Cathy Fitzgerald's programme for the BBC World Service *The Magic Carpet Flight Manual* (24 Sept. 2010). http://www.bbc. co.uk/worldservice/documentaries/2010/09/100923-magic-carpet-flight-manual.shtml (accessed 16/4/10). See also Jorge Luis Borges, 'Tlön, Uqbar, Orbis Tertius' in Borges (2000), 27–43.

79 **Russian astronaut training centre:** Jem Finer and Ansuman Biswas, *Zero Genie* (2006) *http://www.zerogenie.org/zerogenie.html* (accessed 1/5/11). I am very grateful to Jem Finer for giving me a copy of this work to view and discussing it with me.

women's pool: Beckford, ed. Lonsdale, *Vathek* (1998), 58.

80 **a different dénouement:** see Peter Brooks, *Reading for the Plot: Design and Intention in Narrative* (Cambridge, Mass: Harvard UP, 1992)

'...pattern upon another': Vladimir Nabokov, *Speak, Memory: An Autobiography Revisited* (London: Penguin, 2000), 125.

'... some entreaty': Abdelkebir Khatibi 'O tapete no imaginario do oriente' in Alaoui et al, (2005), 40–49: 41; see also idem and Ali Amahan (1995).

81 **figurative elements:** Connoisseurs of oriental carpets, when they began classifying them, borrowed from Italian Renaissance and Tudor paintings where they appear and add aura to their subjects – they can be seen unfolded over tables or unrolled under the throne of a Madonna and Child or underfoot in portraits of kings and queens, potentates and aristocratic children. Scholars gave one pattern the name 'Holbein' after the oriental rug which covers the table in Hans Holbein's painting *The Ambassadors*, 1533 (National Gallery, London) and another pattern the generic name 'Lotto' after a carpet in Lorenzo Lotto's 'The Alms of St Anthony," Church of SS. Giovanni & Paolo, Venice, 1542.

functions and characters recur: Propp (1968) 20–21.

'...fabulous vicissitudes': Italo Calvino, 'La mappa delle metafore', in Calvino, *Sulla Fiaba* (1996), 129–146: 138.

poetic metre: Khatibi, 'O tapete', 40–46.

'...towards the outside.': Cristina Campo, in 'Notti', from *Gli imperdonabili* (Milan: Adelphi, 1987), 67.

82   **Nureyev's tomb:** The artist Mark Wallinger includes a photograph in 'Apotheosis': see Wallinger (2009), exh. cat., 73–77.

birth and upbringing: The family later grew up just this side of the Urals, in Ufa, the capital of Bashkiria, which became the Soviet Republic Bashkortostan, now part of the Russian Federation. See Julie Kavanagh, *Rudolf Nureyev: The Life* (London: Penguin, Fig Tree, 2007), 2–4.

Orientalising scenarios: *Diaghilev, Les Saisons Russes XXI*, London Coliseum, 12–17 April 2011), performed reconstructions of the original productions, including *Schéhérazade* by Rimsky-Korsakov, with designs by Léon Bakst. Several members of the Ballets Russes are buried in the Russian cemetery too.

romantic ballets: Wallinger (2009), 73–77; the origins of the libretto of *Swan Lake* are confused, though a story by Musäus from his collection of German folk tales is usually given. Interconnections with the *Nights* have not been sufficiently acknowledged.

83   **The dancer's tomb:** I went to the Cemetery of Ste-Geneviève-des-Bois with Betty and Omero Aridjis on All Souls' Day, 2009. It was a most inspiring excursion and I am very grateful to them for organising it. The grave was designed by Ezio Fraterio, the Italian stage designer most famous for his collaborations with Giorgio Strehler.

Chapter 4: The Worst Witch

93   **a kind of virtue:** Bencheikh/Miquel, I: 54–64, 1170–1.

94   **religious tolerance:** See Nabil Matar, 'Christians in *The Arabian Nights*', in Makdisi/Nussbaum (2008), 131–152.

Chapter 5: Egyptian Attitudes

97   **'... in the future.':** Herodotus (1983), 152–160.

98   **Christian wisdom and ethics:** Joscelyn Godwin, *Athanasius Kircher* (London: Thames & Hudson, 1979), 19, 56–59, 64–65; idem, *Athanasius Kircher's Theatre of the World* (London: Thames & Hudson, 2009), 59–80.

Emanuel Schikaneder: The 2010/11 production of *Die Zauberflöte* (*The Magic Flute*) by David McVicar with designs by John Macfarlane at the Royal Opera House, London, emphasised the mythological theme of solar and lunar divinities in conflict, and identified Sarastro with Ra/Osiris and the Queen of the Night with Isis by hanging a huge golden sun disc and a vast eye over his realm and a crescent moon over hers; see also Nicholas Till, 'Freemasonry and the Enlightenment' in Royal Opera House, *Die Zauberflöte* programme (2010/11), 19–24.

Egyptomania: Luckhurst, 'The Mummy's Curse: A Study in Rumour', *Critical Quarterly* 52: 3 (2010): 6–22.

costumes to match: Dadswell (2007), 3–24, discusses the orientalism of performing magic with an emphasis on its Indian, rather than Egyptian or Arab, character, but she provides connections to Egypt's great reputation.

papyri and ancient legends: E. Wallis Budge is the author of, for example, *Amulets and Talismans* (New York: New Hyde Park, 1961).

sand fairy: Julia Briggs, *A Woman of Passion: The Life of E. Nesbit 1858–1924* (London: Hutchinson, 1987), 245–253.

'…eating faeces': 'Journey through the Afterlife', exh.cat. Raymond O. Faulkner, trans., Carol Andrews, ed., *The Ancient Egyptian Book of the Dead* [1972, 1984] (London: British Museum Press, 2010), 36; 80; 170; 189. (News on television and occasionally photographs in newspapers casually include unburied corpses within shot, while the reporter stands and speaks, ignoring them.)

99   **Pharaoh's magicians:** Also known as Iannes and Jambres, or Ianne and Mamre, they are not named in Exodus, but in 2 Timothy 3: 8 (as Jannes and Jambres).

'…do good in his life.': BL Cotton Tiberius B.V. *Astrological Miscellany, including the Marvels of the East (991–1016)*, (PI fl. 87); repro. in Warburg Institute Photographic Collection.

literature of the region: Margaret Anne Doody, *The True Story of the Novel* (New Brunswick, NJ: Rutgers UP, 1997), 29.

101   **tales Shahrayad tells:** Eg 'The City of Brass'; 'Alexander and a Certain Tribe of Poor Folk' ANEnc I: 88–89.

***Romance of Alexander*:** Stoneman, Intro. In [Alexander], pp. 1–27 discusses the difficulties of dating the Romance.

is conceived: Ibid., 37–44.

102   **'…experience in the magic art':** Ibid., 37.

103   **'…spirits in the night-time.':** Virgil; *Aeneid*, Bk. IV, lines 558ff. (1969), 112. Traditionally, in illustrations of Virgil, for example, she is assumed to be the same person; however the transition from the distant Massylian to the actual officiant at the pyre takes place without explanation.

black Sibilla Libyca: Peter Dronke, 'Hermes and the Sibyls: Continuations and Creations', in Peter Dronke, *Intellectuals and Poets in Medieval Europe* (Rome: Edizioni di Storia e Letteratura, 1992), 219–44, esp. 223–6; Warner, Marina (2004) 66–70; McGrath (2005).

104   **For 'Aethiopia':** see McGrath (1996).

pugnacious defences of magic: Apuleius of Madauros, *Pro se de magia*, 2 vols, intro. Vincent Hunink (Amsterdam: J. C. Gieben, 1997); http://www.let.kun.nl/v.hunink/documents/apuleius-apol-intro.

htm#a1(2) (accessed 27/11/10); Apuleio (1992); Marchesi, 'Un processo di magia nel secondo secolo dopo Cristo' [1955], ibid., 155–79.

105   **'...he who conjures phantoms':** Apuleio, *Della magia*, 79.

Apuleius's treatise: Marchesi, 'Un processo', 155–79.

...this irrepressible book: Apuleius (1950).

106   **'restless dance':** See Tambiah (1990).

'not of Infidels, but Atheists': Thomas Browne, *Religio Medici* (Oxford: Clarendon Press, 1909) *http://penelope.uchicago:edu/relmed/relmed.html* (accessed 29/4/11), 30. See Michael Hunter, ed., *The Occult Laboratory: Magic, Science and Second Sight in Late 17th Century Scotland*, (Woodbridge: Boydell Press, 2001); also Marina Warner, intro. to Kirk (2007), vii–1.

108   **examined and edited now:** See Professor Rob Iliffe (dir.), *The Newton Project* (University of Sussex, 2011); http://www.newton-project.sussex.ac.uk/prism.php?id=1 (accessed 2/5/11).

A famous watercolour: Paul Hulton, *America 1585: The Complete Drawings of John White* (North Carolina and London: British Museum, 1984), 7–38, Plate 49.

In 2007, the image was catalogued...: 'John White, British/American *Watercolour of Algonquian Shaman in Stylized Pose*, 1585–1593.' See *http://www.britishmuseum.org/research/search the collection* (accessed 29/4/11).

109   **'... they find to be true':** Thomas Harriott, *The published account of A true and brief report of the Newfoundland of Virginia by Thomas Harriot (1590)* in Hulton, *America,* 1585, Fig.15, p. 117 (spelling modernised).

111   **'the Ripley scroll':** George Ripley, *Rotulum hieroglyphicum G. Riplaei Equitis Aurati.* Copy of a Copy made in 1588, of the 'Emblematicall scrowle: supposed to be invented by Geo. Ripley', c.1600, Wellcome Library. MS 692. See Betty Jo Teeter Dobbs, *Alchemical Death and Resurrection: The Significance of Alchemy in the Age of Newton* (Washington, DC: Smithsonian Institute Library, 1990).

112   **'... prophete and nigromancier':** Richard Higden, trans., *Polychron,* BL Harl. Ms. VI.19, *c.* 1425 or 1475.

'Through Nigromancie': Richard Robinson, *The Reward of Wickednesse: Discoursing the . . . abuses of wicked and ungodlye worldelinges, etc.* (London: W. Williamson, 1574). I owe this reference to Steven Connor who discussed uses of nigromancer or necromancer with me most helpfully. Private corresp., Nov. 2002.

uses of darkness and light: Cf. Duke: 'If virtue no delighted beauty lack/Your son-in-law is far more fair than black.' (*Othello*, I. iii. 289–290)

113   **'...out of warrant':** Brabantio repeats the accusation of witchcraft to the Duke (ibid. I.iii. 60–61).

resonates with 'gypsy': Mark Netzloff, '"Counterfeit Egyptians" and Imagined Borders: Jonson's 'The Gypsies Metamorphosed'", ELH, 68, No 4 (Winter, 2001), 763–793; Erwin Pokorny, 'Das Zigeunerbild in der altdeutschen Kunst: Ethnographisches Interesse und Antiziganismus', in Andreas Tacke and Stefan Heinz, eds., *Menschenbilder Bietrage zur Altdeutschen Kunst* (Petersberg: Michael Imhof, 2011, 97–318. I am most grateful to Dr Elizabeth McGrath for these references.

Bizet's vision of Spain: José F. Colmiero, '*Carmen*' and the Construction of Oriental Spain', *Comparative Literature* 54 No 2 (Spring, 2002), 127–144.

...not least by herself: Webster, John, *The White Devil* V:i; in *The Selected Plays of John Webster and John Ford*, ed. G.B. Harrison (London: J. M. Dent, 1969), 68–70

repatriate Africans: See Gretchen Gerzina, *Black London: Life before Emancipation* (London: John Murray, 1995).

114   **his mother's image:** ANEnc I:244–5; Bencheikh/Miquel, 2:651–687; Mathers/Mardrus, 4:70–111.

Dr. Caligari: See Daniel Pick, *Svengali's Web: The Alien Enchanter in Modern Culture* (New Haven and London: Yale UP, 2000), 127–165.

'...read in the Bible.': Lane (1836), 263.

115   ***kihana* (divination):** Savage-Smith, Introduction, in Savage-Smith, ed., *Magic and Divination in Early Islam*, xiii–xliv: xiii.

Tree of knowledge: Toni Morrison, *Playing in the Dark: Whiteness and the Literary Imagination* (London: Picador, 1993); I give examples of such visitors in the history of Victorian spiritualism. See Chapter 21: 'Exotic Visitors, Multiple Lives' in *Phantasmagoria, 277–84*. One of the most significant was W.B. Yeats's 'spirit visitor', the historical figure, Leo Africanus, a Spanish-Arab scholar, traveller and poet who became celebrated in sixteenth-century Italy: he was singularly helpful in lifting Yeats's writer's block.

Chapter 6: Magians and Dervishes

127   **fairy or folktale:** Chraïbi (2008), 11.

when he does not comply: 'Aladdin' contains a non-sequitur: when Aladdin will not give the magician the lamp before he has climbed out of the cave, 'the African magician' loses his temper and leaves, without the lamp. In 'Hasan of Basra', which it closely resembles, Hasan has already thrown down the herbs needed for the magic elixir, so the magician has accomplished his wicked plan.

De Quincey: Jorges Luis Borges, 'The Thousand and One Nights' in (1985), 42–57: 55–56.

fairy romances: The Story of Janshah', or 'The Tale of the Fair Sad

Youth', ANEnc 1:238–44; Mathers/Mardrus 3:269–85; for Sayf al-Muluk, ANEnc 1:362–4.

129 **'Gharib and Ajib'** : see André Miquel, *Un Conte des Mille et une Nuits: Gharib et Ajib* (Paris: Flammarion, 1977); see ANEnc I:193–6.
Persian magians: ANEnc II:629.
'Jullanar the Sea-Born': ANEnc I:248–51; Bencheikh/Miquel 3:55–93.

131 **Zobeide:** 'The Eldest Lady's Tale', ANEnc I:174–5; ANE 125–133; Bencheikh/Miquel I:129–38; Lyons I:106–113.
'...Muhammad's revelations': ANEnc I:196.

134 **'...a full beard':** Bede, quoted in McGrath (*Rubens Bulletin*, 2008), 93–4
Individual 'Moors': McGrath, ibid. Peter Paul Rubens, *Mulay Ahmad, c.* 1609. Museum of Fine Arts, Boston. Rubens, *Adoration of the Magi, c.* 1624. Koninklijk Museum voor Schone Kunsten, Antwerp.

136 **'...recognition by the Gentiles':** McGrath, ibid.

137 **'...Sufis of Isfahan':** Pétis de la Croix, *Les mille et un Jour*, 5 vols (Lyons: Frerès Bruyset, 1717), 1: 2. (2006), 331.
the artist...Vanmour: Duncan Bull, Introduction in Eveline Sint Nicolaas et al., *Jean-Baptiste Vanmour: An Eyewitness to the Tulip Era* (Amsterdam: Kocbank, 2003).
'...whirls out of piety,': Jean-Baptiste Vanmour, 'Air sur lequel tournent les Derviches de Pera', in *Recueil de cent estampes représéntant différentes nations du Levant* (Paris: Sr Le Hay, 1714). Another copy belonged to H.S Ashbee the artist and designer.

138 **first edition:** Jean-Baptiste Vanmour, *Explication des cent estampes qui réprésentent différentes nations du Levant* (Paris: Jacques Collombat, 1715).
fuller commentary: 'Il y a d'autres Devichs [*sic*] qui passent de Pays en Pays, & qui mènent souvent une vie libertine. Il en vient beaucoup à Constantinople, de Perse & des Indes. Le Bonnet de Dervich est un bon passeport pour aller partout où l'on veut; pour s'insinuer même à la table des Grands, qui n'oseraient les en chasser, pour ne point paraître superbes . . . quoy que leur présence leur soit souvent incommode.' Ibid., 12.
'...which is its principle': 'La plupart des Derviches Indiens & Persans adorent le Feu, par conséquent le Soleil qui en est le principe. Ils font toute sorte de figures dans le Monde; & on se trompe presque toujours dans l'estime ou le mépris qu'on fait de leur personne.' Ibid., 24.
'something of the divine': Ibid., 26.

139 **'... mere abstractions.':** Godwin (1834), 189–190.

Chapter 7: Dream Knowledge

143   **'...most famous poets of her time.':** Bencheikh/Miquel I: 35.

144   **only one she has not told:** Kilito (2010), 67–70.

    '...the bard's memory.: Derek Walcott, 'A frowsty fragrance', *NYRB* (15 June 2000), 57–61.

    Ghazoul (1996), 26.

    '...lights in the distance.': Calvino (2009), 51.

    '...foot of the alcove.': ANE: 17; Galland I: 44.

    Shahriyar never sleeps: Kilito (2010), 20.

146   **Adolphe Lalauze (1881–2):** see Irwin (2011), 71, PL. 57.

    Kay Nielsen (1917): see Mathers/Mardrus 1: frontispiece; Irwin (2011), 141–2, Pl. 115.

148   **who gains a fortune**: in 'The Story of Two Dreamers' Borges attributes it to the Arab historian al-Ishaqi, and cites Richard Burton, Night 351. Borges (1998), 56–57.

    both of them have the same dream: ANEnc I:312; 'Conte de al-Mutawakkil et de Mahbuba', Bencheikh/Miquel II: 70–2.

    on oracles: Michael Wood, *The Road to Delphi: The Life and Afterlife of Oracles* (London: Chatto & Windus, 2004).

149   **Buluqiya and Hasib**: *'The Adventures of Buluqiya',* ANEnc I: 130–2; Mardrus/Mathers 3:251–292; Bencheikh (1988), 177–244; Stephanie Dalley, 'Gilgamesh in the *Arabian Nights'*.

    '...three beautiful doves': Mardrus/Mathers 3: 278–9.

150   **'Second Sight':** See Kirk (2007), 7–29, 30–63.

    ANEnc I: 392–3.

151   **'...transitory window.'** Proust, *À la Recherche du temps perdu*, 1: 20–21; Proust, Moncrieff, trans., et al., *In Search of Lost Time*, 1: 8.

152   **Something I need to know.:** Stephenson, *Possession: Jung's Comparative Anatomy of the Psyche*, pp.42–71.

153   **Jackson Pollock:** Steph Polcari 'Contexte, Influences, Références', in *Jackson Pollock et le Chamanisne'*, 11–16, 25. Pollock undertook Jungian analysis intermittently, 1938–43.

    Russian empire's march eastwards: Johannes Scheffer, *History of the Lapps: A most true description of their origin, superstition, magical rites, nourishment, culture, and trade of the Lapps, etc. etc.'* (Frankfurt, 1673). *Shaman* is first cited in 1698 in the *OED*, designating a healer from the many nomadic peoples living in the regions on the outer perimeter of the Arctic circle in steppes and forests of the subpolar regions from Lapland to Mongolia to Alaska; the etymology is uncertain but it probably enters English via Ger. *Schamane*.

    '...''safety value'' of the clan.': See 'A Yakut Shaman', in Anatole Lewitsky, 'Shamanism', in *The College of Sociology (1937–39)*, ed. Denis

Hollier, trans. Betsy Wing (Minneapolis: Univ. Minnesota Press, 1988), 248–261, 255.

154 **current familiarity:** When *The Rite of Spring* was first choreographed by Nijinksy for the Ballets Russes in Paris in 1913, it included the figure of a priest who presides over the frenzied sacrifice of the Chosen Maiden. The dance was a re-enactment - fanciful and wishful - of primitive, authentic Russian culture. In 1984, when Martha Graham revised the original, she saw through to the mythical core of the piece; herself enthralled by atavistic symbolism, she knew she would bring its scandalous fertility cult drama closer to a more recognisable North American tradition by using the Russian term, 'shaman', for the celebrant of the rites. See, *Diaghilev* exh. cat. I am grateful to Rosella Simonari for her account of Martha Graham's *Rite of Spring, And Dance Shaped the Wor(l)d: Relationship Between Dance and Literature in the Work of Martha Graham* in her Ph.D., Univ. Essex, 2011.

155 **'...as if I were breaking apart...':** Barack Obama, *Dreams from My Father: A Story of Race and Inheritance* [1995] (New York: Three Rivers Press, 2004), 372.

writers' methods: Naddaff (1991), 13–57.

156 **uses of performative speech:** Judith Butler, *Excitable Speech: A Politics of the Performative* (New York and London: Routledge, 1997), discusses the reverberations in contemporary definitions of 'hate speech', for example.

157 **'In the Penal Colony.':** Kafka (1999), 140–67.

'...impose him on reality': Jorge Luis Borges, 'The Circular Ruins', in *Ficciones*; trans. Anthony Bonner (New York: Grove Press, 1994), 52–58: 53.

'...dreamed him asleep.': Ibid., 55.

158 **'...dreaming him':** Ibid., 57–8.

'...boy's soul out of them.': Lewitsky, 'Shamanism', 248–61, 253. The Collège de Sociologie was founded by Georges Bataille and Roger Caillois. Caillois was visiting Buenos Aires in 1939 and so found himself there when Paris fell to the Nazis; he spent the war years in Argentina in close contact with Borges and his friends, the Ocampo sisters, Silvina and Victoria. The latter was the editor of *Sur*, the literary magazine which published Borges, and Caillois's lover and patron. Lewitsky was shot as a member of the Resistance in 1942.

'...already halfway gone.': Ibid., 254.

159 **'...thing in his dream!.':** Lewis Carroll, *Through the Looking Glass*, in *Alice's Adventures in Wonderland* and *Through the Looking-Glass*, [1871], ed. Hugh Haughton, (London: Penguin, 1998), Ch. 4, 164–5.

Part III: Active Goods

161 **Epigraph:** Jan Švankmajer, *The Complete Short Films*, DVD (2007); idem, *Decalogue* (1999).

Chapter 8: 'Everything You Desire to Know about the East...'

163 **Epigraph:** Hugo van Hofmannsthal, 'Letter', in *The Lord Chandos Letter and Other Writings,* ed and trans. Joel Rotenberg (New York: *NYRB*, 2005), 117–128: 125, 128.

164 **'...hearing them speak.':** Antoine Galland, 'Avertissement', in Galland/Sermain I: 21–22.

'...manners of orientals.': Ibid., p. 21.

'...manners here.': Mary Wortley Montagu, 'Letter to Lady Mar, 10 March 1718', in Montagu (1994), 118; Ballaster, *Fables* (2005b), 65–90, 179–192.

166 **'Thing Theory':** Brown (2001), 1–22.

'... subject-object relation.': Ibid, 4.

167 **Gentile Bellini:** He may have painted the beautiful if faded portrait of the Sultan Mehmet II in the National Gallery, London. It is only attributed to him now. See http://www.nationalgallery.org.uk/paintings/attributed-to-gentile-bellini-the-sultan-Mehmet-ii (accessed 11/4/11).

tapestry weavers: Coecke's wife Mayken Verhulst later made a remarkable album of woodcuts from the drawings he brought back, which depict busy scenes, packed with typically down-to-earth details of Turkish table manners and toilette (*Les Moeurs et fachons de faire des Turcz*, 1553); these prints come closest to Lorck's enterprise.

On Lorck see: [Lorck] (2009); Warner (2010), 15–17.

168 **water supplies:** These prints appeared eventually in a suite known as 'The Turkish Publication', which was published in 1626, nearly forty years after Lorck's death: [Lorck] (2009), Vol.3.

'...booties from the combat': [Lorck] (2009) 1.116.

areas of sensibility.: Borges proposes that once Kafka had appeared he created retrospectively a recognisable family group of like-minded sensibilities across time and geography. See 'Kafka and His Precursors', in Borges (2000), 234–6.

170 **'...weird and sinister.':** Peter Ward-Jackson, 'Some Rare Drawings by Melchior Lorichs in the Collection of Mr John Evelyn of Wotton, and now at Stonor Park, Oxfordshire', *Connoisseur*, 135: 544 (March 1955), 83–93: 87, 90.

172 **portraits of Suleiman:** It was enough to recreate afterwards two different prints, each of them extraordinarily impressive, revealing the artist's under-used capacity for psychological insight: a head and shoulder portrait of Suleiman, and the full-length figure. (It is a shame

that the painted version, which Lorck later sent to the Emperor Maximilian II, has vanished.) Suleiman's mausoleum stood near another for his Sultana, Roxelana, who had begun life as a slave, and to whom he wrote some blazing poems.

artists condense images: 'At brande Frederik 2. Om Melchior Lorcks kobberstik-portræt a Frederik 2', *SMK Art Journal*, 2006: 22–35, trans. English on website of Statens Museum für Kunst, Copenhagen.

illusionistic verismo: Cf. The exhibition *The Sacred Made Real*, (National Gallery, London, 2010).

Prospect of Constantinople: The full reference in the Leiden Library catalogue is: *Byzantium sive Constantineopolis.* [Door] Melchior Lorichs. [Constantinopel/Wenen, 1559 [1561(?)] – (BPL 1758); reproduced in facsimile in [Lorck] (2009), 4. See Marco Iuliano, 'Melchior Lorck's Constantinople in the European Context', in [Lorck] (2009), 4: 25–60: 51–60.

173   **blazons of scripture:** See Mia Mochizuki, *The Netherlandish Image after Iconoclasm 1566–1672: Material Religion in the Dutch Golden Age* (Burlington, VT: Ashgate, 2008).

174   *A Song of...Antichrist:* This was written and printed separately, not to accompany the engravings.

plight...under the ottomans: Erik Fischer, Lorck's editor, points out that no prisoners fared well then, and calls the work 'larmoyante' (elsewhere he describes it as 'slightly hypocritical').

'gruesome and evil.': This edition of 1574 was known in a single copy, which went up in flames during the Allied bombing of Hamburg, known as Operation Gomorrah; [Lorck] (2009), 1: 124.

'iconoclash': See Bruno Latour et al, *Iconoclash. Beyond the Image Wars in Science, Religion and Art* (Cambridge, Mass.: MIT Press; Germany: ZKM Karlsruhe, 2002).

'...would restrain me.': Melchior Lorck: 'An Autobiographical Letter', written on Jan 1 1563, *Melchior Lorck in Turkey,* Copenhagen, 1990, p. 13. This is a better translation; see [Lorck] (2009), I:xx, for a 'paraphrase'.

175   **envision the stories:** Lorraine Daston and Peter Galison explore, *in extenso*, the ambition and the failure of the different claims to scientific objectivity in *Objectivity* (New York: Zone Books/MIT Press, 2007).

178   **'...made to talk.':** Daston, 'Speechless', in (2004), 20.

'... they are enlisted.': Ibid., 14–15.

formidable team: see [*Description*] in *Abbreviations*; also Laissus (1998) and Grigsby (2002).

179   **Mme de St Morien:** I have not been able to find anything more so far on the women artists and engraver working on the *Description*.

180   **For Edward W. Lane:** Ahmed (1978); Irwin (2004), 23–8.

182   **storytellers in Cairo:** Lane (1836), Chapters XXII-XXIII; Ahmed (1978), 195.

    very expensive: The Arabic manuscript Lane worked with is now in the Cambridge University Library.

    William Harvey: Jenny Uglow, *Nature's Engraver: A Life of Thomas Bewick* (London: Faber & Faber, 2006), 345–350; Irwin (2011), pp. 31, 38–44. Ahmed (1978), 144.

183   **'...or in China.':** Lane, Preface to *Arabian Nights*, 1: viii; quoted in Ahmed (1978), 128.

    '...no trace of imagination': MacDonald (1900), 167; Ahmed (1978), 165–166.

    reality bodily before us: *Dublin Review*, 8 (Feb. 1840), 127; Ahmed (1978), 145.

184   **'...an Eastern tale.':** Caracciolo (2004). Scott in turn 'derives from' Richard Hole (1797), where Hole compares Sinbad's relation with the *Odyssey* to the resemblance of a Saracenic building to a Greek temple.

185   **'...year of 1842.':** Gautier (2003), 11. (My translation)

186   **'...trembling shoulders.':** ibid, 39.

187   **'...for the sewers.':** *Edinburgh Review*, 164 (July 1886), 166; quoted in Ahmed (1978), 163.

    Albert Letchford, Irwin (2011), 102–3, Pls. 58, 68–72, 164.portfolio (1897), The Arcadian Library.

189   **Claudius as CEO:** *Hamlet*, dir. David Birkin, Old Fire Station, Oxford (1998). On historical *anachronism*: See Michael Neill, introduction, *Antony and Cleopatra* (1994), pp. 29–67.

Chapter 9: The Thing-World of the *Arabian Nights*

195   **Epigraph:** Ursula Marx et al., eds, Esther Leslie, trans., 'Scrappy Paperwork', in *Walter Benjamin's Archive: Images, Texts, Signs,* (London and New York: Verso, 2007), 45.

    through the pages of a book: The tale of the poisoned book is told with variations by Alexandre Dumas in *La Reine Margot* (1845). He dramatises a legend that the queen coated a book with arsenic intending to kill her husband, but her son opened the book instead.

197   **continuing to speak:** The stories of St Edmund, St Kenelm, St Osyth and St Sidwell in England, St Denis in France, St Melor and St Winifred in Celtic territory, preserve the pattern and strengthen the link between legend and folklore. Beatrice White, 'A Persistent Paradox', *Folklore*, 83:2 (Summer 1972), 122–31: 123. cf. *The Divine Comedy: Inferno*, Canto 28, 121–3.

    not quite a thing: see Bill Brown, 'Reification, Reanimation, and the American Uncanny', *Critical Inquiry*, 32:2 (Winter 2006), 175 ff.

sign of a fortune-teller: Daniel Defoe, *A Journal of Plague Year* (London: 1840), 54.

198 **'...of the playground.':** S.T. Coleridge, 'The Friend', in B.E. Rooke, ed., *The Collected Works of STC*, Bollingen Series 75 (London, 1969), **'..thrall over him':** Ballaster (2005), 360–5.

199 **'Things quicken.':** Brown, 'Reification,' 175.

luxury hotel: It is called Peri Palas - every name in this tale reverberates with a delighted self-reflexiveness about the genre of fabulous storytelling (the heroine's name sounds like Perrault).

'...out of the bathroom.': Byatt (1995), 190–1.

201 **Grimm Brothers' stories:** For example, 'The Magic Table, the Gold Donkey, and the Club in the Sack', in *The Grimm Reader*, trans. and ed. Maria Tatar (New York: Norton, 2010), 113–125.

Russian Fairy Tales: Afanase'ev is usually credited with pioneering these records of the tradition, but in fact he combed earlier field collectors' works, and, like Italo Calvino later in his corresponding enterprise, *Fiabe italiane* (1956), re-voiced oral folk material. When Roman Jakobson made a tally of stories he considered unique to the Russian repertory, he decided 30 per cent of them did not appear in Western European tradition. Some of these, such as 'Prince Ivan', 'The Firebird and the Gray Wolf' and 'Koschey the Deathless' were interpreted by the Ballets Russes. See Afanase'ev (1973), 612–620.

202 **besom as she goes:** See 'Baba Yaga', ibid., 363–5. See also review essay, Marina Warner, 'Witichines' on Dubravka Ugrešic, *Baba Yaga Laid an Egg* (Edinburgh: Canongate, 2009), *LRB*, 31:16 (27 Aug. 2009), 23–4.

203 **'tournament of value':** Appadurai, 'Introduction: Commodities and the Politics of Value', in Appadurai (1986), 21–2.

204 **'Playing is reality'.** D.W Winnicott, *Playing and Reality* [1971] (London: Routledge, 2006), 38–64; see Warner 'Out of an Old Toy Chest', *Journal of Aesthetic Education*, 43: 2 (Summer 2009), 3–18; also Warner, cur., *Only Make-Believe,* exh. cat., 4–19.

'...to the collective.': Susan Stewart, *On Longing: Narratives of the Miniature, the Gigantic, the Souvenir, the Collection* (Durham, NC and London: Duke UP, 1993), 173.

'...animate things.': See Victoria Nelson's original and inspired study, *The Secret Life of Puppets*.

'...tell *their* stories.': Svankmajer, *Decalogue*, see note to epigraph above, p. 163.

205 **'...a corpse out of him.':** Simone Weil, 'The Iliad: Poem of Force', in Simone Weil and Rachel Bespaloff, *War and the Iliad*, trans. Mary McCarthy, intro. Christopher Benfey (New York: 2005), 3.

206 ***eidola:*** Daston (2004) 12–24. Kenneth Gross has followed his 1992

study *The Dream of the Moving Statue* with *Puppet: An Essay on Uncanny Life* (Chicago: Univ. of Chicago Press, 2011).

uncanny: E.T.A. Hoffmann, 'The Sand-Man', in *The Best Tales of Hoffmann* trans. E.F. Bleiler, 183–214.

a powerful *eidolon*: Daston brings in Heidegger's essay on 'Das Ding', which is self-sufficient, and contrasts it to Kant's object or *Gegenstand*, which is the product of ideas and representations of the thing. Daston (2004), 16.

her father's photograph: Georges Brassaï, *Proust sous l'empire de la photographie* (Paris, 1997) 94–106 See Warner, 'Double Vision' in (2000) 185.

'...a thing, *predmet*.': Mickhail Epshtein, 'Things and Words: Towards a Lyrical Museum', in *New Paradoxes* (Moscow: Sovetskiy Pisatel, 1988); ed. and trans. Alla Efimova and Lev Manovich, in *Tekstura: Russian Essays on Visual Culture* (Chicago: Univ. Chicago, 1993), quoted in Tim Travis, 'Things with Souls: The Object in Late Soviet Culture', *Things*, 12 (Summer 2000), 37–55: 41–42.

'...go to make friends.': Charles Fernyhough, *The Baby in the Mirror: A Child's World from Birth to Three* (London, 2008), 135.

'...furniture, clothes.': *Benjamin Archive*, Marx/Leslie, 110.

207   **'...with others and oneself.':** Epshtein, 'Things and Words', see also Daston (2004), 42.

they *charm* them: William Christian, Jr., 'Yard Sale: Activation and Loss of Personal Value in Objects', kindly lent by the author, 26 April 2004; William Christian, Jr., 'The Presence of the Absence: Transcendence in a Mid-West Household'.

fetish: The word derives from Portuguese for a made thing, and was introduced by le Président de Brosses in 1760 in a study of animism; Goethe and Coleridge both adopt the concept, before Marx and Freud's influential enrichments of the term in relation to their own societies. Karl Marx, 'The Fetishism of Commodities and the Secret thereof', *Capital* (2008); see Pietz. (1985), 5–17; (1988): 121–2 and Van Eck, forthcoming, kindly lent by author.

209   **painted white:** The Bulgakov Museum http://www.ukraine.com/museum/bulgakov (accessed 10/5/11).

Chapter 10: The Word of the Talisman

215   **Abu Mohammed the Lazy:** The story appears in the Egyptian manuscripts of the *Nights*, and in the 14th century, a different version is told in *Kitab al-Hikayat al-'ajiba*; André Miquel considers it originated in 13th- or 14th-century Iraq. See ANEnc I: 71–73; Ulrich Marzolph, 'Narrative Strategies in Popular Literature: ideology and ethics in tales from the *Arabian Nights* and Other Collections', *Middle Eastern Literatures*: vol. 7: Issue 2 (2004), 171–182; Bencheikh/Miquel I: 1211.

impressive of the plots: Roger Lonsdale gives several examples, including James Ridley, *Tales of the Genii* (1764), I: 129, in notes to Beckford (1998), 130.

217 **'the zodiacal circle.':** 'Tilsam', *Encyclopaedia of Islam*, new edn. Th. Bianquis, et al., Vol. X, fascicules 171–2 (Leiden: Brill, 1999), 500–502.

suspected of necromancy: Abbé Fauvel, *Talisman magique et superstitieux de Catherine de Médicis, Reine de France etc.* (Paris, ?1770), (British Library).

other languages in the same period: For example, in Spanish dictionaries the word *talismán* does not appear in *Covarrubias* of 1610 (Tesoro de la lengua castellana), but does appear in the *Diccionario de Autoridades* of 1737. Information kindly given by Trevor Dadson, 30 Nov. 2009.

218 **The new printing presses:** See Falk Eisermann, 'The Indulgence as a Media Event: Developments in Communication through Broadsides in the Fifteenth Century', in *Promissory Notes on the Treasury of Merits*, ed. R.N. Swanson (Leiden and Boston: Brill, 2006); 309–330.

Substitutes for the pilgrimage: Rogers, *Arts of Islam*, exh. cat.,

a subset of amulets: Venetia Porter, (2011): kindly lent to MW Nov. 2009.

be captured: The exhibition also included 'Le Soleil de sciences majeures' of al-Buni, a compendium of amulets and talismans, with explanations how to make them, copied in Marrakesh, 25 July 1868, for the future Sultan Hasan I.

219 **non-sense...crucial to magic:** Colla (2009) quotes Edward Westermarck, 'The Evil Eye', in *Ritual and Belief in Morocco* (London: Macmillan, 1926), 414–78, and James Trillaing, 'Medieval Interlace Ornament: The Making of a Cross-cultural Idiom,' *Arte médiévale*, 9: 2 (1995), 59–86.

these different kinds of thing: On exhibition in Case 45, 'Magic and Divination', in The Middle Eastern Room, British Museum, Nov. 2009.

child's...jacket: This example was included in Feeke and Putnam, curs., 'A Kind of Magic' exh. Henry Moore Institute, Leeds, and the British Museum's Contemporary Arts and Cultures Programme.

220 **'...illicit talismans.':** Venetia Porter, (2011), 131–2.

remedy or a poison: Jacques Derrida, 'Plato's Pharmacy', in *Dissemination* (New York : Continuum, 2004).

221 **talismanic clothes:** Hulya Tezcan, 'Les Vêtements talismaniques', in *A la cour du Grand Turc: Caftans du Palais de Topkapi,* Musée du Louvre, Paris *11 Oct 2009–18 Jan 2010* (Paris: Cinq Continents, 2009), 48–55.

parental wishing: Chemise talismanique, Inde, 15th-16th centuries, Maison du monde arabe, Paris, 2009.

with his brothers: 'Joseph', Sura 129: 2–96 [Koran], trans. Abdel Haleem, 15. Inscriptions also include vows and prayers and invocations – to the saints, to the Seven Sleepers of Ephesus, and the Fourteen Immaculates (the Twelve Imams, plus the Prophet and his daughter Fatima).

222   **particular detail:** Tezcan, 'Vêtements talismaniques', 48–55.

      exchange of rings: Doniger (2000).

223   **'..had it about her.':** ANE, 357–410.

223   **aptness for carving:** Elliott Colla, personal communication, 21 Dec. 2009.

      seduction scene: Doniger (2000) interprets the scene more critically, as Badoura's revenge on Camar's neglect and misogyny.

226   **'...peace of mind.':** Genlis (1803), 87.

      truth-telling dress: Mlle l'Héritier, *La Robe de sincerité*, see Warner, *Beast*, 177–9; Andersen, *The Emperor's New Clothes*, (1979) 77–86

      '...Allah's name invoking': Goethe, 'Charms', in Goethe (1998), 8–9. It is interesting that 'Talisman' is italicised here, as an imported foreign word.

      '...in various manners.': Walter Scott, *The Talisman* [1819] 4.

227   **'...mad dogs.':** Ibid., 5.

228   **'...so many wonders.':** Wedgwood (1887), 72.

229   **'...follow his directions.':** Ibid., 76.

      '...talisman's deep bane.': Libretto downloaded from web. The opera premiered in 1887.

230   **superfluity and plenty:** Michael B. Miller, *Au bon Marché 1869–1920: Le Consommateur apprivoisé* (Paris: Armand Colin, 1987), 9, 155–177; see also Rachel Bowlby, *Just Looking: Consumer Culture in Dreiser, Gissing, and Zola* (London: Methuen, 1985).

231   **'. . . wear it with confidence.':** Jean-Marie Aladel, *Notizia storica sopra l'origine e gli effetti della nuova medaglia coniata in onore dell'immacolata concezione della Santissima Vergine* . . . trans. Dott. G. Panini (Perugia, 1836); ('Sainte Catherine à Paris au XIXème Siècle'; 'Le Don de la Médaille'; 'Histoire de la Médaille', leaflets (Chapelle Notre Dame de la Médaille Miraculeuse, 140 rue du Bac, 75340 Paris). I am grateful to Fr. Tom Davitt for his help.

232   **enigmatic inscriptions:** Pope John Paul II used a slight variation of the reverse image as his coat of arms, the Marian Cross, a plain cross with an M underneath the right-hand bar (which signified the Blessed Virgin at the foot of the Cross when Jesus was being crucified).

      The Virgin's promise: The Lazarists, known in English as Vincentians, were a very successful global missionary order, who were active in the Middle East. The French colonised Algeria in July 1830. For the complex early history of the medal see C.M. Stafford Poole, 'Pierre Coste and Catherine Labouré: The Conflict of Historical Cricitism and Popular Devotion', *Vincentian Heritage Journal*, Vol. 20 Issue 2, Article 3. Available at http://via.library.depaul.edu/vhj/vol20/iss2/3 Accessed March 20 2011.

John Henry Newman: personal communication, John Cornwell, to whom I am most grateful. See his *Newman's Unquiet Grave: The Reluctant Saint* (London: Continuum, 2010).

free from original sin: St Bernadette received her visions of the Virgin Mary at Lourdes, in 1858; during these Mary called herself the Immaculate Conception and in this way confirmed the doctrine.

'...produce miracles': 'The correct use of a miraculous medal', from Histoire de la Médaille (leaflet).

233   **St Thérèse's relics:** The UK tour took place 17 Sept.–15 Oct. 2009; Michael Whyte has made a documentary film, *Relics and Roses* (2011). [See *http://www.carmelite.org/index.php?nuc=content&id=52* (accessed 6/4–11)] For Pope Benedict's revival of indulgences, see Paul Vitello, 'For Catholics, a Door to Absolution Is Reopened', *New York Times*, 10 Feb. 2009. See 'Pilgrim Saint: St. Thérèse's Relics on Tour England and Wales, (Sept. and Oct. 2009) http://www.thereseoflisieux.org/ pilgrim-saint-thereserelicsont/ (accessed 10/5/11).

Chapter 11: The Voice of the Toy

240   **out of thin air:** For *Enron* (2009), which I saw at the Royal Court Theatre, London, that year, Lucy Prebble drew on several writers' and historians' investigations of that collapse, which her play anatomised, lucidly and ludically. She personified the accumulating debt as velociraptors - not hostile jinn, but fabulous monsters nonetheless.

242   **The Love of Three Oranges:** Giambattista Basile, 'I tre cedri' in *Il Raconto dei racconti* ed. Ruggero Gharini (Milan: Adelphi, 1994) 582–94.

243   **privy things:** See Jacques Rustin, Préface, to Diderot, *Les Bijoux indiscrets,* (1981), 7–33.

'...only truth there is.': Claude Crébillon, fils, *Le Sopha: Conte moral* (1742), ix. The novel was translated by Eliza Haywood and William Hatchett the same year. Bonamy Dobrée re-translated it in 2000.

'...is still missing.': Antoine Bret, *Le B . . ., ou Histoire bavarde* (Paris, 1748; London, 1749, 1751). See Jacques Rustin, Préface, to Diderot, *Les Bijoux indiscrets,* 7–33, and Fanny Beaupré and Roger-Henri Guerrand, *Le Confident des dames: Le bidet du XVIIIème au XXème siècle, histoire d'une intimité* (Paris: La Découverte. 1997), 18–19.

244   **The Vagina Monologues (1996)** by Eve Ensler, has been a success worldwide, performed by Oprah Winfrey, Jane Fonda and Glenn Close amongst others.

'**...dualism of soul and body.**': Anne Deneys, *Diderot Studies*, Vol. XXXI (Geneva: Droz), 83–95: 85.

true reports: *Anecdotes sur Mme la Comtesse du Barry* (London, 1775), probably written by Mathieu-François Pidansat de Mairobert: see Robert Darnton, *The Forbidden Best-Sellers of Pre-Revolutionary France* (London: 1996), 337. ff; on D'Aulnoy, see Warner (1994), 285–6.

245   **even a hackney coach:** See Blackwell (2008); reviewed by Sophie Gee, 'Things into People', *TLS*, 9 Jan. 2008, 23.

in a chicken yard: However, she reminds them of their own childish 'amusements, which, you frequently call making believe.' Mary Jane Kilner, *The Adventures of a Pin-Cushion* (London, 1780), 15. It was reprinted in 1788, 1780, ?1810, 1815 and 1818. She followed this success with *Memoirs of a Peg-Top* (c. 1794).

against beating children: Anon., *The Adventures of a Whipping-Top. Written by itself.* (London, c. 1780).

246   **into a heavy sleep:** Charles Dickens, *A Christmas Carol,* ed. Andrew Lang (London: Chapman and Hall, 1897), 47–9.

247   '**...Crying of Lost Things.**': Lamb (2004), 949–67: 950.

'**...accounting for it.**': Lamb cites Ian Watt writing that the advertisements of the kind Wild pioneered were precursors to or outriders of the formal realism of the early novel, exhibiting in miniature the techniques of narrative developed by authors concerned to 'bring an object home to us in all its concrete particularity'. Ian Watt, *The Rise of the Novel* (Berkeley: Univ. California Press, 1957), 29, in Lamb (2004).

'**autonomous glamour**': Lamb (2004), 954.

régime of value: Arjun Appadurai, 'Introduction: Commodities and the Politics of Value', in Appadurai (1986), 3–63.

'**...of another man.**': Lamb (2004), ed. Burke *On the Sublime* (1787), 70.

248   '**I know...I am you.**': Jonathan Lamb, 'Gulliver and the Lives of Animals', in Frank Palmeri, ed., *Humans and Other Animals in Eighteenth-century British Culture* (Aldershot: Ashgate, 2006), 169–77, further developed in Jonathan Lamb, *The Evolution of Sympathy* (Pickering & Chatto, 2009), 117–28, see his *The Things Things Say*, chapter 9, Princeton U.P, forthcoming 2011.

Hans Christian Andersen: 'The Snow Queen: A Tale in Seven Stories', in Andersen (2004), 175–204.

249   '**...all her soul.**': Ibid., 179.

'**broken mirror**': A. S. Byatt, 'Out of the Shadows', *Financial Times* Jan. 15 2005.

250   '**...said the glass splinter.**': Hans Christian Andersen, 'The Darning Needle', in Andersen (1975), 271–4: 272–3.

'**... in every story!':** 'The Flying Trunk', 'The Fir Tree', 'The Collar', in Andersen (2004), 125–32, 163–74, 261–66.

'**...to suffer.':** Dinah Birch, 'A Poker Inside Him', *TLS,* 20 May 2005: 3–4.

'**faced and mastered.':** W. H. Auden, 'Grimm and Andersen', in *Forewords and Afterwords* (London: Faber & Faber 1979), 198–208: 200.

251   '**...trials are real.':** Ibid., 201.

'**...not foolproof.':** Ibid.

glamour of possessions: Marx (2008); Lynn Festa, 'The Moral Ends of Eighteenth- and Nineteenth-century Object Narratives', in Blackwell (2008).

Chapter 12: Money Talks

252   **Epigraph:** Lucy Prebble, *Enron*, 59.

louis d'or: [Charles Gildon] *The Golden Spy. The Introduction, or the First Nights Entertainment* (1710, on title page, but BL catalogue gives 1709). BL has another, full copy (304 pp.), with the different title, *The Golden Spy: or, A political journal of the British nights entertainments and love and politics: wherein are laid open, the secret miraculous power and the courts of Europe, etc.* (London, 1710).

'**...Loquacious dumb....':** [Gildon] 'The Introduction; or the First Nights Entertainment' (London: 1710 on title page, but BL catalogue gives 1709.) 2–4.

253   '**...which I was brought.':** Joseph Addison, 'The Adventures of a Shilling', *Tatler*, 249 (Nov. 1710).

'**...of subjectivity.':** Greg Afinogenov, 'Addison's Peregrinating Shilling', in *Slawkenbergius's Tales* (7 Nov. 2007) http://slawkenbergius. blogspot.com/2007/11/addisons-peregrinating-shiling.html (accessed 21/11/10).

254   **died forgotten:** Walter Scott introduced the novel, with a memoir of the author, in 1822.

garrulous money: Anon., *The Adventures of a One Pound Note; a poem, Written by Myself* (London, 1819). The conceit also listened in on metal coin: for example, Helenus Scot, *Adventures of of a Rupee* (1783).

255   '**...had collapsed.':** 'Object 72: Ming Banknote', in MacGregor (2010), 465–9. Listen to the podcast: MacGregor, *No. 72: A History of the World in 100 Objects* (BBC Radio 4, 15 Sept. 2010).

value...inscribed into them: Joe Cribb, ed., *Money: From Cowrie Shells to Credit Cards* (London: British Museum Publications, 1986), 116–19, 135, 151, 158–59, 163, 168–69, 171–89. Balzac recognises the relation between inscription and value in *La Maison Nucingen* (1837), in which Rastignac's sudden wealth has been achieved through the new medium of the lithographic press, on which his collaborator the financier M. de Nucingen prints money to issue to investors. I am very grateful to Stephen Bann for this reference.

…within a rational state: Frederick Tristan, 'Les Enfants d'Hermès et de Salomon', in Alain Bauer et al., *Le Manuscrit Graham. Les Constitutions d' Anderson. Le Discours de Ramsay: Franc-Maçonnerie Les textes fondateurs,* Paris: Le Point, 24, hors série (Sept.-Oct. 2009), 49–51; and Victoria Gairin, 'Les Symboles de la franc-maçonnerie', ibid. 108–113. Margaret C. Jacob, *Living the Enlightenment: Freemasonry and Politics in 18th Century Europe* (New York and Oxford: OUP, 1991), 23–39, 166–7.

256   **'…impervious to moral law.':** Cribb, ibid. 121.

ban on usury: 'Obect 99: Credit Card. Issued in the United Arab Emirates, AD 2009', in MacGregor (2010), 647–651.

'…son of Time.': [Gildon], (1710), 6.

'… teeming populations.': Buchan (1997), 19–20.

258   **'…by fits and starts.':** David Luke, 'Chronological Summary of the Composition and Publication of *Faust Part Two*', in Goethe (1994), lxxxi-lxxxii.

'…bore me, as they often do.': Goethe (1994), 'An Imperial Palace: A Pleasure Garden' 4: 6031ff: 45

259   **'…series straightaway.':** Ibid., 46.

'…anything/You please.': Ibid., 4: lines 6119ff. 47.

'…who are magicians.': Ibid., 4: lines 6141–2: 48

260   **OMC:** For example, on 17 Dec. 2004, BBC News reported, 'A 22-year-old gamer has spent $26,500 (£13,700) on an island that exists only in a computer role-playing game (RPG). The Australian gamer, known only by his gaming moniker Deathifier, bought the island in an online auction.

'The land exists within the game *Project Entropia*, an RPG which allows thousands of players to interact with each other. *Entropia* allows gamers to buy and sell virtual items using real cash, while fans of other titles often use auction site eBay to sell their virtual wares.

'Earlier this year economists calculated that these massively multi-player online role-playing games (MMORPGs) have a gross economic impact equivalent to the GDP of the African nation of Namibia.' Investment prospects : "This is a historic moment in gaming history, and this sale only goes to prove that massive multi-player online gaming has reached a new plateau," said Marco Behrmann, director of community relations at Mindark, the game's developer.' See, 'Gamer buys $26,500 virtual land' 17 Dec. 2004). http://news.bbc.co.uk/1/hi/technology/4104731.stm (accessed 16/4/11).

launder money: Anastasia Trombly, 'OMC hypergrid currency

gained popularity in 2010', *Hypergrid Business*, 15 Feb. 2011. http://
www.hypergridbusiness.com/2011/02/omc-gained-popularity-
in-2010/ (accessed 16/4/11) see also Doug Tsuruoka, 'Cash in the
Millions Circulating via Games', *Investor's Business Daily*, 23 Dec. 2010.
http://www.actimize.com/index.aspx?page=news353 (accessed
16/4/11).

Mezzotint ... enchanted whistle: M.R.James, *Count Magnus and
Other Ghost Stories*, ed. S.T. Joshi (London: Penguin, 2005), 2 vols.,
1:25–36; 81–100.

other freedoms: 'Theresa May to scrap asbos', *Guardian* 28 July 2010.
Since then, in the wake of the UK riots in August 2011, the discussion
about disciplining young people by controlling their personal devices
has become fierce, though the proposals remain unresolved.

Chapter 13: Magnificent Moustaches: Hamilton's Fooling, Voltaire's Impersonations

265   **Epigraph:** Quoted by Said for his Introduction to Auerbach (2003).
Masquerade: The literature is rich, with Joan Rivière's essay,
'Womanliness as Masquerade', *International Journal of Psychoanalysis*, 10
(1929), 303–313, as an influential departure. See Terry Castle, *Masquerade
and Civilisation: The Carnivalesque in Eighteenth-Century English Culture
and Fiction* (Stanford: Stanford UP, 1986); the concept of 'perpetual
masquerade' in an orientalist context has been richly explored in
Srinivas Aravamudan, 'Lady Mary Wortley Montagu in the Hammam:
Masquerade, Womanliness, and Levantinization', *ELH*, 62: 1 (1995),
69–104.

Mahometan whiskers: Daniel Defoe, *Robinson Crusoe* (London:
Penguin, 2003), Chapter 11; I was reminded of this by Rajani Sudan,
Fair Exotics: Xenophobic Subjects in English Literature, 1720–1850,
(Philadelphia: Penn University Press, 2002), pp. 2, 13.

266   **'The plumage of love'**: Mozart, *Così fan tutte, ossia La Scuola degli
Amanti*, trans. anon., http://mrwolfgangamadeusmozart.blogspot.
com/2010/07/cosi-fan-tutte-libretto-english.html.

thoughts on late style: Michael Wood, intro. to Said (2006), xiii.

267   **'...in the actual world'**: Ibid., 66.

268   **'...patterns and conceits.'**: Ibid., 65.

another environment: 'Reflections on Exile', in Said (2000), 173–86:
186.

other borders: Max Saunders, *Self-Impression: Life-writing,
Autobiografiction, and the Forms of Modern Literature* (Oxford: OUP,
2010) has explored very richly the continuity between the performed
selves of earlier writers and the insights into plurality and fluidity
ascribed to modernists.

269   **great ladies:** His audience included, for example, Henrietta Bulkeley, sister-in-law of the Duke of Berwick, the son of King James II, and therefore a claimant to the English throne during Cromwell's Protectorate.

269   **Horace Walpole:** He translated and 'augmented' *Princess Mayblossom*, which was published by William Dodsley in 1783.

    '…early ages.': Hamilton (1849), Lewis, Preface, v–vi.

    playful experimenter: See Jean-François Perrin, 'Les Contes d'Hamilton: une lecture ironique des Mille et une nuits à l'aube du XVIIIe siècle', in Chraïbi, 2004, 270–297.

270   **'…pleasantry throughout.':** Scott, intro. to Anthony Hamilton, *Memoirs of Count Grammont* (New York: H.M. Caldwell, nd), vii–xxi; xvii–xviii.

    '…as they do these days.': Le Bélier, *Le Cabinet des Fées* (Amsterdam and Paris, 1785),Vol. XX, 49.

    Fleur d'Épine (c. 1704): Anon. trans into English, 1793; 'The History of May-Flower', trans. M. Lewis, 368–444; it enfolds 'The Story of Pertharites and Ferandina', which Andrew Lang excerpted as 'The Comb and the Collar', in *The Olive Fairy Book* (1907): Hamilton, trans. Lewis, 474–508.

271   **'…gives way to laughter':** Clark (1921), 256; see R. Robert…., ed. *Contes parodiques et licentieux du 18e siècle* (Nancy, 1987), 144–46.

    '…say what they think.': Anon. Ed., Bidpai, 1697, quoted in Warner (1994), 165.

272   **'…right to err.':** Voltaire, R. Pearson, ed., and trans. *Candide and Other Stories* (Oxford: 2006) 178–189:189.Voltaire's contes were translated into English soon after their first appearance. See H.N. Brailsford, ed., *Candide and Other Tales*, trans., Tobias Smollett, revised by James Thornton (London: Everyman, 1937.)

    'fables of reason.': Pearson (1993) and idem, *Voltaire Almighty: A Life in Pursuit of Freedom* (London: Bloomsbury, 2005).

    limits of knowledge itself: See "Micromegas: A Philosophical Story", in Voltaire, *Candide and Other Stories*, 89–106. This tale does not bring in direct oriental allusions (except in the name of one of the protagonists, who comes from the star Sirius, and is hence 'le Sirien', homonymous with 'Syrian.'

273   **'…sultanas' reply.':** Voltaire 'Zadig or Destiny: A Tale of the Orient' in Voltaire (2006), 177:108 Voltaire was going to subtitle it 'The Plaything of Providence'.

274   **'But….':** Ibid., 165–168.

275   **incidents in the Koran:** Sura 18, 'The Cave', Qur'an, trans. Abdel Haleem, 187–188. Philip Kennedy first point ed out to me the closeness of the passages, and suggested that Voltaire even chose to position

it as his Chapter 18 to rhyme with the Koran. The possibility is only conjecture, and the editing history of *Zadig* is complex. I am grateful for Roger Pearson's elucidations. Private correspondence, 30 May 2011.

a Man of Envy: Voltaire, *Zadig or Destiny,* in Voltaire (2006), 120–121.

276 **château at Sceaux:** Roger Pearson, 'White Magic', Kennedy/Warner.

'Le Crocheteur borgne.': For further discussion of this story see Pearson (1993), 41–48.

'...white magic of the oriental tale.': Pearson, 'White Magic', op. cit.

277 **against small-pox:** See Aravamudan, 'Lady Mary Wortley Montagu in the Hammamn,' 88–90; idem, 'Womanliness, and Levantinization', *ELH* 62: 1 (1995), 69–104: 88–90. Edward Jenner discovered how to 'vaccinate', using dead cells, in 1798; see *Arabick Roots*, exh. cat., 54, 58–61.

'...the wine of Surinam.': Voltaire, *La Princesse de Babylone*: http://www.voltaire-integral.com/Html/21/09BABYLO.html (accessed 2/10/10).

278 **brazen blasphemy:** Voltaire, *The White Bull* (2006), 254–86; see also, 'The whole faithfully done into English.' Jeremy Bentham, trans. (London: John Murray, 1788).

279 **'...wants to be mine.':** Voltaire, trans. Pearson (2006), 256.

'...been thanked.': Voltaire, *The White Bull*, 260–263.

280 **'...plays of Oscar Wilde.':** Hugh Haughton, 'Introduction', in Hugh Haughton, ed., *The Chatto Book of Nonsense Poetry* (London: Chatto & Windus, 1988), 16.

use of this trope.: Felicity Nussbaum, 'British Women Write the East after 1750: Revisiting a "Feminine" Orient', in *British Women's Writing in the Long Eighteenth Century: Authorship, Politics and History*, eds. Jennie Batchelor and Cora Kaplan (London: Macmillan, 2005), 121–139.

...eagerly with them.: Mary Wortley Montagu, 'The Sultan's Tale', in Montagu (1996), 16–27.

'...non-punitive story.': Isobel Grundy, Introduction, in Montagu (1996), ix–xv.

Oriental style: See Ballaster (2005a); Chawton House Library has useful digitised indexes of *The Lady's Magazine* 1770–1837.

281 **stage machinery:** It was thought to be by Byron, even though one might have thought her son, Richard Brinsley, would have made sure she was credited.

in a Montgolfier: I am indebted to Elizabeth Kuti for telling me about Inchbald and her play, *The Mogul's Tale, Or, The Descent of the Balloon* (1784) in *Collection of farces and other afterpieces* (New York: Blom, 1970). Inchbald was revisiting *The Sultan, Or, A Peep into the Seraglio* (1775), written by Bickerstaffe after an earlier French play,

Charles-Simon Favart's *Soliman II, ou les trois sultanes*, itself adapted from the story by Jean-François Marmontel (1723–99), about a spirited Christian beauty, Roxelana, who reforms a Sultan; Mozart's opera, *The Abduction from the Seraglio* is based on the Marmontel, which also inspired Hannah Cowley, *A Day in Turkey, or The Russian Slaves* (1791), first performed 1827. See Angela Escott, *Generic Diversity in the Dramatic Work of Hannah Cowley* (London: Univ. London Press, 2005); idem (2010), and Daniel O'Quinn, Intro. (2005). Many thanks, also, to Laurence Williams for this reference.

in the repaired balloon: He tells them, 'Yes, from you Christians, whose laws teach charity to the world, have I learned these virtues. For your countrymen's cruelty to the poor Gentoos has shewn me tyranny in so foul a light, that I was determined henceforth to be only mild, just, and merciful . . .' (Inchbald, ibid.).

Chapter 14: 'Symbols of Wonder': William Beckford's Arabesque

289 **Epigraph:** Leslie Marchand, ed., *Letters and Journals of Lord Byron*, 12 vols. (London 1973–82), III: 101, quoted in Nigel Leask, '"Wandering through Eblis":Absorption and Containment in Romantic Exoticism', in Fulford and Kitson (1998), 165–188: 178.

'...Egyptian Prince.': 'Elouard Felkanaman et Ansel Hougioud', in Beckford (1992), 99–171.

as you please: Jorge Luis Borges, 'The Translators of *The Thousand and One Nights*', in Borges (1999), 92–109.

290 **'...fusion...':** Laurent Châtel, 'Re-Orienting William Beckford: Translating and adapting the Thousand and One Nights', Kennedy/ Warner.

scholarly editions: see E.Shaffer, 'Composing and decomposing the corpus of William Beckford: French and English Beckford', *Comparative Criticism* XXV: 255–265; Laurent Châtel, 'Les sources des contes orientaux de William Beckford: *Vathek* et la *Suite des contes arabes* bilan de recherches sur les écrits et l'esthétique de Beckford, Gilbert, Kepler', in *Etudes Epistèmé*, no 7 (printemps 2005).: 93–106.

'...some arabesque': Beckford (1992), Préface, np.. The oriental stories of contemporaries also inspired Beckford; besides Hamilton, Walpole, and Pétis de la Croix, he shows signs of having read the burlesque tales of Thomas Gueulette. See Tania Collani, 'Le merveilleux allégorique dans *Vathek* de William Beckford', *Séminaire d'analyse textuelle, L' objectalité du texte* (Bologna, 2005), http://www.rilune.org/dese/tesinepdf/Collani/

Collani-merveilleux-allegorique-Vathek.pdf (accessed 24/4/11). See also Ballaster (2006b), 364–370.

291   **'...carbuncles.':** Mario Praz, intro. to *Three Gothic Novels* (London: Penguin, 1988), 21.

'...in Paradise.': W.B. to Henley, 26 Jan. 1782, Lewis Melville, intro. Frank T. Marzials, *The Episodes of Vathek* (London, 1912), viii. Beckford was a distant cousin of Hamilton's, and proud of the connection.

'...modern imagination.': 'A [kind of] poetry, quite unforgettably bound up with the book, appears in a rather strange juxtaposition of quasi-idyllic innocence with enormous or futile magical solemnities: like the dark vibrations of a star, this then colours and quickens the freshness of the natural scenes to the point of discomfort; but not without giving this approximation of a dream something more simple and more extraordinary.' Stéphane Mallarmé, 'Préface à Vathek' [1876], in *Vathek et ses épisodes*, ed. Didier Gérard (Paris: José Corti, 2003), 419–435: 421, 433.

'...cruelty...': Shaffer, 258.

292   **if not the richest:** Beckford's grandfather established the family's estates in the West Indies; the property was increased by his father.

demons and jinn: See Warner (2001), 119–160, for Southey and Coleridge, and on the influence of Caribbean magic on psychic explorations.

'The Spider Negress.': Beckford (1992), 194–214.

'Messac': Ibid., 194, footnote.

293   **'Fountain of Merlin.':** Beckford (1992), 35–42.

frenzied writing: He seems to have abandoned fiction around 1790.

'dear Arabian.': See Katherine Turner, 'Elizabeth Craven', *DNB* (Oxford: OUP, 2004); http://ezproxy.ouls.ox.ac.uk:2117/view/article/576 (accessed 4/12/10).

'...old Mohammedan.': Châtel (2005), 93–106; also Châtel, Kennedy/Warner. Another aspiring orientalist in the group was Marianne-Agnès Fauques de Vaucluse, whose husband taught French to the great scholar Sir William Jones, translator of the *Rig Veda* and other sacred Sanskrit texts. The orientalist Jonathan Scott acquired part of the *Nights* in manuscript from Dr White. See Scott (1800).

to this material: See Appendix I, Concordance, ANEnc II: 743–782 for clear and useful tables of the different stories in different translations and manuscripts.

'wandering imagination.': Beckford, Préface (1992), 23; Beckford (1998), 163–164.

294   **hospitable structures.:** See Kilito (2001) for a brilliant exploration of this question.

294	**his oriental tales:** [William Beckford], *Vathek: Conte Arabe* (Paris, 1787), 1–2; idem (2003), 7; idem (1998), 163–4.

'**...Pandemonium':** Austin Dobson, 'Exhibitions of the Eidophysicon', in *At Prior Park and Other Papers* (London Chatto, 1912), 277–81.

295	'**...Halls of Eblis.':** Note dated 1838, quoted by Lonsdale, intro. to Beckford (1998), xi–xii; see Leask, '"Wandering through Eblis", 165–188: 169–175 for connections between exoticism and panoramic display.

295	'**...moving among men.':** Cyrus Redding, 'Recollections of the Author of "Vathek"', *New Monthly Magazine* (June 1844), quoted by Melville, intro. to Beckford (1912), vii.

'**...bestreaked with green.':** Beckford (1998), 5, 11.

296	'**...control the world':** Ibid., 22. Beckford and Henley's notes connect the talismans to two stories in the *Nights* and refer to encrypted Arabic alphabets, 'the *prophetical*, the *mystical*, the *philosophick*, the *magical*, the *talismanick*, etc.', Beckford (1786), note to 10: 220.

'**...distortion and metamorphosis.':** See Châtel (2010): 140–141; also Rebecca Johnson, 'The Cutting Edge of Translation: Ambivalence and Intercultural Exchange in Vathek'. Paper given at MLA Annual Meeting, Washington, DC, 28 Dec. 2005.

'**...Hell in literature':** Borges (1999), 236–9: 238.

297	'**...of childhood.':** Beckford (1998), 120.

'**...perseverance.':** W.B. Letter of 21 March 1785, quoted in Melville, intro. to Beckford (1912), ix.

298	**not the only...fictions:** William Beckford, *The Story of Al Raoui [or, The Tale-Teller], A Tale from the Arabic* (London, 1799), one of the few published in his lifetime in English; a copy is in the British Library. It includes a German translation and some verses. The story is included in vol. 4, Wortley Montagu mss of the *Nights*, which were copied in 1764 in Egypt, and entered the Bodleian Library in 1802. See Jonathan Scott's notes, to Or. Ms 455. In the Dedication (to Mrs Cuthbert), Beckford says that he worked on it '16 years before', ie. in 1783 (ibid., v–vii). For Beckford's publication history, see Shaffer (2003), 255–265.

'**...to determine.':** Beckford (1786), vii.

299	'**...of a thousand.':** Melville, intro. to Beckford (1912), xi.

footnoting the footnotes: Beckford drew especially on Barthélemy d'Herbelot's monumental work of orientalism, *Bibliothèque orientale, ou dictionnaire universel contenant généralement tout ce qui regarde la connaissance des peoples de I'Orient. Leurs Histoires et Traditions véritables ou fabuleuses* . . . (Paris: Compagnie des Libraires, 1697). Galland had finished this after D'Herbelot's death.

use of fans: Beckford (1786), 316–317.

scholarly depths: Beckford (1787). Lonsdale edits Henley's edition and draws from Beckford's 1816 edition, where he expanded the notes to 56 pages. See Beckford (1998), 121–161.

'Genii': Beckford (1786), 218; Beckford (1787), 169, note 8, p. 7. Ibid., 304–305; Beckford (1787), 187.

300   **'...devour the dead.':** 'The Story of Sidi Nouman', ANE, 737–745; ANEnc I: 380–381; Beckford (1786), 304–5 continues: 'That kind of insanity called by the Arabians Kutrub (a word signifying not only a wolf, but, likewise, a male goul) which incites such as are afflicted with it, to roam howling amidst those melancholy haunts; may cast some light on the possession recorded by St Mark ch V.1.&c...' This passage does not appear in Beckford (1787).

'...more than a translation.': Byron, *Poetical Works*, 895, quoted in Nigel Leask, '"Wandering through Eblis",' 165–188: 180.

301   **'Episodes.':** It is not inconceivable that they might retell some part of the missing volume of the Wortley-Montagu manuscripts. See Beckford (2003), 149–352.

'Prince Alassi': 'Histoire des deux princes amis', 149–194.

302   **'To shear believers...':** Beckford (1786), 304–305; this passage does not appear in Beckford (1787).

God of Fire: 'From time to time we were enveloped in a whirlwind of sparks, which the Mage regarded as graciously emitted in our honour . . . In the portion of the temple where we stood, the walls were hung with human hair of every colour; and, from space to space, human hair hung also in festoons from pyramids of skulls chased in gold and ebony. Besides all this, the place was filled with the fumes of sulphur and bitumen, oppressing the brain and taking away the breath. I trembled, my legs seemed to give way; Firouzhah supported me. "Take me hence," I whispered; "take me from the sight of thy god . . ."' Beckford (1912), 40.

The pervasive impression of stench from the burning hair has also been scientifically researched: 'costus', the chemical released from old hair, produces one of the smells that is most revolting to humans, coded to keep anything and anyone at bay. See Nadia Wagner's 'Recent Addition to the Permanent Collection [of the Library of Scents]', *Cabinet Magazine* Event (Brooklyn, 18 July 2009). See *http://www.cabinetmagazine.org/events/wagner.php* (accessed 5/12/10).

English version: 'The Story of Prince Alassi and the Princess Firouzhah', in Beckford (1912), 1–52: 29–31 (revised as 'Histoire du Prince Alassi et de la princesse Firouzka', 1837).

303   **missing an ending:** Beckford (2003), 195–238; Beckford (1912), 53–178.

Barkiarokh: Beckford (1998), 239–79; Beckford (1912), 179–227.

'**...humble and ignorant.**': Beckford (1998), 120.

304   **Bentley's Standard Novels:** Lewis Melville, intro. to Beckford (1912), xx–xxi.

305   **consigned them:** Ibid., v–xxiv. Two of the shorter tales, which Frank Marzials translated into English from the original French, were published in the *English Review* in 1909–10.

uniting the novel: William Beckford, *Vathek,* with *The Episodes of Vathek,* ed. Kenneth W. Graham (Peterborough, Ont.: Broadview Press, 2001). The full set of stories were gathered together for the first time in 1912, but still had to wait until 1929 to be included within the frame of the novel in a French edition; Beckford (1929).

'**...Romantic solitary.**': Donna Landry, 'William Beckford's *Vathek* and the Uses of Oriental Re-enactment', in Makdisi/Nussbaun (2008), 167–194: 192.

306   **many advocates:** Fatma Moussa Mahmoud, 'Beckford, *Vathek* and the Oriental Tale', in Mahmoud (1960) 63–121. Moussa's daughter is the novelist and activist Ahdaf Soueif.

On Fonthill: See Châtel (2005), 93–106; idem, Kennedy/Warner; Landry, 'William Beckford's *Vathek*', *passim.*

James Wyatt: Worked at Lee Priory, and at St George's Chapel, Windsor, Durham and Salisbury cathedrals; Chris Brooks, *The Gothic Revival* (London: Phaidon, 1999), 153; see also 'William Beckford', exh. Dulwich Picture Gallery, London, 6 Feb.-14 April 2002.

Chapter 15: Oriental Masquerade: Goethe's *West-Eastern Divan*

309   **Epigraph:** Johann Wolfgang von Goethe, 'Talismane', in *Poems of the West and East: West-Eastern Divan - West-ostlicher Divan, Bi-lingual edition of the Complete Poems* (Germanic Studies in America 68). Verse trans. by John Whaley, ed. Katharina Mommsen (New York, Paris et al.: Peter Lang, 1998), 8–9; 14–15. (WED/Whaley)

'**...younger than his.**': Goethe, 'Unbegrenzt (Uncircumscribed)', in Goethe (1986), 237.

another, new being: See Reed (2009).

310   **Hefiz...died in 1389:** The date of his death is not certain. See Vesta Sarkhosh Curtis and Sheila R. Canby, intro. to *Persian Love Poetry* (London: British Museum, 2008), 7.

'**...cannot be equalled.**': Ibid., Mommsen, 'Introduction' to WED/ Whaley, xvii–xviii.

311   '**...could be a Moslem** Ibid., xvii.

'**...newly evolving poetics.**': Jaroslav Stetkevych, 'Arabic Poetry and Assorted Poetics', in Malcolm Kerr (ed.), *Islamic Studies: A Tradition and its Problems* (Malibu: Undena, 1980), 113.

'**...slinking whisperer**': 'People', in [Koran] trans. Abdel Haleem, 446.

'**...embodied together.**': Katharina Mommsen Ibid., xvii.

312   '**...Paradisal quality**': WED/Whaley, xi. Avery and Heath Stubbs, Intro, *Hafez of Shiraz*, 1–22: Curtis and Canby, 'Introduction', in *Persian Love Poetry*, 9.

picnics in Paradise: Yet, in some ways, it must be admitted that Hafiz today does not have all the right enemies: like Rumi and Kahlil Gibran, he appeals to the Californian school of libertarian hedonism, and to New Age cultists of intoxication and Eastern mysticism. The veteran American poet Robert Bly, a guru of the new masculinities and author of *Iron John*, a riposte to feminism, spent fourteen years translating some of Hafiz's *ghazals*. The translations are uneven and often wilfully determined to suit Bly's modern purposes, but Hafiz's characteristic tone can be heard. Robert Bly, 'Some Thoughts on Hafez', in *The Angels Knocking on the Tavern Door. Thirty Poems by Hafez*, trans. Robert Bly and Leonard Lewisohn (Harper Collins 2008), ix-xi.

'**...strand of silk.**': Hafiz of Shiraz (1952), 56.

313   **Abu Nuwas:** Philip Kennedy, *Abu Nuwas: A Genius of Poetry* (Oxford: Oneworld, 2005), 25–26; ANEnc II: 468–69; See Bencheikh/Miquel 3:1023. In real life, Abu Nuwas was court poet to Hanin's son, Caliph al-Amin, who was something of a rake.

Barmecides: ANEnc II: 487–489

Pier Paolo Pasolini: *Il fiore delle mille e una notte* (*The Arabian Nights*, 1978).

boys and girls: Kennedy, *Abu Nuwas* esp. Ch. 2, '"Love, Wine, Sodomy . . . and the Lash" - the lyric poetry of Abu Nuwas', 29–78.

'**...in writing.**': Maurice Pomerantz, Letter to *LRB*, 20 Jan. 2011: 4. I am grateful to him for his clarification of the word's history.

314   **oriental sayings:** WED/Whaley, xx.

'**...Barmecides once knew.**': WED/Whaley, 2–3: 14–15.

Victorian monument: Warner (2009) *LRB*, 31: 7 (9 April 2009), 13–14.

'**...one's own worse Life...**': FitzGerald, Letter to Cowell, quoted Annmarie Drury, 'Accident, Orientalism, and Edward FitzGerald as Translator', *Victorian Poetry*, Spring 2008, Vol. 46, Issue 1: 37–55.

'**...residence in Fitzgerald's.**': Borges (1999), 'The enigma of Edward Fitzgerald', 366–8.

315   '**...course of history.**': W. G. Sebald, *The Rings of Saturn*, trans. Michael Hulse (London: Vintage, 2002), 200.

'**...against the mimetic.**': Stetkevych, 'Arabic Poetry,' 103–123:104.

316   **the poetry breaks into the stories:** see Geert Jan Van Gelder, 'Poetry and the *Arabian Nights*', ANEnc 1: 13–17.

personal and social: See Cave (2011).

317 **praise to the beloved:** See Hendrik Birus, 'Goethe's Approximation of the *Ghazal* and its Consequences', in *Ghazal as World Literature: Transformations of a Literary Genre* I, ed. Th. Bauer and A. Neuwirth (*Beiruter Texte und Studien* 89, 2005), 415–429: 424.

Hatem: In full Hatem Zograi's. Goethe seems to have made up the name, perhaps invoking Abu Ismail al-Tughra'i, a vizier under the Seljuks, who was charged with setting the ruler's cipher on official documents, and Hatem al-Ta'i, the pre-Islamic poet.

'Joseph': [Koran] Sura 12: 29–34 trans. Khalidi, 185–186; *Falnamah*, MS 979: fol 68, in Rogers, *Arts of Islam*, no. 245, 220.

318 **beautiful song:** [Schubert] sleeve notes, trans. Keith Anderson, *Deutsche Schubert-Lied.*

among Germanists: See T. J. Reed, 'Was hat Marianne wirklich geschrieben?' Skeptische Stimmen aus England', in '*Liber Amicorum:*' Katharina Mommsen zum 85. Geburtstag,' eds. Andreas & Paul Remmel (Bonn: Bernstein Verlag 2010).

319 **dissident Muslim:** Lewisohn, 'Hafez and his Genius', in Bly and Lewisohn, *Angels Knocking on the Tavern Door*, 67–70.

'...by a puritan.': 'The Man Who Accepts Blame', ibid., 21–22.

320 **'...other people.':** ibid., 21.

ideals more fully: Mommsen (1960) pp. 185–299; and lecture (2008).

321 **than a sorcerer's:** See Gloria Flaherty, *Shamanism and the 18th Century* (1992), 168–72.

'...making peace.': Daniel Barenboim, 'Bonding across Cultural Boundaries', in Edward Said, *Music at the Limits* (New York: Columbia UP, 2007), 259–264.

'...European culture.': Daniel Barenboim and Edward W. Said, *Parallels and Paradoxes: Explorations in Music and Society* (London: Bloomsbury, 2002), 7.

322 **'...strategies of power.':** Edward Said, 'Orientalism Reconsidered' [1986], in Said (2000), 198–215: 200.

'...located and interpreted': Said (1983), 4.

'...aesthetic of resistance.': Said (2006), 25–47.

strategy for survival: *Knowledge is the Beginning*, DVD, sleeve notes.

Part V: Flights of Reason

323 **Epigraph:** Thomas Campanella, *De sensu rerum et magia* (On the Sense of Things and Magic) Bk IV, Ch 161.

Chapter 16: Thought Experiments: Flight before Flight

330 **Epigraph:** Félix Nadar, epigraph to *Droit au vol* (Paris, 1866), n.p.

'Camar al-Zaman.': I have not included the second part of the romance, about Camar's sons. Each of the mothers falls in love with the other's son, in a plot that doubles the story of Phaedra, and catches the earlier echoes in the vows of chastity Camar and Badoura made in their youth. Some scholars, like Mia Gerhardt, believe this sombre resolution of the romance was grafted on; Mardrus leaves it out of his translation, but the Pléiade editors argue for the depths it adds to the romance.

331   **'the invisible worm':** William Blake, 'The Sick Rose', in *Songs of Innocence and Experience*, in *The Complete Poetry and Prose of William Blake*, ed. David V. Erdman (New York: Anchor, 1988), 23.

'fable of modernity.': Laura Brown, *Fables of Modernity: Literature and Culture in the English Eighteenth Century* (Ithaca, NY: Cornell UP, 2001).

'...manipulate the other.': Brian Vickers, 'Analogy versus Identity: The Rejection of Occult Symbolism, 1580–1680', in *Occult and Scientific Mentalities in the Renaissance*, ed. B. Vickers (Cambridge: CUP, 1984), 95. Quoted in Thomas M. Greene, 'Language, Signs and Magic', *Studies in the History of Religion*, 75, *Envisioning Magic: a Princeton Seminar and Symposium*, ed. Schafer and Kippenberg (Leiden: E.J. Brill, 1997), 255–272.

333   **flying ointment.':** Ginzburg (1991); Steven Connor, *The Book of Skin* (London: Reaktion, 2003), 192–203.

féerie **tradition:** Anne E. Duggan, 'Women and Absolutism in French Opera and Fairy Tale', *The French Review*, Vol. 78, No 2, 2004, 302–15:305.

334   **huge slippers:** Wilhelm Hauff, *Little Mook* [and *Dwarf Longnose*], trans. Thomas S. Hansen and Abby Hansen (Boston: David R. Godine, 2004); *Der kleine Muck* appeared in Hauff's first collection *The Caravan* (1826), see Thomas S. Hansen, intro., *Little Mook*, v–xvi.

Eastern soaring: Illustration by Boris Pak, ibid., 17.

'The Frog Princess': Afanase'ev (1973), 119–123; thanks to Robert Chandler for help, corresp. 29 July 2009; and to Dubravka Ugrešic, corresp. 17–18 Oct. 2009.

'...once a fairytale.': Velimir Khlebnikov, 'Iranskaya pesnya' (1921), in *Collected Works*, trans. Paul Schmidt, Vol. III (Harvard UP, 1997), 84; this version quoted in Roman Jakobson, 'On Russian Fairy Tales', in Afanase'ev (1973), 631–651: 650.

335   **flight before flight:** For background see Clive Hart, 'A Directory of Heavier-than-Air Flying Machines in Western Europe 850 BC–1783 AD', in idem, *The Prehistory of Flight* (Berkeley: Univ. California Press, 1985), repri. *Cabinet Magazine*, 11 (Flight) (Summer 2003); Marina Warner, 'That Soaring Feeling', review of Hart, *Images of Flight* (Berkeley, 1988), *TLS* (2–8 Dec. 1988), 1331–1332; Jules Duhem, *Histoires des idées aéronautiques avant Montgolfier* (Paris, 1943); idem,

Musée aéronautique avant Montgolfier and *Histoire des origines du vol à reaction* (Paris, 1959); Anne McCormick and Derek McDonnell, eds, *Imaginary Voyages & Invented Worlds* (Sydney: Hordern House Rare Books, 2002); Keen (2006), 507–535; Richard Holmes, *The Age of Wonder* (London: HarperCollins, 2008), 125–162; also Richard Holmes, produced by Tim Dee, 'A Cloud in a Paper Bag', BBC Radio 3 (23 Dec. 2009).

'heuristic…fiction': Aït-Touati (2005), 15–31: 25.

male absolutism: Anne E. Duggan, ibid., 306.

True History: [Lucian] 1988.

336   **folly and arrogance:** François de Polignac, 'Alexandre entre ciel et terre: Initiation et investiture', *Studia Islamica*, 84 (1996), 135–144.

wonders of the universe: The *Romance* also describes Alexander's other quests and adventures: how he travelled to India to talk to the Gymnosophists, holy men who, to contemplate the deepest mysteries, stood on one foot under a banyan tree, lived on air and never cut their hair. Nor did his exploits end with his success at scaling the skies; he had earlier designed a diving bell to take him down to the ocean floor: 'I stepped into a glass jar,' he writes, 'ready to attempt the impossible. As soon as I was inside, the entrance was closed with a lead plug . . . I got down to a depth of 464 feet . . . and behold, an enormous fish came and took me and the cage in its mouth and brought me to land a mile away. There were 360 men on the ships from which I was let down, and the fish dragged them all along. When it reached land, it crushed the cage with its teeth and cast it up on the beach. I was gasping and half-dead with fright.' [Alexander] (1991), Book 2: 118–119. Polignac, 'Alexandre', 136–137, 143.

337   **Godwin:** D.R. Woolf, 'Godwin, Francis (1562–1633)' *Oxford DNB* (OUP, 2004) http://www.oxforddnb.com/view/article/10890 (accessed 5/1/08).

the seated Domingo: R.B., *English Acquisitions in Guinea and East India*, printed for Nathaniel Crouch, at the Bell in the Poultry near Cheapside (London, 1700). Includes 'A Description of the Isle of St Helena, where the English usually refresh on their Indian voyages. With an account of the Admirable Voyage of Domingo Gonsales, the Little Spaniard, to the World in the Moon, by the help of several Ganza's or Large Geese. An Ingenious Fancy, written by a late learned Bishop.' [1638] (London, 1700), 58–100: 68. The arrangement prefigures the aeronautical experiments of the philosopher Ludwig Wittgenstein with man-lifting kites at the beginning of the 20th century. The philosopher studied aeronautics at the University of Manchester in 1908–11 and began seriously to construct kites at the Kite Flying

Upper Atmosphere Station near Glossop. He was influenced by the military inventions of Samuel F. Cody, who built kites for the British army, intended to lift soldiers. I am entirely indebted to the artist Alastair Noble for this fascinating historical connection. Noble revisited 'Wittgenstein's Flights' in a series of sculpture installations. See Alastair R. Noble and Michael J. Howard, *Wittgenstein's Flights* (Albuquerque: The Land/an art site, (c. 2008).

338   **"serious fiction":** Aït-Touati (2005), 15–31: 18.

'**...attributed to him.'**: Godwin, *Man in the Moone* (1700), 88.

'**...new philosophy'**: Aït Touati, ibid., 26.

339   **bodily in the air:** Cyrano de Bergerac, *L'Autre Monde: l'Histoire comique des Estats et empires de la Lune,* written 1650, published posthumously, censored (1657), ed. Margaret Sankey (Paris: Minard, 1995).

340   **John Wilkins:** Wilkins was also, briefly, Master of Trinity College, Cambridge, and Oliver Cromwell's brother-in-law: he married his sister Robina in 1656. J. T. O'Connor and E. F. Robertson, 'John Wilkins', *MacTutor History of Mathematics* http://www-history.mcs. st-andrews.ac.uk/Biographies/Wilkins.html (accessed 28/11/07).

'**...distempered fancy'**: Wilkins (1691), p. 197.

even ringtones: Wilkins (1640); I also read the BL copy of the French trans. *Le Monde dans la lune* (Wilkins, 1656) (the English vols were available on microfilm only); also John Wilkins, *Mercury, or the secret and swift messenger: showing how a man may communicate his thoughts to a friend at any distance* [1641] (London, 1694).

'**...do a Mouse.'**: Wilkins (1656), 268.

'**...in this enterprise!'**: Wilkins (1656), 269.

341   '**...so much despised'**: Wilkins (1691), A4 [sic].

in its body: Ibid., 173–4.

'**...ten yards at a time'**: Ibid., 195.

Intro, in Paltock (1928), Ibid., 207 quoted Bawden, xii.

'**...regularly attempted'**: Wilkins (1691), 205–207.

342   '**...in the spring'**: Ibid., 202.

'**...by common consent.'**: Wilkins (1640), aa.

'**...good of mankind'**: Quoted O'Connor and Robertson, 'John Wilkins' (see note to p. 340 above).

'**...resemble flies'**: Jorge Luis Borges, 'John Wilkins' Analytical Language' [1942], in Borges (1999), 229–232: 229: 231.

343   **merely fanciful:** Jules Duhem, *Musée Aéronautique avant Montgolfier: Recueil de figures et de documents pour servir à l'histoire* (Paris, 1944, PhD thesis, 2 vols) begins with 'L'aviation fabuleuse', gives an invaluable inventory, and includes fumigations and salves used in magic, but leaves out the *Nights.*

Daedalus/Leonardo approach: Wilkins has a less fortunate percursor in the Arabic lexicographer al-Jawari (d.c. 1002) who attempted to fly but fell (thanks to Geert Jan Van Gelder for this information).

The founders of Google, Larry Page and Sergey Brin, are keen kite-surfers; Brin is now spending 'increasing amounts of time' building a kite-powered sailing boat. Ken Auletta, 'Searching for Trouble', *New Yorker*, 85: 32 (12 Oct. 2009), 52; in James Cameron's *Avatar* (2010), which magnificently transposes an underwater and bioluminescent world to the surface of the utopian planet of Pandora, the CGI visions of flying show men and women plugging themselves into imaginary creatures as if they were electronic, and then standing on them as they spread their vast wings, like albatrosses or giant rays, and riding them as if they were surfboards.

'…of Abyssinia': S. Johnson (1994), 3.

'half-dead': Ibid., 13–15. Dr Johnson had already scoffed at the idea of human flight seven years before in *The Rambler*, 199 (1752). R. C. Johnson, 'Flying Machines and Other Spectacular Objects: The Oriental Tale and Epistemologies of Scale', paper given NYU Abu Dhabi, Dec 15 2009.

344   ***Peter Wilkins:*** [Paltock, Robert] *The Life and Adventures of Peter Wilkins A Cornish Man* (London: J. Robinson and R. Dodsley, 1751). The book was announced in the *Gentleman's Magazine*, Nov. 1750; further editions followed in 1783 and 1784; it appeared in *Weber's Popular Romances*, 1812, and was illustrated by Robert Stothard in 1816. In France, the first translation of 1763 was also followed by later editions; it appeared in German in 1767. I have read in the British Library: [Robert Paltock], *The Life and Adventures of Peter Wilkins* (London, 1860). Other editions include idem, *The Life and Adventures of Peter Wilkins* (London, 1854); and idem, intro. Edward Bawden (London: Dent, 1928).

     unknown lawyer: For a long time the identity of the joking author remained unknown, but in 1994, a scholar was able to show that he was a certain John Elliott (1759–1834), who had indeed been a member of the crew of the *Resolution*, Cook's own boat on the second voyage. Paltock has left one interesting trace – he sold some manuscripts containing some 'fanciful engravings' to the famous bookseller William Dodsley, Bawden, Intro, pp.

345   **'…perished by it':** ANE, 107.

     '…verdure…ever seen': Peter Wilkins [Robert Paltock], *The Life and Adventures of Peter Wilkins*, illus. Phiz (London, 1860), 21.

346   **'…she could fly':** Ibid., 30–31.

348   **'…buxom air':** Charles Lamb, *London Journal*, 5 Nov. 1834, quoted Bawden, intro, Paltock (1928), xi.

     '…a naturalist': Charles Lamb, *Book for a Corner* (1868), I. 68, quoted Bawden, ibid., xi.

349   **present-day society:** *The Travels of Hildebrand Bowman, esq. Written by himself* (London, 1778), 265–266.

       ...one of these women: The author provides an engraving from memory of this unforgettable highlight of his adventurous life, ibid., f. p. 275.

       '...all that saw it': Ibid., 275–276.

350   **Alae-putae:** *Travels of Hildebrand Bowman*, 269–271.

       ...the French Daedalus: N**** [Restif de la Bretonne], *La Découverte australe par un homme-voland, ou le Dédale français* . . . 4 vols (Leipzig/Paris, 1781), I, 101.

       hominid elephants: (2002), no. 66.

352   **Patagonian giantess:** Ibid. I: 235.

       '...white and fluffy': Ibid. IV: 18.

       Louis Binet: See Wyngaard.

353   **crinoline petticoat:** *Découverte*, I: 101.

       not so successful: See BL Ms Add. 34113, folios 189r and 200v, in 'Parachutes, sponges, and tenuous air', in Hart, *Prehistory*, Appendix II, 209–210. This is an indispensable and hugely enjoyable compendium of early experiments, attempts and failures. See also Jules Duhem, *Histoire des origines*.

354   *Flying Indians:* Mr Farley's Night, Theatre Royal, Covent Garden, June 19, 1827. Collection Marina Warner.

       extraordinary ascension: Playbill, JJC.

       'manfully active': Poster for *Queen Topaze* (1861), JJC London Playbills folder 8 (14).

355   **Winsor McKay**, *Little Nemo in Slumberland*, Vol. 1 West Carrollton, Ohio: Checker Books, c. 2010); *passim*, but esp. Oct 15 1905–Aug 15 1909. 62–73.

356   **'wonderful thoughts.':** J. M. Barrie, *Peter Pan and Wendy* (London: Hodder and Stoughton, [1911], rep. 1981).

Chapter 17: Why Aladdin?

357   **Epigraph:** BL Evan, 2477 I am most grateful to the curator of the Evanion Collection, BL, Helen Peden, for showing me this rare playbill.

       bill of entertainments: Playbill, Suffolk County Council Archives.

358   **casts his spells:** *Aladdin, Or The Wonderful Lamp* (London: New Juvenile Library, 1816), 10. (BL. 12202.aa.32); *Aladdin, or, The Wonderful Lamp An Eastern Tale by a Lady* (London c. 1840), sets the story on stage with foldout vignettes; Dean & Son's Pantomime toy books 'with five set scenes and nine trick changes' include *Aladdin or the Wonderful Lamp* (London, 1880). JJC Miniature Theatre 1 (41a–52).

359   **different plays:** The John Johnson Collection of Ephemera at the

Bodleian Library, Oxford includes lovely fresh prints of popular toy theatre cut-outs, by other manufacturers as well as Pollock's, the most famous today. The toy theatre designs still survive, and can be bought from Pollock's Toy Museum, London.

Aladdin **dominates the scene:** *Aladdins* I looked at in the BL include: *Harlequin Aladdin with Inkle and Yarico* (Edinburgh, 1820). This is the same text as New Juv. Lib. (see note above) but with different cut-outs; George Soane, *Aladdin A Fairy Opera*, (1826), same as above but with songs by Henry R. Bishop (c. 1860); Webbe and P. J., illustrated tale, *Aladdin and the wonderful Lamp! Or, Harlequin and the flying palace* 1866; Cruikshank illus., *Aladdin, and the wonderful lamp; or, The Willow pattern plate and the flying Crystal Palace.* (before 1876). Irwin (2004), p. 17–18, 47–48, 57–58, 101.

360   **Royal Shakespeare Company:** see Cooke.

Hanna Diab's stories: Jean-Paul Sermain, Notice, in *Galland* 3: I-XIV: II.

Galland's journal: May 27 1709, Bencheikh/Miquel 3: 1002.

361   **'...anti-Semitic':** Robert Irwin, 'There's the rub ... and there too', *TLS* (24 Dec. 1993), 14–15.

362   **'...slaves of that ring.':** ANE, 661.

'...genie disappeared.': ANE, 722–724.

363   **'...that mortal be.':** O'Keeffe, *Aladdin Songs*, Theatre Royal, Covent Garden London, 1788.

364   **'...China-ware':** Ibid.

killed him: John O'Keeffe, *The Little Hunchback; or, A Frolic in Bagdad*, in John O'Keeffe, *Dramatic Works,* 4 vols. (London, 1789), II: 281–334.

mild and clement: see p. 475: note on Inchbald.

See O'Quinn, 'Introduction: The Supplementation of Imperial Sovereignty' in O'Quinn (2005), 1–32; see Ch. 14.

Imperial Gothic mode: *Obi, or Three-Finger'd Jack* (1800), for example, draws directly on the account the doctor Benjamin Moseley gave of local obeah medicine, starred the black actor Ira Aldridge, and was performed 'with Songs and Choruses' at the Theatre Royal, Haymarket around 1800. Other titles in this odd, mixed genre branch of entertainment include *Pizarro* (1814), *The Black Princess (1814 – featuring the heroine Jettiana and the Usurper O'erwhelmo*; *The Slave* (1816); *Paul and Virginia* (1818); *Inkle and Yarico* (1819). See also Alan Richardson, 'Romantic Voodoo: Obeah and British Culture, 1797–1807', in *Sacred Possessions: Vodou, Santeria, Obeah, and the Caribbean*, eds. Margarite Fernández Olmos and Lizabeth Paravisini-Gebert (New Brunswick and London: 2000), 171–194.

365   **closer to home:** Bridget Orr, 'Galland, Georgian Theatre, and the Creation of Popular Orientalism', Makdisi/Nussbaum (2008) 103–130.

the slave trapped within: See Warner (2001), 141–150. The associations must have been picked up by the audience at that time. See Henry R. Bishop, *Songs, Recollections, Duels. Choruses, in the Fairy Opera of Aladdin* (Theatre Royal Drury Lane, 29 April 1826), 18; George Sloan, *Aladdin: A Fairy Opera in Three Acts* (London, 1826), 65.

a poetic drama: Adam Oehlenschlager, *Aladdin, or The Wonderful Lamp*, trans. Henry Meyer (Copenhagen:Glydendal, 1968); see John L. Greenway, 'Acoustic Figures and the Romantic Soul of Reason', *European Romantic Review* (2000), 11, 2, 214–222, accessed 25 June 2010. H. C. Orsted was a friend of Hans Christian Andersen and played a crucial part in stopping him writing tedious tragedies and take up fairy tales instead. See also Margaret Sironval, 'Écritures européennes du conte d'Aladin', *Féeries* 2, 2004–2005: 245–256, 248–249.

366   **'...end to every dissonance':** Orsted, quoted Greenway, op. cit., 219.

'...a sedan chair': JJC: London Playbills folder 8 (14).

Great Exhibition: Armstrong (2008). 190–192, 218–221.

367   **mass entertainment:** Bolossy Kiralfy, *Constantinople at Olympia Superb Spectacle*, libretto (London, 1894), JJC, London Play Places 5 (55).

to stage the Orient: Barker (1988), 49–50.

'...backward or forward.': Ibid., 234.

'...spoils of war.': 'The "Arabian Nights" Tableaux. Invented and Produced by Herman Hart', ibid.

368   **'...Mrs Cookesley.':** Barker, ibid., 253.

369   **'military manoeuvres':** Barker (1988), 117.

'...stage pageant.': 'The Sketch', (2 Jan 1895), in Barker (1988), 256.

370   **'...the world go round':** Paolo Giorza, *The Orient Spectacular Entertainment* arranged by Bolossy Kiralfy. The Lyrics written by Horace Lennard (London: Metzler & Co., 1895), 46.

Chapter 18: Machine Dreams

371   **Epigraph:** Michael Powell, *A Life in Movies:An Autobiography* (London: Heinemann, 1986) no p. no; Hein Heckroth (1901–70) was costume and set designer for *The Red Shoes* (1948), *Tales of Hoffmann*, and several other films created by Michael Powell and Emeric Pressburger.

'diurnal variations.': Michaud (2006), 53, quoting Dickson and Dickson (2000), 19–20.

372   **evolution of photography:** See Ian Christie (1994), for early history of cinema and its relations with theatrical showmanship.

'...surfaces in motion.': Philippe-Alain Michaud, notes towards an exhibition of oriental carpets, kindly lent by the author.

373 **'...disequilibrium:** ibid.

'and beyond it.': Michaud (2004), 56. In their artist's book, Lawrence Norfolk and Neal White, *Ott's Sneeze* (London: Bookworks, 2002), the authors point out that nothing of the sneeze itself is visible; they re-enacted the sneeze in laboratory conditions and filmed it split into milliseconds in order to make visible the *pneuma* of which Michaud speaks.

374 **'...Ghost Dance.':** The films are preserved in Library of Congress. and can be viewed online.

summoning of spirits: See Chapter 15: 'The Camera Steals the Soul', in Warner (2006) 189–202.

'...being in an image.': Michaud (2004), 66.

375 **escape to freedom:** John C. Eisele, 'The Wild East: Deconstructing the Language of Genre in the Hollywood Eastern', *Cinema Journal*, 41: 4 (Summer 2002), 68–94.

George Méliès: *The Invention of Hugo Cabret* (for release 2011), directed by Martin Scorsese after the children's novel by Brian Selznick, explores the later years of Méliès, when he was forgotten. Here a famous film director pays tribute to one of his great precursors. Simon During has termed them 'secular enchantments' in *Modern Enchantments* (2002); see also Jack Zipes, 'Georges Méliès: Pioneer of the Fairy-Tale Film and the Art of the Ridiculous', in *The Enchanted Screen: The Unknown History of Fairy Tale Films* (New York and London: Routledge), 31–48; *Georges Méliès: First Wizard of Cinema*, DVD, essays by Norman McLaren and John Frazer (2009).

376 **'authentic Oriental artefacts':** Fritz Lang and Thea von Harbou, *Der müde Tod* (Destiny) (1921). Robert Irwin alerted me to the pioneering scene with the carpet. See Robert Irwin, 'Flying Carpets,' *Hali*, March-April 200: 109, 164–165.

'trick' films to date': R.W. Paul, 'The Magic Sword' [1901], in *R.W. Paul: The Collected Films 1895–1908*, ed. with intro. Ian Christie, 'Robert Paul: Time Traveller' (London: BFI, 2006); Frank Gray, 'Innovation and Wonder: Robert Paul in 1896', in John Barnes et al, *Hove Pioneers and the Arrival of Cinema* (Brighton: Univ. Brighton, 1996), 16–23; Ian Christie, (2004).

378 **the magic vehicle:** See Marco Formisano, 'Macchina', in *Dizionario dei temi letterari*, ed. Remo Ceserani et al. (Turin: Unione Tipografico-Editrice Torinese, 2007), II: 1341–1344.

379 **have them for himself:** Fairbanks is suspected of holding back the opening of the rival film in the US, though this is denied by his biographer, Jeffrey Vance, *Douglas Fairbanks* (Berkeley: Univ. California Press, 2009), 169; see Frederic Raphael, 'Douglas Fairbanks the Fraud', review of Vance, *Douglas Fairbanks* (2009), *TLS* (24 April 2009), 9–10.

382 **sympathetic East:** Eisele, 'Wild East'.

Mongol Prince: The other two princes also represent oriental decadence: 'the Prince of the Indies', one of the princess's three suitors, keeps falling asleep; the Prince of Persia, played by a woman, is ridiculous, fat and foolish. See Robert Irwin, 'Delhi dreadful', review of Reeva Spector Simon, *Spies and Holy Wars: The Middle East in twentieth-century crime fiction*, *TLS* Aug 19 and 26 2011: 3–4, for a witty account of oriental villainy in popular culture.

'…"unseen" enemies.': Eisele, 'Wild East', 71.

383 **script alongside Fairbanks:** Achmed Abdullah, *The Thief of Bagdad. Based on Douglas Fairbanks's Fantasy of the Arabian Nights.* Illustrated with scenes from the Photo Play (London: Hutchinson, n.d.).

pulp fiction writer: John F. Barlow, *Mini-Bio of Achmed Abdullah*; http://www.imdb.com/name/nm0008280/bio (accessed 18/4/11).

anthology of poetry: Achmed Abdullah, *Lute and Scimitar: Being poems and ballads translated out of the Afgan, the Persian, the Turkoman, the Tarantchi, the Bokharan, the Balochi and the Tartar tongues, together with an introduction and historical and philological annotations by Achmed Abdullah; and with a preface by Harvey Allen* (New York: Payson & Clarke, 1928).

purpling the Orient: *The Swinging Caravan* (1911), *The Red Stain* (1915), *The Blue-Eyed Manchu* (1916), *Bucking the Tiger* (1917), *The Trail of the Beast* (1915), *The Man on Horseback* (1919), *The Mating of the Blades* (1920). He also wrote *Dreamers of Empire* (London: Harrap, 1930), which explores the lives of romantic explorers and soldiers of fortune who made their lives in the Middle East, inc. Burton; also *A Buccaneer in Spats* (1924).

The orient in modernity: Amit Chaudhuri, op. cit, (2008), 91.

385 **1940 fantasy epic:** See Anon, *Alexander Korda's Thief of Bagdad, Authorized Edition, adapted from Alexander Korda's Technicolor Production* (Akron and New York: Saalfield, 1940).

'….Winged Imagination.': Abdullah, *The Thief of Bagdad*, 201.

Chapter 19: The Shadows of Lotte Reiniger

390 **Epigraph:** Junichiro Tanizaki, trans. Thomas J. Harper and Edward G. Seidensticker, *In Praise of Shadows* (New Haven: Leete's Island Books, 1977), 27.

feature to survive: Two films – of a political and satirical character – made in 1917 and 1918 by the Italo-Argentinian director Quirino Cristiani, are thought to be contenders, but have not been traced. Reiniger's original was burned in a fire; the existing restoration by the BFI was made from a copy.

'....**Was of brass**.': Quick-eyed, as horsely as a horse can be,
Like an Apulian steed, as highly bred.
And I assure you that from tail to head
Nothing could be improved by art or nature,
So they supposed at least who saw the creature.
But yet the wonder nothing could surpass
Was how it went if it were made of brass . . .
Geoffrey Chaucer, trans. Nevill Coghill, 'The Squire's Tale'. V. 194–198
(Harmondsworth: Penguin, 1971), 412.

scholarly translations: Irwin, Intro., Lyons 3: IX–XIII; ANEnc. I:
172–4; also Robert Irwin, 'The Arabian Nights', programme note to
Al layla wa-Layla, dir. Tim Supple, Edinburgh Festival, 2011.

391   **died in London 1981:** Sources are not clear about whether they
were Jewish, but they were certainly leftist, and opposed to Fascism;
many of their friends, if not they themselves, were under threat. Carl
Koch and Lotte Reiniger began a wandering life after they closed
their Berlin studio in 1935; they travelled to Britain to make two
films in the historic GPO series commissioned by the innovative
documentary producer John Grierson, while Koch also worked for
Jean Renoir in Rome. In 1948 they were given permission to stay
in England, and remained (Koch died in 1963).

accuracy and confidence: John Isaacs, *The Art of Lotte Reiniger*
(1970) documentary film, included in Lotte Reiniger, *The Fairy Tale
Films*, DVD (2008). See Christie (2004); 163–171: 170.

'...**all vanity**.': R. L. Stevenson. 'A Penny Plain and Twopence
coloured,' in *Memories and Portraits* (1887), 134, 392.

movements with the music: Margit Downar, *Lotte Reiniger:
Silhouettenfilm und Schattentheater*,Austellung des Puppentheatermuseum
im Münchner Stadtmuseum 2 June-17 Aug. 1979 (München: Lipp,
1979), 27–30. Carl Koch operated the rostrum camera above her
play-table; others assisted, as photographs of Reiniger at work reveal.
John Isaacs, personal communication, 2006.

flights of fancy: Isaacs, *Art of Lotte Reiniger*; Reiniger collaborated
as illustrator with Eric Walter White, who provides a useful early
filmography in the children's story, *The Little Chimney Sweep*, which
he wrote after her eponymous 1935 film (Bristol: White & White,
1936); see also William Moritz, *Lotte Reiniger*: http://www.awn.com/
mag/issue1.3/articles/moritz1.3.html (accessed 27/10/08).

'...**they appear**': Jean-Paul Sartre, *The Psychology of Imagination*, anon.
trans. (New York: Farrar, Straus, Giroux, 1991), 177.

revenge on him The libretto is by Colette. See [Ravel] *L'Enfant et
les sortilèges*, sleeve notes by R. Nicholas.

'...**real people**': John Isaacs, email to Marina Warner, 24 Sept. 2009.

393 **demons of Waq-Waq:** In *Seelische Konstruktioner* (1927–29), Ruttmann created a brilliant small shadow puppet sequence with the epigraph 'How very strange, as if the whole world were drunk'. Ian Christie, lecture at Synapsis, Bertinoro, 2009.

Berlin in 1926: 'Collaborators' named in the credits are Berthold Bartosch, Alexander Kardan and Walter Turck, who helped with the technical aspects. The film was lost for many years; a silent version was found and a score commissioned from Freddie Phillips in the 1950s; in 1991, the whole film was restored in Germany, and reunited with the original score by Wolfgang Zeller which had been discovered in an archive in New Zealand; the BFI issued the DVD in 2001.

394 **'...flesh and blood.':** Mathers/Mardus, 'The Magic Tale of the Ebony Horse', III: 392–424: 394; ANE: 796–819; Lyons II: 127–51; Bencheikh/Miquel: II: 81–103.

395 **'...'Second Dervish.':** ANE, 94–105.

397 **shadows with darkness:** Warner (2006), 159–166; see also Ernst Gombrich, *Shadows: The Depiction of Cast Shadows in Western Art* (London: National Gallery, 1995); Michael Baxandall, *Shadows and Enlightenment* (New Haven: Yale UP, 1995); Victor Stoichita, *A Short History of the Shadow* (London: Reaktion, 1997).

art of shadowplay: See for example: Jeanne Cuisinier, *Le Théâtre d'ombres à Kelantan* (Paris: Gallimard, 1957).

398 **Mahabharata:** In 1972, when I spent several weeks on Bali, I used to bicycle along the beach at night until I saw the flaring torches in the palm groves and turned inland to follow them, to find the gathering under the trees of a hamlet where the show was taking place.

missing elements: See Jackie Wullschlager, intro. to Andersen (2004), xv–xlvi; also website of Andersen Museum, Odense, Denmark.

movement of the story: Kenneth Gross, *Puppet: An Essay on Uncanny Life* (Chicago: Univ. Chicago Press, 2011).

several early films: Hoffmann, 104–129; see Warner (2006), 181–6.

seen in so little: One of Hans Christian Andersen's most sinister and depressing stories, 'The Shadow' develops a variation on the theme of the *Doppelgänger*, as a man finds himself replaced by his own shadow and eventually eclipsed and destroyed by him/it: Andersen (2004), 223–236.

400 **artist in this vein:** *The Art of Tim Burton*, MOMA, New York, 22 Nov. 2009–26 Apr. 2010.

films for children: *Rose Red and Snow White* in *Lotte Reiniger The Fairy Tale Films* DVD (2008).

form of portraiture: Lotte Reiniger, *Shadow Theatres and Shadow Films* (London: Batsford), 11–12.

disregard for realism: Leask, '"Wandering through Eblis"', 165–188, discusses what he calls 'panoramic' viewing re Loutherbourg, and optical entertainments.

'…what is this thing…?: Hollis Frampton, quoted by Ian Christie during his seminar, Bertinoro, 9 Sept 2009.

401   **'filtow':** Roy A. Sorensen, *Seeing Dark Things: The Philosophy of Shadows* (NY: OUP, 2008), quoted Christie.

402   **entrench anti-Semitism:** See the powerful article by Patrick Colm Hogan, 'Narrative Universals, Nationalism, and Sacrificial Terror: From *Nosferatu* to Nazism, *Film Studies*, 8, Summer 2006, 93–105; Pick, *Svengali's Web*, 1–15, 127–165.

Aladdin, 1954 *The Fairy Tale Films*, DVD (2008).

Chapter 20: The Couch: A Case History

405   **Epigraph:** Paul Valéry, 'Mauvaises Pensées et autres' (May 1899), in Valéry, *Oeuvres* (Paris: Gallimard (Pléiade), 1983), 1461.

historical setting: Nabil Matar, 'Christians in *The Arabian Nights*', in Makdisi/Nussbaum (2008), 131–152.

406   **'…gesture in fiction.':** Philip Kennedy, 'The True Aladdin', Kennedy/ Warner.

407   **wedding to another man:** Boccaccio (1980), 794–812, 807.

408   **'…earth in Alexandria.':** Mardrus/Mathers, 3:50.

no exception: See Gerhardt (1963), 93–103 for a fierce criticism of Mardrus's translation, and Jorge Luis Borges, 'The Translators of the Thousand and One Nights', in *The Total Library* 101–106 for a different approach.

stories themselves: For example, 'Histoire de Bohetzadm & et de ses Dix Visirs' in *Suite des Mille et une Nuits,* in *Le Cabinet des fées*, Vol. 40, 6–39, and engraving on p. 34 of the 'sopha', a double bed and the scene of the [supposed] crime.

'Sofa ou Sopha.': Fréd. Godefroy, *Dict. de l'ancienne langue française et de tous ses dialectes.* (Paris 1881–1902).

409   **stays and corsets:** Montagu (1994), 58–59.

'a Volume.': Cowper, 'Advertisement' to (1994).

'…Sofa last.': Cowper, 'The Sofa', ibid., 6.

'…made the town.': Ibid.

410   **'…loveliest lines.':** Elif Batuman, *The Possessed: Adventures with Russian Books and the People who Read Them* (New York: Farrar, Straus, Giroux, 2010), 205–06.

411   **'…mortal control':** Lydia Marinelli, *Die Couch: Vom Denken in Liegen*, exh., Sigmund Freud Museum, Vienna, 5 May - 5 Nov. 2006. (Munich: Prestel), 13.

'**...illegitimate sexuality.**': Ibid., 24.

'**Smyrna Rug.**': a Ghashgh'i carpet, from Iran, 1880s, (?) (165 x 277cm): The Freud Museum, London, LDFRD 6410. With thanks to Michael Molnar, who showed me Erica Davies's inventory of the rugs in the museum. (A friend of mine, Dr Estela Welldon, who is a practising psychotherapist in London, recently sent me a note on a new writing card, and her couch appears floating, as if in flight on the page.).

412   **to his friend Fliess:** Lydia Marinelli, "'Meine ... alten und dreckigen Götter". Aus Sigmund Freuds Sammlung' ('My Old and Dirty Gods' – From Sigmund Freud's Collection) (Freud Museum, Vienna, 1998), quoted by Andreas Meyer, 'The Shadow of a Couch', *American Imago* 66: 2 (Summer 2009), 137–147: 143.

to be decoded: See Eleanor Cook, *Enigmas and Riddles in Literature* (Cambridge: CUP, 2006).

'**...feel of things.**': H.D. visited him both in his Vienna consulting rooms and at his country house in Dobling; she also visited him in Hampstead shortly before his death; H.D., 'Writing on the Wall', in H.D. [Hilda Doolittle] (1985), 3–12: 116. My thanks to Joan Jonas for this inspiring quotation.

413   '**...cave of treasures.**': Ibid., 23.

'**...implicit in the process.**': Ibid., 132.

414   **Vienna in 1891:** Alberto Manai, 'Nota del Curatore', in Riegl (1998), 179–200: 179.

small, browny-grey...on the wall: Yuruk rug early 19th century, from Anatolia, Turkey. (The Freud Museum, London) LDFRD 6426. The most valuable of the oriental carpets which Freud owned is 'a particularly beautiful example' of a rare Tekke Bird Asmalyk rug, 18–19th century, sprinkled with crested birds. It is draped over the table opposite the foot of the couch; Gillian Cutbill, 'An Obsessive Collector', *Hali: The International Magazine of Carpets and Textiles*, 33 (Jan.-Feb.-Mar. 1987), 10–12, 105.

propped position: H.D., 'Writing on the Wall', 17.

415   '**...died on rugs.**': Anon. quotation, in Bettini, 234–5.

Gabbeh, dir: Mohsen Makhmalbaf (1996); Makhmalbaf's most famous film is *Kandahar* (2001).

416   **destroyers of fantasy:** The late Shusha Guppy first introduced me to the culture of this pastoral people when she travelled with them on their annual transhumance, c. 1975. Makhmalbaf and his family were active in the struggle during the elections of June 2009 against Ahmadinejad's continued repression. See Bari Weiss, 'Finding Missing Persians', *Wall Street Journal*, 17 Feb. 2010. *http://online.wsj.com/article/ SB10001424052748704804204575069323196402004.html* (accessed 26/4/ 11).

417   **'...with our own youth.':** Sigmund Freud, Letter to his fiancée, 14 Aug. 1882; John Forrester found this for me. Michael Molnar pointed out the change of image that took place in the passage from German to English.

     sea depths: H.D., 'Writing on the Wall', 75, 82–83.

     '...precious it would be!': Goethe, 'Outside the City Gate' in *Faust: Part One*, (1994) lines 1110–25. Three years later, Freud again writes how he wants to fly to Martha: 'Zu Ostern' (Freud to Martha Bernays 3 Apr. 1885.

418   **'...infinite combination grows.':** Goethe, *Faust's Study (iii)* in *Faust Part One*, trans. Bayard Taylor, quoted in Sigmund Freud, *The Interpretation of Dreams*, trans. James Strachey [1953] (Harmondsworth: Penguin, 1980),), S.E. IV. 388–389]; Goethe, *Faust: Part One*, trans. (1984), 94–5.

     'nodal points.': 'The Dream Work', in Freud, *Interpretation of Dreams*, S.E. IV: 388–389.

     pennants and signs: H.D., 'Writing on the Wall', 69.

419   **of a single night:** Ferial Ghazoul, 92, quoted in Colla (2009), note 8.

     The Confidant: Crabbe (1967), 298–312. The tale within a tale is in lines 47–567.

421   **another riddle:** The warning on French level crossings has become proverbial: I saw 'Un fasciste peut en cacher un autre', on a wall at Bures-sur-Yvette in 2009, for example.

     glimpses from the wings: Peter Brooks, *Henry James Goes to Paris* (Princeton: Princeton UP, 2007).

422   **'...proves useless.':** Freud, 'Theory of Dreams'; Paul Federn, 'On the Sensation of Flying in Dreams', Scientific Meeting, 31 Jan. 1912, *Minutes of the Vienna Psychoanalytic Society*, IV (1912–18), ed. Herman Nunberg and Ernst Federn, trans. M. Nunberg with Harold Collins (New York: International Universities Press, 1975), 28–34: 30.

     '...family manner.': Sigmund Freud to Martha Bernays, 30 Nov. 1883. For a nuanced account of relations between Sigmund and both Moritz and Mitzi Freud, see the letter of Lilly Freud-Marlé to Ernst Freud, 4 Dec. 1958 in Lilly Freud-Marlé and C. Tögel, eds., *Mein Onkel Sigmund Freud*, (2006), 45–8.

423   **Judaica:** He translated and published the Kabbalistic work, *The Book of Zoha* (reprinted Nabu Press, 2010), for example.

     double horror: Michael Molnar, '. . . das Kind soll wissen . . .', *Luzifer-Amor: Zeitschrift zur Geschichte der Psychoanalyse*, 36 (2005), 134–148. He lent me the English version, '. . . the child should know . . .' In relation to Tom Seidmann-Freud, he expresses his debt to Barbara Murken: '"die Welt ist so uneben" - Tom Seidmann-Freud

(1892–1930). Leben und Werk einer großen Bilderbuch-Künstlerin.'
In: *Luzifer-Amor: Zeitschrift zur Geschichte der Psychoanalyse.
Themenschwerpunkt Familie Freud*, 33: 17 (Tübingen: edition diskord,
2004), 73–103: 89.

but flying: 'Dies Kind, statt auf dem Diwan zu liegen, beginnt im
Zimmer umherzufliegen.' Seidmann-Freud (1929). On the wall behind
the child on the 'couch' there is a picture of a pelican, inscribed Abu.
The children in the Wunderhaus are called Hobu and Tobu, and so
the bird's name follows suit. But according to the laws of psychopathology, I couldn't help but think that this might be an oblique
allusion to the print of Abu Simbel which hung over the Couch in
Freud's consulting room in Vienna (!). Furthermore, Michael Molnar
informs me that the first psychoanalytical 'ambulatorium' for out-
patients in the 1920s was on the Pelikanstrasse in Vienna.

Freud's other sisters: Rosa died in Treblinka in 1942; Mitzi and
Pauli disappeared after being deported to Theresienstadt and then, in
1942, to Maly Trostinec; Dolfi died in Treblinka in 1943; only Rosi
survived the camps, and emigrated to the US.

Conclusion: 'All the story of the night told over . . .'

429   **Epigraph i:** Marcel Proust, *Time Regained*, in *In Search of Lost Time*,
trans. Moncrieff/Kilmartin, 6 vols. (London: Chatto, 1992), VI: 446–447.

Epigraph ii: Introduction, trans. George Martin (London: Penguin,
1982), xviii-xix.

to defer the hour: 'Histoire du fils du roi, de la femme et de l'Ifrit',
Bencheikh-Miquel II: 640–643.

430   *regressus ad infinitum:* Irwin, 283–284. Evelyn Fishburn, 'Readings
and Re-Readings of Night 602', *Variaciones Borges, Journal of Philosophy,
Semiotics and Literature*, Aarhus, 18 (2004), 35–42. This article is the
fruit of fine detective work, in which Fishburn shows that Burton
included this recursive loop, often cited admiringly by Borges, in the
Supplemental Nights (c. 1919), VI: 257–272. See also Evelyn Fishburn,
'Traces of the *Thousand and One Nights* in Borges', in Van Gelder and
Ouyang, *New Perspectives*, 81–90.

possibility of recognition: See more on this in Cave (1988); also
Marina Warner, *Mirror-Readings*, Philip Kennedy and Marilyn
Lawrence, eds., *Recognition: The Poetics of Narrative* (2010), 227–34;
Borges, 'Translators of the 1001 Nights', 'Emma Kunz', 'The Partial
Magic of the Quixote,' and several other allusions. See Fishburn,
Reading and re-readings', ibid., 36.

431   **'...view to beginning.':** Paul Ricoeur, 'The Symbol Gives Rise to
Thought', in *The Symbolism of Evil*, trans. Emerson Buchanan (Boston:
Beacon Press, 1969), 349.

'**...among savages.**': R. G. Collingwood, *The Philosophy of Enchantment: Studies in Folktale, Cultural Criticism, and Anthropology*, ed. David Boucher, Wendy James and Philip Smallwood (Oxford: Clarendon Press, 2005), 195.

Why the attraction?: See Steven Lukes, 'The Problem of Apparently Irrational Beliefs,' in *Handbook of the Philosophy of Science, Philosophy of Anthropology and Sociology*, eds. Stephen P. Turner and Mark W. Risjord, (Elsevier, 2007), 591–606 for a helpful and rich discussion of various approaches to the problem of other people's belief systems; see also Saler (2006) for an overview.

We cannot know See Paul Veyne, *Did the Greeks Believe in Their Myths?*, trans. Park Wissing (Chicago & London, 1988).

432 '**...is not true.**': Wallace Stevens, 'The Pure Good of Theory' in *The Collected Poems* (New York: Vintage, 1990), 332. See Warnes (2009) for a good discussion of religious ontology v. scepticism.

'**...what it aims at.**': Ricoeur, *Symbolism*, p. 351, quoting Bultmann, *Glauben und Verstehen*.

'**reasoned imagination.**': Borges, Introduction, to Bioy Casares (2003), 5.

433 '**...cognition and verification.**': Calvino (1999), 26–7.

'**...literature perpetuates.**': Ibid.,

434 '**...it corresponds.**': Ibid., 27.

'**...we can *hear* again.**': Ricoeur, *Symbolism of Evil*, 351.

magic agency: See Gell (2009), 208–228.

435 '**...would be kept.**': Ludwig Wittgenstein, *Remarks on Frazer's Golden Bough*, ed. Rush Rhees (Nottingham: Brynmill, 1979), p. vi, quoted in Thomas de Zengotita, 'On Wittgenstein's Remarks on Frazer's Golden Bough', *Cultural Anthropology*, 4: 4 (Nov. 1989), 390–398: 390.

'**...its depth**': *Remarks*, p. 13e, quoted de Zengotita, 394.

'**is *ethics*.**': Wittgenstein's Lectures on Ethics, *Philosophical Review*, 74: 1 (1965), 3–16: 12–13. Emphasis in original. Quoted in de Zengotita, 397.

436 **alternative to...war:** Cf. Nacer Khemir says of his fabulist and poetic film, *Bab Aziz*, that it is 'a highly political film, and deliberately so. It is a duty nowadays to show to the world another aspect of Islam, otherwise each one of us will be stifled by his own ignorance of "The Other". It is fear that stifles people, not reality.' Interview in *Nacer Khemir: Das Verlorene Halsband der Taube*, eds. Bruno Jaeggi and Walter Ruggle (Baden: Verlag Lars Muller/Trigon Films, 1992), 108; quoted Roy Armes, 'The Poetic Vision of Nacer Khemir', *Third Text*, Vol. 24, Issue 1, 2010: 69-82:81.

A SCHOOLBOY LEARNING THE ALPHABET.

Bibliography

Arabian Nights: editions and translations

Arabian Nights' Entertainments [c.1706–21], Mack, Robert L. ed., (Oxford: Oxford University Press, 1998) **[ANE]**

Les mille et une Nuits, Bencheikh, Jamel Eddine and Miquel, André, trans. and ed., 3 vols. (Paris: Gallimard, 2005) [**Bencheikh/Miquel**]

Burton, Richard, *Arabian Nights, The Marvels and Wonders of the Thousand and One Nights,* ed. and trans. Jack Zipes (New York: Signet, 1999)

Burton, Richard, *The Arabian Nights: Tales from A Thousand and One Nights,* intro. A.S., Byatt (New York: Random House, 2001)

Burton, Richard, *The Arabian Nights,* 13 vols. http://www.manybooks.net/authors/burtonri.html (accessed 26 April 2010) **[Burton]**

Le Cabinet des fées; ou Collection choisie des contes de fées, et autres contes merveilleux, ed. Charles Joseph Mayer, 41 vols (Amsterdam, 1785–89 and Geneva, 1789–93)

Chauvin, Victor, *Bibliographie des ouvrages arabes ou relatifs aux arabes,* Vols. 4–7 (Liège 1900–03, repr. London, 2003)

Dixon, E., ed. *Fairy Tales from the Arabian Nights,* illust. J. D. Batten (London: J.M. Dent, 1893)

[Encyclopaedia] *The Arabian Nights Encyclopaedia,* Van Leeuwen, Richard, and Marzolph, Ulrich, eds with Hassan Wassouf, 2 vols (Santa Barbara, Denver and Oxford: ABC Clio, 2004) **(ANEnc)**

Gabrieli, Francesco, trans. and ed., *Le Mille e una Notte* [1948], intro. Tahar Ben Jelloun, 4 vols (Turin: Einaudi, 2006)

[Galland] *Les mille et une Nuit: contes arabes,* 3 vols. Antoine Galland, trans., and eds., Sermain, Jean-Paul and Chraïbi, Aboubakr (Paris: Flammarion, 2004) **[Galland]**

Haddawy, Husain, trans., *The Arabian Nights,* based on the text of the fourteenth-century Syrian manuscript edited by Muhsin Mahdi (New York: Norton, 1990) **[Haddawy/Mahdi I]**

Haddawy, Husain, trans., *The Arabian Nights II: Sindbad and Other Popular Stories* (New York: Norton, 1995) **[Haddawy/Mahdi II]**

Housman, Laurence, *Stories from the Arabian Nights,* illus. Edmund Dulac (London: Hodder & Stoughton, 1907)

Lane, Edward William, trans., *The Arabian Nights' Entertainments; or, The Thousand and One Nights With six hundred woodcuts by William Harvey,* 3 vols. (London: John Murray, 1850) **[Lane]**

500 *Bibliography*

Lang, Andrew, ed., *The Arabian Nights' Entertainments*, Illus H.J. Ford (London:Longmans, 1898)

Lyons, Malcolm C. with Lyons, Ursula, trans., *The Arabian Nights: Tales of 1001 Nights*, intro. Robert, Irwin. 3 vols (London: Penguin, 2009) **[Lyons]**

Mathers, Powys, *The Arabian Nights: The Book of the Thousand Nights and One Night*, from the translation of Dr J. C. Mardrus. 6 vols. (London: The Folio Society, 2003) **[Mathers/Mardrus]**

Scott, Jonathan, *Tales, Anecdotes, and Letters translated from the Arabic and Persian* (Shrewsbury: T. Cadell, 1800)

Weber, Henry, *Tales of the East*, 3 vols (Edinburgh: Ballantyne, 1812)

Primary sources

Afanase'ev, Aleksandr, *Russian Fairy Tales*, trans. Norbert Guterman (New York: Pantheon, 1973)

[Alexander], *The Greek Alexander Romance*, trans. Richard Stoneman (London: Penguin, 1991)

Andersen, Hans Christian,*The Complete Stories*, trans. Erik Haugaard (London: Victor Gollancz, 1975)

Andersen, Hans Christian, *Fairy Tales*, trans. Tiina Nunnally, ed. and intro. Jackie Wullschlager (London: Penguin, 2004)

Apuleius, *The Transformations of Lucius, Otherwise Known as the Golden Ass*, trans. Robert Graves (London, Penguin Classics, 1950)

Apuleio [Apuleius], *Della Magia*, trans. Concetto Marchesi (Palermo: Sellerio, 1992)

Ashour, Radwa, *Siraaj: An Arab Tale*, trans. Barbara Romaine (Austin: University of Texas Center for Middle Eastern Studies, 2007)

D'Aulnoy, Marie-Catherine, *Contes*, ed. Philippe Hourcade, 2 vols (Paris: Société de textes français modernes, 1997)

Auster, Paul, *The Invention of Solitude* [1982] (London: Faber & Faber, 2005)

Ballaster, Ros, *Fables of the East: Selected Tales, 1662–1785* (Oxford: Oxford University Press, 2005a)

Beckford,William, ed. William Henley, *An Arabian Tale, from an Unpublished Manuscript* (London: J. Johnson, 1786)

Beckford, William, *Vathek Conte arabe* (Paris, 1787)

Beckford, William, trans F.T. Marzials, *The Episodes of Vathek* (London, 1912)

Beckford, William, ed. Guy Chapman, *Vathek with the Episodes of Vathek*, 2 vols (London: Constable, 1929)

Beckford, William, ed. Didier Girard, *Suite de contes arabes* (Paris: José Corti, 1992).

Beckford, William, *Vathek*, ed. Roger Lonsdale (Oxford: OUP, 1998)

Boccaccio, *The Decameron*, trans. G.H. McWilliam (Harmondsworth: Penguin, 1980)

Bioy Casares, Adolfo, *The Invention of Morel*, trans. Ruth L.C Simms (New York: New York Review Books, 2003)

Bioy Casares, Adolfo, *Asleep in the Sun*, trans. Susanne Jill Levine (New York: New York Review Books, 2004)

Borges, Jorge Luis, *Fictions*, ed. Anthony Kerrigan (London: John Calder, 1962)

Borges, Jorge Luis, *Labyrinths*, ed. Donald A. Yates and James E. Irby (London: Penguin, 1964)

Borges, Jorge Luis, *Collected Fictions*, trans. Andrew Hurley (London: Penguin, 1998)

Bushnaq, Inea, trans. and ed., *Arab Folk-Tales* (New York: Pantheon, 1986)

Byatt, A.S., *The Djinn in the Nightingale's Eye: Five Fairy Stories* (London: Chatto & Windus, 1995)

Calvino, Italo, *Invisible Cities* [1972], trans. William Weaver (London: Vintage, 1974)

Calvino, Italo, *If on a Winter's Night a Traveller* [1979], trans. William Weaver (London: Vintage, 1998)

Carter, Angela, *Nights at the Circus* (London: Chatto & Windus, 1985)

Chandler, Robert, ed. and trans. *The Magic Ring and Other Russian Folktales* (London: Faber & Faber 1979)

Chaucer, Geoffrey, *The Riverside Chaucer*, ed. Beson, Larry D. (Oxford: OUP, 2008)

Chelkowski, Peter J., *Mirror of the Invisible World: Tales of the Khamseh of Nizami* (New York: Metropolitan Museum of Art, 1975)

Cowper, William, ed. James Sambrook, *The Task and Selected Other Poems* (London: Longman, 1994)

Crabbe, George, *Tales, 1812, and Other Selected Poems*, ed. Howard Mills (Cambridge: Cambridge University Press, 1967)

Crébillon, Claude, *Le Sopha: Conte moral* (Paris, 1742)

[Dante] Alighieri, Dante, *The Divine Comedy*, trans. John D. Sinclair, 3 vols (London: Macmillan, 1956

Diderot, Denis, *Les Bijoux indiscrets*, ed. Jacques Rustin (Paris: Gallimard, 1981)

Fitzgerald, Edward, The *Rubáiyát of Omar Khayyám*, ed. Daniel Karlin (Oxford: OUP, 2009)

Gautier, Théophile, ed. Romain Pehel, *La mille et deuxième Nuit* (Paris: Editions Mille et une nuits No. 427, 2003)

Genlis, Stéphanie Félicité (Mme) de, *Le Saphir merveilleux, ou Le Talisman du bonheur* (Paris: 1803)

Ghitani, Gamal al-, *Zayni Barakat* [1971,], ed. and trans. Farouk Abdel Wahab (London: Penguin, 1990)

[Gildon, Charles], *The Golden Spy; or, A political journal of the British nights entertainments and love and politics: wherein are laid open, the secret miraculous power and the courts of Europe, etc.* (London, 1710)

[Godwin, Francis], *The Man in the Moone; or A Discourse of a Voyage Thither*. By Domingo Gonsales [pseud.]. (London: John Norton), in R.B., *English Acquisitions in Guinea and East India*, Nathaniel Crouch, (London: 1700)

Goethe, Johann Wolfgang von, *Faust, Part One*, ed. and trans. Philip Mayne (Harmondsworth: Penguin [1949, 1959], 1984).

Goethe, Johann Wolfgang von, *Selected Verse*, intro. and ed. David Luke
    (Oxford: OUP [1964], 1986)
Goethe, Johann Wolfgang von, *Faust, Part One*, and *Faust Part Two*, ed. and
    trans. David Luke, 2 vols (Oxford: OUP, 1994)
Goethe, Johann Wolfgang von, trans. Whaley, John, *Poems of the West and East:
    West-Eastern Divan - West-östlicher Divan*, bilingual edition of the Complete
    Poems. (Germanic Studies in America 68), ed. Mommsen, Katharina (New
    York, Paris et al.: Peter Lang, 1998) (WED/Whaley)
Gonzenbach, Laura, *Beautiful Angiola* and *The Robber with a Witch's Head*, ed. and
    trans. Jack Zipes, 2 vols. (New York and London: Routledge, 2004)
[Grimm] *The Complete Fairy Tales of the Brothers Grimm*, trans. and ed. Jack
    Zipes. (New York: Bantam, 1992)
Grimm, Jacob and Wilhelm, *Selected Tales*, trans. Joyce Crick (Oxford: Oxford
    World's Classics, 2005)
Hafiz of Shiraz: Thirty Poems, trans. P. Avery, and J. Heath-Stubbs. (London:
    John Murray, [1952], repr. New York: Other Press, 2003)
Hamilton, Anthony, *Princess Mayblossom*, trans. Horace Walpole (William
    Dodsley, 1783); *History of May-Flower: A Fairy Tale* (London: G. and T.
    Wilkie, 1793)
Hamilton, Anthony, 'Le Bélier', *Lé Cabinet des Fées,* Vol. 20 (Amsterdam and
    Paris, 1785)
Hamilton, Anthony, *Fairy Tales and Romances*, trans. M. Lewis, H. T. Ryde and
    C. Kenney (London, 1849)
Hariharan, Githa, *When Dreams Travel* (London: Picador, 1999)
Herodotus, *The Histories*, trans. Aubrey de Sélincourt (Harmondsworth:
    Penguin [1954], 1983)
Hoffmann, E.T.A, ed. E.F. Bleiler, *The Best Tales* (New York: Dover, 1967).
Inchbald, Elizabeth, *A Mogul's Tale, Or, The Descent of the Balloon* (1784)
Johnson, Samuel, *The History of Rasselas Prince of Abyssinia* [with Ellis Cornelia
    Knight, *Dinarbas: A Tale*] ed. Lynne Meloccaro (London: Everyman, 1994)
Kafka, Franz, *The Complete Short Stories*, ed. Nahum N. Glatzer (London:
    Vintage, 1999)
Khoury, Elias, *Gate of the Sun* [1998], trans. Humphrey Davies (London:
    Vintage, 2005)
Kirk, Robert, *The Secret Commonwealth of Elves, Fauns, and Fairies*, intro.
    Marina Warner (New York: New York Review of Books 2007)
[Koran] Abdel Haleem, M.A.S. trans., *The Qur'an* (New York: OUP 2008)
[Koran] Khalidi, Tarif, trans., *The Qur'an* (New Delhi Penguin, 2009)
[Lucian] Lucien, *Histoire véritable*, trans. and intro. Perrot d'Ablancourt [1654],
    ed. Sabine Wespieser (Paris: Actes Sud, 1988)
Mahfouz, Naguib, *Arabian Nights and Days*, trans. Denys Johnson-Davies (New
    York: Anchor Books, 1995)
Marlowe, Christopher, *Doctor Faustus and Other Plays* (Oxford: OUP, 2008).

Montagu, Mary Wortley, *The Turkish Embassy Letters,* ed. Jack Malcolm and Anita Desai (London: Virago, 1994)

Montagu, Mary Wortley, *Romance Writings*, ed. Isobel Grundy (Oxford: OUP, 1996)

Nesbit, E, *The Phoenix and the Carpet* (London: T. Fisher Unwin, 1904)

Oehlenschlager, Adam, *Aladdin, or The Wonderful Lamp*, trans. Henry Meyer (Copenhagen: Gyldendal, 1968)

Paltock, Robert, *Les Hommes volans ou les aventures de Peter Wilkins*, trans. P.F. de Puisieux, 3 vols (Paris, 1763)

Paltock, Robert, *The Life and Adventures of Peter Wilkins*, intro. and illus. Edward Bawden (London: Dent, 1928)

Perrault, Charles, *Contes*, ed. Gilbert Rouger (Paris: Garnier, 1967)

Pétis de La Croix, François, *Les mille et un Jours. Contes persans.* ed. Pierre Brunel, Christelle Bahier-Porte and Frédéric Mancier; with idem, *Histoire de la Sultane de Perse et des Vizirs*, ed. Raymonde Robert, and Abbé Bignon, *Les Aventures d'Abdalla*, ed. Raymonde Robert (Paris: Honoré Champion, 2006)

Potocki, Jan, *Manuscript Trouvé à Saragosse*, ed. Roger Caillois (Paris: Gallimard, 1958)

Potocki, Jan, *The Manuscript Found in Saragossa*, trans. Ian Maclean (London: Viking, 1995)

Qur'an, see [Koran]

Restif de la Bretonne, Nicolas-Edmé, *La Découverte australe par un homme-volant, ou le Dédale français* (Leipzig, 1781)

Rushdie, Salman, *Haroun and the Sea of Stories* (London: Picador, 1990)

Sarkhosh Curtis, Vesta and Canby, Sheila, eds, *Persian Love Poetry* (London: British Museum 2008)

Scott, Walter, *The Talisman* in *Tales of the Crusaders* (Edinburgh: Archibald Constable, 1825)

Seidmann-Freud, Tom, *Das Wunderhaus.* (Berlin: Ophir, 1927)

Seidmann-Freud, Tom, *Das Zauberboot* (Berlin: Ophir, 1929)

Shakespeare, *Anthony and Cleopatra*, ed. Michael Neill (Oxford: 1994)

Shakespeare, *Othello*, ed. Michael Neill (Oxford: 2006)

[Shakespeare] *The Riverside Shakespeare*, ed. G. Blakemore Evans, et al. (Chigago: Houghton Mifflin, 1974)

Shaykh, Hanan al-, *One Thousand and One Nights* [Alf layla wa-Layla] (London: Bloomsbury, 2011)

Sheridan, Frances, *The History of Nourjahad: The Persian* (1767) in *Oriental Tales*, ed. Robert Mack (Oxford: OUP, 1992)

'The Testament of Solomon', trans. F.C. Conybeare, *Jewish Ouarterly Review* (October 1898); digital version Joseph H. Peterson, ed., http://www.esotericarchives.com/solomon/testamen.htm (1997). Also M. R. James, ed. and trans., *Ghosts & Scholars 28*, http://www.users.globalnet.co.uk/~pardos/ArchiveSolIntro.html (1999)

Ugrešic, Dubravka, *Baba Yaga Laid an Egg*, trans. Ellen Elias-Bursac,
    Celia Hawkesworth and Mark Thompson (Edinburgh: Canongate, 2009)
Virgil, *Aeneid*, trans. W.F. Jackson Knight [1956] (Penguin, 1969)
Voltaire, *The White Bull*, trans. Jeremy Bentham (London: John Murray, 1788)
Voltaire, *Candide and Other Stories*, ed. and trans. Roger Pearson (Oxford:
    OUP, 2006)
Voltaire, *La Princesse de Babylone*, archived online at: http://www. voltaire-
    internal.com/Html/21/09BABYLO.html (accessed 2 October 2010)
Walpole, Horace, *Hieroglyphic Tales* [1785] (London: Pallas Athene, 2010)
Weber, Henry W., *Tales of the East Comprising the most popular romances of*
    Oriental origin, and the best imitations by European authors, with new translations
    and additional tales, never before translated, 3 vols (Edinburgh, 1812)
Wedgwood, Henry Allen, 'The Bird Talisman: An Eastern Tale', reprinted from
    The Family Tutor, Vol. 3, 1852 (Cambridge: C.J. Clay at CUP, 1887)
Wilkins, John, *The Discovery of a New World in the Moone. Or, a Discourse*
    tending to prove that there may be another habitable World in that Planet, 2 vols.
    (London: E.G. for Michael Sparke and Edward Forrest, 1640)
Wilkins, John, *Le Monde dans la lune*, trans. Sr de la Montagne (Rouen: Chez
    Jacques Caïlloüé, 1656)
Wilkins, John, *Mathematical Magick* (London: for Ric. Baldwin, 1691)
Wonder Tales: Six French Stories of Enchantment, ed. Marina Warner, (London:
    Chatto & Windus, 1994)
Yunis, Alia, *The Night Counter* (New York: Crown, 2009)
El-Zein, Amira, *The Unseen and the Seen: Jinn among Mankind* (Louisville, Kty:
    Fons Vitae, 2002)
Zipes, Jack (ed.), *Spells of Enchantment: The Wondrous Fairy Tales of Western Culture*
    (New York: Viking, 1991)

Background and critical works

Ahmed, Leila, *Edward W. Lane: A Study of his Life and Works and of British Ideas*
    of the Middle East in the Nineteenth Century (London and New York:
    Longman and Librairie du Liban, 1978)
Aït-Touati, Frédérique, 'La Découverte d'un autre monde: Fiction et théorie
    dans les oeuvres de John Wilkins et de Francis Godwin', *Études Épistémè* 7
    (printemps 2005), 15–31
Altick, Robert, *The Shows of London* (Cambridge, Mass.: Harvard 1978)
Appadurai, Arjun, ed., *The Social Life of Things* (Cambridge: 1986)
Apter, Emily, *The Translation Zone: A New Comparative Literature* (Princeton
    and Oxford: Princeton UP, 2006)
Armstrong, Isobel, *Victorian Glassworlds: Glass Culture and the Imagination,*
    1830–1880 (Oxford: OUP, 2008)
Ballaster, Ros, *Fabulous Orients: Fictions of the East in England, 1662–1785*
    (Oxford: OUP, 2005b)

Barenboim, Daniel and Edward W. Said, *Parallels and Paradoxes: Explorations in Music and Society* (London: Bloomsbury, 2002)

Barker, Barbara M., ed., *Bolossy Kiralfy: Creator of Great Musical Spectacles: An Autobiography* (Ann Arbor: Univ. of Michigan Press, 1988)

Bencheikh, Jamel Eddine, *Les Mille et une Nuits ou la parole prisonnière* (Paris: Gallimard, 1988)

Bencheikh, Jamel Eddine, Claude Brémond and André Miquel, *Mille et un Contes de la nuit* (Paris: Gallimard, 1991)

Blackwell, Mark, *The Secret Life of Things: Animals, Objects, and IT-Narratives in Eighteenth-century England* (Bucknell Univ. Press, 2008)

Borges, Jorge Luis, *Seven Nights*, trans. Eliot Weinberger (New York: New Directions, 1985)

Borges, Jorge Luis, *Altre Inquisizioni* (Milan: Feltrinelli, [1963], 2000); *Other Inquisitions 1937–52* (NY, 1966)

Borges, Jorge Luis, *The Total Library: Non-Fiction 1922–1986*, ed. Eliot Weinberger (London and New York: Penguin, 1999)

Brooks, Peter, *Reading for the Plot: Design and Intention in Narrative* (Cambridge, Mass.: HUP, 1992)

Brown, Bill, 'Thing Theory', *Critical Inquiry*, 28: 1 (Autumn 2001) Candlin and Guins, pp. 139–153.

Buchan, James, *Frozen Desire: An Inquiry into the Meaning of Money* (London: Picador, 1997)

Butler, E.M. *The Myth of the Magus* (Cambridge: CUP 1948)

Caillois, Roger, *The Edge of Surrealism: A Roger Caillois Reader*, ed. Claudine Frank, trans. Claudine Frank and Camille Naish (Durham, N.C.: Duke UP, 2003)

Calvino, Italo, *Sulla Fiaba* 1996 (Palermo: Solleno)

Calvino, Italo, *Six Memos for the Next Millennium*, trans. Patrick Creagh (London: Jonathan Cape, 1999)

Candlin, Fiona and Guins, Raiford, eds., *The Object Reader* (London and New York: Routledge, 2009)

Caracciolo, Peter, *The Arabian Nights in English Literature: Studies in the Reception of the 1001 Nights into British Culture* (Basingstoke: Macmillan, 1988)

Caracciolo, Peter, 'The House of Fiction and *le jardin anglo-chinois*', *Middle Eastern Literatures* 7: 2 (2004), 199–211.

Cave, Terence, *Recognitions: A Study in Poetics* (Oxford: Clarendon Paperbacks, 1990)

Cave, Terence, *Mignon's Afterlives: Crossing Cultures from Goethe to the Twenty-First Century* (Oxford: OUP, 2011)

Châtel, Laurent,' Les Sources des contes orientaux de William Beckford. (*Vathek* et la 'Suite des contes arabes'): bilan de recherches sur les écrits et l'esthétique de Beckford, *Études Épistèmè*, (7 2005), 93–106.

Châtel, Laurent, 'Of Greeks and Goths in the English Garden', *RSÉAA XVII-XVIII*, 60(2005), 217–242

Châtel, Laurent, 'The Lures of Eastern Lore: William Beckford's Oriental
   Dangerous Supplements', *RSÉAA* XVII–XVIII, 67 (2010), 127–144.
Châtel, Laurent, 'Re-Orienting William Beckford : Translating and Adapting
   the *Thousand and One Nights*, in ed. Kennedy/Warner (New York:
   NYUP, forthcoming)
Chaudhuri, Shohini, 'Visit of the Body Snatchers: Alien Invasion Themes in
   Vampire Narratives', *camera obscura* 40–41 (May 1997): 180–199.
Chebel, Malek, *Dictionnaire amoureux des mille et une Nuits* (Paris: Plon,
   2010)
Chraïbi, Aboubakr, ed., *Les mille et une Nuits en partage* (Arles: Actes Sud/
   Sindbad, 2004)
Chraïbi, Aboubakr, *Les mille et une Nuits: Histoire du texte et classification des
   contes* (Paris: L'Harmattan, 2008)
Christian, Jr. William, 'The Presence of the Absent: Transcendence in an
   American Midwest Household', in Vargyas, Gábor ed., *Passageways: From
   Hungarian Ethnography to European Ethnology and Sociocultural Anthropology*.
   Studia Ethnologica Hungarica 12. Budapest: Department of European
   Ethnology and Cultural Anthropology, The University of Pécs and
   L'Harmattan 2009 [2011], 221–238
Christie, Ian, *The Last Machine: Cinema and the Birth of the Modern World*
   (London: 1994)
Christie, Ian, 'The Magic Sword: Genealogy of an English Trick Film', *Film
   History*, 16:2 (2004), 163–171
Clark, Stuart, *Thinking with Demons: The Idea of Witchcraft in Early Modern
   Europe* (Oxford: Clarendon Press, 1997)
Clark, Ruth, *Anthony Hamilton: His Life and Works and Family* (London and
   New York: John Lane, 1921)
Codrescu, Andrei, *Whatever Gets You Through the Night* (Princeton: Princeton UP,
   2011)
Colla, Elliott, *Conflicted Antiquities: Egyptology, Egyptomania, Egyptian Modernity*
   (Durham, N.C. and London: Duke UP, 2007)
Colla, Elliott, 'The Ladies and the Eye: Figure and Narrative in the Porter's Tale'.
   (Kennedy/Warner, NYUP, forthcoming)
Colla, Elliott, 'Magical Ethic: Wonder and Advice in *Alf layla wa-Layla*', Paper
   given at BA workshop *The Compass of Story*, 2009
Coppola, Al, 'John Rich and the Eighteenth-Century English Stage: Commerce,
   Magic and Management', in *The Stage's Glory*, eds. Jeremy Barlow and Berta
   Joncus (Newark: Univ. of Delaware Press, 2010)
Corso, Simona, *Automi, Termometri, Fucili: L'Immaginario della macchina nel
   romanzo inglese e francese del settecento* (Roma: Edizioni di storia e
   letteratura, 2004)
Dadswell, Sarah, 'Jugglers, Fakirs, and Jaduwallahs: Indian Magicians and the
   British Stage', *New Theatre Quarterly* 23:1 (February 2007), 3–24.

Dalley, Stephanie, 'Gilgamesh in the *Arabian Nights'*, *Journal of the Royal Asiatic Society*, 3:1 (1991), 1–17.

Daston, Lorraine, *Things That Talk: Object Lessons from Art and Science* (New York: Zone Books/MIT Press, 2004)

Doniger, Wendy, *The Bedtrick: Tales of Sex and Masquerade* (Chicago: Univ. of Chicago Press, 2000)

Dronke, Peter, *Sources of Inspiration: Studies in Literary Transformations, 400–1500* (Rome: Edizioni di storia e letteratura, 1997)

Dupont, Florence, *The Invention of Literature: From Greek Intoxication to the Latin Book*, trans. Janet Lloyd (Baltimore, Md and London: Johns Hopkins 1999)

During, Simon, *Modern Enchantments: The Cultural Power of Secular Magic* (Cambridge, Mass.: UP, 2002)

Escott, Angela, 'The Imperial Project: Resistance and Revolution in Hannah Cowley's *oriental musical comedy*.' *Restoration and Eighteenth-Century Theatre Research*, 20: 1 and 2 (2005)

Eisele, John C., 'The Wild East: Deconstructing the Language of Genre in the Hollywood Eastern', *Cinema Journal* 41, No.4, Summer 2002: 68–94.

Fulford, Tim and Kitson, Peter J., *Romanticism and Colonialism: Writing and Empire, 1780–1830* (Cambridge: CUP, 1998)

Gell, Alfred, *Art and Agency: An Anthropological Theory* (Oxford: Clarendon Press, 1998)

Gell, Alfred, 'The Technology of Enchantment and the Enchantment of Technology', in F. R. Candlin and Guins, eds., 208–228.

Gerhardt, Mia, *The Art of Story-Telling. A Literary Study of the Thousand and One Nights* (Leiden: Brill, 1963)

Ghazoul, Ferial, *Nocturnal Poetics: The Arabian Nights in Comparative Context* (Cairo: American University in Cairo Press, 1996)

Ginzburg, Carlo, *Ecstasies: Deciphering the Witches' Sabbath*, trans. Raymond Rosenthal (Univ. of Chicago: Chicago Press, 1991)

Godwin, Joscelyn, *Athanasius Kircher: A Renaissance Man and the Quest for Lost Knowledge* (London: Thames & Hudson, 1979)

Godwin, Joscelyn, *Athanasius Kircher's Theatre of the World* (London: Thames & Hudson, 2009)

Godwin, William, *The Lives of the Necromancers* (London: Frederick J. Mason, 1834)

Goody, Jack, *Myth, Literature and the Oral* (Cambridge: CUP, 2010)

Greenway, John L., 'Acoustic Figures and the Romantic Soul of Reason', *European Romantic Review*, 11 2 (2000), 214–222.

Grigsby, Darcy Grimaldo, *Extremities: Painting Empire in Post-Revolutionary France* (New Haven: Yale UP, c. 2002)

Grosrichard, Alain, *The Sultan's Court: European Fantasies of the East*, trans. Liz Heron (New York: Verso, 1998)

Hamilton, Alastair, *The Arcadian Library* (Oxford: The Arcadian Library/OUP, 2011)

Hart, Clive, *Images of Flight* (Berkeley: Univ. of California Press, 1988)

H.D. [Hilda Doolittle], *Tribute to Freud* [1956] (Manchester: Carcanet, 1985)

Heath, Peter, 'Romance as Genre in "The Thousand and One Nights"', in Marzolph, 170–225.

Hole, Richard, *Remarks on the Arabian Nights' Entertainments, in which the Origin of Sindbad's Voyages and Other Oriental Fictions is particularly considered* (London: T. Cadell, 1797)

Hovannisian, Richard C. and Georges, Sabagh, eds, *The Thousand and One Nights in Arabic Literature and Society* (Cambridge: CUP, 1997)

Hunter, Michael, ed. *The Occult Laboratory: Magic, Science and Second Sight in Late 17th Century Scotland* (Woodbridge: Boydell Press, 2001)

Irwin, Robert, *The Arabian Nights: A Companion* (London: Allen Lane, 1994; London and New York, Tauris Parke, rev. edn., 2004) [Irwin]

Irwin, Robert, *Visions of the Jinn* (Oxford: Arcadian Library with OUP, 2011)

Jackson, Rosemary, *Fantasy: The Literature of Subversion* (London and New York: Methuen, 1981)

Johnson, Barbara, *Persons and Things* (Cambridge, Mass.: Harvard UP, 2008)

Johnson, Rebecca Carol, Maxwell, Richard and Trumpener, Katie, 'The *Arabian Nights*, Arab-European Literary Influence, and the Lineages of the Novel', *Modern Language Quarterly* 68:2, (June 2007), 243–79.

Johnson, Rebecca, 'On *Tristram Shandy* and the Nineteenth-Century Arabic Novel', in *The Compass of Story: The Oriental Tale and Western Imagination*, (British Academy, 28–29 March, 2009)

Kabbani, Rana, *Europe's Myths of Orient: Devise and Rule* (London: Macmillan, 1986)

Keen, Paul, 'The "Balloonomania: Science and Spectacle in 1780s England', *Eighteenth Century Studies*, 39:4 (Summer 2006), 507–535

Kennedy, Philip and Warner, Marina, eds, *Arabian Nights: Encounters and Translations* (New York: NYUP [Kennedy/Warner]

Khatibi, Abdelkebir and Amahan, Ali, *Du signe à l'image: Le Tapis Marocain* (Casablanca: Edition Lak International, 1995).

Kilito, Abdelfattah, *L'Oeil et l'aiguille: Essai sur Les mille et une nuits* (Paris: Éditions Le Fennec, 1992)

Kilito, Adbelfattah, *The Author and his Doubles: Essays on Classical Arabic Culture*, trans. Peter Cooperson (New York: Syracuse UP, 2001)

Kilito, Abdelfattah, *Dites-moi le songe* (Arles: Actes Sud, 2010)

Kristeva, Julia, *Strangers to Ourselves*, trans. Leon S. Roudiez (New York: Columbia UP, 1995)

Kwiatkowski, Will, *The Eckstein Shahnama: An Ottoman Book of Kings* (London: Sam Fogg, 2005)

Lewis, Dr G. Griffin, *The Practical Book of Oriental Rugs* (Philadelphia and London: J. P. Lippincott, 1920).

Laissus, Yves, *L'Egypte, une aventure savante avec Bonaparte* (Paris: Fayard, 1998)

Lamb, Jonathan, 'The Crying of Lost Things', *ELH* 71:4 (Winter 2004), 949–967.

Lane, Edward W., *An Account of the Manners and Customs of the Modern Egyptians, written during the Years 1833–34 and 1835*, 2 vols (London: Charles Knight, 1836)

Lanier, Jaron, *You Are Not A Gadget* (New York: Knopf, 2010)

[Lorck] Fischer, Erik et al. *Melchior Lorck,* 4 vols (Copenhagen: The Royal Library and Vandkunsten, 2009).

Lowe, Lisa, *Critical Terrains: French and British Orientalisms* (Ithaca: Cornell UP, 1991)

Luckhurst, Roger, *The Mummy's Curse: A New Cultural History* (Oxford: OUP, forthcoming, 2012)

MacDonald, Duncan, Black 'On Translating the Arabian Nights: I', *Nation*, 71, b, 167–8, 185–6. (September 1900)

MacDonald, Duncan, Black 'The Thousand and One Nights', *Enc. Brit.* (Chicago and London, 1950), Vol. 22: 157–9.

MacGregor, Neil, *History of the World in 100 Objects* (London: Allen Lane, 2010)

Maclean, Gerald, *The Rise of Oriental Travel: English Visitors to the Ottoman Empire, 1580–1720* (Basingstoke: Palgrave Macmillan, 2004)

Maclean, Gerald, Introduction to Gerald Maclean, ed., *Re-Orienting the Renaissance: Cultural Exchanges with the East* (Basingstoke: Palgrave Macmillan, 2005), 1–28.

Mahmoud, Fatma Moussa, ed. *William Beckford of Fonthill 1760–1844.* Cairo Studies in English (Cairo: Casta Tsoumas, 1960)

Makdisi, Saree and Nussbaum, Felicity, eds, *The Arabian Nights in Historical Context: Between East and West* (Oxford: OUP, 2008) [Makdisi/Nussbaum]

Mashek, Joseph, *The Carpet Paradigm: Integral Flatness from Decoration to Fine Art* (New York: Edgewise Press, 2010)

Malti-Douglas, Fedwa 'Shahrazad Feminist', in *The Thousand and One Nights in Arabic Literature and Society*, ed. Hovannisian and Sabagh (Cambridge: CUP, 1997), pp. 40–55.

Marks, Laura U., *Enfoldment and Infinity: An Islamic Genealogy of New Media Art* (Boston: MIT Press, 2010)

Marx, Karl, *Capital*, ed. and trans. David McLellan (Oxford: OUP, 2008)

Marzolph, Ulrich, ed. *The Arabian Nights: Past and Present, Marvels & Tales* Special Issue, 18: 2, (2004)

Marzolph, Ulrich, See Abbreviations: ANEnc and Marzolph

McCown, Chester Charlton, 'The Christian Tradition as to the Magical Wisdom of Solomon', *Journal of the Palestine Oriental Society*, 2 (1922), 1–24.

McGrath, Elizabeth, 'Rubens and his Black Kings', *Rubens Bulletin Koninklijk Museum voor Schone Kunsten Antwerpen*, Jrg.2, 2008 87–101

McGrath, Elizabeth, 'The Streams of Oceanus: Rubens, Homer and the boundary of the ancient world.' *Ars naturam adiuvans. Festschrift für Matthias Winner*, zum II Marz eds., Victoria v. Flemming and Sebastian Schütze, 1996, 464–76.

McGrath, Elizabeth, 'The Black Andromeda'. JWCI, vol. 55, 1992: 1–18.

McGrath, Elizabeth, 'Sibyls, Sheba and Jan Boeckhorst's *Parts of the World*', in *Florissant. Bijdragen tot de kunstgeschiedenis der Nederlanden (15de-17de eeuw). Liber Amicorum Carl Van de Velde*, eds. A. Balis et al. (Brussels, 2005), 357-70.

McGrath, Elizabeth, 'Jacob Jordaens and Moses's Ethiopian Wife', JWCI, Vol. 70, 2007:247–85.

Michaud, Philippe-Alain, *Aby Warburg and the Image in Motion,* trans. Sophie Hawkes (New York: Zone Books, 2004)

Michaud, Phillippe-Alain, *Sketches: Histoire de l'art, cinéma* (Paris: Kargo et l'Éclat, 2006)

Miller, Daniel, *The Comfort of Things* (Cambridge: Polity, 2008)

Miquel, André, 'The Thousand and One Nights in Arabic Literature and Society', in *The Thousand and One Nights in Arabic Literature and Society*, ed. Hovannisian and Sabagh, (Cambridge: CUP, 1997), 6–13.

Mommsen, Katharina, *Goethe und 1001 Nacht* (Berlin: Surhkamp, 1960) (and lecture, 'Goethe and the 1001 Nights', SOAS, 3 December, 2008.

Moretti, Franco, ed. *The Novel* Vol. 1: *History, Geography and Culture;* Vol. 2: *Forms and Themes* (Princeton and Oxford: Princeton UP, 2006)

Morrison, Toni, *Playing in the Dark: Whiteness and the Literary Imagination* (London: Picador, 1993)

Mottahedeh, Roy P., ''Aja'ib in *The Thousand and One Nights*', in Hovannisian and Sabagh, 29–39.

Naddaff, Sandra, *Arabesque: Narrative, Structure and the Aesthetics of Repetition in 1001 Nights* (Evanston, Ill: Northwestern UP, 1991)

Nance, Susan, *How the "Arabian Nights" Inspired the American Dream 1790–1935* (Chapel Hill: Univ. of North Carolina Press, 2009)

Nelson, Victoria, *The Secret Life of Puppets* (Cambridge, Mass: Harvard UP, 2001)

Nelson, Victoria, *Gothicka* (Cambridge, Mass: Harvard UP, forthcoming, 2012)

Oliver, Susan, *Scott, Byron and the Poetics of Cultural Encounter* (Basingstoke: Palgrave Macmillan, 2005)

O'Quinn, Daniel, *Staging Governance: Theatrical Imperialism in London, 1770–1800* (Baltimore, Md: Johns Hopkins UP, 2005)

Orlando, Francesco, 'Forms of Supernatural in Narrative', in F. Moretti, *The Novel*, Vol. 2, 207–243.

Orr, Bridget, 'Galland, Georgian Theatre, and the Creation of Popular Orientalism, in Makdisi/Nussbaum, 103–130.

Ouyang, Wen-chin and Hart, Stephen M., eds, *A Companion to Magical Realism* (Woodbridge: Thamesis, 2005)

Owen, Alex, *The Place of Enchantment: British Occultism and the Culture of the Modern* (Chicago and London: Univ. of Chicago Press, 2004)

Pearson, Roger, *The Fables of Reason: A Study of Voltaire's Contes Philosophiques* (Oxford: Clarendon Press, 1993)

Pearson, Roger, *Voltaire Almighty: A Life in Pursuit of Freedom* (London: Bloomsbury, 2005)

Perrin, Jean-François, ed., *Le Conte oriental*, in *Féeries,* No. 2, 2004–5 (Grenoble: Univ. Stendhal-Grenoble)

Pietz, William, 'The Problem of the Fetish, I,' *RES*, 9 (1985): 5–17, 'The Problem of the Fetish, II', *RES*, 13 (1987): 23–45.

Propp, Vladimir, *Morphology of the Folktale,* trans. Laurence Scott [1928] (Austin: Univ. of Texas Press, 1984)

Quayson, Ato, 'Fecundities of the Unexpected: Magical Realism, Narrative, and History', in Moretti, *The Novel,* Vol. 2: 726–756.

Riegl, Alois, *Antichi tappeti orientali*, ed. Alberto Manai (Quaderni 4, Macerata: Quodlibet, 1998)

Said, Edward, W., *Orientalism: Western Conceptions of the Orient* (London: Penguin, 1978; revised ed. 1995)

Said, Edward W., *The World, the Text, and the Critic* (London: Vintage, 1983)

Said, Edward W., *Culture and Imperialism* (London: Chatto & Windus, 1993)

Said, Edward W., *Out of Place: A Memoir* (London: Granta, 1999)

Said, Edward W., *Reflections on Exile and Other Literary and Cultural Essays* (London: Granta, 2000)

Said, Edward W., Introduction, in Erich Auerbach, *Mimesis: The Representation of Reality in Western Literature* (Princeton: Princeton UP, 2003)

Said, Edward W., *On Late Style* (London: Bloomsbury, 2006)

Savage-Smith, Emilie, *Magic and Divination in Early Islam,* in *The Formation of the Classical Islamic World*, vol 42, gen. ed. Lawrence I. Conrad (Aldershot, Ashgate, c.2004)

Schwab, Raymond, *L'Auteur des mille et une nuits: Vie d'Antoine Galland* (Paris: Mercure de France, 1964)

Schwab, Raymond, *The Oriental Renaissance: Europe's Rediscovery of India and the East, 1680 to 1880* [1950], trans. Gene Patterson-Black and Victor Reuking (New York: Columbia up, 1987)

Seymour, St John D., *Tales of King Solomon* (Oxford: OUP, and London: Humphrey Milford, 1924)

Shalev-Eyni, Sarit, 'Solomon, his Demons and Jongleurs: The Meeting of Islamic, Judaic and Christian Culture', *Al-Masaq* 18: 2 (September 2006), 145–160.

Sironval, Margaret, 'Écritures européennes du conte d'Aladin', *Féeries*, 2 (2004–05), 245–256.

Sironval, Margaret, *Album: Mille et une Nuits* (Paris: Gallimard, 2005)

Stephenson, Craig, *Possession: Jung's Comparative Anatomy of the Psyche* (London: Routledge, 2009)

Stoneman, Richard, *Alexander the Great: A Life in Legend* (New Haven and London: Yale UP, 2008)

Sudan, Rajani, *Fair Exotics: Xenophobic Subjects in English Literature, 1720–1850* (Philadelphia: Univ. of Pennsylvania Press, 2002)

Tambiah, Stanley Jeyaraja, *Magic, Science, Religion, and the Scope of Rationality.* (Cambridge: CUP, 1990)

Thomas, Nicholas, *Entangled Objects: Exchange, Material Culture and Colonialism in the Pacific* (Harvard: UP, 1991)

Todorov, Tzvetan, *Nouvelles Recherches sur le récit* (Paris, 1978)

Todorov, Tzvetan, *The Fantastic: A Structural Approach to a Literary Genre*, trans. Richard Howard (Ithaca, NY: Cornell UP, 1973)

Todorov, Tzvetan, *Poétique de la prose* (Paris: 1971), inc. 'Narrative-Men', in Marzolph (2006), 226–238.

Torijano, Pablo A., *Solomon the Esoteric King: From King to Magus - Development of a Tradition* (Leiden: Brill, 2002)

Tromans, Nicholas, *Richard Dadd: The Artist and the Asylum* (London: Tate, 2011)

Turkle, Sherry, *The Second Self: Computers and the Human Spirit* (Cambridge, Mass.: MIT Press, 2005)

Turkle, Sherry, ed., *Evocative Objects: Things We Think With* (Cambridge, Mass.: MIT Press, 2007)

Van Eck, Caroline, '"L'idole se prend pour la chose même, la figure est souvent confondue avec la chose figurée": On the Early History of Fetishism as a Way of Understanding Living Presence'. Kindly lent by the author. To appear as *François Lemée et la statue de Louis XIV sur la Place des Victoires: aux origines de la réflection ethnographique et esthétique sur le fétichisme,* Paris: Centre Allemand d'Histoire de l'Art and the École des Hautes Études en Sciences Sociales, 2012.

Van Gelder, Geert Jan, *Close Relationships: Incest and Inbreeding in Classical Arabic Literature* (London: I.B. Tauris, 2005)

Van Gelder, Geert Jan, 'Naming of parts – or not', review of **Lyons**, TLS 23 Jan 2009:7–8.

Van Gelder, Geert Jan and Ouyang, Wen-chin, *New Perspectives on Arabian Nights: Ideological Variations and Narrative Horizons* (London: Routledge, 2005)

Van Leeuwen, Richard, See Abbreviations: ANEnc

Vanmour, Jean-Baptiste, *Explication des cent estampes qui représentent différentes nations du Levant* (Paris: Jacques Collombat, 1715).

Vanmour, Jean-Baptiste, *Recueil de cent estampes représentant différentes nations du Levant* (Paris: Sr Le Hay, 1714).

Vernant, Jean-Pierre, 'The Reason of Myth', in *Myth and Society in Ancient Greece*, trans. Janet Lloyd (London: Methuen, 1980)

Warner, Marina, *From the Beast to the Blonde: On Fairy Tales and Their Tellers* (London: Chatto & Windus, 1994)

Warner, Marina, *No Go the Bogeyman: Scaring, Lulling and Making Mock* (London: Chatto & Windus, 1999)

Warner, Marina, *Fantastic Metamorphoses, Other Worlds: Ways of Telling the Self* (Oxford: OUP, 2001)

Warner, Marina, *Phantasmagoria: Spirit Visions, Metaphors, and Media* (Oxford: OUP, 2006)

Warner, Marina, 'Ghosts and Daemons: The Revival of Myth and Magic'. Presidential Address, 23 October 2004, printed in Proceedings of *The Virgil Society*, 26 (2008), 17–31.

Warner, Marina, 'Ventriloquism: Dear Old Khayyám', *LRB*, 31: 7 (9 April 2009): 13–14

Warner, Marina, 'View of a View: Melchoir Lorck', 32: 10 (27 May 2010): 15–17

Warnes, Christopher, *Magical Realism and the Postcolonial Novel between Faith and Irreverence* (Basingstoke: Palgrave Macmillan, 2009)

Willemen, Paul, ed., *Pier Paolo Pasolini* (London: 1977)

Wyngaard, Amy S., 'The Fetish in/as Text: Rétif de la Bretonne and the Development of Modern Sexual Science...', *PMLA*, Vol 121, no. 3, May 2006: 662–686.

Yeazell, Ruth Bernard, *Harems of the Mind: Passages of Western Art and Literature* (New Haven and London: Yale UP, 2000)

Zein, Amira, El- *Islam, Arabs and the Intelligent World of the Jinn* (New York: Syracuse UP, 2009)

Zipes, Jack, *The Enchanted Screen: The Unknown History of Fairy-Tale Films* (London: Routledge, 2011)

Zamora, L. P., and Faris, Wendy, eds., *Magical Realism* (Durham, N.C.: Duke UP, 1995)

Art: exhibitions and catalogues

The Age of Enchantment. Beardsley, Dulac and Their Contemporaries 1890–1930. Essay by Rodney Engen, cur., Dulwich Picture Gallery, London, 28 Nov. 2007–17 Feb. 2008.

Alaoui, Brahim et al., *Espelhos do Paraíso Tapetes do mundo islâmico, séc. XV-XX* exh. cat. (Lisbon: Fundaçao Calouste Gulbenkian, 2005).

Arabick Roots, cur. Rim Turkomani, The Royal Society, London, June 2011.

Arts de l'Islam: Chefs-d'oeuvre de la collection Khalili, Institut du monde arabe, Paris, 6 Oct. 2009–14 March 2010.

À la Cour du Grand Turc: Caftans du Palais de Topkapi. Essays by Hulya Tezcan, et al., Musée du Louvre, Paris, 11 Oct. 2009–18 Jan. 2010, exh. cat. (Paris: Cinq Continents, 2009)

[Beckford]: *William Beckford 1760–1844: An Eye for the Magnificent*, curs. Philip

Bibliography

Hewat-Jaboor and Bet McLeod (Dulwich Picture Gallery, London, 6 Feb. -14 April 2002).

Buvoli, Luca, *Flying: Practical Training for Beginners*, Boston: MIT List Visual Arts Center, 2000.

Falnama: The Book of Omens, eds.Massuma Farhad with Serpil Bagci. Arthur M. Sackler Gallery, Smithsonian, Washington DC, Oct 24 2009-Jan 24 2010.

Diaghilev and the Golden Age of the Ballets Russes, 1909–1929, exh. cat. (Victoria & Albert Museum, London, 25 Sept. 2010–9 Jan. 2011).

L'Étrange et le merveilleux en terres d'Islam, exh. cat. (Louvre, Paris, 23 April-23 July 2001).

Jackson Pollock et le chamanisme, ed. Marc Restellini, exh. cat. (Paris: Pinacothèque de Paris, 2008).

Journey through the Afterlife: *The Ancient Egyptian Book of the Dead*, John M. Taylor, cur., British Museum, 4 Nov. 2010–6 March 2011.

A Kind of Magic: Talismans, Charms and Amulets from the British Museum, Henry Moore Institute, Leeds, 2 April -29 June 2003.

Napoleon on the Nile: Soldiers, Artists, and the Rediscovery of Egypt. Essay by Lisa Small. Dahesh Museum of Art, New York, 31 Dec. 2006.

[Kay Neilsen] The Unknown Paintings, ed. David Larkin (Toronto & London, 1977)

Porter, Venetia, *Arabic and Persian Seals and Amulets in the British Museum* (London: British Museum Publications, 2011).

Rogers. J. M. ed., *The Arts of Islam: Treasures from the Nasser D. Khalili Collection*, Art Gallery of New South Wales, Sydney, 22 June-23 Sept 2007.

Sciences and Arts in the Islamic World [Al-Mizan], Museum of the History of Science, Oxford, 26 Oct 2010–20 March 2011.

Stoichita, Victor, *La Sombra*, Museo Thyssen-Bornemisza, Madrid, 10 Feb -17 May 2009.

The Sacred Made Real: Spanish Painting and Sculpture, 1600–1700, ed. Xavier Bray, National Gallery, London, Feb. 28-May 31 2010,

Tromans, Nicholas, *The Lure of the East* exh. cat., London, Tate Publishing, 2008.

Venice and the Islamic World 828–1797, Institut du Monde Arabe, Paris, 2 Oct. 2006–18 Feb. 2007; Metropolitan Museum of Art, New York, 27 March-8 July 2007, exh. cat., (Paris: Gallimard and New Haven: Yale UP, 2006).

Wallinger, Mark, *The Russian Linesman: Frontiers, Borders and Thresholds*, exh. cat. (Hayward Gallery, London, 18 Feb.-4 May 2009)

Only Make-Believe: Ways of Playing, Warner, Marina, cur. Compton Verney 25 March-5 June 2005.

Films and related media

Clements, Roy and Musker, John, *Aladdin* [1992] (USA: Disney, 2008).

Dickson, W. K. L. and Edison, Thomas, *Buffalo Dance* (United States: Edison Manufacturing Co., 1894).

Dickson, W.K.L. and Edison, Thomas, *Ghost Dance* (United States: Edison Manufacturing Co, 1894).

Finer, Jem and Biswas, Ansuman, *Zero Genie* (artists' film, 2006) www.zerogenie.org

Fitzgerald, Cathy, *The Magic Carpet Flight Manual* (BBC World Service, 24 Sept. 2010) Archived at: http://www.bbc.co.uk/worldservice/documentaries/2010/09/100923-magic-carpet-flight-manual.sh tml (accessed 16/4/10).

Has, Wojcieck J., *Manuscrit trouvé à Saragosse* (1964), CD enclosed in Potocki, Jean *Manuscrit trouvé à Saragosse*, ed. Roger Caillois (Paris: Gallimard, [1958] 1972)

Khemir, Nacer, dir., *Les Baliseurs du désert* (The Wanderers of the Desert) (1984); *Le Collier de la colombe* (The Dove's Lost Necklace) (1991), and *Bab'Aziz: Le Prince qui contemplait son âme* (*Bab'Aziz:* The Prince who contemplated his Soul) (2008), typecastfilms.com; *En Passant avec André Miquel* (2011).

Korda, Alexander, dir. (with Michael Powell et al.) *The Thief of Bagdad* (1940)

Lang, Fritz and Harbou, Thea von, *Der müde Tod (Destiny)*, dir. Fritz Lang, (Germany, 1921. Reissued Magic Entertainment, Inc. 2000).

Makhmalbaf, Mohsen, *Gabbeh*, (MK2 Productions, 1996).

[Méliès] *Georges Méliès: First Wizard of Cinema (1896–1913)*, essays by Norman McLaren and John Frazer. Los Angeles: Film Preservation Associates, 2008.

Ocelot, Michel, dir., *Azur et Asmar*, 2006.

Pasolini, Pier Paolo, dir., *Il fiore delle mille e una notte* (*The Arabian Nights*), script by Pier Paolo Pasolini and Dacia Maraini (Produzioni Europee Associati [PEA], 1978).

Paul, R.W., *The Collected Films 1895–1908*, with commentary by Ian Christie (London: BFI, n.d).

Reiniger, Lotte, *Die Abenteuer des Prinzen Achmed* (*The Adventures of Prince Achmed*), dir. Lotte Reiniger (London: BFI, 2001).

Reiniger, Lotte, *The Fairy Tale Films*, (London: BFI, 2008).

[Reiniger] Moritz, William, *Lotte Reiniger* http://www.awn.com/mag/issue1.3/articles/moritz1.3.html

Smaczny, Paul, *Knowledge is the Beginning: Daniel Barenboim and the West-Eastern Divan Orchestra*, Euroarts 2007–08.

Švankmajer, Jan, *The Complete Short Films*, (London: BFI, 2007).

Walsh, Raoul, *The Thief of Bagdad: An Arabian Nights Fantasy* [1924], script by Douglas Fairbanks and Achmed Abdullah. (USA: Eureka Films 2001).

Theatre, Opera and Music

Cooke, Dominic, *Arabian Nights*. First performed Young Vic 16 Nov. 1998, revived Royal Shakespeare Company, Stratford-on-Avon, 5 Dec. 2009. (London: Nick Hern Books, 2009).

Mozart, Wolfgang Amadeus, *Die Zauberflöte* (The Magic Flute). Interpretation by David McVicar, conducted by Colin Davis and David Syrus, Royal Opera House, London, Winter Season, 2011.

Mozart, Wolfgang Amadeus, *Così fan tutte*. dir. Peter Sellars (Emmanuel Music, Austria: ORF recording, 1989).

Mozart, Wolfgang Amadeus, and Da Ponte, Lorenzo, *Così fan tutte*. Trans. Marmaduke Browne, adapted by John Cox, with Charles Mackerras conducting the Orchestra of the Age of Enlightenment. (Chandos, 2008).

Mozart, Wolfgang Amadeus, *Die Entführung aus dem Serail* (The Abduction from the Seraglio), ed. H.C. Robbins, Vienna Philharmonic, conducted George Solti, Dec. 1985. 2 CDs: London 417 402.

Mozart, Wolfgang Amadeus, *Don Giovanni*. Dir. Peter Sellars, Monadnock Music Festival, Manchester, New Hampshire, 1980.; featured in Mike Dibb, *In Pursuit of Don Juan*, BBC 1988, 1989.

Mozart, Wolfgang Amadeus, *Zaide*. Dir. Peter Sellars, *Mostly Mozart* Festival, Lincoln Center, New York, and Barbican, London, 2006.

Prebble, Lucy, *Enron*. Dir. Rupert Goold, Royal Court Theatre, London, 2009.

Ravel, Maurice, *L'Enfant et les sortilèges: Fantaisie Lyrique* [1925]. Libretto by Colette. CD notes by Nicolas Rodger, *Deutsche Grammophon 457 589–2*.

Rimsky-Korsakov, Nikolai, *Schéhérazade*, in *Diaghilev: Les Saisons Russes XXI*, Coliseum, London, 12–17 April 2011.

Schubert, Franz, *Deutsche Schubert-Lied* (Edition-13, Goethe Lieder, trans. Keith Anderson, Vol. 2. Naxos 8.554663).

Shaykh, Hanan al-, *One Thousand and One Nights (Alf Layla wa-Layla)*. Dir Tim Supple, Edinburgh Festival, 23 Aug.-3 Sept. 2011; London: Bloomsbury, 2011.

Index